PRAISE FOR *BLACK LONDON*

"Marc Matera offers us a vibrant and sophisticated history of the people of African descent, both famous and fugitive, who coursed through the heart of the British Empire in their quest for personal, professional, and political recognition in the twentieth century. Part social history, part collective biography, this genealogy of peripatetic black political formation reveals London as a bustling global portal for some of the most inspiring people who championed anticolonial modernity. *Black London* archives the often terrible, troubling contradictions at the heart of racialized and sexualized imperial encounters and asks us to rethink both the makers and the tempos of decolonization."

—Antoinette Burton, author of *Empire in Question: Reading, Writing, and Teaching British Imperialism*

"Marc Matera's vibrant and kaleidoscopic excavation of black London traverses a stunning range of domains (from political activism to newspaper editing, from jazz performance to sexuality) to explore in admirable detail the complexities of what it meant to be black in the English metropole in the interwar period. If the book is a nuanced study of the emergence of black internationalism at the height of empire, it is also a marvel of rediscovery, bringing back to light a number of overlooked or understudied figures, including Una Marson, Amy Ashwood Garvey, Coleridge Goode, and Ras Prince Monolulu. Simply put, *Black London* is a must-read."

—Brent Hayes Edwards, author of *The Practice of Diaspora: Literature, Translation, and the Rise of Black Internationalism*

"This engaging and lively book, richly peopled and powerfully situated in time and space, brings the multiple worlds of black Londoners vividly to life. *Black London* charts a web of black intellectuals, performers, and ordinary citizens who saw London as the place in which they might remake themselves, along with transforming the core of imperial thought and policy. Marc Matera's account of the diverse sights and sounds—along with politics and personal relationships—of the late imperial metropole explains much about the complex dynamics of race and urbanity not only in the twentieth century but in the twenty-first as well."

—Jordanna Bailkin, author of *The Afterlife of Empire*

"Marc Matera's carefully historical and deeply researched study places figures and events familiar in pan-African history in a richly textured setting. Reaching far beyond political protests against imperialism and racism, Matera traces the lives of women and men moving from Soho music clubs to Speakers' Corner, from film sets to university seminars, through interracial sexual liaisons and diverse alliances with British activists. He reveals how, despite much disagreement and difference, black London gathered people and influences from Africa and its diaspora and generated both powerful alternate views of the future and cultural forms which later found new homes around the Atlantic world. Many stories within black Atlantic history will be enriched by this book."

—Philip S. Zachernuk, author of *Colonial Subjects: An African*

THE GEORGE GUND FOUNDATION
IMPRINT IN AFRICAN AMERICAN STUDIES

The George Gund Foundation has endowed
this imprint to advance understanding of
the history, culture, and current issues
of African Americans.

The publisher gratefully acknowledges the generous support of the African American Studies Endowment Fund of the University of California Press Foundation, which was established by a major gift from the George Gund Foundation.

Black London

THE CALIFORNIA WORLD HISTORY LIBRARY

Edited by Edmund Burke III, Kenneth Pomeranz, and Patricia Seed

Black London

THE IMPERIAL METROPOLIS AND DECOLONIZATION IN THE TWENTIETH CENTURY

Marc Matera

UNIVERSITY OF CALIFORNIA PRESS

University of California Press, one of the most distinguished university presses in the United States, enriches lives around the world by advancing scholarship in the humanities, social sciences, and natural sciences. Its activities are supported by the UC Press Foundation and by philanthropic contributions from individuals and institutions. For more information, visit www.ucpress.edu.

University of California Press
Oakland, California

Library of Congress Cataloging-in-Publication Data

Matera, Marc, 1976– author.
   Black London : the imperial metropolis and decolonization in the twentieth century / Marc Matera.
     p.   cm.—(The California world history library ; 22)
   Includes bibliographical references and index.
   ISBN 978-0-520-28429-6 (cloth : alk. paper)
   ISBN 978-0-520-28430-2 (pbk. : alk. paper)
   ISBN 978-0-520-95990-3 (ebook)
   1. Blacks—England—London—Social conditions—20th century   2. Postcolonialism—England—London—History—20th century.   3. Decolonization—Great Britain—History—20th century.   I. Title.   II. Series: California world history library ; 22.
   DA676.9.B55M38   2015
   305.896′04210904—dc23
2014035966

Manufactured in the United States of America

24   23   22   21   20   19   18   17   16   15
10   9   8   7   6   5   4   3   2   1

In keeping with a commitment to support environmentally responsible and sustainable printing practices, UC Press has printed this book on Natures Natural, a fiber that contains 30% post-consumer waste and meets the minimum requirements of ANSI/NISO Z39.48–1992 (R 1997) (*Permanence of Paper*).

CONTENTS

ILLUSTRATIONS

ACKNOWLEDGMENTS

This book is more than ten years in the making. I have accrued more debts in completing it than I can acknowledge adequately here. Its flaws reflect my own limitations and failings, not a deficit of assistance or guidance. In an indirect but profound sense, the influence of my lifelong friends Lucas Blalock and David Schultz suffuses this text. Without them in my life, I would not have taken the paths that I have, and I first experienced the transformative impact of fortuitous encounters and of love and friendship among intellectual fellow travelers with them. They inspired me in our youth, and even now, when large distances separate us, they continue to do so. Many other dear friends and critical interlocutors have shaped me since my first faltering steps into the world of books and learning—too many to mention by name—but I trust that you know who you are and how much you've meant to me.

Carlton Wilson first exposed me to the history of a black presence in Britain while I was an undergraduate at the University of North Carolina, Chapel Hill. I became a history major after taking his class. I would have never considered going to graduate school or thought myself capable of the endeavor without the mentorship and encouragement of Angelika von Wahl. My first graduate adviser at the University of Colorado, Boulder, and later my collaborator, Susan Kingsley Kent, remains a very important person in my life. I continue to benefit from her intellectual acumen, irrepressible spirit, and boundless generosity to this day.

Like the ideas and figures that fill the pages that follow, this book is the product of heterogeneous spaces and networks of sociality and intellectual exchange, so it is important to acknowledge here some of the most formative ones. I started the project as a doctoral student in the History Department at Rutgers University, New Brunswick, New Jersey, where the influence of the outstanding historians, anthropologists, and literary critics on the faculty as well as my fellow graduate students shaped both it and me. A predissertation award from the Rutgers Graduate School supported my early research in the United Kingdom. I had the good fortune to work as an editorial assistant at the *Journal of the History of Ideas* under Donald R. Kelly, from whom I learned the true meaning of erudition. Carolyn Brown and Allen Howard were patient and generous guides through the richness and complexities of African histories and encouraged this interloper's efforts at every point along the way. Like the other graduate students who have had the privilege to learn from and with her, Joan W. Scott taught me to question the old shibboleths of the discipline of history, as well as the necessity and pleasures of unending critique. Peers such as Kris Alexanderson, Brian Connolly, Andrew Daily, Jennifer Miller, Sandrine Sanos, and Michal Shapira both challenged and sustained me. They continue to surprise and amaze me with their brilliance, and I beam with pride at each of their triumphs and eagerly await those to come. I wrote much of the dissertation as a graduate fellow at the Institute for Research on Women and Gender ("Diasporas and Migrations," 2005–2006) and the Center for Cultural Analysis ("Cultures of Circulation," 2006–2007). Their directors—Nancy Hewitt and Michael Warner, respectively—and the faculty and graduate fellows offered incisive comments and suggestions for refining my arguments and conceptual frameworks. Belinda Edmondson shared not only her considerable insights but also her own research on the Jamaican poet and playwright Una Marson, saving a cash-strapped graduate student untold time and money. My dissertation committee members—Bonnie G. Smith, Allen Howard, Temma Kaplan, and Brent Hayes Edwards—suffered through an overly long thesis and often multiple versions of the chapters therein, offering the ideal combination of encouragement and criticism. Most of all, I owe a tremendous debt of gratitude to my mentor Bonnie G. Smith. At our first meeting when I was a prospective student, she challenged me to venture into the "mean streets" of New Jersey, a life-changing provocation for which I will be eternally grateful. In the years thereafter, she regularly nourished my mind, body, and soul. Bonnie remains my guiding star, the model of what a scholar and person should be.

The participants in the 2007 seminar in modern British history at Columbia University, organized by Susan Pedersen and supported by the Andrew W. Mellon Foundation, helped me revise an early draft of chapter 1. Some of the material contained in chapter 6 was published in the article

"Colonial Subjects: Black Intellectuals and the Development of Colonial Studies in Britain," in the *Journal of British Studies* (April 2010). It and, by extension, the revised and expanded chapter included here benefited greatly from the feedback and suggestions of then-editor Anna Clark, her successor Elizabeth Elbourne, and the journal's anonymous readers. An offer to participate in the "Unconventional Wisdoms" conference at Newnham College, Cambridge University, in April 2009 provided the opportunity to reassess the interwar British Empire through the medium of imperial cinema and the social and political world of black London. A slightly expanded version of that paper appears in the collection *Brave New World: Imperial and Democratic Nation-Building in Britain between the Wars,* edited by Laura Beers and Geraint Thomas (London: Institute of Historical Research, 2012). That contribution in turn, became the germ of chapter 7.

Without the intrepid sleuthing and painstaking research of numerous, often underappreciated scholars and archivists in the United Kingdom and elsewhere, the lives and stories recounted in this book would have been beyond my reach. Gretchen Holbrook Gerzina's seminal *Black London: Life before Emancipation* illuminates the hitherto forgotten lives and labors of people of African descent who populated the city during the late eighteenth and early nineteenth centuries. This book echoes her powerful evocation of the diversity of black contributions to life in the imperial capital and contributes a later chapter in the history of black London. Marika Sherwood encouraged my efforts from the beginning, and this book stands on the shoulders of the foundational scholarship that she, Hakim Adi, Peter Fryer, Bill Schwarz, and Winston James have produced. LaRay Denzer, Alison Donnell, Delia Jarrett-Macauley, and many others have demonstrated that it is possible to tell different, more complex stories about black internationalism and anticolonialism through the lives, art, and activism of African and Afro-Caribbean women. Without their work, many of the details about such women that fill the following pages, especially chapter 3, would have remained beyond my grasp. Jeffrey Green, Paul Oliver, Val Wilmer, Stephen Bourne, and Andrew Simon have recovered, recorded, and archived the largely forgotten lives of the denizens of black London, as well as the music and art they generated. It would have been impossible to produce the account of the sounds and rhythms of black London without the direct assistance of the latter in particular. I would also like to thank the dedicated archivists and staff at the Schomburg Center for Research in Black Culture, New York Public Library, in Harlem; the School of Oriental and African Studies

Library, the British Library, and the National Archives in the United Kingdom; and the other unsung experts who made this work possible.

A constellation of friends and friendly spaces kept me going through recurrent moments of doubt and the book's multiple iterations. The rotating cast of our Tuesday group in New York, especially Isra Ali, Harper Gould, and Aaron Windel, injected warmth and laughter into my graduate-student years and taught me a great deal about the joys, challenges, and responsibilities of teaching. My former colleagues at Northern Arizona University, especially Scott Reese, Susan Deeds, Sanjam Ahluwalia, Sanjay Joshi, Eric Meeks, Leilah Danielson, and my first department chair, Cynthia Kosso, not only showed me the ropes but also opened their hearts and homes to me from the moment I arrived in Flagstaff. Our running conversations about scholarship and much else greatly enriched my thinking and my life. Their unflagging faith in me during my four years at NAU propelled my work, while their delicious cooking kept me well fed. The Intramural Grant Program and Dean of Arts and Humanities Michael Vincent provided summer funding to support my ongoing research and writing as the dissertation metamorphosed into a book manuscript. Most of the hard work of writing actually took place in coffee shops in multiple cities—Jersey City, New York City, London, Flagstaff, Santa Cruz, and San Francisco—and I also owe thanks to the legion of baristas and night owls of these haunts.

Since I joined the Department of History at the University of California, Santa Cruz, in 2012, I have had the great privilege and joy of working with and establishing friendships with some of the sharpest minds and some of the funnest people anywhere, including my fellow newcomers Jennifer Derr, Maya Peterson, and S. A. Smythe. A veritable supernova, Gail Hershatter has inspired and challenged me in more ways than she will ever know. Catherine A. Jones is a rare treasure, a person as kind and as humble as she is brilliant. With her typical mixture of generosity and acuity, she read and offered invaluable suggestions for revising the penultimate draft of the introduction. Mark Anderson in the Anthropology Department became not only my chief interlocutor on all things related to soul music but also something of a secondary editor who helped me pare down and focus the first two chapters of the book. The conveners of and participants in the "Sex and the Archive" workshop at UCSC in 2014, especially Mayanthi Fernando, Anjali Arondekar, Judith Surkis, Michael Allan, and Gina Dent, were incredibly generous in providing thoughtful critiques and practical guidance for final revisions to chapter 5.

My hardworking editors at the University of California Press, Niels Hooper, Kim Hogeland, Bradley Depew, and Steven Baker shepherded this work through the long publication process with undeserved care and patience. Niels also secured the two best readers an author could hope for, and I want to thank Antoinette Burton and Minkah Makalani for wading through the unwieldy manuscript and for offering insightful and detailed suggestions for revisions that enabled me to improve the final product immensely.

My family has supported me throughout these journeys and my transformation from a boy growing up in the mountains of western North Carolina to a wandering graduate student and then professor. Both of my grandfathers valued education and instilled in me a deep appreciation of the importance of teachers to our world. One of them, Vincent Matera, for whom learning was a lifelong pursuit, first exposed me to a university campus, and in a sense, I've never left. I cling to the hope that my meager efforts will make them proud. From the women in my family, I learned that women make the world go round long before I began my engagement with feminist theory and histories and, from my grandmother Dorothy Matera, that there is nothing wrong with being a "freak" of the family. Although I will never be as strong as my grandmothers, mother, or sister, I will never cease trying to be. Most of all, I want to thank my parents, Mike and Charlene, and my dear sister, Michelle. They taught me to trust my intellect and to follow my convictions even if they did not share them. This book is dedicated to you for standing by me especially when, as I suspect was (and is) often the case, you did not understand me. Finally, Zoe Whitehouse has given me more than words can capture. She has been my toughest reader and my biggest champion, my inadvertent coauthor and partner in crime.

ABBREVIATIONS

APU	African Progress Union
ARPS	Aborigines' Rights Protection Society (Ghana)
ASAPS	Anti-Slavery and Aborigines' Protection Society
ACAE	American Council for African Education
BCL	British Commonwealth League
CFU	Colonial Film Unit
CSA	Colonial Seamen's Association
CWAE	Committee for the Welfare of Africans in Europe
CPGB	Communist Party of Great Britain
CAA	Council on African Affairs
FCB	Fabian Colonial Bureau
HMV	His Master's Voice
IAFE	International African Friends of Ethiopia
IAWSEC	International Alliance of Women for Suffrage and Equal Citizenship
ILP	Independent Labour Party
KCA	Kikuyu Central Association
KUTVU	Communist University of the Toilers of the East
LAI	League Against Imperialism
LCP	League of Coloured Peoples
LSE	London School of Economics

NCBWA	National Congress of British West Africa
NCCL	National Council of Civil Liberties
NWA	Negro Welfare Association
NWL	Nigerian Women's League
SLWM	Sierra Leone Women's Movement
SOAS	School of Oriental and African Studies
UCL	University College of London
UCWI	University College of the West Indies
UNIA	Universal Negro Improvement Association
USAD	Union of Students of African Descent
WANS	West African National Secretariat
WAS	West African Society
WASU	West African Students' Union
WAYL	West African Youth League
WINC	West Indian National Council
WISU	West Indian Students' Union
WSF	Workers' Social Federation

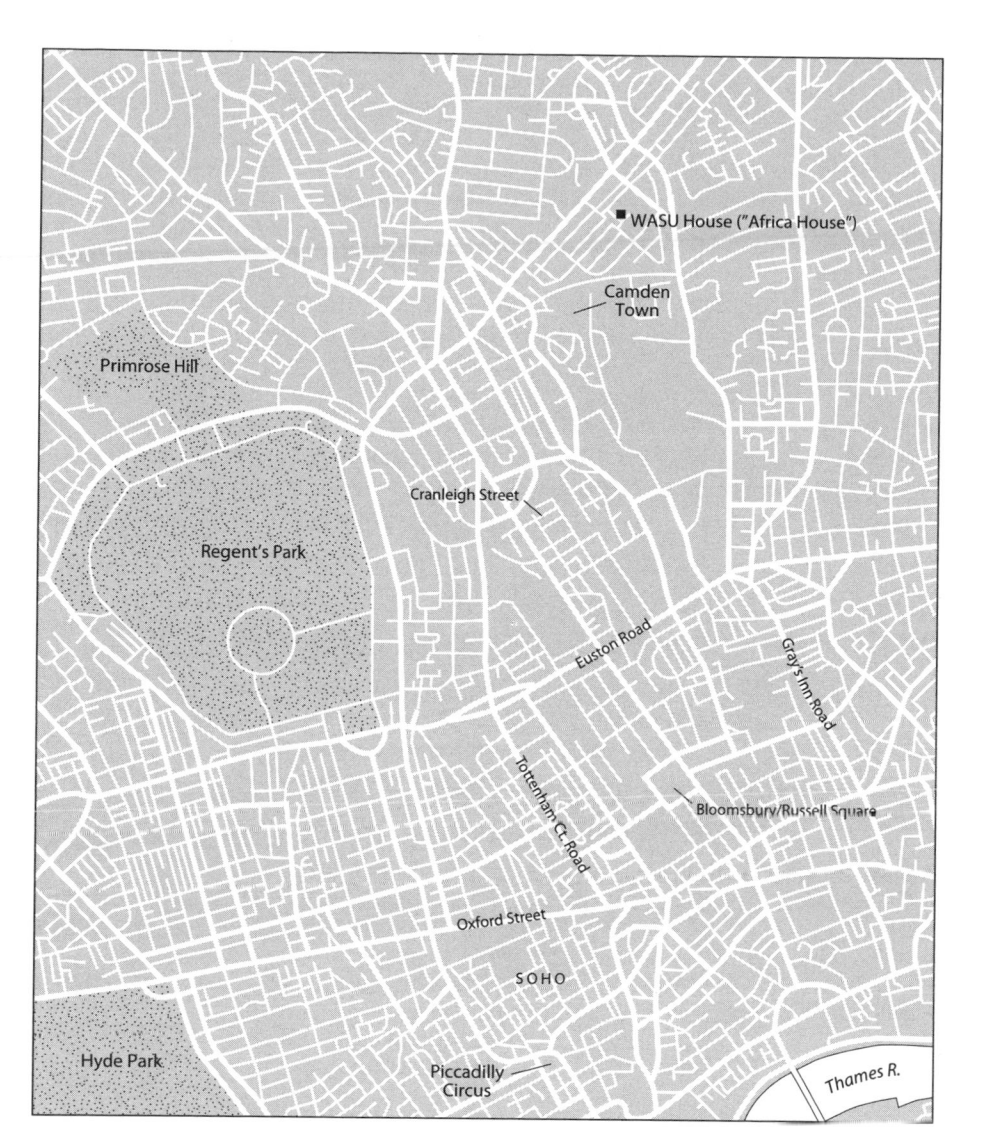

Spaces of Black London. Map by William L. Nelson.

Introduction

THE IMPERIAL AND ATLANTIC
HORIZONS OF BLACK LONDON

THE UBIQUITOUS PRESENCE OF AFRICA in 1930s London, especially when compared to the United States, astounded Eslanda Goode Robeson, the wife of the African American singer and movie star Paul Robeson: "There is news of Africa everywhere: in the press, in the schools, in the films, in conversation. English people are actively interested in Africa economically and politically."[1] Her observation is incongruous with historians' associations of interwar colonial troubles and metropolitan anxieties with Ireland and India. Her narrative of life in London also contradicts most narratives of the rise of multiethnic Britain, which trace the presence of people of African descent to migration in the decades after World War II. The early twentieth century witnessed a sustained, if much more limited, influx of Africans and Afro-Caribbeans into Britain. Goode Robeson pointed to Africa's presence in domestic imperial culture—in schoolbooks and newspapers, on the radio and the big screen. The Robesons soon discovered a different "Africa" in London, one whose rhythms and modes of expression overlapped with but also exceeded the "dark continent" of the imperial imagination, an Africa that hailed and challenged them in unexpected, life-altering ways.

This book is the story of the intellectual, cultural, and social worlds of black London during the three decades after World War I. It is equally a story of the ideas and political projects those worlds generated. *Black London* examines the efforts of people of African descent to organize across colonial boundaries against racism and empire, as well as the many cultural and intellectual expressions of this desire and will to unity. It does so by tracking black Londoners in three-dimensional space and reconstructs a set of diverse but interconnected sites of intellectual and cultural production in the imperial metropolis. The texture of daily interaction and the organization of social relations within these sites, as well as the affective investments they engendered, molded the art, scholarship, and politics of black sojourners and migrants.

During this period, the administrative center and capital of the British Empire became a locus of resistance to empire. It served as a meeting point of intellectuals, artists, revolutionaries, and movements for colonial freedom. There, people from diverse colonial settings exchanged ideas and devised plans for a transformed global order in private homes, clubs and political organizations, universities, and bars. Some of these individuals returned to Africa or the Caribbean to become leaders of incipient independence movements and postcolonial nations. Their sojourns in London had a transformative impact on their intellectual and political development and helped propel some of them to prominence. Many more produced works of scholarship, literature, and music of enduring relevance. Others were more in the way of organizers of ideas and action among London's small black community of student sojourners, professionals, artists, and agitators. The city functioned as both facilitator and provocateur, providing the context and "the resources for the creation of a rich array of subaltern networks of the colonised" and "an effervescently hybrid political culture."[2] The prevalent racism in the metropole and the conversations, alliances, and boundary crossings that it made possible, as well as the tensions and conflicts such encounters produced, influenced the changing political commitments and personal identifications of Africans and Afro-Caribbeans. As the South African writer Peter Abrahams later recalled, "London was the critical point of contact where Pan-African, socialist and anti-colonial ideas were shared and enlarged." Intellectuals and activists from the colonies "shared classes, meals, parties," and much more, and in the process, they "got to know each other and each other's problems intimately and personally." Quotidian encounters and activities yielded capacious political imaginaries and rerouted lives. "Only in England," C. L. R. James wrote, "did I learn to break through the inherited constraints of my environment."[3] This book examines black cultural and intellectual production that emerged from the social geography of black London and the imperial and transatlantic networks that shaped the contours of that geography. The city provided the material conditions for organizing people of African descent into a transnational force in the making of a world after empire.

Reconstructing the rich social and intellectual world of black London challenges long-standing characterizations of black nationalism as a movement of national self-determination. In practice, a more nuanced political vision emerged from the complex range of possibilities for affiliation and sovereignty that empire unwittingly propagated. Most studies continue to reduce the political imaginaries and struggles produced during the twilight of European imperialism to a nationalist teleology, reducing black internationalism after World War I to a Wilsonian rhetoric of self-determination, "a profound investment in the ideal of racial sovereignty," and "black freedom grounded in and embodied by a vision of the independent black state." The political possibilities envisioned by black intellectuals and activists in late imperial London challenge this conflation of resistance to imperialism with the pursuit of independent nation-states and force us to rethink "the symmetry between nationality and citizenship" and "the scale and composition of political terrains, public spheres, discursive communities, and intellectual fields."[4] Up to the 1950s, black intellectuals and activists in London maneuvered and articulated their demands in a world of empires in which *sovereignty* was a relative term, and within the political and conceptual framework of the British Empire, in particular. Empires incessantly managed, manipulated, and reproduced difference on multiple levels, but they did so within the context of a larger unity. The British imperial polity constituted a highly differentiated series of discontinuous structures and spaces as well as an interconnected "unit of political and ethical debate." Negotiation between colonizers and the colonized centered not only on the meaning and implications of differences among cultures and bodies but also the application of ostensibly universalizing discourses—of citizenship, self-government, and development, to name only a few. In taking up these categories and the practices of liberal citizenship, black critics of the empire changed their meaning.[5] As Kevin Grant, Philippa Levine, and Frank Trentmann observe, empires "not only produced struggles for racial equality and, ultimately, independence from colonial rule," but were also "sites of social and political movements that developed critiques of national sovereignty and explored transnational identities of citizenship and belonging."[6] However, very little of the recent scholarship associated with the so-called new imperial, international, and global histories considers the networks forged or traveled by colonial subjects. A perspective that assumes the fundamental Britishness of the British Empire, treating it as a projection of national culture, and that slots all anticolonial critiques of it into the nationalist plot occludes whole realms of political imagination and struggle.

The majority of Africans and Caribbeans in London sought a radical transcending of the empire, not a complete severing of ties with it. The shifting rationales for the British Empire and what Mrinalini Sinha describes as the global "restructuring of the interwar imperial social formation" informed their political goals and their conceptions of what black liberation might entail in an increasingly interdependent world.[7] The 1931 Statute of Westminster, which ratified the principles outlined in the Balfour Declaration at the 1926 Imperial Conference, codified the legislative independence of the self-governing dominions. In bifurcating the polity into the Commonwealth of Nations with legislative equality and an empire of colonial dependencies and protectorates, the act effectively institutionalized the color bar at the imperial level at a time when fears of "a rising tide of color" and "race war" abounded.[8] The law also reaffirmed responsible self-government and dominion status as goals for non-European colonial subjects. In the eyes of most Africans and Afro-Caribbeans, the road ahead required, not a Manichean choice between remaining subjugated colonies or becoming independent nation-states, but navigating the tension between national/racial chauvinism—which fueled expansionist ambitions whether in liberal democratic or fascist guise—and the necessity of international organization and cultural exchange. Africans and Caribbeans in London demanded a meaningful form of imperial citizenship, internal self-government, federation at the regional level, and democratic, mutually beneficial relations at the level of the empire-cum-commonwealth as a whole. They endeavored, in Gary Wilder's words, "to institute forms of *non-national* colonial emancipation"; they leave us with "histories of colonial overcoming" that were also "histories of negotiation with colonial modernity" and visions of alternative "futures that were once imagined but never came to be."[9]

Black London demonstrates that the imperial metropolis was also a site of African diasporic formation, intellectual production, and political organizing where the larger context of empire represented the generative common ground for African and Afro-Caribbean intellectuals' and artists' imaginings of a global black community. Many Caribbean and African men and women came to see themselves as "black intellectuals" and devoted their energies to fostering greater cooperation between people of African descent around the globe. As Winston James suggests, "The story of the black experience in twentieth-century Britain . . . is one . . . of Jamaicans, Barbadians, and other Caribbeans along with Ghanaians, Nigerians, and other continental Africans—meeting one another"; "of tensions as well as self-identifications and solidarities formed among these groups"; "of Guyanese and Kenyans not only becoming Caribbeans and Africans, respectively, but also their embrac-

ing more expansive and inclusive identifications as 'Negro' and 'black.'"[10]
London was not only the hub of very powerful imperial structures and networks enabling and regulating the circulation of people, ideas, and wealth,
but also a node in cross-cutting conversations among people of African
descent. The burgeoning literatures on the African diaspora and the "black
Atlantic," a term coined by Robert Farris Thompson and popularized by Paul
Gilroy, highlight the rhizome, or web of networks, formed by ongoing interactions between communities of African descent across political boundaries
and oceanic space during the nineteenth and twentieth centuries.[11] Too
often, however, studies of the black Atlantic and African diaspora fail to pay
adequate attention to the continuing participation of Africans or to the
effects of late-nineteenth- and twentieth-century colonization in Africa. As
J. Lorand Matory argues, "The 19th- to 21st-century dialogue among the mas-
sive urban black populations of the Atlantic perimeter has ... done as much
to constitute the Africanity and the creativity of these populations as has any
ancestral African or plantation culture." Matory and others have shown how
transatlantic religious connections and intellectual exchange yielded extra-
territorial notions of African "nations" and nationalities on both sides of the
Atlantic.[12] Between the 1920s and 1940s, West Africans, especially Nigerians,
in London further elaborated the conception of Yorùbá identity that developed in these exchanges. It became one among several touchstones of an
expansive understanding of the horizons of West African history that animated their demand for a self-governing regional federation within the
empire. West African intellectuals and artists traced a deep history of African
cultural unity from the ancient intracontinental migrations to the more
recent effects of the slave trade and post-abolition patterns of return and
resettlement that gave rise to the Krio and other creole communities in
Freetown, Sierra Leone, and Lagos, Nigeria, and to the ongoing circulation
of people and ideas under colonial rule.

Africans and Afro-Caribbeans thought and acted as participants in two
different extranational "affective communities": as aspirational imperial citizens within the juridical and political space of the British imperium, and as
members of a transimperial collectivity of people of African descent.[13] Black
university students, professionals, artists, and activists established a number
of organizations and publications, which are the primary focus of chapters 1
and 2. Through them, Africans and Afro-Caribbeans pressured British colonial officials, politicians, and others interested in Africa and the colonies,
contributing to the major fluctuations in colonial policy and the development

of colonial studies during the empire's final decades. While serving as new means of voicing social commentary and political dissent, black organizations also became homes away from home and centers of cultural and intellectual exchange, facilitating the circulation of ideas and news around the Atlantic and throughout the British Empire. As British power in Africa reached its precarious apex after the First World War, black intellectuals and activists in these groups resituated Africa and the Caribbean at the forefront of a worldwide trend toward cultural hybridity and internationalism in their scholarship, art, and political protest. Shunning narrowly racial or nationalist conceptions of community as dangerous illusions, intellectuals and cultural producers of African descent articulated theories of internationalism based on centuries of cultural exchange, encompassing the Atlantic slave trade and British colonialism in Africa and the Caribbean, and claimed that the cumulative weight of this history prepared them collectively to assume the lead in bringing about a radically transformed global order.

THE TOPOGRAPHY OF BLACK LONDON

This book presents a history of black politics as it emerged in multiple spheres and from an array of intellectual and cultural sources in London; as such, it is an intellectual history grounded in social relationships and spaces. It lingers on and moves among particular centers of interaction across colonial boundaries and the personal relationships formed in them. African and Afro-Caribbean intellectuals considered a more variegated range of political possibilities as the context of their daily lives came to include different groups and different formations of blackness. Ideas, practices, and cultural forms were domesticated, transformed, and produced within patterns of daily interaction and the defined spaces where it occurred. The cumulative effect of encounters among people of African descent shaped the perceived horizons of political struggles, scholarship, and art. Far from simply responding to British caprice, black thinkers, artists, and agitators elaborated a sense of interiority and an expansive conception of Africanity built out of their own public spaces, cultural resources, and networks of sociality. As Bill Schwarz notes, "Uneven though the geographical existence of the black metropolis was, it possessed both a reality and a powerful symbolic register."[14] To appreciate the reach, evolution, and limits of their intellectual and political imagination requires careful attention to where these intellectuals lived, ate, danced, debated, studied, and loved in the metropolis—in sum, to the "political and affective consequences of social embeddedness."[15]

London, Liverpool, Manchester, Bristol, South Shields, Glasgow, and Cardiff are home to Britain's oldest black communities, in some cases dating back several centuries.[16] In the port cities, the development of a largely working-class black presence was tied to the British shipping industry. Small pockets of university students and professionals from Africa and the Caribbean also formed in places like Oxford, Cambridge, Newcastle, and Edinburgh beginning in the nineteenth century. For an array of reasons, the majority of migrants and sojourners increasingly gravitated to London in the twentieth century. Notting Hill/Ladbroke Grove and Brixton in west and south London, respectively, became centers of black settlement during the unprecedented migration that followed World War II, and even today serve as metonyms for the Afro-Caribbean presence in particular.

During the quarter century before the war, however, many newcomers of African descent made Camden Town and surrounding areas in north and central London their "home." The appellation *Camden Town* entered common parlance in the years preceding the First World War in connection with a cohort of post-Impressionist artists known as the Camden Town Group. Today, the neighborhood is probably best known for its sprawling markets and as the former stomping grounds of the now-deceased singer Amy Winehouse, its history as a base of black life and politics largely forgotten. Unlike the later pockets of predominately, though hardly exclusively, Afro-Caribbean settlement, this social world in Camden Town was built by West Africans, especially Nigerians. In a 1998 photo-essay, Lola Young juxtaposes contemporary real estate ads for properties in the north London neighborhoods of Camden Town and Primrose Hill with Femi Franklin's personal photographs of family and friends from the 1940s, which chronicle and pay homage to the area's small, close-knit Nigerian community. As Franklin explained in 1991, during the early 1940s, "I cycled from Trinity College Cambridge to Camden Town at weekends to meet the Nigerians. They were eating and making merry." "They continue to do so till today," he added, "except that only a few are left in Camden Town, the single rooms are now beyond means."[17] For many Africans and Afro-Caribbeans, the area was a center of their social and private lives during the 1930s and 1940s. The headquarters and hostel of the West African Students' Union—first established at 62 Camden Road in early 1933 and, from 1938, located at 1 South Villas, Camden Square—played no small part in drawing them to the neighborhood. Scores of new arrivals spent their first nights in the city at the WASU hostel, the most enduring black institution in the city. Most moved to more permanent residences, usually in close proximity to friends or bases of activity such as the union. Many more spent their Saturday nights at its dances.

When the Trinidadian radical George Padmore first settled in London mid-decade, he stayed with Jomo Kenyatta on Vauxhall Bridge Road before moving to Guilford Street just off Russell Square. Kenyatta, who would become the first prime minister and then president of Kenya after independence, first traveled to London in 1929 under the name Johnstone to deliver a protest petition on behalf of the Kikuyu Central Association to the Colonial Office. He returned to Kenya in September 1930, only to begin a fifteen-year sojourn in the metropole the following year. He traveled across Europe to Moscow twice, meeting Padmore along the way, and attended the Comintern's school the University of the Toilers of the East (KUTVU). During his years in London, Kenyatta mingled with West Africans, Afro-Caribbeans, and African Americans and participated in multiple black organizations and in the agitation in defense of the Scottsboro Boys in the United States and Ethiopia. He published in black and left-wing journals, trained with and advised or translated for anthropologists at the London School of Economics, and produced an ethnography of the Kikuyu, *Facing Mount Kenya*. During this same period in the mid-1930s, he appeared alongside Paul Robeson in the interwar years' most popular empire film, *Sanders of the River*. Though in the minority as an East African, Kenyatta's trajectory through and activities in the imperial metropolis resembled those of the Afro-Caribbeans and West Africans who formed his closest associates. In the late 1930s, Padmore and his partner Dorothy Pizer moved to Cranleigh Street behind Euston Station, where Kenyatta spent many evenings. The couple regularly entertained black agitators, artists, intellectuals, and trade unionists for nearly two decades, including the young Trinidadian historian Eric Williams, who lived with his first wife, Elsie, on King Henry's Road in South Hampstead while completing his Ph.D. thesis in 1937.

In the mid-1940s, the self-named "Primrose gang," which consisted of Nana Joseph Emmanuel Appiah and several other West African radicals mainly from the Gold Coast, shared a residence at 37 Primrose Gardens. The Barbadian communist Peter Blackman lived a half-mile south at 3 Primrose Hill Road, and the South African novelist Peter Abrahams around the corner from him at 98 King Henry's Road. Further to the north, the Ghanaian intellectual K. A. B. Jones-Quartey resided at 25 Laurier Road adjacent to

Parliament Hill. When Kwame Nkrumah came to London from the United States at the end of World War II, this densely clustered group of black agitators and thinkers guided his entry into life in the city. He initially stayed at the WASU's Africa House and spent much of his time at either Padmore's flat or Primrose Hill. He eventually found more permanent accommodations with Ako Adjei, a fellow Ghanaian whom he knew from his time as a student in the United States, at 60 Burghley Road in Kentish Town. The choice of location was no accident; the one-room apartment lay equidistant to the WASU, the Primrose gang, and Padmore's flat, about a half-mile from all three. "Although the room was smallish and the house was without a bath," Appiah recalled. "Kwame could take his daily baths, his meals and haircuts at Primrose Gardens, where he could also hold discussions with Kankam Boadu, Bankole Akpata and myself far into the night and to his heart's content."[18] When they were not busy plotting the downfall of British colonialism in Africa, the "gang" often hosted racially mixed parties where guests mingled and danced through the night to the sounds of the African diaspora on gramophone records. Nkrumah's part in the creation of Ghana began in the black organizations and their informal adjuncts of the imperial metropolis.

During the Jazz Age, images of "savage" Africa increasingly jostled for cultural ground and consumers' attention with sounds and performances of modern blackness from across the Atlantic. Music, in particular, supplied an alternative "arena of Black Atlantic intellectualization," providing resources for novel conceptions of association and new political imaginaries, and a number of black musicians and their families settled in north London as well.[19] The black Welsh guitarist Francis Antonio (Frank) Deniz began his career as a professional musician with the Sid Clements Society Band in his hometown of Cardiff during the mid-1930s. He soon developed a love of jazz, and "people would say 'if you want to play that you've got to go to London.'" Soon after they married, he and his wife, Clare, a pianist whom he met while she was playing with his brother at a local club, did precisely that. The Nigerian composer, organist, and longtime WASU member Fela Sowande and his wife eventually convinced the couple to move to Camden Town to be closer to them. Fela and Frank had worked together in New York City, and Sowande's wife, who came to Britain as a member of the choir in the musical *Blackbirds* but returned to the United States at the start of the Second World War, tutored Clare in jazz piano. The Nigerian drummer and dancer Billy Olu Sholanke's address at 18 Eton Road, a block from Primrose

Hill Road, appears in Nkrumah's diary, which colonial officials confiscated when he returned to the Gold Coast.[20] In the 1940s, the Nigerian innovator Oladipupo "Ambrose" Adekoya Campbell, whose band, the West African Rhythm Brothers, supplied the entertainment for many WASU events, lived in a flat in St. Pancras. Campbell's friend and bandmate Brewster Hughes (Ignatius Abiodun Oke) settled in Camden Town at the end of World War II. If the city's growing music scene was the primary draw for musicians, their ties to other members of London's black community, along with factors such as cost and the willingness of landlords to rent to people of color, guided their choice of residence in the city.

Heading south across Euston Road, a number of a black musicians and club owners lived in Bloomsbury and on or near Tottenham Court Road, while many African and Afro-Caribbean students attended the area's institutions of higher education. The former often worked in or ran establishments in Soho farther to the south, where the latter flocked to relax, socialize, and dance to jazz, rumba, calypso, and early West African highlife. Students from Africa and the Caribbean enrolled at universities across England and Scotland, but the majority studied at one of the cluster of schools that constitute the University of London. African, Afro-Caribbean, and African American students and scholars attended the seminars of eminent anthropologists, historians, and political scientists at the London School of Economics and lectures at the International Institute of African Languages and Cultures alongside students from South and East Asia, colonial service personnel, and budding Africanists. As chapter 6 demonstrates, the struggle for recognition within the university, especially in the fields of social anthropology and imperial history, became part of the battle against imperialism. Black scholars wrote within and against colonial historiography, positioning themselves among an expanding body of colonial "experts" both within and outside academia, while exposing the linkages between the racial foundations of British colonialism and knowledge production in the metropole. The university also served as an important site of black intellectual exchange, and black organizations regularly circulated the work of fellow black intellectuals and cited it in their memoranda and letters of protest to the Colonial Office, British politicians, and the press. Their publications served as outlets for politically engaged scholarship as well as mouthpieces of anticolonialism and an emerging black internationalist perspective.

Outside the university, black students and intellectuals congregated at Bloomsbury cafés and pubs or at the Student Movement House at 32 Russell

Square. A few, such as the Kenyan Peter Mbiyu Koinange (born Koinange Wa Mbiyu), were boarders at the latter. A goodly number of other black and South Asian students, including the first female barrister in West Africa, Stella Thomas, and several black musicians lived in private apartments in the area as well. In the late 1920s, one of the first West Africans to record in Britain, Roland C. Nathaniels, lived on Russell Square. The Jamaican jazz musician Leslie Thompson had an apartment nearby on Marchmont Street. The daily movements of these black Londoners linked the seminar rooms and literary salons of Bloomsbury to the more democratic and volatile black dance clubs of Soho a few blocks away. Musicians from Africa often supplemented their incomes with work as translators for university faculty and researchers.

The music of black Atlantic cultures, jazz above all, emanated from the shabbier and more diverse spaces of Soho as nowhere else in Britain. Consisting of the area below Oxford Street wedged between Tottenham Court Road/Charing Cross Road at its eastern terminus and Regent Street to the west, Soho was home to successive waves of immigrants and, in the early twentieth century, a louche nightlife scene. The singer and multi-instrumentalist Augustus Kwamlah Quaye was a true product of Soho and, performing and recording under the name Cab Kaye, one of the most recognizable figures in British jazz during the 1940s and 1950s. He was born in the small enclave of black entertainers on St. Giles High Street, just east of Soho, in 1921. His mother, Doris Balderson, was a music hall singer; his father, Caleb Jonas Kwamlah Quaye, was a drummer from the Gold Coast known professionally as Mope Desmond; and his paternal grandfather had been a church organist in Accra. Desmond played with such African American jazz greats as the clarinetist Sidney Bechet but died in a rail accident when his son was only four months old, forcing the family to relocate to Portsmouth. By the age of fourteen, Kaye was frequenting black nightclubs in Soho such as the Shim Sham and the Nest, where he met the African American trombonist Ellis Jackson, the first black musician to gain a permanent spot in a high-society band in Britain as a member of Billy Cotton's band. Jackson convinced Cotton to add Kaye as a singer and dancer. In the following years, Kaye performed with some of the era's most popular white bands and is credited with breaking the color bar at the Paramount Dance Hall on Tottenham Court Road by refusing to play after a black patron was denied entry. However, he increasingly sought the company of other black musicians. He briefly joined Ken "Snakehips" Johnson's band, Britain's premier all-black orchestra, at the Café de Paris during the early years of the Second World War. Kaye enlisted in the merchant navy three days before a German bomb claimed the lives of Johnson and bandmate David "Baba" Williams at the club. While on leave, he had a brief stint with Don Marino Barreto's Cuban band in London. In a series of calamities that befell him in 1942, he was torpedoed at sea, then survived a plane crash. While convalescing in New York, he encountered trailblazers of improvisational modern jazz such as the trumpeter Roy Eldridge. In 1946, Kaye joined Leslie "Jiver" Hutchinson's all-black band on a government-sponsored tour for armed forces in Egypt and India and then spent much of the late 1940s and 1950s in France, Belgium, and the Netherlands. As London's black population swelled during the mid-1950s, he returned to Soho. Settling in East Finchley for a decade, he performed and recorded with a number of Afro-Caribbean musicians, including the trumpeter Dave Wilkins, the saxophonist George Tyndale, and the singer Mona Baptiste, and led his own "All-Coloured Band" at the Fabulous Feldman Club at 100 Oxford Street. From 1961 until the coup that brought down Kwame Nkrumah, Kaye served as Ghana's entertainments officer, working by day and playing in Soho's jazz clubs at night. In private, he reverted to his Ga name, Nii-lante, and began wearing kente cloth, and he added highlife music to his performance repertoire. In the early 1960s, Ghana's most popular highlife band, the Ramblers Dance Band, covered his song "Beautiful Ghana" under the new title "Work and Happiness" for the Decca recording company, and it became a staple of the Nkrumah government's "Work and Happiness" events and radio broadcasts. To the end of his life, he believed in Nkrumah's vision of a united Africa. Kaye's public career, his musical influences and output, and his changing sense of self encapsulate black Soho's mix of diverse musical forms and pan-African political visions and its links to points across the Afro-Atlantic world.[21]

Inside the clubs of Soho, black agitators and students danced and chatted alongside bohemian artists, homosexuals, prostitutes, gamblers, and internationalists of various types, while black musicians sweated out the vernacular sounds of African America, the Caribbean, and West Africa. These usually modest establishments assumed unique significance for performers and patrons of African descent as sanctuaries from white hostility and, in some cases, as sites of political organizing. In them, musicians, listeners, and dancers produced sonorous and embodied performances of the black international, and circular breathing complemented and, at times, competed with the circulation of written texts. Chapter 4 traces musicians' networks and enters into these spaces of black sociability and musical innovation and consumption. It presents a history of listening in black London, the global entanglements that shaped musical life-worlds, and the political imaginaries that emerged, in part, from these soundscapes. The Soho–Camden Town axis oriented the daily routines of many black intellectuals, artists, and agitators; the clustered points of convergence along and around it facilitated pan-African connections, the development of a sense of common political purpose, and survival in a harsh setting.

Part intellectual history, part sociocultural history, and part prosopography, this book follows black men and women primarily but not exclusively from Africa and the Caribbean through the private rooms and public squares, streets and estuaries, of black London, where black intellectuals, activists, and artists met and confronted their differences. It emphasizes the imperial metropolis's history as a site of black cultural and intellectual production and illuminates the social relations and spaces that generated this work and precarious political solidarities, from the WASU's Africa House to Soho's nightclubs and, finally, the set of an imperialist film where the Robesons met Kenyatta and many other Africans and Afro-Caribbeans.

BLACK INTERNATIONALISM AND
THE IMPERIAL METROPOLIS

In *International Government* (1916), the socialist and former colonial servant in Ceylon (Sri Lanka) Leonard Woolf cited the growth of international organizations as a significant feature of the modern world. A resurgence and proliferation of internationalisms occurred across the political spectrum and around the world in the wake of the Great War. Socialist and communist internationalisms developed alongside and in tension with liberal capitalist and imperialist forms. The new League of Nations and its various programs, from the mandate system to the Committee on Intellectual Cooperation across national boundaries, institutionalized aspects of both of the latter varieties. The dangers of nationalism and imperial rivalries and the challenge presented by "racial" or "cultural" differences, used virtually as synonyms at the time, preoccupied advocates of international organization of all stripes. In the years before the war, a number of "international" or "world" congresses, including the 1911 Universal Races Congress in London, took up these issues, but, as Akira Iriye notes, "before World War I few in Europe or North America developed a conception of global internationalism, embracing different races and peoples."[22] Such a conception began to emerge, if only slowly and through the initiative of non-European thinkers and activists, during and after the Paris Peace Conference. Most radically, the Communist International (or Comintern) declared its commitment to the liberation of people of African descent and colonial peoples at its founding in 1919, sponsored a number of conferences directly or through affiliated groups like the League Against Imperialism, and brought African Americans, Asians, and anticolonial activists to Moscow to study and exchange ideas.

Imperialism also assumed an increasingly internationalist guise during the interwar period, in part because of the new communist challenge, the spread of fascism, and with it, the reemergence of virulent nationalisms and territorial aggrandizement. In bringing different races and cultures together within a political structure, however unequal, empire represented a type of internationalism by another name. Many British internationalists looked upon their empire as a model and building block for greater international organization. As early as 1905, John Coatman, the chair of imperial economic relations at the University of London, suggested "that the political theory which is based on the sovereign nation-state as the natural and inevitable political unit must be thought out again ... and rewritten," and contended that "the British Commonwealth is a microcosm ... of the world community of the future."[23] Following the peace settlement, "new internationalists" disaggregated the nation-state and argued that its component terms represented "different types of community and identity: social ethnic identity (the nation) versus political rights and allegiance (the state)." In a Foreign Office memorandum from 1918, the classical historian and liberal internationalist Alfred Zimmern advocated an international organization that would "ultimately resemble less a centrally organized bureaucracy and more a loosely associated version of the existing British Commonwealth." Far from abandoning the framework and practices of empire, as Frank Trentmann remarks, this "new global vision of coordination was often seen as a global extension, even a historical culmination of the British Empire." Conservative advocates of "Greater Britain" such as Leo Amery, who served as colonial secretary from 1924 to 1929, pressed for empire-strengthening initiatives to bind Britain and the empire, especially the dominions and white-settler colonies, more closely together. He maintained that the "process through which the loyalties of individuals and states within the empire were expanded to encompass the national loyalties of each nation as well as a wider loyalty to the empire as a whole could be replicated in ways that would promote world harmony." Between the wars, imperial Britain and France mobilized new global communications technologies and staged their largest imperial exhibitions, spectacles celebrating vast multiracial empires that, in turn, became the occasion for shadow gatherings of colonial peoples. Internationalist causes and organizations also attracted mass participation among an imperial public. The British Commonwealth League, League of Nations Union, Anti-slavery and Aborigines Protection Society, and internationalist feminist and pacifist groups held rallies and conferences and spawned international petition movements and local branches throughout the empire. These groups attracted non-European colonial subjects to varying degrees and sometimes became avenues of anticolonial dissent, but nearly all of them advocated an internationalized, coordinated form of colonial administration or interimperialism in the face of the predations of white-settler communities within the empire and outside imperial rivals.[24]

Colonial dissidents and opponents of empire and white supremacy also internationalized their efforts between the world wars.[25] Though dominated by African Americans and Afro-Caribbeans in the United States, both the Pan-African Congresses led by W. E. B. Du Bois and Marcus Garvey's much larger Universal Negro Improvement Association depended on and extended migratory patterns and channels of communication among people of African descent.[26] These well-studied movements constituted only the tip of an iceberg. In his 1962 essay on the diversity of pan-Africanisms in the early twentieth century, George Shepperson urged historians to situate them within, and to examine the intermingling of, a larger field of internationalisms, including the rise of regional, ethnic, and religious movements (from pan-German and pan-Slavic movements to pan-Islamism, pan-Arabism, and pan-Asianism); federalism (as exemplified by the United States); and "the appearance of multi national states often out of European colonialism" like the British Commonwealth of Nations and the French Union. The events of the 1930s, especially the Italian invasion of Ethiopia and unrest in colonial Africa and the Caribbean, centered Africa as a crucial pivot of the global imperial order, creating new openings for black interventions in metropolitan debates about internationalism and colonial reform, particularly on the left. Brent Hayes Edwards and Minkah Makalani have shown how African Americans, Afro-Caribbeans, and Africans in interwar Paris, Harlem, and, to a lesser extent, London envisioned a "'Black International,' an explicitly anticapitalist alliance of peoples of African descent from different countries around the world." They call attention to "the ways that expression was molded through attempts to appropriate and transform the discourses of internationalism" that predominated during the period: "the discourse of international civil society as embodied in the League of Nations, the counter-universalism of proletarian revolution envisioned by the Communist International, and the globe-carving discourse of European colonialism." The majority of extant work focuses on networks of black male intellectuals, workers, and revolutionaries; male-dominated black organizations and institutions; or black activism within the international communist movement. Moving beyond these confines, Lara Putnam reconstructs the circuits of the "circum-Caribbean migratory sphere" and the flowering of more eclectic expressions of black internationalism in popular culture in response to "emerging populisms," "international mobility control," and "an unprecedented crisis of empire itself."[27] As the main exponents of antifascism shelved the issue of colonial freedom or openly defended the empire by distinguishing British and French colonialism from the Nazi racial politics in the 1930s, black intellectuals and activists in London and elsewhere attempted to forge an anti-imperialist cultural front, one in which collaboration and shared struggle among disparate communities of African descent constituted part of a broad anti-imperialist movement encompassing and linking Britain's colonies in Africa and the Caribbean and, ultimately, other colonial and semicolonial populations.

Whereas black nationalists focused on organizing around race either to co-opt existing political structures or to build new ones to exercise collective sovereignty, black internationalists directed their efforts at the global color line, necessitating a radical overhaul of the structures of white supremacy on a supranational scale and of prevailing understandings of sovereignty. "At the core of black internationalism," as Michael O. West, William G. Martin, and Fanon Che Wilkins put it, "is the ideal of universal emancipation, unbounded by national, imperial, continental, or oceanic boundaries—or even by racial ones." In practice, like imperialism and nationalism (or internationalism), black nationalism and internationalism were not mutually exclusive. Indeed, as Edwards observes, "for most of the anticolonial activists . . . who worked in the metropole in the post–World War I period, nationalism only arose as a discourse contiguous with the heady and ambitious *inter*nationalisms of the time."[28] The thinking and aspirations of African and Afro-Caribbean intellectuals and activists in London developed in conversation with a wide array of internationalist movements and institutions—liberal, socialist, communist, Christian, feminist, and imperialist in their orientation—offering models of extranational community. They collaborated with potential British allies and drew on the ideas and precedents of Irish, Indian, and Egyptian nationalists and, above all, African Americans. Their articulations of black internationalism were complex amalgams of regional and colony-level mobilizations mediated by crosscurrents of internationalism and transatlantic black organization and formed in the crucible of their encounters in the city where they all met, revealing a greater diversity of pan-African thought and action.

As I use it here, *black internationalism* connotes multiple formations, heterogeneous but unified in opposition to the racial order of empire and in a desire to transcend prevailing geopolitical divisions through an embrace of cultural differences. Black internationalism morphed and evolved not only in response to crises and the course of events but also in relation to different contexts and audiences.

Movement across racialized settings within and beyond the empire, as well as changing patterns of sociability and correspondence and of book and periodical circulation, compelled black intellectuals and agitators to reconceive the composition and extent of their audiences and spheres of action. In London, they addressed a shifting constellation of publics simultaneously. Public discourse does not merely speak to an already existent constituency, but constitutes a "subjunctive-creative project" of world making and a social act summoning the collectivities it presupposes. As subjects of the British Empire, black sojourners and migrants imagined themselves and acted as participants in an imperial public as well as various colonial and regional publics. They contributed to mainstream public discourse in Britain—in the British press, Parliament, and many other forums. They appropriated the practices of liberal civil society—speaking to crowds at political rallies or in Hyde Park, petitioning the Colonial Office, and publishing books, small tracts, and journals—performing citizenship in advance of its formal achievement. African and Caribbean intellectuals often mobilized the very terms of the colonial regime—concepts such as *partnership, self-government,* and *the Commonwealth*—to make political and material demands on the imperial state. At the same time, through small journals, conversations in private spaces, and a variety of public forums, they formed ties of mutual influence with other black scholars and activists and participated in a vibrant transatlantic black public.

Black London explores a multiplicity of black internationalisms articulated within and beyond black organizations and the internationalist left; in texts, sounds, self-presentations and collective performances of blackness; and in the organization of social spaces. The visions of political community beyond empire conveyed in anticolonial agitation and the writings of black intellectuals were only part of a larger cultural and intellectual ferment linking the imperial metropolis to cities around the Atlantic. The circuits of empire and of transatlantic black intellectual and artistic cultures relied increasingly on new audio and visual recording and broadcasting technologies in addition to print culture, at once enabling and constraining black internationalist activity. Black musicians and, via records and the airwaves, their music circulated alongside fugitive publications through networks spanning the Afro-Atlantic world and the British Empire, constituting publics of performers, listeners, dancers, and consumers. In some cases, these might be seen as forming radical counterpublics insofar as they rerouted imperial and diasporic connections, elaborated "different ways of imagining stranger-sociability," and generated commonality out of "embodied sociability, affect, and play."[29] Nevertheless, diasporic ties and imperial networks also constrained and delimited the extent of transcolonial alliances and anticolonial solidarities. Although some had personal ties to South Asians or came from areas in East African and the Caribbean with sizable South Asian populations, Africans and Afro-Caribbeans spent much more time with each other and African Americans than with South Asians or other groups of colonial students and intellectuals in the metropole. Likewise, notwithstanding a few notable exceptions, connections were far weaker, and political collaboration remained more limited, between West Africans from British- and French-controlled territories than interaction among West Africans within these empires. Substantive efforts at forming a wider "colored internationalism" or transimperial Afro-Asian solidarity emerged periodically—on the eve of the Second World War and at war's end, for example—but were intermittent at best.[30] For all its expansive, even utopian, qualities, the black international that was envisioned and, to some extent, formed in London reproduced or erected barriers and hierarchies even as it challenged others.

Black internationalism developed as much through the negotiation of difference among people of African descent as against shared racial oppression. Metropolitan encounters sparked heated political disagreements and revealed biases, power inequalities, and differential experiences of racialization between black subjects of the British Empire and African Americans, Caribbeans and Africans, West and East Africans, and those hailing from different ethnic groups and colonies. If the city became, as James puts it, one of "the planet's primary crossroads at which black people came to a greater sense of group consciousness," political activism and daily life exposed ideological, class, regional, and colonial divisions. The "cultures of black internationalism," Edwards reminds us, not only enabled "new and unforeseen alliances and interventions on a global stage," but also entailed "unavoidable misapprehensions and misreadings, persistent blindnesses and solipsisms, self-defeating and abortive collaborations, a failure to translate even a basic grammar of blackness."[31] In the realm of queer theory, Lauren Berlant and Lee Edelman have theorized this inherent instability and the constant "undoing of the stabilizing frameworks of coherence"—"from the unbearable, often unknowable, psychic conflicts that constitute the subject to the social forms of negation that also, but differently, produce subjectivity"—as the "negativity" of relation. By undermining the transparency of operative categories and fictions of individual and collective sovereignty, negativity presents an obstacle to organizing political action. Yet, in disturbing the totalizing frameworks that sustain the existing hierarchical order, it "enacts the dissent without which politics" or the possibility of other forms of social relation "disappears," and "in this sense, is inseparable from the struggles of the subordinated." More than mere barriers to unity, internal strains, fractures, and "the myriad misrecognitions that inform the encounter and define its limits" provided the inescapable conditions of possibility for black internationalist political imaginaries—their visionary qualities, their failings, and all.[32]

London's black population remained overwhelmingly male until the late 1950s. Homosocial bonds and a redemptive model of black masculinity provided social cohesion and undergirded the black internationalism of black pressure groups. These factors also exacerbated tensions between individuals and contradictions in personal conduct while marginalizing African and Afro-Caribbean women. Chapter 5 looks more closely at the "sexual politics of black internationalism."[33] Sexual relationships between black men and white women were more common at the heart of the empire. White women often helped newcomers navigate the difficulties that confronted them in the metropolis, and most African and Afro-Caribbean men developed close personal and sexual relationships—in some cases, marriages—with white women who helped them in both their personal lives and political activism.

Representations of black male bodies as both predatory, even "demonic," and exotic objects of desire pervaded popular culture and public discourse in interwar Britain. Colonial officials and others attempted to use black men's sexual behavior to police their activities in general. The fraught topic of inter-racial sexuality was also the subject of debate among men of African descent. Black men articulated their anticolonial politics and differences within their ranks in part through the various meanings they attached to it and to con-duct of the self more generally.

Ultimately, the views and self-conceptions of most black activist-intellec-tuals reaffirmed gender hierarchy and rested on the construction of a self-determining, heterosexual, and male subject. In this sense, revolutionary black masculinity varied little from bourgeois British masculinity or subse-quent anti- and postcolonial nationalist masculinities. Meanwhile, African and Afro-Caribbean women labored on the margins and in the gaps between groups, both black pressure groups and white-led feminist and international-ist organizations, articulating feminist visions of black internationalism that are the topic of Chapter 3. These women were major contributors to and helped sustain and expand black pressure groups and other centers of black cultural and political life in the city, extending their reach while often mar-ginalized within them. Many of the social spaces of black London were the products of women's labors, but they often reflected a conventional gender hierarchy. Limited in number and often circumscribed to what their male peers perceived as positions appropriate to their gender, women sojourners, nonetheless, performed vital roles in mounting resistance to racism and imperialism in the metropole. Such women as Una Marson, Amy Ashwood Garvey, and Constance Cummings-John traveled widely, forming alliances that were never limited to black male intellectuals and activists. In fore-grounding the needs of and unity among women of African descent, their black internationalism exceeded the terms and goals of their male contempo-raries and white feminists in Britain. Their analyses of how colonial racial categories and the gender norms avowed by white colonial officials and the male colonial elite overdetermined the exploitation of darker-skinned women, and their various efforts to define black liberation in light of feminist concerns expose the limits of male-dominated organizations and a historiog-raphy that continues to grant them pride of place, implicitly gendering the local/national/specific as feminine and the global/transnational/hybrid as masculine.[34] Examining black women's intellectual production and organ-izing activities among themselves or within feminist internationalist groups, through literature and popular culture as well as political tracts and periodical culture, not only changes the gender profile of black internationalism but also reveals an array of black internationalisms in conversation that were discrepant and often incommensurable in content and molded through a variety of cultural forms and modes of address.

ONE

Afro-metropolis

BLACK POLITICAL AND CULTURAL
ASSOCIATIONS IN INTERWAR LONDON

DURING THE EARLY DECADES of the twentieth century, the black population in London consisted largely of black workers and a much smaller number of black professionals and artists born in Britain and the colonies; colonial students from Africa and the Caribbean; and African American entertainers and intellectuals passing through and sometimes settling in the city.[1] From the mid-nineteenth century, a steady stream of university students from South and West Africa and the Caribbean entered Britain, most to pursue degrees in law or medicine. African rulers and the mission-educated African elite, especially in coastal towns like Freetown, Lagos, and Accra, sent their children to British schools and universities, as did their counterparts in the Caribbean. Island scholarships brought a handful more each year. Although most returned home after completing their studies, others remained and formed some of the earliest black pressure groups in Britain, such as the short-lived African Association.[2]

The First World War brought significantly larger numbers of Afro-Caribbeans and Africans to the metropole as both laborers and military personnel. After the war, despite growing antipathy to their presence, some stayed in Britain, leading to new organizing efforts. Still, the censuses of 1911, 1921, and 1931 indicate that the total number of Africans and Caribbeans in Britain remained less than 14,000, though these figures included Caribbean-born whites and excluded the British-born black population.[3] A series of "race riots" in 1919 targeted non-European and mixed-race working-class communities in the seaside and riverside districts of London, Liverpool, Cardiff, South Shields, and Glasgow. The government's response in the form of the Coloured and Alien Seaman Order of 1925 and the Special Certificate of Nationality and Identity in 1932 effectively institutionalized a color bar in the British shipping industry. African seamen found themselves stranded in Britain and, like their British-born black counterparts, unable to find work.[4] By the late 1920s, the communist-affiliated Negro Welfare Association and the Colonial Seamen's Association ministered to the needs of black workers.

There was a simultaneous rise in the numbers of Afro-Caribbean and West African university students, the vast majority of whom were men, in Edinburgh, Oxford, Cambridge, and especially London during the interwar years. A mix of British- and Caribbean-born professionals created the African Progress Union (APU) and Society of Peoples of African Origin near the war's end, and growing numbers of Caribbean and especially West African students joined the Union of Students of African Descent (USAD) in the early 1920s. Avowedly apolitical, as the *African Times and Orient Review* reported, the USAD sought to bring "together all Africans in statu pupillaris resident in England," to keep "African students in London in a condition of active intellectuality," and to encourage the study of "African history and sociology." The APU participated in the Pan-African Congresses of 1921 and 1923. The USAD sent delegates to the latter as well, invited W. E. B. Du Bois to address its members, and became more outspoken by the mid-1920s in denouncing racism in the metropole. Although their activities focused primarily on student sojourners and educated elites, these groups provided important models for more ambitious and enduring projects.[5]

In the 1920s and 1930s, as Britain consolidated its grip on West Africa and amid mounting protest in the Caribbean and the ongoing disposition of the local population at the hands of white settlers and businesses in South and East Africa, London became an important locus of black resistance to racism and empire, a place where transatlantic and imperial networks of people, information, ideas, and cultural forms overlapped and converged. Life in the imperial metropolis had a transformative effect on many African and Caribbean sojourners, and they, in turn, altered the city's cultural landscape and the tenor and substance of resistance to empire. Black intellectuals established new organizations and publications to pressure the imperial state and to engage with British and imperial publics, academicians, and people of African descent around the Atlantic. These institutions became beachheads for a growing black presence, first stops for newcomers and visitors to the city, and generated dreams of pan-African solidarity.

The West African Students' Union and League of Coloured Peoples (LCP) emerged among a variety of transimperial, internationalist movements taking pan-ethnic, feminist, pacifist, communist, socialist, and liberal forms, and the unique sight lines, new opportunities, and obstinate difficulties of the imperial metropolis shaped their black internationalism. A growing interest in black unity on both sides of the Atlantic and new expressions of resistance in the colonies informed the political aspirations of Africans and Afro-Caribbeans who increasingly viewed themselves as representatives of a renascent Africa and global black community. Their political visions and the audiences they addressed expanded as they came into contact with others of African descent and various currents of internationalist and anticolonial thought in London. Building on early organizing efforts among people of African descent in the city and the colonies, these organizations provided an institutional basis for a sustained engagement with and onslaught against the imperial state. They alternately exploited and circumvented the networks of empire to connect black intellectuals around the Atlantic, sympathetic groups in Britain, and burgeoning anticolonial movements. From their position at the heart of the British Empire, the WASU and LCP functioned as relay points, linking protests, disseminating news and ideas, and organizing political action. Ever-present tensions within and among groups and individuals threatened practical unity and the larger political projects that it represented; alliances were formed, renegotiated, and abandoned as each passing crisis or issue presented new openings and challenges. Nevertheless, black sociality, critical debate, and the accretion of even fleeting moments of cooperation led many to identify with an extranational conception of blackness and encouraged regional ambitions in the form of a West Indies Federation and United West Africa.

WEST AFRICA IN LONDON

Andrea Levy's award-winning novel *Small Island* (2004) opens with an English female narrator's memory from her childhood. "I thought I'd been to Africa. Told all my class I had. Early Bird, our teacher, stood me in front of the British flag. . . . And I stood there as bold as brass and said, 'I went to Africa when it came to Wembley.'" The teacher admonished her pupil: "'You're not usually a silly girl, Queenie Buxton . . . but you did not go to Africa, you merely went to the British Empire Exhibition, as thousands of others did.'" Twenty-six million people visited the British Empire Exhibition in the north London suburb of Wembley, "the largest of Britain's great imperial pleasure parks," during 1924–1925, and the West Africa pavilion was one of its popular attractions, according to estimates, drawing as much as 60 percent of all visitors. Queenie's error was the mistake of a young child, but eminent imperialists also marveled at the exhibition's technological grandeur and verisimilitude. According to the governor of Nigeria, Hugh Clifford, Rudyard Kipling declared after touring the exhibition grounds: "It's the biggest thing man ever set to hand, in design and in a certain grandiosity. . . . The West Africa building is full of spirit. One almost smells the nigger passing by."[6] "Africa" was an object of the popular and political imagination designating a whole field of competing representations, and the staging of West Africa at Wembley "demonstrated that the city and colony were intertwined spectacles." As Paul Landau observes, "There were two interfaces for Westerners' contacts with Africans during the colonial era. The first was actual: trading, working, having sex, sharing a joke or a beer; policing, killing, and negotiating; requesting, releasing or denying consents and licenses, paying taxes; prevaricating, appealing, judging, and so on. The second was virtual: the paper-thin barrier composed of photographs, words on stationery, and images projected onto screens. Both interfaces supported a kind of two-way traffic." For Africans in London, Wembley demonstrated the ways in which the virtual undergirded and sustained actual relations between Britain and West Africa.[7]

The activism of black intellectuals in interwar London often centered on representation in both the semiotic and political senses of the term, and the exhibition sparked renewed attempts at organizing West Africans in London across colonial divisions. In the months leading up to and during the exhibition, Felix Oladipo (Ladipo) Solanke, a Nigerian law student from Abeokuta and a member of the USAD, gained notoriety for a series of letters published in *West Africa* criticizing racist and often salacious depictions of Africans. In "An Outrage," Solanke condemned a recent article in the *Evening News* under the headline "Cannibalism." The latter quoted a lengthy footnote from a report titled "Empire Making in Nigeria" by Governor Clifford in which he claimed that British rule eliminated the "cannibalism, slave-trading, obscure black-magic rites . . . that uncounted centuries of barbarism had bred." Solanke charged that both the article and the governor's remarks were "calculated not only grossly to mislead the British public, but to do serious harm to those of us from Nigeria who are now in London for educational purposes." His criticisms linked the racism of average Britons to official complicity in propagating the image of a savage precolonial Africa redeemed by

British colonialism, casting doubt on the espoused intention of the upcoming exhibition, "which no doubt will be visited by many Nigerians who may be looked upon as cannibals by the British public."[8] For many like Solanke, who felt daily the effects of British ignorance, such pronouncements belied the inclusive rhetoric around Wembley. As he noted, the danger was precisely that most Britons would believe they experienced the real Africa there.

The exhibition's organizers envisioned it as a tribute to the dominions' and colonies' contributions to the war effort and as a means of restoring "public faith in the direction of progress damaged by the war." After the imperial conference of 1923 and the defeat of imperial trade preferences in that year's elections, they hoped it would stimulate investment in the colonies and British consumers' interest in empire products. The meticulously crafted displays at the exhibition reflected the liberal internationalist ethos of the postwar years, as well as the lessons of wartime experience regarding the importance of imperial coordination and colonial resources. The exhibition handbook heralded the promise of "empire strengthening," "empire consolidation," and "empire development" based on the application of modern science and new communication and transport technologies. Colonial participation was the largest ever for a British exhibition, and in return, organizers promised (and spent enormous sums of money) to offer something more than the same racial stereotypes that had characterized previous imperial spectacles, advertising the event as "a family party, to which every part of the Empire is invited, and at which every part of the Empire is represented." Nigeria, Sierra Leone, and the Gold Coast contributed sums in excess of what the British government requested, funds raised through taxation on imports and exports. Record numbers of West Africans traveled to London for the occasion. Roughly sixty Hausa, Yorùbá, Mendi, Asante, and Fanti speakers worked and lived in the "native village" and "native workshop," and many more African dignitaries, planters, and members of the British-educated commercial and professional elite made the journey.

"Princess" Akosua Baa, a member of the Asante royal family who brought a Golden Stool from the community's women to Queen Mary as a wedding gift, "became one of the sensations of the exhibition." The anthropologist Robert Sutherland Rattray, recognized as the foremost authority on the Asante in Britain, introduced her to the press, noting in an interview that she carried a special charm "because she hoped it will bring a little one." His *Manual of the Gold Coast,* which was distributed to visitors at the Gold Coast pavilion and which described in detail the practice of "wife purchasing" in the colony, framed and contextualized her presence in the exhibition. Symbols of African backwardness and sexual innuendo pervaded press coverage of Baa. "When West Africa Woos," which appeared in the *Sunday Express* on May 4, 1924, began: "One of the features of Wembley is a West African village ruled by a native princess. Below she tells the story of love as it is made in Akropong." The first half of the article took the form of an interview between the author, Charles Graves, and Baa, whose attire he described as consisting of "downtrodden, men's boots" and "a section of carpet and part of a curtain." She reappeared in the piece's closing vignette, but this time her husband accompanied her. "Apparently," Graves wrote, "the princess was explaining my presence with some difficulty." "Then," he continued, "the prince walked slowly over to the [West African] sergeant and spoke to him. 'He asks . . . whether you wish to know more.' I looked at the princess, coyly hiding her blushes with the fringe of her beloved carpet. No I did not."[9]

Africans in London scrutinized and challenged the version of Africa presented for public consumption in the West Africa "village" and in the press, mounting effectively their own miniature shadow exhibition. Both before and after Wembley opened, the USAD was a hub of activity. Solanke recorded a talk entitled "An Instance of Mortality" in èdè Yorùbá for broadcast as part of a BBC feature on African languages in early 1924, and the USAD held a series of lectures and cultural events featuring prominent visitors to coincide with the official opening. After the exhibition opened, the USAD initiated an extensive letter-writing campaign led by Solanke and Joseph Boakye Danquah from the Gold Coast. The union passed a resolution condemning "When West Africa Woos," and sent copies of it to Colonial Secretary J. H. Thomas, West African newspapers and *West Africa*, the prince of Wales (the president of the Wembley exhibition), the four West African governors, and the proprietor of the *Sunday Express*. It denounced representations of Africans that "hold up to public ridicule citizens of countries whose money has been voted in large sums for the purpose of the exhibition." In a letter to *West Africa*, Danquah challenged the veracity of Rattray's portrayal of Asante social practices, citing several instances of mistranslation, and Solanke delivered a series of lectures "on Egba people and their customs" at the Student Movement House at 32 Russell Square, much of which focused on marriage practices and the position of women in Yorùbá society. Both men devoted significant energy to studies of West Africa in the mid-1920s; Danquah published his own ethnography of the Asante (*Akan Laws and Customs*) in 1928. In so doing, they asserted their expertise against that of recognized British authorities and challenged the latter's monopoly on the production of knowledge on Africa. By rallying to the defense of African womanhood and presenting reasoned arguments in various public forums, they also demonstrated their capacity to perform the rights and responsibilities of liberal citizenship.[10]

According to Solanke, the outrage over the coverage of West Africans at the Wembley Exhibition led directly to the creation of the Nigerian Progress Union and the West African Students' Union the following year. He would later claim that the inspiration for his organizing work came from a "dream one night during which Almighty God graciously revealed to me ... that until Africans at home and abroad, including all persons of African descent, organise and develop the spirit of the principles of self-help, unity and cooperation among themselves, and fight to remove the colour bar, they would have to continue to suffer the results of colour prejudice."[11] Solanke's protests in *West Africa* thrust him to the forefront of black activism in London just two years after his arrival and precipitated gestures of solidarity from others of African descent. Amid the uproar over Wembley, the Jamaican Amy Ashwood Garvey, cofounder of the Universal Negro Improvement Association and Marcus Garvey's first wife, wrote to express her support. They shared, in particular, a belief in the importance of education, for women and men, as a prerequisite to political and social advancement. Drawing on her organizing experience, in July 1924, Ashwood Garvey, Solanke, and thirteen other Nigerian male students formed the NPU in London. Aided by a letter of introduction from Ashwood Garvey to the editor, Solanke contributed a series of pieces to the African American journal *The Spokesman* in 1925. In "Nigeria: Its Institutions and Customs," he argued "that when we talk or write about any Yourba [*sic*] custom or institution we are speaking about a people who to-day are to be found playing a great part among all Negroes the world over," and he listed the contributions of people of Yorùbá descent across West Africa and in the Americas. In an "Open Letter to the Negroes of the World," he laid out the NPU's platform and called for greater coordination of black struggles around the globe. While demanding the full benefits of imperial citizenship and dominion status for West Africa, he insisted that the continuation of attempts at "enslaving us ... commercially, industrially and economically" linked West Africa, "especially ... Nigeria the mighty home of the American and West Indian Negroes," to people of African descent across the Atlantic. With the Garveyite movement in steep decline in the United States, he wrote, "it is important for the assistants and

FIGURE 1. "Two Lawyers" (October 12, 1936), Ladipo Solanke on right. Topical Press Agency/Springer, Hulton Archive, Getty Images.

successors of Mr. Marcus Garvey to note that their organisation . . . has aroused in us . . . our race consciousness although we may disagree with some of the methods of that great Negro organiser." Solanke's political vision already extended far beyond Nigeria's boundaries, a sign of Ashwood Garvey's influence on his thinking.[12]

While in London for the Empire Exhibition, J. Ephraim Casely Hayford and Dr. H.C. Bankole-Bright, the president and chairman, respectively, of the faltering National Congress of British West Africa (NCBWA), encouraged students and professionals to consolidate existing organizations such as the USAD, NPU, and recently formed Gold Coast Students' Union into a single organization dedicated to promoting West African unity. After much debate, on August 7, 1925, a small group of law students from West Africa, led by Solanke and Danquah, established the West African Students' Union. Though ostensibly an association of and for West African university students, the union adopted an expansive view of its purpose. The NCBWA, the first political organization claiming to represent all four of Britain's West African colonies, influenced its ambitions. As Frederick Cooper notes, the organization's "political focus was not Nigeria, the Gold Coast, or Sierra Leone, but the cosmopolitan space that connected all of them." Between the

1880s and 1910s, as Vivian Bickford-Smith puts it, the British "betrayed" creole and educated Africans in favor of white settlers in southern and eastern Africa and "traditional" rulers in West Africa as partners in colonial administration. The NCBWA emerged from the ranks of the former and in response to the way that indirect rule "established and reinforced ethnicized (and religious) collectivities." As Jemima Pierre observes, "Nativization was racialization, but this racialization worked through ethnicization—the constitution and organization of a constellation of tribal groupings" that became the basis of their incorporation into colonial administration and the empire as a whole. The NCBWA sought "to ensure local rights," including participation within the colonial legislative council and employment opportunities for qualified Africans, "while acting as representative to natives as a *racial* collective."[13] Plans for the first NCBWA conference, held in Accra in March 1920, developed alongside the peace talks at Versailles, and the model of the Indian National Congress and the liberal internationalism of U.S. president Woodrow Wilson, in particular, informed its demands. The resolutions passed at the conference asserted "the right of the people to self determination" and their claim to "all and every right of free citizenship of the Empire." Under the leadership of the Nigerian Herbert Macaulay, the Sierra Leonean Bankole-Bright, and Casely Hayford, Thomas Hutton-Mills Sr., and Kobina Sekyi from the Gold Coast, the NCBWA ratified its own constitution covering the entirety of British West Africa at a second meeting in early 1923. The document emphasized "the promotion of the common interests of the British West African Dependencies politically, economically, educationally, socially . . . to promote and effect unity of purpose and of action among them."[14] By 1924, support for the NCBWA in West Africa had begun to wane significantly, but it revived the dream of a United West Africa associated with earlier intellectuals such as the Sierra Leonean Africanus Horton and the Afro-Caribbean émigré to Liberia Edward Wilmot Blyden.

The WASU pursued the NCBWA's goals, including imperial citizenship and dominion status for a West African state, long after the latter organization's demise and used the union's position in London to protest the injustices of colonial rule and publicize those struggling against them in the colonies. The founding members included men from all four of the British colonies in West Africa. Bankole-Bright was among the cofounders, and Casely Hayford became its first "patron." On September 27, 1926, the WASU held a reception for the latter at Pinnoli's Restaurant. In his remarks, published in the second issue of the group's journal, Casely Hayford told its members that the "Congress expresses British West African nationality" and argued that a unified West Africa represented only the first step in the advancement of "African international union and sentiment," by which "Africans... scattered all over the world" would "in time acquire experience of African nationality." While noting that "the object of the African ... is the attainment of nationality, the possibility of raising his head among the other peoples of the world, and of commanding his national and racial opportunity," Casely Hayford urged his audience to repudiate the imposed territorial boundaries that separated them under British rule and "to stretch out a hand to our brethren over the Atlantic who have brotherly yearnings for us, as we have for them."[15]

In 1927, the WASU published a speech by Bankole-Bright, then a member of the Legislative Council in Sierra Leone, as a pamphlet. The inside cover featured a photograph of the speaker in profile, dressed in a fashionable double-breasted suit with a cigar dangling from his mouth. In his address, Bankole-Bright maintained that, contrary to the claim that Britain was expanding liberal freedoms and extending the reach of the rule of law, recent events showed growing discrimination and autocracy in the colonies. He called on his audience to "cry aloud in this Metropolis" for "the rights of true citizenship."[16] Bankole-Bright's accusations became a source of concern for the governor of Sierra Leone and the Colonial Office after WASU reprinted them and excerpts appeared in West Africa and Truth.[17] Hereafter, agents of the imperial state increasingly, if only begrudgingly and paternalistically, engaged in a dialogue with the WASU and especially Solanke, illustrating a growing appreciation of the heightened costs of anticolonial protest in the imperial metropolis.

Under Solanke's leadership as its general secretary, over the following three decades the WASU became the most important pressure group devoted to African issues and a center of black social and political activity in London. Several generations of prominent West African intellectuals, artists, and politicians passed through its ranks.[18] The WASU issued the first number of its journal, Wāsù (Preach), in 1926. By 1933, the union claimed that it circulated widely throughout Britain's four West African colonies, the United States, and the Caribbean and was "well-known in East and South Africa, especially in Kenya and Uganda."[19] In the inaugural issue, the Sierra Leonean H.J.L. Boston proposed a self-governing federal state in West Africa as a means to satisfy the "desire [for] union but not unity," and asserted that the West African increasingly "centres his interests, not only on the Colony from which he hails, but also on that part of the continent designated West Africa; *to him West Africa has a meaning*; to him West Africa has a future."[20] Danquah described the WASU's purpose as helping "to create a healthy national sentiment throughout the whole of West Africa," but the WASU was not nationalist in the usual sense of the term. As James Coleman states, its activities focused on "the awakening of a racial, not a territorial, consciousness." Nigerians like Solanke often outnumbered other West Africans in the union, but "in no instance were native-born Nigerians encouraged ... to think of Nigeria as an individual national entity or to feel that they were Nigerians." For the WASU, "'Race,' 'African,' and 'nationality' were interchangeable, almost synonymous, terms."[21] The factors leading to the founding of the union, and the intellectual and political tributaries that shaped its aims, were imperial, regional, and transatlantic in nature.

The group's members crafted a capacious political imaginary that encompassed the whole of British West Africa and a wider black Atlantic world from a number of different sources, including the regional federalism of the NCBWA, liberal and socialist variants of internationalism, and the ideas of African American intellectuals. Solanke read the NAACP's *The Crisis* for the first time in London and corresponded with and forwarded copies of *Wāsù* to its editor, Du Bois. Marcus Garvey was an important source of inspiration and ally to the WASU in its early years. He helped to finance the launch of its journal and transferred the lease on his residence in West Kensington to the union when he left London in 1928.[22] Yet the WASU's interpretation of African history and culture and its political vision for West Africa more closely resembled the ideas of Alain Locke. Employing Franz Boas's notion of cultural diffusion in the elaboration of his own ideas, Locke insisted on an analytical approach that highlighted the "reciprocal cultural interchange and influence, of Negro on white, and white on Negro."[23] As early as 1916, he argued that when "modern man talks about race," he is really talking about ethnicity and, what is more, that ethnic groups might be termed more accurately "ethnic fictions," as such groupings were "the products of countless interminglings ... the result of infinite crossings."[24] In 1928, Locke addressed the WASU in London. He claimed that racism and nationalism were two sides of the same coin, the one depending on the other for its coherence, and that internationalism would be the defining feature of an emerging "new world." "In this time of revolution," he argued, "our racial thinking must rise to a higher plane; and just as there is no room in progressive thought to-day for narrow and selfish nationalism, so there is also no

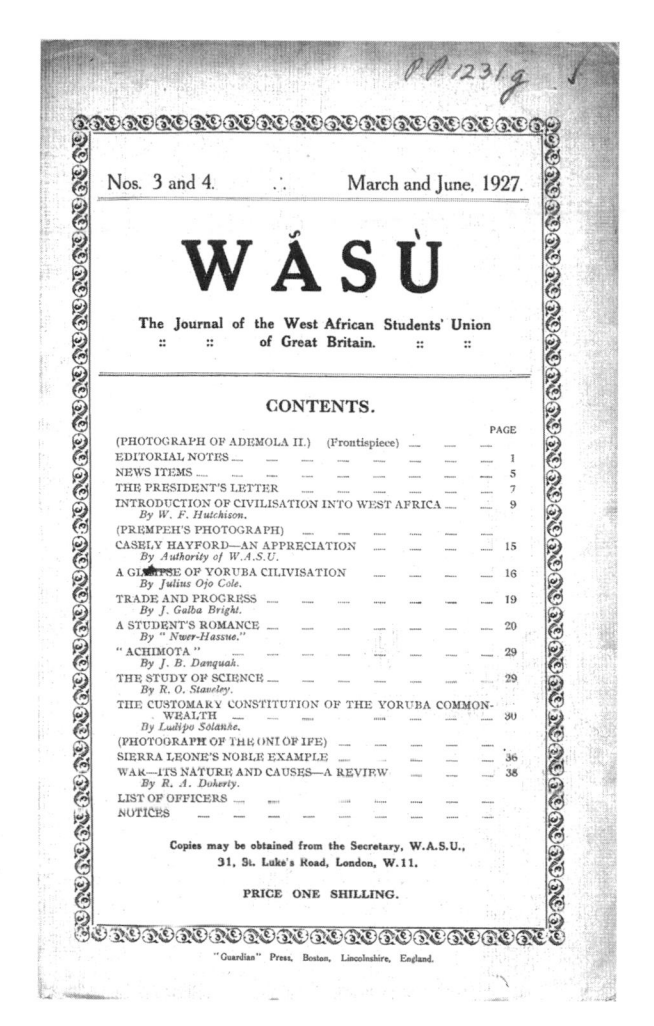

Nos. 3 and 4.   ∴   March and June, 1927.

WÅSÙ

The Journal of the West African Students' Union
::   ::   of Great Britain.   ::   ::

CONTENTS.

Copies may be obtained from the Secretary, W.A.S.U.,
31, St. Luke's Road, London, W.11.

PRICE ONE SHILLING.

"Guardian" Press, Boston, Lincolnshire, England.

FIGURE 2. Cover of *Wāsù: The Journal of the West African Students' Union of Great Britain* 3–4 (March–June 1927). © The British Library Board.

proper place for narrow and selfish racialism." Far from representing a retrograde turn to ethnic separatism or chauvinism, the movement toward pan-African cooperation epitomized the "new internationalism" of the age. Locke conceded that mutual ignorance and vast differences in history and circumstance continued to divide, as he put it, "the now separated branches of the Negro peoples." Nevertheless, he insisted, "people will be most efficient who live in terms of the greatest possible synthesis of civilisations, and we welcome this difficult task which our peculiar heritage and history imposes [*sic*] upon us."[25]

The WASU interpreted Locke's vision of black internationalism through the lens of the union's understanding of West Africa's past. Reiterating Locke's arguments but placing greater emphasis on cultural exchange in Africa (as opposed to the Americas), the editorial that prefaced his reprinted speech declared: "Throughout her history Africa seemed to have been nature's experimental ground for the fusion of various cultures and civilisations.... Thus to-day Africa is the richest continent in racial types and harbours ... the greatest conglomeration of men of all shades of colour, custom and cultures." This long history of ethnic and cultural blending represented Africa's unique "spiritual heritage" and Africans' primary contribution to human civilization, the quality that both defined and secured their place in the "family of nations."[26] To the extent that the WASU celebrated a distinctive Africanness, it was one defined by continuous, if varying, patterns of cultural mixture, not an innate racial essence. Locke's notion of modern New Negroes as a racial avant garde paralleled union members' self-presentation as the leaders of a new Africa, and the WASU's journal offered copies of the *New Negro* for sale to its readers, but the subtle differences between their ideas reflected the greater importance that the WASU accorded to the agency of Africans, past and present.

Through *Wāsù*—especially the writings of Solanke and its early editors Danquah, Melville C. Marke, Julius Ojo-Cole, and Ohenenana Cobina Kessie—and pamphlets like Joseph William de Graft Johnson's *Towards Nationhood in West Africa* (1928), the WASU disseminated a regional and circum-Atlantic perspective on the West African past as part of a comprehensive view of the region's place in an interconnected world. Originally from the Gold Coast, de Graft Johnson wrote: "The hope and desire of Africa is the same throughout the length and breadth of the continent. It is concentrated in the great yearning for freedom" and for "recognition in the Comity of Nations." The WASU contributed to this struggle by "correlating lines of thought and action."[27] Steeped in a West African intellectual tradition stretching back to Dr. James Africanus Beale Horton and Bishop James Johnson in the mid-nineteenth century, Solanke lectured and produced writings on West African history, culture, and customs, based in part on research for his MA thesis on Yorùbá marriage practices.[28] In his short history of West Africa, *United West Africa (or Africa) at the Bar of the Family of Nations* (1927), he drew upon forerunners such as Blyden and Samuel Johnson, as well as racist imperial historiography, to demonstrate the existence of a common ancient culture in West Africa, a "separate sort of civilization [that] Africa had since given to the Family of Nations," and "to prove that all the various peoples inhabiting Abyssinia, the Sudan, Egypt, North Africa, and all along the Mediterranean shores have from the earliest times been so closely connected with the inhabitants of West Africa." On the basis of their linked histories, he asserted, "the more we are together the happier we shall be." Believing that the WASU and its published organ had an important role to play in the "complete Restoration, Regeneration, and second Rise of West Africa," Solanke stressed the need for an African hostel in London as "a training ground for practical unity and effective co-operation" and an expression of "West African individuality." "The time has come," he argued, "when West African nationality must find a permanent foothold in Great Britain.[29]

A particular conception of Yorùbá-ness, itself the product of the transatlantic traffic among Africans linking British West Africa to Brazil and the Caribbean, lay at the heart of Solanke's analysis and the WASU's distinctive brand of internationalism. As J. Lorand Matory has shown, mission-educated African, Afro-Brazilian, and Afro-Caribbean returnees to towns along the West African coast, especially Lagos, cultivated this notion of Yorùbá identity beginning in the 1890s.[30] The ongoing dialogue between people of African descent in the diaspora and the West African intelligentsia shaped Solanke's perspective on West African history, and a congratulatory reader's letter indicates that *Wāsù* circulated in Brazil. Solanke contributed the article "Unity and Co-operation" to the journal's fifth issue. As in *United West Africa,* he drew on a wide array of sources—from ancient texts to more recent works such as Leo Frobenius's *The Voice of Africa* (1923), Joseph Thompson's *Mungo Park* (1898), Martin S. Kisch's *Letters and Sketches from Northern Nigeria* (1910), and Samuel Johnson's *The History of the Yorubas from the earliest times to the beginning of the British Protectorate* (edited by Obadiah Johnson, 1921)—to trace a history of contact and mutual influence stretching from Egypt, Abyssinia, and eastern Sudan to the coast of Benin and Nigeria. Mobilizing Frobenius's notion of a unique "Atlantic Civilisation" emanating from Ife, the ancient Yorùbá city in southwestern Nigeria, Solanke suggested that the Atlantic trade in enslaved Africans marked a tragic departure from this history of intra-African exchange whose consequences, including British colonization, nonetheless created the conditions for West African unity in the present, because of the resettlement of liberated Africans like those who became the Saro of Nigeria and Krio of Sierra Leone.[31] In "The Solidarity of the African Race," Prince Adetokunbo

Adegboyega Ademola, the son of the Alake of the Egba, maintained that "the West African tribes have from time immemorial been closely related one with the other," and cited the demographics of the slave trade and extant traces of Asante and Yorùbá cultural practices and folklore in Jamaica and the United States to establish an analogous connection between West Africans and people of African descent in the Caribbean and the Americas.[32] Similarly, the Sierra Leonean Krio (or Creole) Robert Wellesley Cole claimed that an experiential "West African sense" had developed in conjunction with an appreciation of these deep historical linkages and an awareness of the necessity for "self-help" and cooperation in the present.[33] West African intellectuals in the WASU, especially self-identified Yorùbás and Krios, pointed to cultural blending as the hallmark of African history. Connected to each other and an array of non-African cultures by processes of long duration, Africans and dispersed populations of African descent around the world were cultural hybrids and embodiments of internationalism.

In the late 1920s, West Africans were the primary catalysts behind black internationalist thought and activity in London. The members of the WASU articulated and performed a conception of *Africanness* that was both modern and cosmopolitan, a conception that contradicted the one on display at Wembley. They attached particular significance to the long history of cultural mixture in West Africa, extending to the region's links to people of African descent across the Atlantic, as the cornerstone of a philosophical and political commitment to internationalism. Citing the examples of a broad resurgence throughout the Afro-Asian world, Danquah asked in the inaugural issues of *Wàsù*, "What then . . . has he [the Negro] contributed?" He suggested that people of Africa descent had "aroused the world to a higher level of ethical idealism and to a far deeper humanitarian conception of life. . . . A new humanity of Negroes is rising from the forsaken ashes of the past."[34] In the near future, African intellectuals in the WASU argued, the accumulated weight of these historical connections would give rise to a regional federation in West Africa—an entity capable of accommodating difference within a unified structure, of serving as a building block for a transformed British Commonwealth, and of facilitating lateral connections still farther afield. They argued that the choice was not between remaining subjugated colonies and becoming independent nation-states along colonial lines, but rather between exclusionary nationalisms that bred racial hatred, on the one hand, and internationalism based on formal equality and an embrace of cultural differences and exchange, on the other.

Contrary to the image of a happy imperial family projected at Wembley, racial barriers hardened in both Britain and the colonies after 1919. Everyday manifestations of racism increased, such as denying people of African descent service at hotels and restaurants, demonstrating that a de facto (if not de jure) color bar operated in the metropole as well as the empire. In 1929, the *Times* reported that London's Savoy Grill had refused to serve the African American entertainer Paul Robeson, causing a minor scandal, but for most of the city's black residents this type of incident was all too familiar.[35] The Joint Council to Promote Understanding between White and Coloured People in Great Britain found in 1933 that "London hotels are quite prepared to receive coloured visitors from the East as guests either to sleep or take meals but . . . did not feel able to receive persons of Negroid race." The same pattern would persist in the market for long-term rentals for decades to come.[36] The prevalence of racism shocked newcomers who arrived with idealized visions of the "mother country" as the home of fair play and gentlemanliness. Writing in 1934, Nyasilie Magxaka recalled, "I thought that on leaving South Africa for England, I was at the same time leaving the infamous colour bar behind and was coming to the paradise of freedom." To the contrary, "the treatment of coloured people in London almost forces one to believe that [the] colour bar is the policy of the British Empire."[37]

Discrimination forced qualified black professionals into private practice and brought them together in organizing efforts that yielded some of the earliest black organizations in Britain. The Trinidadian physician John Alcindor, who maintained a private practice in London, participated in the African Association's Pan-African Conference in 1900 and served as president of the short-lived African Progress Union. Dr. Cecil Belfield Clarke from Barbados practiced medicine in the London Borough of Southwark for nearly fifty years between the 1920s and 1960s. He was active in the WASU, a founding member of the League of Coloured Peoples, and in the late 1930s, worked with the Trinidadian radicals George Padmore and C. L. R. James in the International African Service Bureau.

The Jamaican physician Dr. Harold Arundel Moody came to England in 1904 as a twenty-two-year-old student. He settled in London, in part to help his younger brothers through King's College: Ludlow Moody, whose first wife, Vera, was Norman Manley's sister, returned to Jamaica and became a government bacteriologist, and Ronald Moody became a dentist and a renowned sculptor.[38] Moody later admitted that his perception of Africa and his African ancestors reflected the racial hierarchy in colonial Jamaica when he arrived: "I had been educated away from my heritage and towards the country which I had learnt to call 'home.' My desire then was to have as little as possible to do with my own people and upon Africans I looked down as a species too low in the rank of human development for me in any way to associate with. I was black indeed but I was not African, nor was I in any way related to Africa. . . . At heart I really believed I was English."[39] Moody does not appear to have participated in the few existing black associations while in medical school during the war or following his graduation in 1919. Years of exposure to racial prejudice in Britain gradually altered his understanding of the relationship between his racial identity and Britishness. In December 1927, he addressed the USAD in London in a speech that focused on the problems to which he would devote the remainder of his life—racism and self-determination for the Caribbean and Africa.[40] By the 1930s, he identified with a color-blind conception of imperial citizenship and a transnational conception of blackness, linking him to others of African descent. Moody presided over the League of Coloured Peoples from its founding in 1931 until his death in 1947. From his Victorian home and medical practice at 164 Queen's Road in the southeastern suburb of Peckham, he managed the league's activities and hosted scores of African, Afro-Caribbean, and African American visitors and sojourners.

Though occasionally disparaged by British officials and more radical black activists in his own time, Moody made an enduring contribution to black cultural and political life in London. As David Killingray points out, he likely addressed more white Britons than any of his contemporaries, and he wrote at least four short books or pamphlets on race relations in Britain. He lectured Britons on the evils of racial prejudice in letters to newspapers and as a lay preacher.[41] Moody became a champion of unity among people of African descent but continued to emphasize the necessity of interracial cooperation throughout his life. His religiosity underlay his reformist politics, pacifism, and liberal internationalism, and his standing as a medical expert was central to his self-identification as an intellectual and exemplary representative of his race. Moody converted to Congregationalism in his school days and remained active in the church thereafter, delivering sermons nearly every Sunday and serving as chairman of the London Missionary Society in 1943. The nonconformist tradition's emphasis on redemption for all through Christ dovetailed with his message of inclusiveness and equality. He frequently used his scientific knowledge and medical metaphors in his writings, speeches, and sermons, describing racism, for example, as the "infection in the blood stream" of the British Empire. During a speech in Wolverhampton in October 1929, he described Africa as the cradle of humanity and argued that "examined scientifically, anatomically, or physiologically, there is nothing in the organic make-up of coloured people that implies inferiority."[42] As Moody and officials in the Colonial Office recognized, the respect and authority that accrued from his status as an educated professional and an upstanding Christian lent considerable weight to his appeals to white audiences.

In 1931 Moody began meeting with a group of black and South Asian professionals, British liberals and feminists, and the Society of Friends to consider new initiatives to address the color bar in Britain. The immediate result was the Joint Council to Promote Understanding between White and Coloured People in Great Britain, a public relations and charitable organization with strong ties to several religious groups. The founders modeled the body on the multiracial joint councils in South Africa, reflecting the connections between South African and British liberal critics of racism and colonialism. The Quaker John Fletcher headed the council, and Moody served as vice-chairman. The non-Europeans in the group argued in favor of a separate organization under their control. South Asians, including the former member of the Legislative Council in Kenya R. S. Nehra, wanted it to address the concerns of all non-Europeans in Britain, but Moody insisted that the plight of people of African descent deserved special attention. The NAACP in the United States inspired his efforts, due in part to the presence of the Harvard-educated African American historian from Howard University Charles Wesley, who was in London on a Guggenheim fellowship. Wesley and Moody spoke at a series of YMCA-sponsored functions in early 1931 to rally support for the proposed organization.

On March 13, Moody chaired a meeting at the Central London YMCA on Tottenham Court Road, where "some seventy coloured people and others" formed the League of Coloured Peoples, citing "the desire, born of an innate sense of independence and racial pride, to help ourselves." The LCP became the first multiracial organization in Britain led by people of African descent. The new organization held its first official meeting at London's Memorial Hall on June 5. In addition to black professionals and students, sympathetic politicians such as Ellen Wilkinson and representatives of British missionary organizations, the Friends Society, and the Anti-Slavery and Aborigines' Protection Society (ASAPS) took part. The LCP declared its aims: "To promote and protect the Social, Educational, Economic and Political interests of its members. To interest members in the Welfare of Coloured Peoples in all parts of the World. To improve relations between the Races. To co-operate with organisations sympathetic to Coloured People." The word *coloured* never lost its broader connotations as encompassing all non-Europeans, and a few South Asians participated in the league for extended periods. Nehra was a member of the league's executive committee and its first treasurer, and the Sri Lankan Pastor Kamal Chunchie served as its vice president from 1935 to 1937. During the early 1930s, Moody collaborated with Chunchie, R. K. Sorabji, and the Christian Sikh Shoran Singha in the Coloured Men's Institute, a religious and social center for non-European seamen in London. The LCP held social events jointly with India House and the Commonwealth of India League and hosted receptions for visiting members of the Indian National Congress such as Gandhi and Nehru. Nevertheless, Moody envisioned it as an organization dedicated, first and foremost, to giving a voice to people of African descent around the world, and advocating on their behalf occupied the bulk of the league's efforts throughout its existence. "As far as we are concerned," Moody explained, "this term includes everybody, because there are no WHITE people. . . . We therefore admit all people as members. For practical purpose[s] . . . , however, our work is mainly confined to people of African descent—at present mainly West Indian and West African—although we have some Indians in our ranks."[43]

Afro-Caribbeans predominated within the LCP, but it was hardly an exclusively Caribbean group. Its membership reflected the increasing interaction among Africans, Caribbeans, and African Americans, especially visiting scholars and entertainers, in the city. In addition to Moody as president, the LCP's executive committee consisted of George Roberts (Trinidad), Dr. Belfield Clarke (Barbados), Samson Morris (Grenada), Robert Adams (British Guiana), and Desmond Buckle (Gold Coast). C. L. R. James attended early LCP conferences and contributed to its journal. The group's founding members also included the Grenadian politician and early champion of the West Indies Federation Theophilus Albert Marryshow, who was in London to lobby the Colonial Office. The Barbour James family was a prominent presence in the league. John Alexandra Barbour James, originally from British Guiana, worked for the post office in the Gold Coast between 1902 and 1917, while his wife and family lived in London. After his wife Caroline

FIGURE 3. Group photograph from League of Coloured Peoples Conference, including *(seated first row)* Dr. Harold Arundel Moody *(center)*, founder and president of the league, Una Marson *(right of Moody)*, and C. L. R. James *(far right)*. *The Keys* 1, no. 1 (July 1933): 3. © The British Library Board.

died, in 1920, he married Edith Rita Goring, a teacher from Barbados who had also worked in the Gold Coast. Both became central figures in the LCP; John held the office of vice president and remained active in the group until he returned to the Caribbean in 1938. His London-born daughter Amy Barbour James, a concert singer who studied with Amanda Aldridge, helped organize many of the group's events and served on its executive committee.[44] West Africans such as Dr. Crispin Curtis Adeniyi-Jones from Sierra Leone, Stephen and Stella Thomas from Nigeria, and Kobina Sekyi from the Gold Coast participated in its activities, and the Kenyan Johnstone (later Jomo) Kenyatta contributed to its journal. The African American actors Paul Robeson and Beresford Gale also joined the organization.

In the early 1930s, the LCP intervened in issues as diverse as discrimination in the professions in Britain, the plight of black seamen and children of working-class interracial couples in Cardiff and Liverpool, and censorship in the colonies. The league assisted individuals with securing housing and employment, raised funds for hurricane victims in British Honduras, and joined the international campaign in defense of the Scottsboro Boys in the United States. Within months of establishing the organization, Moody began corresponding with Walter White of the NAACP and Dr. Carter G. Woodson of the Association for the Study of Negro Life and History. The *Journal of Negro History* published a letter from Moody recounting the league's work to date. By the beginning of 1934, the LCP had small branches in Liverpool, Cardiff, British Guiana, Jamaica, Panama, and Sierra Leone.[45]

Through its various activities and particularly its quarterly journal, *The Keys,* the LCP lobbied for equal rights for British subjects of all races while elaborating a vision of black unity that extended beyond the British Empire. A critique of the color bar as a global phenomenon linked these two aspects of its work. The opening editorial of *The Keys* declared: "Our task lies in stating the cause of our brothers and sisters within the British Empire. We cannot afford however to ignore the claims of the peoples of colour who owe allegiance to a flag other than our own. All along the line there is the same tale. . . . Recent happenings in England, Kenya and the U.S.A. show . . . that we have reached a critical period in the history of our race. Never was there a greater need for unity within our ranks." The journal's title referred to Dr. James Emman Kwegyir Aggrey's use of piano keys as a metaphor for inter-racial harmony, but it also positioned the journal as the proverbial key that would open the door barring black advancement. "Our plea . . . is for equality of opportunity. We are knocking at the door and will not be denied. 'The Keys' will, we trust, be an open sesame to better racial understanding and goodwill."[46] To the end of his life, Moody maintained his belief that the imperium could be reformed into a mutually beneficial association built on the celebration of cultural differences. Though shaped by different circumstances in Jamaica and less confrontational in its tactics than many of the African intellectuals in the WASU, the LCP championed black unity in terms broadly commensurate to the latter, as part of a global movement toward greater cooperation and integration, and maintained that an extensive history of Atlantic exchange placed people of African descent at the forefront of this development, making them the avant garde of the age of internationalism. As Clare McFarlane put it in his remarks at a Wilberforce centenary celebration in Port Maria, Jamaica, which appeared in *The Keys*: "By the very circumstance of being cut off from our natural or racial origins, we, in these West Indies, are favourably placed for leading the way in the acquirement of an international consciousness . . . the outlook which will regard the world as a single place and all men as brothers." This, he argued, "is the peculiar task allotted to these islands and the distinctive contribution to world affairs which it is their privilege to make."[47] McFarlane's outline of Caribbean history paralleled Solanke's view of West Africa's past, and they came to broadly similar conclusions regarding the international importance of black struggles in the present.

During its early years, the LCP provided greater opportunities for women's involvement than did other London-based organizations such as the WASU, but its male leadership, starting with its president and patriarch, conformed to a middle-class ideal of respectability that in certain ways restricted women's participation and engagement with its journal's readers. Whereas male members and officers presided over meetings and wrote editorials and essays on history, economics, and political issues for *The Keys,* women's public contributions to the league were overwhelmingly social and artistic. By embracing the cultural project associated with black internationalism, women established a position from which to counter British racism, to contribute to the creation of a black public sphere in London and new transatlantic connections, and to link black unity to feminist concerns. Moody and his English wife, Olive Mabel Tranter, opened their Peckham home to a succession of female new arrivals, providing appropriately respectable lodgings to Afro-Caribbean and African women, from Una Marson in the early 1930s to Irene Cole, Robert Wellesley Cole's younger sister, in the early 1940s. In the mid-1930s, the league's executive committee included Barbour James, Dorothy Clarke (Bermuda), Sylvia Lowe (Jamaica), and Viola Thompson (Sierra Leone). Constance Horton (Sierra Leone), Dulcina Armstrong (British Guiana), Audrey Jeffers (Trinidad), and Dr. Hyacinth Lightbourne (Jamaica) participated in the group as well. Stella Thomas studied law at the Middle Temple and was active in both the WASU and LCP before becoming the first female barrister in British West Africa. The Jamaican writer Una Marson volunteered as the LCP's unpaid secretary in autumn 1933, becoming the first in a series of Caribbean women whose labor maintained the organization throughout its existence. Until 1935, she was the primary editor of *The Keys,* handled the group's correspondence, and organized its varied social calendar, which allowed her to establish connections among London's black cultural producers and organizations that she would utilize throughout her career.

Marson and other women in the league broke new ground for black art in the imperial metropolis. An all-black cast of predominantly league members, starring the brilliant Stella Thomas, performed Marson's drama *At What a*

Price at the YWCA Central Club Hall and then London's Scala Theatre. Other LCP functions featured performances of spirituals and poetry readings, and *The Keys* celebrated the accomplishments of black recitalists.[48] Marson organized a league concert at the Indian Students' Hostel on October 21, 1933, at which the Alabama native John Payne, Ike Hatch, and Amy Barbour James sang a program of spirituals, accompanied by the Guyanese musicians Rudolph Dunbar and Bruce Wendell on the clarinet and piano. The same year, Dunbar and his orchestra, which *The Keys* described as "the finest coloured Orchestra in London," provided the music at the group's farewell dance for the West Indies cricket team. Paul Robeson was scheduled to open the league's "bazaar" in March 1935, organized by Sylvia Lowe. When he had to cancel, Payne and Sail Rodgers sang in his place.[49]

Marson established *The Keys* as the most prominent black publication in Britain, with a monthly worldwide circulation of more than two thousand by 1934. She also made it a rare forum for black literature in Britain, exposing readers to the work of contemporary African American authors, and Caribbean women contributed much of its original literary content.[50] Poems like Marson's "Nigger" and Lowe's "Disillusionment (After seeing the Trooping of the Colour)," in which the narrator is "For ever broken by our welcome here," captured the mix of pain and anger shared by many black sojourners.[51] Poems denouncing the color bar appeared alongside inspirational verse such as Margaret R. Seon's "Vision," addressed to an emerging transatlantic "nation . . . but within its springtime." In Lowe's "The Stamp of Freedom (Written by the great-grand-daughter of a West Indian slave, on meeting an African girl)," two black women separated by an ocean and "concourse" with "other men" enact the pan-African embrace, equating liberation with collaboration among women of the black world: "O daughter of a grand and ancient race, / . . . You come, swift from the waking Afric dawn. / . . . Long have we wandered far beyond your shores, / With other men had concourse; but your arts / Move kindred feelings in us, . . . You call us back. Within us something stirred."[52] Like the writings of male pan-Africanists, Lowe's poem centered on the themes of dispersal and return, but she used interactions among black women, facilitated by art, to represent the reunion of diasporic blacks and Africans.

The LCP became a mainstay of black London and a functional link between agitation in the colonies and the metropole. Fortnightly events offered a rare social outlet for its denizens. Soon after Marson resigned from her post as editor in March 1935, however, the league lost several of its most active women, and though *The Keys* continued an uninterrupted run until the start of World War II, its literary content declined sharply after its first three years.

BLACK PROTEST AND THE BRITISH LEFT

The memberships of the LCP and WASU overlapped considerably in the early 1930s. WASU members published in *The Keys,* and the union sent the league copies of *Wāsù.* The groups focused their protests on many of the same issues, establishing the coordinates of a political imaginary largely shared by them despite their differences, and their social functions attracted the relatively small pool of student sojourners, hungry for interaction and a sense of belonging. The international campaign in defense of the Scottsboro Boys and agitation against growing government censorship in the Caribbean and Africa galvanized black intellectuals and linked their efforts in London to the struggles of Africans and others of African descent elsewhere. These causes also brought them into greater contact with potential allies associated with the Second (socialist) and Third (communist) Internationals, often via black radical intermediaries.

Black activists' and intellectuals' connections to the international communist movement varied widely but tended to be intermittent and pragmatic.[53] From its inception in 1919, the Third International espoused anti-imperialism, and in 1928, the Sixth Congress of the Comintern reaffirmed its commitment to the liberation of colonized populations throughout the world and the subjugated black masses of the American South. "In doing so," as Hakim Adi writes, the Comintern "became, perhaps, the era's sole international white-led movement to adopt an avowedly antiracist platform, and it was certainly the only one formally dedicated to a revolutionary transformation of the global political *and* racial order."[54] But the Sixth Congress also directed national communist parties to treat socialists and race-based organizations as enemies, exacerbating sectarian in-fighting and greatly limiting the possibilities for collaboration on the left. The small size of the Communist Party of Great Britain (CPGB), racism among the party rank and file, and the failure of operatives to engage systematically in organizing efforts among colonial workers greatly limited the Comintern's achievements. In the late 1920s and early 1930s, the Afro-Caribbeans George Padmore, Arnold Ward, and Chris Braithwaite (alias Jones) worked through the institutions and infrastructure of the Communist International to forge networks among people of African descent, but all three ultimately severed their ties with the Comintern in the mid-1930s following the advent of the new Soviet Popular Front policy, which sacrificed anti-imperialism for anti-fascist solidarity in Europe.

The British branch of the communist-affiliated League Against Imperialism (LAI), formed in Brussels in 1927, became the center of a great deal of anticolonial and antiracist activity until 1937. Under the former diplomat Reginald Bridgeman, the LAI actively cultivated allies among liberals, socialists, and Asian, Caribbean, and African agitators, representing something of an exception to the "class against class" policy of the "Third Period" after 1928. At its annual meeting in 1933, the LAI passed a resolution that pledged its support to the campaign for the release of the Scottsboro defendants and the "struggles of the Negro Workers in Africa and the West Indies for complete freedom and self-determination." The Barbadians Ward and Braithwaite had ties to Bridgeman and other communists in the LAI such as Hugo Rathbone. In 1931, Ward formed the Negro Welfare Association (NWA) with their assistance, and directed the group's political and social welfare activities as its secretary until 1936, coordinating the greater part of the Scottsboro agitation in London. Braithwaite, a former dockworker who lived with his white wife in Stepney, served on the NWA's executive committee and ran the Colonial Seamen's Association.

The most influential Afro-Caribbean communist operating in Europe during the early 1930s was George Padmore. Born Malcolm Nurse, he traveled from Trinidad to the United States in 1924 to study medicine and later entertained plans to study law, but he became immersed in politics and joined the communist party. He worked briefly in Harlem with African American radicals formerly associated with the African Blood Brotherhood before moving to Washington, D.C., where he participated in communist organizing at Howard University. Padmore became a full-time Comintern publicist and organizer for the next four years. The Red International of Trade Unions (the Profintern) appointed him head of its tiny Negro Bureau (officially known as the International Trade Union Committee of Negro Workers), and he directed it and edited its journal, *Negro Worker,* from Hamburg until the Nazi's rise to power. As Susan Pennybacker writes, "It is no exaggeration to suggest that Padmore himself *became* the Negro Committee in the few short years of its greatest prominence, years encompassing the early campaign around Scottsboro." Circulated clandestinely by black and colonial seamen, often disguised as religious tracts, Padmore's writings on Scottsboro helped publicize the case and the international movement to free the victims throughout the black world.[55]

A number of Africans also had at least a passing engagement with communism, but very few maintained a lasting affiliation with the party. Beginning in the late 1920s, Bridgeman and Rathbone of the LAI were in contact with the WASU, hoping to reach African students in Britain as well as anticolonial and trade unionist movements in West Africa. Jonathan Derrick estimates that several dozen Africans attended the KUTVU, or Communist University of the Toilers of the East, during the late 1920s and 1930s. Bankole Awoonor-Renner from the Gold Coast, who published an anthology of poems (*This Africa*) in Moscow in 1928, was one of the first. The Sierra Leonean trade unionist Isaac Theophilus Akunna Wallace-Johnson spent several months there at about the same time. Kenyatta first came to London in 1929 as the general secretary of the Kikuyu Central Association to deliver a petition to the Colonial Office demanding the release of the imprisoned Kikuyu leader Harry Thuku. He met Padmore in Frankfurt later that year, and the pair traveled together to Moscow. In London, he connected with Solanke and the WASU as well as socialist critics of settler colonialism in Kenya such as Norman Leys and Isabel and William McGregor Ross and communists in the LAI. He contributed to the *Sunday Worker* and the new *Daily Worker* before returning to Kenya in September 1930. By mid-1931, Kenyatta was back in London to testify before the Parliamentary Joint Committee on East Africa and made a second trip to the Soviet Union in 1932–1933. Both he and Wallace-Johnson continued to publish in communist outlets during the mid-1930s. Wallace-Johnson organized protests in support of the Scottsboro Boys in Lagos and sent news of them to Padmore in Hamburg. After colonial authorities deported him from Nigeria, he and the former WASU president J. B. Danquah addressed a Scottsboro meeting in Accra on February 6, 1934.[56]

A younger group of Africans and Afro-Caribbeans established ties to the communist party in the late 1930s and 1940s. Desmond Buckle from the Gold Coast, who was active in the LCP in the mid-1930s, became the first African member of the CPGB in 1937. The Barbadian Peter Blackman studied at Durham University and was posted to Gambia as a missionary, but he soon soured on missionary work because of discrimination in pay and other "unchristian racist practices." He returned to Barbados for a time before settling in London in 1938, where he gravitated to Dr. Moody and the LCP because of his missionary background. With the start of *The Keys*' sixth volume, he assumed the roles of editor and general secretary of the LCP. However, Blackman became increasingly involved in the LAI and NWA, headquartered in the office of the CPGB's Colonial Bureau. Although Moody eventually expelled him from the LCP for expressing "anti-British" views, for a time he helped push *The Keys* in a more critical direction and strengthened ties between the NWA and LCP.[57]

The international campaign in support of the Scottsboro Boys—the nine black youths who had been accused, then hastily convicted, with all but one sentenced to death, for raping two white women on a train en route from Chattanooga, Tennessee, to Paint Rock, Alabama—provided the occasion for momentary collaboration as well as the airing of mutual suspicions between the far left and the two main black organizations in London. Both the WASU and the LCP officially opposed communism, and the deeply religious president of the league rejected it on moral as well as political grounds. Party operatives, in turn, derided these groups as bourgeois opportunists or imperialist lackeys, especially Moody and the league. Nevertheless, the WASU collaborated with and enjoyed the support of the LAI and the few black communists working for the Comintern. Even Moody proved willing to work with communists via the London-based Scottsboro Defence Committee.

In June 1932, Ada Wright, the mother of two of the defendants, arrived in London. She visited Parliament and addressed crowds throughout the British Isles to launch a European publicity tour by the communist International Labor Defense. She spoke to a crowded LCP meeting. Moody corresponded with Walter White of the NAACP about the visit, and the two shared information on their parallel efforts and the communist-led legal defense team in the United States. As financial secretary of the LAI, Bridgeman served as her host and formed a loose alliance including black activists of various political persuasions alongside white and Asian communists, socialists, and liberals. Kenyatta and Cobina Kessie, the current editor of *Wāsù*, were among the Scottsboro Defence Committee's vice presidents and secretaries. The African American singer and stage performer Isaac "Ike" Hatch was the only other black member of the executive committee. A New York City native, Hatch had settled in London in 1925, and worked as a nightclub host and singer in Soho, often alongside Caribbean, African, and black British musicians. In the summer of 1933, he presided over a Scottsboro gala at the Phoenix Theater. A diverse roster of black entertainers took part, including black minstrel acts like the Mississippi Page Boys and the Black Flashers, the classically trained musicians John Payne and Rudolph Dunbar, the Gold Coast Quartet, and the then-relatively unknown Guyanese dancer Ken Johnson. The next year, the *Daily Worker* reunion party boasted Hatch and the Kentucky Minstrels as well as a "carnival Dance Band." As Pennybacker notes, Hatch "helped to create the vogue of Scottsboro," but working behind the scenes, Arnold Ward remained at the center of Scottsboro activity in London.[58]

Both the WASU and LCP compared white supremacy in the United States to the racial politics undergirding the British Empire. The long editorial that opened the first issue of *The Keys* connected the Scottsboro case to racial discrimination and violence in British colonies in South and East Africa and "on our very doorsteps in Cardiff, Liverpool, and London and elsewhere." The author declared: "Scottsboro is a challenge to the Coloured Races. It is just as much our case, and cause, as it is the case of the prisoners, and we, like them, are on trial." Despite Moody's personal misgivings and Ward's distrust of him, the liberal reformer and the communist collaborated publicly. At a meeting in December 1933, Ward proposed a resolution on Scottsboro, which the league passed, forwarded to the U.S. consul in London, and published in *The Keys*. The resolution registered the members' "unanimous protest against the recrudescence of the Lynching of Negroes in the United States of America," which produced "race friction not only in America but throughout the world," and called on "the United States Government to put an end to this incident which has stirred the emotions of the whole world white and black alike."[59] In a 1934 editorial under the heading "'Nigger' Hunting in America and Africa," *Wāsù* compared the British suppression of the Women's War of 1929 in southeastern Nigeria to the lynching of African Americans in the United States. "British justice" in the empire, the WASU suggested, was little better than lynch law.[60]

With the Scottsboro campaign in Britain nearing its peak in early 1934, protest erupted in the Gold Coast over a proposed extension of the criminal code targeting seditious materials. First instituted in Nigeria by Governor Graeme Thomson in 1929, "sedition ordinances" banned a variety of "suspect" publications, including the *Negro Worker* and other left-wing periodicals, in most British colonies in Africa and the Caribbean by the late 1930s. With the full backing of the conservative secretary of state for the colonies Philip Cunliffe-Lister (Lord Swinton), Governor Shenton Thomas instituted the Gold Coast Criminal Code Amendment Ordinance No. 21 on March 31, 1934, which mimicked the Nigerian ordinance, in what the government had characterized as a model colony. The move appalled defenders of free speech in Britain and the Gold Coast. The Fabian Society and the newly formed National Council of Civil Liberties (NCCL) took up the issue. Two separate delegations made the journey from the Gold Coast to London to protest the sedition ordinance and a new Waterworks Bill in mid-1934. One of the most powerful native rulers in the colony, Nana Ofori Atta, led the main delegation, known as the Gold Coast and Asante Delegation; Danquah, his brother and the editor of the *Times of West Africa,* served as its secretary. The second delegation consisted of the former secretary of the NCBWA Samuel R. Wood and George E. Moore, representing a group of younger, more vocal critics of the government in the Aborigines' Rights Protection Society (ARPS). The two delegations brought similar petitions opposing the bills and calling for an elected unofficial majority in the Legislative Council. The secretary of state and colonial office refused to give either a hearing, and the new legislation went into effect later that year.

To black intellectuals in London, these actions seemed part of a concerted effort to silence the colonial intelligentsia and buttress autocracy across the non-European empire. The WASU had protested first the imposition and then the revision of the Nigerian sedition ordinance. The arrival of the two Gold Coast delegations strengthened ties between London-based black organizations and resistance movements in West Africa, enhancing the groups' prestige in the colonies while amplifying the effects of the latter. Both the WASU and LCP held receptions for the Gold Coast and Asante Delegation and wrote letters to the Colonial Office and members of Parliament on their behalf.[61] Nana Ofori Atta, who had been a patron of the WASU since the late 1920s, sat with members for a group photo, graphically illustrating unity between a prominent "traditional" ruler and the African students and intellectuals in the union, and he spoke at a league conference on "the negro in the world today." In an article in *The Keys,* the Nigerian Louis Nwachukwu Mbanefo, who was also a WASU member, compared recalcitrant local publishers and critics of the colonialism in West Africa to Thomas Paine and William Cobbett. Efforts in support of the ARPS representatives Wood and Moore continued well into 1935, and after a series of meetings organized by the WASU, NCCL, and LAI, the Colonial Office finally granted Wood and Moore an interview. Danquah, Wood, and Moore remained in London for several years, and despite their differences, all three joined Amy Ashwood Garvey and C. L. R. James's International African Friends of Ethiopia; Wood and Moore also served on the executive committee of its successor, the International African Service Bureau.[62]

The agitation on behalf of the Gold Coast delegations in Britain was, as Derrick notes, "among the biggest anti-colonial lobbying efforts in the 1930s." The NCCL saw the sedition ordinances as "symptomatic" of an "increasing repressive tendency" as observable at home as in the colonies.[63] Its leadership left unquestioned the assumption that true British ideals were democratic and color-blind. Black critics, by contrast, viewed the legislation as symptomatic of a uniquely imperial problem—the undemocratic foundations of the colonial state—and used the issue of censorship in the colonies to highlight the deepening racial divide within the empire. Writing in *The Keys*, Danquah maintained that "now it is clear every Governor in a Crown Colony cannot stand one step below the greatest autocrats of the world." He cited a sequence of recent developments suggesting that the empire was increasingly a bifurcated entity, divided between, on the one hand, white populations in Britain and the dominions, which enjoyed the rights of democratic citizenship, and, on the other, the millions of non-Europeans subjected to increasingly extreme forms of control and exploitation. The Statute of Westminster, Danquah argued, "which ... substituted for it [the second British Empire] a ghostly entity called the British Commonwealth of Nations, ... led to a greater tightening of Imperial control over the Colonies, born of a dread that ... the red and white yolk of Empire would slip from their hands."[64] Far from supporting the progressive development of democratic civil society and self-government, Britain employed force to stamp out organic expressions of them. Connecting the plight of the Scottsboro defendants, violence and suppression of dissent in the colonies, and their local struggles against racism in the city, the Africans and Afro-Caribbeans drew attention to an increasingly stark color line within and beyond the British Empire.

AN "AFRICAN HOME" IN THE METROPOLIS

During the flurry of activity related to Scottsboro and the sedition ordinances, a new controversy developed over competing attempts to establish a place for people of African descent in London. Within the context of these broader campaigns, the effort to maintain a social center and hostel assumed symbolic as well as practical significance as a battle for freedom of action and city space. Protest against Colonial Office interference rippled through overlapping networks of black activists and leftist groups.

The goal of creating a hostel for people of African descent was not new. The black Liverpudlian and politician John R. Archer established the African Progress Union (APU) in London at the end of the Great War. A fixture in local left-wing politics, he had been elected the mayor of Battersea in 1913, making him the first black mayor in Britain. In the years that followed, Archer became a dedicated pan-Africanist, a member of the United Irish League (a gesture of allegiance to his mother's side of the family), and a major supporter of Shapurji Saklatvala, the first Communist MP in the House of Commons. Archer acted as the APU's president from its founding in 1918 until 1921, when the physician John Alcindor succeeded him following an internal shake-up. The group's constitution included the goals of establishing a "'Home from home,' where the members of the Association may meet for social recreation and intellectual improvement" and maintaining "a magazine or other publications . . . to promote the general advancement of African Peoples."[65] A few years later, Solanke and Ashwood Garvey proposed opening a hostel in London under the NPU's management not only to fill a pressing need but also to serve as a site of knowledge production and a demonstration of Africans' capacity for self-government. Like the APU and NPU before them, both the WASU and LCP sought to establish a residence and social space in the city.

Publishing *Wâsù* initially consumed the bulk of the WASU's limited resources, so its campaign for the creation of a hostel did not begin in earnest until 1927. Solanke proposed a cooperative scheme to the Colonial Office whereby the colonial governments of West Africa would fund a hostel for African students. Some officials in London seemed receptive to the idea, especially after the difficult time they had securing housing for African visitors during Wembley, but most within the Colonial Office and their colleagues in the colonies rejected it as a needless expense. Left to its own devices, the WASU initiated an independent fund-raising campaign. In "An Appeal—Need for a Central Home in London for African Students," Solanke described the proposed venture as an "'African home' in London, the management of which should be chiefly in the hands of the Africans themselves," and citing the example of the Indian hostel's influence on "the heterogeneous tribes of India to-day," he stressed the hostel's potential for fostering African unity.[66] The WASU occupied a house in West Kensington for a year in 1928 after Marcus Garvey secretly transferred the lease to them.[67] The following year, Solanke set out for West Africa to raise funds for a more permanent home. During his three-year absence, he cultivated stakeholders among local rulers and the coastal colonial elite, and started twenty new branches of the WASU in British West Africa and one in the Belgian Congo, where the British Leverhulme conglomerate operated with a virtual free hand.[68]

While keeping a close watch on Solanke's movements, the Colonial Office seized the opportunity to expand its oversight of student sojourners through a seemingly benevolent gesture. Major Hanns Vischer, secretary-general of the International Institute of African Languages and Cultures and a former director of education in Northern Nigeria, organized a committee including Dr. Moody to develop plans for a small social club and hostel. When he returned to London, Solanke found the union riven by internal divisions and financial problems that forced the group to stop publishing its journal for a time. Perceiving Vischer's initiative as a deliberate attempt to exclude the WASU, he publicly opposed the committee's scheme.

In the face of this new threat, the union closed ranks and moved forward with its plans. The WASU rented a house at 62 Camden Road on January 1, 1933. Over the next few months, the Nigerian Opeolu ('Olu) Obisanya, Solanke's soon-to-be wife, transformed the large house into a comfortable "home from home," and the hostel accepted its first guest, Prince Ademola, in early March. Vischer and Moody visited the hostel soon after it opened, and *Wāsù* reported that the LCP's president "burst into a hearty congratulation for ... this great monument."[69] The WASU's hostel and headquarters became a point of entry into the city for African students and numerous other visitors, as well as a popular rendezvous for London's black residents. It served as a site for the exchange of ideas among black intellectuals from around the Atlantic, and like the union's journal, it became a space for the performance of a modern but distinctive Africanness. The hostel's facilities were open to anyone of African descent, not just members or West African students, and overnight or short-term lodgers included African Americans, Afro-Caribbeans, and prominent African visitors. By staying at the WASU hostel, even for a short period of time, new arrivals entered the subculture of black sojourners and migrants in the imperial metropolis. The Guyanese T. Ras Makonnen remembered the hostel as "much more of a social outlet, for WASU House was a homely place where you could always get your groundnut chop, and there would always be dances on Saturday night."[70] The future president of Nigeria Benjamin Nnamdi Azikiwe, who studied in the United States and spent several weeks in London on his way back to West Africa to edit the *West African Pilot,* stressed its significance as a clearinghouse of news and ideas. It was, he recalled, "the headquarters of most West African students in London, where we congregated and devoured West African newspapers. I also had the pleasure of giving a series of talks to the students there."[71] The union also hosted officials in the Colonial Office, members of Parliament, and colonial experts, providing a rare setting in which African intellectuals could engage them in substantive debate. It was through the WASU that many future political leaders in West Africa first met the British politicians and colonial administrators who would one day hand over the reins of the colonial state.

Everyday life at the hostel became part of the union's struggle against racist portrayals of Africans and colonialism. *Wāsù* featured photographs of both the exterior and interior of the house, as well as group photographs of members and various important "friends" in which the former appeared in fashionable dress, presenting a picture of refinement and respectability. While emphasizing the unique contributions of African culture, pictorial and narrative depictions of the hostel adhered to middle-class British notions regarding the proper ordering of domestic life, particularly in terms of prescribed gender roles and sexual behavior. Group shots invariably featured 'Olu Solanke seated beside the group's guest in the center of the frame. Management of the hostel reflected the patriarchal organization of the middle-class home, complete with a married couple as "warden" and "matron" (usually Ladipo and 'Olu Solanke). The WASU constitution prohibited "non-residents" from entering the "residential quarters of the hostel without permission of the Warden" and "opposite sexes other than a husband and his wife" from either entering or remaining "together in any of the BEDROOMS." "Admission to girl students as residents" was dependent upon "the Warden's wife or a Matron being also resident at the Hostel, at the same time."[72] The WASU's founders consisted exclusively of men. As small numbers of African women joined the union thereafter, their gender continued to limit their influence in the group and even access to its hostel.

Nevertheless, in the mid-1930s, West African women, including many of the first African women to earn professional degrees in Britain, became a prominent and vocal presence within the union. Women members supplied important organizational labor, often filling the post of librarian or treasurer, contributed to its journal, and were instrumental in spreading the WASU's message beyond London to West Africa, the Caribbean, and the United States (activities discussed further in chapter 3).[73] Ironically, given that boarding at the hostel was not an option for most, women arguably had the greatest impact by building the WASU House into a center of black cultural and social life in London. In 1935, 'Olu Solanke, Ibidun Doherty, Victoria Omolara Bucknor, Irene Howe, Mrs. G. Nigretti, and 'Remi Ademola formed a "social committee" that organized and hosted regular dances and concerts, where a diverse mix of people mingled and danced to gramophone records or live performances. "Over fifty, irrespective of class, colour or creed, attended" the WASU's first social on September 14, 1935, including several prominent Afro-Caribbeans, such as the famous cricketer Learie Constantine, his wife, Norma Constantine, and H. O. Beresford Wooding, a barrister and the first new Caribbean member of the WASU since 1926. A varied cast of musicians performed a mix of black Atlantic styles, from the jazz and rumba to guitar-based West African palm-wine and highlife music popular in port cities up and down the coast. Besides entertainment, the social boasted a buffet of "tasty refreshments and other delicacies" prepared by Howe.[74] Operating within gendered constraints, WASU women used the social committee to carve out a semiautonomous space for themselves within the organization and created a setting where Africans and others of African descent in London enacted black internationalist solidarity through cultural expression and sociability, as much over a spicy rice dish and on the dance floor as through political organizing. Nigerian, Ghanaian, and Sierra Leonean women, including new arrivals Tinuade Adefolu, Adenrele Ademola (the daughter of Alake Alaiyeluwa Ademola II and Prince Ademola's sister), and Titilola Folarin (the daughter of the prominent barrister Adebesin Folarin), continued to direct the social committee into the late 1930s, but women members remained excluded from the top positions on the WASU's executive committee until the war years.

The WASU aimed to "present to the world a true picture of African life and philosophy," to "promote the spirit of self-help" and unity, and to foster "inter-racial understanding." The WASU House and *Wāsù* became related instruments for achieving these goals and demonstrated the fallacy of popular representations of African backwardness. As a functioning display of African initiative and intelligence, the hostel was the WASU's most consistent argument for self-government and colonial reform.

With Moody as the public face of the project, Vischer's committee moved forward with funds provided by the colonial governments in West Africa and the Caribbean, philanthropic and religious organizations in Britain, and several commercial firms with significant interests in the colonies. In October 1934, "Aggrey House," named in honor of the recently deceased educator from the Gold Coast Dr. Kwegyir Aggrey, began accepting members, and the space became fully operational in early 1935. Of its fifty members, roughly half were West African; the remainder consisted of Afro-Caribbeans and a few South and East Africans. The WASU's publicity onslaught against Aggrey House scheme began in the spring of 1934. Although they criticized Moody for his involvement, Solanke and the union focused the brunt of their attack on the Colonial Office, which they accused of attempting to establish indirect rule over Africans in London. They published a pamphlet by Solanke titled "The Truth about Aggrey House: Government Plan for Control of African Students." "The British Government which has absolute control over the lives of these peoples in their native lands," he charged, "has deemed it fit to seek a plan whereby it might exercise the same control over those studying in England." Linking Aggrey House to government "oppression" in the colonies and the "indignity" of racism in Britain, he appealed "to every lover of freedom to help us check this scheme of Imperialism which would strangle the very thought of its subjects and control their every action and opinion." The defense of WASU House was "a necessary preliminary to the greater independence."[75] In "The Year End Open Letter to the Educated Youths in West Africa" from January 1935, Solanke compared Aggrey House to the "system of Indirect Rule," and an editorial in *Wāsù* urged: "It is not enough for us to fight in the colonies for freedom. It is of the utmost importance that in the heart of the Empire we own and man a Hostel which will fight our cause *on the spot* and give the lie to traducers of the race whenever they say that we have not the capacity to manage our own affairs. It is for this reason that the white man of the imperialist school is doing his utmost to ruin the movement."[76] The LAI backed the WASU's position in the dispute over Aggrey House, which it characterized as a medium for "imperial propaganda." The same month that "The Truth about Aggrey House" appeared, the WASU held a protest meeting in which representatives of the LAI, NCCL, NWA, and Society of Friends took part. The participants declared a boycott of Aggrey House and formed the Africa House Defence Committee, which included the countess of Warwick as its president, the journalist Kingsley Martin, Julian Huxley, Norman Leys, and William M. Macmillan.[77] Writing in the *Negro Worker,* Padmore demonized the Colonial Office's attempt to "set up a little Jim-Crow hostel" in London and endorsed the WASU hostel.[78] In the months and years that followed, the union relentlessly challenged the notion that Aggrey House addressed the needs of African students in London, but Solanke continued to seek recognition and financial support from the parties behind the scheme.

The WASU hostel at 62 Camden Road hosted more than 160 guests, but by the end of 1936, it was clear that the group could not sustain the financial burden of rent on its current location. *Wāsù* did not appear in 1938 and 1939, but reemerged with a new format the following year. Solanke repeatedly requested Hanns Vischer's assistance with obtaining support from the West African governments and began courting John Harris, head of the Committee for the Welfare of Africans in Europe (CWAE). His persistence and fear that the controversy would push the WASU further toward the radical left led Vischer to appeal within the Colonial Office for subtle intervention in the form of assistance with fund-raising. He suggested that a form of benevolent paternalism vis-à-vis the WASU would give the government at least some hope of channeling members' energies into more moderate outlets and cited the pacifying influence of Aggrey House on those who joined it. "I have often seen Kenyatta Johnstone there meek and mild and very happy," he wrote, "and I am sure that the influence of Aggrey House on him and other wild lads from Africa . . . cannot be overestimated." While in London for the coronation in 1937, the Alake of Abeokuta arranged a meeting between Harris and representatives of the WASU at which it was agreed that the CWAE would lend the group £750 to purchase a new home. The Alake contributed an additional £100. Vischer ultimately prevailed within the Colonial Office, and the same year, the union received the first annual grant of £250 from the Nigerian government for the maintenance of its hostel. This represented only a partial victory given that the WASU had solicited funds—and the recognition they implied—from all four of Britain's West Africa colonies; two years later, the Gold Coast awarded the group a onetime grant of £100. Nevertheless, after an intensive appeal campaign, aided by Vischer and Harris, the WASU hostel fund grew to £1,500 by 1938, making the CWAE loan unnecessary, and the group acquired a freehold property on Camden Square. Free from the burden of rent or mortgage payments, the WASU's finances improved dramatically, and the new hostel heightened the union's profile and secured, in physical form, recognition of the African presence in the imperial metropolis.[79]

The WASU moved to 1 South Villas, Camden Square in mid-1938. The new hostel, which the members dubbed Africa House, had twelve beds, a café, a small library with a wide range of newspapers and books related to Africa and black history, and several recreational rooms for public lectures, debates, and other social events. Not only did women members continue to sustain the group financially, but it was largely through their labors that the male-dominated WASU made its greatest mark on the cultural life of the city. After the union moved into the larger location in 1938, 'Olu Solanke ran a small restaurant where she and other WASU women served lodgers and outside patrons "Joloff Rice" and other African dishes made with ingredients sourced through female relatives in Nigeria.[80] The popularity of the WASU's biweekly Saturday-night dances, where a diverse mix of "merry-makers" mingled and danced, grew steadily over the following decade, becoming an escalating source of income, and the group became more widely known for these events than for any of its other activities. Black musicians, both professional and amateur, frequently provided the music at these and other functions, and some became longtime members and engaged in the group's political activities. On rare occasions, the WASU hired professional dance bands like E. Child's Six Spirits of Swing, but the union usually relied on talent within its own ranks. Due to "these organised social, intellectual and spiritual functions," the WASU's annual report for 1938 declared, "'colour prejudice,' which is recently becoming rife in other parts of Great Britain, may now be considered as having died a natural death at the Hostel, ... enabling the white and black subjects of His Majesty the King to look and treat one another as brethren and equal citizens of the same Empire and at the same time promoting the spirit of universal brotherhood among all the races."[81] In addition to socials and dances, the union hosted receptions for visiting dignitaries and its annual WASU Day celebration, which involved more elaborate programs. The 1934 WASU Day festivities at St. Martin-in-the-Fields featured a program of traditional West African airs and melodies with piano accompaniment. The WASU celebrated the coronation of King George VI in 1937 with a dance featuring an orchestra led by O. A. Adeyin, and a sákárà band, including singers, drummers, and a *goje* or fiddle player, provided the entertainment at a reception for the Alake of Abeokuta during his visit to London.[82] The WASU feted Eslanda and Paul Robeson in 1935 in honor of their patronage of the group, and the members greeted them at the union's anniversary celebration the following year with a sákárà band followed by a dance performance by a group of women members. The Nigerian jazz organist and composer Fela Sowande, who served, in effect, as the WASU's music director, was one of the African musicians Robeson encountered at the hostel. During the reception for the Robesons, he accompanied G. Biney (most likely J. Kwesi Biney) in an "African ceremonial air" and a program of "Negro spirituals" on piano.[83]

The controversy over Aggrey House divided the WASU and LCP, as well as members from Nigeria and the Gold Coast within the union, and all but one of the members from the latter country left it for a time. The dispute magnified the ever-present tensions between Afro-Caribbeans and Africans that expressions of unity glossed over but never exorcised entirely. In spite of the differences in the composition of their membership and the public dispute over Aggrey House, the two most enduring black pressure groups during the interwar period increasingly appealed to the same publics and shared a set of political and intellectual concerns—above all, racism, the place of Africa and people of African descent in world history, and unity and cooperation within and among large and diverse black and colonial populations. Although their members came to London from varying circumstances and approached these issues from different perspectives and sources, they often arrived at similar conclusions, in part because of their encounters and struggles in the imperial metropolis. The organizations' political goals were remarkably similar—namely, the promotion of Africans and Afro-Caribbeans "to positions of authority and trust" and "federation, self-government, … and economic development" in British West Africa and the Caribbean. In immediate political terms, the horizon of their black internationalism was largely coterminous with the boundaries of the empire, and in this sense, their members remained "British" in their self-presentation and political assertions. But for the members of both groups, these steps were prerequisites to fostering greater interracial understanding and a transformed social order on a global scale. The WASU's "nationalism" was, at base, fundamentally internationalist, articulating regional, continental, and pan-African registers of belonging. At the same time, its members insisted that their identities as black and African made them more, not less, suitable for the full measure of imperial citizenship, and they envisioned a reformed multiracial federation based on relations of equality in which a self-governing West Africa would take its rightful place. The union viewed its hostel, in Solanke's words, as "a miniature West African Federal State under the management of a miniature West African Federal authority popularly known as WASU."[84] Africa House encouraged this political imaginary and its pan-African attachments by giving it quotidian substance. Due especially to the efforts of their women members, the WASU and LCP formed new spaces of interaction among people of African descent in London that were keys to their longevity and, ironically, platforms for their male leadership to mobilize universalist but fundamentally gendered ideals of citizenship with which to argue for representation within the British Empire on more equitable terms. As new crises emerged in the mid- to late 1930s, the tensions over Aggrey

House subsided, and it and WASU House developed into significant centers of black political activity.

．　．　．

In early July 1938, Lady Kathleen Simon, the Irish wife of the chancellor of the exchequer and stalwart of the Anti-Slavery and Aborigines' Protection Society, presided over the official opening of Africa House. It was a momentous occasion for the union and, indeed, for black London. The WASU's annual report for 1938 described the hostel as an "important and purely-African institution," "the first of its kind in London and the first in the history of New Africa." Lady Simon's presence as the keynote speaker, acting as a representative of the CWAE, attests to the WASU's rising public stature in the years leading up to the war, but it also illustrates the connections—and ultimately the disconnect—between black activism and internationalist groups in Britain. Simon was a committed antislavery activist, a Scottsboro signatory, and an advocate of colonial reform. Besides the WASU, both she and Harris had ties to Padmore and Dr. Moody. Lady Simon's devotion to antislavery work colored her view of the Italo-Ethiopian conflict and later appeasement; like Harris, she attributed the Italo-Ethiopian war to slave raiding and slavery. In her address, she expressed admiration for W. E. B. Du Bois and Paul Robeson, but she also declared, "We are glad to be British citizens and this Hostel is to help us be better citizens. The greatest thing about the British Empire is that it stands for equal citizenship." Her appearance at Africa House led to an interview with the Jamaican journalist Gwen Edwards during which she asserted "that only under European rule would Abyssinia be better off." She was more evasive on the subject of the recent disturbances in the Caribbean, stating that the "matter had to be judged on its own merits as the standard of living was different among the different peoples in the world." "The colored people will take their place in the world," she added, "but only by virtue of their own efforts." Simon saw no contradiction in asserting, on the one hand, the necessity of European stewardship, even at the expense of a fellow member of the League of Nations, and, on the other, that only the independent initiative of "colored people" could improve their lot within the British Empire. She simultaneously advanced an image of a color-blind empire based on equality and introduced cultural difference as a mitigating factor in access to wealth, political power, and social services.

As she spoke at Africa House, her husband, Sir John Simon, Prime Minister Neville Chamberlain, and the rest of the cabinet contemplated relinquishing African territories to placate Hitler's demand for colonies. As early as November 1937, citing the bloody record of German colonialism in Africa, the WASU passed a resolution stating in unequivocal terms that "we strongly protest against any ... scheme whereby any portion ... of African colonies, British, French or otherwise, shall be handed over now or at any future date, to Germany." In early December, the press reported John Harris's call for collective administration of former German colonies in Africa in place of rule by individual mandatory powers under the current League system. As Pennybacker observes, his and the WASU's "positions were directly counterposed."[85] The circumstances surrounding the opening of Africa House provide a glimpse into the complex and often-contradictory relationship between black activist-intellectuals and their white allies, between anti-imperialism and antifascism, as the decade progressed.

In a final twist that again exposed the way imperial interests and racial paternalism undermined the potential for cooperation, the WASU immediately entered into a protracted dispute with Harris and the CWAE over ownership of its new home. The CWAE and WASU had agreed that the former would hold the property in "nominal trust," while the union retained the exclusive power to nominate the non-African trustees and to oversee the day-to-day management of the hostel. The WASU rejected the initial draft of the trust deed, which "gave the Trustees very wide powers of control of W.A.S.U." As with the earlier controversy over Aggrey House, union members believed that assistance seemingly offered in the spirit of cross-cultural, interracial cooperation merely cloaked a scheme to limit their autonomy and freedom of expression. The two sides negotiated a compromise, and four representatives of the union agreed verbally to a revised draft. However, the WASU never received the new version, and the dispute remained unresolved well into the following decade, even after Harris's death in 1940. By the time Solanke finally agreed to pay £500 toward the £800 mortgage on the hostel to have ownership transferred to the WASU in 1944, plans for the opening of another, much larger hostel at Chelsea Embankment in southwest London preoccupied the group.[86]

Black Internationalism and Empire in the 1930s

IN 1935, AS KWAME NKRUMAH PASSED through London en route to the United States, where he would study at Lincoln University and the University of Pennsylvania, he saw a newspaper placard that announced "MUSSOLINI INVADES ETHIOPIA." He remembered feeling "as if the whole of London had suddenly declared war on me personally."[1] After the Second World War, Nkrumah returned to London for an extended sojourn. During the intervening decade, many of his friends and future collaborators mobilized existing institutions and formed new organizations in the city to combat the combined forces of imperialism and the global color bar. While Paul Robeson and his close friend the British actress and film critic Marie Seton chatted as they waited for his wife, Eslanda, on a train station platform in Berlin in 1934, the two noticed a group of Nazi storm troopers gathering around them. Robeson immediately made the connection to the Jim Crow South. "This is like Mississippi," he told Seton. "It's how a lynching begins. If either of us moves, or shows fear, they'll go further. We must keep our heads."[2] George Padmore was arrested in Hamburg soon after the Nazis' rise to power in 1933, and not long before his split with the Comintern. In a piece titled "Fascist Terror against Negroes in Germany," published in the *Negro Worker,* he compared Nazi racial violence to the treatment of the Scottsboro Boys. He warned, "Most Negroes in Europe and America as well as in the colonies do not yet fully realize that fascism is the greatest danger which confronts not only white workers, but it is the most hostile against the Negro race."[3] On tour with the Trinidadian calypsonian and stage performer Sam Manning, Amy Ashwood Garvey witnessed the brutality of occupying Nazi forces in the Sudetenland. Returning to London, she and C. L. R. James formed the

International African Friends of Ethiopia (IAFE) to organize propaganda efforts in defense of the African state in the weeks before the Italian invasion. Una Marson and many others of African descent joined the throng that greeted the exiled emperor Haile Selassie when he arrived at London's Waterloo Station in 1936. Marson had poured herself into managing the day-to-day affairs of the Ethiopian embassy in the months before Selassie's arrival and would accompany him to Geneva to issue a final plea for assistance in the name of "collective security."

A constellation of causes and ideas, as well as overlapping chains of personal ties, connected these individuals, and the 1930s dramatically altered their individual trajectories. They experienced the rise of fascism in a personal way and linked it to other instances of racial oppression and imperial aggression around the world. Their paths crossed in the imperial metropolis, where their attention turned increasingly to Africa, and they played significant roles in the intellectual and political elaboration of black internationalism in 1930s London. Metropolitan encounters at a historical conjuncture defined by competing imperialisms and internationalisms encouraged people of African descent to think in terms of their shared circumstances and challenges and to see themselves as representatives of an extranational racial community and a transcolonial opposition to empire. With the final stuttering expressions of old-style imperialist expansion focused on Africa, black intellectuals and agitators argued that their own freedom was key to world peace and stability and that antifascism was inseparable from anti-imperialism and the fight for racial equality within and between states.

Mussolini's grab for the African horn positioned colonial Africa at the forefront of political debate during the era of the Popular or "United Front" against fascism, and as Pennybacker observes, "London served as an unofficial center of colonial and antifascist exile." Ras Makonnen recalled that "Britain was really in a ferment—seething, in fact, like an African pot."[4] He not only emphasized the politicizing influence of metropolitan location but also claimed that the struggle for African liberation developed in part through relationships formed in Britain. During the 1930s, Cedric Robinson notes, "the radical nationalists were really internationalists, settling into variants of Pan-Africanism or socialism," and of James, Padmore, and Makonnen, in particular, he observes, "Together, they helped to constitute that generation of Black intellectuals that—at their historical conjuncture—presumed or perhaps understood that the project of anti-imperialism had to be centered in the metropole." Yet Robinson suggests that Makonnen's remarks, particularly his emphasis on the relative freedom these intellectuals enjoyed in the metropole, and similar ones by Padmore evidence "self-delusion" rooted in a "near-reckless admiration" for British liberal ideals; "their social and psychological identifications with European culture," in turn, "made the analytical and theoretical authority of European socialism almost irresistible." While it is certainly inaccurate to suggest that black anticolonialism developed first and foremost in London, Robinson's critique is rooted in a binary opposition between Anglophilia and engagement with the European left, on the one hand, and an essentialized "Black Radical Tradition," on the other.[5] Compared to the colonies, London offered greater freedom of expression and association and gave Africans and Afro-Caribbeans a privileged vantage point concerning the growing menace of fascism and the machinations of the British government in response to it. The importance of the imperial metropolis had less to do with a British commitment to individual liberties, which authorities regularly ignored when it came to anticolonial agitators, or left-wing opposition there than with the opportunities it presented for exploiting imperial connections in the cause of African freedom and the city's function as a transcolonial, transatlantic crossroads. In London, Makonnen believed, "Africans were not only compelled to think out the position of their own people, but were forced by the pressures of the times into making alliances across boundaries that would have been unthinkable back home." In contrast to Robinson, Makonnen consistently foregrounded the agency and contributions of African intellectuals in the city.[6]

The late 1930s was a time of possibility and of danger. Many black activist-intellectuals believed that the moment required and would initiate transformative political projects and a new epoch of world history, contributing to the conviction that their actions in the metropole could have far-reaching consequences. Their interactions in London and the "pressure of the times," including Britain's complicity in fascist expansion and the limits of antifascism on the left, convinced them of the necessity of thinking and acting across and through a multiplicity of "decided differences." In articulating their opposition to fascism and empire, Africans and Afro-Caribbeans borrowed from, expanded upon, and critiqued extant conceptions of internationalism to make material and political demands on the imperial state and to articulate a basis for intercolonial cooperation and a unified front against empire.

In thunderous tones, Amy Ashwood Garvey declared from the plinth at Trafalgar Square to a large demonstration organized by the IAFE on August 25, 1935: "No race has been so noble in forgiving, but now the hour has struck for our complete emancipation." She situated the crisis in Ethiopia within the context of interimperial relations and a history of black suffering and perseverance. In doing so, she placed the struggles of colonized peoples around the globe at the forefront of the fight against fascism. "You have talked of 'The White Man's burden,'" she noted wryly, but "now we are . . . standing between you and Fascism."[7] Originally from British Guiana, Thomas Griffiths first came to London that year, and during his brief stay before proceeding to Denmark, he came across a newspaper announcement for the rally and decided to attend. He listened as Ashwood Garvey, Jomo Kenyatta, and a number of others denounced the Italians' designs on Ethiopia, a member of the League of Nations. After the speakers concluded, he asked to address the crowd, claiming to be an Ethiopian. He recalled, "I linked up the struggle in Ethiopia with the larger struggle against imperialism in Africa."[8] During the Italo-Ethiopian War, Griffiths restyled himself T. Ras Makonnen. He returned to Britain two years later and remained for twenty years, collaborating closely with many of those he met that day in Trafalgar Square, until he followed George Padmore to Ghana to assist with the preparations for independence. As for the rest of these intellectuals, Makonnen's time in London, especially his interactions with African intellectuals there, led him to a deeper investment in Africa as the forefront of opposition to empire. The Italian invasion of Ethiopia created an opening for black intellectuals to engage with a range of white sympathizers, but ultimately, it exacerbated the fissures between them, engendering new attempts at organizing people of African descent autonomously.

During the reign of Menelik II (1889–1909), the kingdom of Abyssinia had rebuffed Italian encroachments. When Mussolini amassed his forces in the Italian colony of Eritrea after a border skirmish with Ethiopian troops, the Great Powers failed to respond decisively. Instead, France signed a secret agreement with Italy in early 1935, transferring a portion of northern Chad to Italian Libya. In the months leading up to the invasion in October, the British government offered a self-serving proposal amounting to collective colonization via the League-appointed Committee of Five. Eventually, roughly a month after the war began, both Britain and France voted in support of League sanctions against Italy. In December, they rejected a proposal to extend these to oil imports, and the French and British foreign ministers, Pierre Laval and Samuel Hoare, concluded a secret pact essentially conceding the majority of Ethiopia to Mussolini. When the specifics of the agreement came to light, the ensuing public outcry in Britain forced Hoare to resign, but the backroom dealings between the upstart Italians and representatives of the British and French empires continued. The Ethiopian emperor, Haile Selassie, delivered a stirring defense of his country's sovereignty before the League of Nations in Geneva, but the body rejected both his resolution denying Italian claims on Ethiopia and his request for a loan to fund the resistance movement. The Soviet Union joined the League in the autumn of 1934 but, as some black intellectuals noted in anger, continued to supply Italy with petroleum and other war materiel. On July 4, 1936, the assembly voted to lift the sanctions on Italy, and in November 1938, a little more than a month after the signing of the Munich Agreement, Britain officially recognized Mussolini as "Emperor of Abyssinia" by treaty.

The war in Ethiopia provoked a public outcry from people of African descent around the Atlantic and reaffirmed their conviction that the quest for global peace and stability could not be separated from the struggle for racial equality. Not only did many view Ethiopia as the only remaining independent African state, but as an ancient empire with a recent history of successful resistance to European invasion, it was also a potent symbol of African defiance in the face of imperialism and of an emerging modern Africa.[9] Imperiled by a conflict that, as the Africanist scholar William M. Macmillan observed, many interpreted as a "racial war," it inspired a "tremendous awakening" among black people around the globe. The editor of the *Ethiopian Observer* received thousands of letters of support. Both the African American mass press and such movement-oriented publications as the NAACP's *Crisis* carried extended coverage of the war and reprinted readers' letters expressing solidarity with the beleaguered Ethiopians. African Americans wrote to the Ethiopian Research Council in Washington, DC, to volunteer for military service, declaring, "We are Ethiopians." In Harlem, Erik McDuffie notes, "nationalist stepladder orators enjoyed renewed visibility on the neighborhood's streets," and the communist Provisional Committee for the Defense of Ethiopia enjoyed broad-based support in the local community. For Paul Robeson, "it was a watershed for black American consciousness, since it exposed 'the parallel between [black American] interests and those of oppressed peoples abroad.'" In British-controlled West Africa, a mass meeting in Lagos in late September 1935 attracted more than two thousand people, and leading members of the Nigerian Youth Movement formed the Lagos Ethiopia Defence Committee three months later. Makonnen remembered hearing that schoolchildren wept in the Gold Coast when Italian troops entered Addis Ababa. There were expressions of outrage throughout the Caribbean, including boycotts of Italian-owned businesses. While European leaders and the British left debated the merits of sanctions, dockworkers in South Africa and Trinidad imposed their own by refusing to offload Italian cargo. The crisis in Ethiopia precipitated a rush of activity in cities across Europe as well, particularly among Africans and Antilleans in Paris. The first meeting of the Comité International pour la Défense du Peuple Ethiopien drew a crowd of eight hundred blacks, Arabs, and whites, bringing together black intellectuals and workers, pacifists, antifascists, and an array of international, colonial, and metropolitan feminist organizations.[10]

Black women were at the center of much of this activism on both sides of the Atlantic and used the moment to forge new links between black organizations as well as with white and mixed-race internationalist groups. In Paris, Paulette Nardal served as secretary of the pacifist Comité Mondial contre La Guerre et le Fascisme as well as the Comité International pour la Défense du Peuple Ethiopien, founded by the labor organizer Tiemoko Garan Kouyaté from the French Sudan (Mali). She established ties to the male-dominated Union des Travailleurs Nègres and became the first female contributor to its journal, *Le Cri des Nègres*. Her article included a telegram sent to the League of Nations in which she decried the Italian assault on Ethiopia in the name of "the colored peoples [*les groupements de couleur*] of the entire world, without distinction of nationality, party or class." Fluent in English, she also became the "primary relay point" between the Comité International and Ashwood Garvey's IAFE in London, and when local committees in the Gold Coast, Nigeria, and Sierra Leone raised £500,000 for the Ethiopian cause, she tried to use the Comité International to deliver the funds to Emperor Selassie. While maintaining close ties to these other groups, she formed her own, the Comité d'Action Ethiopienne.[11]

Like Nardal, Ashwood Garvey launched a new black organization dedicated to the defense of Ethiopia while collaborating with a mix of groups in Britain. Many Britons opposed Mussolini's assault on Ethiopia, though primarily in the name of liberal internationalist principles enshrined in the notion of collective security; the vast majority also opposed retaliatory measures that might further destabilize relations in Europe. The crisis inspired the creation of nonaligned pressure groups devoted to publicizing Ethiopians' plight, which opened new avenues for cooperation between blacks and whites. Ashwood Garvey and other black activists worked with the Abyssinian Association and Sylvia Pankhurst's Workers' Social Federation (WSF). Pankhurst had been interested in the issue of colonial freedom for quite some time, but the major European powers' impassive response to Italian aggression against Ethiopia underscored its salience for her. She became close friends with Ashwood Garvey and a supporter of the IAFE and the League of Coloured Peoples. In 1936, she launched the staunchly anti-imperialist *New Times and Ethiopian News*.[12]

The Italo-Ethiopian War provided an issue around which moderate and more radical black intellectuals—Afro-Caribbean, African American, and African—in London could unite and had a radicalizing effect on existing black organizations. Ethiopia preoccupied the WASU during the second half of 1935. The union's journal published "The League, Italy and Abyssinia" in July, which argued the crisis demonstrated that the international body was "most ineffectual." A month later, the WASU forwarded a resolution to the British foreign secretary stating that "this union views with horror, alarm and indignation the contemplated aggression of Italy on Abyssinia and it most strongly protests against it." Beginning in September, it held weekly religious services to "invoke divine intervention" on behalf of Ethiopia that combined theology, political analysis, and music. The WASU compared the diplomatic maneuverings around Ethiopia to the hollowness of British claims to "benevolent trusteeship," and cast the Italian invasion as part of a larger struggle between humanistic cosmopolitanism and narrowly national or racial interests. An article in the November issue of *Wāsù* dismissed any notion of a fundamental difference between Italian aggression and the actions of other European empires, which "subscribe to a form of society based on the exploitation of the many by the few for the enrichment of the latter. . . . What Italy is doing today the other 'great' nations had done in the past." The author expressed hope that "the Ethiopian disaster may yet prove a blessing in disguise if it succeeds in uniting the black peoples of the world." African and Afro-Caribbeans in the imperial metropolis aligned themselves with Ethiopia "against what they saw as the common front of imperialism."[13]

C. L. R. James came to Britain in 1932 at the urging of the Trinidadian cricketer Learie Constantine, who lived and played professionally in Nelson, Lancashire. A product of Trinidad's elite Queen's Royal College, James had been a colonial schoolteacher and had established a reputation as a short-story writer in Trinidad and a member of the avant-garde Beacon Group. He arrived in London with two book manuscripts, "The Life of Captain Cipriani" and "Minty Alley," the latter a novella set in the gritty but vibrant markets of Port of Spain. As his funds began to dwindle, he made his way to Constantine's home in Nelson in late May, where the two collaborated on the latter's biography, *Cricket and I* (1933). Over the next two years, James's attention turned increasingly to politics, and he commenced a lifelong engagement with Marxism. He reported on cricket for the *Manchester Guardian* and used the off-season to study the Marxist canon. His reading left him convinced that Stalin had betrayed communist internationalism and its early anti-imperialism. In mid-1933, James returned to London, where he met a number of African intellectuals and activists. He took part in several LCP functions and published two pieces in *The Keys*. At an early league conference, he characterized the crown colony system as a "cancer" and argued, "Any united movement in the West Indies had to be based on the black masses, or it was doomed."[14] The Ethiopian crisis erupted at a moment of personal and political transition for James, sparked in part by his growing contacts with Africans in the city. "Gradually, . . ." he later recalled, "I began to gain a conception of black people which I didn't possess when I left the Caribbean." The Italian invasion pushed him further in the direction of both Africa and the radical, nonaligned left.[15]

In July 1935, James and Ashwood Garvey formed the IAFE at the latter's International Afro Restaurant "to assist by all means in their power in the maintenance of the territorial integrity and political independence of Abyssinia." Kenyatta tersely summarized the IAFE's position in the communist party's *Labour Monthly*: "To support Ethiopia is to fight Fascism." James chaired the new body, and Dr. Peter Milliard from British Guiana and T. Albert Marryshow, the head of the Grenada Workers' Association, served as vice chairpersons. The group also included Kenyatta, Sam Manning, the St. Lucian economist W. Arthur Lewis, and the African American singer John Payne; J. B. Danquah, Tufuhin Moore, and Samuel R. Wood from the Gold Coast joined as well. Ashwood Garvey was the center of gravity, mobilizing and extending her international network of contacts. She organized a series of protests and spoke at rallies held by the Labour Party, Independent Labour Party, and LAI.[16] She approached her friend Ladipo Solanke and addressed a meeting of the WASU on the subject of Ethiopia in October 1935. Soon thereafter, a group of women within the union answered her call to action by forming the Ethiopia Defence Fund. In publicizing the new initiative, its journal acknowledged that the "W.A.S.U. ladies" were the motive force behind this and many of the group's other activities: "If anyone wishes to know how in these hard times *WASU* is still forging ahead, our answer is that it is mostly due to the activities of our women members. Their motto seems to be (excuse the Mussolinian ring): With the men, without the men or against the men, *WASU* must be maintained. Our Socials Committee and the W.A.S.U. Ethiopia Defence Fund are entirely composed of our women. . . . While the men were discussing, the women had acted."[17]

The Italian invasion of Ethiopia and the placid response of Britain and the League of Nations precipitated the LCP's most outspoken statements against imperialism to date. Despite the pacifism of its founder and president, in the summer of 1935, Claude Cummings, an "African correspondent" in Wales, suggested "that an urgent appeal be sent forthwith . . . for all the manhood of our race who are fit to rally round Abyssinia so that the Italians may be given a sound drubbing," adding that "we shall never be free until we unite among ourselves." On September 4, 1935, the league passed a resolution expressing solidarity with the Ethiopian people and forwarded the document to the Ethiopian legation, the British and Italian governments, the League of Nations Union, and "all European Governments now operating in Africa." It charged "that this attitude of a European country towards an African people is expressive of a deeply seated conviction in the minds of most European peoples that African peoples were ordained to be their serfs," and it called upon "the European countries which now wield authority in Africa and . . . the League of Nations . . . to consider a plan for the future of Africa which . . . should be nothing less than the ultimate and complete freedom of Africa from any external domination whatsoever."[18] Protests and organizing efforts continued throughout 1936 and 1937. In the spring of 1936, *The Keys* published James's "Abyssinia and the Imperialists," which was markedly more provocative in its tone than the journal's usual content. "Africans and people of African descent, especially those who have been poisoned by British Imperialist education," he wrote, "needed a lesson. They have got it." In March 1937, the LCP collaborated with several groups to organize a fund-raiser for Ethiopian refugees and invited the visiting African American scholar Ralph Bunche to preside. Bunche declined but attended, and Padmore assumed the responsibility in his place. At its annual general meeting in 1938, the league called "the attention of His Majesty's Government and Parliament to the great movement of solidarity which the Italian

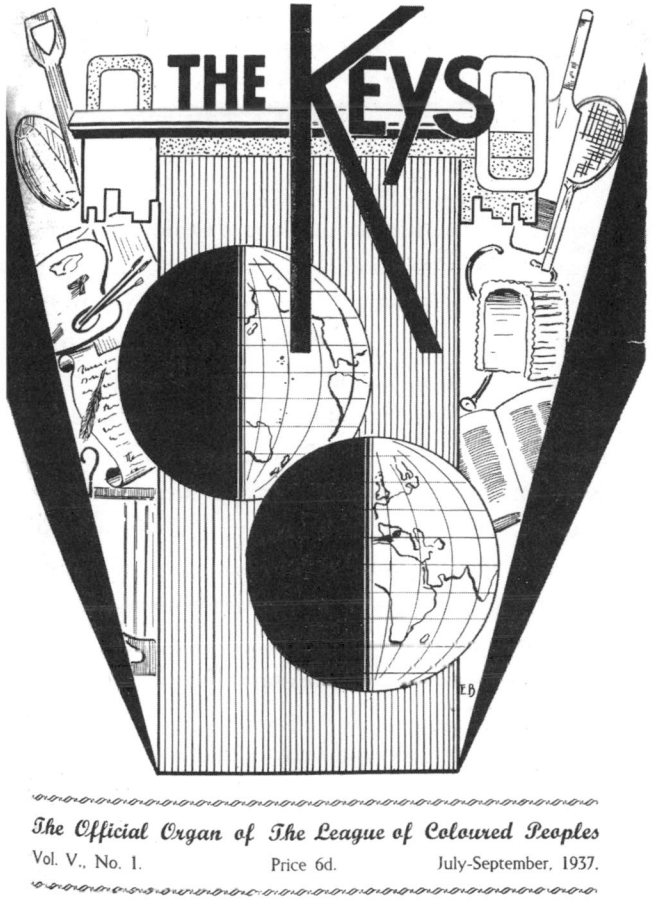

The Official Organ of The League of Coloured Peoples

Vol. V., No. 1.   Price 6d.   July-September. 1937.

FIGURE 4. Cover of *The Keys* 5, no. 1 (July 1937). © The British Library Board.

attack upon Abyssinia has brought about among the African and African-descended peoples in reaction against European violence, conquest and domination."[19]

As the situation worsened in Ethiopia, Emperor Haile Selassie fled Addis Ababa for London. For those who met him in person, the experience provoked feelings of sympathy and pride. Makonnen recalled forcing his way through the throng of onlookers at Waterloo Station on June 3, 1936, to get a glimpse of the arriving delegation. Chris Braithwaite's daughter presented the exiled emperor with a bouquet of flowers, and Ashwood Garvey and the IAFE hosted a reception for the emperor and his party.[20] Hezekiah Oladipo Olagunju Davies, a Nigerian student who had helped form the Lagos Youth Movement, became active in the WASU soon after he arrived in London in 1934. In anticipation of Selassie's first press conference in the city, Davies secured credentials as a correspondent for the *Nigerian Daily Times*. The only African among the large group of reporters, he "was ushered in first before [Selassie]." Davies had little knowledge of Ethiopian history and, as he recalled, assumed that Ethiopia had also "come within the operation of the Berlin Conference." When he asked "whether Ethiopia was or had ever been an Italian colony," Selassie "sat upright" and replied, "The Ethiopian empire has always been a sovereign state, and has been so for eight thousand years; no power on earth can convert Ethiopia into a colonial possession."[21] In the weeks ahead, Davies noted the British government's growing discomfort with Selassie's presence, which deepened his apprehension about its willingness to pursue a policy of colonial appeasement. Una Marson had the closest view of the emperor's travails. While working in the information section at the League of Nations, she approached the head of the country's legation, Tekle Hawariat, to offer her assistance, and he sent her to Dr. Azaj Workneh Martin, the Ethiopian ambassador to Britain. On October 2, 1935, the day before Italian troops crossed into Ethiopian territory, Marson returned to London. Although the embassy could pay her little to nothing, she eagerly worked for long hours in its office, handling the bulk of its growing correspondence, and chose to return to Geneva as Selassie's personal secretary. Exhausted and distraught, she returned to Jamaica in late September 1936, where she told the *Daily Gleaner* in an interview the day of her arrival that "the position of Ethiopia is very heart-breaking and the tribulations of the Ethiopians have cracked me up." Marson compared the British response to the violation of a fellow League member's sovereignty to the discrepancy between British imperial rhetoric and practice, chastised her fellow Jamaicans for not joining the diasporic outcry, and called for concerted action among those in London to pressure the government. "The Colonial office," she maintained, "is not going to lift a finger to work out a clear and definite Colonial policy until it has to do so."[22]

Certain patterns recurred in the reactions of black intellectuals and activists to events in Ethiopia, especially a tendency to cite Italian aggression as part of a general critique of empire and as evidence of the need for greater levels of cooperation among people of African descent. Marson's identification with Ethiopia and her relationship with Dr. Martin reaffirmed her commitment to black unity and informed her perspective on the events of the late 1930s, including the labor unrest that gripped the Caribbean. She penned a moving poem, "To Joe and Ben (Brutally murdered in April 1937 at Addis Ababba [sic] by the Italians)," in response to news of the executions of two of the Ethiopian ambassador's sons, Joseph and Benjamin Martin. Educated in Britain, both young men had been on the platform with Ashwood Garvey at the aforementioned IAFE demonstration in Trafalgar Square, and Marson had gotten to know them personally. They returned to Ethiopia to join the underequipped forces resisting the Italian advance. The brothers' sacrifice resonated with her growing attachment to Africa and people of African descent around the world and with her own commitment, as she put it, "to fight for a country / yours, and yet not yours."[23] Her poem also highlights how gender discourse inflected responses to the war. Marson, Ashwood Garvey, and women within the WASU and LCP emphasized Italian atrocities against women and children and organized to collect funds for Ethiopian refugees. By contrast, most black men around the Atlantic, including the African and Caribbean men who dominated London-based organizations, consistently represented the conflict in terms of sexual assault, describing it as the "rape" of Ethiopia, and some proposed armed struggle there and throughout the colonial world. If, as some scholars suggest, this was the more radical position, it also reflected a conception of pan-Africanism as a response to the emasculating effects of European imperialism.[24]

INTERNATIONAL AFRICANS AND
THE GLOBAL IMPERIAL ORDER

The Ethiopian crisis became the lens through which black intellectuals viewed global politics and the British Empire, particularly its racist foundations, on the eve of the Second World War, and their activism reached new levels in London. As existing organizations such as the LCP and WASU rallied to the cause of Ethiopia, first the short-lived IAFE and then the International African Service Bureau emerged as further expressions of the desire for unity and fostered new links between people of African descent in the city and beyond.

Upon his release, the German authorities deported George Padmore to Britain, but he soon returned to Paris. While in London, he reconnected with his contacts among the city's black population and delivered several public lectures. After one of these at the London headquarters of the League Against Imperialism, he encountered his childhood friend James, a fortuitous reunion that would prove to be significant for both men. Padmore, in James's words, "was tied up with Moscow," while he had become a Trotskyist since his arrival in Britain the previous year. But, James recalled, "that didn't trouble us. That night we ... stayed up talking till about 4 o'clock in the morning."[25] Writing in the NAACP's *The Crisis* in late 1937, Padmore noted, "The Italo-Ethiopian War and the demand of Hitler for the return of the former German colonies in Africa has [*sic*] served to focus attention on the question of the 'Haves' and 'Have Nots.' ... It is no exaggeration to say that there never was a period in the history of post-war Europe when the issue of peace or war has been so inseparably bound up with the scramble for colonies in Africa as at the present time." Two months later, in the *Chicago Defender*, he claimed to have returned to Germany and compared "the position of the Jews under the Nazi regime" to "the conditions of the Negroes in the Southern States of America and South Africa."[26] In the shadow of the Italo-Ethiopian War, the political activities of Afro-Caribbeans and Africans and the level of collaboration between them grew considerably, filliped by the arrival of new personalities such as James and Padmore.[27] The chance encounter between the latter two and the years of collaboration it initiated illustrate how black intellectuals formed connections—in this case, reconnected—on the margins of leftist political activity in the 1930s, while maintaining their autonomy from the organized left.

Black activist-intellectuals interjected their perspectives into imperial and transatlantic debates over imperialism and the coming war, and helped force a major reformulation of the espoused goals of colonial governance. In a world in which empire was the greatest destabilizing force, and Africa the focus of renewed imperial ambitions—as white internationalists whether liberal, socialist, or communist recognized—the dual themes of imperialism and internationalism as much defined the field of political discourse in which black intellectuals formulated their goals as did the more commonly posited binaries of nationalism and imperialism or nationalism and internationalism.[28] Representatives of black organizations participated in countless events sponsored by center-left internationalist groups including the Independent Labour Party (ILP), Union for Democratic Control, National Council for Civil Liberties, Antislavery Society, Fabian Society, Friends Society, and LAI. The LCP and WASU held summer schools, study groups, and conferences. An impressive array of intellectuals from Britain and the colonies presented papers at the LCP's third annual conference in 1936, most notably James, H. O. Davies of the WASU, the African American economic historian George Brown, Leonard Barnes, Norman Leys, and William M. Macmillan.[29] In 1938, Peter Blackman addressed a crowd of ten thousand at a rally in London's Empress Stadium organized by the League of Nations Union's National Youth Executive. At the instigation of James Desmond Buckle, the small Gold Coast Students Association (GCSA), NWA, CPGB, and London Federation of Peace Councils cosponsored a public "Colonies and Peace" meeting later that year, and representatives of the NWA, GCSA, LCP, and the Coloured Film Artistes Association participated in the conference "African Peoples, Democracy and World Peace" in July 1939.[30] In their speeches and writings, black intellectuals situated conditions in the colonies within a constitutional struggle for meaningful citizenship in the British Empire and a global band of color facing worldwide white supremacy.

The main leftist parties in Britain did not form a Popular Front comparable to the one in France in the 1930s, and after the Labour government resigned in 1931, fractured over management of the growing economic and budgetary crisis, the center-right National Government remained in power until 1940. Nevertheless, internationalist ideals and symbolism suffused public rituals and political culture in Britain. Support for the League of Nations, in particular, ran high until the end of the 1930s and transcended partisan political divisions. Pacifism was a prominent feature of liberal and socialist variants of internationalism. In late 1935, the British public reacted to Italian aggression with a mixture of outrage and expressions of support for the League of Nations, but as fears of military escalation mounted over the coming months, attention to Ethiopia's plight abated.[31] The country's fate foreshadowed that of anti-imperialism in the era of antifascism. In practice, socialists, communists, League of Nations Union members, and antislavery and other human-rights activists frequently worked together on particular causes, from the Scottsboro petition movement to aiding Spanish republicans and refugees. During the final years of the decade, however, the issue of appeasement undermined this incipient unity, often making for odd bedfellows. Debates over international organization and appeasement were also about imperialism and the structure and goals of the British Empire. The notion of an egalitarian British Commonwealth of Nations gradually supplanted the old "language of empire," particularly in socialist and antifascist circles. The colonial secretary and former Labour Party member Malcolm

MacDonald told colonial administrators at the 1938 summer school at Oxford: "The trend is towards the ultimate establishment of the various colonial communities as self-supporting and self-reliant members of a great commonwealth of free peoples and nations." A term used originally to distinguish between the self-governing white dominions and colonial dependencies with large non-European majorities, in its new guise, *the Commonwealth* reflected a new imagining of the British Empire as a family consisting of "trustees" and "wards" but devoid of the explicit racial chauvinism of Victorian and Edwardian imperialism.[32]

While a small minority opposed internationalism to empire, many others, including British socialists and proponents of the new Commonwealth ideal, advocated the internationalization of colonial administration or interimperialism to ease competition for resources and territory between the major powers. Whereas the notion of the Commonwealth wrapped the self-serving, hierarchical relations of empire in an illusory façade of equal partnership, the internationalism espoused by groups from the center to the left of British politics amounted to little more than a coordinated imperialism and the ratification of the color line on a global level. As early as 1933, the Labour Party "declared ... that the mandate system should be accepted for all colonies inhabited mainly by peoples of primitive culture ... such as certain African and Pacific territories." The British League of Nations Union championed a resolution in 1938 advocating "the transfer where practicable of non-self-governing colonial territories ... to the mandate system" to "secure equal opportunities for trade and commerce of all Members of the League." In a speech the same year, John Harris of the Anti-Slavery Society and the Committee for the Welfare of Africans in Europe revealingly (but inaccurately) linked the Berlin Treaty of 1885 to the 1919 Treaty of Saint Germain, which included the Covenant of the League of Nations, as progressive steps toward international administration in Africa. He proposed the creation of a vast territory under international control in Central Africa as "an instrument with which to begin a new era in colonial affairs." Like the new idealized vision of the Commonwealth, the proposal, as Pennybacker notes, "encouraged optimism in Britain's imperial future and her role as a sensible, adjudicating power," but "severely compromised any notion of independent African agency and fostered illusions."[33]

Afro-Caribbeans and Africans denounced these proposals as a betrayal of the spirit of internationalism and the continuation of imperialism in a more coordinated form. When a majority at the "The Colonial Problem and Peace" conference organized by the National Peace Council and Anti-Slavery Society in 1935 endorsed collective administration of the colonies by the world's industrial powers, Arnold Ward "accused liberal delegates of being preoccupied with peace in Europe and showing little real concern for the problems of Africa and the threat to Ethiopia." In *How Britain Rules Africa,* published the following year, Padmore condemned the Peace Council's proposal to share colonies as "collective imperialism," pointing to racial prejudice and capitalist exploitation of colonial resources as the real barrier to meaningful reform within the British Empire. "Even in London, the heart of the Empire," he wrote, "men and women of color are often ostracized and humiliated in such a way as to destroy whatever early love and affection they might have had for the Commonwealth of which they are supposed to be citizens."[34] Collective administration, he asserted in a piece for *The Crisis,* rationalized the continuation of colonial subjugation and capitalist extraction into a "Utopian" future. Whereas European communists and socialists attributed war and economic exploitation to capitalism, of which imperialism was but an epiphenomenon, black intellectuals centered empire in their analyses as the driving force behind an increasingly monopolistic form of capitalism and the most resolute barrier to cross-cultural cooperation and socialism. When the European powers, specifically Britain and France, sacrificed Ethiopia, they legitimated the pursuit of empire and set Europe on the path to another war. As they "scurried away like rats from a drowning ship," the liberal empires of Western Europe deserted "not only . . . the victim of aggression, but the League and collective security. But little did they realise that when Addis Ababa fell the peace of Europe would go down with it." The "irreconcilable clash of interests among the imperialist powers" rendered the League, as Padmore put it, echoing Lenin, nothing more than a "thieves kitchen."[35]

By the start of the war in the fall of 1935, James was head of the Finchley/ Hampstead branch of the ILP. As the main institutional bases of the left became increasingly quiescent and accommodationist on the question of empire in the name of antifascist collaboration, the war in Ethiopia divided the ILP. James called on the "workers of Europe, Peasants and workers of Africa and India, sufferers from Imperialism all over the world" to "organise yourselves independently, and by your own sanctions, the use of your own power, assist the Ethiopian people." He traveled throughout the British Isles, making the case to local party branches for autonomous internationalist action. "In a typically torrential speech" during the ILP's annual conference in Keighley, Fenner Brockway remembered, James "appealed as a black worker for help for the black population of Abyssinia," but the party's leadership remained resistant to the idea. Two of the ILP's three members of Parliament, the pacifists George Buchanan and John McGovern, opposed direct action on the grounds that the Abyssinian cause was nationalist, not socialist, in nature and suggested that Haile Selassie was as much a dictator as Mussolini. The third, James Maxton, maintained "that 'working-class sanctions' . . . would help to create a psychology of war against Italy." In the end, due largely to James's impassioned plea, the rank and file voted to adopt a resolution supporting workers' sanctions. However, he soon led an exodus of the Trotskyist "Marxist Group" from the party after it refused to join the Fourth International.[36]

James devoted much of 1936 and early 1937 to developing the Trotskyist movement in Britain, called first the Trotsky Defence Group and then the Revolutionary Socialist League. He became the intellectual center of gravity in the small group of communist dissidents and edited their journal, *Fight*. He regularly denounced Stalinism and the Popular Front as communist complicity with imperialism. With the financial assistance of two of Constantine's English neighbors in Nelson, Harry and Elizabeth Spencer, James traveled to France in 1936 to conduct research for his history of the slave revolt and revolution in Saint Domingue and spent part of the next year in Brighton writing the manuscript.

As James moved away from the ILP in the late 1930s, Padmore became a larger presence within it. More than James, he experienced the new Soviet Popular Front policy as a betrayal on a personal level and embodied the growing spirit of independence among black activists and intellectuals in the late 1930s. Padmore condemned socialists and communists alike for failing to rally around the cause of Ethiopia, noting that "bourgeois humanitarians did more . . . to help the Abyssinians than any of the national sections of both Internationals." After his departure from the international communist movement, he embarked on a new career as a freelance journalist and agitator, focusing on organizing outside the confines of the established left. He never again joined a political party but worked in partnership with an array of groups and individuals to gain the widest possible hearing for colonial abuses. If, as Pennybacker suggests, "Padmore's departure from the communist movement beckoned a greater ecumenism of purpose on the antiracist left," he also helped generate a new level of cooperation among people of African descent across political and regional differences. Though often focused on the British Empire, his writings covered the pan-African world, and they traversed much of it in published form, facilitating communication and debate between black intellectuals and anticolonial activists in Britain, Africa, the Caribbean, and the United States.[37]

Padmore shuttled between Paris and London for nearly two years before finally settling in the latter by late 1935. He assisted the English shipping heiress Nancy Cunard, whom he first met in London through Ward in 1932, with the completion of her remarkable *Negro: An Anthology,* a sprawling compilation of black writing and culture tracing the contours of diasporic Africa. While in Paris, he caught up with Kouyaté, who had recently split with the Comintern and was coordinating much of the activity regarding Ethiopia in France. Padmore and Kouyaté collaborated on plans for an abortive Negro World Congress (Congrès Mondial Nègre), part of their broader efforts, as Edwards explains, "to *institutionalize* a new International, a working organization channeling and linking the networks of activists and information they represented."[38] In London, Padmore initially stayed with Kenyatta and soon began working closely with other Afro-Caribbean and African intellectuals, including several associated with the IAFE. Not long after his split with the communists, he wrote to Solanke, "All the young African friends made a great impression on me. I now feel that despite all our difficulties and the terrible plight of our fatherland, there is a future for Africa."[39] Padmore's encounters with African intellectuals in the WASU reinforced his commitment to organizing people of African descent independently. At about the same time, he became a contributor to several African American publications. In 1935, *The Crisis* published a series of pieces on Ethiopia and Africa. Padmore urged African Americans to organize "common action. . . . For when all is said and done, the struggles of the Abyssinians is [*sic*] fundamentally a part of the struggles of the black race the world over for national freedom, economic, political, social and racial emancipation." Between 1938 and the late 1940s, he wrote on a near-weekly basis for the *Pittsburgh Courier* and *Chicago Defender,* through which his words reached millions of black readers in the United States and, von Eschen suggests, "crafted a popular language for the international movement that animated black American discourse" during these years.[40]

Not only did James's views go beyond the cautious anti-imperialism of the ILP, with its significant faction of pacifists, but in rejecting League sanctions against Italy as a ruse, he was also at odds with his peers in the IAFE. At a meeting of the group on October 2, 1935, he resigned over the issue. Two days later, the ILP's *New Leader* ran an article by James in response to the recommendations put forward by the League of Nations' Committee of Five, which involved handing over key state functions related to the military, policing, economic policy, public finance, and social welfare services in Ethiopia to European experts and advisers appointed by and answerable only to the League. He critiqued the committee's report as a roadmap to what J. A. Hobson had termed "inter-imperialism" and characterized the plan as "the greatest swindle in all the living history of imperialism." He situated the crisis in Ethiopia within a longer history of imperialism, refusing to distinguish between the imperialism of individual nations and coordinated, international forms of external control. "Let us fight not only Italian imperialism," he exhorted, "but the other robbers and oppressors, French and British imperialism." The following year, James put forward similar arguments in a review for the *New Leader* of Padmore's *How Britain Rules Africa* and the Ugandan Prince Hosea Akiiki Nyabongo's *Africa Answers Back*. He criticized Padmore's conclusions regarding the "future of Africa," particularly his appeal to "'enlightened far-sighted sections of the ruling classes of Europe with colonial interests in Africa' to co-operate with Africans." "Africans must win their own freedom," he insisted. "Nobody will win it for them. They need co-operation, but that co-operation must be with the revolutionary movement in Europe and Asia."[41]

The IAFE seems to have become moribund soon after James's resignation. Kenyatta told Ralph Bunche that "James ran out on him."[42] By autumn of 1936, Kenyatta and several others associated with the IAFE joined Padmore in a new working group called the Pan-African Federation for the Defence of Africans and People of African Descent. Padmore, Kenyatta, Cunard, and a few others met informally at Bogey's Bar in the Royal Hotel and the bar at the Regina Hotel, both in Bloomsbury, until the group eventually secured a meeting place at 2 Calthorpe Street on the corner with Grays Inn Road. Robert Broadhurst, a merchant who had earlier acted as a liaison between the NCBWA and the London-based APU, was elected president, and fellow Ghanaians Samuel R. Wood and George E. Moore, the Somali Mohamed Said, J. J. Magade of South Africa, and Kenyatta served as vice presidents. After Ras Makonnen arrived in London, he, Kenyatta, and Padmore frequently visited the LCP, Aggrey House, and the Student Movement House to draw more Africans and Afro-Caribbeans into the group's activities, and various members soapboxed in Hyde Park on Sundays. Special Branch reported that the group also distributed a small news bulletin titled the *Voice of Africa,* but lack of funds soon forced the federation out of its premises, allegedly in arrears. In early 1937, Padmore moved to 42 Alderney Street in Pimlico, which doubled as a headquarters for the group and his residence. At about the same time, Nyabongo returned to Britain to continue his studies at Oxford, living briefly with Padmore.[43]

In March, the Sierra Leonean I. T. A. Wallace-Johnson arrived in London from Accra to appeal his sedition convictions before the Privy Council. Moving between Europe and West Africa during the early 1930s, Wallace-Johnson had worked with the Comintern in Moscow and Hamburg, corresponded frequently with Padmore, and maintained contact with the LAI and NWA in London. In June 1935, he established the West African Youth League (WAYL) in the Gold Coast. Largely because of its campaign in support of Ethiopia, the WAYL soon had more than twenty branches across the colony. Just weeks earlier, on May 15, 1935, the *African Morning Post* had published "Has the Africa a God?" written anonymously by Wallace-Johnson. In it, he declared, "The European ... believes in the god whose law is ... Ye 'Civilised' Europeans, you must 'civilise' the 'barbarous' Africans with machine guns. Ye 'Christian' Europeans, you must 'christianise' the 'pagan' Africans with bombs, poison gases, etc." Both Wallace-Johnson and the paper's Nigerian editor, Nnamdi Azikiwe, were arrested for the piece, and the former convicted of two counts of sedition, carrying a £50 fine or three months in jail. Wallace-Johnson paid the fine but appealed unsuccessfully before the West African Court of Appeal, leaving the Privy Council as his only recourse. Upon his arrival in London, he contacted Reginald Bridgeman at the LAI and Arnold Ward of the NWA and floated the idea of a central bureau for agitators from the colonies, but he received little encouragement or support from the CPGB. He then turned to Padmore and the Pan-African Federation.[44]

On the evening of April 5 or 6, 1937, Padmore convened a meeting of the Pan-African Federation to discuss the formation of a committee "embracing radical Colonial elements." Wallace-Johnson, James, Makonnen, Nyabongo, and the Nigerian Louis Nwachukwu Mbanefo, a member of the WASU and LCP, were present. Bunche, who came to study anthropology at the London School of Economics (LSE) in preparation for an extended research trip to East Africa, met Padmore at an Ethiopia event in late March, and at the latter's urging, he attended the gathering as well. The conversation, Bunche noted, was spirited and "centered on" developing a "program for Africa." Mbanefo suggested organizing an "African Bureau and Journal for [the] exchange of information regarding African problems and all exploited black peoples"; "all agreed that African liberation must depend on socialization thru revolution of Europe and socialization of Africa." The group elected Wallace-Johnson, James, Kenyatta, Nyabongo, and Braithwaite to a planning committee. At a follow-up meeting in mid-April, the committee decided to organize a demonstration to arouse sympathy for Ethiopian refugees and "to start a publication ... dealing with colonial matters especially in relation to South and West Africa." By June 1937, the International African Service Bureau (IASB) established a small headquarters at 94 Gray's Inn Road, a short walk from the LAI's offices at 53 Gray's Inn Road, but relocated to 12a Westbourne Grove in Bayswater sometime in 1938, where Makonnen and William Harrison, an African American student at the LSE, reportedly lived.[45]

Chaired by Padmore, the IASB assembled an impressive mix of black intellectuals and activists who had far-reaching connections and traveled to London in the service of myriad causes. According to James, "The basis of that work [in the IASB] ... was Padmore's encyclopedic knowledge of Africa, of African politics and African personalities, his tireless correspondence with Africans in all parts of the continent, the unceasing stream of Africans who made the Bureau and its chairman their political headquarters when in London." "Revolutionaries and bourgeois nationalists," he recalled, "all came."[46] Wallace-Johnson acted as the group's general secretary. Ashwood Garvey and Kenyatta served as co-vice-chairpersons, Broadhurst as treasurer, and Makonnen as the publicity secretary. The remainder of its executive committee consisted of a mix of West Africans (Mbanefo, Azikiwe, and Kouyaté) and Afro-Caribbeans (James, Braithwaite, and the Jamaican Aida Bastian, who helped form the Ethiopian World Federation in Harlem in 1937). Three of the WASU's most prominent members—Mbanefo, Adetokunbo Adegboyega Ademola, and Laminah Sankoh, the Sierra Leonean editor of *Wāsù*—were involved in the group. Arnold Ward joined after his expulsion from the Communist Party for refusing to carry out a reorganization of the NWA, and the Sierra Leonean Constance Horton (later Cummings-John) after her trip to the United States in early 1937. Black entertainers such as Sam Manning and the African American pianist Lawrence Brown attended some of the group's early meetings. The Guyanese Peter Milliard, James Headley, and the Nigerian Babalola Wilkie (or Wilkey) participated in its activities.[47] The young St. Lucian economist W. Arthur Lewis advised the IASB on economic issues in the colonies. Padmore lived with Dorothy Pizer in a flat in Cranleigh Gardens, where their neighbors included for a time

Kenyatta and the English socialist Dinah Stock, and where they hosted a rotating cast of black intellectuals, including the historian Eric Williams, for evening tête-à-têtes.

The IASB's aims were internationalist in scope and content. An early leaflet characterized it as "an organisation representing the progressive and enlightened public opinion among Africans and Peoples of African descent," devoted to the development of "a stronger and more intimate feeling of international solidarity and inter-racial unity." During late 1937 and early 1938, the bureau published the *African Sentinel* as well as a shorter, mimeographed news bulletin entitled *Africa and the World,* both edited by Wallace-Johnson. In mid-1938, *International African Opinion* replaced the *African Sentinel.* James edited the journal until his departure for the United States in October, after which Harrison and Makonnen shared the duties. The *International African Opinion*'s masthead announced the IASB's "motto": "EDUCATE— CO-OPERATE—EMANCIPATE, Neutral in nothing affecting the African Peoples." A lengthy editorial—unsigned but likely written by James—opened the inaugural issue, amounting, in Edwards words, to "a call to internationalization" explicitly addressed to a transcolonial audience. James characterized the bureau's purpose as assisting "by all means in our power the uncoordinated struggle of Africans and people of African descent against the oppression from which they suffer in every country." Although the challenges "differ from country to country," he asserted, "there is a common bond of oppression, and as the Ethiopian struggle has shown, all Negroes everywhere are beginning to see the necessity for international organisation and the unification of their scattered efforts." Although many of its members were Afro-Caribbeans, James touted the IASB as an "AFRICAN" organization, and advertisements for the group claimed it was "run solely by Africans." But if, as James put it, the group "styles itself African," he insisted, "the reason for this is not racial chauvinism. We repudiate the idea of substituting a black racial arrogance for a white." As Edwards suggests, "'African' here indicates ... a claimed identity," not an appeal to a primordial blood bond. James repudiated the idea that "African emancipation is to be achieved in isolation from the rest of the world" and argued for the necessity of international organization "of all forms of struggle," while distinguishing the IASB's internationalism from that of the main founts of left-wing politics in Europe.[48]

Although the bureau limited "active membership" to people of African descent, it welcomed white allies as "associate" members. Padmore's close friends Cunard and Ethel Mannin supported the group's activities. Its white

PRICE 3d. (10c. U.S.A. and Canada)

INTERNATIONAL

AFRICAN OPINION

Motto :

EDUCATE—CO-OPERATE—EMANCIPATE

Neutral in nothing affecting the African Peoples

VOL. I.   No. I.   JULY, 1938.

INTERNATIONAL AFRICAN OPINION is the monthly organ of the International African
Service Bureau.   Views expressed by contributors are not necessarily endorsed by either the
Bureau or the Editorial Committee.   No payment is made for MSS. submitted, and such
contributions as are sent must include a self-addressed stamped envelope to ensure their return;
the Editorial Committee will not undertake correspondence concerning MSS. otherwise sent.

Annual subscription is 3/6, while single copies are 3d. each.

All communications should be addressed to: Editorial Committee, International African
Opinion, 12a, Westbourne Grove, London, W.2.

CONTENTS

FIGURE 5. Cover of *International African Opinion* 1, no. 1 (July 1938).
United Kingdom, The National Archives, Kew, CO 323/1610/2.

patrons eventually included Sylvia Pankhurst, the left-wing publisher Victor
Gollancz, Dorothy Woodman of the Union of Democratic Control, and
several Labour and ILP MPs, among them Arthur Creech Jones, Ellen
Wilkinson, Noel Baker, and Reginald Sorenson, who was also a trustee of the
WASU. The IASB met regularly with the Labour Commonwealth Group in
the House of Commons, and members addressed branches of trade unions
and the League of Nations Union, peace and antifascist rallies, and ILP and
Labour Party functions. During the second half of 1937 alone, the IASB held
demonstrations in Trafalgar Square, Hyde Park, and Memorial Hall, passed
resolutions protesting the treatment of strike leaders in the Caribbean, and
planted more than twenty-five questions with their contacts in the House of

Commons on such subjects as "repressive legislation" and the confiscation of "progressive literature," the cocoa planters' boycott of monopolistic European firms in Nigeria and the Gold Coast, and working conditions for African miners in the Gold Coast. James later recalled, "We allowed no opportunity of putting our case to pass us by."[49]

The IASB was never an institutional base akin to the WASU or LCP but rather a nodal point in shifting sets of relationships and networks that outlasted it. It was an unstable product of the tense international and domestic atmosphere, mounting anticolonial protest in the empire, and, more than most scholars have acknowledged, a grafting of Padmore's web of contacts onto well-established connections among African intellectuals in London. Makonnen claimed that the "whole movement towards the IASB derived directly from the Ethiopian crisis, and although our interests now became broader, a link was maintained with Ethiopia right through the period in London."[50] Nevertheless, significant ideological divisions marked relations among groups and individuals even at the height of agitation in support of Ethiopia, and differences of perspective and experience remained a significant stumbling block to effective political unity. Working relationships both within the IASB and between it and other black organizations were fragile and frequently strained. The IASB brought together black activists with markedly different relationships to organized communism. Unlike James and Padmore, Makonnen and Kenyatta had little interest in Marxism. James recalled Kenyatta as "an African nationalist, a man who when you told him something, as long as it was against imperialism and for the Africans, could be depended upon." Pizer later told St. Clair Drake "that any visits Kenyatta made to Moscow certainly had no effect on his ideology, nor did any 'education' that she and Padmore tried to give him." Bunche deemed him an "intense racial chauvinist" who had little to no faith in whites and noted that Wallace-Johnson seemed at least "mildly left-wing," but "quite a blatant 'I' man." Some of the Africans Bunche met shared their suspicions that certain West Africans in IASB were looking only for an opportunity for "grafting." James remembered that he, Padmore, and Braithwaite attended LCP events "chiefly with the idea of asking inconvenient questions" and communist meetings solely "to criticize their policy," despite Wallace-Johnson's ties to the LAI.[51]

Despite their personal and political differences, Afro-Caribbeans and Africans found a basis for cooperation in a set of core principles that emphasized cooperation, equality, and self-determination for all colonial peoples.

In the fall of 1936, *The Keys* publicized a recent debate held at the WASU's hostel on "the advantages of greater cooperation between Africans and West Indians—a subject as vital as it is longstanding." Although "West Indians came in for the usual trouncing for their vanity, their ignorance of the cultures of their forefathers, their desire to be imitation Europeans, and their blindness to the advantages of mutual understanding," the author (likely Lewis) noted that the "lively" debate "itself showed signs that these charges are beginning to lose their original validity." He implored Afro-Caribbeans "to break through the anti-African propaganda with which their educational system is saturated, and . . . to re-establish contact with the civilisations in which they have their roots."[52] Internal divisions and differences of opinion never disappeared, but personal relationships forged through interaction and debate in London bred a sense of participating in a pan-African struggle. Padmore and James followed very different trajectories through the worlds of organized Marxism in Europe, but Ethiopia led them to similar conclusions regarding the relationship between imperialism, nationalism, and fascism, and both men turned to revolutionary internationalist solutions that placed unique importance on Africa. Their substantive differences and the extended debates that followed from them centered on means, not their diagnosis of moment, and contributed to the development, as Adi puts it, of "a new Marxist and anti-imperialist as well as a Pan-Africanist political milieu" in London during the late 1930s.[53]

James met African scholars such as H. O. Davies in the WASU and developed close friendships with Mbanefo and Kenyatta, contributing to his growing identification with the anticolonial struggle in Africa. In a review of Kenyatta's ethnography of the Kikuyu, *Facing Mount Kenya* (1938), James invited the book's author to engage in a public exchange of ideas not only because they shared the goal of African liberation, but precisely because of their differing opinions as to the road ahead. "All friends of the African know the first necessity," he wrote. "But for what? . . . How does he [Kenyatta] see the future of free Kenya? He must let us know, so that all of us, Africans and friends of Africans, can thrash the problem out." James addressed his friend and fellow traveler as a participant in a wider public constituted through "exchange and argument," not unanimity or an innate racial affinity, and the circulation of texts like the *International African Opinion* and *Facing Mount Kenya*. The textual manifestations of this conversation were only the tip of the iceberg. James ("Nello") closed a lengthy and impassioned letter to Padmore, written in 1953 after a fifteen-year separation: "I have never had for you anything else but admiration and respect. You and I know more than most the long way we have travelled from the little capital in the little West Indian Island ... let me send my warmest good wishes to yourself, Dorothy, the indomitable Ras, and all other friends. I cannot tell you how pleased and proud I was to see that in all those disputes I used to have with him, Jomo was right and I was wrong."[54]

After Wallace-Johnson and then James left London for Sierra Leone and the United States, respectively, in 1938, financial difficulties, reportedly due to the erstwhile member Babalola Wilkie's misappropriation of funds, precipitated the IASB's decline. Makonnen resigned from the group later that year and attempted to form a West Indian Co-operative Alliance. By 1939, the IASB relocated to 35 St. Bride's Street, the offices of the ILP, and the Colonial Office and Special Branch reported that Padmore ran the ILP's colonial bureau. He contributed regularly to the *New Leader, Left,* and *Controversy,* and he and Kenyatta kept the issue of colonial violence on the ILP's agenda and in the pages of its publications. The two lectured at ILP summer schools and as part of Workers' Educational Association programs. Allies on the British left who refused to see anti-imperialism as marginal to antifascism were increasingly rare, and although the ILP was more anti-imperialist than ever, it was in decline as the war approached. In 1944, Padmore officially dissolved the IASB, only to rehabilitate the Pan-African Federation with his close collaborators Kenyatta and Makonnen in order to organize the 1945 Pan-African Congress in Manchester. Working from London, he remained an important facilitator of black internationalist activity into the 1950s. Continuing the work of the IASB, the tireless Padmore would have a profound influence on a new generation of African student agitators during the 1940s.

AFRICA AND THE CARIBBEAN

In the late 1930s, articles on the "rape" of Ethiopia regularly appeared in *Wāsù, The Keys, African Sentinel,* and *International African Opinion* alongside pieces on the disturbances in the Caribbean and Africa, the draconian pass system instituted by the Smuts regime in South Africa, and the possible return of mandate territories such as Togoland to Nazi Germany. Collectively, these issues focused black internationalist activity in London and reaffirmed the conviction that the remedy for the abuses of British "trusteeship" consisted of democratic self-government, economic development, and federation in West Africa and the Caribbean. The convergence of these events enabled black critics of empire to position struggles in the colonies within the larger context of the crisis initiated by the global economic downturn and spread of fascism.

In the mid-to-late 1930s, a rash of major strikes and demonstrations erupted in the Gold Coast, Nigeria, Kenya, Tanganyika, the Copperbelt of Northern Rhodesia, and throughout the British Caribbean. Beginning in Trinidad as early as 1933, the official centennial of the abolition of slavery, and erupting sporadically in other locales including British Honduras (Belize), British Guiana (Guyana), Barbados, and Jamaica in the years that followed, the disturbances were, as Mary Chamberlain explains, "the culmination of a century of frustration, and a watershed marking the transition from the struggle for emancipation to one for independence."[55] These expressions of discontent also reflected the deepening effects of the Depression, which, in the Caribbean and the coast of West Africa, resulted in declining earnings as the price of sugar, cocoa, palm oil, and other exports plummeted, and a steep rise in jobless rates and the cost of staple goods. British papers such as the *Reporter* attributed the unrest largely to local anger over Ethiopia. Three weeks into the 1937 strike in Trinidad, the governor convened a special session of the Legislative Council during which he listed "racial feeling engendered by sensational reports of the Italo-Ethiopian War" as one of the main causes. Sir Selsyn Grier reiterated this view in his remarks at the 1938 summer school for colonial administrators at Oxford.[56] Black agitators were not the only ones to draw a connection between Ethiopia and unrest in the colonies.

The first rumblings of trouble in Trinidad overlapped with a series of celebrations across the British Isles, cosponsored by the Anti-Slavery Society and League of Nations Union, to mark the centennial of emancipation, inciting public discussion of the achievements and failings of colonial rule since the end of slavery. Among Afro-Caribbeans and Africans in Britain, even political moderates like Dr. Harold Moody of the LCP highlighted the discrepancy between the rhetoric of British benevolence that characterized the festivities and current conditions in the Caribbean. At the Wilberforce centenary celebration in Hull, he urged his audience, "Please do not lose sight of the fact that Wilberforce's work was made essential, not on account of the sins of my own people, but mainly or entirely because of the sins, selfishness and short-sightedness of your own people—sins from which, as a race, you have not, even yet, altogether delivered yourselves." He added: "I would . . .

remind you that the Englishman is so proud of himself and of his achievements and has such a consciousness of race superiority that he will do and does do everything in his power to establish this fact—the one fact on which the whole of his existence seems to depend." In a piece on the Wilberforce Centenary in WASU's journal, Modjaben Dowuna observed, "The principle for which the abolitionists stood requires constant reiteration to-day, for the danger of it being undermined, is as great to-day as ever." Because the "spirit which brought slavery into being is far from being dead," he argued, "it should be the business of future African leaders to extend their interests beyond their local communities" to "the conditions ... of other parts of Africa" and "in America and the West Indies." Ignoring the self-congratulatory tone of the centennial festivities, Dowuna cast people of African descent as the abolitionists of the 1930s and insisted that the task before them required greater "cultural contacts" and international organization.[57]

The near-simultaneous occurrence of the centenary with the unrest across Britain's "tropical empire," a term used to encompass Britain's colonies in sub-Saharan Africa and the Caribbean, led both critics and agents of empire to link these regions within a single imaginative and analytic framework.[58] The work of the historian William M. Macmillan and the appearance of the first installment of Lord Malcolm Hailey's sweeping *African Survey* helped legitimize a more holistic approach to the tropical empire and encouraged black intellectuals' tendency to think in terms of the similarities between their circumstances. A self-described "lib-lab," Macmillan lived from the age of six in South Africa and produced two critical, if paternalistic, works on the position of Africans in the Union of South Africa—*Bantu, Boer and Briton* (1929) and *Complex South Africa* (1930). Following a trip to the Caribbean in 1934, he cautioned that the "groundswell of discontent" in Jamaica should be taken as an ominous portent of things to come in colonial Africa. Although "I was trying to find a model colony," he wrote to Leys, "I'm sadly dashed and much more unrepentant socialist."[59] In 1936, he published *Warning from the West Indies: A Tract for Africa and the Empire,* which examined the economic and social causes of the unrest in the Caribbean. As the title indicates, he believed the work stoppages and ensuing violence presaged future developments in Britain's African colonies. "My visit [to the West Indies] early this year," Macmillan explained in the preface, "was undertaken ... to get new light on the study of the African colonies."[60] In his subsequent book, *Africa Emergent* (1938), he compared racial segregation in the Union of South Africa to "the racial decrees of Nazi Germany" and stressed the need for a new approach to the colonies that included investment in development and the incremental introduction of democratic self-government. *Warning from the West Indies* and *Africa Emergent* influenced an entire generation of Africanist scholars in Britain and provided both colonial reformers and black critics with a set of powerful arguments.[61]

The conservative Malcolm Hailey borrowed heavily from Macmillan in his comprehensive *African Survey,* the first edition of which appeared in 1938. Hailey's text immediately superseded the extant standards, Frederick Lugard's *The Dual Mandate in British Tropical Africa* (1926) and the American Raymond Leslie Buell's *Native Problem in Africa* (1928), as the primary reference on colonial Africa. Though hardly a radical, Hailey maintained that recent events in the Caribbean and the growth of anticolonial movements across Britain's African colonies exposed the erroneous "assumptions of trusteeship," which "failed to place on the colonial power any direct obligation to assist in the material or social development of the indigenous population."[62] Although, as R. D. Pearce observes, Hailey "had no wish for a uniform pan-African policy towards the British territories," his *African Survey* did "much to encourage a pan-African approach to the administration of the continent" and laid the foundation for a "new [intellectual] mapping of the continent" as the object of development and welfare schemes. In this sense, as Pearce suggests, Hailey "effectively destroyed indirect rule as a system."[63]

Black intellectuals in London read Macmillan's work approvingly, if not without criticism; they were even more ambivalent about Hailey's work. Macmillan participated in conferences organized by the LCP and WASU on several occasions, and Marson reportedly distributed copies of *Warning from the West Indies* during the violent suppression of strikes and protests in Jamaica in 1938. W. Arthur Lewis reviewed the book in *The Keys.* Although he applauded Macmillan's attention to the poverty that "reflects itself in every aspect of life," the economist disagreed with the latter on the form that development should take. Whereas Macmillan proposed "intensive cultivation" of agricultural goods for export and "the formation of large capitalist companies able to afford machinery and trained agricultural staffs," Lewis argued that such a program would only deepen economic dependence and further reduce prices and wages, virtually guaranteeing that any wealth produced would continue to flow outward. He proposed a "policy of extending peasant cultivation" as a more favorable alternative. In 1937, Lewis spoke on the topic "African Economic Problems" alongside Macmillan at an LCP conference. "The prime object in developing Africa," he maintained, "should be the increased welfare of Africans . . . ; exactly the same process is going on today in Africa as went on in the West Indies in the eighteenth century—vast wealth is being poured out in dividends, leaving the country impoverished, and the people with little to show for their labour." During the years that followed, in addition to land redistribution, Lewis increasingly emphasized state-directed industrialization and the growth of secondary industries, as evidenced in his first major work, *Labour in the West Indies: The Birth of a Workers' Movement,* published in 1939 as part of the Fabian Research Series. Yet he remained critical of the top-down, technocratic orientation of the emerging development paradigm and identified racial prejudice as a barrier to development "from below." Lewis and his peers in London went much further than either Macmillan or Hailey in challenging the reputed peculiarity of the black laborer and insisted that economic development must proceed in conjunction with the extension of the franchise to a mass electorate and other constitutional reforms.[64]

The work of Macmillan and Hailey contributed to the emergence of a new language of colonial development within official circles during the 1940s. Black intellectuals in London were critical interlocutors in this process. Communist internationalism and the rise of expansionist fascist regimes in Europe and Asia heightened the stakes in the debate over British imperialism, and the activities of Africans and Afro-Caribbeans at the heart of the empire amplified the effects of protest in the colonies. In fact, colonial officials erroneously suspected IASB involvement in the wave of strikes that rocked the Caribbean as well as the cocoa holdup in the Gold Coast. The often-brutal response of local officials and police to expressions of deprivation and political discontent in the British Caribbean brought black organizations together in a working alliance. From their seat in the imperial metropolis, they scrutinized the proceedings and findings of the commissions of inquiry charged with investigating the disturbances, and like Macmillan and Hailey, they connected events in the Caribbean to emerging struggles in colonial Africa.

Beginning in 1936, *The Keys* featured a series of articles defending the oil field strikes in Trinidad as expressions of "genuine" hardships and legitimate grievances. The Barbadian H. W. Springer insisted, "To put the blame on 'agitators' is to shrink criminally and perilously from the real situation." He maintained that the islands' status as crown colonies entitled them to make material claims upon the British state and, by extension, "every British voter." The journal also published an address to the LCP by Grantley H. Adams, a member of the House of Assembly in Barbados, that systematically examined the causes of the disturbances in each case.[65] On August 8, 1937, the IASB held the first of several meetings and demonstrations in Trafalgar Square to publicize the plight of Caribbean workers, an event that attracted a crowd of roughly two hundred people. James delivered a sweeping overview of Caribbean history, and Kenyatta compared recent events in the islands to "instances of oppression by white settlers in Kenya."[66]

In response to the most recent strike in Trinidad during 1937, Secretary of State for the Colonies W. Ormsby Gore appointed a commission chaired by Sir Murchison Fletcher to investigate its causes. As the commissioners prepared their findings, Padmore decried the government backlash in Trinidad as "Colonial Fascism." "After 140 years of Crown Colony rule," he wrote, ". . . [i]t is high time for a fundamental change in the political constitutions . . . along the road of self-determination." When the commission released its report, signed by Sir Arthur Pugh of the general council of the Trade Union Congress, he described it as "an outrage," "truly Fascist" in character, that "would do credit to Mussolini." Wallace-Johnson asked in the *African Sentinel,* "Is the Secretary of State for the colonies prepared to accept the West Indian affair as a sort of warning against future occurrences of a similar nature in any other section of the Colonial Empire?" "Labour unrest is not confined to the West Indies alone," he pointed out. Lewis also excoriated the commission's findings in *The Keys.* He blamed the recent unrest on the government's "policy of 'provoke and shoot'" and the oil companies that were "prospering exceedingly" and "taxed too lightly" but refused to raise wages despite the ballooning cost of living. "Having . . . set itself up to champion the oil interests even at the cost of inaccuracy," he argued, "the Commission could not but produce a report in the main useless to the cause of social progress in Trinidad."[67]

Despite the ideological differences among their members, the LCP, NWA, and IASB collaborated with increasing regularity to step up the pressure on Parliament and the Colonial Office. During the spring of 1938, Padmore watched from the gallery as the House of Commons debated the appointment of a second commission of inquiry and reported on it in the *Chicago Defender.* When strikes in Jamaica culminated that summer in mass protests, rioting, and violent clashes with police and troops resulting in numerous casualties, the three organizations reacted swiftly. In June, the LCP held a meeting at Memorial Hall where the speakers included Lewis, Peter Blackman, Ronald Kidd of the National Council for Civil Liberties, and

Reginald Bridgeman, who was at the time a Labour Party candidate for the House of Commons. The league passed a resolution asking for farther-reaching reforms than the group had proposed in the past. Expressing "horror at the bloodshed in Jamaica," it demanded that the British state act immediately "to improve the economic condition of the population," provide "universal free education up to University standard," and create a University of the West Indies. The resolution also called for "the same constitutional rights and the same civil liberties as are enjoyed by the people of Britain, including universal adult suffrage," the removal of property qualifications for members of the colonial legislatures, and the formation of a "Federation of the West Indies with complete self-government." Moody wrote three letters published in the *Times* and represented the LCP in a deputation to the Colonial Office that included Kidd, Bridgeman, Dorothy Woodman of the Union of Democratic Control, and the communist Ben Bradley. The IASB organized another protest in Trafalgar Square, and its executive committee passed a resolution that demanded the immediate release of the labor organizers Uriah Butler and James Barrett in Trinidad and Ulric Grant in Barbados. It enumerated specific reforms such as "land settlement schemes, improvement of housing conditions, abolition of child labour, ... and, above all, a fully democratic constitution."[68] Before summer's end, Parliament announced the creation of a West Indian Royal Commission headed by Lord Moyne (Walter Guinness) to investigate the larger economic and social causes of the disturbances across the Caribbean. The move was due in part to the agitation of black intellectuals in London and their mobilization of support from segments of the British left. Nevertheless, Blackman immediately criticized its guidelines in *The Keys,* particularly the "significant omission from the terms of reference ... for enquiry into the political aspect of the life of these territories." He argued that "only when economic improvement goes hand in hand with political freedom will the West Indies be freed from the stultification of all progress by those who at present ... prevent even the most elementary change in the lot of the W. Indian people."[69]

Before the Moyne Commission left for the Caribbean, the LCP, IASB, and NWA presented it with a joint memorandum on "economic, political and social conditions in the West Indies," and in response, the commissioners agreed to hear testimony from Moody and Blackman. The lengthy document was sweeping in its scope and the product of a remarkable instance of intellectual and political collaboration. Multiple drafts circulated among Moody, Blackman, Makonnen, Padmore, James, and Lewis, and the parties solicited reports and advice from other experts and eyewitnesses to events in the Caribbean before submitting the final version. "To assert that the West Indian colonies have not sufficient men of talent to manage their own affairs," the document's authors claimed, "is absurd." They insisted on universal suffrage and democratic government as the "first step on the road towards ... *Federation and Dominion status.*" In closing, the signatories evoked the history of emancipation and linked the disturbances to the outrage provoked by the Italian invasion of Ethiopia: "In 1833, there was reason to apprehend a universal Negro rebellion for freedom, and emancipation was granted from above to prevent the cataclysm of emancipation from below.... Similarly today, when the rape of Ethiopia has given a great stimulus to growing Negro consciousness, it is not a question of rebellions if, but rebellions unless, democratic government is granted."[70]

With fascism on the march in Europe and the African horn, and unrest spreading in the Caribbean, questions arose regarding the British government's willingness to concede territory in Africa to avoid a military conflict in Europe. By 1936, rumors of overtures offering part or all of the southern Gold Coast, the Gambia, Nigeria, Cameroon, or Togoland to Germany sparked a flurry of accusations in Parliament and a series of scares among Africans in Britain and the colonies. As war drew closer, erstwhile critics of colonialism and pacifists like Roden Buxton pleaded with the Nazis to accept compensatory African colonies.[71] Africans and Afro-Caribbeans in London fiercely opposed colonial transfers in any form. At its founding, the IASB listed as one of its primary aims "arousing public interest around ... the question of the transfer of colonies to Fascist powers and/or collective mandatory system ... advocated among sections of British opinion." The *African Sentinel* reprinted letters of protest and resolutions against colonial transfers from Cameroon, Basutoland in South Africa, Trinidad, L'Union des Travailleurs Nègres in Paris, the Federation of French Colonial Workers (Rassemblement Colonial), and Braithwaite's Colonial Seamen's Association (CSA). In 1937–1938, the IASB organized protests, including a shadow exhibition in Glasgow to counter the Empire Exhibition there, and published a pamphlet titled *Hands Off the Protectorates.* Representatives of the bureau addressed numerous branches of the Labour Party, trade unions, cooperative societies, League of Nations Union, and Peace Council on "the colonies in relation to the 'Have' and 'Have Not' struggle over Africa." Padmore published "Hands off the Colonies!" in the *New Leader,* contributed to an ILP course on "imperialism and war," and delivered a lecture to the GCSA on "Africa, a pawn in European politics." The *Negro Worker* published Wallace-Johnson's aptly titled "'No Sir! No Colonies Back' for Germany." Blackman declared in *The Keys*, "African and other inhabitants of the British Empire can only give their support to a policy which secures peace, neither at the expense of the weaker peoples, nor by the complete abolition of every vestige of freedom . . . in the world." The WASU's annual report for 1938 noted that the threat of colonial transfers to Germany "caused so great a consternation and unrest among the students that they took every step, in their power and in co-operation with . . . peoples in West Africa, to protest against . . . any such scheme." Between late 1938 and autumn 1939, the union repeatedly requested and received assurances from Colonial Secretary Malcolm MacDonald that these rumors were unfounded.[72] These groups also agitated against the transfer of the southern African protectorates Bechuanaland, Basutoland, and Swaziland to the Union of South Africa, condemning it as an instance of fascist expansion within the British Empire and evidence of the imperial government's readiness to sacrifice Africans' rights to secure its interests. Writing in *Controversy*, Padmore described the Union of South Africa as "the world's classic Fascist state" and observed that, while "public attention is so firmly engaged with Fascist depredations in Abyssinia, Spain, China and South-Eastern Europe," the "quieter Fascist tendencies within the British Empire are ignored." The government's machinations on the imperial and international level mirrored one another.[73]

Padmore wrote to W. E. B. Du Bois in 1946: "The points of view which we seek to present in a hostile white world have to be put forward at psychological moments, so when one can get a publisher receptive to the idea of presenting our manuscripts, one has to . . . seize the opportunity." The mid- to late 1930s briefly presented black activist-intellectuals with such a moment. "As far as political organisations in England were concerned," James later observed, "the black intellectuals had not only arrived but were significant arrivals."[74] By 1938, with events in central Europe increasingly commanding the conscience of the British left, the need to defend the British Empire (rhetorically and militarily) overshadowed the concerns of Afro-Caribbeans, Africans, and other colonial subjects. When Padmore submitted a manuscript entitled "The Black Man's Burden" to George Allen and Unwin in 1939, it was rejected as much for its timing as for its content: "Whether it is wise or even practicable to publish what is in effect anti-British propaganda at the present time seems to me more than doubtful; Mr. Padmore should have spoken earlier—or hereafter; there would have been a time for such a word. But now?" The moment had passed. As Padmore recalled in *Pan-Africanism or Communism* (1956), communists and socialists abandoned "anti-imperialism . . . for anti-fascist and anti-war" activism, but right up to the start of the war, he and other black activist-intellectuals continued to insist that anti-imperialism was intrinsic to the battle against fascism.[75]

. . .

For Africans and others of African descent in London, appeasement began in Ethiopia, long before the surrender of Czechoslovakia at Munich in 1938; its roots lay in the deep affinity between imperialism and fascism. One did not need to look to Europe for examples of the racism and Herrenvolk nationalism characteristic of fascism. "From time to time," a piece on the Caribbean in the *International African Opinion* began, "we read sentences passed upon workers in Germany and Italy and are appalled by their severity. 'That could only happen in a Fascist country,' smugly declares the Communist, the Socialist, the Liberal, and even Tory humanitarians. . . . But could it? What about this 'democratic' British Commonwealth of Nations?"[76] During the late 1930s, black intellectuals couched their antifascism in terms of a general critique of empire and called for progressive forces in Europe and colonial territories to form a united front against empire. The *International African Opinion* lauded the Indian National Congress leader Jawaharlal Nehru for his remarks at the "Peace and Empire" conference at Friends' House in London in July 1938. Nehru asserted: "Anti-Fascist British people should realize that it is not possible to conduct the anti-Fascist struggle successfully, if the anti-imperialist struggle is ignored. . . . [O]ur problem, therefore, is to work for the independence of all subject peoples, not to make them narrow-minded nationalist units, but free partners in this larger order."[77] In early 1939, Padmore, Kenyatta, Wilkie, and their allies in the ILP Fenner Brockway and Dinah Stock formed the British Centre Against Imperialism, which resumed the work formerly done by the LAI without the latter's communist ties. An executive council of nineteen members, consisting of ten representatives of colonial territories and nine British anti-imperialists, headed the group. That August, the group released "A Warning to the Colonial Peoples," most likely penned by Padmore, and the *International African Opinion* published largely the same text as a "Manifesto against War" in October. It exclaimed: "We denounce the whole gang of European robbers and enslavers of the colonial peoples—German Nazis, Italian Fascists,

French, British, Belgian and Dutch democrats—all are the same IMPERIALIST BANDITS." Even if appeasement proved successful in the short term, the manifesto cautioned, it would "only delay . . . the threatening conflict. The next issue will be the Colonial question." As Padmore bluntly put it in *Africa and World Peace,* "Empire and peace are incompatible."[78]

During the 1930s, black intellectuals and activists linked British colonialism in Africa and the Caribbean to developments and settings *beyond* the British Empire, from the Jim Crow–era United States to the growing fascist threat to Africa and Europe. The major imperial powers' response to the Italo-Ethiopian conflict and the willingness of many at the highest reaches of the British government to contemplate the transfer of African colonies, protectorates, or mandate territories to Nazi Germany, the Union of South Africa, or some system of international administration informed how these activist-intellectuals viewed the government's response to events in the Caribbean and Africa, and vice versa. The confluence of events encouraged people of African descent in London to see events in Africa and across the Atlantic as related, provided a basis for cooperation between black radicals and moderates, and sparked new attempts to link agitation across colonies and even empires. Despite their divergent agendas, in the wake of the disturbances in the Caribbean and Africa, black intellectuals from the colonies and a range of white advocates of colonial reform in Britain shared a certain pan-African outlook, articulating their object of analysis and imagined field of activity in ways that linked the Caribbean to an "emergent" Africa. "The prevailing feeling in these last few months before the war," Makonnen recalled, "was that we should insist on seeing the colonial world as a whole. So if there was to be a commission sent out to investigate trade union conditions in Trinidad, . . . we were determined to submit a manifesto . . . that did not restrict itself to one small fragment, but showed what was happening in West Africa as much as in the West Indies." "The same grasp of the wider issues," he added, "brought us into close touch with other coloured groups in London."[79]

Although Africans and Afro-Caribbeans remained committed to furthering cooperation and mutual understanding across racial and ethnic divisions, they increasingly focused their efforts on organizing people of African descent outside the institutions of the European left and endeavored to create, as Makonnen put it, an "international African" movement "free from entanglements."[80] On the eve of the Second World War, the LCP began planning a world conference of Africans and people of African descent to be held in 1940.[81] The IASB issued a manifesto calling for the creation of a "World Socialist Federation of Equal Nations and Peoples, regardless of race, colour or creed." Padmore wrote in the ILP's *New Leader* in 1941, "We demand full self-determination not as an end in itself—for we are not narrow nationalists—but as the historic prerequisite for the free and voluntary co-operation between all nations and peoples and races."[82] Transatlantic print culture in the form of books, small pamphlets, and serial publications was at the heart of these attempts to forge a black international. The journals and other publications of London-based black organizations linked geographically discontinuous movements in their content and circulation. In doing so, they drew on both imperial and transatlantic networks of information and support that converged in the imperial metropolis—networks that shaped the political vision outlined in their contents.

The majority of these black intellectuals and organizations rejected nationalism as a divisive and obsolete paradigm for political community. Like many of their British contemporaries, ranging from the center to the left wing of the political spectrum, they mobilized the language of internationalism, but unlike the former, they used it to articulate, on the one hand, black and colonial unity and, on the other, a vision of global community that acknowledged and embraced cultural difference and exchange. In a 1937 editorial in *Wàsù* responding to a piece by Malcolm Hailey on "Nationalism in Africa," Solanke declared, "Our nationalism is with a difference. It is not of the Mussolini-Hitler-Franco or the 'Ethiopian' type which may be termed rabid nationalism. Ours is based on justice. . . . We do not believe in the parrot-cry, 'Africa for the Africans,' but rather Africans for Africa—a great difference."[83]

Most agreed that British colonialism was only slightly better than fascism, but the question of whether or not to support Britain in another interimperial conflict divided them. In September 1938, the IASB published a pamphlet titled *Europe's Difficulty Is Africa's Opportunity,* which implored "Africans, people of African descent, and colonial peoples all over the world . . . not to be caught by the lying promises" and "to organize yourselves and be ready to seize the opportunity when it comes."[84] The question split the GCSA. In October, Desmond Buckle proposed a motion stating "that this Association refuses to fight for the British Empire" and, a month later, helped defeat another, put forward by William Ofori Atta, to the effect "that the salvation of the Gold Coast lies in close co-operation with the British Labour Party." In the end, the majority in London reaffirmed their commitment to a radically transformed Commonwealth. In November, with rumors swirling of a possible transfer of west Cameroon, which had been incorporated into Nigeria, the WASU organized a protest meeting at which more than seventy students passed a resolution that declared: "We prefer to continue to remain under His Majesty's Government protection and tutelage until we are able to stand for ourselves within the British Commonwealth of Nations."[85] Such expressions of loyalty to Britain contained a clear statement of expectations for the future, demonstrating that the union's members recognized the moment as an opportunity to press for substantive change. H. O. Davies, the president of WASU in 1935–1936 and later warden of Africa House, articulated the sentiments of many of his contemporaries when he wrote from Nigeria in fall 1938, "'British Empire deserves nothing but extinction as complete as that of the Dodo,'" while arguing that Nigeria could "live and flourish" within the Commonwealth.[86]

THREE

Black Feminist Internationalists

THE NUMBER OF WOMEN from the Caribbean and Africa in London remained small until the 1940s. No aggregate figures are available for women from the colonies studying in Britain, but a proposal to establish living accommodations for Caribbean women students at College Hall reported yearly totals of no fewer than seven and as many as seventeen at the University of London between 1923 and 1933.[1] Although wealthy families along the coast of West Africa increasingly sent their daughters to study in Britain from the nineteenth century onward, there remained a huge gender discrepancy in access to education, especially higher education abroad, throughout the first half of the twentieth century. Unprecedented numbers of female students arrived from both regions during the 1940s, some supported by new colonial scholarships. By the end of the decade, the Colonial Office counted a total of 644 West African women students, more than half of whom were from Nigeria. The African American social scientist John Gibbs St. Clair Drake estimated that "perhaps less than a thousand British-born colored women were living in London, as well as a few hundred African and West Indian women and girl students" in the late 1940s. In 1951, the government census found that 63 percent of the 4,216 Afro-Caribbeans and 81 percent of the 2,183 West Africans in Britain were men.[2]

If African and Afro-Caribbean women faced many of the same challenges as their male counterparts, such as discrimination in housing and employment, they were more isolated, and many suffered from intense loneliness that exacerbated the sting of British racism in its many forms.[3] Black organizations such as the WASU and LCP provided some solace, gathering spots, and, to some extent, even a voice, and black women played an integral role in their development and helped mend the internecine rifts that emerged within and among them. Seizing the gendered ground consigned to them by their male counterparts, WASU women built the union's hostel into a center of black sociability and were behind its most popular attractions—its African restaurant and recurrent dances. These and other black women worked across organizations and imperial boundaries to organize opposition to the Italian invasion of Ethiopia. However, their male peers frequently excluded women from major debates and subordinated them within the organizational structure, while criticizing them for supposed backwardness. It became even more difficult for women to assert their influence as these groups assumed a more nationalist stance in the late 1940s. As a result, male-dominated black pressure groups were rarely the sole focus of African and Caribbean women's energies. Many moved among several groups, while also participating in largely white feminist internationalist organizations. Both settings supplied frustration as well as inspiration and invaluable contacts. Women of African descent relied on and formed connections that were personal and informal— and, thus, more flexible, dynamic, and tenuous—creating, in Jennifer Boittin's words, "not so much a core as a tangle of connections" whose reach extended far beyond the metropolis.[4]

Scholars have begun to trace the emergence of women-qua-women politics and various instantiations of the "new woman" and "modern girl" as, at once, culturally and geographically specific and inextricably tied to transnational processes.[5] "The modern girl heuristic," Lynn Thomas argues, "elucidates how female figures identified by a cosmopolitan look, an explicit eroticism and the use of specific commodities surfaced in many parts of the globe," and how "their near-simultaneous emergence was tied to the international circulation of commodity cultures, mass media and political discourses." Although whites commonly used the words *girl* and *boy* in a derogatory manner to refer to black adults, "when black writers prefaced 'girl' with 'modern,'" Thomas observes, "they signaled something unsettlingly progressive rather than decidedly pejorative," a sense that women were acquiring a degree of "contingent independence from conventional female roles." The modern girl became "a social category and performative style, a style that could be adopted by married and unmarried women alike, and interpreted as anything from disreputable to respectable." Black women in Africa, Europe, and the Americas engaged with the figure of the modern girl, variously identifying as such or criticizing this new and potentially disreputable interloper. The founder of the Women's Party in Nigeria, Oyinkan Abayomi, and others published pieces in the West African press on "modern womanhood" and the ways educated women could contribute to social and political change.[6] A whole range of issues, including women's roles in politics and racial uplift, women's education, fashion and new consumption patterns, and domesticity, marriage, and changing sexual mores, cohered around the modern black girl. In 1932, Mabel Dove, who wrote the "Ladies' Corner" in the Accra-based *Times of West Africa* under the pseudonym "Marjorie Mensah," urged her readers to support the WASU's hostel campaign in London and "do something that will be a monument of African effort and endeavour." "We women," she wrote, "should show our men their duty."[7] Women on both sides of the Atlantic debated these subjects and others in person and in published exchanges, editorials, women's pages, and readers' response columns as growing numbers of them entered internationalist, regional, or pan-Africanist organizations.[8] Afro-Caribbean and African women in London joined this dialogue and were critical interlocutors and conduits in the transnational flow of ideas and cultural practices.[9]

In simply walking the streets of London, women of African descent became a spectacle of sorts. The city's other residents conflated them with a litany of popular images of black female bodies, from Jazz Age performers to representations of African women in cinema, ethnographic photography, and exhibitions. The intense public scrutiny inspired reflection on the corporeal and sartorial content of women's embodiment of black femininity. In 1935, Titilola Folarin, a Yorùbá-speaker from Nigeria, described a new attitude to fashion among her "WASU lady colleagues." Folarin and her peers attempted "to modernise our present style to induce our educated girls and others to have more love and respect for their own native dress culture" in the hope "that our girls in West Africa will now begin to realise that the time has come when we should not only respect but also improve our own culture, whether it be in the line of dress or otherwise." Folarin asserted that "systematic refinement" was the best way to pay "respect" to their African cultures. When they walked the West End in their revised "native costumes," she wrote, "many of our English friends who saw us expressed their pleasure and satisfaction at the show." This "show" continued a pattern of African contributions to Britain's consumerist society and the metropolis's increasingly cosmopolitan flavor. "About a week after whilst passing through Regent Street in the West End of London," Folarin added, "we discovered in some of the shop windows a certain number of ladies' hats, almost exactly in the same style and shape of how we tied up our 'Gele' on the day we passed through . . . a week before."[10] The appearance of their creative handiwork in the posh boutiques of Regent Street highlighted the subsumption of black women's labor and bodies within the imperial culture industry, and the economic structures of colonial rule more broadly, on fundamentally exploitative terms. Nevertheless, in recounting this quotidian instance of appropriation and mimicry, Folarin portrayed the city as an eminently performative space marked by global, though unequal, flows of goods, styles, and people, and African women *dans la rue* as cultural intermediaries who engaged in deliberate self-fashioning through a creative process of retention and selective borrowing rather than avatars of "tradition."

This chapter looks more closely at a group of African and Afro-Caribbean women, their challenges to the strictures imposed on black women's bodies in the name of respectability, and their engagement with feminism, a significant and varied field of internationalist thought and activity in its own right.[11] It presents their lives in varying degrees of detail depending on the availability of sources, which range from a few fugitive archival traces to the considerable literary oeuvre of Una Marson. By examining how these women articulated feminism and a positive investment in blackness, what follows charts alternative trajectories and visions of black internationalism instantiated in art as well as activism. Many histories of pan-Africanism and anticolonialism pursue their intellectual resources, manifestations, and modes of address solely within black organizations or the equally male-dominated structures of the radical left. In the most thoroughgoing study of West Africans in Britain, Hakim Adi notes that as late as 1957 the *West African Student,* the journal of the WASU, "could still complain about the 'apathy of the West African woman,' and . . . that 'our society has not been able to produce women of our mothers' caliber.'" Adi devotes less than two pages to the subject of women, and this statement appears at the end of the section, seemingly confirmed by the larger narrative. Our understanding of the history of black internationalism will remain inherently androcentric and reproduce the gender politics that structured the WASU and other race or anticolonial groups if black internationalism is taken to be synonymous with political protest that emanated from such organizations. As Lara Putnam suggests, once we "shift from tracking a few leaders to exploring the cultural ferment of the world they came from" and "set aside the Great Man theory of history that still shades some accounts of political change in the African diaspora, we see active women everywhere." If we look beyond the numbers and the proclamations of male activist-intellectuals, the same is true of the black world of the imperial metropolis.[12]

Movement across the different political, cultural, and racial geographies of the Caribbean, Africa, Europe, and the United States shaped the lives as well as the gender and racial consciousness of the Afro-Caribbean and African women considered here. As Elleke Boehmer and Bart Moore-Gilbert suggest, such movement "allowed these transnational women travelers opportunities of self-expression and group-identification which would have been comparatively limited, even unacceptable," in the colonies.[13] London exposed them to the scrutiny of white strangers, colonial officials, and their black male contemporaries as well as different currents of internationalist thought and antiracist and anticolonial movements throughout the empire and the Atlantic world. Their sojourns yielded connections that they would draw upon for the remainder of their lives, often leading to opportunities to travel further afield, geographically and intellectually, and they, in turn, formed connections between anticolonial and feminist networks, local and transcolonial struggles. Experiments at the fringes of feminine "racial respectability" became part of a larger critique of the ways that racism operated in conjunction with sexism and economic exploitation in both metropolitan and colonial settings. Their constructions of and appeals to black womanhood developed in opposition not only to the sexism of white and black men but also to the imposed racial and ethnic categories of colonial rule. Agitating on multiple fronts, in- and outside the city's black organizations, they elaborated black feminist internationalisms and imaginings of a political collectivity of black women across divergent conditions and barriers of class, ethnicity, and colony.

THE MIGRATIONS OF AMY ASHWOOD GARVEY AND THE HISTORY OF PAN-AFRICANISM

Very much has been written and spoken of the Negro, but for some reason very little has been said about the black woman. She has been shunted into the social background to be a child-bearer.

AMY ASHWOOD GARVEY, 1945 PAN-AFRICAN CONGRESS[14]

In terms of the sheer breadth of her activities alone, Amy Ashwood Garvey is a singular figure in the history of the black Atlantic. Knitting together Kingston, Jamaica; New York; Kumasi, Ghana; and London—and many stops in between—as her most recent biographer Tony Martin states, "her itinerant life weaves like a thread connecting an amazing array of major personalities and events in the history of the African world of the twentieth century." In short, as Marika Sherwood puts it, "if there was ever a life of lived Pan-Africanism, it was that of Amy Ashwood Garvey."[15] If it is no longer possible to say that "very little has been said about the black woman," as Ashwood Garvey did in her remarks at the 1945 Pan-African Congress, she and other Afro-Caribbean and African women remain in the "social background" in most renderings of the pantheon of pan-Africanism. In Simon Gikandi's otherwise insightful essay "Pan-Africanism and Cosmopolitanism," as Alison Donnell notes, "she is just the backdrop, her restaurant the venue for the real story that is to be told, the story of meetings of men and men's minds."[16] Martin, at times, falls prey to the same tendencies, subsuming the diversity of Ashwood Garvey's activities within the larger story of an overwhelmingly male struggle. Of her time in London during the 1930s, he explains, "She became a pivotal figure around whom revolved a brilliant coterie of young African and Caribbean activists. These were mostly young men who were destined to be among the heirs to the struggle that Garvey had waged so magnificently in the 1920s, . . . men who before long would see that struggle through to political independence in the Pan-African world." Ashwood Garvey's male associates, Martin tells us, made up a "who's who" of pan-Africanists and black anticolonialists, but he reduces her significance to the male company she kept in his repeated use of the labels "Mrs. Marcus Garvey No. 1" and "Wife No. 1" to describe her.[17] So long as black internationalism is conceptualized solely in terms of the intellectual and political projects of male pan-Africanists, women such as Ashwood Garvey can only appear as marginal and allusive figures, dilettantes even.

In her public and private conduct, Ashwood Garvey repeatedly broke with middle-class norms of feminine respectability. She eschewed expectations by participating in political organizing and marrying Marcus Garvey, a dark-skinned partner of humbler origins. After meeting Garvey at the age of seventeen, she helped launch the Universal Negro Improvement Association (UNIA) in Jamaica.[18] By early 1919, she had joined him in New York City, where they laid the foundations for a black organization of unprecedented size. In December, the couple married in a much-publicized service in Harlem, but only months later, they separated, each citing the infidelity of the other as the reason. Ashwood Garvey later recalled that she felt stifled by Garvey's autocratic style and conservative views on women. She rejected his demands

FIGURE 6. Amy Ashwood Garvey on stage at the 1945 Pan-African Congress in Manchester. The original caption accompanying the photograph in *Picture Post* stated, incorrectly, "On the stage is Amy Jacques Garvey, the second wife of Marcus Garvey." John Deakin/Stringer, *Picture Post* Collection, Getty Images.

of dutiful servitude in marriage and politics, but she continued throughout her life to claim a stake in his name and the project it represented.

In 1922, Ashwood Garvey left for London and a tour of Europe. She helped form the Nigerian Progress Union in 1924, and for her efforts, the other founders named her Iyalode (queen of the ladies), a chieftaincy title bestowed on Yorùbá women in Egbaland. She may have met Charlotte Olajumoke Obasa because, the same year, she wrote a letter in support of a petition from the latter's Lagos Women's League calling for more and better education facilities and employment opportunities for girls and young women—causes she pursued for the remainder of her life.[19] After touring the

United States and the Caribbean during the late 1920s and early 1930s, Ashwood Garvey was back in London by mid-decade. She reconnected with old friends such as Solanke and met the feminist and anti-imperialist Sylvia Pankhurst, who found in her an inspiring and, if anything, more radical collaborator. In 1935, Ashwood Garvey opened the International Afro Restaurant beneath her residence at 62 New Oxford Street, and then the Florence Mills Social Parlour, a restaurant and nightclub on or near Carnaby Street, the following year. Her menu of largely Caribbean cuisine attracted African and Caribbean students, intellectuals, and activists. Caribbean musicians such as Rudolph Dunbar and Sam Manning performed regularly to a mixed but disproportionately black crowd of dancers at the Florence Mills club. From her Soho outposts Ashwood Garvey organized the bustle of activity around the IAFE in the months leading up to and during the Italo-Ethiopian War, as well as, to a lesser extent, its successor the IASB. Her male associates attested to her mental acuity and boundless energy. Makonnen remembered her as "quite a spellbinder." At the end of his semiautobiographical *Beyond a Boundary,* James remarked of the cricketer Frank Worrell, "His responses to difficult questions were so unhesitating, so precise, and so took the subject on to unsuspected but relevant areas, that I felt it was I who was undergoing examination . . . I have met only three such persons, two men and one women." The two men were Leon Trotsky and a young Hungarian refugee in London during the late 1930s; the woman, Ashwood Garvey. James hastened to add: "This is not a register or appraisal of capacity in general. . . . What I am dealing with here is a unique capacity to concentrate all the forces available and needed for the matter in hand."[20] Yet Ashwood Garvey appears fleetingly in the recollections of these men and often in ways that distance her from their activities. Neither she nor any other woman of African descent appears in James's short essay "Black Intellectuals in Britain," written in the early 1970s. George Padmore referenced Ashwood Garvey twice in passing in his monumental *Pan-Africanism or Communism?* In the second instance, he referred to her as a representative of the "Jamaica Women's Movement" at the 1945 Pan-African Congress. Peter Abrahams notes only, "She was a gay spirit filled with appealing laughter, and she used men as men usually used women."[21]

The lively but decidedly middlebrow atmosphere at night at the Florence Mills—and likely its overwhelmingly black clientele—led Ashwood Garvey's white neighbors to file a lawsuit against her. She closed her businesses by the end of 1938 and left London the following year. She traveled to the Caribbean and then continental Europe with Manning before spending the war years in Jamaica. Her attention turned increasingly to the plight of black working women. She blasted the schoolgirl system of domestic service in Jamaica, which she described as "quasi-slavery under a thin camouflage of philanthropic solicitude"; campaigned for a minimum wage and better working conditions for female domestics; and attempted to start a school of domestic science, a scheme that ultimately failed for lack of funding. Of the last-named project, Ashwood Garvey explained, "I lay claim, in this venture, to a sincere and fervent desire to help the women of my race. I am battle-scarred in their service, and have known and felt what it is to have the iron pierce my soul."[22] Through the travails of poor working women in the Caribbean and elsewhere, Ashwood Garvey called attention to the blind spots and contradictions in the dream of pan-African unity she had pursued since her youth. Her changing views on the relationship between race and class were part of an emerging feminist perspective that increasingly guided her energies.

In 1953, she again left Jamaica to join her brother Claude in Harlem. She threw herself into Adam Clayton Powell's campaign for a seat in the House of Representatives and joined in the New York–based West Indian National Council (WINC) and the Council on African Affairs (CAA). Ashwood Garvey's involvement with the CAA introduced her to Kwame Nkrumah and reunited her with Paul and Eslanda Goode Robeson, whom she first met in London. She participated in and helped compile the proceedings of the CAA's conference "Africa—New Perspectives," and she spoke at a WINC meeting at which the group adopted resolutions demanding, among other things, the "right of self-determination and self-government for the peoples of Africa." Looking to the postwar period, she told the *New York Amsterdam News* of her plans to launch an international women's publication to "bring together the women, especially those of the darker races, so that they may work for the betterment of all," and declared: "There must be a revolution among women. They must realise their importance in the post-war world. . . . Women of the world must unite."[23] Women of African descent around the world represented the living bridge between the struggle for black liberation and this "revolution."

In late summer 1945, Ashwood Garvey headed for Britain en route to realizing her lifelong goal of visiting West Africa. She chaired the opening day of the Fifth Pan-African Congress in Manchester, and before a gathering of predominately male would-be nation-builders and trade unionists from Africa, the Caribbean, the Americas, and Europe, she lauded women teachers as a "progressive" force and denounced the marked imbalance in wages for Jamaican men and women for which, she charged, "the Negro men of Jamaica are largely responsible."[24] She also became interested in the Scottish nutritionist John Boyd Orr's World Movement for World Federal Government, especially its potential for advancing the position of non-European women on a global level. Ashwood Garvey left for West Africa in 1946 and spent the late 1940s and early 1950s traveling, speaking to women's groups, visiting old friends such as former WASU president J. B. Danquah, and experimenting with a girls' school and several failed business ventures in Liberia, the Gold Coast, and Nigeria. She would return to take part in the independence celebrations in Ghana in 1957.[25]

Ashwood Garvey's understanding of the prospects for black collaboration and unity evolved with her increasingly feminist stance. Gender and class hierarchies came to inflect and complicate her understanding of race, and she moved from the narrowly black nationalist politics of her youth to a more expansive and explicitly feminist internationalism focused on the needs of black women. Martin points to the influence of her interactions with Caribbean Marxists like James and Padmore, but the latter focused on the black male toilers of the world.[26] Her writings and her relationships with black and white feminists indicate the importance of "cross-border and multi-axial alliances" and connections beyond the male-dominated centers of black activism to her personal and political journey and, more broadly, to feminist formations of the black international.[27] During her travels and wide-ranging activities, she conducted fieldwork and research for a number of book manuscripts that situated the struggles of women of African descent within the history of feminist and women's suffrage movements around the globe, and located the rise of black feminism within that of the black Atlantic world. She envisioned a four-volume "Mother Africa Series" that included a biography of the late Marcus Garvey, variously entitled "Marcus Garvey, the Man of Destiny" or "Black Man of Destiny"; a study of Liberia based on her interviews with local informants; an ambitious history of West Africa and the African diaspora, "My Mother Africa" or "Africa Speaks," which the *Barbados Advocate* characterized as an "almost complete history of the African Peoples"; and "Women of Colour," a comprehensive account of the lives and labors of women of African descent on both sides of the Atlantic. The contours of the latter can be discerned from a speech she delivered in Barbados in 1953 titled "The Rise of Woman." Ashwood Garvey covered the "history of women of African descent and the part they had played in the progressive march of man through classical, medieval, feudal and modern times." She completed large portions and, in some cases, multiple drafts of these books but never succeeded in getting them published. Sylvia Pankhurst released a short overview of "Liberia, Land of Promise" in pamphlet form as a preview of the larger text. The two first met in the 1930s when both were heavily involved in the agitation on behalf of Ethiopia, and they forged a friendship and alliance in the service of an African cause. Pankhurst was one of the suffragists that Ashwood Garvey referenced by name during her address in Barbados. In her short introduction to the pamphlet, she described Pankhurst as "a very trusted friend of mine," "the outstanding feminist of the century," and a "staunch friend of Ethiopia in its hour of need, and, we may add, of all Africa in its present difficulties."[28]

Back in London during the late 1950s, when blacks in Britain faced the worst racially motivated violence since 1919, Ashwood Garvey was at the forefront of community activism in London's Notting Hill area, one of the largest centers of black settlement after the Second World War. She served on the editorial board of the *West Indian Gazette and Afro-Asian-Caribbean News,* Britain's first nationally distributed independent black monthly newspaper, launched in 1958 by the Afro-Caribbean communist Claudia Jones. She once again established a home for people of African descent in London, but one oriented this time to the needs of black women— the Afro-women Service Bureau. Soon thereafter, with financial assistance from the MP Sir Hamilton Kerr, she purchased a house at 1 Basset Road in Notting Hill that became the Afro-women's Centre, a hostel and advice office offering practical services such as mending and laundry. The center also served as the headquarters of the Association for the Advancement of Colored People, which she founded shortly after returning to London. Ashwood Garvey went home to Jamaica in 1965 after a two-decade absence. Thereafter, she continued to travel widely despite her failing health, even undertaking a lecture tour in California at the invitation of the Black Panthers the year before her death in 1969.[29]

Ashwood Garvey's globe-trotting; her public feuds with Garvey and later with his second wife, Amy Jacques Garvey; and her on-again, off-again relationship with Sam Manning reversed prevailing gender norms. She combined the roles of entertainment impresario, entrepreneur, and political organizer, linking the discontinuous but overlapping realms of transatlantic black performance and black political discourse. In the late 1930s and 1940s, she expanded the scope of black internationalism to address the particular exploitation of black working women. In this sense, and in the way in which gender and class hierarchies forced her to confront the limits of racial unity, her political journey paralleled that of many Caribbean and African women who passed through and sustained black London.

"TO AFRICAN WOMANHOOD"

The position of women in African societies figured heavily in British imperial discourse as well as the counterarguments of African men. The former frequently claimed that misogyny suffused traditional African societies, while the latter held that the deleterious effects of British colonialism and capitalism, not African men or cultures, had degraded African women. Most men in the WASU reaffirmed the need for a hierarchical division of the sexes and posited women as, alternately, repositories of tradition, a yardstick of racial consciousness and development, or even a fetter or obstacle to the latter. In a piece from 1928, "Ade" insisted: "African women are not downtrodden. Native custom gives them a high place." Ade attempted to demonstrate that the status of women in precolonial African societies compared favorably with that of contemporary European women, but he and other WASU men embraced gender norms consistent with the Victorian doctrine of separate spheres for the sexes. "The sphere of the woman is the home," he explained. "The sphere of the man is outside."[30] Alongside several references to the women's diverse contributions to the union, *Wāsù* featured Anthony Abiodun's article "Education of Women and Employment in Africa." Abiodun asserted that the "division of labour" between the sexes was the "root principle" of "our ancient customary law," the "first axiom" of which was "that women are fundamentally different from, if not inferior to, men in matters physical, emotional and intellectual" and that their roles "must be regulated . . . in conformity with these differences." For Abiodun, women's education should consist of training in practical skills to help them fulfill their roles as wives and homemakers, perform "lighter forms of factory and farm work," or become secretaries, "making them fit and capable future mothers of a future virile people . . . without coming into clash with our men."[31] Like British colonial officials, WASU men espoused an approach to economic development premised on an assertion of inherent differences between the sexes, a hierarchical arrangement of gender roles, and the need to balance limited modernization and the maintenance of tradition.

African women used this constrained rhetorical ground to place social issues of importance to women on the agendas of the WASU and LCP, while challenging their male contemporaries' views on the proper roles of women. They sought to dismantle precisely the "colonial structures of nativism" and ethnic differentiation under indirect rule.[32] Many argued that education was the key to improving the plight of women in the region and to furthering cooperation—between men and women, among Britain's four West African colonies, and among different races around the globe. After an address by Margery Perham at the Royal Society of Arts on March 24, 1934, Stella Thomas, who was active in both the WASU and the LCP, criticized Lugardian indirect rule for "making puppets of African chiefs" and insisted that Africans "wanted sound education, to be able to understand and then express themselves as they would like to, . . . to look after their own institutions and to judge for themselves the merits of those institutions."[33] The Nigerian Kofoworola Aina Moore, the first African woman to graduate from Oxford University, was active in the WASU during the mid-1930s and married a fellow member, Adetokunbo Adegboyega Ademola. Ignoring pressure from her father to follow in his footsteps and enter the legal profession, Moore decided to pursue teaching because, as she later explained in her autobiography, education was essential "to the development of . . . the 'sense of the modern world in all its intricacies,' with which we are by natural force of circumstances to come into contact."[34] These women maintained that equal access to rigorous education was essential to producing citizens of a self-governing West Africa and the modern world. They founded new branches and established ties to other black organizations around the Atlantic, and those who became educators inspired a generation of young women who participated in postwar anticolonial movements. Moore returned to Nigeria with "high ambitions" for increasing the membership of local WASU branches and organizing women locally, and she published didactic pieces directed toward women newspaper readers.[35] Beatrice Vigo, who was married to Arthur Vigo, the vice president of the WASU branch in Zaria, Nigeria, acted as the organization's representative in the United States during the early 1930s before traveling through the Caribbean and London on her way back to Nigeria. Thanks to her efforts, the WASU found a distributor for its journal in New York City, expanding its reach beyond West Africa, the Caribbean, and Britain. All the while, Vigo pursued her own feminist agenda, situating her "plan for the promotion of the status" of West African women within the larger spectrum of the union's activities.[36]

The Sierra Leonean Constance Horton was active in the WASU, LCP, and IASB during the mid-1930s. Born into a prominent Krio family of intellectuals and professionals in Freetown, she received an elite mission education and, like her mother before her, came to Britain in 1935 to continue her education. Her time in London marked the beginning of an itinerant existence that linked the struggles of people of African descent and women at three points around the Atlantic. Within a year of her arrival, she earned her qualification as a teacher, and she received a grant to travel to the United States in September 1937 to study the possible application of the Jeanes-school model of adaptive education to the Sierra Leone Protectorate. While there, she attended Cornell University and visited the Jim Crow south. Her exposure to the U.S. variant of racism had a radicalizing effect on her thinking, and her relationship to the centers of black activism and others of African descent changed when she returned to London. She became increasingly impatient with the complacency and prejudices of many of her West African and Afro-Caribbean male colleagues in the LCP and WASU. She joined the IASB, read Padmore's *How Britain Rules Africa,* and listened to Wallace-Johnson's fiery tirades in Hyde Park against the abuses of British imperialism. Soon after her return, Horton married Ethnan Cummings-John, a barrister who was a member of the LCP's executive committee and the warden of Aggrey House, in a ceremony in North London. After the wedding, Major Hanns Vischer threw a dinner party for the newlyweds. "He slapped me on the back," she remembered, "and told me, 'Constance, I am so proud of you. It's the best thing you could have done, marrying a man like Ethnan. Now you must go home and be quiet. Ethnan is a lawyer and will look after you.'" Vischer's advice succinctly expressed the expectations for a woman of her background held not only by British colonial officials but also by many African men, but she had different ambitions: "All I could do at the time was laugh and agree with him, but I had no intention of remaining 'quiet.' Politics was now in my blood. Marriage to me did not mean keeping out of political affairs."[37]

The couple returned to Freetown soon thereafter. Cummings-John's experiences abroad and the connections she formed in London guided her professional and political ambitions in Sierra Leone. She declined a post as a government school inspector to become principal of the African Methodist Episcopal Girls' Industrial School, which thrived under her direction. In February 1938, she established a local branch of the LCP, the first in West Africa. The LCP's annual report noted "that the Sierra Leone [Sedition]

FIGURE 7. Constance Cummings-John. *The Keys* 5, no. 1 (July 1937): 4. © The British Library Board.

Ordinances were made the subject of a recent deputation to the Secretary of State" thanks to her efforts. Removed from the oversight and control of Dr. Moody, Cummings-John tried to take the branch in more radical directions, but the elitist stance of many members, for example in reaction to her attempts to organize among the protectorate population, frustrated her hopes of turning the organization into a catalyst of broad-based political mobilization. She soon joined the recently established Freetown branch of the West African Youth League (WAYL), founded by Wallace-Johnson.[38] Organizing across ethnic and confessional lines, the WAYL established trade unions and satellite branches in the protectorate, included Muslims and members from the protectorate on its various committees, and quickly attracted significant popular support. Cummings-John served on the group's executive committee as vice president, and she garnered the highest number of votes overall as one of the four WAYL candidates elected to the Freetown municipal council in 1938, becoming at just twenty years of age the only African woman to win an election in British colonial Africa. She held her seat on the council until 1942, despite growing pressure from colonial officials to renounce her ties to Wallace-Johnson and thus avoid "preventive detention" during the war. During these years, Cummings-John focused on issues that impinged directly on women's lives, such as education, sanitation, and regulations in the local markets. She framed these issues as part of building unity between the inhabitants of the Sierra Leone Colony and Protectorate on the local level and the larger battle against global white supremacy. She decried the elitism and sexism of many West African men in London as well as of the Krio elite in Freetown, and repeatedly traversed and formed connections across not only geographical boundaries but also ethnic, class, and sectarian lines and divisions between Africans, Afro-Caribbeans, and African Americans.

As the number of African women in London expanded in the 1940s, so did their presence in the city's black organizations, transforming these groups and resulting in new links among them. The WASU's annual report for 1941 noted the growing influence of women within the organization, and members soon elected Aduke Alakija as the WASU's first female vice president. The union began demanding not only self-government but also universal adult suffrage and greater educational and employment opportunities for women. For the first time, it protested discrimination against African women in Britain, especially in the nursing profession, forcing the colonial secretary and Colonial Office to address the issue. African and Caribbean women also contributed to the emergence of new organizations after the war, such as the West African Society and West African National Secretariat (WANS). Writing in the inaugural issue of the WANS's *New African* in 1946, Edith H. Wallace-Johnson, the wife of I. T. A. Wallace-Johnson, issued a call "to African Womanhood" to "bring ourselves to the forefront" of "work towards the great goal of self-determination and complete and absolute independence for Africa." Mrs. O. Alakija Renner, who was married to the vice chairperson Bankole Awooner-Renner, served as joint-treasurer and handled the financial business of the cash-strapped organization alongside Kwame Nkrumah's white partner, Florence Manley.[39]

West African women persisted in pressing their own agendas within predominately male organizations such as the WASU and WANS, as well as feminist and leftist groups in Britain. As their numbers grew, they also formed the first autonomous African women's organizations in London. Irene Cole, a Krio from Sierra Leone, and Folayegbe M. Akintunde-Ighodalo, a Yorùbá-speaker from Nigeria, came to Britain as students in the 1940s. Both women participated in the WASU, indeed became prominent voices within it, while launching new women's groups. Cole joined the union as a medical student. She read widely and had strong political convictions, especially concerning the need for expanding women's educational opportunities in British West Africa.[40] In August 1942, she addressed the WASU Conference on West African Problems, at which the union passed a resolution demanding "INTERNAL SELF-GOVERNMENT NOW." Cole covered problems associated with household economics, trade, education, religious differences, and the lack of adequate public health services, but she focused particularly on the role of women "at a critical stage" in African history. She argued that European colonialism had diminished the social, economic, and political standing of African women even more than that of their male counterparts, adding, "If this vague or negative idea of a woman's position becomes a real fact it will mean the passing away of one of the finest specimens of woman-hood in the world."[41] Cole remained active in the WASU for most of the decade. She served on the executive committee of the LCP in 1945–1946, while managing her brother's surgical practice during his extended trip to West Africa as a member of the Colonial Advisory Committee on the Welfare of Colonial People in the United Kingdom. After he returned to Britain, Dr. Wellesley Cole established the West African Society (WAS) in 1947 with a small group of African intellectuals, including Irene Cole, her friend Lottie Hamilton-Hazeley, and Olive H. Johnston. Hamilton-Hazeley established and chaired the Freetown branch of the organization and contributed a piece, "Female Education in Sierra Leone," to WAS's journal, *Africana*. Amid her participation in these groups, the tireless Cole helped organize the West African Women's Association, the first group of its kind in London. Though apparently short-lived, the association organized women's study groups and a support network to facilitate women's entry into British universities and to generally assist them in navigating the challenges of life in the metropolis.[42]

Folayegbe Mosunmola Akintunde-Ighodalo lived in London between 1948 and 1955. She studied economics at Regent Street Polytechnic and earned a degree conferred by the University of London. She joined the WASU soon after her arrival, but she also participated in women's and socialist organizations and, like Cole, cofounded a new African women's organization. Embarrassed by her lack of familiarity with the major political issues of the day and events in other parts of the empire, Akintunde-Ighodalo spent hours poring over pamphlets and African newspapers at Africa House and the library at the Colonial Office. Already somewhat familiar with Padmore's ideas from his contributions to Nnamdi Azikiwe's *West African Pilot,* she read his books and met him and numerous other black intellectuals and visiting African dignitaries through the union. By the early 1950s, she had become the most prominent female member in the WASU, and in 1953, its members elected her its second female vice president.[43] In September, she helped launch the Nigerian Women's League of Great Britain and Ireland and was elected its first president.

Akintunde-Ighodalo's experiences as a member and representative of the WASU revealed, in both positive and negative ways, the need for and potential of women's activism. That summer, when the Nigerian delegation came to London to participate in talks on the colony's new constitution, she met its two female members, Mrs. Margaret Ekpo and Mrs. Comfort Tanimowo Ogunlesi (née Okusanya). Ogunlesi encouraged her to organize Nigerian women in Britain, and this initial encounter marked the beginning of a friendship and working alliance between them.[44] The same year, Akintunde-Ighodalo developed a close relationship with the Scottish feminist Mary Elizabeth Sutherland. As the WASU's vice president, Akintunde-Ighodalo attended conventions and conferences of all the major British political parties, and she met Sutherland and a number of other Labour women at party functions. Sutherland "often invited her young Nigerian friend to her home, encouraging her to participate in Labour Party activities, including political campaigning and writing for its publication, *Labour Women.*" Akintunde-Ighodalo addressed the annual conference of the party's women's wing and attended its International Women's School at the Beatrice Webb School in July 1953. "I came away ... with a renewed hope in the salvation of the world," she recalled. "Here for a week, I had been among people with the right vision and the will to bring into reality the socialist ideal of the brotherhood of man regardless of race, creed or colour." For Akintunde-Ighodalo, the gathering of women captured the spirit of socialist internationalism and provided an example of cooperation across barriers of class, race, and ethnicity, as well as the power of organized womanhood to affect change. As she wrote in *Labour Women,* "My experience at the school has filled me with a new courage in the power women can wield in a society. It has shown me that it is possible to have one of my life's ambitions fulfilled, that is, to help, when I get back to my country, the women to find their place and status in our rapidly changing society."[45]

If the WASU opened new doors for Akintunde-Ighodalo, her seat on the group's executive committee did not guarantee her right to participate in its decisions. By the end of the 1940s, a group of young radicals led by Joseph Appiah dominated the committee. "Unquestionably chauvinistic," her biographer LaRay Denzer notes, "the radical members of the executive tried to neutralize her influence." Assuming that her responsibilities as a young mother and full-time student would prohibit her attending meetings late into the night, Akintunde-Ighodalo remembered, "they would call a meeting of the executive," and "for the first three hours they would discuss non-issues. . . . Then by midnight, when many members had left, they would at last deliberate on major issues." Undaunted, she made arrangements with her husband, Jerry Ighodalo, to allow her to stay at the meetings until the executive committee finally voted on weightier issues. Eventually, she forced her male peers to conduct the meetings at a more practical hour.[46]

In late 1953, Akintunde-Ighodalo, Olu Olaniyan (née Dare), and several other Nigerian women formed the Nigerian Women's League (NWL). They envisioned the organization not only as a means of fostering community among and ameliorating the daily challenges of African women sojourners and migrants, directly linking their plight in London to the future prospects of Nigeria, but also as an expression of Nigerian women's unique contributions to the global community. A series of tragic stories about West African women in London that focused attention on the relative lack of services available to them provided the immediate impetus for the creation of the new league, and its founders cited their own feelings of isolation and loneliness in London to underscore the need for such an organization. At the same time, the NWL claimed the authority to translate and represent Nigerian womanhood to Britons and the world. The group officially launched its activities with a New Year's dance at Hampstead Town Hall that attracted a diverse crowd, reproducing a strategy used with success by successive generations of WASU women. "Above all," the author(s) of a statement issued at the dance declared, "we were fortunate to be given a small opportunity of interpreting Nigerian women to the British and the many other nationals who by the very position of London congregate there." They situated the group's pursuits and, more broadly, the unique burdens and contributions of Nigerian women within an international feminist tradition: "We believe that the women of Nigeria are capable of following in the courageous footsteps of the many brave women of other lands who have in the past fought against prejudice and overcome overwhelming obstacles in achieving great victories in the field of human endeavour. . . . Ours is the cause of Nigerian womanhood."[47]

While aligning themselves with "brave women of other lands," including Britain, NWL members also asserted the distinctiveness of their circumstances and, thus, their "cause." Their vision of political and social change exceeded those of male contemporaries and of socialist feminists in Britain, who invited them to speak as "little sisters." In mid-1954, *West Africa* published a letter from Akintunde-Ighodalo responding to those who viewed women's suffrage in Nigeria as a premature development or a deviation from African gender norms. "The argument," she wrote, "has often been advanced by many of our men that if Nigerian women want the vote they must fight for it just as the suffragettes did in Britain." Akintunde-Ighodalo countered this contention by refusing to accept Britain as the yardstick against which Nigeria should be measured. "Nigeria," she argued, "is, unlike Britain, not content to take hundreds of years to evolve a democratic system of self-government," adding, "There seems a lot to be said for Nigeria aiming at contributing something to the course of world development instead of being a mere copyist."[48] In defending her position, she reversed the charge more commonly leveled against colonized women to present women's struggle for the vote and social reform as an alternative to, rather than an instance of, mimicking their colonial rulers. Local misogyny and the imperial order, she suggested, were of a piece.

Informed by their own experiences in the white metropolis, the feminism of West African women like Akintunde-Ighodalo developed within the context of their involvement in the male-dominated centers of black activism and their encounters with European-run feminist and internationalist groups. Operating in the interstices between these realms, African women extended their reach while challenging their internal hierarchies. As their numbers grew, the apathy, if not the antipathy, of British officialdom and African men brought them closer together in autonomous organizing efforts. For them, improving the plight of African women necessitated meaningful cooperation among the colonies of West Africa and among different groups within each colony. At a time when forces in Britain and the colonies increasingly channeled internationalist aspirations into more narrowly nationalist goals, Akintunde-Ighodalo criticized the trend toward abandoning broadly defined black organizations in favor of balkanized ethnic associations.[49]

The lives of these West African women followed transcolonial paths, and they applied the organizing skills and contacts accumulated along the way in later endeavors. The connections they formed in London became the basis for personal relationships and future collaboration, and sent them in new directions, to new locales, or shaped their subsequent lives in still other ways. According to Denzer, as a student at Queen's College in Lagos before she departed for London, Akintunde-Ighodalo revered her teacher and WASU stalwart Kofoworola Moore, whom she viewed as the "epitome of woman-hood" for her "ideas of equality," "demeanor," and "fashionableness."[50] In the late 1950s and 1960s, Akintunde-Ighodalo worked alongside Irene Cole in Nigerian women's groups. Gender and racial discrimination thwarted Cole's goal of becoming a surgeon like her brother, so she settled on gynecology as her field of specialization because it would allow her to do the most good for West African women. The decision took her to Brighton in early 1947 to complete her training, and at about the same time, she married the Nigerian Samuel Osarogie Ighodaro.[51] At the end of the decade, the couple left for Ibadan, Nigeria, where Cole-Ighodaro applied both the professional exper-tise and organizing experience that she had acquired in Britain throughout a long public career. During the 1950s, she worked for the Ministry of Health, the YWCA, and as a private practitioner; gave Red Cross lectures; and helped establish several women's organizations, including the National Council of Women's Societies and the Nigerian Association of University Women. Collectively, these women helped establish women's branches of political parties and autonomous women's organizations across coastal West Africa in the decades before independence.

Under growing pressure from colonial officials to renounce her associa-tion with the WAYL in Sierra Leone, in 1946, Cummings-John, now a wid-owed mother, traveled with her two sons to New York City, where her half brother, the celebrated dancer Asadata Dafora (born Austin Horton) lived, and settled in Brooklyn. Unable to find a job as a teacher, she supported her family by working in local hospitals, while once again devoting considerable time to activism. She served on the executive committees of the anti-imperi-alist Council on African Affairs (CAA) and the American Council for African Education (ACAE), founded by the Nigerian Nwafor Orizu to organize a scholarship program for African students to attend U.S. colleges and universities. The CAA brought Cummings-John into contact with the Robesons, Alphaeus Hunton, and African American women activists such as Charlotta Bass, and she used the organization to raise funds for "the cause of free education for girls in Sierra Leone."[52] Cummings-John returned to Freetown in 1951 to build a girls' school named after Eleanor Roosevelt, whom she had met while in the United States, and re-entered politics. She doggedly pursued the same concerns that had preoccupied her in 1938—the political and social position of women, equal rights for the protectorate population, and self-government for a unified Sierra Leone. She also launched the Sierra Leone Women's Movement (SLWM) with her childhood friend Lottie Hamilton-Hazeley and her cousin Mabel Dove, who was visiting from the Gold Coast. Between them, these women had extensive experience with organizing on behalf of notable black associations in London during the 1930s and 1940s. The SLWM included protectorate women at all levels, published a newspaper, created a women traders' cooperative, and pressed for greater educational opportunities for women. Throughout the 1950s and early 1960s—in various capacities as an elected representative of the Sierra Leone People's Party, the head of a thriving girls' school, and the leader of a mass women's organization—Cummings-John continued to travel abroad, establishing ties to international organizations and pursuing fund-raising options around the world. She contributed to black cultural and political life in London from afar; the program "Presenting the Negro World," a festival of black art, literature, films, and music organized by the London branch of the Society for African Culture in April 1959, credited her as one of the event's sponsors. Five years after Sierra Leonean independence, in 1966, Prime Minister Albert Margai appointed her the first mayor of Freetown, but, shortly thereafter, a military coup toppled the government, forcing her into exile in London. Back in Britain after nearly thirty years, she formed Women for Disarmament and became active in the larger Campaign for Nuclear Disarmament as well as local branches of the Labour Party and Co-operative Society.[53] As Cummings-John moved between London, New York, and Freetown, her political activities connected global struggles against racial and gender-based oppression, movements for colonial freedom, and the more immediate concerns of women in each of these locales.

THE BLACK FEMINIST INTERNATIONALISM OF UNA MARSON AND THE LIMITS OF SISTERHOOD

Originally from Jamaica, Una Marson traveled across Europe and traversed the Atlantic multiple times during the 1930s and 1940s. As a poet, dramatist, editor, activist, and radio personality, her activities on both sides of the ocean were at once integral to the development of black internationalism and a critical intervention in the gender politics enveloping it. In London from 1932 to 1936 and from 1938 to 1946, she participated in a wide range of black political and cultural initiatives and became the most prominent black feminist in the imperial metropolis. The LCP initially consumed the bulk of Marson's time and energy, but she also moved in other circles, especially feminist internationalist groups, and confronted the limits that the color line imposed on international sisterhood.

Marson's feminist politics and peripatetic style led many of her male contemporaries to view her with suspicion, even scorn, and to characterize her as a "loner" or as "extremely charming, but not one of us." Some of them vilified her personally and politically during the war years, even as her office at the BBC and her flats in Hampstead and then Bayswater became important gatherings spots for people of African descent traveling through, stationed in, or living in the city. As Jarrett-Macauley notes, quoting Jeffrey Green, respectable "black middle-class women . . . 'were not expected to fully participate in political matters but to be artistic and civilised, ideal wives for professional men.'" Provocative and iconoclastic, Marson "didn't fit anywhere" in the male world of black activism or the white women's movement.[54]

The youngest daughter of respected middle-class parents, Reverend Solomon Isaac and Ada Marson, Una attended one of Kingston, Jamaica's elite high schools. During the late 1920s and early 1930s, she earned growing acclaim for her literary efforts while working as a journalist, social worker, and secretary. She published two collections of poetry, *Tropic Reveries* (1930) and *Heights and Depths* (1931), and her first play, *At What a Price,* appeared at Kingston's Ward Theatre in June 1932.[55] Marson also developed a reputation as an outspoken feminist and fought passionately for the cause of women stenographers. In 1928, she founded and edited the women's journal and published organ of the Kingston Stenographers Association, *Cosmopolitan,* becoming at the age of twenty-three the first female editor-publisher in Jamaica. Its mission, Marson explained, was "to foster 'COSMOPOLITAN' spirit, a wider vision, a more tolerant attitude" and, at the same time, to contribute to the development of "a clean, thoughtful and artistic Island literature." She presented the publication as a counterpoint to the masculinist perspective of the colonial press and an agent of a dawning "age of woman." In one piece, Marson defended the "poor modern woman," whose appearance she linked not only to fashion but also to women's heightened political and economic demands, against the recent invectives of "eloquent, strong old-fashioned young men" in the *Daily Gleaner*: "We need no victory over short skirts and bobbed hair half as much as we need a victory over selfishness and lack of enthusiasm in ourselves and in our country." "A big rally of women workers," she suggested, "would be the best thing to sweep the cob-webs from certain brains."[56]

Marson was exposed to the UNIA at a young age in Jamaica. She was one of many girls who participated in its elocution contests and later defended the famed pan-Africanist Garvey in the *Cosmopolitan*.[57] In reference to the 1931 Miss Jamaica contest, she admonished, "Some amount of expense and disappointment could be saved a number of dusky ladies . . . if promoters of the contest would announce in the daily press that very dark or black beauties will not be considered." Nevertheless, the views expressed by the publication closely resembled those of feminist internationalists in Britain. The *Cosmopolitan* espoused liberal internationalism, envisioning the rise of a "world-wide commonwealth" from a reformed British Empire. As Astley Clerk wrote in the May 1929 issue, "Empire does not mean Jamaica, England or one or two other countries under the British flag—it means more—it means Greater Britain, including every country which flies the Union Jack." Marson's contributions to the *Cosmopolitan* in the late 1920s advocated the expansion of educational and employment opportunities for women, women's self-help groups, and women's suffrage, but rarely touched upon issues related to race, cultural identity, or racism. She read and admired Harlem Renaissance authors Zora Neale Hurston, James Weldon Johnson, and Claude McKay, but feminism preoccupied her more than racial conscious-ness in the years prior to her departure for Britain. As her biographer Delia Jarrett Macauley observes, "her culture, as far as she had been aware, was English" when she left Jamaica.[58]

For someone with Marson's literary ambitions, particularly with new immigration restrictions limiting Afro-Caribbeans' entry into the United States, the next logical step was to test her fortunes in Britain. Instead of opportunity, she found disappointment and racial arrogance. After a lonely and frustrating first year engaged in a futile search for employment, she began working as the LCP's unpaid secretary in early 1933, representing the league at a variety of forums, managing its day-to-day business, and editing *The Keys* for the following two years. The relatively high quality of the journal owed a great deal to Marson's previous experience in Jamaica, and the job demanded that she be familiar with such diverse topics as the Scottsboro Boys case in the United States, the plight of black seamen and their families in England and Wales, and the expropriation of Kikuyu lands by white settlers in colo-nial Kenya. Marson met prominent activists, artists, and student sojourners from Africa and the United States. She attended WASU events and talks on

African art and drama at the International Institute of African Languages and Cultures, read the books of African intellectuals such as Akiki Nyabongo, and visited the set of the film *Sanders of the River,* where she met and discussed literature with its star, Paul Robeson. She also frequented the growing number of nightclubs in Soho featuring black musicians and, in her capacity as social secretary, booked a number of them for league functions.

Marson used the LCP and *The Keys* as a platform for black art and to initiate a transatlantic dialogue around literature. In addition to publishing original works by Afro-Caribbean writers, she commissioned the Guyanese author and former Harlem resident Eric Walrond to review Zora Neale Hurston's *Jonah's Gourd Vine* and Langston Hughes's *The Ways of White Folk.* In November 1933, Marson directed a league production of her play *At What a Price* at the YWCA Central Club, to positive reviews from the *Manchester Guardian* and *West Africa.* The all-black cast of LCP members included a young W. Arthur Lewis, Stella Thomas, Viola Thompson, and Sylvia Lowe, and Bruce Wendell's Coloured Orchestra provided the music. The successful performance led to a three-night run at the West End's Scala Theatre, marking, as *The Keys* reported, "the first time that a play written and performed by Coloured Colonials had been staged in London." Marson donated the meager proceeds to the LCP's fund to establish a black cultural center in the city, a cause that she championed for the following decade.[59]

Although Marson eventually drifted away from the LCP, her exposure to Africans and other black intellectuals through the league left an indelible mark on her thinking and writings. When Sir Nana Ofori Atta Omanhene, the African king of Akyem Abuakwa, arrived in London as the head of the Gold Coast and Asante delegation in July 1934, she assumed responsibility for officially welcoming the African dignitary on behalf of the LCP, and the pair enjoyed each other's company throughout the summer. As Marson later recalled, "He was gleaning Western ideas and I was probing the mind of an African Paramount Chief." Her relationship with Ofori Atta deepened her conviction "that Africa mattered," and she altered her appearance to reflect her ongoing personal and political transformation. To the chagrin of some of her female peers, Marson stopped straightening her hair and took to wearing vibrant colors, distinctive patterns, and bold accessories and developed an interest in Africa and African cultures. Sylvia Lowe recalled, "She liked to look African. She put her hair as they did . . . natural not plaited, and combed out." She "was more interested in them [Africans] than in our own affairs . . . she was a bit ahead of most people but we didn't think of that in those days."

In early 1935, Marson denounced global white supremacy and issued a stirring call to action in *The Keys*. Rejecting communism, she noted: "We don't want to fight, we are pacifists," and insisted, "We must work out our own salvation.... Then, and only then will the Negro race be a race contributing richly to the world." Rather than deploying a primordial racial essence or universal black experience, she cited mutual ignorance and variations in the form and degree of racial oppression as significant obstacles to fostering intraracial cooperation, but she maintained that cooperation among people of African descent was both necessary and a reflection of the larger drift toward internationalism: "The whole world is coming closer together ... and the Negro world must come together."[60]

Marson's association with the league also allowed her to establish ties to largely white, middle-class feminist organizations like the Women's International League for Peace and Freedom, the British Commonwealth League, and the International Alliance of Women for Suffrage and Equal Citizenship, while bringing individuals such as the journalist and novelist Winifred Holtby and the feminist Margery Corbett Ashby into the black-run LCP as members and patrons. Founded in 1925, the British Commonwealth League (BCL) attempted to develop women's organizations throughout the empire and dedicated itself to raising the "status of women of the less forward races" in particular. Both it and the Women's International League weighed in on colonial questions, and the latter petitioned successfully for the inclusion of women on the League of Nations Mandate Commission. Whereas British feminists before and immediately following World War I had tended to focus on the plight of Indian women to the extent that they considered the colonies at all, their attention thereafter turned increasingly to Africa and such issues as prostitution and female initiation practices in the 1930s. They approached African and other non-European women with the same air of cultural, if not racial, superiority as their Victorian and Edwardian predecessors, and like other white internationalists and antifascist partisans, most "were believers in empire" who called for an extension of the mandate system, not colonial freedom.[61]

Marson joined the BCL soon after her arrival and remained a member for six years. As her knowledge of conditions in colonial Africa and experiences with racism in Britain propelled her in more radical directions, she became more confident and outspoken. In June 1934, she attended a league conference accompanied by Jomo Kenyatta. Marson spoke on the topic "The Colour Bar in England" as part of a panel titled "Bars to Careers," which also

included Winifred Holtby. While the latter decried the racism of white settlers in South Africa, Marson pointed to specific instances of racial discrimination against qualified black women in the metropole. As Bush notes,
"Holtby's attitude to blacks was less patronising than those of her white,
middle-class male co-activists," but even she retained "an emotional commitment to empire and the higher ideals of trusteeship." From their first meeting
at the conference, Marson challenged Holtby to think beyond the BCL's
liberal maternalism. She had read *Mandoa, Mandoa,* the novelist's anticolonial parody of white-settler society racism in South Africa, the previous year
and deemed it "a most brilliant satire," and the two remained in touch until
the latter's death in September 1935. On one occasion, Holtby, who often
entertained intellectuals from the colonies and bohemian artists, hosted a
literary tête-à-tête that included Marson and Walrond. The conversation
began over afternoon tea but stretched late into the evening, covering, as
Holtby wrote to Vera Brittain, "the colour question, miscegenation, birth
control and race prejudice inside out."[62] In November 1934, Marson spoke on
"social and political equality in Jamaica" at the Women's International
League's conference "Africa: Peace and Freedom," produced a report on the
event for the LCP, and contributed a poem to *The Keys* to mark the occasion.
An epigraph by the Scottish trade unionist William Ballinger citing the
enormous discrepancy in government expenditures for schooling white versus black children in South Africa frames the poem, "Education," which then
proceeds to highlight the role of education in the formation of racialized
subjects: "The abuse of learning is when it is given / To subject races . . . And,
since the quarrel / Will bear no colour for the thing they are, / Fashion it
thus; . . . And keep them ignorant."[63] The Women's Social Service Club of
Jamaica invited Marson to represent it at the Twelfth Annual Congress of
the International Alliance of Women for Suffrage and Equal Citizenship
(IAWSEC) in 1935 an international feminist conference in Istanbul attended
by 280 delegates representing thirty countries. Although participants hailed
from around the globe, the chair of the congress, Margery Corbett Ashby,
noted that Marson, who participated in the session "East and West in
Co-operation," was the "first delegate from Jamaica and the first woman of
African race."[64] In her speech, Marson identified British colonialism and the
legacy of slavery in the Caribbean as the two main factors shaping Jamaica's
history and the problems of Jamaican women. Claiming to "talk on behalf of
all the Negroes of the world not only Jamaicans," she lauded the work of the
NAACP and condemned the "barbarism" of lynching. "Even in London,"

she told her audience, "one sometimes sees discrimination against black people, even those who are British subjects. Negroes are suffering under enormous difficulties in most countries in the world."[65]

Marson universally impressed her listeners in these forums. The *Manchester Guardian* reported that she "astonished the [IAWSEC] Conference by her intellectual vigour," and after meeting her, Corbett Ashby joined the LCP and became a "liberal subscriber" to the organization. These conferences heightened Marson's profile among feminists in both Britain and Jamaica and affected her deeply, reaffirming her commitment to internationalism; but she consistently raised awkward questions and connected seemingly disparate forms of oppression in a manner that exposed white feminists' investment in empire. Whereas leading feminists like Corbett Ashby argued that women should "take their share in building up the work of the Empire" instead of dismantling it, for Marson, Christine Bolt observes, "internationalism brought an increased awareness of the racial and gender problems generated by imperialism." She delighted in meeting and learning from women from India and other colonies, but the hubris of white women, especially those who claimed to speak with the authority of experience on colonial conditions but ignored the perspectives of women of color, increasingly angered her. In reference to an event at the Royal Empire Society, she sneered, "I gathered from the speech by the white Rhodesian that African women did not exist in Rhodesia; in any case, they did not loom largely enough on her horizon for even a casual mention." Ultimately, Marson was no more at home in internationalist women's organizations than in the LCP, and her views regarding the prospects for a fuller realization of the Commonwealth ideal changed accordingly. Surveying the empire, she wrote in 1937, "The Statute of Westminster which has given the Dominions complete freedom, the agitation in India, the demand of Egypt for independence, the delegations from West Africa—all these things tend to show that there can be no true Commonwealth of Nations . . . until the liberty, well-being and advancement of all peoples under the British flag are more satisfactory."[66]

Several of her poems register her ambivalence toward the white feminists she met in Britain. She penned sonnets in tribute to her deceased friend Holtby and the British feminists gathered at the 1935 IAWSEC conference. "To the I.A.W.S.E.C" addresses the "Women of England who in freedom's name / Work with courageous women of all lands," and ends: "What bitter struggles have their spirit known / So that just rights to womanhood should come: / For lands can only reach the greater good / When noble thoughts inspire sweet womanhood." The poem appears opposite "To Joe and Ben," Marson's moving requiem for the sons of the Ethiopian ambassador to Britain, in her third collection of poetry, *The Moth and the Star* (1937). Suggestively juxtaposing the gathering of feminist internationalists in Istanbul and resistance to the Italian invasion of Ethiopia, the placement posits a connection between these examples of service to internationalist causes, "yours, and yet not yours," while calling attention to the destabilizing force of imperialism—"This hate and greed / That brings forth war"—in a manner rarely seen in the writings of white feminists. The poem for Holtby attributes her singularity as a "valiant woman, author, speaker, friend" to her cosmopolitan sympathies, "as wide as they were true." Marson originally intended to dedicate "Little Brown Girl," which appears earlier in the volume, to Holtby as well. The poem reenacts the moment when the white feminist gaze attempts but ultimately fails to apprehend the eponymous "girl" who remains voiceless throughout. As Anna Snaith notes, "The narrator gropes towards a position of empathy and understanding of the 'brown girl's' simultaneous alienation and racial pride, but this is undercut by her construction of the girl and her homeland." Unable to locate this "exotic" woman walking the streets within her mental geography of the city or the empire, she asks:

> And from whence are you
> Little brown girl?
> I guess Africa, or India,
> Ah no, from some island
> In the West Indies, But isn't that India
> All the same?

The contrast between the "White, white city" of "coated people" and the brown (i.e., mixed-race) girl, which conjures the ethnic diversity of the Caribbean, parallels the irreducible distance between the observer and observed. The poem's closing lines foreclose the possibility of mutual recognition in the imperial metropolis:

> What are you seeking
> To discover in this dismal
> City of ours?
> From the look in your eyes
> Little Brown girl
> I know it is something
> That does not really exist."[67]

The growing threat of fascism, especially after Italy's invasion of Ethiopia, and the unrest in Britain's African and Caribbean colonies increasingly preoccupied Marson during the late 1930s. As discussed in chapter 2, she was closer to these events than most of her contemporaries. She worked in the League of Nations' information section for three months in 1935—the first black woman to do so—which gave her a unique perspective on the diplomatic posturing as Italy prepared to invade Ethiopia. She returned to London to volunteer for the Ethiopian ambassador and accompanied Emperor Haile Selassie back to Geneva as his personal secretary. She sorted mountains of letters from well-wishers across the black world and then watched as Selassie's appeals to the international body fell on deaf ears. Nancy Cunard, who covered developments in Geneva for the Associated Negro Press, recalled Marson as a "capable well-informed secretary" wearing a "golden dress, a figure of . . . 'oriental splendor.'" In September 1936, Marson returned home, physically and emotionally exhausted but emboldened. Amid the anxious atmosphere in Jamaica during 1937 and 1938, she achieved her greatest literary triumphs to date with the production of two plays and the publication of a new collection of poetry, *The Moth and the Star,* and helped launch the Readers and Writers Club, which injected a critical edge and appreciation of Afro-Caribbean vernacular culture into the relatively small literary scene. Isobel Seaton recalled, "I went to the club three or four times and could see that Una was the prime mover in it. She felt intensely about everything and had a very good sense of humour."[68] Marson's second play, *London Calling,* presented to Kingston audiences a picture of Caribbean students' lives abroad. Soon after its run at the Ward Theatre in 1937, she founded the Kingston Dramatic Club. The latter staged *Pocomania,* her third drama, at the Ward Theatre in January 1938; it was, as she put it in private correspondence, "the biggest success of all."[69]

Marson also worked as a journalist for the *Jamaican Standard* and contributed to *Public Opinion,* a weekly publication affiliated with Norman Manley's People's National Movement. "As both catalyst for change and recorder of it," Jarrett-Macauley explains, "*Public Opinion* would over the next twenty years remain at the centre of Jamaican political life, taking up radical and left-wing positions on domestic and overseas issues." Although the paper's editorial board later included prominent Jamaican women such as Amy Bailey, Gloria Escoffery, and Edna Manley, Marson was initially its sole female contributor.[70] In "Feminism," published in May 1938, she challenged men who suggested that women were intellectually inferior and drew attention to the capricious nature of standards for feminine respectability. "The very word conjures up in their minds chatty meetings of frustrated spinsters who are sublimating their normal instincts," but, she maintained, "the idea of feminism is not to make a woman more conscious of her sex but to develop that within her which will make for a live, active mental and physical personality." As in her earlier writings, she referenced the gains of British feminists, but now she cited African women "who are equal to any emergency" alongside them.[71]

Marson's experiences abroad introduced to her writing a new emphasis on racial unity and a transcolonial perspective. In her pieces for *Public Opinion,* she maintained that colonialism continued to retard the development of a national culture in Jamaica and the progress of women in all fields. She linked racial and gender hierarchies in colonial Jamaica by tracing the roots of both to the sexual exploitation of enslaved women. "Educated Jamaicans," she charged, "spend their whole lives thinking they are not coloured, and it is an insult to call them 'Negro' because one or two generations back they had some white ancestor of the male sex. Now we can never be free from inhibitions, complexes, indecision and lack of confidence until we accept ourselves for what we are." Marson contrasted middle-class Jamaicans' imitation of all things English, their obsession with fine gradations in skin color, and their failure to rally around the cause of Ethiopia to working-class popular traditions that celebrated the island's historical connection to African cultures. She cited the poetry and novels of James Weldon Johnson and Claude McKay, and W. E. B. Du Bois's *The Souls of Black Folk,* which "should take pride of place in every coloured home," the books of Nyabongo and Nnamdi Azikiwe, and Indian artists and intellectuals such as Gandhi, Nehru, and Rabindranath Tagore as potential models for Jamaican cultural producers. "It is not that we should abhor other races and idolise our own," she explained, "but ... that we should admire the work of other races, reverence that of our own heroes and build something that is essentially our own."[72] Marson insisted that if Jamaicans were not, as she put it, "to remain strangers in [their] own land," they had to embrace their place within a global band of color and, in politics as well as the arts, pursue an agenda based at once on racial pride and cultural internationalism.[73] However, she rejected simplistic notions of a return to Africa, and a pronounced ambivalence suffused her writing. In dialect verse, blues poems, and her third play, *Pocomania,* she staged the quandary of diasporic relation in terms of a cross-class conversation among black women forged through the arts and subaltern culture.

English Romanticism and, via the orientalist reveries of Coleridge, Yeats, and the Shelleys, Indian love poetry and Hindu devotional literature heavily influenced Marson's poetry from the 1920s and early 1930s. "A Dream" in *Heights and Depths* begins with the first line of Percy Bysshe Shelley's "The Indian Serenade," and a footnote to "Summer Days" reads "To the tune of the Indian Love Lyric 'The Temple Bells.'"[74] She took the title for *The Moth and the Star*, and included an epigraph, from Shelley's poem of the same name. Notes of melancholy, longing, and mystical experience reemerge, but, as Mary Lou Emery remarks, "the social relationship and psychological condition constituted through the racialized gaze . . . drives this new period in Marson's poetry." Marson linked the racism that confronted people of African descent in London to depictions of blacks in books, on stage, and on screen. The poem "Nigger," published in the first issue of *The Keys*, prefigures Fanon's famous passage in *Black Skin, White Masks*. An incident in which passing children on the street "flung" the epithet at her opens a meditation on the history of the word, from slavery to minstrelsy: "'Nigger' was raised then to a Burlesque Show / And thus from Curse to Clown progressed." The poem comes full circle in a closing, ironic prayer. The "little white urchins" give way to adult racists whose hypocrisy reveals the relationship between whiteness, imperial power, and metropolitan space: "God keep my soul from hating such mean souls, / . . . Those who preach Christ / And say with churlish smile / 'This place is not for 'Niggers.'"[75]

Street scenes recur in Marson's poetry and in her second play, *London Calling*, which she began writing soon after Ofori Atta's departure in 1934. Couched in a comedy of manners with a conventional romantic plot, *London Calling* highlights the unstable relation between racial markers and masquerade, difference and desire, in the highly stratified interactions between colonial subjects and British "hosts." The plot repeatedly underscores the importance of performance in the negotiation of social identity. It revolves around a series of competing racial performances involving a group of drama students, Rita and Sydney Fray and Alton and Frank Lane, from the fictional island colony of Novoka ("no voice") during 1934–1935. Life in "a city of walking iceboxes" forces them to grapple, on the one hand, with the ignorance and racism of the English upper classes, represented by the Burtons, and, on the other, with their own sense of being culturally rudderless in relation to their African friend Prince Alota Bayo, inspired by Ofori Atta. Even Rita's surname, Fray, suggests the unraveling of self and its attendant cultural moorings, which accompanied transcolonial encounters in the metropole.

In private, the Novokans discuss the cold weather, subtle and not-so-subtle social rebuffs, the men's popularity with white women, Lady Burton's brother (the anthropologist Larkspur), and his courtship of Rita. Early on, they accept invitations to perform a "native sketch" for the "International Society" and to spend the Christmas holiday at Lady Burton's aristocratic home in Kent, Stonehurst. The near-simultaneous arrival of these invitations and the Novokans' reaction to them imply that the Novokans view the scenarios as essentially similar. Sydney laments, "One never knows when those kindnesses are sincere or merely patronising." Alton recounts an incident earlier that day: "Some kids shouted 'Hello Snowball' at the me this morning." Rita interjects, "And you said 'Hello Shine,'" to which Alton replies, "Exactly. How did you guess?"[76]

Rita at first recoils from Lady Burton's invitation as well as the International Society's proposition ("What do they take us for? Cheap entertainers?"), but with the help of Alota, Alton convinces her and Sydney to join him in some "pranks." When Frank expresses concern that their audience might see through the farce, Sydney interrupts, "I never get a crowd that knew the difference between Nevada and Timbucktoo—as for Novoka, it would take them too long to find it on the map." His reference to a "crowd" invokes the stage but also recalls the black agitators and performers soapboxing weekly before British onlookers in Hyde Park. Like those outdoor orations, the Novokans' own performance blurs the line between the reproduction of imperial stereotypes, on the one hand, and a positive investment in blackness and opposition to colonial categories, on the other. Alton tells Alota, "As we have only English customs in Novoka we want to borrow from you." The latter agrees to help and jokes that he is taking them "back to Africa" as he dresses them in colorful robes and beads and teaches them dance steps. Rita is reticent throughout, but Alota encourages her, admires her beauty in the faux African garb, and refers to her as his African "Princess."[77] Amid the play of racial parodies, Rita simultaneously discovers and invents a connection to Alota and his culture.

The Novokans' spectacle, which occurs offstage between acts, is apparently a success, confirming Sydney's suspicions. When the students arrive at Stonehurst, their host encourages them to don their "native costume," and they continue their act by speaking pidgin English and extolling the wonders of the "dark miracle country." The Burtons' feigned hospitality belies profound anxiety over the family's declining fortunes and deep cracks in the empire's edifice, which figure in the play as two sides of the same coin.

Obliged to countenance the presence of "negroes" in the family home because of their financial dependence on his "Crazy Uncle" Larkspur, the Burtons' son, Douglas, protests: "It [is] bad enough about the men, but a negro woman in our house, why, it isn't decent." When his sister, Elsie, points out that he is only making a "fuss" because of their guests' skin color, he explodes, "It will mean the end of the great British Empire. There will be no subject peoples any more." After Larkspur outs the family to a local reporter, photos of the family dancing with their black visitors appear in the newspaper, and social ostracism looms, Douglas pleads with Rita "to promise not to marry" his uncle in England. In the end, she announces that she will marry Alton, who has also courted her from the start, instead.[78]

Both "Nigger" and *London Calling* link racial caricatures on stage to racism on the street and ultimately to the private world of a declining ruling class clinging with renewed ferocity to its investment in imperial whiteness. As Emery points out, Marson's writings dwell on the visual as a modality of social relationships, particularly "the dynamics of seeing . . . in colonial relations." However, as if functioning as a critical counterpoint, music and the aesthetics of aurality frequently appear as means of imagining community beyond the phenotypical grounds of white supremacy and empire. The voices of black working women surface with increasing regularity as carriers of alternative performance traditions, conceptions of value and beauty, and ripostes to the racial optics of colonial society. The poems in *The Moth and the Star* oscillate formalistically and thematically. A number of them deal with the "self-destructive internalization of colonialist values and racist standards of beauty" and respectability as a part of a general critique of the representation of black female bodies in imperial visual culture. Others show the influence African American writers as well as the jazz, swing, and calypso Marson heard in Soho nighteries or on 78 records in London, and she draws on popular cultural forms such as the ballad and the blues to enact a "new black poetics."[79] Marson dedicated the collection "to you whose voice called me back to the green pastures of song." In "Cinema Eyes," a mother refuses to allow her daughter to go to the cinema until "black beauties / Are chosen for the screen," recounting the painful personal and psychological consequences of growing up "with a cinema mind": "I saw no beauty in black faces, / The tender light and beauty of their eyes I did not see; / . . . The mellow music of their voice." "Black Burden" expresses the dream of global black unity and collective liberation, foregrounding the agency of black women while suggesting that the "burden" of color prejudice falls heaviest on their shoulders:

I am black,
And I have got to travel
Even farther than white folk,
For time moves on—[. . .]

Black girl—what a burden—
But your shoulders
Are broad.
Black girl—what a burden—
But your courage is strong—
Black girl, your burden
Will fall from your shoulders,
For there is love
In your soul
And a song
In your heart.

Song and vernacular speech in Marson's poetry often signal entry into the world of black working women and their private thoughts and conversations. The final section of *The Moth and the Star*, "Poems of Life," features a number of blues poems and Marson's earliest experiments with dialect verse. In examples of the latter such as "Gettin' de Spirit," "The Stone Breakers," and "My Philosophy (As expounded by a Market Woman)," working-class Jamaican women express their views and articulate their struggles. "Black Is Fancy," "Brown Baby Blues," and "Kinky Hair Blues" implicate standards of beauty in the reproduction of gender and racial hierarchies, and implicate black men in the pressure for women to conceal the markers of their blackness.[80] The latter two poems take the form of classic blues tunes. The recordings of women blues singers such as Bessie Smith, Angela Davis argues, represented a rare public expression of working-class African American women's concerns during this era and, like Marson's poetry, "challenged the gender politics implicit in dominant representations of marriage and heterosexual love relationships." Given that Smith was a personal favorite of Marson, her blues poems can be read as a black feminist gesture across class and national lines, one grounded in the gendered experience of racialization.[81]

Written in 1937, Marson's third play, *Pocomania,* bears signs of the circumstances in which she produced it, particularly the expressions of discontent sweeping through the Caribbean. Soon after completing it, she initiated a correspondence with James Weldon Johnson of roughly two years. At turns playful, self-deprecating, and, as she admitted, "garrulous," her letters conveyed pangs of self-doubt but also the importance of literature to her personally and as a vehicle for forging a distinctive Jamaican culture and for facilitating dialogue among people of African descent. She mentioned that the League of American Negro Writers inspired the Readers and Writers Club, discussed the writing process and her recent work, and sent him press reviews of *Pocomania*. In a letter from late January 1938, Marson situated Jamaica within the context of a global movement against racism that inspired her hopes for the future. "I think of our struggles in America—of Africa—the coming country—of the West Indies in her birth struggles—and I say, to borrow from Wordsworth—'Bliss is it / In this dawn to be alive / And to be young is very heaven!'" Describing the situation on the island as "a case of 'Jamaica Aroused,'" she added, "Our most pressing need is that labour should be organised, especially with regard to wages."[82] "Jamaica Aroused" is a clear reference to Edna Manley's sculpture *Negro Aroused* (1935). As David Boxer observes, "The half figure of an unmistakably *black* man, his gaze turned skywards, is a symbol of a search; a vision of a new social order." It became "the very icon" of the political stirrings of the late 1930s.[83]

Both Manley and Marson drew inspiration and source material from pocomania, a new form of ecstatic revivalism that spread rapidly in Kingston in the 1930s. As Putnam remarks, "The cosmopolitan ports, economic crises, and xenophobic ultimatums of the late 1920s seem to have acted as a kind of crucible for race-conscious revivals." Most scholars connect pocomania to the pukumina tradition that developed among post-emancipation African immigrants in Jamaica during the nineteenth century, but it was likely filliped by the return of 25,000 Jamaicans who worked alongside Afro-Haitians and Afro-Cubans in Cuba between 1930 and 1935, as well. Often accompanied by drumming, worshippers engaged in "shouting and singing throughout the night, with children and adults lying upon the earth, night and day, in a 'trance.'" The prominence of lower-class Afro-Jamaican women as leaders and participants in the movement linked it to other cultures of myalism or Obeah worship and distinguished it from Rastafarianism. Manley later recalled "the trips I was taking at night listening to the Pocomania meetings," and she introduced others, including Zora Neale Hurston, to them. *Negro Aroused* appeared alongside twelve other sculptures, including *Pocomania,* at her first solo exhibition in Kingston in 1937.[84]

Like Manley, Marson gravitated to the female-led spiritual manifestations of mass disaffection from the colonial order. Her play was seminal in its incorporation of antiphony, popular spirituals, calypsos, and orature, and in its treatment of vernacular cultural forms in the Caribbean as the product of the historical ties linking Africans and people of African descent across the Atlantic. The play presents pocomania as an expression of a hybrid Afro-Caribbean culture, one in which working-class women occupy a central position. Women are the primary participants in an ongoing transatlantic dialogue between West Africa and the Caribbean, which the play extends. (Indeed, a theater group in Nigeria staged it in Lagos in May 1940.)[85] "Our Pocomaniacs," Marson wrote to Weldon Johnson, "must be something like the 'Shakers' used to be in your Southern states or perhaps like the 'Holy Rollers' in Nassau. I think the word means 'a little madness.'"[86] "In spite of the medley of people and the strong British influence," she explained on a 1939 BBC radio broadcast, "the heart of Africa still beats loud and insistent in this isle of the west. The frenzied shouts in mystic dances of Africa live in the Pocomania religious cult."[87] During an interview with the West African journalist Victor Delumo six years later, she again suggested that pocomania was "the nearest thing to Africa that we have in the West Indies," and evidence that "our African ancestry is with us still."[88]

Pocomania is equally notable for its exploration of the potential for cross-class alliances among Afro-Jamaican women through the relationship between the working-class leader of the pocomaniacs, Sister Kate, and the middle-class protagonist, Stella Manners. The play offers a critical picture of middle-class society in Jamaica but, paradoxically, reaffirms class-based norms in the end. After Sister Kate's death, the final resolution of the multiple disturbances within the play—in the social fabric of Jamaica as well as inside Stella—involves the substitution of a union with David Davis, a physician who returns transformed by years of studying abroad in England, for Stella's attraction to pocomania. Belinda Edmondson suggests that this implies that the "spirit," "vitality," and "little madness" of Caribbean folkways had to be subdued and disciplined to serve the nation just as heterosexual marriage reins in unruly female desires. However, an element of ambiguity persists in this seemingly conventional ending. Though more sympathetic than the men associated with the Christian church, David is ambivalent toward pocomania and, as her doctor and suitor, tries but fails to stop Stella from attending the Ninth Night Celebration. At one point, he confesses to feeling "out-paced by Pocomania" in his pursuit of Stella, and in the play's final lines, concedes, "We all need a little madness in our lives," to which Stella responds: "Now you have admitted that, it will be so much easier to love you."[89]

In her prose and poetry, fiction and nonfiction from the late 1930s, Marson exposed the constraints of middle-class respectability in a racially stratified social formation while plumbing the potential for cross-class identification among black women. Many of her contemporaries in Jamaica "based their demands for reform on a careful pattern of identification and difference between themselves and lower-class women," but as Honor Ford-Smith observes, "Marson's struggle was different. With very little support, she questioned how knowledge was linked to power and identity, and began the work of creating a language that could address discursive absences." If Marson never resolved the class tensions explored in *Pocomania,* "she nonetheless named the conflict." In a letter to Weldon Johnson, Marson characterized poetry writing as compulsion rather than a choice. "Sometimes," she confided to him, "I am not sure that I am a true poet in feeling and execution, feeling, well yes—but I have not written a line since I published *The Moth and the Star.* The impulse ... comes on like a madness and I write furiously for a couple months, usually in the Spring, then I go to sleep again!" In describing pocomania and poetry writing as madness, she posited a connection between them as potentially subversive modes of discourse and aligned herself with the still-beating African "heart" of Jamaican popular culture.[90]

Marson condemned the injustice of colonial officials' violent response to the unrest in Jamaica in 1938, which *Pocomania* and her poem "At the Prison Gates" presaged. "In Africa today," she remarked in one opinion piece, "a warning is being taken from the West Indies," appropriating the title of William M. Macmillan's book but modifying it in a subtle but revealing manner; the presumed recipients of the "warning" were Africans, not the imperial ruling classes of Britain.[91] Marson returned to London in late summer to raise funds for a new charitable organization and offshoot of the internationalist Save the Children movement, the Jamaica Save the Children Association. In September 1938, she spoke at an LCP conference and submitted a memorandum to and testified before the Moyne Commission investigating the disturbances in the Caribbean. At the LCP gathering, she attributed the strikes and rioting "to the inconceivable poverty of the people, who must continue to agitate for a remedy to their deplorable condition." In her submission to the commission and her subsequent testimony, Marson focused on factors contributing to the "suffering" of poor Afro-Jamaican women, such as limited educational opportunities, the social and legal stigma attached to concubinage and illegitimacy, and mass unemployment. Noting the prevalence of racial prejudice across the empire, she stated, "We are handicapped for our colour in Jamaica and in London."[92]

The onset of World War II brought not only danger and hardship but also new opportunities and purpose for Marson. She watched as the dislocation of war scattered the community of black students and intellectuals in London, many of whom evacuated to the north, returned home, enlisted, or otherwise contributed to the war effort. Soon, thousands of colonial troops, including many from the Caribbean, poured into the city, and the sight of people of African descent doing their part in the "People's War" provoked a sense of pride. In her poem "The Convoy," a moment of mutual recognition between the narrator and a passing convoy of black troops disrupts the former's feelings of isolation and alienation on the streets of "the great white busy mart":

> There I stood, moved, yet unmoving,
> Weeping with no sign of tears,
> Greeting all these unknown soldiers
> I had known a thousand years.
> For they were my blood brothers,
> Brown like me, as warm of heart,
> And their souls were glad to greet me
> In the great white busy mart.
> Our gay hearts grown sad and wiser
> Stirred to life a second then,
> A thousand words unsaid, were spoken—
> And we each took heart again.
> Oh my brothers, in the conflict
> Of our own bewildered life,
> How much strength we bring each other,
> What fine courage for the strife.[93]

In one sense, the "strife" in the poem refers to the war, but the allusion to the "strength we bring each other" suggests that the narrator and troops share a different and wider "conflict," the struggle against racism around the world.

With the government under pressure to maintain loyalty and support for the war in the colonies, the dearth of BBC broadcasts to the Caribbean and Africa became a source of increasing concern. Under these circumstances, Marson and the Guyanese journalist and musician Rudolph Dunbar pushed for more varied programming tailored specifically to a Caribbean audience. After contributing to several BBC specials and the television show *Picture Page,* in March 1941, she became the full-time program assistant for and the voice of *Calling the West Indies.* Though ostensibly a propaganda tool and means for Caribbean troops to reconnect with home, the protean West Indies Service broadcasts allowed Marson to venture beyond these parameters. The inclusion of her poem "At the Prison Gates, Jamaica, 1937," depicting the dire condition of poor workers, on a "Salute to the British West Indies" program in 1942 provoked the ire of officials in the Caribbean and the Colonial Office, particularly for its last verse:

> Crowds marching—every day
> More hungry—every day more sad;
> And I hear a great stir of voices
> Among those who rule the land
> In politics and those who rule in gold.
> But the tramp of the weary feet still sound,
> On they march—must they march on forever?[94]

On *Calling the West Indies,* Marson publicized the achievements and efforts of people of African descent as well as the activities of British feminists in war-torn London, and aired in-studio performances by black musicians. During a program on the Women's Institute movement in Britain, she told listeners, "I am convinced that the future progress of the West Indies is largely in the hands of women; though women can contribute a good deal to their country's welfare individually, it is through solid organisation that they can be most useful." As the war concluded, she established *Caribbean Voices,* which became an indispensable vehicle for the dissemination of the work of Caribbean authors.[95]

Marson's home and, before a German bomb destroyed it, her tiny office at Bedford College, the temporary headquarters of the Empire Talks Department, became common ports of call for Afro-Caribbeans and others of African descent.[96] The trade unionist Maida Springer, who was born in Panama to Afro-Caribbean parents and migrated to Harlem at the age of the seven, was among the many black artists, professionals, and soldiers whom Marson interviewed. Yevette Richards claims that Springer's encounters with Marson and Padmore in London "marked the beginning of her contact with the pan-African leadership" and her "passion for African labor development," inspiring her to press for greater AFL-CIO involvement in Africa when she returned to the United States.[97] The evening gatherings at Marson's flat at 14 The Mansions, Mill Lane, in West Hampstead made a great impression on Springer. Afro-Caribbeans and Africans, mainly male service personnel and students, gathered there to eat Marson's Caribbean fare, chat, and

FIGURE 8. Una Marson broadcasting from a London theater, February 23, 1942. Original caption: "Girlfriend of the Forces." Photograph by Fred Ramage. Hulton Archive, Getty Images.

debate in a salonlike atmosphere.[98] Springer recalled: "I think Una was very selective about the people she invited—these were men who had a vision of the future, and they were looking forward to the day when they were going to have a country, not a colonial dependency. So it was very good talk at night. Very explosive talk! (laughs) Had they been heard, they would all have been court-martialed."[99] Marson and her guests discussed politics, read poetry aloud, and shared their hopes for a transformed postwar world, and the night often culminated in her taking them on a tour of Soho's hottest black nightspots.

In 1941, Marson met and fell in love with Dudley Thompson. Born in Panama but raised in Jamaica, Thompson had worked briefly as the headmaster of a rural school before the war. He came to London as a member of the Royal Air Force and served in Europe as a flight lieutenant in the Bomber

Command.[100] In terms of societal norms for a woman of her background and intelligence, Thompson represented the perfect man for Marson—her real-life David. After they met, he became a regular at Marson's evening soirées, and the two spent nearly two years together. In 1943, the relationship ended, leaving Marson heartbroken and distraught. "At that stage of the war," Thompson later recalled, "I was preoccupied with the Pan-Africanist movement and I got deeper into its activities. My circle has included Kenyatta, Padmore, Nkrumah. . . . I grew away from the literary group."[101]

The split occurred during an increasingly vicious campaign against Marson and her work for the BBC by two markedly different, even directly opposed, parties: Lady Davson of the West India Committee, which represented the white elite and their commercial interests in the Caribbean, and a group of Caribbean radicals at Aggrey House, including Thompson's associate Peter Blackman. By March 1942, the BBC's African Service director, John Grenfall Williams, noted that the Aggrey House group was "out to get Miss Marson and anyone who protected her . . . at all costs" and, to this end, "collected ammunition" in the form of the "foulest" allegations.[102] Despite his veiled phrasing, Williams made it clear that the attacks on Marson focused on her personal life as much as her politics and execution of her professional duties. These Caribbean men's criticisms of her representativeness included questions about the suitability of a woman for the position and slanderous accusations about her sexuality.

Wounded but undeterred, Marson threw herself into a new project, launching *Caribbean Voices* in March 1945. As Snaith notes, "The program's importance in establishing a Caribbean literary presence and in creating a network of writers on both sides of the Atlantic cannot be underestimated and is often stressed, but rarely is Marson's name mentioned." She traveled to Kingston to recruit talent in mid-1945, passing through the United States and making stops in New York, Washington, D.C., and Miami, and continued to produce Sunday-evening broadcasts until she left her post at the BBC in July 1946. Nevertheless, there is something ironic, even tragic, about Marson's characterization of her urge to write, and of pocomania (and Stella's attraction to it and Sister Kate), as madness because rumors had begun to circulate, even making their way across the Atlantic to Jamaica, regarding her deteriorating mental state. The combined effects of personal disappointment, loneliness, and public humiliation worsened the recurring bouts of depression that plagued Marson during her years in London, and she returned to Jamaica to restore her health.[103] The Anglo-Irish radio-producer Henry

Swanzy, who commonly receives credit for building the platform, assumed direction of *Caribbean Voices*.[104]

. . .

One evening at George Padmore's flat while St. Clair Drake was in Britain in 1948, the dinner conversation turned to the subject of a West African artist in London who wanted to marry a white woman because she would "understand him." Drake noted that Padmore "was quite sympathetic to his point of view." He asked if "colored women over here object to Negro [men] who marry white [women]," to which Padmore replied, "There are no colored women over here to marry." Drake then "mentioned the rarity of colored girls in [the] U.S. who are leftist and movement oriented." Padmore concurred: "Yes. Just imagine we married one of those Fisk girls I knew. After I read that section of your book [*Black Metropolis*] on the Negro upper class I was trying to think of myself married to one of those women—going to sorority dances, playing bridge—ha!"[105] Drake and Padmore, central figures in the intellectual elaboration of pan-Africanism and the notion of an African diaspora, found common ground in what they perceived as commensurate experiences vis-à-vis black women and a shared conception of the black activist-intellectual as heterosexual and male. As McDuffie observes in his study of African American feminists in the Communist Party, "Black radicalism has always been gendered; that is, the political programs, articulations, and 'freedom dreams' of black radical activists and intellectuals are invariably informed and shaped by a complex interplay of gender, race, sexuality, class, and politics." Padmore's erasure of African and Caribbean women in London, as well as both men's attribution of political backwardness to African American women, reveal that black internationalist activity reproduced gender hierarchy in ways that mimicked nationalist ideology. Despite their avowal of internationalism, Padmore, Drake, and their male associates' conception of revolutionary black masculinity differed little from bourgeois nationalist masculinity. Male anticolonialists in London equated black liberation with the rehabilitation and assertion of an "autonomous, self-determining black revolutionary manhood," displacing women from the political realm. Afro-Caribbean and African women in London often found that their pursuit of feminist social, economic, and political objectives ran up against opposition not only from colonial authorities but from many black men as well. They remained, at best, "sister outsiders" in relation to the main institutional bases of black activism, even when their labor built them. Women such as Marson, whom Thompson distinguished from male pan-Africanists as a "literary" artist, become avatars for the limits of politics. The comments on Ashwood Garvey's personal life, the attacks on and attempts to neutralize the influence of Marson and Folayegbe M. Akintunde-Ighodalo suggest that they represented something disruptive and threatening.[106]

For the women considered here, the process of their disappearing from the annals of anticolonial pan-Africanism began during their lifetimes.[107] Thompson won a Rhodes Scholarship in 1946 and went on to become a lawyer, serving as part of Kenyatta's defense team during his trial for allegedly inciting rebellion in Kenya. In the only reference to Marson in his autobiography, *From Kingston to Kenya: The Making of a Pan-Africanist Lawyer,* Thompson noted in passing that, "for a short time while the Emperor [Haile Selassie] was in exile in London, the Jamaican writer, Una Marson was his secretary."[108] Thompson's casting of Marson as a minor figure defined solely by her subordinate relationship to a great man corresponds to the position given to Caribbean and African women by many of their male contemporaries and successive studies based on their accounts. The elision of black feminists' activities continues to serve as the basis for genealogies of the black radical-intellectual tradition that posit as its inevitable culmination the attainment of independent nation-states by African and Caribbean men. Not only are women absent from most accounts, but the erasure of their unwieldy lives and influence obscures the gender and sexual politics of black anticolonialism. Within many histories, opposition to empire and antiracism are reduced to masculinist expressions and forms of political struggles, and as the views and actions of such women as Ashwood Garvey become more explicitly feminist, they recede beyond the horizon of pan-Africanism and anticolonial nationalism.

Soon after Drake and Padmore's evening chat, A. A. Y. Kyerematen, then a doctoral student in anthropology, reported an episode in *Africana* that belied their assertions. He wrote, "in a conversation with some Gold Coast women students in England, I made the remark that when I returned to the Gold Coast, I was going to see to it that women out there resumed their proper place. This, of course, invited sharp and violent protests and cries of: 'What a waste, after all your education!'"[109] Kyerematen (and, his phrasing implied, his readers) expected a hostile response to such a comment. Women of African descent established a vocal presence in London, playing significant, if circumscribed, roles in every black organization. They challenged both racist stereotypes and the gender biases of their male peers. But more than that, they developed feminist analytics that grappled with multiple axes of oppression on a variety of fronts and forged transnational networks of mutual aid and discussion and eventually the first black women's groups in Britain. Many moved on to burgeoning anticolonial movements and to organize women of African descent on both sides of the Atlantic. From relatively privileged backgrounds, African and Afro-Caribbean women such as Cummings-John, Ashwood Garvey, and Marson applied the skills acquired in their upbringing as young women of the educated elite to expose the racist underpinnings of extant models of colonial respectability and femininity and to challenge the categorical distinctions of the racializing project of colonialism. They charted new possibilities for conceptualizing the black international through art, music, and the needs of black women, and their thought and wide-ranging activities reveal oblique intersections of women-qua-women politics and black internationalism.

FOUR

Sounds of Black London

MUSIC WAS AN EVER-PRESENT PART of black sociability and anticolonial activity in early- to mid-twentieth-century London, and nowhere more so than in the Soho establishments of Amy Ashwood Garvey. In 1935, she opened the International Afro Restaurant beneath her residence at 62 New Oxford Street and, not long thereafter, the Florence Mills Social Parlour, a restaurant and nightclub on or near Carnaby Street.[1] Black internationalist activity consisted of more than organizing protests, writing books, and publishing journals and small tracts. Music and its sponsorship was another example of the ways that black women generated new political imaginaries and solidarities.

The Florence Mills club was a product of Ashwood Garvey's personal, political, and business partnership with the Trinidadian actor, vaudeville comedian, and calypsonian Sam Manning. The two met in New York City around 1920, when Ashwood Garvey secured Manning a position in the UNIA's musical department, beginning a relationship that stretched over three decades. In the late 1920s and 1930s, the pair joined the growing ranks of transatlantic entertainment impresarios. Their many shared endeavors included a series of successful musical revues in the United States during 1926–1927. The same year, the Parlophone label released nine calypso recordings, the first available in Britain, including seven that Manning had made in New York in 1924. Manning embarked on a Caribbean tour with the New Orleans native Syd Perrin in 1929, making stops in Jamaica, Trinidad, Barbados, and British Guiana. Ashwood Garvey joined them, busying herself with booking arrangements, speaking engagements, and interviews with the local press. Back in New York in early 1930, Manning produced a new batch of records before returning to the Caribbean. He later claimed to have performed in *Kykunkor* (The Witch Woman), a drama by the Sierra Leonean musician, dancer, and choreographer Asadata Dafora, which had a successful run on Broadway in 1934 and helped to introduce African music and dance to the United States. Throughout their travels, Ashwood Garvey and Manning relied heavily on UNIA contacts to secure performance spaces, publicity, and information on local political developments.[2]

Manning arrived at the Port of Southampton on June 27, 1934, accompanied by the Trinidadian pianist and bandleader Lionel Belasco. In August, they recorded twelve sides for the Decca label. Belasco returned to New York shortly thereafter, and Manning and Ashwood Garvey began recruiting talent from the black communities of London, Liverpool, and Cardiff for a new musical comedy. Heralded in the press as "the first [British] negro revue," *Harlem Nightbirds* toured for two seasons in the provinces and Ireland with a weeklong run in London sandwiched in the middle. Afterwards, they approached potential financial backers for another Caribbean tour, during which Manning planned to recruit musicians and performers for an all-black band and stage show in Britain; but in the end their departure was delayed until 1939.[3]

During the intervening years, Ashwood Garvey's London establishments became regular haunts of African and Caribbean students, intellectuals, and activists. C. L. R. James recalled that the International Afro Restaurant was "very important to me, because from those early days to this day, I find English food uneatable." It was also "the center of a good deal of West Indian agitation." In a piece the *Chicago Defender* reprinted, the *Sunday Express* reported that "race intellectuals from all parts of the world [were] wont to gather" there.[4] As news of Italy's preparations for war filtered back to London, in August 1935, James and Ashwood Garvey formed the International African Friends of Ethiopia at the restaurant, which continued to serve as the organization's headquarters in the coming months.

Named after the African American singer and dancer who became a transatlantic sensation after the first of Lew Leslie's *Blackbirds* revues opened at the London Pavilion in 1926, the Florence Mills club became a hangout for people of African descent in the metropolis and a hotbed of political activity as well. Ashwood Garvey's friend and earliest biographer, Lionel Yard, described it as "a calypso club with bamboo decorations, creole food, and the haunting melody of American jazz and blues." The menu featured Caribbean specialties like peas and rice alongside "American and Chinese dishes." According to Yard, "prices were variable to suit the circumstances of the poor and the more prosperous patrons," making the club an "economic turnstile that earned from the rich and fed the poor."[5] At night, the staff cleared the tables to make room for dancing to performances by Caribbean musicians. The Guyanese clarinetist and bandleader W. Rudolph Dunbar hosted "dance cocktail parties" on Thursday evenings, but on most nights Manning took charge of the club's entertainment, interleaving Jamaican mento, calypsos, blues, and jazz with the occasional comedic skit in his band's performances.[6] A talented singer, Ashwood Garvey occasionally contributed to the show. When live music was not on offer, the 78 records of African American, Caribbean, and African musicians "spun late into the night."[7]

The Florence Mills attracted visiting black celebrities, agitators, and cash-strapped students, as well as "curiosity seekers" eager "to see what the new importation from the colonies had to offer." Amid the dancers and other merrymakers, on any given night, one could find, as Yard put it, "prominent race leaders hotly engaged in ideological disputes while sipping a pot of tea. . . . All the activities that stimulate political thinking, economic planning for a free Africa, received their impetus and the blessing of Amy and Sam at this retreat." A "restaurant by day," it often became a darkened "planning institution by night." According to Ras Makonnen, it was "one of the most famous" of the small, often short-lived black clubs in Soho. "You could go there after you'd been slugging it out for two or three hours at Hyde Park or some other meeting, and get a lovely meal, dance and enjoy yourself." While helping to coordinate the public campaign against imperialism, Ashwood Garvey feted the African American track star Jesse Owens, fresh from his triumph at the 1936 Munich Olympics, with calypsos and Caribbean cuisine. As late as 1947, the *Ashanti Pioneer* in the Gold Coast reported that Ashwood Garvey was "remembered in London as a mother of African and West Indian students," because she "opened a Restaurant and Club for them."[8]

Ashwood Garvey left London near the end of 1939, by which point she had closed her restaurant and nightclub. But the Florence Mills was only one of a growing number of establishments in Soho specializing in the presentation of African diasporic sounds during the 1930s and 1940s, and only one of many places where politics rubbed shoulders with leisure, artistic production, and consumption. By the early twentieth century, London was a common stop on transatlantic tours that brought generations of African American and Afro-Caribbean singers, dancers, and musicians to Europe and often points far beyond. For some, the city became a long-term residence; for many more, it was a familiar port of call. Like many African and Caribbean intellectuals and activists, black entertainers had transnational careers. Some individuals, such as Ashwood Garvey and Manning, lived the lives of both. The imperial metropolis became an important node of the circuits traveled by black musicians and black expressive cultures, facilitating musical exchange, the creation of innovative hybrid forms, and expansive visions of the African world.

The late nineteenth and early twentieth centuries saw the emergence of an array of new musical styles across the Afro-Atlantic diaspora: the blues, ragtime, jazz, and swing in the United States; *paseo* and calypso in Trinidad; tango in Argentina; *son* and *danzon* in Cuba; and palm-wine, jùjú, konkoma, highlife, and Muslim sákárà music in West Africa, to name only a few. All of these forms traveled to and, to varying degrees, found a home in London. Black musicians sojourning or based in Europe transformed these styles in ways reflecting their new setting. Musicians and composers routinely moved between styles and produced compositions combining diverse elements even as they labored under conditions that restricted their professional opportunities. Music and musicians contributed to black internationalism in multiple, mutually reinforcing ways. First and most obviously, black musicians often developed close ties to black pressure groups in the city, becoming fixtures at their social and fund-raising events. Antiracist and anticolonial causes provided the occasion—and black organizations the setting—for interactions among black musicians from different corners of the Atlantic. These encounters, in turn, transformed their compositional politics, even as their involvement extended the reach and raised the tenor of black protest. While black musicians used lyrics and the composition of their bands to express a desire for black unity and a commitment to antiracist, anticolonial politics, as Paul Gilroy has argued, an analysis of such overt political statements and activities must be combined with a "consideration of inferred and immanent political positions, specifically of the *musical* forms involved and the social relations in which they are produced and consumed."[9] This chapter embeds the lives and professional trajectories of black musicians within a close analysis of the politics of musical composition and performance, on the one hand, and the social spaces in which black music was performed and consumed in London, on the other.

The chapter considers the links among imperial and transatlantic networks, particular sites of black cultural production and consumption, and the politics of the sound itself—interconnected elements of the relationship between black music and black struggle in London. African American, Afro-Caribbean, African, and black British musicians played a seminal and consistent role in the introduction and development of jazz in Britain. As Jeffrey Green points out, an overreliance on sources such as Jack Hylton's recollections of the 1930s, bandleader Ted Heath's 1959 autobiography, and catalogues of recordings released on disc at the time has led many historians of early jazz in Britain to claim, as Jim Godbolt does, that "the black contribution to British jazz was slight."[10] Often barred from the best-paying gigs, black jazz musicians made a universe centered on Soho. By the 1930s, the area was notorious for illicit activities of all sorts and a metonym for the growing popularity of jazz and black dance styles. For both reasons, it earned a reputation among white Britons as the heart of the "Black Mile," and a mélange of white sophisticates, left-wing intellectuals, Jewish musicians, socialists, homosexuals, and transsexuals frequented Soho's black clubs. The area had a different resonance or, at the least, carried additional meanings for people of African descent. While, for black musicians and bands, Soho offered employment (though little compensation) and a platform for creative expression within a profession in which they remained marginalized, it also provided an affirming sanctuary in a hostile city. Casual encounters in the area's clubs and the sounds that enveloped patrons within their doors reinforced the sense of unity in blackness, lending it imaginative content and a quotidian reality. As Putnam observes, "It is far easier to trace the history of the print-centered public and its particular black internationalisms; but the international consciousness generated by the black performative realm may have mattered more, and mattered to many more."[11]

London was a crossroads of musical cultures. African, Caribbean, and African American musicians regularly met, collaborated, and shared the bandstand, and the music that they played was never limited to jazz. They borrowed and reworked lyrics, melodies, and instrumentation from multiple black communities, and their genre-blurring experiments helped produce new styles that would be redomesticated as "Caribbean" and "African" (or "Trinidadian" and "Ghanaian") during and after the era of decolonization. Their evolving sounds were artifacts and articulations of black internationalism, even when not explicitly political or oriented toward an immediate agenda.

EMPIRE JAZZ

By the 1930s, London was "swinging" to the sounds emanating from black America, which spurred a fad for players of African descent who were believed to have an innate knack for navigating syncopated rhythms. Many of the prominent white orchestras added not only African American tunes and arrangements but also musicians of color, and negrophilia provided a commercial incentive for the first attempts to form all-black dance bands. Yet imperial networks and boundaries shaped the development of jazz in London as much as African American models did. In 1935, the Musicians Union in Britain, with the support of the Ministry of Labour, imposed a virtual ban on jazz musicians from the United States. African American musicians and entertainers continued to come in the years that followed but were limited to the popular stage and had to rely on local talent for band support. The ban dramatically curtailed the presence (except in record form) and the artistic influence of the era's leading African American bands and cleared the way for inferior-quality white swing outfits to monopolize the pop music market. It also opened limited opportunities for black musicians from Britain's colonies. In effect, the Musicians Union's ban introduced imperial preference to the British jazz scene, if not a complete embargo on American imports. Nevertheless, even as witnessing the "real thing" came to mean seeing at least some black faces on the bandstand, there remained significant obstacles to black incursions into the British music business and especially to maintaining a degree of autonomy from white promoters and bandleaders. As Paul Oliver explains, "While denying entry to American musicians the Musicians Union ban may even have assisted to a certain extent, in the creation of an audience for black musicians . . . it did not create many opportunities for British black musicians." According to the jazz archivist and historian Andrew Simons, union reps "did not intervene on behalf of Negroes!" The Jamaican multi-instrumentalist Leslie Thompson's stint as the only nonwhite member of the band at an exclusive club in Mayfair ended in 1934 when their trombonist, "who had some influence in the Musicians' Union," pressured the bandleader to "sack one of the band and distribute that fellow's money to the others. . . . I assume that the fellow said 'You can sack the black one.' And I was the first trumpet, too." After their set that night, Thompson sarcastically "thanked him for his loyalty to members of his union." He never paid union dues again, and union representatives, seemingly uninterested in organizing black musicians, never said anything about it.[12]

The backgrounds and skill levels of black musicians varied widely. For many, the paths by which they made their way to London involved either sojourns in the United States or work with African American musicians.

After serving in the merchant navy, the Trinidadian Cyril Blake stayed in Britain at the end of the Great War. His first professional break came when he joined Will Marion Cook's Southern Syncopated Orchestra as a guitarist. Soon thereafter he switched to the trumpet at the urging of Egbert Thompson, the orchestra's conductor and the former bandleader of the 369th Infantry "Hellfighters." Between 1919 and 1921, the Southern Syncopated Orchestra enthralled audiences and critics alike across the British Isles. As Alyn Shipton points out, "The majority of jazz histories draw attention to the Original Dixieland Jazz Band, as the white New Orleans ensemble arriving in London in April 1919 and 'bringing jazz to Europe.' In reality the syncopated orchestras had got there first."[13] Although, strictly speaking, the orchestra was not a jazz band, it provided many Britons' first exposure to the syncopation that would become the genre's most identifiable trait. Despite the band's accolades and Cook's meticulously crafted image of respectability, its performances also laid the foundation for the association, in the British imagination, of authentic blackness and "primitive" culture with jazz and ragtime music. During two years of extensive touring in Britain and Western Europe, the African American musicians in the group trickled back to the United States, and Thompson filled their slots with a growing number of Africans, Afro-Caribbeans, and the black British violinist James Horton Boucher (grandson of Sierra Leonean Dr. James Africanus Horton). By October 9, 1921, when a collision at sea sank the SS *Rowan* while en route from Glasgow to Derry, killing nine of the band's thirty-two members, it included the Jamaican trumpeter Joe Smith, the Sierra Leonean pianist Frank Lacton, the Ghanaian William Martin Ofori, and the Nigerians Gay Bafunke Martins on banjo and Akinlawon Olumuyiwa on vocals, in addition to Cyril and his older brother, George "Happy" Blake. Lacton, a founding member of the APU, and the Barbadian singer Frank Bates were among those killed in the disaster. Following the tragedy, the organist Bruce Wendell from British Guiana joined the reconstituted orchestra; only the conductor Thompson remained from the orchestra that had performed at the Philharmonic Hall in 1919. Between 1919 and 1922, more than one hundred musicians passed through the band, producing numerous new offshoots and music teachers who made a tremendous impact on the development of jazz in Britain.[14] After Egbert Thompson's death, Cyril Blake assumed leadership of Thompson's Negro Band (the successor to the Southern Syncopated Orchestra). The group that started as the Southern Syncopated Orchestra became progressively a unit of players from the British Empire. The Blake

Connections to musicians already in Britain lured others, and once there, these contacts eased the newcomers' entry into life in the city and brought them into contact with other black musicians from around the Atlantic. When Thompson moved to Britain in 1929, Joe Appleton sent him to stay at a friend's place in Fulham his first night, and he met a number of prominent African American artists during his visits to John Payne's flat in the weeks that followed. The Blake brothers recruited several Jamaicans who went on to become some of the era's top jazz musicians. Stephenson and de Souza arrived in London on November 9, 1935; Hutchinson and Bertie King landed in the city ten days later. All four immediately joined Cyril and Happy in the band at the Cuba Club on Gerrard Street, which also included Joe Deniz and the black Briton Robert Mumford-Taylor. Soon thereafter, Deniz followed the Blake brothers to the Shim Sham Club, while Mumford-Taylor stayed at the Cuba Club, where Clare Deniz (Frank's wife) joined him on piano. Although black women singers and dancers took the stage in growing numbers, female instrumentalists such as Clare and Lily Jemmott were rare on the interwar jazz circuit.[17]

This disparate but overwhelmingly male group of black Britons, Caribbeans, and Africans formed the core of a small but tight-knit circle of black jazz players in London from which Leslie Thompson formed an all-black swing orchestra in 1936. During the early 1930s, Thompson played first trumpet in a string of popular African American musical revues, and in 1934, he supported Louis Armstrong on his European tour. Plans for the creation of an all-black dance band arose from casual chats between Thompson and Ken "Snakehips" Johnson at the former's apartment. Born Kenrick Reginald Huymans, Johnson was the son of the Minister of Health in British Guiana and had come to Britain as a student. In 1934–1935, he traveled to the United States, where he perfected the hip-swiveling dance move invented by the Harlem native Earl "Snakehips" Tucker (from whom he derived his moniker, as well). He had the opportunity to see the great black swing bands of the day firsthand in New York City and later claimed that Fletcher Henderson encouraged his aspirations as a bandleader and even allowed him to lead his famed orchestra on one occasion. When his visa expired, Johnson went to Trinidad and formed a dance band that included Dave Wilkins, Carl Barriteau, and David "Baba" Williams. In January 1936, Johnson returned to London, but he needed a veteran musician to get his scheme off the ground. At the time Thompson met him, "he was ignoring" his studies and "taking lessons from Buddy Bradley," the African American choreographer who revolutionized dance on the London stage.[18]

Thompson was close with Rudolph Dunbar and knew of his earlier attempt at maintaining an all-black ensemble, African Polyphony, as well as the difficulties that ultimately confounded his efforts. Although faintly aware of Marcus Garvey's activities during his youth in Jamaica, Thompson recalled that "Jamaica was dominated by a culture from England and America, and like many I accepted it without thinking." It was only in London, listening to Garvey at Speakers' Corner in Hyde Park, that he experienced a political "awakening."[19] Inspired by Garvey's message and the outpouring of black protest over Ethiopia, he began to assemble the best black talent in town. The band consisted of King, Stephenson, Appleton, and Mumford-Taylor on saxophones and clarinet; Thompson, Hutchinson, Wally Bowen, and Arthur Dibbin on trumpet; the South African Bruce Vanderpoye or Abe "Pops" Clare on double bass; de Souza on piano; Joe Deniz on guitar; and Tommy Wilson on drums. Because the only serviceable black trombonist in London, Frank Williams, had no interest in the long separations from home required of touring, the band also included the white trombonists Reg Amore and Freddie Greenslade, who, in an ironic twist on the minstrelsy tradition, appeared in blackface on the bandstand to maintain the appearance of an all-black ensemble. According to the industry magazine *Melody Maker*, however, Williams appeared with the band during at least one of its early performances in Stepney.[20]

Not content to simply produce a novelty act, Thompson mimicked the style and sound of American big bands and used the same arrangements: "I made them rehearse to get that lift that Jimmie Lunceford and Ellington were getting on their records."[21] In late spring 1936, the band began performing at movie theaters and dance halls across Britain, variously billed as the Aristocrats of Jazz, the Emperors of Swing, or the Jamaican Emperors of Jazz. Although the group barely made enough to cover its expenses in the early days, it quickly built a reputation among audiences and fellow musicians as one of the swingingest bands in Britain. The band's big break came in early 1937, when it secured a six-week trial engagement at the upmarket Old Florida Club in the West End and, with it, wages three to four times higher than the average nightclub acts made.

With the band's popularity growing, Johnson and his manager, Ralph Deene, signed a contract formalizing their joint ownership of the group and, at the same time, excluded Thompson from any financial stake in it. The move precipitated not only the latter's exit but also that of most of the other band members.

After the breakup, Thompson returned to the theater world, while the others moved on to performing and recording opportunities with various other bands for a time. Nonetheless, the Thompson-Johnson band's stint at the Old Florida had been an unqualified success and led to an indefinite contract from the club's management. Johnson quickly reconstituted the orchestra by recruiting a quartet of old friends and bandmates from Trinidad: Carl Barriteau, Dave Wilkins, George Roberts, and Dave "Baba" Williams. When they arrived in London, Johnson threw a party at the Nest in Soho and found accommodations for them. Former members eventually rejoined the group as well. The new-look ensemble, now called Ken Johnson and His Rhythm Swingers or His West Indian Dance Orchestra, remained at the Old Florida until April 1939, when it moved to Willerby's for six months, but neither club offered arguably the most important ingredient in propelling a dance band to stardom—frequent radio broadcasts. As hostilities broke out in Europe and nightspots closed their doors, the Johnson orchestra secured a new residency at the exclusive subterranean supper club the Café de Paris. Located on the corner of Coventry and Wardour Streets, the oval, two-tiered space featured a revolving dance floor and catered to "the aristocracy, millionaire industrialists, American play boys, Conservative M.P.'s and daring debutantes." The club's management and elite clientele compelled Johnson's band to perform a fairly mundane mix of conventional dance music. However, the BBC regularly used the Café de Paris for live broadcasts, and when the musicians finished their night's work, they were only a short stroll from Soho's jazz clubs.[22]

Johnson's band kept a tiring schedule, continuing to tour variety theaters across Britain on top of its regular engagement. At many shows, in addition to their core lineup, the group featured other black artists, such as Cyril Blake, Frank Deniz as a second guitarist, and singers such as the Cardiff native Don Johnson and Cab Kaye (Augustus Kwamlah Quaye), a black Londoner whose father came from the Gold Coast. For radio broadcasts, Johnson commonly added a female vocalist, such as Betty Dale. While de Souza was away on tours with Benny Carter in France and Nina Mae McKinney in Australia, Clare Deniz filled his seat at the piano until pregnancy forced her departure. Later remembering, "I was sad that I was pregnant and had to leave," she maintained that the Johnson orchestra was the best jazz band in London, even though it had to play mainly standard dance material at most venues.[23]

The Johnson orchestra made commercial recordings for British Decca and HMV in 1938 and 1940, respectively, and the band's tenure at the Café de Paris led to session work with smaller, mixed-race groups for its members. Bertie King and Dave Wilkins recorded with the pianist and jazz critic Leonard Feather's Ye Olde English Swinge Band on September 12, 1938, a collaboration that grew out of their appearances at Feather's No. 1 Rhythm Club in London. Based on the model of Feather's original, established in 1933, rhythm clubs, in which white, largely male jazz aficionados listened with rapt attention to "record recitals," sprang up across Britain; by 1935, more than a hundred existed throughout the British Isles, and *Swing Music* and *Hot News,* Britain's first jazz magazines, catered to this growing audience. The No. 1 Rhythm Club also hosted Sunday-night jam sessions, where visiting musicians demonstrated their chops for club members. Although Feather charged admission, the talent received no financial compensation for playing, only a 78 record of their choice from his collection of new releases. Several black musicians recalled that, to their annoyance, club members had little interest in their live demonstrations of technique compared to the records that Feather and others played. Despite their rather exploitative nature, the rhythm clubs became another avenue for the transatlantic circulation of records, as well as a meeting place for musicians, which led to recording opportunities such as Wilkins's studio sessions with Una Mae Carlisle and Fats Waller. Moreover, there is evidence to suggest that the Johnson band's sound circulated farther afield and that—even while performing for white, largely upper- and middle-class patrons and, via the radio, a wider British listening audience—its members continued to have other publics in mind. In addition to producing records for the commercial market, Johnson had his band's broadcasts from the Café de Paris recorded on acetate discs and distributed copies to its members.[24] The group's rhythm section—Yorke de Souza, Joe Deniz, and Tommy Wilson—with the addition of the white bassist Tommy Bromley rented a West End studio and recorded four tracks. While commercial recordings and radio broadcasts reached a broader segment of listeners in Britain, these unreleased records circulated privately among black musicians and their families and friends.

New opportunities for black musicians to broadcast to Africa and the Caribbean augmented the distribution of music on records. During the Second World War, the BBC's West African and Caribbean services expanded dramatically, and for the first time, performances by black musicians in London could be heard in the colonies. Una Marson's *Calling the West Indies* program was particularly significant in this regard. She invited a succession of black musicians into the studio and publicized their movements and triumphs, bringing the music of black London to listening audiences in the Caribbean. In fact, her familiarity with "all the West Indian Bandsmen" helped her secure a position at the BBC in the first place. Marson interviewed Ken Johnson, the black British composer Reginald Foresythe, and a number of other musicians and played their commercial recordings on air. *Calling the West Indies* featured in-studio performances by such jazz players as de Sousa and Wilkins and organ recitals by the Nigerian Fela Sowande. The BBC broadcast spirituals and hymns by Dunbar's London Negro Choir on Sundays. Marson regularly presented jazz alongside renditions of popular calypsos by the singers Edric Connor and Freddy Grant, and she proposed hiring Cyril Blake's band to perform a program of circum-Caribbean numbers, "Jamaican songs and Trinidad Calypsos and perhaps a Rumba or two." Initially, popular orchestras, including Johnson's and Edmundo Ros's, performed on air twice a month, the latter a mix of swing and Latin numbers, but as the programming expanded to four days a week, Marson relied on a smaller combo, Harry Gold and the Pocomaniacs, joined by rotating musical guests.[25] Through this combination of personal ties, recordings, domestic and imperial broadcasts, and the clubs that linked them all, jazz produced in Britain circulated among and helped establish the contours of a layered but growing black listening public of transatlantic reach. At the peak of his band's popularity, Johnson and the trombonist Baba Williams were killed, and several other band members injured, when a German bomb crashed through the Rialto Cinema above the Café de Paris on the night of March 8–9, 1941, bringing the most successful attempt at maintaining an all-black dance orchestra to a tragic end.[26] Harry Gold and the Pocomaniacs performed "Dear Old Southland" during *Calling the West Indies* on June 2, 1945, as a tribute to the deceased bandleader and dancer. Marson explained to her listeners: "This number always holds a very special memory for all West Indians because we remember it as the signature tune of that popular maestro, Ken Johnson."[27]

From the 1930s through the 1950s, the overwhelmingly white orchestras of bandleaders like Bert Ambrose and Gerald Walcan Bright, known simply as "Ambrose" and "Geraldo," enjoyed the luxury of sold-out tours with multinight stops or extended residencies at high-society spots such as Ciro's Embassy Club and the Savoy Hotel, where the BBC broadcast their performances. The relative success of Johnson's orchestra notwithstanding,[28] their black counterparts usually found themselves cloistered in the capital's humble nightclubs on Tottenham Court Road or in Soho and their touring limited to one-night engagements—the bane of the professional musician given the rigors and dangers of constant travel. All of the black musicians interviewed as part of the National Sound Archive's Oral History of Jazz in Britain project discussed the scarcity of qualified players as one obstacle to forming all-black bands, but most also cited discrimination in hiring practices. Thompson recalled that Dunbar "did his best to gather musicians to form a coloured orchestra but couldn't get work." In 1929, the pianist George Ruthland Clapham from St. Kitts attempted to form an all-black ensemble, including Thompson, Joe Appleton, Isaac Augustus "Gus" Newton, Lily Jemmott, Al Jennings, and Monty Tyree.[29] The group rehearsed, and Clapham approached booking agents, which led to a short stint at a dance club substituting for the resident band. However, in Thompson's words, "it was an ambitious failure." Around the same time, the Afro-Caribbean drummer Oscar Dawkins made a separate attempt to form a black orchestra but met with the same result. The number and quality of black players in Britain grew in the years that followed, and similar efforts continued throughout the 1940s. According to Frank Deniz, "After Ken Johnson, everybody wanted to form a coloured band, . . . and we used to rehearse," but, he added, "we never got paid." In 1944, Leslie "Jiver" Hutchinson left his well-paying job as a soloist with Geraldo's band to launch a new group with his business partners and former bandmates King, Wilkins, de Souza, and Clinton Maxwell. Like the Johnson bands before it, Hutchinson's All-Coloured Orchestra consisted of the top black jazz musicians of the day, including the relative newcomer Coleridge Goode. Despite assistance with bookings from one of the biggest names in the business, Bert Ambrose, and a two-month tour for British troops in India in 1945, discrimination consigned the band to an endless string of one-nighters. Writing in *Melody Maker* in 1946, Hutchinson decried the racism that excluded him and his orchestra from professional associations and quality bookings. The Trinidadian guitarist and bandleader Gerald "Al" Jennings echoed his sentiments two weeks later. Jennings had performed in the capital in 1927 and 1936, but in both instances, soon moved on to Europe, where, as he explained, "everything. . . was so different, from a coloured musicians point of view, from conditions obtaining in London." After serving as a petty officer in the British navy during which time he played for injured black troops, Jennings returned to the city with his All-Star Caribbean Orchestra in 1945, only to find racial prejudice still pervading the profession. The experience left him wondering "whether now would be a good time for him to lay down his baton for good." "I have listened with disgust," he explained, "to the petty objections raised by managements, their clienteles, and even white musicians, against the engagement of an all-coloured band." Hutchinson tried to keep his band afloat throughout the late 1940s and 1950s, but financial difficulties often forced its members and even the bandleader himself, who rejoined Geraldo's orchestra from 1949 to 1956, to moonlight with white-led orchestras to make ends meet. Amid constant touring with the latest iteration of the band, he died in November 1959 when the group's bus overturned en route between engagements—a victim, indirectly at least, of the color bar in the British music industry. *Melody Maker* noted in its obituary, "When he again left the Geraldo band to try to get back to session work, he found the doors closed. He maintained that this was because of his colour and was rather bitter about it."[30]

If personal contacts and professional opportunities attracted black musicians and entertainers to London, barriers to black achievement and success helped solidify the bond among them once they were there. Discrimination exposed commonalities between musicians' professional struggles and the position of others of African descent in the imperial metropolis. Thompson always preferred working with other black entertainers or, as he put it, "people who were seeing life as I too [did]." As he recalled of Johnson's first band, "With all these fellows it might seem odd that we got on so well—African, Welsh, Jamaican, Londoners—and Tom [Wilson] from Birmingham, I think—but in Britain you are black or you are white. And we weren't white. We all expected different treatment, and that united us, as it were." Although they continued to "define themselves by stating where they were from," for Thompson and many of his contemporaries, "the thing that dominated was the pigment, especially in dance music," and "we coloured chaps, united by our colour and by our ambitions, had a group feeling even if we came from Guiana, Jamaica, Africa, Barbados, Cardiff, and London." British racism contributed mightily to the development of a "group feeling" among black musicians and, through the 1950s, motivated continued efforts at forming black bands. Black Soho nurtured this bond and celebrated it as an elective affinity. When jobs were scarce, which was most of the time, the area's clubs were the center of their daily lives. After the white American owner of Ciro's refused to allow Ambrose to use Joe Deniz as a substitute for his usual white guitarist, Deniz moved on to a job with Happy Blake's band at the Cuba Club.[31]

A live BBC broadcast on December 12, 1941, began with a simple walking piano line over the hum of voices and clinking glasses before the announcer's voice intruded: "Hello, Rhythm Club. This is Harry Parry speaking and presenting Cyril Blake and his band from Jig's Club, London, playing 'Cyril's Blues.'" As the players alternated solos before converging in a raucous climax, the revelers in the background grew louder. A bandleader, impresario, and Benny Goodman devotee, Harry Parry built his reputation as one of the "kings of swing" in Britain in large part through his popular weekly broadcasts featuring his Radio Rhythm Club Sextet and other predominately white swing bands at exclusive supper clubs. The broadcast from Jig's Club was Parry's first and only remote broadcast from a nightclub serving a largely black clientele, and the recordings from it are "the only aural evidence of what the scene was like at the Afro-Caribbean West End clubs during the original swing era."[32]

Earlier that year, Cyril Blake formed a new four-piece house band at Jig's. On the night of the live broadcast from the club, the band consisted of the drummer Clinton Maxwell, pianist Errol Barrow, and the Trinidadian "ace frettist" Lauderic Caton. After spending the late 1930s in Europe where he played with the Belgian Django Reinhardt among others, Caton had made his way to London in 1940, and he pioneered the use of electric guitar in British jazz.[33] Jim Godbolt claims that Alec and Rose Ward ran the club, but Happy Blake reputedly had an ownership stake or some other connection to it, as he did with many of the era's black dance clubs in Soho. Over the years, the Blake brothers' bands and the various clubs that Happy owned or managed acted as a turnstile for new arrivals from the Caribbean. Unlike the smart hotels and clubs of the West End where the white orchestras of the day played strictly formal dance music with rigid tempos and soft, understated orchestration, musicians sweated out tunes "with more percussion than discretion" in the cramped quarters of Soho's after-hours clubs.[34] The music that patrons listened and danced to at Jig's and other black clubs was not limited to jazz and swing. Blake's bands performed a mix of songs as diverse as their audience. Some of his bandmates hailed from Guyana or Trinidad and had listened to the styles of the Spanish-speaking western Caribbean from a young age; others had toured extensively throughout the Caribbean and beyond before coming to Britain. Blake's bands regularly interspersed Venezuelan *paseos,* Trinidadian calypsos, and Jamaican mentos among jazz favorites and jam sessions in which soloists alternated swinging out. In addition to Jig's, Blake's rotating cast of musicians held residencies at the more upscale Havana and Cuba Clubs, where their sets included mainly Latin-inflected material.

Located on Wardour Street at the entrance to St. Anne's Court, Jig's Club was called "London's Harlem" by the music press, both for the music played there and for its clientele. One critic described the recordings of Blake's band at Jig's as capturing the atmosphere in which jazz was born. A modest bandstand lay to the right as you entered Jig's, the bar stood at the far end against the back wall, and at the center of the one-room club was a full-sized billiard table. The British jazz musician Jack Glicco described it as "a death-trap . . . so badly ventilated that it was always thick with tobacco smoke." When Godbolt visited the club in 1941, signed photographs of esteemed visitors like Louis Armstrong "adorned the grimy walls." As "cue-holders sized up their shots," "energetic and graceful jitterbugging" continued all around them, and "Steve, a diminutive black waiter, wheeled and ducked through the swirling dancers triumphantly holding his tray of drinks high."[35]

Jig's attracted blacks of all classes and jazz aficionados as well as homosexuals, socialists, and young white Britons drawn by the mix of exotic pleasures it offered. Visitors from as close as the suburbs and as far away as the Continent, North America, and the colonies and dominions cavorted with same-sex dance partners, bohemian writers and artists, pimps, prostitutes, and gamblers. For many, especially younger Britons in search of a taste of the low life or some vaguely defined authenticity, jazz music and the dingy night-clubs of Soho provided the setting for their first interactions with people of African descent. Decades later, Beryl Bryden, who later became a popular singer in Britain, still recalled the thrill of her first trip to Jig's. Noting that the neighborhood had an unsavory reputation, Bryden described the scene as she and her companions entered the club: "There's this not very big room and almost half of it is a huge billiard table. I should think that about 80% West Indians mostly, and there in the corner is this wonderful little jazz band, and, oh, it was absolutely fabulous because we'd never heard any live colored jazz before apart from records, and we really had a ball." Jig's was also a popular rendezvous for musicians looking to hone their improvisational skills in a jam session or merely searching for a casual conversation after finishing their paying gigs elsewhere. *Melody Maker* declared the club "the mecca of West End jamsters." Visiting African American musicians as well as black players from Africa, the Caribbean, and Britain frequently "jumped in" or took the stage while the house band was on break.[36]

But, above all, during its thirteen-year existence, Jig's Club was a haven for people of African descent in London, whether or not they had a passion for jazz. Within its confines, artists and audience members exercised black creativity and urbanity in a collective performance, and black sociability transpired with an ease and relative lack of self-consciousness largely impossible outside its walls. The club's name was an ironic gesture to the complex, even contradictory, associations of blackness for Soho's diverse habitués. An obvious play on the racial pejorative *jigaboo,* the word *jig* assumed new connotations in the hands of black musicians who employed it as a term of self-identification, perhaps in reference to Louis Armstrong, who "impishly changed one of the lines . . . to 'Just a Jig I Know'" in his 1931 recording of the song "Just a Gigolo."[37] The term also referred to a popular African American dance. The apostrophe-*s* at the end of the name, signifying possession and marking a social space of and for the cultural expression of blackness, said it all. Late nights spent mingling and dancing with one another to an eclectic mix of black diasporic sounds at Jig's, the Nest, or other Soho haunts substantiated, if only in fleeting and unstable ways, fairly abstract and utopian notions of pan-African unity. Many more of London's black residents visited these lowbrow establishments than joined or participated in black organizations like the WASU, LCP, or IASB. For those who partook of both, the cacophony of black sounds emanating from Soho provided an ethereal analogue to their political activism.

The extraordinary broadcast of Blake's band at Jig's lived on in record form. In early 1941, the Gramophone Company launched the Regal-Zonophone label to release swing records at the more affordable price of two schillings, which made them accessible to a wider segment of the listening public in wartime Britain—including the Caribbean and African student population. Two sides from "the famous Jig's Club Session," "Cyril's Blues" and "Frolic Sam," were among the new imprint's first releases.[38] Black musicians, dancers, and audiences; clubs, records, and the radio; race, sex, cosmopolitanism, and internationalism. That night at Jig's Club in 1941, as well as the connections and visions of community it encouraged and projected, illustrate essential lineaments of black Soho.

Consisting of the area to the south of Oxford Street wedged between Tottenham Court Road and Charing Cross Road at its eastern terminus and Regent Street to the west, Soho housed an incomparably diverse social milieu in the imperial metropolis, where black music, jazz in particular, was on display like nowhere else in Britain and few places in Europe. In many respects, the area's raucous, smoke-filled outposts, where a variety of clandestine activities were readily available, appeared the opposite of the concert hall, the church, or the purposefully respectable atmosphere at the WASU House. Yet there was considerable overlap between these spheres, and black musicians habitually moved between them. The nightclubs of Soho—several of which were owned or managed by individuals of African descent, often in partnership with people of other ethnic minorities—became important sites of interaction between black musicians, intellectuals, and activists. As with black organizations, a combination of imperial and transatlantic ties shaped these spaces. The clubs attracted white Britons and individuals from elsewhere in the British Empire who had an interest in colonial issues or black culture, and encouraged interracial interaction. But the associations and experiences of black people with jazz and the places it inhabited in the city differed significantly from those of whites. For black sojourners and migrants, whether musicians or nonmusicians, Soho clubs provided a refuge from the racism pervading British society, and many identified the sounds that filled the air in these often down-at-the-heel sanctuaries as "our" music.

From the Edwardian period onward, Londoners came to recognize cosmopolitanism as a distinctive feature of life in a global city. Beginning in the years before the Great War, Soho became one of the principal sites associated with the pleasures and anxieties sparked by the consumption of imported cultural forms and the presence of foreign bodies. As Judith Walkowitz observes, "Dance was a major cultural expression of this double-edged cosmopolitanism."[39] Dance "crazes" swept through Britain as never before during the interwar years. Dances like the shimmy, the Black Bottom, the Charleston, and, in the 1930s, the Lambeth walk and jitterbug—all developed by African American women dancers and choreographers, and introduced via the popular stage—became symbols of the era's modernity and one way in which the post–World War I "new woman" defined herself.[40] Businesspeople, from lowly entrepreneurs to entertainment mogels, rushed to meet the public's seemingly insatiable demand for this quintessentially modern form of amusement, opening dance halls and nightclubs throughout the country.[41] In the capital, social dancing was one of Soho's main attractions, and for some, the racial mixing within its boundaries symbolized the transformative potential of internationalism.

As one jazz historian puts it, white Britons reacted to jazz and swing with a mixture of "fear and fascination."[42] These sentiments extended to black players and derived much of their force from the eroticism attributed to the music and the space of the club. In the 1920s, public officials, from Whitehall and the commissioner of the London Metropolitan Police down to beat cops patrolling the streets, expressed fears, using racial and sexualized terms, that the popularity of dancing, especially in clubs, signaled a more general deterioration of morals and imperial decline. The press fueled similar concerns among the general public. The *Daily Mail* characterized the Charleston as "reminiscent of Negro orgies." As George McKay notes, "Black jazz was articulated as a threat within the framework of the imperial experience," and the "public racialized discourse of the consumption of jazz in Britain was frequently channeled through the (dancing) body, (black) masculinity, and the fascinating threat to white female sexuality." Even those who dismissed nightclubs' reputation "as seats of Satan" noted the prominent black presence as part of their appeal and exoticism. In his contribution on London nightlife to the 1924 visitors' guide, *Brightest Spots in Brighter London,* W. W. Seabrook highlighted the diversity among patrons of the city's nightclubs: "The types of frequenters are as diverse as are their races, colors and creeds." White jazz musicians and writers tended to conflate virtuosity, sexual prowess, and blackness. The British saxophonist Max Jones claimed, "You never found a great jazz musician who wasn't also sexually vital." When the *Blackbirds* revue of 1935 visited London, its star, the African American instrumentalist and singer Valaida Snow, attracted Jones's attention for a mix of erotic and artistic reasons or, as he put it, because she was the "female Louis Armstrong" and "looked good to us; you know, sexual charm had a lot to do with it."[43]

Although London was home to a wide variety of niteries spread across the city, ranging from posh supper and dance clubs to illegal dens of gambling and prostitution with more working-class and racially diverse clienteles, public jeremiads and policing efforts focused on Soho in particular. As Frank Mort states, "Cosmopolitan bodies and spaces came to mark Soho as a site of both pleasure and danger."[44] The growing popularity of jazz and swing music, and the perception of these styles as distinctly black forms, benefited its black clubs while attracting scrutiny to them. Attempts to clamp down on Soho nightspots produced grist for sensationalist newspaper articles, furthering, for patrons and detractors alike, the close association between the new musical import and the district's racially and sexually promiscuous spaces.[45] The lurid picture of Soho presented in the mainstream press was openly racist, but its reputation as a center of vice in a multitude of forms contained an element of truth. By the 1920s, a range of criminal activities—from the sale of alcohol and holding dances without a license to petty larceny, drug dealing, gambling, and prostitution—were part of its atmosphere and, indeed, its allure. "Dance hostesses," nude tableaux, and striptease acts as well as female and male prostitution were common features of the area's nightlife. Like Storyville in New Orleans, the Tenderloin and Greenwich Village in New York City, and Montmartre in Paris, Soho "was a sanctioned zone of legal and sexual transgression," as well as "a major site for cultural and sexual experimentation." The former police superintendent Robert Fabian characterized Soho as a "Square Mile of Vice . . . where you can buy anything and see everything." Commentators attributed much of the criminality, especially the sex trade and dope peddling, to non-European men. Thus, as Catherine Parsonage observes, "due to the increasing representation of jazz as black music, and the concurrent move of black musicians into the nightclubs, . . . jazz was firmly positioned, metaphorically and literally, as the musical accompaniment to the other perceived evils of the underworld of London." [46]

If the sparkling department stores of nearby Oxford Street offered a scrupulously packaged image of imperial modernity beyond the means of most to acquire, Soho evinced a grittier, more visceral cosmopolitanism. In the novelist and essayist Alec Waugh's view, Soho's ethnic and cultural diversity lent the area "a swarthy duskiness, an Oriental flavour," "a cringing savagery . . . [and] a quality peculiarly un-English." Homosexuals, the literati of bohemia, Greeks, Cypriots, Italians, Russian and Polish Jews, and East and South Asians all established a presence and intersected in Soho's labyrinthine streets and alleyways. Artists, actors, models, and screenwriters from Strand Films on Soho Square rubbed shoulders with celebrities, royalty, and members of high society in the area's clubs and the pubs of Fitzrovia, just north of Oxford Street. Soho was a center of queer sociability as well, and by the late 1930s, a "queer migration" to its black after-hours clubs was well under way. The presence of black bodies and music in the district's nightclubs also linked these urban spaces to colonial settings across the empire, underscoring the intimate relationship between them as if instantiating a sort of return of the repressed colonial Other. The specters of unconventional sexuality and of blacks mixing with whites threatened to invert the racial order of empire.[47]

The dance-band veteran Jack Glicco described "the nightly scene in the average club":

A single room, most about 25 feet square, crammed with smoke, noise and people. A few tables round the walls; a curtained alcove at one end; a small rostrum on which the band played like men possessed. Bottles and glasses on the tables; people laughing and talking; couples dancing so thickly on the floor that no flooring could be seen. And over all, an air of jollity and merriment that had a slightly hysterical quality, as if at any moment the gaiety would crumble to anger or tears. It often did.

Kate Meyrick, "the queen of London's nightclubs" in the 1920s, owned the 43 Club at 43 Gerrard Street. According to Glicco, "There was nothing pretentious about the club, . . . yet here came peers and commoners, famous jockeys and the top names in stage and variety. . . . Here you could hear the world's greatest artists at jazz—all for the price of the entrance fee and a drink." London-based jazz musicians, especially young Jewish musicians like Harry Gold and Billy Amstell, frequented the 43, which afforded them the rare opportunity to play with visiting American jazz greats.[48] Despite the calculated "louche cosmopolitanism" of the 43, the club catered primarily to an elite, heterosexual clientele; "interracial couples were a rare sight on Mrs. Meyrick's dance floor, as were same-sex couples."[49] Just outside its door, street prostitution was plainly visible on Gerrard. The socialist 1917 Club, cofounded by Leonard Woolf, lay across the street, and the Tea Kettle, a queer café, lay around the corner on Wardour Street. South Asian students gathered at Shafi's, one of the first Indian restaurants in London, at 18 Gerrard Street, and Fabian socialists at the 1917 Club. The Big Apple, with its largely black clientele, was down the street from Meyrick's club. There, Fabian recalled, "I learnt all about jazz, boogie-woogie and calypso from my colored friends years before they became known outside the murky little 'colored clubs.'"[50] To a much greater extent than at the 43 Club, these other elements of Soho's social pastiche—internationalist politics, black cultural expression, and "outsiders" of various stripes—collided in the more democratic confines of the area's black nightclubs.

The first establishments catering to a black clientele opened in central London during the 1920s. There were the Erskine Club on Whitfield Street behind Tottenham Court Road and the Black Man's Café on White Lion Street. Sam Minto and Edward Felix, who later served as secretary of the British Colonial Club for African and Afro-Caribbean military personnel and students near St. Martin's Lane, ran a small club on Denmark Street, just east of Charing Cross Road and Soho, a few doors down from a notorious gambling spot. At roughly 2 A.M. on November 30, 1924, police raided the

Erskine Club, where they found the establishment filled with apparently intoxicated revelers dancing to a jazz band consisting of several "men of colour." They arrested the proprietor, Uriah Erskine, for the illegal sale of liquor, but it was the spectacle of white women carousing with black men and the potential for interracial sexual liaisons that, as Martin Pugh notes, "really caused the outrage . . . for which the owner was prosecuted." In their evidence against Erskine, the police stated that "the dancing was most objectionable from the suggestive movements," and reported other offensive sights, such as a white woman seated on a black man's knee.[51]

Because of strict wartime regulations against the sale of alcohol after a certain hour, most establishments took the form of "bottle parties," especially after a judge upheld their legality in 1932. This practice involved forming a partnership of sorts with a local wine or liquor shop. In theory, as callers at a private party, guests could bring or order a bottle in advance, which would be reserved at the liquor store and then delivered when they arrived. In practice, bottle parties were clubs in which, for the price of a membership or admission fee, patrons could order drinks all night.

The most popular and fondly remembered black clubs were clustered on the western, southern, and eastern fringes of Soho. They included, moving clockwise, the Blue Lagoon and Frisco's on Frith Street just south of Soho Square; the Shim Sham at the southern terminus of Wardour Street and the Big Apple and Cuba Club on Gerrard Street; and the Nest and Bag O' Nails on Kingly Street, one skinny block west of Ashwood Garvey's Florence Mills club. Jig's Club lay near the center of this triangular zone of black frivolity and musicianship.[52] Jack Isow, a Polish Jew born in Russia, and the African American singer Ike Hatch opened the Shim Sham at 37 Wardour Street in 1935. Isow brought significant capital and experience to the venture; well known from the variety stage, records, and radio, Hatch served as the host and public face of the club. Unlike the cramped rooms and cellars that housed most of Soho's clubs, the Shim Sham had a street-level façade that led downstairs to "an expansive and brilliantly lit room" with an elevated rostrum and thirty-by-twenty feet of dance floor surrounded by tables. Joe Deniz described it as "the first real effort to make [a black club] look like a place, not thrown together."[53] Before the Shim Sham, Hatch had emceed and presided over the nightly jam sessions at the Nest, which opened its doors in 1933. By comparison, the Nest was smaller and grittier, and the music and atmosphere there more raucous and improvisational. Although the Nest had "no official cabaret," in Glicco's estimation, "it produced the finest impromptu cabaret in town." The club's owner, Meyer Cohen, embraced its reputation as one of the city's liveliest black clubs. He stationed a Barbadian bouncer at the door, supplied free whiskey to black patrons with the understanding that they would converse or dance with his white customers, and even paid cab drivers to divert black fares from other nightspots. Frisco Bingham, rumored to be from Jamaica, had owned clubs in Paris before relocating to London and opening Frisco's. Fabian described it as "a poky little cellar, decorated with five pounds' worth of painted hessian and dried-up palm leaves," which nevertheless helped its owner "become one of the great names of Europe as a club proprietor." Thompson, however, recalled that Frisco's "was really run by a girl named Lydia," a black British dancer and former member of the chorus line in Will Garland's *Brown Birds*.[54]

Despite the differences among these clubs, the relatively small group of black musicians who played in them and the diverse but distinctive composition of their clientele linked them, and the Blake brothers were usually at the center of it all. Though a multi-instrumentalist who played the alto saxophone, violin, and drums, Happy Blake made his greatest impact on the London music scene as a club manager-owner and recruiter of talent, earning him the nickname "the Captain" in musician circles. If black Soho was London's Harlem, Happy was its unofficial mayor. Nearly all of the Caribbean musicians who came to London during the 1930s and 1940s, and several Africans and black Britons, passed through the Blake brothers' bands. Happy performed or booked the entertainment at the Cuba Club, the Shim Sham, and the Nest, and owned the Rendezvous des Artistes in the late 1930s, the Barbarina in St. John's Wood during the war, and the Trade Winds Club at 74 Jane Street in the East End in the late 1940s. After Hatch's split with Isow and the Shim Sham, Norris Smith assumed his responsibilities, but the Blake brothers remained the creative masterminds behind the entertainment, with Cyril leading the house band and Happy securing new talent for its ever-changing roster. In addition to his stint at Jig's and Cuba Club, Cyril's bands held residencies at the Havana Club (1941–1942), West One (1942), Bag O' Nails (1942), Barbarina (1942–1943), Chesterfield (1944), Panama (1946), Goose and Gander (1947), and Blue Lagoon (1948).[55]

Eroticism, unconventional sexuality, and the blurring of gender lines accompanied the sounds of the musicians and the spectacle of interracial mixing at black clubs. Despite the close quarters, the dancing was more spontaneous, athletic, and provocative, and less couples-oriented, than in the exclusive nightspots of the West End. At the Shim Sham, young black women, including dancers from the variety stage, replaced the white dancing hostesses of Meyrick's 43 Club, but the Shim Sham was also known as "an establishment where a man could even get hooked for the evening if so inclined." The black Welsh pianist Lily Jemmott performed solo at one club "dressed like a man . . . with an Eton crop, collar and tie, and clothes like a barrister." Plainclothes police who infiltrated black clubs frequently noted the presence of "Lesbian type[s]" and "women dancing together" amidst interracial couples on the dance floor. An anonymous complaint to the police about the Shim Sham reported that "there is a negro band, white woman [sic] carrying on perversion, women with women, men with men," and described, in thinly veiled terms, same-sex liaisons in the lavatories. An announcement in the entertainment weekly *Night and Day* characterized Frisco's as "the real thing (Dress optional)" and noted the "cheerful staff (black) and clientele of exquisite young men (white)" at Jig's Club. Glicco remembered "Sonia," an "outstandingly lovely" lesbian bartender at the club. "Men held no interest for her," and using her tips and gifts from her "ritzy" women admirers, "she befriended a number of girls who had got themselves into trouble and never asked for repayment." He also recounted watching a black dancer perform an amateur "strip-tease act" at Jig's one evening. A "coloured girl, who was very drunk, climbed on the billiards table and started to do a dance called the 'Suzy Q.'" When "some of the men . . . demanded to know why she did not take the dress off," the woman "told the crowded room that she would do a strip-tease act for them if they would con-tribute to a charity she named" and "then did the promised act." After "she had finished stripping," Glicco added, "she completed the dance that had started the whole affair before she stepped down off the table and dressed." The dance step that the woman performed (the Suzy Q) was immortalized in the 1936 song "Doin' the Suzy Q" by Lil Hardin Armstrong, Louis Armstrong's second wife, and incorporated into the Big Apple, Lindy Hop, salsa, and other dances. Her impromptu performance may be read as a blend of artistry and farce. The bottle party, hot jazz, and striptease shows were the three great additions to nightlife in Soho between the wars. As she danced on the billiard table before a presumably mixed-race audience, the unnamed black woman parodied the aping movements of the white burlesque dancers who catered to elite white men and the debutantes and scions of high society who crowded the dance floor at posh London niteries, while demonstrating her expertise with the black dance du jour.[56]

Soho's most popular black clubs were not only music and dance venues but also gambling spots and bases of both legal and illegal sex work. The Nigerian seaman "Gentleman" Thomas, who settled in London after the First World War, was "well-known at the gambling tables of Soho." He owned several "shortlived dives" in Soho and Stepney, while advising the anthropologist Margery Green on Igbo language and culture. Glicco recalled that, "while the band played [at Jig's], gamblers would play games of snooker for £100 and more a side," and "prostitutes came to hand over their earnings to their men at around three in the morning." Fabian claimed that the Nest was the "first place in Britain where reefer cigarettes . . . were smoked." Eventually, crime gangs infiltrated the club, and it closed in 1939 after police discovered a ring of jewelry thieves operating out of it.[57]

The diverse crowd and illicit practices at these clubs were part of their appeal, but they did not make for longevity. If you owned one club in Soho, chances were you had owned several. Clubs closed with regularity because of police raids, gang fights, or some combination of calamities, only to be replaced by others. When one venture met with disaster, the club owner set up shop in a new location nearby; sometimes she or he merely reopened under a new name in the same spot. Police raided twenty-seven bottle parties in Soho and the West End as part of a major crackdown in December 1936, including the Shim Sham, the Cuba Club, the Nest, and Frisco's.[58] The upscale Old Florida Club and Café de Paris both fell victim to German bombs during the war, but many of Soho's other black nightspots closed in these same years as part of a renewed police onslaught. Still, some clubs enjoyed relative success and staying power and developed reputations for catering to a particular group—as a "West Indian," "hot jazz," or "bohemian" spot, for example—though they usually attracted far more varied clienteles than these labels suggested. On February 7, 1942, police raided Jig's, and the club affectionately known among the "swing fraternity" as "Harlem in London" closed. By that time, the peripatetic Blake had moved on to the West One Club in Grafton Street and the Bag O' Nails, where some of the first modern jazz combos in Britain later debuted.[59]

Black musicians mingled in each other's homes, the orchestra pits of West End theaters, and rhythm clubs, as well as the backing and session bands of white British headliners and visiting African American entertainers. But, most of all, they came together in Soho. As Coleridge Goode put it, "A kind community of black musicians, especially West Indians, centred on those clubs." They were spaces of creative freedom where black musicians, as Simons observes, "often stifled in their regular dance band employment, could join after-hours jam sessions to better their improvisational abilities." The hours were long, the wages were low, and job security was minimal for dance band musicians, so they tended to change posts frequently or hold down several at one time. Most clubs allowed musicians to enter without paying the membership or entrance fee in hopes that they would sit in with the band. If they received any compensation for playing, it usually came in the form of food or drink. "We'd do them [performances] seven nights a week," playing until seven or eight in the morning or "'til the last customers came in," Clare Deniz remembered, but "never got paid." At one club called Tractors, she and her husband, Frank, played for a simple meal of curry and rice. Nevertheless, the black dance clubs of Soho were the last—and usually the most enjoyable—stop of the night, even for outstanding players whose services were in high demand such as Bertie King, whom Thompson compared favorably to the legendary African American saxophonists Coleman Hawkins and Benny Carter. Although the musicians worked at different paying gigs all over town, Thompson recalled that "see you at the Nest, Jig's, etc." remained a common refrain among them. "Certainly," he explained, they were "the best place to meet and talk . . . and have nothing to worry about."[60]

African American expatriots and visitors also gravitated toward Soho's black clubs, and many jammed with the house band or performed solo sets. The pianist Garland Wilson played as a second pianist with Happy Blake's band at the Shim Sham when it opened. While working with the resident band at the Nest, Glicco met "all the famous coloured stars," including the Mills Brothers, Elisabeth Welch, Paul Robeson, and Cab Calloway. "Cab," he recalled, "would play with us regularly." Deniz encountered the French swing violinist Stephen Grappelli and Adelaide Hall at the club. Thompson saw socialites such as the shipping heiress Nancy Cunard and her African American companion Henry Crowder and met Sam Manning, the African American blues singer Alberta Hunter, and pianist Art Tatum at Soho niteries. He spotted Coleman Hawkins at the Nest when he visited London in 1934. Louis Armstrong and Dizzy Gillespie also visited the club. "Denied any solo opportunity" in the *Cotton Club Show* at London's Palladium, according to Jim Godbolt, Gillespie "sat in" with the house band. While Fats Waller was in London in 1938, Thompson heard him play a forty-five-minute set "in the small hours of the morning, around four or five o'clock," at Jig's. The opportunity to watch, listen to, and even play with African American stars not only provided a type of professional development for London-based black musicians but also instilled a sense of coparticipation in a shared idiom. Some got jobs touring with famous African American artists after these Soho encounters. The Trinidadian drummer and percussionist Edmundo Ros worked at the Nest and Jig's, and Thompson averred that Waller must have heard him at one of them, which led to a spot on one of the latter's London recording sessions.[61]

For many white musicians and leftists, these clubs cemented the association of black music with antifascism and internationalism in the late 1930s and 1940s. As Walkowitz suggests, "The gathering in the Shim Sham [and other black clubs] of Jewish anti-fascists and Communists, as well as black pan-Africanists," transformed them into "'democratic' and 'international' space[s] of the Cultural Front." Jazz became so popular on the left that, notes Kevin Morgan, CPGB officials in London criticized "communist spectacles . . . for featuring 'hot trumpeters' at the expense of political propaganda." The founder of Mass Observation, Tom Harrison, "hoped that jazz could be a 'crystallizer of feeling' on behalf of progressive internationalism," and Jewish jazz players like Amstell and Gold, who regularly performed jazz and calypso on Marson's broadcasts, frequented black nightclubs. Max Jones recalled that his time in Soho's clubs was an "eye-opener" in ways not limited to music. Listening to the records of African American bands like the Duke Ellington Orchestra and playing with black musicians "not only removed [the] colour prejudice" instilled in his youth; his interactions in black clubs also eroded his homophobia. One night Jones met Garland Wilson in the dressing room at the Shim Sham. Wilson played new records from the United States for him, and they soon became "bosom buddies." Jones recalled, "he was very gay," so "people would say 'you didn't go out with him,' or '[I hope] you kept your back against the wall with him.'"[62]

Soho's clubs were sites of cultural and political innovation, where black and white intellectuals, artists, and activists converged. For devotees, they were spaces of possibility, including the possibility of indulging in illicit pleasures and cultural experimentation or envisioning new forms of community. Many of the city's black residents embraced the clubs' cosmopolitan atmosphere and the notion that jazz was, in the words of Alain Locke, "the characteristic musical speech of the modern age." Like the progressive and jazz press, black Londoners associated the space of the club with internationalist politics, but they also characterized these jazz cellars as rare places of black expression and sociability in the white metropolis. This double-understanding of jazz as both distinctively black and, as Eric Porter puts it, "an articulation of a broader human community and consciousness" mirrored the worldview animating black internationalist activity.[63] As jazz and black bodies became a part of Soho's cultural and social makeup, the music heard within the district's clubs provided an aural complement and stimulus to the political imagination.

The clubs brought black musicians together with students, activists, and workers of African descent in an atmosphere where blackness was celebrated as modern and cosmopolitan. For the nonmusician, the would-be student agitator as well as the casual pleasure-seeker, the niteries provided meeting grounds and a welcome respite from the racism pervading daily life in Britain. In a piece for *Melody Maker* titled "Harlem in London: Year of Advancement for Negroes" from 1936, Rudolph Dunbar declared that the Shim Sham "represents the new outlook on the colour question." He emphasized the presence of "white and coloured people together" on the dance floor, and situated the club's arrival on the scene within the context of a series of developments that exercised black organizations and activists in London during the mid-1930s, including the Italian invasion of Ethiopia, the opening of a new hostel for black university students in London (presumably the first WASU House), and the film *Sanders of the River*, which starred Paul Robeson and featured dozens of other black actors and extras. The Nest was particularly popular among West African students in London. While Nnamdi Azikiwe was in London in 1936, he stayed at the WASU House, reconnected with Louis Mbanefo, Fela Sowande, and other old friends, and ate Caribbean fare with black radicals at Ashwood Garvey's Florence Mills club. Azikiwe's childhood friend H. O. Davies noted that "'Zik' was a tireless dancer," and the two friends "spent many nights together at various night clubs." In his autobiography, Azikiwe recalled the Nest in particular: "Hatch's singing and dancing coupled with the bevy of beauties who flocked there transformed it into 'a second Harlem.'" As places where "confraternity between blacks and whites was encouraged," Soho's black nightclubs were unique in London. Ras Makonnen remembered the Nest as a rare place where blacks of different classes and from different regions mixed. When Ralph Bunche asked Eric Williams for club recommendations, the latter suggested the Shim Sham, the Nest, and Frisco's; his wife, Elsie, made Ruth Bunche a "black wool dress" for their night out. During World War II, the former IASB member Babalola Wilkie opened a club on Greek Street in Soho, where, according to Laurie Deniz, the regulars included black and white musicians as well as colonial students and agitators. For the South African writer Peter Abrahams, Soho "had the feel and air of a cosmopolitan village." There, "blacks congregated to eat and drink and pass the time and exchange news from 'home'" at "small nightclubs and little restaurants." "This, looking back," Abrahams claimed, "was the seedbed of the later unity of African, American, and Caribbean black folk."[64]

This is not to say that all black intellectuals and activists spent their nights carousing in nightclubs or saw Britons' enthusiasm for black music as entirely unproblematic. Rather, Soho's black nightclubs existed in symbiotic, if agonistic, relation to the WASU House and other centers of black activism and social life. As Putnam points out, "it is no coincidence that black internationalism surged within the transatlantic print and performative realm simultaneously... the two kinds of black internationalisms were driven by some of the same geopolitical developments—and spurred each other on (at times by duking it out) as well."[65] The association of blackness with the clubs' legal shadiness threatened the image of racial and gendered respectability crafted by groups like the WASU and LCP, and some, especially older, members fretted over the way that the commercialization of black dance music perpetuated common stereotypes of mindless sensuality and lasciviousness. Discussions of jazz in the early issues of the LCP's journal were limited—at times even disparaging—and tended to lump it together with the vaudeville and minstrel traditions. Ladipo Solanke of the WASU chastised some African students for spending their time dancing with white women in clubs instead of focusing on their studies and race work. Yet both groups regularly featured well-known nightclub musicians at their functions, and *The Keys* included articles celebrating the genius of such artists as Duke Ellington. The annual WASU Day festivities in 1937 opened with a ball at the Northumberland Rooms in Trafalgar Square. Cyril Blake and his Mad Lads provided the music for an evening "packed with gaiety and joy."[66] In 1946, the WASU hosted the Gold Coast Police Band's farewell concert, concluding an extended tour of Britain during which the band recorded for HMV. During the 1940s and early 1950s, the Nigerian Ambrose Adekoya Campbell and his West African Rhythm Brothers often headlined the union's social events while holding a residency in Soho and playing at jazz festivals across Britain. When Ken Johnson died in 1941, friends, colleagues, and other mourners gathered for his funeral at Aggrey House, the social center for students of African descent that had become a base of political organizing.[67]

The activities of some musicians and entrepreneurs bridged the worlds of black activism and the jazz club. The son of a priest and a middle-class Lagosian family, Charles Olufela "Fela" Sowande received his early music education at Christ Church Cathedral in Lagos under Ekundayo Phillips, who introduced him to European church and classical music. He also led two of the most popular early highlife dance bands in Lagos, the Chocolate Dandies and the Triumph Club Dance Band. In 1934, Sowande left for London, where he initially planned to study civil engineering. He joined the WASU and soon returned to music as both a source of income and the focus of his studies. He played in or led some of the city's best jazz bands at Frisco's, Chez Louis, and other clubs. In 1938, he succeeded Johnson on the bandstand at the Old Florida Club and formed a new, seven-piece "All-Coloured" group, featuring several of the musicians discussed above. Sowande formed a friendship and professional partnership with the African American singer Adelaide Hall after her husband, the Trinidadian Bert Hicks, took over the club. He went on to make numerous recordings with Hall, "attaining the reputation of being the finest Hammond jazz organist in the world."[68] In addition to jazz and dance tunes, Sowande's band performed his arrangements of spirituals with a five-person choir. He also began composing during his lengthy sojourn in London and produced a series of orchestral works that incorporated African melodies. As in Lagos, Sowande moved between the hazy environs of clubs and the somber atmosphere of the church and concert hall in London, and due to his influence, WASU dances and events featured a range of Afro-Atlantic styles. There was, as Bode Omojola suggests, "something decidedly political in Sowande's 'intentional hybridity.'" As with his peers in the WASU, his "nationalism" was "a supranational concept, which, rather than merely focus on the projection of one country," crafted "a holistic representation of African music" that was inseparable from his broader cultural internationalism. His African sound was "a means towards demonstrating the cross-cultural potential of musical communication," "not a mere ambassadorial projection of native or national identity."[69]

In 1945, the LCP began soliciting talent for its own dance orchestra under the direction of Geoffrey Bond, but Happy Blake and Al Jennings soon took charge of the project. Jennings, who chaired the group's entertainment and dance committee, formed and directed the League Dance Band. As he had done for so many Soho clubs, Blake handled "all their musical engagements, such as dances and socials," during the mid-1940s. Through their efforts, a 1948 LCP report announced, "the League has been able to re-muster the coloured musicians in the London area and by this means has served in procuring engagements, acting as Commission agent for such bands thereby providing a source of income." At that time, Blake also owned and operated the Trade Winds Club on Jane Street in London's East End. *Checkers*

Magazine described the club as "a home to all coloured artistes, musicians, students and seamen . . . in and around London town" and noted that Blake "can be identified with every organization whose aims are for the advancement of the Negro race."[70]

Coleridge Goode made the voyage to Britain from Jamaica on a banana boat in August 1934. After a few days in London, he took the train to Glasgow, where he began studying electrical engineering at Glasgow University. He soon became involved in the city's music scene, playing standard dance fare with the house band at the Charing Cross dance hall and jazz on Sundays at the Queen Mary Club. Goode arrived with an excellent music education. From 1911 to 1934, his father, George Goode, had directed the Kingston Choral Union in Jamaica. When his son was born in 1914, George named him Coleridge in honor of the great black British composer Samuel Coleridge-Taylor, whose works, including his magnum opus *Hiawatha's Wedding Feast,* the choir regularly performed. In Glasgow, Goode met a number of touring musicians. "One of the very first visitors I got to know," he remembered, "was the [black British] pianist/vocalist Cab Kaye." He admired Ken Johnson's orchestra from afar: "For me, it was *the* band, the biggest inspiration at the time." He wrote to the bandleader in early 1941, just weeks before his death. Early the following year, Goode moved to London, where he initially lived with Una Marson in her West Hampstead flat. (Her sister, Ethel Marson, was his father's secretary in Kingston.) In the following three decades, he played the bass in many of the era's top jazz and calypso bands and became known as one of the most skilled black musicians in the country. This brief biographical sketch reveals some of the imperial and transatlantic networks, as well as the mixing of genres and forms, that shaped the development of black music in London.[71]

During the Second World War, the circle of Caribbean musicians around the Blake brothers, as Jones put it, "branched off into a little West Indian nightlife lot [at] a little place called the Caribbean Club" on Denman Street in Soho. Owned by Rudolph "Rudy" Evans (aka André Dakar), an Afro-Caribbean actor, singer, and former tenor saxophonist in Sowande's band at the Old Florida Club, the Caribbean opened its doors around the time that Jig's Club closed. Following a brief spell with Leslie Hutchinson's all-black band, Goode moved to the club in 1944, in part because he knew the establishment's manager, whose brother was his family's dentist in Jamaica. The Caribbean Trio, consisting of Goode, guitarist Lauderic Caton, and pianist Dick Katz, a Jewish exile from Nazi Germany, built a reputation as jazz experimentalists. The band moved to the Rose Room in late 1946 and added the drummer and singer Ray Ellington after working with him on a recording session in support of Stephen Grappelli. The London-born son of the African American comedian Harry Brown and a Russian Jew, Ellington had played with musicians such as Rudolph Dunbar in London nightclubs before serving in the British Royal Air Force during the war. The charismatic and well-regarded drummer—of whom Spike Milligan said, "if he hadn't been black, he would have been the best white drummer in the country"—assumed the responsibility of fronting the group, now billed as the Ray Ellington Quartet. The ensemble embarked on a ceaseless and highly successful touring schedule and made a number of radio broadcasts and recordings in the late 1940s. When health problems forced Caton to quit touring, Laurie Deniz replaced him on guitar. In 1951, the band joined BBC Radio's *The Goon Show.* Despite their sophisticated, modern jazz sound, the quartet achieved mainstream success by adding comedy and an element of playfulness to their on-air performances.[72]

Goode went on to an illustrious career, playing and recording with such modern-jazz musicians as the trumpeter Ellsworth McGranahan "Shake" Keane from St. Vincent and the Jamaican alto saxophonist Joe Harriott's free-jazz quintet. Nevertheless, he later recalled his time with the Caribbean Trio as "a highlight of my career," both for the music they played and the setting. The lack of drums in the trio shifted the rhythmic burden to the other instruments but freed the musicians to explore new roles and timbres. The instruments became almost interchangeable, each alternating between rhythmic and melodic functions. As Goode explained, "We put together intricate arrangements, using all the resources you could get from a piano-guitar-bass trio . . . and tried to make everything fresh with new voicings and textures of sound." The format allowed for the assertion and melding of distinct musical personalities, the expression of unity *through* difference. "But," Goode recalled, "there were other things too [about the Caribbean Club] that were perhaps as important as the music." For him, the tenor of social relations within the club encouraged the inventiveness and "intellectual quality" of the trio's sound. "There," in Val Wilmer's words, "Caribbean and African-American officers rubbed shoulders with Whitehall mandarins," aristocrats, and "Soho's raffish element." Josie Miller, the British-born daughter of a black circus hand, worked as a waitress at the Caribbean; the experience "changed her life." She met the future president of Botswana Seretse Khama, Django Reinhardt (who sat in on Caton's oversized electric guitar), and the painters Frank Auerbach, Lucian Freud, and Pablo Picasso. She taught "Cockney rhyming slang" to the African American singer Lena Horne. While in London in 1947, Horne also visited the WASU and made financial contributions to it and Nkrumah's West African National Secretariat. Although Ras Makonnen spent most of the war in Manchester, he had fond memories of the Caribbean Club as well, and Una Marson mentioned it on air during one of her broadcasts. Despite its eclectic mix of patrons, Goode remembered the Caribbean as "homely in a way" because "most of the clientele were regulars and knew each other well." Like his contemporaries, he looked to the postwar period with optimism, anticipating significant social and political change, and saw its promise instantiated on a nightly basis inside the Caribbean. "The Caribbean Club was a kind of ideal of how people could mix without tensions and trouble. As the war ended we were looking ahead to the way things might be better . . . It was a genuinely mixed club in terms of race and class." He added, "We could do interesting things with the music because we felt completely relaxed playing there."[73] The London-based trio rerouted jazz through an international(ist) Caribbean.

On May 8, 1945, VE Day, another, more spontaneous expression of hope for a transformed postwar social order erupted in Piccadilly Circus, just yards from the Caribbean Club, when the Nigerian Ambrose Adekoya Campbell and an "ad hoc mix of students and seamen" treated the throng of revelers to the sounds of West Africa's port cities. "Imagine," Campbell reminisced more than sixty years later, "four or five drummers and two or three guitars and these voices singing. . . . We had a huge crowd following us around Piccadilly Circus. You could hardly move." According to lore, this moment marked the first public appearance of the group later known as the West African Rhythm Brothers, the most popular African band in mid-century London and a major influence on the development of postcolonial Nigerian music. These performances of unity with other races and classes in the Caribbean Club and Piccadilly were exercises in political imagination, as well as artistic creativity, forged in a city marred by modern imperial warfare and racial violence, nurtured in its "homely" spaces, and freighted with larger histories of black struggle and "of listening, echoing, and sounding." As wartime destruction reduced the city's housing stock, exacerbating the effects of racial discrimination, it became even more difficult for people of African descent, especially mixed-race couples, to secure accommodations. Campbell, his English partner, Ida Gould, and the drummer Ade Bashorun shared a coal cellar in a condemned building for a year, and the members of the West African Rhythm Brothers rarely worked solely as musicians. Goode also had trouble finding a place to live. Ultimately, Evans gave him a tip on a place that had been requisitioned for service personnel but was partially vacant, and he and his family settled in Notting Hill, foreshadowing the postwar transformation of the geography of black London. Goode's family lived in the house for the remainder of the twentieth century. "I was the second West Indian in the neighbourhood," he noted. "Rudy was the first."[74]

At the Caribbean Club, Goode began to "feel and understand the idiom of modern jazz," but after his band's departure, it became associated almost exclusively with calypso, albeit calypso performed with the addition of African hand drums and Latin American percussion instruments such as the maracas, bongos, and congas. African, African American, and Afro-Caribbean musicians and styles intermingled in the imperial metropolis. Whereas in France, where the market for the beguine from Martinique developed alongside a taste for jazz and Cuban music, as John Cowley observes, "in Britain there was little or no interest in vernacular music from the English-speaking West Indies." However, consumers in the British Isles represented only part of a larger imperial marketplace and soundscape. London served as an important early base for the recording and distribution of African and Caribbean music on record, drawing pioneers of these forms, and BBC broadcasts beamed these sounds to British colonies in West Africa and the Caribbean, with significant consequences for the development of local musical cultures.[75]

Most scholars link the introduction of Caribbean and African music to the arrival of unprecedented numbers of migrants from these areas and "the irresistible rise of multi-racial Britain" in the late 1940s and 1950s.[76] Newcomers played an important role in expanding the audience for these styles, but familiar faces produced much of these ostensibly new sounds from Trinidad, Cuba, Brazil, and West Africa, and tutored the new arrivals from Africa and the Caribbean. During the 1930s and early 1940s, the live performance of Caribbean and Latin American styles developed on the margins of Soho's music scene. As noted above, the Blake brothers' bands regularly included popular calypsos in their sets, and they moved between residencies at jazz spots and Latin-themed clubs. *Melody Maker* noted of the band at

Jig's: "Cyril Blake and the boys have an extensive repertoire of West Indian calypsos, apart from the swing style which they feature for dancing." Marson described Blake's band at the Havana as "very very good on West Indian music, the very best I have heard in London." While leading his own bands at these clubs, Blake, Maxwell, and Frank Williams, a veteran of Johnson's group, also played with the "brilliant rumba pianist" from Cuba Don Marino Barreto at the Congo Club on Denman Street. The year after his band's historic on-air performance from Jig's, he composed a set of topical calypsos for a BBC broadcast to Caribbean service personnel. Until his death in 1951, Blake continued to perform in jazz clubs while playing and recording calypso with his Calypso Serenaders, which included his brother Happy on violin. When the Trinidadian calypsonian George Browne (aka Young Tiger) came to London in 1942, he "sang for his supper" in a minstrel show, worked in the chorus of the 1943 revival of *Show Boat,* and led a Caribbean vocal group through renditions of popular American hits. After the war, he started learning the double-bass with Lauderic Caton. The two men shared a flat for two years and worked together at the Club du Faubourg in Soho. Browne absorbed many of Caton's "aesthetic and philosophical beliefs" and "credited [him] as his mentor and guru." Other mainstays of the jazz and dance-band world, such as Freddy Grant, Brylo Ford (the Iron Duke), Bertie King, Clinton Maxwell, Dave Wilkins, and the Nigerian drummer Billy Olu Sholanke, accompanied calypsonians and singers such as Lord Kitchener (Aldwyn Roberts), Lord Beginner (Egbert Moore), and Mona Baptiste—all of whom arrived on the *Empire Windrush*—at nightclubs, at dances for black students, or on recordings like Kitchener's epochal "London Is the Place For Me" (1951). Grant, Leslie Hutchinson, and Norbert Payson, a former member of Al Jennings's orchestra, backed the Jamaican dialect poet and singer Louise Bennett on her first recordings of folk songs for Melodisc Records in 1950. Hutchinson's West Indian Orchestra played behind her on a second session for the Tri-Jam-Bar label soon thereafter.[77]

The "Old Brigade," as Cowley terms them, also helped introduce Latin American music to British listeners and more famous white popularizers. While a student at the Royal Academy of Music, in 1938, the percussionist Edmundo Ros joined Marino Barreto's band at the Embassy Club. Shortly after the start of the war, Ros formed his own group, which included Frank Deniz and, before he was called up in 1942, Leslie Thompson. The band performed Latin American music as a cabaret act at the Mayfair Hotel and for radio broadcasts, introducing dances like the samba and mambo to Britain, and Ros gained a reputation as London's premier Latin percussionist. "I can truly say," Thompson wrote, "that we started Latin American dance music in London!"[78] Ros graduated from the clubs to decades-long success. In 1962, he appeared at the annual Royal Variety Show performing the calypso "London Is the Place for Me" in tuxedo and tails for the royal family.

Black British musicians encountered these same forms via members of Britain's mixed-race seafaring communities. Frank Deniz learned Latin styles firsthand during his days in the shipping industry. In Brazil, he heard performances by samba bands and visited samba schools. He later claimed that Stanley Black, the individual most often credited with introducing Latin American music to Britain, and others attracted to the music of Brazil and Cuba thought it was universally "fast and furious" before he and other black musicians corrected them. Calypso was one of Joe Deniz's earliest musical influences as a youth in Cardiff. After serving in the merchant navy until his ship was torpedoed, he formed the Spirits of Rhythm with Frank and Clare. The group recorded jazz for UK Decca and performed alongside the American bandleader Glenn Miller at the Jazz Jamboree of 1944. At the same time, all three brothers performed as the Hermanos Deniz Cuban Rhythm Band, which (despite its name) played mainly Brazilian music.[79]

These examples highlight not only the presence of black music other than jazz well before the 1950s but, more important, London-based musicians' underrecognized contributions to the "acoustic motions of Black Atlantic sound[s]" in the twentieth century. The remainder of this chapter examines the music produced by people of African descent in London as, to quote the anthropologist Steven Feld, "a nonlinguacentric arena of Black Atlantic intellectualization," "performances and imaginaries of connectedness," and products of "detoured . . . pathways storied and traveled from X to Y by way of Z."[80] Within the context of decolonization and the Cold War, the musical styles discussed here—jazz, calypso, highlife—and many others were nationalized in ways that effaced the transatlantic traffic that shaped them, even as artists continued to use them to critique political oppression and economic exploitation and to dialogue across national boundaries.[81] A number of scholars have noted the immense popularity of Afro-Caribbean and Latin American music in West Africa, citing the circulation of records and musicians between these regions, but the role of London and its small diasporic community receives little to no attention. The city functioned as an important site for the cross-fertilization of these ostensibly distinct(ive) regional musics. In addition to their involvement in political organizations and activism, black musicians in London, predominantly a mix of British-born, Caribbean, and African subjects of the empire, self-consciously combined Afro-Atlantic forms, expressing in another register solidarity and mutual influence within an interconnected black world. Their convergence in the imperial metropolis, and the intermingling of the musical cultures that traveled with them, produced pan-African performance settings and hybrid compositions that articulated alternative histories and political imaginaries. Their sounds transported performer and audience to many different but interconnected locales and provided a way of inhabiting simultaneously "the what is, the what once was, and the what *may be.*"[82]

Calypso—a popular song form whose lyrical content ranges from social commentary to hypermasculine verbal jousting, and from bawdy talk to political protest—developed in the English-speaking Caribbean during the late nineteenth and early twentieth centuries, beginning first in Trinidad. Dense rhythmic patterns and African-style antiphony characterized the earliest examples of calypso, but lyrical content and jazz instrumentation with guitar and horns assumed greater prominence in the early decades of the twentieth century. Due to both Trinidad's proximity to Venezuela and circum-Caribbean migration, Latin American music was a prominent component of early calypsonians' repertoires. Regional networks connected port cities in the British Caribbean to Spanish-speaking islands and Central and South America, producing a degree of cultural intimacy rare even among the territories of the British colonial Caribbean. Putnam points out that "Limón in 1930 was as tightly linked to Kingston as was Colón, Bocas del Toro, Santiago de Cuba, or Havana—which is to say, far more tightly linked than Kingston was to any port in any British Caribbean Territory." The pianist and bandleader Lionel Belasco helped popularize calypso outside Trinidad, but he recorded nearly as many Venezuelan tunes and Jamaican mentos as calypsos between the late 1910s and 1930s. Other pioneers of the form, from Sam Manning to Lord Kitchener, grew up listening to the Spanish-language songs in Trinidad's dance halls, and their travels spread calypso throughout the greater Caribbean, from Jamaica in the north to Aruba and Curaçao to the south, and to New York City and London. Manning recorded for both Okeh's "Race" and "West Indian" series in the mid-1920s, and *Melody Maker* hailed him as a "rumba pioneer" when the Florence Mills club opened. Its proprietor, Ashwood Garvey, spent much of her youth in Panama and returned several times in her lifetime.[83] The Guyanese Ken Johnson likely took the name for his first band with Leslie Thompson from the most popular dance orchestra in Panama during the 1930s, the Aristocrats of Jazz, which consisted mainly of English-speaking Afro-Caribbeans, including several Jamaicans. Edmundo Ros claimed to be Venezuelan. In fact, he was born in Port of Spain to an Afro-Venezuelan mother and Scottish father, and lived in Caracas from 1927 to 1937. Aside from the obvious commercial incentive to do so, in falsely asserting that he hailed from Venezuela, Ros gestured not only toward his family's history but also to the wider horizons of his musical background and that of many Caribbean artists of his generation.[84]

After the Columbia Gramophone Company in Britain purchased the Germany-based Carl Lindstrom Company, acquiring the Odeon and Parlophone imprints, it released the first Caribbean recordings in Britain on the latter in 1927, including seven tracks by Manning, recorded in New York in 1924–1925. In addition to the export market, the label directed its early releases toward British jazz listeners, but sales appear to have been modest. In 1934, Belasco's orchestra recorded twelve sides for Decca, four of which featured Manning on vocals. These were the first recordings of Caribbean music made in Britain, but Decca issued them for export only. Soon thereafter, Belasco produced another set of recordings for the Imperial-Broadcast Company. Juan Harrison provided the vocals on one of these sides, a rumba entitled "Habanerita," which Manning had recorded earlier. Cowley speculates that Harrison's presence "may suggest that the band ... was the 'All British Coloured Band' or 'Rumba Coloured Orchestra' organized in Britain by Rudolph Dunbar." Belasco returned to the United States within a year, but Manning remained in London and recorded several songs with his West Indian Boys for Parlophone, including two spirituals and a *paseo,* "Ara Dada," which featured Gus Newton on vocals in Trinidadian Hindi.[85]

The newcomers of the 1940s also mixed calypso, Latin music, and jazz in their compositions, sessions, and sets. Like Manning and Wilmoth Houdini in the 1920s and 1930s, some took up the themes of racial pride and unity explicitly, as in Kitchener's rebuke of blacks who attempted to pass for white in "If You're Not White You're Black" (1953):

> You hate the name of Africa
> The land of your great-grandfather
> The country where you can't be wrong
> The home where you really belong
> You'd rather be among the whites
> Than stick up for your father's right.

Although calypso attracted only a small number of listeners outside London's black community and received little attention from the jazz press, which, as Oliver notes, "was deaf to the black music in its midst," within six months of his arrival, Kitch was performing regularly at three different clubs, and he recorded for Melodisc in the early 1950s. His "Kitch's Bebop Calypso" and Young Tiger's "Calypso Be" riffed on the developing bebop-calypso schism among black music lovers, while employing straight-ahead jazz for accompaniment; both artists loved bebop and frequently worked with jazz musicians. Kitch's childhood friend Rupert Theophilus Nurse served as the arranger and talent scout for Melodisc, which specialized in Afro-American and African music. Before coming to Britain, Nurse had played tenor saxophone and developed his orchestration skills in the first Trinidadian big band, the Modernaires, in Port of Spain. In 1945, he arrived in London as a member of Jennings's West Indian All Stars. When the group split, he started playing double bass with Fitzroy Coleman's band at a small black nightclub off Leicester Square called the Antilles. He also toured and recorded with Hutchinson's band. As the in-house arranger at Melodisc, Nurse added jazz concepts and jazz players to recording sessions. Thus, many of what are now recognized as early studio recordings of calypso and other Caribbean styles in Britain were in fact politically inspired hybrids that borrowed heavily from jazz, Latin American, and African styles. These songs combined phrasing, instrumentation, and arrangements from different idioms in, to borrow the Trinidadian singer and actor Edric Connor's words, an "experiment of freedom." The calypso produced in London increasingly featured African percussion instruments, melodies, and rhythmic patterns. Young Tiger and Rupert Nurse's Caribbean Rhythm Band produced adaptations of the Yorùbá chant "Oken Karange" in the 1950s, titled "African Dream" and "Song of Joy," respectively. In a slip that attests to its genre-straddling qualities, Melodisc mislabeled the latter's instrumental version by attributing it to the Sierra Leonean singer Ali Ganda (or Lord Ganda). In his rendition, Browne sings "in my dream I had traveled far and gone to my home back in Africa."[86]

A number of African musicians settled in London even before these first self-conscious stirrings of a Caribbean music scene in the city. While some, such as the composer and jazz organist Fela Sowande, introduced African elements into African American and European forms, others produced variations on the popular music of port cities in British West Africa. In the early twentieth century, coastal West Africa gave birth to an array of new musical styles, including Yorùbá *agidigbo* hand-piano music, the *konkoma* street parade music of the Gold Coast, and *asíkò* (or *ashiko*) street drumming, variants of which spread throughout the region. Lagosians traced *asíkò* to the arrival of the Àgùdà, or Amaro, emancipated Africans and their descendants from Brazil and Cuba. As Christopher Waterman explains, "Asíkò was symbolically associated with various predominately Christian black immigrants," but "elderly Lagosian informants point to a relationship between asíkò rhythms and the Afro-Brazilian samba" and "sometimes use the terms . . . interchangeably." Kru mariners transplanted the Liberian, two-finger style of guitar playing to ports of call such as Accra and Lagos, while mercantile networks made an affordable acoustic guitar, known as a box guitar, available to a wider segment of the population. Both greatly influenced the development of early palm-wine music. Early African brass band and ballroom dance music, the antecedents to highlife, mixed arrangements and instrumentation imported from the European military and dance-band traditions with African and diasporic elements. Whereas "Sákárà [of the predominately Muslim and Hausa areas of northern Nigeria] and asíkò were modernized African musics," the latter connected intimately to the consolidation of Yorùbá identity, protohighlife groups such as the Calabar Brass Band in Nigeria "performed Africanized Western music." The "demographic flow linking colonial entrepôts" spurred "the growth of pan–West African urban musical traditions," and gramophone discs and visiting regimental and Salvation Army bands from the Caribbean brought European, Afro-Caribbean, and other styles to the region, which African players incorporated into their music. In the 1920s and 1930s, European firms like the British United Africa Company distributed recordings of Hawaiian guitar music, the string music of Jimmie Rodgers and the Woodie Brothers from the southern United States, and Afro-Cuban bands. In sum, patterns of migration and imperial trade networks connected the West African colonies to one another and to musical cultures across the Atlantic, shaping the development of popular music across the region.[87]

During these same years, London emerged as a significant locus of the production and exchange of African popular music, and African musicians produced new amalgams of black Atlantic forms that record companies and returnees then reexported to the continent. In the early 1920s, the Zonophone label, owned by parent company Gramophone and Victor, began issuing the first discs of African music recorded in Britain—indeed, the first significant collection of African recordings produced anywhere. The label's first West

African releases, recorded in London in 1922, consisted of twenty-two couplings of Christian hymns in Yorùbá by the Reverend J.J. Ransome-Kuti, grandfather of the international Afrobeat star Fela Kuti. In October of the following year, Zonophone recorded a group of songs for its South African series. Often accompanied by Sylvia Colenza on piano, the black South African activist and first secretary of the African National Congress Sol Plaatje provided the vocals for six, including "Nkosi Sikeleli Afrika," the ANC's official anthem.[88] Technological advances in the recording process led the company to make a concerted push into the African market, and it greatly expanded its offerings during the late 1920s. Musicians hailing from the Gold Coast featured disproportionately in Zonophone's catalogue, but by the end of the decade, it boasted an impressive selection of music in seventeen different West African dialects as well as "Coast English," and an even larger number of recordings by South African musicians. Although a few groups, such as the Ga Quartet and the Kumasi Trio, traveled to London specifically to record, the label relied predominately on Britain's existing West African population, including student sojourners, for recording artists. In March 1927, the German Artiphon imprint released ten double-sided 78s by university-educated Roland C. Nathaniels, who lived on Russell Square; and soon thereafter, Zonophone issued several tracks by him in the Ewe language of southeastern Ghana, Togo, and Benin—the first African recordings produced using the new electrical recording process. Nathaniels also served as a talent scout and consultant for the label.[89] The same year, the imprint launched a new series under the prefix EZ with twenty-five double-sided records: sixteen by George Williams Aingo's band, most of them consisting of drums, guitar, and various accoutrements such as kazoo, concertina, tambourine, and castanets; the remainder, guitar and vocal tracks by Harry Eben Quashie. Zonophone went on to issue call-and-response chants by Ben Simmons, as well as recordings by the singer J. Kwesi Biney and the virtuoso guitarist Nicholas de Heer, all of which, like Aingo and Quashie's first releases, featured vocals in Fante, an Akan dialect. Ga speakers such as Edmund Tagoe, Frank Essien, and the Ga Quartet also recorded for Zonophone, the quartet using less conventional instrumentation, including piano, while Quashie and the Kumasi Trio produced a number of sides in Twi, another Akan dialect. In 1929, the label released ten double-sided records by the West African Instrumental Quintet. In addition to these musicians from the Gold Coast, it offered recordings by M. Cole in Igbo and by Isaac Jackson and the guitarist Domingo Justus in Yorùbá.[90]

Although relatively little is known regarding the lives of these West African musicians, the considerable overlap between recording ensembles suggests that ties among them transcended colonial and ethnic boundaries. The Yorùbá-speakers Justus and T. K. Browne accompanied Cole in Igbo and E. O. Martin in Fante on recordings. Aingo recorded in a number of different languages, including Hausa, and Nathaniels even in Swahili, the hybrid vernacular of East Africa. Zonophone advertised these records as examples of "traditional" music, but the melodic content and instrumentation, the prevalent use of guitar and piano, evidenced the fusion of diverse elements that produce jùjú, highlife, and other popular genres. Some of these early African recordings were politically inspired. In 1927–1929, as he established the WASU, Solanke produced a selection of Yorùbá songs, proverbs, and "philosophy," reflecting his conviction that Yorùbá culture provided a basis for a wider West African unity. These recordings contributed to the production and dissemination of a pan-Yorùbá identity that became a cornerstone of the union's efforts and circulated alongside its journal as well as the records of Marcus Garvey. Some of these West African musicians later played at the WASU hostel or at political rallies, and they were conduits for the African-derived material that African American concert recitalists such as Roland Hayes and Paul Robeson incorporated into their repertoires during the interwar period. "G. Biney," who serenaded the Robesons during a ceremony held in their honor at the WASU house in 1935, was probably J. Kwesi Biney. The Gold Coast Quartet, mentioned in chapter 2 as part of the line-up for the 1933 Scottsboro Defense Gala organized by Ike Hatch, most likely included the musicians who had earlier recorded under the name West African Instrumental Quintet. Roland C. Nathaniels took part in the WASU-organized prayer meetings on behalf of Ethiopia two years later.[91]

A regular column in *West Africa,* "EC's Gramophone Notes," publicized new releases from Zonophone's catalogue to readers in West Africa and Britain. The records seem to have sold well in both locales, but the label released its last London recordings of West African musicians in June 1930.[92] The end of Zonophone's EZ series and the advent of field recording in West Africa by the EMI subsidiaries Parlophone, Odeon, and after 1931, His Master's Voice (HMV) eliminated recording opportunities for African musicians in Britain for a decade. Beginning in 1929, EMI produced scores of double-sided, ten-inch discs of sákárà, jùjú, and àpàlà percussion-based music recorded in the Gold Coast and Nigeria in the HMV JL, HMV JZ, and Parlophone B series. Of the aforementioned West African musicians who recorded in London, only the lead guitarist of the Kumasi Trio, Kwame Asare, returned to the Gold Coast, and he appeared in HMV's growing catalogue of local recordings under the name Jacob Sam in the 1940s. From 1933 to 1958, the HMV GV series distributed 250 double-sided discs in western and central Africa, consisting almost exclusively of Cuban and, to a lesser extent, Puerto Rican and Brazilian musicians recorded in Havana, New York, or Paris. The series released its first recordings by African and Afro-Caribbean musicians in London only in the mid-1950s, one of which was the Ghanaian band the Quavers' bluesy homage to the great calypsonian, "Kitch" (1953).[93]

With few public venues for the performance of African music besides the WASU in Camden Town, African music went back underground for a time. Like other working-class blacks in Britain, these musicians faced a hard life, especially during the depression years. They sought out work and sustenance wherever they could find it. Billy (or Willy) Olu Sholanke boxed professionally, performed as a fire-eater, and worked as a translator. Both he and Quashie played bit parts in imperialist films, as did a number of other African musicians. Living in Lambeth and destitute, Ben Simmons landed in court in 1931 after he kept the money from a saxophone that a tobacconist had given to him to sell. The magistrate presiding over the case noted that he had served as a corporal in a white regiment during the war and exclaimed, "Then they say it isn't a free country! ... That couldn't have happened in America." He proceeded to sentence Simmons to three months' hard labor and to issue a deportation order.[94]

A new crop of West African musicians arrived in the late 1930s and 1940s. British and American soldiers stationed in West Africa during the Second World War brought the latest popular styles from the other side of the Atlantic. For many of the most influential players of the period, however, contact with Afro-American forms came not merely via gramophone records and foreign soldiers but through personal interactions in London as well. These musicians attempted to Africanize the highlife dance music popular among urban elites in West Africa, while borrowing elements and sometimes tunes from the jazz, calypso, and Latin music canons. Like their predecessors, they performed at Soho nightclubs and often headlined WASU events. The percussionists Ola Johnson and Emmanuel Ade arrived in Britain in 1938, and the guitarists Rans Boi and Brewster Hughes (Ignatius Abiodun Oke), from the Gold Coast and Nigeria respectively, the following year. The son of a Muslim cleric, Folorunso "Ginger" Johnson was born in Ijebu, Nigeria, but claimed both Brazilian and African ancestry. After he was orphaned at a young age, his sister raised him in Lagos, where he learned the basics of drumming and eventually entered the city's jazz scene. Both Johnson and Hughes served in the merchant navy and worked in munitions factories during the war. Johnson settled in London around 1943. He began a long association with Edmundo Ros in the late 1940s and picked up the congas. He joined the tenor saxophonist Kenny Graham's Afro-Cubists between 1951 and 1954, and played in African and modern jazz clubs throughout the decade. Johnson made a number of recordings for Melodisc that mixed popular Latin American dance music with highlife. By the early 1960s, he had earned a reputation as the best Afro-Latin percussionist in Britain, though he never played one style exclusively.[95] Oladipupo "Ambrose" Adekoya Campbell also joined the merchant navy at the start of the war. After a two-day stop in Liverpool during his first voyage, he jumped ship on a second visit in 1940 and made his way to London. Campbell was a product of the educated, Christian coastal elite. The son of a preacher, he gained his early musical education in the church choir. From a young age, he stole away to the nightclubs and stalls of the Lagosian docklands, where he imbibed the lowbrow forms popular among itinerant laborers. His early days in London were challenging, but he found succor in playing this music with West African friends in Camden Town. At the end of the war, Hughes moved from Manchester to Camden Town and joined Campbell's ad hoc band. This cohort introduced the urban sounds of West Africa to a broader segment of British musicians and listeners than ever before, and Campbell, as a composer, bandleader, guitarist, percussionist, and singer, became the driving force behind, and the most recognizable figure in, the city's small but vibrant West African music scene.[96]

Campbell and the schoolteacher and standout guitarist Brewster Hughes had been bandmates in the Jolly Orchestra, the most popular band performing palm-wine music in Lagos during the late 1930s. Its personnel included a mix of Yorùbá, Kru, Asante, and Saro musicians, playing guitars, banjo, and mandolin accompanied by pennywhistle, drums, and other percussion. Some of their songs, including "Wallace Johnson," which honored the Sierra Leonean agitator, carried a political message and expressed working-class concerns. The Jolly Orchestra launched the careers of some of the era's most influential musicians, including that of the founder of jùjú music in Lagos, Abdulrafiu Babatunde "Tunde" King, who also left Nigeria for London in the 1940s. Campbell and Hughes represented the group's only Saro members. The Saro were descendants of emancipated slaves who were repatriated to Sierra Leone before eventually returning or migrating to Nigeria in the late nineteenth century. Often ridiculed by local Africans and "paternalistically dismissed by European colonizers as 'inauthentic' Africans," as Michael Veal explains, the Saro community (or "creoles") "bore the brunt of social transformation," but "their intermediate cultural position meant that they were crucial in the appropriation and translation of European cultural elements into African forms."[97] Like those who identified as Àgùdà or Amaro, Hughes and Campbell shared an expansive sense of their "African" musical heritage that mirrored the understanding of West African history undergirding the WASU's black internationalism.

In 1945, Campbell formed a band from his circle of friends to support Britain's first black ballet company, Les Ballets Nègres, led by the Jamaican dancer and choreographer Berto Pasuka. Pasuka established Les Ballets Nègres with the classically trained dancer Richie Riley, an old friend from Jamaica, and the LCP contributed talent and publicity to the enterprise. Pasuka's choreography dramatized a transatlantic pattern of pan-African connections through market scenes set in West Africa and the Caribbean and a tribute to the famous educator Dr. Kwegyir Aggrey. Les Ballets Nègres premiered in London with a cast of several black-British dancers, three Nigerians, two Jamaicans, a Ghanaian, a Trinidadian, a Guyanese, a German, and a Canadian. A tour across the United Kingdom, a trip to Paris, and an appearance on BBC television in June 1946 followed.[98] Writing in the *West African Review* in 1947, Noel Vaz described the company as "the first indication of a theatrical medium African in origin and motif, often West Indian in flavour, . . . which promises to become a serious and permanent contribution to the Theatre, not only as a vital contribution to Ballet, but also to the propagation of Negro ideals, ideas and problems." Pat Brand of *Melody Maker* was effusive in his praise of the show's music, calling it the "biggest thing in pure rhythm that I have ever experienced," and noted the presence of the Jamaican trumpeter Leslie Thompson and other jazz musicians in the "packed audience." "From the moment these five musicians strolled, strumming and chanting, into the little auditorium . . . ," he wrote, "the audience was gripped and moved by a primitive pulsating urge in the face of which the greatest rhythm section on wax pales into emasculated imitation—which, of course, it is." Brand's erroneous characterization of the band's music as the "primitive" source of jazz was symptomatic of most Britons' responses.[99]

The music of the West African Rhythm Brothers, as Campbell's group became known, held different significance for the growing ranks of African students and migrants, namely, as the sonorous projection of West African modernity into the heart of the empire. The band's successful debut with Les

Ballets Nègres led to further engagements at the Chelsea and Hampstead arts balls and jazz festivals across Britain. It toured throughout the late 1940s and 1950s. The West African Rhythm Brothers' recordings became the core of Melodisc's catalogue. The band recorded more singles than any other group and at least one full-length album over a period spanning the end of the ten-inch 78 rpm disc era in the early 1950s to the late 1960s and the advent of seven-inch 45 rpm and long-playing, twelve-inch 33 rpm records.[100] However, the group, which consisted of Ade Bashorun, Latiju Pedro, Salustino Dosangous, and Tunde Cole, in addition to Campbell and Hughes, made its name and developed its innovative sound largely within more modest spaces of black sociability in London. The WASU became one of the group's first and strongest supporters, and the band frequently performed at the union's dances until Campbell left for a West African tour in the late 1950s. In March 1946, the WASU's journal reported that the West African Swing Orchestra, which consisted of the West African musicians around Campbell and Caribbean horn players, "has been a real discovery and they have drawn a good number of dancers."[101] As Stapleton observes, Campbell and his band "played a double role" in the 1940s and 1950s: "adding a new life to a British music scene in the post-war years and sustaining the African community in an often bleak environment" marked not only by the continuance of wartime scarcities but also by a growing racist backlash against the presence of people of African descent, including antiblack riots in 1949 and 1958. In fact, its members were the victims of racial violence only weeks before their impromptu VE Day performance in Piccadilly. Soon after Hughes arrived from Manchester, in February 1945, a group of white men attacked the musicians in an underground station. When one of them tried to push Campbell onto the tracks, Hughes pulled a pistol, shot, and wounded one of their assailants. Afterward, his wife, Betty Ogle, hid the weapon from the police, but Hughes received fifteen months in jail for the incident.[102]

The growing popularity of the West African Rhythm Brothers' guitar-heavy brand of highlife helped encourage the establishment of the first Soho nightclubs devoted to the presentation of African music. As Omojola notes, individuals "such as Campbell, who would later lay the foundation for the emergence of modern Nigerian popular music, ... rose to stardom mainly through their nightclub engagements in London." The drummer Ade Bashorun remembered, "We were playing every night, either at town halls, festivals or the clubs in Soho, like the Abalabi and the Club d'Afrique."[103] Beginning in 1952, the band held a residency at the Abalabi, a basement club

WEST AFRICAN STUDENTS' UNION
present
TROPIC NIGHT DANCE
No. 5

AUGUST BANK HOLIDAY — MONDAY, 3RD AUGUST

CHELSEA TOWN HALL   ::   7-30 p.m.—12 mid-night

Bands:

AMBROSE CAMPBELL & THE WEST AFRICAN RHYTHM BROTHERS

RON SOMERS & HIS MUSIC

Tickets 6/-   *(Members 5/-)*

★ BAR.   NICELY FLAVOURED JOLLOF RICE STRAIGHT FROM THE KITCHEN 2/6 PER PLATE ★

'Buses 11, 19, 22.   Tickets from W.A.S.U., 13, Chelsea Embankment, S.W.3 and at the door.
H. L. O. George, Social Secretary.

Printed by The Hereford Times Ltd., General Printing Works (T.U.), London and Hereford.   L5379.

FIGURE 10. Advertisement for the fifth "Tropic Night Dance" presented by the West African Students' Union and featuring Ambrose Campbell and the West African Rhythm Brothers. School of Oriental and African Studies Library, Archives and Special Collections, London, United Kingdom, Papers of Dr. Robert Benjamin Ageh Wellesley Cole (PP MS 35/6/1/14).

on Berwick Street owned by the Nigerian Ola Dosunmu and his English wife, Irene. The music performed at the Abalabi influenced a generation of British jazz musicians, cutting across the growing divide within their ranks. "Traditionalists delighted in their African authenticity," but modern jazz players such as Kenny Graham also became devotees. The British saxophonist Ronnie Scott told Wilmer that "Ambrose was a bit special, a bit of a musicologist." The Abalabi attracted writers, artists, and other "louche Soho-ites" as well. According to Wilmer, who photographed the staff and bands there in the mid-1950s, Africans, Afro-Caribbeans, and "record collectors rubbed shoulders with debutantes and diplomats, attracted to the rhythmic and cultural diversion." Campbell and the novelist Colin MacInnes, who fictionalized the former as Cranium Cuthbertson and the scene at the Abalabi in *City of Spades* (1957), became close friends; MacInnes was even the godfather of one of Campbell's children. In a 1957 survey of affordable nightlife, he wrote: "One thing is common . . . to all the nicest of these poor man's London night spots—they are conducted by coloured people. Without them, London would be a provincial city. . . . And all of their clubs have that atmosphere of good manners, of fun, of sociability, and of absolute equality for all."[104]

In the 1940s and 1950s, leading practitioners of highlife in London and West Africa adopted Afro-Caribbean instrumentation and songs—calypsos and rumbas, in particular. Calypsos such as Lord Kitchener's "Nora" became huge hits on both sides of the Atlantic. Musicians who traveled to London were a major impetus behind the incorporation and synthesis of these styles in the decades before decolonization. Some of the earliest recordings of West African musicians in London show evidence of cultural borrowing. The 1929 recordings of the West African Instrumental Quintet, comprising two guitars, *cavequinho* (a cross between a banjo and mandolin), tambourine, and other percussion instruments, included "Kara So," which derives its melody from the Caribbean carnival favorite "In the Dew and the Rain," written by Errol Duke, aka the (Mighty) Growler. In its melodic content and instrumentation, "Ader Su—No. 2" recalls Cuban string bands like Trio Matamoros (or Septeto Matamoros); another track is titled "Bra Sil." The quintet also released two different versions of the Jamaican mento "Sly Mongoose": "Tin Ka Tin Ka" and "Almer Bou." The tune and its eponymous chicken-stealing protagonist spread through migratory circuits to Harlem, Colombia, and elsewhere. Phil Madison first recorded the song in 1923, but Belasco and Manning produced more popular calypso versions in 1924 and 1925, respectively. Thereafter, it remained a staple for calypsonians. Marson played a version of the tune with new lyrics mocking Hitler and other Nazi leaders on a broadcast during the Blitz in 1940. Bertie King, a former member of the Johnson-Thompson band, recorded a version for Melodisc in London in the late 1950s.[105]

Initially, the West African Rhythm Brothers were a largely percussion-based ensemble led by Campbell on vocals and African drums on loan from London museums, accompanied by Hughes on guitar and occasionally a pianist.[106] The band performed a mixture of reworked adaptations of traditional songs and original compositions in the style of *asíkò* drumming pieces or slower, guitar-led palm-wine music with minor harmonies and plaintive singing. The group's sound was, as Veal observes, "a conscious reaction to . . . the increasing trend toward westernized highlife and ballroom dancing" in West Africa during the war. It was also a response to conditions and trends in the metropole. In London, Hughes explained, "West African students and servicemen were finding themselves increasingly out of touch with their own music as a result of the war. . . . It was to supply this deficiency, to highlight the diversity of the African dance, so much a part of African culture, that the West African Rhythm Brothers was formed." Ade Bashorun, the only professional musician in the group, recalled that band members "were doing the typical African music: we didn't want to follow the Latin style, like Edmundo Ros."[107]

Yet this was not simply a process of indigenization. African musicians' exposure to Afro-Caribbean music and players in London shaped their novel sound, through both their desire to Africanize highlife and their inclusion of Afro-American styles in compositions and performance repertoires that blurred generic and regional distinctions. The Rhythm Brothers crafted, as Wilmer puts it, "a new African music influenced by their experience as migrants" out of the pan–West African forms they carried with them and elements borrowed from black cultures in the Americas.[108] As their sound became more self-consciously "African," it became progressively more diasporic in its influences. When Campbell arrived in Britain, his abilities on the guitar were limited. Bashorun tutored him in their spare time, but Campbell took up the instrument in a serious way only after he began taking lessons from the Trinidadian virtuoso Lauderic Caton, whom he honored as a respected elder and forebear in a Yorùbá ceremony when they met. In the late 1940s, Campbell added two Barbadian horn players, Willy Roachford on reeds and Harry Beckett on trumpet, as well as the Ijo pianist Adam Fiberesima from eastern Nigeria. The band introduced popular calypsos into their sets and developed a more upbeat, danceable style of highlife like that of some contemporaries in West Africa but with a heavier, pulsating rhythm. Describing the band's performance at a WASU fund-raiser in 1954, a correspondent for the *West African Review* wrote, "I must say their music made me quite nostalgic for Nigeria and as I left I heard them playing Fire Fire[;] it reminded me very much of the days when walking in the garden of the Island Club in Lagos I heard Bobby Benson playing the very same wonderful tune."[109] The song that provoked such intense nostalgia in the author, "Fire Fire," was a calypso first popularized in the Caribbean, which later made its way into the repertoires of highlife bands like Benson's. The Rhythm Brothers produced a string of recordings in the 1950s, including multiple versions of "Ominira" ("independence" in Yorùbá), with and without its Caribbean horn section. They contributed to the late-1950s mambo craze in Britain with "Lagos Mambo," as Kitch and Young Tiger produced their own calypso mambos. Buddy Pipp's Highlifers, led by the Ghanaian drummer George Briggars Awoonor-Williams, produced popular recordings of Afro-Cuban music with some of the era's top Afro-Caribbean horn players, while the jazz trumpeter Shake Keane from St. Vincent fronted his own Highlifers band and released a version of "Fire Fire" with the Guyanese pianist Mike McKenzie's All Stars. Hughes left the Rhythm Brothers in the mid-1950s and formed his own combo, the Nigerian Union Rhythm Group (otherwise known as the International Rhythm Band). His Starlite Tempos alternated with Campbell's group at the Abalabi's more upscale successor Club d'Afrique as the house band during the late 1950s and 1960s. As he and his erstwhile collaborator Campbell had done previously, Hughes added Caribbean horn players to the Starlite Tempos, including the trumpeter Dave Wilkins and the Jamaican saxophonist George Tyndale.[110]

These innovative sounds of African London circulated back to West Africa with musicians and on records. Although largely forgotten outside Nigeria until recently, the music that Campbell, Hughes, and their bands produced profoundly influenced younger musicians in Nigeria, inspiring the syncretic music of such luminaries as Julius Oredola Araba, King Sunny Ade, Ebenezer Obey, and Fela Kuti.[111] With its succession of exceptional West African drummers, including the Ghanaian Guy Warren, followed by the Nigerians Sholanke and Johnson, Graham's Afro-Cubists broke new ground in its melding of modern and Latin jazz. An enthusiast of American culture and the American GIs then flowing into Accra, Kpakpo Warren Gamaliel Akwei was recruited as an undercover agent for the United States Office of Strategic Services, changed his name to Guy Warren, and traveled to Lima, Vera Cruz, Key West, and New York in 1943. After he returned to Accra, he worked as a journalist for the *Spectator Daily* and as a jazz disc jockey for the Gold Coast Radio Broadcasting Service, while continuing to serve in the OSS. In 1947, Warren joined the original Tempos band with Joe Kelley and his former bandmate in the Accra Rhythmic Orchestra E. T. Mensah. A fight with a Canadian patron over a racial slur at the European Club, where the group was the house band, cost him his job, and he left for London in 1950. There, he brought African percussion to the Afro-Cubists, played in an all-

Ghanaian band called the Afro-Cuban Eight, and frequented Soho's black clubs. The Afro-Cubists' mixture of Afro-Cuban and African elements inspired the Nigerian saxophonist Chris Ajilo, then a student at the London School of Music, to form his own group, the Cubanos, in Lagos in 1955. Warren returned to West Africa—and briefly, it seems, to Mensah and the Tempos—in 1951 with bongos, conga drums, calypso records. The music writer Mark Ainley suggests, "Most likely he would have thrown in some of Ambrose Campbell's London recordings of calypso highlife." "I went to the Caribbean Club . . . , the haunt of a lot of West Indians," Warren recalled. "It was all calypso every night. When I came back, I brought some of these records and we learnt to play them [the songs] as I knew straightaway that these musical influences were so highlifish." Warren moved to Monrovia, Liberia, soon after his return, formed his own Afro-Cubist ensemble, and introduced listeners there to jazz, Caribbean, and European classical music as assistant director and DJ for the Eternal Love Broadcasting Corporation. Meanwhile, under E. T. Mensah, the Tempos became the era's most popular highlife band, and Bobby Benson mimicked their laid-back orchestration and shuffling beats to develop his own Nigerian variant of dance band highlife. As Mensah later explained, "We evolved a music relying on basic African rhythms. A criss-cross African cultural sound, so to speak." The Tempos' sound incorporated heavy doses of calypso and Afro-Latin music as well. Their signature tune "All For You," which they recorded during the first session for Decca in 1952, took its melody from "Sly Mongoose," and their long list of hits included numerous calypsos and sambas. Mensah traveled to London in 1953 and 1955–1956, where he visited Soho's clubs and played and recorded with Africans and Afro-Caribbeans including, during his second visit, Hughes's West African Swing Stars. The Tempos' calypso highlife was already a hit at the WASU Africa House. Aliyi Ekineh, who came to London in 1946, recalled, "We sang Mensah songs, and every evening we danced, particularly on Saturdays when we invited outsiders."[112]

CODA: BLACK SOUNDINGS

In 1957, Mensah and the Tempos recorded "Ghana Freedom" to mark independence. The musician and ethnomusicologist Steven Feld spent time with Guy Warren, who changed his name again to Kofi Ghanaba after the birth of Ghana, toward the end of his life. Listening to the Tempos' track on the fiftieth anniversary of the country's independence, Ghanaba "highlighted the presence of the maracas and bongos" and "pointed out the horn-lipping vibrato characteristic of the indigenization of brass band music." He also heard "a generous overlay from the Duke Ellington saxophone section sound." "To hear Ghanaba tell it," Feld writes, "Mensah's highlife sounded the independence moment in the deep cosmopolitan jazz transit of Ghana highlife meeting Trinidad calypso via Caribbean London and African American New York." Wilmer notes that one of the Caribbean horn musicians who played with Hughes, the Guyanese trumpeter Rannie Hart, heard a deep affinity between highlife and the idiom with which he was most familiar: "It's just like calypso, only their language." The standard narratives of the arrival of jazz in Britain, of the introduction of Afro-Caribbean styles to West African music, and of decolonization around the black Atlantic elide these histories of listening, circulation, and circular breathing and the regional and imperial crossings of a wider "world a jazz."[113]

Calypsos and the hybrid sounds of Afro-Caribbean, African, and black British artists in London were part of the soundscape of the decade leading to independence in Ghana. Nkrumah's Convention People's Party in the Gold Coast reportedly preordered some 20,000 copies of Young Tiger's "Freedom for Ghana" in 1952. Lord Kitchener produced "Birth of Ghana" in London in 1956; the Sierra Leonean Ali Ganda also recorded a calypso for Melodisc, "Ghana Forward Forever," and Campbell's band, "Good Luck Ghana," commemorating the event. In contrast to the Tempos' "Ghana Freedom," which features bongos and maracas, Kitchener's calypso employed African-style hand drumming and call-and-response patterns reminiscent of asíkò in a small-combo jazz format. Thus, in Feld's words, "the jazzy diasporic intimacy of the highlife-cum-calypso 'Ghana Freedom' sounding in Accra overlap-echoes the calypso-cum-highlife 'Birth of Ghana' sounding Trinidad back to black London." Ganda also produced songs marking Nigerian and Sierra Leonean independence, titled "Nigeria Is Free" and "Freedom, Freedom Sierra Leone." Fellow Sierra Leonean and calypso-highlifer Bliff Radie Byne released a seven-inch record of "Victory for Sierra Leone" and "Independence Merengue" featuring Ivan Chin and His Rhythm Sextet in support. For musicians in West Africa and London, and for many others before them in the 1920s, 1930s, and 1940s, diasporic forms such as jazz, calypso, and other Afro-American styles could articulate African liberation, and highlife could convey connected histories and related struggles embracing a wider black Atlantic.[114]

The circulation of musicians and new media for the transmission of recorded sound linked urban communities in Africa and Afro-America to London and transformed the city's cultural landscape. Encounters between black musicians shaped their personal and compositional politics as well as the development of jazz, calypso, and highlife music in Britain and their ostensible homelands. They produced hybrid styles, performance formats, and compositions that reverberated back into the Atlantic, and many of them understood their experiments at the boundaries of musical idioms as part of the larger political project of black freedom. In melding and juxtaposing material from disparate black musical cultures, black musicians in London traced a history of connections between people of African descent and formed new ones, articulating a black international in sound.

Black musicians from both sides of the Atlantic congregated in the same places and settled in the same areas of the imperial metropolis as did others of African descent. Many amateur and professional musicians participated in black pressure groups, and these organizations regularly publicized the accomplishments of black performers and hosted them. Career musicians, whose wearying schedule limited their political activities, sought out other black musicians, whether from the Caribbean, Africa, North America, or Britain, guided by a sense of unity in struggle and coparticipation in a musical public. The places where these musicians performed provided refuge and rare public spaces for black sociability. Whether in a nightclub, at a WASU dance, or in front of a spinning record, listening and dancing with others of African descent to black artists perform a mixed bag of styles from around the Atlantic contributed an aural and physical dimension to the dream of collective emancipation through black collaboration. In clubs like Jig's, the Nest, and the Caribbean, "the basement of the white metropolis," black struggle and music collided with other marginalized groups and expressions of internationalist politics. These spaces became models for a more egalitarian social order and for equality across ethnic, racial, regional, and class differences, but like the utopian visions and oppositional subject positions they inspired and articulated, these spaces were fragile, susceptible to internal pressures, co-optation, and outside repression.

FIVE

———

Black Masculinities and Interracial Sex at the Heart of the Empire

I ARGUE IN THE FOREGOING CHAPTERS that interaction in London and intellectual and cultural exchange among people of African descent embedded within particular spaces of sociality both mediated and facilitated the movement of news, ideas, texts, and people along intersecting imperial and transatlantic circuits, generating expansive notions of black unity in response to global political developments and a changing imperial system. London, including many of the spaces examined in the preceding chapters, offered new possibilities of self-invention and love across the color line. Private life and social activities became another arena in which black men contested the limits placed on their existence and expressed their anticolonialism, however differently. Sex between black men and white women was far more common in Britain than in the colonies. Interracial relationships varied drastically, from ephemeral liaisons to lasting partnerships, but most male intellectuals, artists, students, and activists from Africa and the Caribbean formed close ties with white women during their time in the city. This chapter considers the intimate as a particularly fraught and highly scrutinized scene of self-fashioning and diasporic formation in the imperial metropolis.[1]

In the wake of the shattering effects of World War I on millions of British men and the simultaneous liberalization of gender roles, sensationalist press coverage and sexualized representations of blackness circulating in transatlantic popular culture fueled anxieties about the potential for and repercussions of "miscegenation." The term *miscegenation* could connote interracial sex, interracial marriage, or the mixed-race offspring of such relationships, but commentators rarely distinguished between these different meanings. In the late nineteenth and early twentieth centuries, Britons usually associated interracial sex with sexual libertinism in the colonies, and subsequent scholars have depicted the colonies as spaces of relative personal freedom for white men, including the freedom to act on nonnormative desires. The Colonial Office took steps to limit interracial relationships in the years before the war, but as long as these liaisons involved sex between white men and "native" women, they reaffirmed the racial order of the empire in the bedroom. The growth of predominately male black populations in urban areas in the British Isles, filliped by wartime arrivals, brought miscegenation and the fears it conjured home to the metropole at a time when the popularity of American cultural imports, many of which were connected to the United States' large black minority, reached new heights. The sexual potency attributed to black men in much of this imagery only exacerbated anxieties over the state of white manhood provoked by the war experience.[2]

These anxieties surfaced in the war's immediate aftermath with the 1919 race riots and the public controversy over France's use of North and West African forces in the occupation of the Rhineland. In both cases, commentators assumed black men's desire, even preference, for lighter-skinned women. In Liverpool, London, and elsewhere, crowds of white rioters targeted mixed-race neighborhoods, looting and terrorizing the homes of black Britons, not only Africans and Afro-Caribbeans but also Arabs and Asians.[3] The following year, writing in Britain's leading leftist newspaper, the *Daily Herald,* the socialist critic of imperialism and secretary of the pacifist Union of Democratic Control, E. D. Morel, who had earlier denounced torture and other atrocities in the Congo under Belgium's King Leopold II, added his voice to the outcry in Germany over the presence of Moroccan and Senegalese troops. In the weeks that followed, women's groups, representing trade unionist, socialist, and feminist constituencies, and publications such as the *Women's Leader* joined the campaign. During his keynote address at a large demonstration organized by the Women's International League for Peace and Freedom on April 27, Morel raised the possibility of "wars of extermination between the two races," spurred by "the militarised African, who has shot and bayoneted white men in Europe, who has had sexual intercourse with white women in Europe." In a statement of support, Reverend John Harris of the Anti-Slavery and Aborigines' Protection Society echoed this warning. Delegates to the 1920 meeting of the Trade Union Congress received copies of Morel's pamphlet *The Horror on the Rhine,* and the Labour Party and Independent Labour Party passed resolutions against the use of African troops in Europe. The Jamaican writer Claude McKay, who spent a little over a year in London after the war, was one of the few to challenge

Morel's paranoid fantasies of black male sexuality. After the *Daily Herald* refused to publish his lengthy letter, it appeared in Sylvia Pankhurst's *Workers' Dreadnought.* "Why," McKay asked, "all this obscene, maniacal outburst about the sex vitality of black men in a proletarian paper?" Years later, he recalled, "My experience of the English convinced me that prejudice against Negroes had become almost congenital among them. I think the Anglo-Saxon mind becomes morbid when it turns on the sex life of colored people." *The Horror on the Rhine,* which went through eight editions by the spring of 1921, and the larger campaign that Morel spearheaded helped establish a pattern in which interracial sex signified as much a political as a moral threat.[4]

Sexuality was the overdetermined context for the negotiation and performance of black masculinity at the heart of the empire. Britons and black migrants alike often conceived of movement between the colonies and the metropole in sexual terms and specifically, given the skewed gender ratio among the latter, in terms of sex between black men and white women. While often minimizing the broader significance of black students' and scholars' intellectual and professional accomplishments as the work of a talented and exceptional minority, when it came to their sexual habits and the threat they posed, white Britons dissected their behavior as indicative of large colonial populations or even their race as a whole. Thus, in London, an awareness of their heightened visibility and presumed representativeness enveloped black intellectuals' intimate relations as much as their political activities. A didactic editorial in *Wásù* cautioned that, as "the real living link between the two peoples," the West African student's "behaviour and particular idiosyncracies; . . . even his reaction to the fair sex; all are meticulously scrutinised by those around him."[5] In this setting, establishing a private life and, however illusory, a sense of interiority as a self-determining, desiring subject became an act of resistance. In an interview with John Gibbs St. Clair Drake, one "Race Leader" enumerated "1. Finding female companionship," "2. Keeping Alive," and "3. Having 'privacy'" as the main goals and biggest challenges of black men in Britain.[6]

Black male intellectuals devoted considerable attention to interracial sex and the issues it raised in public discourse and private conversations.[7] Racial and gender hierarchies of the British Empire inflected relations between blacks and whites in London and the ways observers interpreted them, but competing conceptions of black masculinity and divergent attempts to reconcile the personal and the political developed as much in relation to other black men as to white Britons and their fantasies of black sex. African Americans, Afro-Caribbeans, and West and East Africans often arrived with very different views on sex, monogamy, and how these were related to masculinity, respectability, and anticolonial politics, while most British-born blacks were the product of interracial relationships and grew up in multiethnic enclaves. George Padmore, Ras Makonnen, and Kwame Nkrumah spent years in the United States before moving to London, and a constant stream of African American intellectuals and entertainers passed through the city between the 1920s and 1940s.[8] Men from different parts of the African diaspora discussed variations in racial taxonomies and debated the relative severity of racism in different locales, as well as other obstacles to forging a united front against empire. When considering these questions, the conversation frequently turned to the topic of sex and personal relationships. The prevalence of interracial relationships within the city's small black community surprised African American visitors. The social scientists Ralph Bunche and St. Clair Drake, who visited London during the late 1930s and late 1940s, respectively, were keen observers of the occurrence of and various meanings attributed to variations in sexual behavior and particularly mixed-race couples. Bunche found it "interesting" that Padmore, in his estimation "a pan-Africanist and a racial chauvinist, ignores the [principle] in . . . his choice of [a] woman."[9] While a student at the LSE in the late 1940s, the Trinidadian sociologist Lloyd Braithwaite also began recording the experiences of Caribbean students in Britain, paying careful attention to their personal and sexual relations with white Britons. Dr. Robert Wellesley Cole produced unpublished works dealing with sexuality or "the problem of sex" among "modern Africans," based on his professional expertise as a physician and his many years in black student and intellectual circles in Britain.[10] Makonnen, C. L. R. James, Peter Abrahams, and Nnamdi Azikiwe addressed the topic in their autobiographies, memoirs, and other written accounts of their time in London. Taken as a whole, this scattered archive forms the basis of this chapter. Sexuality—both sexual behavior and discussion of it—was one way to explore the relationship between race, masculinity, and independence and to voice political, regional, class, and other differences. Precisely because its consequences for anticolonial politics remained an open and hotly debated question, it emerged as a particularly charged and volatile arena for the articulation of difference within a putative unity of blackness.

St. Clair Drake traveled to London to conduct research for his doctoral thesis on the black communities in Britain's port cities. He recorded a joke or, more accurately, a humorous anecdote circulating amongst educated Caribbean and African men in 1948. "A case came to the attention of the LCP in which an African stowaway had been arrested for pandering." When the judge presiding over the case asked, "Why do you come here and exploit our women?" the defendant replied "with sullen belligerence, 'You've been exploiting ours for over 300 years!'" Incensed, the judge issued a harsh sentence and had the African man jailed. At this point, the LCP intervened and approached the magistrate. "The League lawyer pointed out that the sentence was not in accord with strict British justice and indicated that really he had been sentenced for both the crime and contempt of court. The judge was contrite and admitted that such sentences would alienate people in the colonies." He agreed to reduce the sentence if the defendant "purge[d] himself of contempt" before the court, but when the league lawyer reported this to the African man, he remained defiant: "You go back and tell that judge that it's worth spending an extra three months in jail just to let him know what was on my mind, and to speak up for my people. An' you tell him, too, that besides it's winter and it's nice and warm in here. And by the way be sure to tell him that my women are working hard and they'll save my money for me and give it to me when I get out." This story, Drake noted, "when told in colored intellectual circles always brought a laugh." The apocryphal tale draws attention in a quite extraordinary manner to the vexed relationship among race, masculinity, and sexuality, between private lives and political struggles, in imperial London.[11]

Drake offered the joke as evidence of black intellectuals' "very ambivalent attitude toward the Negro pimp." "On one hand," he explained, "there was the feeling that such activities were hurting race relations in Britain and occasionally the 'riff-raff from Africa' was bitterly assailed by West Indian intellectuals. On the other hand there was also a tendency to retell jokes about the brazenness of some of the operators, and the tone of the jokes and the effect on the hearers indicated that the intellectuals were getting vicarious pleasure from accounts of these episodes." "The 'riff-raff,'" he added, "were seen as giving the British a dose of their own medicine." In Britain, "the fact that the men are *colonials* and the women members of the 'imperial race' makes every such alliance a potential symbol of 'table turning.'"[12]

Jokes and satire frequently serve (at least) a dual function: furthering group-identity formation and criticizing existing power relations. As Sigmund Freud observed, a joke "represents a rebellion against" authority on a number of fronts and connects the joke teller and audience in a momentary "liberation from the oppression it imposes." It "will allow us to turn to good account those ridiculous features in our enemy that the presence of opposing obstacles would not let us utter aloud or consciously . . . [and] *get around restrictions and open up sources of pleasure that have become inaccessible.*" Or, in Ralph Ellison's evocative words, "Change the joke and slip the yoke." The joke more recently has been taken as a sign of trauma, the interruption of a narrative that cannot be told or an experience that escapes narrative. Jokes are all the more likely to become a vehicle for inaccessible pleasures and subversive desires, or a means to articulate otherwise unspeakable truths, when the internal obstacle of repression is coupled with external strictures and subjugation. For the joke to resonate, the raconteur and audience must have an analogous position vis-à-vis the barriers the joke circumvents—"every joke demands its own audience."[13] Their black skin and the threat of social censure or more punitive consequences for their sexual conduct transcended and, thus, collapsed the differences between black men. In a sense, British discourses of black male sexuality cast even black male professionals and intellectuals in London in the role of the pimp. The African pimp served as a suitable subject of the joke inasmuch as the narrator and audience felt that they shared a certain history, background, quality, or predicament with him.

Jokes simultaneously can delineate the boundaries of the social group and wring pleasure from their inherent instability and permeability. As Dominick LaCapra explains, "*Identity formation might . . . be defined in nonessentialized terms as a problematic attempt to configure and, in certain ways, coordinate subject positions-in-process,*" including "ones not beholden to victimization." According to Lloyd Braithwaite, "the experience of discrimination [alone] did not confer status within the West Indian group." Rather, "it was the reaction to discrimination which brought status. . . . If the act of discrimination had been successfully countered, or some sort of protest registered, the individual in relating his story could present himself as a hero." Our joke follows this narrative arc, but which protest—that of the defendant or that of his advocate from the LCP—was the more effective or laudable? If the representative of British authority (the judge) was the butt of the joke, who was the hero? The LCP member's selfless devotion to black liberation distinguished him from the African pimp's indolent, self-serving behavior and reaffirmed his status as a legitimate representative of the race. The joke about the African pimp condensed and obliquely referenced well-known individuals and scenarios in the imperial metropolis. With each reiteration, the raconteur and audience reaffirmed their investment in this figuration of black masculinity in resistance to colonial oppression and distanced themselves from the figure of the pimp and from certain other black men in the city. Yet the laughter that the story provoked with each retelling among black male intellectuals called this hierarchy of manhood into question—and with it, the particular "fantasy" of individual and collective sovereignty orienting their conduct and politics—at once, staging and drawing surreptitious pleasure from a certain crisis at the level of identity formation.[14] The joke's efficacy and popularity derived from its capacity both to upend extant racial barriers and to register the dissonance internal to London's black community and what Lauren Berlant terms "the estrangement and intimacy of being in relation," "from the unbearable, often unknowable, psychic conflicts that constitute the subject to the social forms of negation that also, but differently, produce subjectivity."[15] Colonial discourses of black sexual excess and British attempts to police black sojourners and migrants glossed the differences between them and conflated their private lives and political activities. Among men of African descent, variations in sexuality became an unstable and contested signifier of divergent political positions and ways of occupying the metropolis.

In their narratives of life in London, black male activist-intellectuals repeatedly mobilized certain tropes, such as the figure of the black pimp, to signal the possibilities for reinvention and heterogeneous performances of black masculinity in the imperial metropolis, as well as to consider the relationship between the latter and anticolonial politics. In his memoirs, South African writer Peter Abrahams described Bah's Club, where "pretty girls and more black men than I had seen in London up to then . . . fraternised." Mr. Bah, the club's owner, "was a tall, thin, elegantly black-suited West African" who nightly made a grand entrance flanked by two white women. Bah had served a stint in prison but rebounded nicely. In addition to his nightclub, "he had a collection of beautiful young women he had set up at various 'good' addresses as 'sex workers' whom he managed," and "owned a stable of racing dogs, one or two racehorses and several fancy cars." Abrahams found Bah's illicit business dealings reprehensible, describing them as an "expression of black racism." On one occasion, he recalled:

> Bah tried to recruit me into his "business" with the promise of big money and any "beautiful gal" I wanted. . . . When I turned him down, Bah had snapped: "What wrong with you? You John Bull nigger?" "No." "Then what?" I shrugged. "This is not right." "They do it to us. They use our women. Been to Lagos?" "Yes." "Accra?" "Yes." "Freetown?" "Yes." "Cape Town?" "Yes. You

been there?" "Me been everywhere. Cape Town, Cairo, everywhere. They do it with our women, so I do it with their women. Only I treat them good. Join me?" "No." "Damn John Bull nigger!"

Abrahams offered his account of Bah to condemn what he perceived as the substitution of one form of exploitation for another. "There is no virtue," he argued, "no goodness in hurting, abusing, degrading someone white because you have been abused, degraded and hurt by someone white."[16] Like his friend Abrahams, Makonnen expressed disdain for this "dubious business." He was concerned particularly about the manner in which some clubs blurred the line between black political activism and sexual commerce. When he entered the restaurant business in Manchester during World War II, Makonnen recalled, "I wanted no part with this image of the Negro club with its bunch of women packing the place from morning to night. I thought too much was at stake. If we were really ambassadors of our people, we should be able to portray our manhood without any regrets."[17] Although some viewed their sojourns in the metropole as, in part, a sexual rite of passage, black activist-intellectuals like Makonnen and Abrahams used the black pimp as a foil against which they differentiated their own projections of black masculinity, relationships with white women, and views on interracial cooperation.

In many cases, sexual relationships and marriages between men from the colonies and British women developed out of friendships and political alliances. The exigencies of daily life informed the reasons that individuals entered into relationships as well as the ways others perceived them. Most people of African descent in Britain, including students and intellectuals, lived a spartan existence straitened by racial barriers to housing, social services, and professional advancement. For many black men, the assistance, affection, and companionship of white women attenuated the effects of lone liness and racism in London. Public personae and political commitments had to be balanced against an austere existence in the metropolis, and with their ambition far outstripping their means, black intellectuals and agitators frequently relied on the financial support of white partners. These relationships, in turn, fueled debate and anxiety over the nature and substance of black masculinity, individuals' professional and class aspirations, and their connection to black liberation. Relations with white Britons became a symbol not only of the pleasures of the metropolis but also of its perils for men of African descent and for the cause of colonial freedom. Many feared that interracial partnerships, like life in London in general, would lead to new forms of dependency, and talk of the corruption of black men by powerful white men and overbearing white women became a means of expressing this concern.

A set of rhetorical tropes recurred in the writings and conversations of black male intellectuals and anticolonial agitators: the black pimp; the homosexual colonial official, the embodiment of a perverse imperial order; and the pragmatic mixed-race partnership, which helped maintain the anti-colonial struggle at the imperial center but threatened the inversion of gender norms and loss of black male autonomy. If these aberrant figures of black male sexuality were not solely the activist-intellectuals' creations, neither were they wholly imposed upon them. Black men referenced them to reflect upon the geography of desire in London, to position themselves within it, and to express political, regional, and class differences within their ranks. At the same time, the reiteration of these tropes registered in condensed form and served to manage the contradictions of daily life and in the recursive process of self-definition within the context of the novel erotic possibilities and entailments of the metropolis. The ideal of the self-sacrificing male activist-intellectual as the agent of black liberation took shape in relation to these figures, on the one hand, and to a feminized Africa, on the other, displacing black women from politics—discursively and at times literally.

SPECTERS OF BLACK MALE SEXUALITY IN THE IMPERIAL METROPOLIS

Britain never instituted antimiscegenation laws—as, for example, South Africa did from 1927—but a profound investment in the racial categories of empire lay beneath its liberal veneer. To most Britons, the bedroom represented, as Bill Schwarz remarks, "the most resonant frontier of all" between colonized and colonizer. During one evening chat, Padmore told Bunche that "Englishman don't want Negroes to fool with their women—even the radicals." The cricketer and, in 1948, president of the LCP, Learie Constantine, said to Drake, "You American boys came over here and saw that they could go around with the girls and thought all was O.K., but where a Yank would have knocked you down and said, 'Leave her alone,' the Englishman keeps quiet and says to himself, 'She's a black man's woman.' She was marked from then on."[18] Antipathy toward interracial sex was widespread and transcended political divisions, inspiring a range of policing strategies and other interventionist measures.

Throughout the interwar period, miscegenation fears continued to focus, as Schwarz explains, on "three imagined figures: the active black man who had stepped out of place, the sexually active woman wittingly or unwittingly courting danger, and the innocent victims of these turbulent liaisons, the children who through no fault of their own . . . belonged nowhere." While many observers insisted that the only white women attracted to black men were prostitutes and social "misfits"—"whether gold diggers bent on taking West Indians for a ride, perverts seeking 'pleasure from physical punishment,'" or simply individuals "indifferent to or without a reputation to maintain"—others, including prominent liberals, socialists, and feminists, depicted them as "innocents in 'mortal danger' who . . . would be 'enticed into becoming prostitutes and then intimidated into remaining so by Coloured men who live off them.'" In either case, most Britons believed interracial sex and the "occasional accidents" (i.e., mixed-race children) were "the sole cause of hostility" toward black men from the colonies. An English professor whom Drake met "maintained stoutly that there was no 'race problem' in England '. . . except for those African students who are always getting the landlady's daughters with babies.'" In the fall of 1948, the British tabloid *News of the World* publicized Patrick Heather's suit against a Nigerian student "for the seduction of his daughter, Norah, who gave birth to twin boys said to have died later." The pair met at a dance, and the student, Heather's attorney charged, seduced her "by representing himself as a lonely African student without friends in an alien country." "Far be it from me to advocate racialism," he concluded, "but no one can blind himself to the fact that there is in us all an innate feeling of race and colour, and whatever way we look at it it is a slur on a white girl and a blow at the racial pride of a white man that a white girl should be seduced by a person of another colour." Although the presiding judge expressed his regret that "what might be an appeal to racial prejudices had been introduced," he implicitly endorsed this view in assessing damages of £700. While in this case "the locale was Dublin," as Drake noted, "the counterpart . . . had occurred in London."[19] Fines and confinement were only two of the punitive actions directed at black men who transgressed the color line; in other instances, the government deported ("repatriated") individuals.[20]

As interracial sex increasingly became a source of concern for the Colonial Office and an array of other interested parties in Britain, outspoken racists and philanthropic do-gooders alike tended to conflate the political challenge to the empire that the black presence in London presented with the possibility of interracial sex and intermarriage. Working under the auspices of the ASAPS before the First World War, Reverend John Harris championed a hostel or residential club for black sojourners to mitigate both. After the war, as head of the Committee for the Welfare of Africans in Europe, he focused its efforts on African students, who, he believed, "pick up all the worst side of our political and social life and return to the Colonies and Dependencies in anything but a helpful spirit." He led a delegation that visited the Home Office in July 1936 to express concern over sexual relationships between black men and white women. Harris proposed the gradual repatriation of black seamen in Britain and suggested that "steps might be found for raising the standard" of their mixed-race offspring "to that of the white races rather than leave them to drift down to that of the black." As Bush remarks, "Control of sexuality thus became an important adjunct to 'empire strengthening.'"[21] Accusations of sexual deviance could have negative repercussions on individuals' career prospects and on black organizations' relations with the Colonial Office, British philanthropic groups, and contacts such as Harris; any support that had been forthcoming for institutions like the WASU hostel and Aggrey House disappeared when either the tone of political discourse or the nature of social intercourse within them seemed to take a more threatening turn.

The WASU House prohibited female visitors after midnight and even unmarried West African women from staying overnight unless the hostel's matron was present, but the popularity of the union's fortnightly dances and other social functions raised suspicion. With the union engaged in a publicity and fund-raising campaign to secure a freehold property, in August 1937, Mr. Mathias of the Colonial Office relayed a recent conversation with Ivor Cummings, the secretary of the trustees of Aggrey House, that "confirmed" his long-standing suspicions. Cummings "told him . . . that two Africans, who had been residing at Aggrey House, recently absented themselves one night" because "they had met two girls, and that as they could not take them to Aggrey House, they had spent the night with them at W.A.S.U." Cummings was the British-born son of a Sierra Leonean physician and a white woman from Yorkshire, and his aspersions against the WASU may have been related to the strained relationship and competition between the WASU and Aggrey House for limited sources of financial support. They also reflected the distance between his moderate reformist stance and the increasingly outspoken and critical position of the union's membership. His accusation precipitated a request for Scotland Yard's assistance. The inspector dispatched to observe the WASU House reported that "African girls had been seen occasionally visiting the Hostel during the daytime, but none was seen at night or in the early morning either entering or leaving. No *white* women had been reported in connection with the Hostel." Disapproval of relationships between black men and white women was so common, he averred, "that if *white* women had been seen there the neighbors would certainly have complained to the police."[22] Nevertheless, the London Metropolitan Police maintained "continuous observation" of the hostel from 10:00 P.M. to 12:30 A.M. through the weekend. A total of twenty-nine white women visited the hostel during the following three nights—twelve, three, and fourteen, respectively—"all of whom then exited the premises by midnight." The police inspector also noted the popularity of the WASU's regular dances: "I was informed by a Borough Council employee that anyone could gain access to the dancing on payment of 6d on the door."[23] If confirmed, Cummings's accusation would have undermined the WASU's tenuous relationship with Reverend Harris, whose endorsement of their fund-raising campaign to purchase a permanent home was crucial to its success. The preponderance of white women among visitors to the hostel, especially for the WASU's dances, continued to concern colonial officials in the months ahead. Accusations of sexual impropriety and complaints about conditions at the hostel reaffirmed officials' suspicions regarding the disreputable management of the WASU hostel and, by extension, the inadvisability of self-government in West Africa. One member of the Colonial Office reported, "I paid a visit to the hostel about a month ago. It was in a disgustingly dirty condition.... I am aware that they have little money at their disposal but they might make an effort to make the place look respectable." Another official underlined these last words and scribbled "even if it isn't!" in the margin.[24] While the WASU celebrated its headquarters and hostel as the product of African initiative and interracial cooperation, colonial officials disparaged it as the instantiation of African backwardness and sexual wantonness.

A short time after this episode, Aggrey House became embroiled in a public sex scandal that culminated on May 3, 1940, in its closure for a time and the expulsion of its most radical members. To the chagrin of Cummings, the board of trustees (chaired by Mr. Fletcher of the Friends' Society), and former supporters of the initiative such as Hanns Vischer and Dr. Harold Moody, Aggrey House had become an unofficial headquarters for a small cadre of African and Caribbean men with communist ties, including Peter Blackman and Desmond Buckle, who dominated the Aggrey House committee.[25] The Colonial Office issued a statement to the Ministry of Information that outlined its version of the events leading to the rift between the trustees and the committee. "One of the students," the statement alleged, "introduced a prostitute [originally 'woman'] into the Club House and was requested to resign his membership." When the individual in question appealed to have his membership reinstated, the Aggrey House committee endorsed the request, but the trustees refused to allow it, considering "the matter to be serious and symptomatic of the generally unhelpful attitude of the House Committee." "No doubt," the missive continued, "the members of the House Committee ... will probably emphasize the political rather than the moral issue," but "the point on which the conflict has come to a head is ... not in the field of politics, although the trustees are very worried about that."[26] Anticipating the circulation of "incorrect versions" of the dispute beyond the metropole, officials sent letters to the governors of Britain's colonies in West Africa and the Caribbean. "Certain members of the House Committee of Aggrey House ... have in the opinion of the Trustees introduced an undesirable political and social tone into the Club House. The Trustees have not felt able to take any action on these grounds, but recently the House Committee, who are all Africans or men of African descent, came into open conflict with the Trustees in connection with the expulsion of a student member on the grounds that he introduced a prostitute into the Club House."[27] In early May, the conservative *Evening Standard* reported the story under the headline "'Moral Issue' Closes Club." The communist *Daily Worker*, however, claimed "that the real purpose is to make way for an organisation which will be semi-official and will regulate the selection of students who come to Britain, also keeping a close watch on them in this country." Moody suggested that the trustees cede control to the LCP. In the end, the board of trustees and, behind the scenes, the Colonial Office used the dispute to expel the radicals on the committee. In late July 1940, the Colonial Office liaison for colonial students, J. L. Keith, reported that the trustees, facing the threat of legal action, had decided to return the members' subscriptions and intended to reopen Aggrey House, but only on the condition of "excluding those who have caused the recent trouble."[28] Colonial officials consistently conflated the reputed deviant sexuality and "subversive" tendencies of these black men in vague references to the "undesirable political and social tone" at Aggrey House, only to assert that the dispute centered on a moral issue. In

the mid-1940s, as a metropolitan expression of the turn to colonial development, a system of the British Council hostels and the Colonial Office
Advisory Committee on the Welfare of Colonial Peoples in the United
Kingdom superseded Aggrey House, once the model for the strategy of indirect rule vis-à-vis colonial students in Britain.

In the imperial metropolis, the questions of where, how, and with whom
black men from the colonies socialized and had sexual relations were always
political. As Stoler argues, discourses of colonial sexuality "were productive
of class and racial power, not mere reflections of them," linking "subversion
to perversion, racial purity to conjugal white endogamy, and thus colonial
politics to the management of sex."[29] London offered more opportunities for
black men from the colonies to form interracial personal relationships and to
engage in transcolonial agitation, heightening the need to contain both. For
colonial officials, missionaries, and other Britons engaged in race relations
work, accusations of sexual impropriety registered their anxiety about the
limits of their influence and control over colonial subjects as black men
moved across the empire and from colony to metropole, while, they claimed,
demonstrating the necessity of their interventions.

Many Africans and Caribbeans perceived more behind white Britons'
interest in their cause than progressive politics or benevolent intentions,
whether these parties were British politicians or feminist and leftist allies.
Makonnen linked the tendency among some black men to view sex with a
white woman as an inherently transgressive act to the fetishization of black
male bodies. He characterized the latter as an intrinsic part of the racial order
of a global imperial system, calling it "social sex imperialism," and suggested
that many Britons' interest in colonial issues remained limited to "this fascination with black sex." Drake noted that "observers of both races are apt to
make cynical statements of the following sort: 'Those women just hang
around WASU and the Caribbean Club to find themselves a colored man,'
or 'Race relations work is just a cover-up. They're all after something else,' or
'That whole crowd is rotten!'" A "very prominent West Indian male, who
spent much of his time in race relations activity," showed Drake a letter from
a white man and commented, "I usually destroy this man's letters. He's one
of these white men who gets a lot of pleasure out of this business (i.e. race
relations activity)." The letter's recipient "went on to name a number of
prominent Englishmen in the fields of public affairs and letters whom he
claimed 'like colored women'" and "one very prominent individual" who
made a habit of visiting "Soho and the East End where there are pretty half

caste women so he could pinch them on the behind and get a sensation out of it." The existence of various forms of white patronage—and the fact that both individuals and black pressure groups often depended on them—exacerbated black intellectuals' suspicions that "perversion" motivated even their white friends and allies.[30]

The sexual behavior of black men was neither limited to nor discussed solely in connection with heterosex. As discussed in chapter 4, Soho's nightclubs served as outposts for sexual nonconformists as well as the city's black denizens. Same-sex relationships undoubtedly developed between black and white men in Britain, though their prevalence is impossible to ascertain today. For known or suspected homosexuals such as the African American singer John Payne or the Barbadian Dr. Cecil Belfield Clarke, sexual orientation was not a barrier to participation in black organizations and movements. Clarke practiced medicine in Southwark for nearly fifty years between the 1920s and 1960s, caring for many of London's black residents. He was a supporter of the WASU and a founding member of the LCP. During his family's stay in London, Bunche's young daughter fell ill, and Kenyatta referred him to Clarke. When Abrahams arrived in London in 1940, Padmore was recovering from throat surgery to remedy an ailment that nearly cost him his voice. Clarke either conducted the surgery or referred Padmore to a trustworthy colleague, and oversaw his recovery after the operation.[31]

Some white observers claimed that blacks had a predilection for homosexual behavior. A twenty-three-year-old subwarden at an international students' club in London who responded to Mass Observation's 1939 questionnaire on "Race" described black men as "friendly, intelligent, with their great failing, in many, being women and often . . . homosexuality, a failing which is very much encouraged and pandered to by the sort of white women they meet."[32] By contrast, some students and intellectuals from the colonies complained that white men sought out black men as lovers and offered assistance with the expectation of sex in return. "Certain important public officials," Drake noted, "were constantly accused of 'having their colored boys,' and one was belabored continuously on the charge of giving his highest favors to likely young African students." He heard similar stories from a few whites involved in race relations activity. He "was quite surprised" when a "prominent British church woman exclaim[ed] bitterly, 'We convert these boys out in Africa and try to teach them how to be Christian gentlemen and then they come over here and find that the best way to get what they want is to climb into some government official's bed!'" Among black male intellectuals, rumors about rampant homosexuality within the upper echelons of British society coalesced in the myth of a "homosexual clique" within the Colonial Office and British government. Many of the black men whom Drake met insisted "that no colored man could get ahead unless he were inducted into it."[33]

Afro-Caribbean and African men deployed the trope of the homosexual clique to critique the empire's racial hierarchy. Drake concluded that the "facts of the matter are not important for sociological analysis upon one level, for this 'myth of the homosexual clique' whether there was one or not served to explain ... events about which the gossipers could not secure complete factual knowledge, and also acted as vehicle for discharging some rather deep seated hostilities toward the government agency in question."[34] Yet, as with the joke about the African pimp, black men wielded the myth not only to voice their frustrations and to highlight the contradiction between the British rhetoric of fair play and their personal experiences, but also to question the motives and behavior of some of their peers and to differentiate resistance to from complicity with the imperial status quo.

By the 1950s, both the black pimp and the myth of the homosexual clique were well-established devices for representing the growing black presence in and sexual countercultures of the metropolis.[35] Returning from Europe to London after World War II, the writer Colin MacInnes became a habitué of the haunts of people of African descent. He developed a love of jazz and African music as well as close personal ties to black artists and intellectuals, and cruised Soho's clubs "for sexual liaisons with Caribbean men." The first two novels of his London Trilogy, *City of Spades* (1957) and *Absolute Beginners* (1959), revolve around these subterranean clubs, and the black subcultures of which they were a part, in the postwar metropolis. The Trinidadian photographer and filmmaker Horace Ové recalled MacInnes as "the first white to speak honestly to blacks, as an equal," but others were more measured in their appraisal of his racial politics. "Though he fought courageously for their rights," Daniel Farson noted, "he could be as condescending to the black people he befriended as the worst type of English colonial bigot." Francis Wyndham suggested that MacInnes's interest in Africans and Afro-Caribbeans was largely "anthropological," reflecting a tendency to look "at people, not individualistically, but as representative of this or that." In sum, as John McLeod explains, MacInnes "discovered in popular cultural activity in postwar London the potential for envisaging social change in the city ... [and] a way of contesting prejudice and violence," but "there was another side to MacInnes's benign interest in black men which tended towards negrophilia, regarding them as either sexual objects or noble savages."

MacInnes's fiction replicates the contradictions of his personal life and politics. In *City of Spades,* he consistently locates the utopian potential for a new social order—and, paradoxically, forecloses that possibility—through interracial sex. The young white homosexual Alfy Bongo frequents the city's black clubs and openly declares not only his preference for black men but also his desire to *be* black. Black pimping, rich and influential white men lusting after black men, and the courtroom converge late in the novel when the white prostitute Dorothy files fraudulent pandering charges against the West African Johnny Fortune. Despite MacInnes's candid portrait of white racism and fantasies of black sexuality, in the end, not only does *City of Spades* represent true interracial love as impossible, but the white characters attribute the hopelessness of such relationships to the innate qualities of African men who do not "understand" love in the European sense. MacInnes and other bohemian writers in Britain helped popularize the word *ponce* as a synonym for pimp, but in the decades that followed, the term came to refer also to effeminate men and homosexuals, blurring the line between these forms of illicit sexuality. Like so much else in (post)imperial British culture, the slang expression indexed the spectral presence of black male bodies as desiring subjects and objects of desire, alternately exploiting and exploited by degraded specimens of white femininity and masculinity.[36]

AMONG BLACK MEN

The ambivalence manifested in the joke about the African pimp extended to real-life individuals who seized the potential for reinvention and profit from Britons' growing fascination with commercialized representations of blackness. Ras Prince Monolulu was arguably London's most recognizable black resident from the 1920s until his death in 1965. As Stephen Bourne notes, "Monolulu, [the pianist and singer] Leslie 'Hutch' Hutchinson and Paul Robeson were among the most famous black men in Britain." Joseph Appiah recalled that "Prince Monolulu was truly the darling of all Britain and the friend of the great." Two different sets of tobacco trading cards issued in 1938 featured the famous "Abyssinian" racetrack tipster in his colorful silk robes, embroidered waistcoat, breeches, and crown of red, white, and blue feathers. From the 1930s onward, nearly every British film with a horse-racing scene—

some ten in all—featured Monolulu playing himself, and in 1936, he became the first black man to appear on British television. He kept company with the rich and the poor, conservatives and socialists, and regaled crowds at Speaker's Corner in Hyde Park with his unique mix of low comedy and anticolonial politics every Sunday for decades. Bunche heard him speak "in all his glory and plumage" at the Labour Party's May Day demonstration in 1937. He was a visible presence at multiple coronations, and the staunchly conservative Lord Derby mentored him in the equestrian arts. "All Britain was touched," Appiah recalled, "when British Television showed the prince, for a change, dressed in tails and top hat, majestically marching" in Derby's funeral procession in 1948. Val Wilmer recalled the spectacle of Monolulu "busking [for] cinema queues" in Piccadilly as "part of the general panorama of streetlife" in the metropolis.[37]

Born Peter Carl McKay on the island of St. Croix, Monolulu migrated to Britain in 1902. He moved from one menial-labor job to the next for a year before landing a spot in the chorus of *In Dahomey,* the first all-black musical staged in the West End. After the show closed, Monolulu traveled in Europe as an itinerant entertainer, "eating fire in a travelling circus, working in Germany as a model and boxing in France, pretending to be an opera singer in Russia, and becoming a fortune-teller in Italy." He spent much of World War I in a German internment camp outside Berlin. He returned to London afterward and began working with an Irish tipster. As he learned the trade, he also developed his own unique style, adapting elements from black and minstrel stage performers and borrowing his signature refrain, "I gotta horse," from a soapbox evangelical. Monolulu peddled his tips at the track and from his stall in the East End's bustling Petticoat Lane market. In 1920, he reputedly won £8,000 on an unheralded horse at the Derby, but his success and popularity were due more to his carefully crafted exotic image than his ability to pick winners. In the 1930s, Regal-Zonophone released a live recording of a typical monologue in which Monolulu repeatedly contrasted the characteristics of blacks and whites, including their sexual and marriage practices, to differentiate himself from white competitors and sportswriters. One of Monolulu's circulars from the late 1940s featured a satirical poem that concluded:

> Punters always study form
> The Bookie takes the money?
> Black man for Luck,
> White man for Pluck.

Monolulu was also renowned and, at times, fined for his jokes at Speakers' Corner. "He knew the rules of the Corner relating to dirty jokes," Appiah explained, "and yet, occasionally, when his funds were low, he would invite arrest by telling an unadorned dirty joke." As a matter of course, the court gave Monolulu a minor fine, but "all his friends, great and small, would send in their contributions which, in the end, always exceeded the fine by one hundred pounds at the minimum." The press unknowingly acted as his accomplice in this profitable scheme by reporting his arrests.[38]

Monolulu's success spawned a number of imitators. In the early 1930s, the Sierra Leonean Ernest Marke survived on earnings from gambling and various graft schemes. He remembered, "There used to be quite a number of coloured men . . . grafting the markets and race courses." Both the Jamaican Big Morris and the Nigerian Peter Jackson (aka Prince Zalemka) mimicked the style of his "old pal the great Prince Monolulu." Morris "dressed exactly like Monolulu" and "copied every item" of his costume, "even the horse shoe around his neck and the 'I got an 'orse' cry." Marke also remembered "Professor E. B. Knight, the great Abyssinian herbalist," who was actually from Demerara. Although he "had never been in any part of Africa," when "he wasn't immaculately dressed in Western clothes he was dressed in expensive African robes; that was part of his gimmick." According to Marke, Knight believed "he never would have been half as successful if the public had known that he was from the Western World . . . he had to present himself as a son of nature." In neither notoriety nor longevity did any of these "characters" approach Monolulu, who reinvented himself as an Ethiopian prince against the backdrop of the Italian invasion of the African nation.[39]

In the imperial metropolis, even the most absurd and puerile racial stereotypes could be appropriated for alternative purposes. London's self-anointed "Ethiopian" prince made his living and fame through a highly stylized self-presentation that simultaneously exploited and catered to British racial fantasies. Monolulu's performances at the track and in Hyde Park blended politics, humor, and what the anthropologist Ulf Hannerz terms "streetcorner mythmaking." Aside from personal profit, Appiah believed that he used entertainment and even bawdy racial caricatures to "subtly educate his ever-growing [British] audience on the evils of race-baiting."[40] Few, if any, blurred the line between "race work" and self-aggrandizement to such an extent as Monolulu.

Despite many black intellectuals' professed embarrassment at his antics, Monolulu was a regular presence in their circles. He appeared alongside

James, Ashwood Garvey, Chris Braithwaite, and Arnold Ward at an International African Friends of Ethiopia rally in Trafalgar Square on August 25, 1935, waving an Ethiopian flag and the Union Jack before the crowd of onlookers. A month later, he was arrested at an IAFE demonstration in Hyde Park "for using indecent expressions." Nearly all of the sojourners and migrants who produced memoirs or other written accounts of their time in London mentioned him, and those who lived in London invariably recommended that newcomers and visiting sightseers pay a visit to his soapbox in Hyde Park. According to Appiah, Monolulu "remained for years the capital adornment and attraction in that famous corner of London." He credited the "old Maestro" with introducing him to the Sunday crowds in Hyde Park. Monolulu lent "me his soapbox and his vast audience for a few hours each Sunday, so that I might put the case for colonial freedom. . . . He would gather the crowd and an hour later he would introduce me as a little brother with a special message." Bunche first encountered Monolulu while strolling through the park on Easter Sunday 1937. In his diary, he noted the presence of "a miserable looking anti-Semite and Fascist" among the "soapboxers" as well as a "wooly haired, loudly ornamented, but witty and highly entertaining blackamoor," who he later learned was Monolulu. When Bunche and his wife, Ruth, hosted a group of Africans and Caribbeans for tea a month later, Padmore "tickled" them with his description of Monolulu and promised to take Ralph to see him and Marcus Garvey at Speaker's Corner. In February 1948, Drake met him while working alone in the office of the LCP. Even before this encounter, the organization's general secretary, the Trinidadian Dr. M. E. Joseph-Mitchell, had expressed "how embarrassed he was at one of the [LCP's] dances when the Prince had been present, 'acting like a clown.'" Monolulu, Mitchell told Drake, "claims to be an Ethiopian, although everybody knows that darky was born in the West Indies. And that costume of his is more like the Red Indians than any Ethiopian's." Mitchell's public distancing of himself from Monolulu masked a deep familiarity and history of collaboration, even a certain begrudging respect.[41]

Like most men of African descent in London, Monolulu spent much of his life in the company of white women, and in 1931, he married the actress Nellie Adkins. But, befitting his public personae, he was more audacious and outspoken than most of his contemporaries on the topic. "There is some tendency for lower-class Negroes," Drake noted, "to justify both pimping and mistreatment of white women on the grounds that colored men are only 'paying the white man back.'" He recounted one instance in which Monolulu

FIGURE 11. Prince Monolulu and his wife, actress Nellie Adkins (August 21, 1931). Photograph by George Woodbine for the *Daily Herald*. Reproduced with permission of Science and Society Picture Library.

"made [this point] explicit publicly." When a female employee of a hostel for African students took a new arrival from Kenya to Speaker's Corner, they stopped to hear the famed prince. The latter soon noticed the young African in the crowd, and "said, very loudly, 'You in Englishman's country now. He's been exploiting you back home. You exploit him now. Exploit him, I say! Exploit *his women!*'" The flabbergasted student "hastily left the park leaving the woman there." During their initial meeting at the LCP's office, Monolulu shared his views on race relations in London with Drake. "After a forty-five minute conversation with the Prince," the latter believed "it was quite understandable why middle-class Negroes considered him something of an embarrassment." He described Monolulu as "a raconteur of very smutty jokes told with words of Anglo-Saxon brevity and bluntness." Yet, if younger, respectable professionals like Mitchell, who was a lawyer, viewed Monolulu with disgust, the prince was also keen to distinguish himself from them. "His ribald interpretation of race relations was essentially a theory that his generation of colored men living in London had existed by virtue of their alliances with white women and their orthodox sexual virtuosity." By contrast, "the present generation which he professed not to understand, existed with equal ease by alliances with both men and women and by their proficiency at various forms of unorthodox sexual behavior." Before Drake left the office, Monolulu extended an "invitation to visit him in Soho and really learn something about race relations in Britain."[42] What Drake and Mitchell perceived as effects of class difference, Monolulu interpreted as a generational shift, but all of them read sexual behavior as an indication of the differences within their ranks.

Shared oppression and a commitment to black liberation brought together black men with disparate backgrounds, beliefs, and personal circumstances. They incessantly debated the relationship between masculinity, sex, and politics, sometimes in print but more commonly during private conversations in their homes and other spaces of black male sociability. Monolulu used two recurring constructions of black male sexuality—those who exploited ties with white women and those who allowed themselves to be exploited by whites (male and female)—to differentiate among black men in London. Such distinctions, however, often proved difficult to maintain in the face of everyday realities, and both those who celebrated sexual libertinism and those who disavowed it reaffirmed the equation of resistance to racism and empire with autonomous heterosexual masculinity.

Many student sojourners from Africa and the Caribbean associated the metropole not only with educational and professional advancement but also with the possibility of marrying or having sex with white women. Since intermarriage between whites and people of African descent remained rare in the colonial Caribbean, Braithwaite noted, "to many a student, this was ... the symbol and badge of success," and Drake observed that, among "West Indians particularly, it was not [at] all uncommon for a student to, as it was sometimes phrased, 'take home him [*sic*] certificate and English wife as evidence that he had completed his education.'" While some students hoped to fall in love and marry, "a good many more were opposed to it but were anxious to have English girlfriends," some, according to Braithwaite, adopting "as their slogan 'Love them and leave' and another, the more virulent 'None shall escape.'" In the metropole, "intimate relations became almost a revolutionary act, a form of personal self-assertion," that encouraged "a split between tenderness and sex in some." Makonnen also noted that many black and Indian students "felt it was a revolutionary act to get their own back on Europe by seducing white women." "I had to speak about this in Hyde Park

FIGURE 12. Prince Monolulu with British seaman in drag on board the RMS *Queen Mary* (1954). "Prince Monolulu and the Bride," unknown photographer. Southampton City Archives (OH/MAR 1066).

once," he remembered, "and attack these apparently intelligent students who felt that by getting a bastard child they could solve the problem of imperialism." Both Braithwaite and James suggested that this mentality was a by-product of the colonial experience. As James wrote, "Take a boy of eighteen, a coloured boy living in the colonies, where the social question is what we know it is," and "drop him in London . . . at a critical age . . . when he is apt to believe that sex and a woman are one and the same thing. . . . It is not surprising that some of the boys get spoilt." Both African and Caribbean men also claimed that white women were generally more "permissive" and felt they could be more sexually adventurous with them. Afro-Caribbeans, in particular, tended to believe that sex with women from the Caribbean, by contrast, led inevitably to marriage. Some men engaged in ephemeral relations, often with working-class women, while having a steadier relationship with a middle-class woman, whether black or white. One Afro-Caribbean man whom Braithwaite knew "solved the problem" by having two girlfriends, "an English girl with whom he slept" and a Caribbean woman with whom he sustained a more platonic and public relationship.[43]

For many, sexual relations with white women, if not a "revolutionary act," instantiated the possibilities for experimentation and reinvention in the imperial metropolis, and an ongoing revision of self-presentation, borrowing from and mixing heterogeneous cultural elements and images of blackness, accompanied the political activities of African and Afro-Caribbean men. Jomo Kenyatta was unapologetic about having multiple sexual partners and "had a disarming openness about these relationships." He believed that African men were predisposed by their culture to practice polygamy and frequently exclaimed as much. As Murray-Brown puts it, "He was an African; the monogamy of the West was an interesting anthropological phenomenon, no more." Like most of his peers, Kenyatta had few close friends among British men, who, he thought, "found it hard to feel real affection for such a person," but he "had a special appeal" with white women. After a visit with his former pupil in Kenya, then known as Johnstone Kenyatta, in September 1929, the Africa secretary of the Church Missionary Society, Handley Hooper, relayed his concerns to Gideon Mugo of Kikuyu Central Association (KCA). Although Kenyatta had been in London for only a few months, Hooper believed that life in the metropolis had undone the Christian morals and humility inculcated by the missions. He had forgotten how "unimportant" he was as a "mission boy" and how "infinitesimal" the concerns of the Kikuyu were within the British Empire, and "spent money on clothes for himself and for a young prostitute who lived with him." Significantly, Hooper penned these words while Kenyatta was in Moscow, and he linked the latter's perverse behavior and arrogance to his new political contacts. Arthur Ruffell Barlow, who had known Kenyatta for nearly twenty years through the Church of Scotland Mission, also noted with surprise his remarkable transformation. Many of the photographs adorning his room in Victoria were of female acquaintances whom he referred to as "interpreters and guides." Barlow described them as "middle-aged, serious looking, plain and intellectuals," not prostitutes as Hooper had suggested.[44]

Kenyatta's was a life of near-constant transformation and reinvention. His example illustrates the complex negotiations involved in the "cultivation of the individual self" in conjunction with movement across colonial spaces. Orphaned as boy around the age of ten, Kenyatta imbibed the lessons of his paternal grandfather, a Kikuyu healer, before going to live at the Church of Scotland Mission in Nairobi at sixteen. In the bustling city, he began working in a photographer's studio, donning "neat Western garb" that, as Carolyn Martin Shaw points out, was "a far cry from the leopard skin he wears on the cover of *Facing Mount Kenya*." Gradually, as his biographer Murray-Brown observes, "the raffish character in safari outfit gave way to a family man in plus-fours and sun helmet, for all the world one of the tweedy sort at the local golf club." He became increasingly involved in anticolonial politics and, in 1929, traveled to London to submit a petition for the KCA. Soon after the filming of *Sanders of the River*, Kenyatta turned a leg injury that forced him to use a cane into an opportunity to embody the role of the author of *Facing Mount Kenya*. Bunche deemed him "something of an exhibitionist" after seeing him "walking around town with an African spear as a cane."[45] During his sixteen years in Britain, Kenyatta revised the stylish dandyism of his youth to cultivate a self-image as an "authentic [African] native" for his white interlocutors and black friends and coconspirators.[46]

Kenyatta was hardly alone in refashioning himself abroad or in his close attention to his self-presentation among his close interlocutors and fellow travelers. Malcolm Nurse became George Padmore when he entered the international communist movement in the United States, and, like Monolulu, Thomas Griffiths donned the Ethiopian honorific title and became T. Ras Makonnen after Italy invaded Ethiopia. On first meeting Makonnen, Bunche described him as "theatrical," noting that he represented "himself as Abyssinian" and sported a goatee in homage to Du Bois, whom he admired greatly.[47] James and the other Afro-Caribbeans in the IASB "styled" themselves international "Africans." Francis Nkrumah reverted to his day name Kwame during his years outside the Gold Coast. Reinvention of the self was inseparable from the elaboration of black internationalism and of efforts "*to configure and . . . coordinate subject positions-in-process.*"[48] In the 1930s and 1940s, as Hazel Carby observes, "a number of male intellectuals, both black and white, created a historical discourse of black manhood in the service of a revolutionary politics."[49] The unease that Monolulu's presence in their midst provoked in many black intellectuals derived at least in part from the way in which his antics not only profited from racial stereotypes but also highlighted the central role of artifice more generally in fashioning political subjectivities.

In describing the prevalence and severity of racism in London, male sojourners and migrants frequently distinguished between white men and women, depicting the latter as more accepting and sympathetic to their plight, and many black activists considered white women on the left to be markedly more radical than their male counterparts, who often altered or abandoned their critical stance in moments of crisis.[50] According to Braithwaite, "Both working class men as well as students claimed that life would have been intolerable without the sympathetic attitude of the women." In a letter to the *Times* responding to reader correspondence linking the violence in 1919 to white men's "instinctive" revulsion to relationships between black men and white women, the general secretary of the Society of Peoples of African Origin, Felix Hercules, wrote: "All honour to broadminded Englishwomen who can see behind the skin and behind the superficial differences and recognise the man inside." Some credited their white female companions with acts of genuine courage, even at the risk of endangering themselves. "I was saved many many times by women," Marke recalled. "A lot of women used to wear clogs in those days, and they took off their clogs [to beat the men] and started shouting 'leave him alone! He hasn't done any harm!'" "Looking back," Abrahams wrote, Padmore "always got on better with the women of the Communist Party than with the men" and "had a higher regard and healthier respect for the women of the 'movement' than any other Marxist, black or white, I have met." Appiah also acknowledged the litany of ways that British women aided black men and burgeoning anticolonial movements: "To the women of Britain, in particular, we owe a special debt of gratitude for their clerical help, their comforting words of hope in times of frustration and despair and, above all, their love and human affection so freely given, often in the face of opposition from families, friends and workmates." "This recognition was manifestly demonstrated," he recalled, "when in 1945 the West African Students' Union . . . unanimously resolved: 'That at independence of each of our countries of West Africa, two monuments in gold be raised to the eternal honor and memory of (a) the white women of Europe, for making our stay in Europe possible and (b) the Almighty Mosquito, for saving our lands from the settlement of colonial usurpers'!"[51]

White women were at the forefront of the British campaigns in defense of the Scottsboro Boys and Ethiopia, and women such as Nancy Cunard, Sylvia Pankhurst, Dinah Stock, Mary Downes, and Ethel Mannin contributed labor and essential financial assistance to London-based black pressure groups and the men who led them. Downes helped Wallace-Johnson manage the affairs of the International African Service Bureau and edit its first journal, *African Sentinel*. Bunche attended a "garden fête" to raise money for Ethiopian refugees, where he met Downes, her sister Mrs. Palmer, Mrs. Napier of the Friends of Abyssinia, and Pankhurst; he made no mention of white men participating in the event, if, indeed, there were any. Makonnen recalled, "Our contacts with white girls were invaluable" to the activities of the Pan-African Federation and its journal, *Pan-Africa,* in the 1940s. "We didn't have to seek them out either," he added. "They would hear us addressing meetings at Trafalgar Square or in some of the London halls, and they'd come round and ask if there was anything to be done" and "were quite prepared to steal the stencils and other materials from their offices." A small group of white women also handled the correspondence and daily affairs of Nkrumah's West African National Secretariat alongside O. Alakija Renner. Nkrumah wrote, "These girls—most of them of good class families—used to come and type for hours on end in the evenings and they never asked a single penny for their work." Isabel and William McGregor Ross, the latter the author of the short book *Kenya from Within* (1927) and former director of public works in the colony, introduced Kenyatta to the Hampstead leftist set and organizations such as the Union of Democratic Control, through which he met Dorothy Woodman. After meeting Dinah Stock at a rally in May 1937, Kenyatta moved into a room in her flat at 15 Cranleigh Buildings near Euston Station, the same row of homes where Padmore and his partner Dorothy Pizer lived. Stock edited Kenyatta's *Facing Mount Kenya* and helped him get speaking jobs with the Workers' Educational Association, Independent Labour Party, and Rotary Club. As Kenyatta's biographer explains, she "accepted absolutely his position and made no attempt . . . to see that he conformed to the white liberal's concept of ordered, constitutional development." Stock was also the secretary of the British Centre Against Imperialism and editor of the *Socialist Review,* and after World War II, she organized the activities of the Pan-African Federation in London and served as managing editor of *Pan-Africa.* Some women viewed these activities as an extension of their commitment to feminism or socialism, or both. Staunchly independent in her views, Isabel McGregor Ross was an ardent feminist and committed activist. Cunard was a famous iconoclast and negrophile who had ties to black radicals on both sides of the Atlantic; and Pizer, a London-born Jewish socialist. Reflecting on the guiding convictions of Cunard and Stock, Makonnen wrote, "We recognized naturally that the dedication of some of these girls to our cause was an expression of equal rights for women. One way of rejecting the oppression of men was to associate with blacks. . . . But many of them were viciously attacked for this."[52]

Black men readily admitted that "alliances" with white Britons, especially white women, could be both pleasurable and useful—and, some even claimed, necessary to survival in London. Yet, if many believed that white women were less prejudiced than their male counterparts, sexual attraction and racism were hardly mutually exclusive. Braithwaite claimed that certain Caribbean students "love[d] to relate stories" of seducing women who showed signs of racial prejudice as a means of "rejecting the rejection through the 'humiliation' of sexual experience."[53] Although some black men exploited "the belief in the generally greater potency of the Negro," and even suggested that the "sexual performance" of British men was "psychologically and physically" inadequate, others felt trapped, sometimes quite literally, by European discourses of black male anatomy and sexuality. One evening during Bunche's stay in London, Peter Mbiyu Koinange described the predicament of one of their African friends. Two English sisters, Bunche wrote in his diary, "moved in on him and refuse to leave. He has to sleep with both of 'em."[54] Moreover, relationships to white lovers and assistants in anticolonial propagandizing, who were sometimes sources of housing and sustenance, fueled anxieties and debate over whether intimate ties conflicted with a political commitment to subjected homelands, a connection that black men frequently represented as a heterosexual union. Were interracial relationships an assertion of racial equality and an exercise of manly independence, even an inversion of impe-rialist racial hierarchies, or did they ultimately reproduce the colonial order? At what point did black men's relations with white women become a form of decadence or exploitation? Some feared that overreliance on white women transformed black revolutionaries into ineffectual dependents. That many had a girlfriend, fiancée, or wife whom they left behind when they moved abroad raised further questions about the connection between interracial sex, masculinity, and politics. Padmore, for example, left behind a middle-class, Afro-Trinidadian wife and their daughter when he embarked on a career as revolutionary tactician and anticolonial agitator. Kenyatta had a Kenyan wife when he came to Britain, and in the early 1940s, he married an English woman, Edna Clarke, who bore him a son. After returning to Kenya, he married twice more. While sojourners and migrants formed new ties over-seas, other relations fell by the wayside; those who eventually returned home or proceeded elsewhere from Britain frequently left partners behind (yet again). The rhetoric embraced by some black male agitators of manly sacrifice for a higher political cause concealed personal histories of loves lost and promises broken.[55]

Shaped by disparate racialized settings and personal trajectories, individu-als grappled with these issues in their daily lives in varying ways but never in isolation. Those who hailed from or sojourned in the United States imported terminology from black American street slang. A whole lexicon, including terms like "ofay," "Uncle Tom," and "monkey chaser" (Harlem Renaissance–era vernacular for an Afro-Caribbean), entered popular use among black men in London by the 1940s. As they traveled, these words underwent a process of translation, assuming new resonances in the racial landscape of the imperial metropolis as individuals with different backgrounds and political agendas employed them to articulate shared commitments and, just as frequently, to underscore their differences.[56] Drake noted that "American-trained intellectuals living in Britain had imported a rather cynical expression, high class pimping or pimping for the race." At the time, African Americans commonly used the term *pimping* in connection with communists and other leftists who exploited racial issues to attract blacks to their movements. Today, the term is the stock-in-trade of commentators on the far-right wing of the political spectrum in the United States who denigrate virtually any prominent black man who raises the issue of racism by labeling him a "race pimp," the implication being that he does so purely for personal gain. Black men in London used the notion of pimping for the race to describe race leaders and agitators who were married to white women or who lived successively with one or more white women, the implication being, as Drake explained, "that there is no real affection on the part of the male, but rather a calculated attempt to secure a white female companion who will support them or 'the cause.'" Although Drake encountered "certain isolated cases . . . of individuals who were taking money from middle-aged white people [and] women, having sexual relations with them, and laughing at them when among groups of Negro males," he concluded: "Most cases were far too complex in the motivations on *both* sides to characterize them by any term or formula."[57] The reworked notion of pimping for the race provided a conceptual vocabulary for the expression of doubts and anxieties related to interracial relationships and the indeterminable question of both parties' motivations.

Among black male activist-intellectuals, even committed and seemingly loving interracial relationships provoked disquieting suspicions about their impact on political pursuits and individual autonomy. The "intellectual" friends of "Cyril," one of Drake's informants, frequently referred to his wife as that "dumb English woman" and "implied that the only reason he had married her was to have someone to work and support him so he could have the leisure to write." "On the surface," Drake observed, "the couple seemed well-adjusted, and the woman while not college-trained certainly was not 'dumb.'" Privately, however, Cyril confessed his own anxieties about the relationship and admitted "that he was not happy with her, felt that she was domineering," and wished he had married a black woman. "Milton," one of Cyril's close friends, was, like him, a writer married to a white woman. To Drake, they appeared "to be an unusually happy and well-adjusted couple, and no aspersions were ever cast upon her ability or intelligence." Still, "other male members of the clique, as well as colored males not in it," made "friendly 'cracks' such as the following: 'Where would old Milton be if he didn't have that English woman working everyday so he can eat,' or 'Milton's lucky to have Audrey, isn't he. She has a good job and knows how to take care of money.'" Chiding of this nature evinced anxieties regarding how best to negotiate the relation between black masculinity and interracial sex, between visions of black liberation and dependence on white women in a racist society.[58]

African, Afro-Caribbean, and African American radicals frequently suggested that self-interest, not dedication to the struggle, lay behind some of their peers' race work and relations with whites. Even when they did not use the term *pimping* explicitly, they framed such aspersions in gendered terms and highlighted the individuals' dependent relationships with whites. In 1937, a protest meeting on the Italo-Ethiopian crisis, cosponsored by the LCP and the British Abyssinian Society, turned ugly when Louis Mbanefo began "attacking the British record in Nigeria," particularly the violent suppression of the Women's War of late 1929. Donald Cameron, the keynote speaker and former governor of Tanganyika (1925–1931) and Nigeria (1931–1935), responded with a shocking display of racial paternalism. According to Makonnen, who was in the audience with Padmore, "Cameron interrupted him. 'You, Mbanefo, naked boy belonging to the Ibo community, you dare to get up here and speak in such a manner about Britain!'" This, Makonnen recalled, "was too much for me and Padmore," but the latter directed his outrage at Dr. Moody of the LCP as much as Cameron: "What have you organized this meeting for, Moody? To reflect on black people by bringing men like this old colonialist Cameron along? These old people are dying but still holding on to the empire doggedly. This is a reflection on our manhood. How dare you, Moody, who received so much of your money from missionaries and the Colonial Office, use your apparatus to denigrate and defame African people?" While still with the Comintern, Padmore had used contemporary African American lingo in his critique of the Aggrey House scheme. Writing in the *Negro Worker,* he compared the plan to segregation in the United States, describing it as an attempt to "set up a little Jim-Crow hostel" in London and Moody as a "sycophant." Throwing his support behind the WASU hostel and the union's campaign against Aggrey House, he declared that "all self-respecting Negroes, whether they come from Africa or the West Indies, will boycott this 'Nigger-lovers' outfit." Padmore recounted the incident between Mbanefo and Cameron to Bunche a few days after it occurred. The story only confirmed Bunche's suspicions regarding Moody. After first meeting Moody and his wife, Olive Tranter, at their Peckham home, he wrote in his diary: "Big Jamaican married to [a] fat ofay. Smug and thick. No part of a fighter."[59] Bunche ultimately rejected communism, whether of the Stalinist or Trotskyist variety, as well as the radical black internationalism of Padmore and his associates, but both men believed the Jamaican president of the LCP used his status as a race leader for personal advancement, compromising his politics and manhood in the process, and cited his relatively comfy suburban lifestyle with his white wife as evidence. Suspicion fell particularly on those with ties to the Colonial Office or other white benefactors. Bunche dismissed Ivor Cummings as a "métis W. African" and "a terrible poseur and sap," and Cummings remained a target of criticism, particularly after he joined the Colonial Office as a welfare officer during the war. Likewise, Bunche noted that J. W. de Graft Johnson held a "big civil service job on [the] Gold Coast," characterizing him as "a typical Uncle Tom" who was "flattered to death by all the invitations he gets to parties, teas, receptions, etc." but "fakes reluctance to go." During a language lesson with Kenyatta, the pair jokingly gave de Graft Johnson a Swahili nickname, which Bunche translated as "white man's nigger."[60]

Some black activists bragged about their sexual aloofness or discipline as evidence of their autonomy and political commitment, and longtime residents and self-conscious race leaders counseled newcomers on the necessity of sexual restraint. One African whom Drake met "was almost idealized by a number of middleclass women in church circles and liberal circles, who invited him to their homes for tea, arranged speaking engagements where he could pick up a little change, and tendered him financial assistance when he needed it," but he "made it a rule" never to let things proceed further or "to seduce any girls in these circles." The man had his own apartment, so, instead, he frequently entertained "somewhat semi-bohemian/female college students, and an occasional girl from the left-wing orbit." Others attempted to avoid these issues by abstaining altogether from interracial sex. One informant "boasted" to Drake that he had never slept with a white woman during his seven years in Britain. He was active in one of London's black pressure groups and "was sure that an affair with a white woman would weaken his leadership."[61] According to Makonnen, "many of us [were] very careful in associating with white women; otherwise you could have terrible things said of them and of yourself." He recalled that Padmore, in particular, "was very cagey about women," adding, "You could never say that George was around with the girls."[62] In Padmore's view, personal relationships had to be subordinated to and serve the political project of African liberation. Indeed, Abrahams claimed that Padmore attempted to couple new arrivals with white women whom he saw as suitable partners and assistants in the struggle. "When I first met Padmore in 1940 I was still Dorothy's tenant and he knew her, having met her at various meetings. Even before our marriage he approved of her as a 'good comrade.'" "I now realise on looking back," he continued, "he had always wanted me to be more than just Dorothy's tenant. It was a form of control, and it worked for the best part of eight years." For Padmore, a relationship with a woman like Dorothy provided an aide in propagandistic activities and a source of financial support and domestic labor, while preventing Abrahams from diverting his energies in search of other sources of female companionship and sexual satisfaction. Abrahams saw this as evidence of Padmore's authoritarian tendencies, a holdover from his days as a communist functionary that never completely left him. "It was the 'Comintern man,'" he wrote, "who was contemptuous when Jomo had too much to drink. Or when Kwame was late for a meeting because of some woman. Or when I was too caught up in writing fiction to complete an assigned job."[63] As Adi observes, Ladipo Solanke of the WASU, who married a fellow Nigerian Christian, "disliked the corrupting influence of life in London, and . . . the 'characteristic features' of some of his Nigerian friends." He complained that, though they were "polygamous by nature," they often practiced "polyandry among the white girls" in London. Solanke linked the "corrupting influence" of the metropolis—specifically, the inversion of polygynous marital practices of African men of the age of maturity and the patriarchal monogamy of their Christian brethren—to apathy toward the fight against racism and colonial rule. Like Makonnen and Padmore, Solanke believed that sexual promiscuity represented a form of complicity with imperialism, not resistance.[64]

In his autobiography, Appiah described how he and other West African friends helped Nkrumah adjust to life in London when he arrived in 1945. In addition to finding him a place to live, the "gang" took it upon themselves to undo the effects of his time in the United States and "decided that he needed a white girlfriend." Appiah explained:

> We had noticed that during dances and other social activities at the [WASU] hostel—our real home from home—Nkrumah was reluctant or too shy to talk to white girls or to dance with them or even to get too close to them. In our home at Primrose Gardens the old gang were always receiving white girl-friends and, as was usual, cuddling them while Nkrumah looked on embar-rassedly. Besides, as a full-grown normal male he required female touch after daily exertion of mind and body. Greater still was the need to break his dread of white women that the United States had instilled in him.

Nkrumah's friends soon found an appropriate and willing candidate— "Diana P.," a young, blonde Marxist. The British-born daughter of a Russian émigré, she was well known to the group of West African agitators through her involvement in anticolonial activism, and confessed her feelings for the newcomer to Appiah "with Marxist candor." "This alliance," he claimed, "did the trick, and soon Kwame could be seen dancing and chatting with white girls at our socials; more than that, he looked more relaxed than ever before."[65] The "alliance" fit nicely with Padmore's criteria by providing Nkrumah with an assistant in anticolonial propagandizing, companionship, and a modicum of leisure with minimal distractions. But, in addition, for Appiah, an interracial relationship was a means to reclaim and perform an assertive black masculinity in the imperial metropolis, to decolonize mind and body, and, thus, an instrumental step in the evolution of a political leader. In his own autobiography, *Ghana,* Nkrumah presented himself as the self-sacrificing agent of African liberation. He offered a pragmatic reading of his relations with women in London to defend what, he indicated, some took for emotionless or rakish behavior as an act of revolutionary will:

> Unfortunately, the fact that I enjoy women's company has led to a great deal of misunderstanding from those who look at my life from the outside. I have never wanted to become too entangled with a woman because I know that I would never be able to devote enough attention to her. . . . I was afraid too, that if I allowed a woman to play too important a part in my life I would gradually lose sight of my goal. Few people have been able to understand this attitude of mine and I have been described by various people as a Don Juan, an impotent man and even a eunuch! Those who know me, however, probably regard me as a very normal man with probably more than average self-discipline.

Nkrumah acknowledged the potential for his relations with women to be read as perverse in one way or another. In repudiating such accusations, he rehearsed a construction of revolutionary black masculinity common to many would-be liberators of Africa. Devotion to the struggle against imperialism and a feminized imagining of colonial Africa necessitated limiting, if not sexual impulses, one's emotional attachments and foreclosed the possibility of maintaining a long-term relationship. The disaggregation of sex and affect, and the instrumentalization of desire for political ends, became acts of will constituting the anticolonial subject. In this rendering, "Nkrumah stands," in Jean Allman's words, "... as the two-dimensional man: the Moderning Man, the Revolutionary Hero."[66]

Nkrumah and other black radicals constructed the political field as the terrain of masculine virtue. Their articulation of black masculinity as defined by selfless dedication to African liberation glossed deep tensions within and among black agitators. Padmore's meticulous attention to his well-pressed appearance, which a number of his collaborators recalled, belied his avowed political ethos of self-denial. Although he advanced a theory of anticolonial revolution based on the black toiling masses in Africa and elsewhere, Drake noted, "Padmore, in many ways, reveals his admiration of British institutions and customs." On one occasion, Padmore confessed, "Man, I'm used to English ways. I'll fight to liberate 'your people' but I ain't gonna live under 'em. I told Zik [Nnamdi Azikiwe] when he was here, 'Man, I'll fight to help you throw the British out, an' then I'm gonna look for the first boat to get outa there.'"[67]

Like so many other black activists and intellectuals, Abrahams spent many a night in the home that Padmore and Dorothy Pizer made together in London; their partnership produced one of the city's most important centers of black sociality and political organizing. Nevertheless, Abrahams later suggested that Padmore's instrumentalist perspective on relationships with women was a convenient rationale concealing a more profound attachment to Britishness. In *A Wreath for Udomo*, he fictionalized Padmore as Thomas Lanwood, a tragic figure of impotent black masculinity beholden to abstract political and economic theories as well as an overbearing English woman, both of which left him disconnected from conditions in the colonies and even the reality of his own situation.[68] Here, Padmore's prolonged exposure to the communist international and his dependence on a white woman, his longtime partner Pizer, confounded his commitment to African liberation.

Upon his arrival in London, the novel's protagonist, Michael Udomo, whom Abrahams modeled on Nkrumah, views Lanwood as the greatest patriot "Panafrica" had produced to date. The attitude of the more seasoned revolutionaries in the group complicates this view from the start. After David Mhendi, a character based on Kenyatta and the architect of a failed uprising in his native "Pluralia," shares news of his wife's murder for defending their land from the encroachments of white settlers, he tells Lois, the English woman who introduced Udomo to Lanwood: "Tom's the luckiest. . . . For him it's an impersonal game of chess. He doesn't really care about people. He hates imperialism impersonally and wants African power impersonally."[69] The difference between Lanwood and his African collaborators emerges most clearly in the depiction of his relationship with Mary Feld, a scathing caricature of Pizer. When Udomo meets Feld, he notes the unfeminine qualities of her body: "She was tall, as tall as himself and terribly thin. But she looked strong; big nose and sticking-out chin; heavily-lidded eyes; an old-looking face set on a long, graceful, young girl's body; only, the body was flat-chested enough to be that of a young boy." Feld's boyish appearance corresponds to her imperious personality and effeminizing influence on men. Inside the couple's flat, Mhendi and Paul Mabi,[70] a sculptor and painter from Panafrica, lounge as Lanwood lectures the newcomer. Things go awry when he singles out Mhendi's penchant for drinking in warning Udomo to avoid needless distractions. Cautioned by Mabi to "stay out this," Feld shouts: "'Why should I? Or is the fight for freedom the preserve of men only? Many women have died in the struggle without whining or self-pity.'" After she and Lanwood leave the room, Udomo asks about Feld; Mhendi laughs "bitterly" and directs him to the dedication in Lanwood's most recent book, *The End of Empire*: "For my dear friend and comrade, Mary Feld, without whose sustained and sustaining support neither this nor any of my other works could have been completed." Dumbfounded, Udomo thinks, "But she has no respect for him." Lanwood himself wrestles with self-doubt and regret as he settles in to complete a piece of writing after his guests leave. "There's no time for sentimentality," he reassures himself. "A man must do what he must. And to do it he must keep alive. And to keep alive he must have food and a home and leisure. That was most important and she'd supplied that."[71]

Abrahams's novel is notable for its frank representation of the ideal of revolutionary pan-Africanism as an ethical act of will and the nagging questions that constantly threatened to undo this ideal in African and Caribbean men's everyday lives. Yet *A Wreath for Udomo* correlates Lanwood's compromised politics with the disruption of proper gender relations resulting from dependence on Feld and her deviant sexuality, which become metonyms for embourgeoisification and Europeanization. When Udomo and fellow sojourner Dr. Richard Adebhoy reunite in their native Panafrica, the former recounts his final days in London, including his time living with Lanwood and Feld. Udomo laments to his friend, "'He's dependent upon her,'" adding, "'You know she even tried . . .'" Adebhoy chuckles "without humour" and interjects, "'with all of us, home-boy!'" Selina, the leader of the market women of Panafrica and chief representative of the African masses in the book, reaffirms this appraisal of Lanwood. When Mhendi and Lanwood arrive in Panafrica, where Udomo is leading the burgeoning independence movement, she welcomes the former by finding him a female companion for the night, "'someone to make your sleep more restful.'" Mhendi inquires if she has done the same for Lanwood, and she replies, "'That one is white for all his black skin. He would not understand.'" Selina asks if Lanwood had a white woman back in London. When Mhendi affirms, "'We all did,'" she interrupts, "'That is not what I mean. You and Udomo and Adebhoy had them to sleep with, but always your hearts were in Africa.'"[72] Selina, like the novel as a whole, conflates the movement of black male subjects between Britain and a fictional Panafrica with sexual relations with European and African women. The degree of sojourners' deracination corresponds to the length and nature of their exposure to white women. Lanwood's didactic style alienates him from local elites until, distraught, he returns to London a physically and emotionally broken man. Because he is dependent on a white woman who loathes him, a life dedicated to African freedom becomes a farce.

In their private conversations and daily lives, men of African descent negotiated and debated endlessly, but never fully resolved, the tensions inherent in crafting personal and collective identities as black men in the imperial metropolis. In their autobiographies and memoirs, they often claimed that their personal lives came second to their political, educational, or intellectual pursuits, scripting themselves as self-sacrificing architects of a new Africa. Like many of his contemporaries, Abrahams articulated the anticolonial struggle as one to shore up an embattled black masculinity in relation to men's most intimate relationships, particularly those with women of the "imperial race." If, for some, the untenable situation of black men in London excused rather cavalier treatment of British women or demanded a degree of emotional aloofness, in its representation of Lanwood, his novel staged the potential costs, in both personal and political terms, of dependence on white women, voicing anxieties that hovered over all such relationships.

· · ·

The context of empire and the racial geography of London politicized the choice of sexual partners and the articulation of black masculinities. Both white Britons and men of African descent framed the movement of black male bodies to the heart of the empire in terms of sexual possibility and danger, if in different ways and for different reasons. The joke about the African pimp and stories about a homosexual clique in the colonial service and British high society drew on shared experiences, but in reiterating these tropes, black male intellectuals called attention to what divided them as much as what linked them, underscoring the ambivalence intrinsic to identity as an always-unfinished social process. Some African and Afro-Caribbean men equated sexual freedom or the exploitation of British women with anticolonial resistance and colonial liberation, or embraced the former in lieu of a fuller realization of the latter. Others decried this behavior as reprehensible and counterproductive to their political aspirations. In both cases, sexuality was central to the reconstitution of gendered selves in opposition to empire, and black masculinity was the presumptive staging ground of anticolonial political subjectivity. In response to representations of pathological black manhood, these self-conscious representatives of the race understood resistance to empire as principally a quest for manly independence and fashioned themselves as selfless agents of African freedom. However, this limited political vision not only replicated the gender norms of the existing social order but also foreclosed the possibility of a black internationalism not inherently masculinist in its orientation and goals.

This model of black revolutionary masculinity dimly reflected the complex realities of black activist-intellectuals' lives in London, which consistently threatened to expose this ideal as a fiction. Most of these men shared their time in London and the battle against British imperialism with white women. The self-presentation of men like Nkrumah hid a history of difficult personal choices and loves forsaken. While in London, Nkrumah formed a close relationship with Florence Manley. She was inconsolable in the days after he returned to the Gold Coast in late 1947, but shortly thereafter his friend and collaborator Bankole Akpata wrote to Nkrumah: "I know how very much she misses you, but she is now adjusting herself to the changed circumstances in order to utilize her energy in the creative task of helping in any way she can in our common struggle." The couple corresponded for a time, and in one heartrending letter, Manley wrote longingly about their reunion and pleaded: "Please soon as you are settled send for me . . . remember all that took place between us, nothing can break that very special bond." In the end, "changed circumstances" and the anticolonial struggle interceded. We have these letters only because colonial officials in the Gold Coast seized them along with copies of the WANS's journal, the *New African,* and other "subversive" materials among his belongings.[73]

SIX

_____

Black Intellectuals and the Development of Colonial Studies in Britain

COLONIAL AFRICA ASSUMED GREATER PROMINENCE in metropolitan imaginings of the British Empire between the 1920s and 1940s. The increased attention to Africa took popular as well as intellectual forms—from colonial exhibitions and imperialist films such as *Sanders of the River* to the African Research Survey, which culminated in Lord Malcolm Hailey's encyclopedic *An African Survey.* An increase in the production of knowledge on colonial Africa, in particular, accompanied the institutionalization of colonial studies in Britain, and the foremost personalities in the fields of anthropology and imperial history had a significant impact on the major policy shifts of the period. These decades saw the flowering of social anthropology's close relationship with colonial administration, and by the late 1930s, officials within the Colonial Office placed much greater emphasis on research and data collection as the handmaiden of colonial development.[1] This opened new opportunities and funding streams for scholars whose work helped justify the maintenance of the imperial status quo.[2] Black intellectuals were critical interlocutors in the development of colonial studies. With few exceptions, however, their engagement with the disciplines of anthropology and imperial history has been expunged from the early history of these fields. As Frederick Cooper notes, it was only during the era of decolonization in the 1950s and 1960s that African scholars became a recognized segment of the community of Africanists, a period in which those scholars increasingly distanced themselves from the study of colonialism.[3]

The production of knowledge on Britain's "tropical empire" was never a one-way street. Although most white "experts" ignored or dismissed their work at the time, Afro-Caribbean and African intellectuals were witnesses to and often critical, if marginalized, participants in this new intellectual mapping of Africa and the formation of colonial studies in Britain. They embraced the professional protocols of these disciplines and produced truly groundbreaking scholarship from within them, even as they criticized some of the most prominent historians and anthropologists of the day on political and intellectual grounds. An editorial in the WASU's journal in 1933 declared, "The aim of *Wasu* is not only to foster West African nationalism . . . but also to combat the false and exaggerated views given to the world by strayed European travelers, anthropologists, missionaries, officials and film producers, who to their own good and aggrandizement embellish . . . the so-called difficulties and dangers they come across in their duties towards their 'Brother Africans.'" However, the author went on to recommend the London School of Economics (LSE), particularly the courses of Bronislaw Malinowski, to students interested in "African Anthropology and kindred subjects."[4]

International relations as a field and the internationalist political theorist Harold Laski, in particular, were also popular with students from the colonies. The threat that imperialism posed to international stability preoccupied major figures in the development of international relations, from John A. Hobson and Alfred Zimmern to Leonard Woolf and Laski. Raymond Leslie Buell produced seminal works in international relations and African studies, including *International Relations* (1925) and *Native Problem in Africa* (1928). Laski held the prestigious Chair of Government at the LSE from 1926 until his death in 1950 and became a major intellectual influence on the Labour Party's socialist internationalism in the late 1930s and 1940s.[5] In *A Grammar of Politics* (1925), he argued for a "new political philosophy" and the creation of a democratic international government to meet the exigencies of a world in which "the unity of interdependence" rendered state sovereignty a dangerous illusion. The "technical pivot upon which our power to end aggression turns," he argued in 1939, "is the abolition of sovereignty."[6] *Wāsù* recommended *A Grammar of Politics* to readers in 1934, and Padmore later recalled, "From what I know of colonial students, few university professors have had a greater influence on their political development than Professor Harold J. Laski."[7]

The Nigerian H. O. Davies was a student of Laski's during the mid-1930s. In an address to the WASU in 1935, he considered the appeal of the new "world religion" of nationalism for colonized peoples, concluding that nationalism was increasingly an "anachronism." "Man has reached that stage of development," he explained, "where he must realise that bonds of blood, of language and tradition are mere accidents which can be put aside in favour of a larger unit—the world-state—or it must perish." Davies elaborated on these ideas while serving as the WASU's general secretary and the warden of Africa House at the end of World War II. In a speech reprinted in *Wāsù*, Davies transformed the political valence of Laski's socialist-internationalist theory by tracing the development of "the capitalist conception of labour," modern nationalism, and the "whole structure of Hitler's race theory" to the transatlantic slave trade and the history of European imperialism. For Davies and other black intellectuals in London, internationalism was the "task which the revolutionary nature of our circumstances set for us," and knowledge production was a weapon in the cause.[8]

As colonial Africa became central to public ruminations on the British Empire, students and intellectuals from Africa, the Caribbean, and the United States increasingly entered the fray in academic as well as other public forums. They gravitated especially toward those fields that spoke most directly to the "revolutionary . . . circumstances" of the moment and to the colonial situation in Africa specifically. Collectively, the work they produced demonstrates that the contribution of Afro-Caribbeans and Africans in Britain during the 1930s and 1940s was as much intellectual as political. Their seminal scholarship was often the product of intellectual collaboration and debates with others of African descent, and in some cases it has had a lasting and transformative impact on anthropology and history, foreshadowing and helping to inspire recent theoretical developments in both disciplines. For many Caribbean and African intellectuals, their sojourns in London proved to be a prodigious experience that transformed their politics and self-conception. As C. L. R. James famously put it, whereas many black students, artists, and professionals thought of themselves as "British intellectuals" when they arrived in the metropole, they came to see themselves as representatives of a global black community and their efforts as having significance beyond their individual aspirations.[9] Sojourners and migrants enjoyed a unique position in the struggle for colonial reform and refashioned themselves as the educated vanguard and "natural leaders" of Africa and the race as a whole—both imaginative constructs that their presence in Britain and interactions with one another helped to consolidate. In the imperial metropolis, they became black intellectuals.[10]

THE EMPIRE IN THE UNIVERSITY

The intellectual crosscurrents linking people of African descent from the colonies to colonial experts in Britain grew stronger in the 1930s, and the former found new, if frustratingly limited, opportunities to participate in scholarly discourse and influence colonial policy. As pressure from the colonial intelligentsia for substantive reform mounted in the 1930s, particularly after the labor disturbances in the Caribbean and Africa, the tropical empire garnered greater attention within Britain's top universities, including Oxford, Cambridge, Edinburgh, and the LSE. This development was linked to the rationalization of the colonial service as well as the professionalization of anthropology, which oriented itself, as the discipline took shape in the 1930s and 1940s, toward the needs of a restructuring British Empire. Advocates of colonial reform and officials in the Colonial Office drew increasingly on the methodological tools of or spoke from within the social sciences. Led by Ralph Furse, the director of recruitment and training for the colonial service from 1919 to 1948, the Colonial Office began to take a more systematic approach to colonial administration, creating a unified service for the whole of the empire in 1930 and instituting Tropical African Service courses at Oxford, Cambridge, and, beginning in World War II, the LSE. Reginald Coupland, who succeeded H. E. Egerton in 1920 as only the second Beit Professor of Colonial History, played a significant role in shaping the new curriculum at Oxford, which included his own courses on the history of the British Empire. Margery Perham, a recognized expert on Africa and tireless defender of the colonial governments and indirect rule, taught some of the courses for colonial service personnel in 1927–1929 and 1933–1934 in addition to her course "Native Administration." Soon thereafter, she was elevated to the position of research lecturer in colonial administration, one of five new research lectureships at Oxford funded by the Rockefeller Foundation in the United States and devoted to advancing social science research. During the late 1930s, Perham and the anthropologist Lucy Mair at the LSE pioneered a new discipline devoted to the "art and science" of colonial administration, an ill-defined program designed to meld the Lugardian ideal of the colonial officer who ruled intuitively and by strength of personality with the methodological precision of the social scientist. By the start of the Second World War, Perham had become reader in colonial administration and a founder-fellow of Nuffield College at Oxford. Perham and Coupland also organized the annual summer program for colonial officers on leave in 1937 and 1938.[11]

Africans and Afro-Caribbeans gravitated toward those scholars with an interest in colonial affairs for a number of reasons. Their curiosity and concern alone distinguished them from the average Briton, who knew comparatively little about conditions in the colonies. Moreover, as Zachernuk observes, "the notion of belonging to an expert community which might better guide colonial policy" appealed to African and Caribbean students and intellectuals.[12] Exploiting their proximity to the seat of governmental and cultural power in the empire, black students and intellectuals increasingly attempted to intervene in public as well as scholarly debates on the future of the colonies. Intellectual discourse, a free and equal exchange of ideas evaluated according to established standards of expertise, offered both a model for relations of "reciprocity" and "co-operation" and a means by which progressive change might be achieved within the empire.[13]

Beginning in the 1930s, a growing number of students went into fields concerned with the history, economics, and social organization of colonial societies in addition to the established bastions of the educated elite, legal and medical studies. Some—such as the Afro-Caribbeans W. Arthur Lewis, Elsa V. Goveia, Lloyd Braithwaite, and Gladstone E. Mills, who earned advanced degrees in Britain during the 1930s and 1940s in economics, Caribbean history, sociology, and public administration, respectively—went on to illustrious careers in academe, holding positions in Britain, the University of the West Indies system, or both.[14] Aduke Alakija, who became the first female vice president of the WASU during World War II, completed a degree in social science at the LSE. Dr. Eric Williams, the first prime minister of Trinidad and Tobago, was an Oxford-trained historian of the British Empire. The first postcolonial leaders of Nigeria and Kenya, Dr. Benjamin Nnamdi Azikiwe and Jomo Kenyatta, were trained anthropologists, as was Kofi Abrefa Busia, Kwame Nkrumah's successor in Ghana.[15] African anthropologists held other important posts within these newly independent states, such as the expert on Asante royal culture Dr. Alex Atta Yaw Kyerematen, who became director of the Ghana National Culture Centre.[16] Still others, such as Nkrumah and Peter Mbiyu Koinange, a high-ranking official in the Kenya African Union, began but never completed advanced-degree programs in the field. Thus, many within the generation of black leaders who oversaw the transition to independence in Africa and the Caribbean studied and wrote within academic disciplines linked to the development of colonial studies in Britain.

Although as late as 1946 50 percent of African university students still entered law or medicine, the remainder pursued training in education, science, and a range of other fields.[17] In addition to the privately funded students and Rhodes and colony or island scholarship holders who traveled to

Britain each year, the introduction of new scholarships as part of the Colonial Development and Welfare Act (passed in 1940 and renewed with additional funding in 1945) facilitated the entry of more students from the colonies, including 200 Africans, into metropolitan universities during the last two years of the war. The number of Caribbean students in Britain grew more dramatically, rising from 166 to 1,114 between 1939 and 1950.[18] Among its wide-ranging activities, the West Indian Colonial Development and Welfare Organization, headquartered in Barbados, awarded scholarships to address the need, underscored by the Moyne Commission's report, for trained personnel in a variety of fields. Initially, medical students predominated, reflecting the overwhelming focus on social welfare (as opposed to economic development) initiatives during the war years, and in 1943, all fourteen hailed from Jamaica. The awards were distributed more equitably among Britain's Caribbean territories the following year, and after the war the Colonial Office allocated more of the scholarships from development funds for training in the social sciences.[19] At the same time, the British Further Education and Vocational Training Scheme funded the education of a number of Caribbean ex-servicemen and -women, including the economist U. V. Campbell and the historians F. Roy Augier and John Hearne. The British Council and other cultural institutions in Britain also sponsored colonial students in the arts, such as the Nigerian sculptor and painter Ben Enwonwu. In rare instances, these new sources of funding supported black intellectuals in their pursuit of advanced degrees, but most funded only shorter, vocational training programs, such as the two-year certificate course in Social Science Administration at the LSE, and political considerations colored the selection process for awards.[20] In 1945, the British Council awarded the Ghanaian economist J. C. de Graft Johnson a scholarship to complete his PhD studies at Edinburgh University. De Graft Johnson helped organize the Pan-African Congress and worked in the Colonial Office between 1946 and 1948. Enwonwu and de Graft Johnson shared the WASU's expansive vision of West African history, but as sponsored students turned government employees, they sometimes faced accusations that they placed personal ambitions before political concerns.[21]

In the 1930s and 1940s, African and Caribbean students entered and contributed to a changing intellectual setting in Britain's universities. The growth of colonial studies, evidenced in the creation of new lectureships, readerships, and professorships, held out the promise that colonial problems might receive the sustained intellectual treatment that many viewed as a prerequisite to reform. The new emphasis on expertise in policy making and on practical relevance in academic colonial studies provided black intellectuals with a set of theoretical tools and a new basis for their political demands and claims to represent colonized populations. British universities also became an important site of interaction and intellectual exchange between people of African descent from around the Atlantic. Davies, Lewis, and the African American economic historian George Brown met at the LSE in the mid-1930s. Brown served as publicity secretary in the LCP before departing for Liberia in late 1935 to "conduct an economic survey." In 1935, Davies was president of both the WASU and the Cosmopolitan Club, an organization at the university, while Lewis remained active in the LCP throughout the 1930s. Their friendship helped to reinvigorate the ties between the WASU and the LCP in the late 1930s, despite the quiescent rivalry between the organizations' foremost personalities, Ladipo Solanke and Dr. Harold Moody, and the rift over Aggrey House. In 1936–1937, Davies served on the league's executive committee, and Lewis as its publicity secretary and editor of *The Keys*.[22]

As Eric Williams observed in the wake of decolonization in West Africa and the Caribbean, "My university generation has taken over not only in the West Indies but also in many of the countries emerging from colonialism. . . . Many West African friends in my university days are today in politics, some on the side of the Opposition, others holding high office in the new Ghana and the new Nigeria." Williams maintained that those in Trinidad who bemoaned the "intellectualism" of his party, the People's National Movement, failed to appreciate one of the key features of the transition to independence throughout the British Empire. "Our PNM Movement," he argued, "is part of the world movement against colonialism. Those who oppose PNM's intellectualism seem ignorant of the fact that the leaders of [anti-]colonialism the world over are the very colonials who formed part of the university generation of the thirties."[23] For many like Williams, their university experience in Britain had a profound impact on their political development both for the frustrations it provoked and for the chance encounters and collaborations it fostered.

THE VOICE OF AFRICA

Working in a discipline still in search of a professional identity, many social anthropologists in Britain set out for Africa to conduct their fieldwork dur-

FIGURE 13. W. Arthur Lewis. *The Keys* 5, no. 1 (July 1937): 3. © The British Library Board.

ing the 1930s and 1940s. As the first chair of anthropology at the LSE from 1927 to 1938, Bronislaw Malinowski built Britain's most rigorous graduate program in anthropology. He had an unparalleled influence on the development of the discipline during the interwar years not only through his seminars and scholarship but also because of his influence within the International Institute of African Languages and Culture (later known as the International African Institute). From the start, the institute epitomized the "complex intertwinings between the needs of colonial administration and the interests of anthropologists and other scholars of Africa."[24] Created in 1926, the institute and its journal, *Africa,* which first appeared in 1928, represented a significant step toward consolidating an amorphous group of individuals with an intellectual or professional interest in Africa into a recognized community of experts. In the inaugural issue of *Africa,* Lord Lugard described the institute as "a connecting link between science and life." Due in large part to Malinowski's efforts, it became an important vehicle for the professionalization of the discipline of anthropology in Britain. The institute established a grant program funded by the Laura Spellman Rockefeller and Carnegie Foundations in the United States and, after the Second World War, the

Colonial Social Science Research Council. The program supported much of the new anthropological work on Africa produced over the following two decades. The first batch of Rockefeller fellows at the institute in 1931 included future luminaries in the field such as Meyer Fortes, Gordon Brown, Audrey Richards, and Perham, and with the exception of Brown, all were Malinowski's students. In the following years, the institute assembled an impressive roster of international scholars with widely varying backgrounds and interests. "Although," as Goody notes, "many of them had little previous experience of anthropology they were to form much of the core of the teaching of African studies for the next thirty and more years." The creation of new sources of financial support related to colonial development schemes further fueled the growth of social anthropology in Britain. By 1945, the Colonial Social Science Research Council supported a number of "surveys" of areas for future research. These surveys—an intellectual mapping of existing lacunae carried out by the Australian Raymond Firth in West Africa, the South African Isaac Schapera in East Africa, and Edmund Leach in Borneo—helped to establish the research parameters for a generation of anthropologists in Britain and the United States.[25]

Anthropology emerged as a popular field among African intellectuals in the 1930s and 1940s. After receiving a master's degree at Harvard University in the United States, Prince Hosea Akiiki (or Akiki) Nyabongo from Uganda earned a PhD in anthropology at Oxford University.[26] Nyabongo's *The Story of an African Chief*, which appeared in the United States in 1935, was reprinted in Britain the following year under the title *Africa Speaks Back*, and in 1937, he published *The "Bisoro" Stories*. Alex A.Y. Kyerematen and Kofi Abrefa Busia also attended Oxford, and both went on to produce significant ethnographic studies on Ghana. Busia studied under the South African anthropologist Meyer Fortes during the late 1940s and published his PhD thesis as *The Position of the Chief in the Modern Political System of Ashanti* in 1951. He subsequently became the first lecturer in African studies at the University of the Gold Coast, the first African to hold an academic chair at the institution, and the first Ghanaian professor at Oxford, where he held the chair in sociology.[27] When Nkrumah arrived in London in 1945, he registered as a PhD candidate in anthropology at the LSE, where he met Harold Laski, but withdrew after only one term.[28] At a time when the Colonial Office began to place a greater premium on the anthropologist's skill set and insights, African anthropologists such as Kyerematen, Busia, and Jomo Kenyatta worked within the discipline whose fortunes were tied most directly to colonial Africa. While numerous scholars have noted the importance of colonialism to the development of anthropology, this point has obscured the ways in which students from the colonies found the discipline enabling, as well as the significance of the intellectual friendships that developed among black scholars around the seminars of Malinowski and other anthropologists in Britain during the 1930s.

The LSE was *the* place to study anthropology in the 1930s. The International African Institute and especially the seminars of such prominent anthropologists as Malinowski and Raymond Firth brought together black intellectuals from both sides of the Atlantic and European colonial officials and anthropology students in a stimulating, and often contentious, intellectual atmosphere. Malinowski's seminar in 1932–1933 consisted of Africanists, including Fortes, Richards, Perham, Mair, Siegfried F. Nadel, and Margaret Read, and the African American anthropologists William Boyd Allison Davis and Elizabeth Davis. The WASU welcomed the arrival of this "bright couple" in London and lauded the Davises' research into the connections between African cultures and "Negro life in the Southern States."[29] The black presence in the seminars grew in the mid-1930s. In 1934, the Nigerian Nathaniel Akinremi Fadipe returned to London and enrolled at the LSE to pursue his doctorate under Malinowski and the sociologist Morris Ginsberg. Fadipe had been an undergraduate at the school between 1925 and 1929, and then spent two terms at Quaker-run Woodbrooke College in Birmingham, Alabama, where he studied internationalism and history. He then joined the faculty at Achimota College in the Gold Coast for three years as its sole African instructor. Fadipe eventually completed his PhD at the LSE and spent the remainder of his short life in London.[30] Eslanda Goode Robeson audited the seminars of Firth and Malinowski in 1934, where she met Fadipe and Kenyatta. Kenyatta also worked intermittently as a translator for Malinowski, the institute, and Ida Ward at the School of Oriental and African Studies, where he interacted with the African American linguist Lorenzo Turner and Paul Robeson.[31] With Malinowski's assistance, Kenyatta and Fadipe received grants from the institute to support their research on the Kikuyu and Yorùbá, respectively, and Malinowski contributed the introduction to *Facing Mount Kenya,* based on Kenyatta's papers from Malinowski's seminars. In 1937, *Africa* published his essay "Kikuyu Religion, Ancestor-Worship, and Sacrificial Practices."[32] When Ralph Bunche came to London in 1937, he visited Africanists and African students at Cambridge and Oxford, but he spent the majority of his time at the LSE, where he attended the seminars and lectures of all of the anthropologists on the faculty, Malinowski's most consistently. On any given day, his peers in the latter's seminar might include Kenyatta, Fadipe, Turner, Koinange, J. W. de Graft Johnson, Cobina Kessie, and the South African educator Donald G. S. M'Timkulu. Bunche also ran into Lewis, then completing his doctorate in economics at the LSE, on several occasions.[33] Discussions in the seminar room and around the university often produced heated disagreements and led, in some cases, to fierce rivalries. But they also created the possibility for intellectual collaboration, personal friendships, and even political alliances that extended beyond the university.

The new emphasis on the study of "culture contact" and "diffusion" in Malinowski's work and, more generally, in Anglo-American anthropology informed many African intellectuals' understandings of race, colonialism, and cultural change, and supported their attack on the color bar. In their writings on West African history and the impact of European imperialism, Nnamdi Azikiwe and Ladipo Solanke used anthropological work to challenge the notion of intractable racial differences. At the same time, they found in these and their own studies of West African cultures and institutions sources of unity and evidence of Africans' capacity for self-government. Citing Franz Boas, the principal of Achimota College Reverend A. G. Fraser, and others, Azikiwe claimed that "no reputable anthropologist to-day entertains the notion of a racial inferiority for government or other institutions of society," while, as we've seen, Solanke and others in the WASU identified a consistent pattern of cultural synthesis or "re-admixture" as the distinguishing feature of West African history and the basis of a growing sense of "universal brotherhood" among Africans.[34] Similarly, Nkrumah, who earned a bachelor's degree in sociology at Lincoln University and then an MS in education and an MA in philosophy the University of Pennsylvania, recalled how his political investment in pan-African unity led him to the study of "cultural contact" and, in particular, the debate between Melville Herskovits and E. Franklin Frazier. In sharp contrast to the prevailing view, articulated by Frazier in various forums during the 1930s, that African American culture developed in imitation of the dominant European American culture, Herskovits, a former pupil of Boas, emphasized, in *The Myth of the Negro Past* (1941) and a number of shorter pieces, the survival of "Africanisms" or West African elements within African American cultural practices. Amid a discussion of his activities and associates in London, Nkrumah tellingly turned to this debate. "We believed," he wrote, "that unless territorial freedom [in

West Africa] was ultimately linked up with the Pan African movement for the liberation of the whole African continent, there would be no hope of freedom and equality for the African and for people of African descent in any part of the world." "At that time," he continued, "I was interested in two sociological schools of thought in the States, one represented by the Howard Sociologists led by Professor Fraser [*sic*], and the other led by Dr. M.J. Herzkovits [*sic*]. . . . I supported, and still support, the latter view and I went on one occasion to Howard University to defend it."[35] On both sides of the Atlantic, Africans and people of African descent eagerly followed anthropological debates about cultural change in Africa and the historic bonds between Africans and those in the diaspora. Africans in Britain were attracted to Malinowski, in particular, insofar as he moved toward incorporating the effects of colonial rule and the perspective of educated colonial subjects into the study of culture change and his functionalist method during the mid-1930s.

In a pair of programmatic essays that appeared in *Africa* in 1929 and 1930, Malinowski championed a conception of anthropology as a practical science and outlined a new research agenda that emphasized "relevance" and privileged "culture contact" within a rapidly changing colonial scene. He sought to demonstrate the necessity of incorporating anthropological knowledge in the administration of the British Empire. "Whether we adopt in our practical policy the principle of direct or indirect control," Malinowski asserted, "it is clear that a full knowledge of indigenous culture . . . is indispensable." He opposed his vision of the "science" of practical anthropology and the work of the International African Institute to the extant "antiquarian" studies of African customs and institutions associated with the African Society, founded in 1901 in memory of Mary Kingsley. In his 1929 essay, "Practical Anthropology," Malinowski maintained, "A new branch of anthropology must sooner or later be started: the anthropology of the changing Native," and he envisioned an instrumental role for the new institute in the advancement of this field of inquiry. Gesturing toward the recent work of Boas, he observed, "Nowadays, when we are intensely interested . . . in problems of contact and diffusion, it seems incredible that hardly any exhaustive studies have been undertaken on the question of how European influence is being diffused into native communities." For Malinowski, anthropologists relinquished any claim to relevance as long as their research continued to be based on the fiction of hermetically sealed cultural units. He argued that "the study of the diffusion of Western cultures among primitive peoples" would not only "throw an extremely important light upon the theoretical problem of the contact of cultures, transmission of ideas and customs, in short, on the whole problem of diffusion," but also produce knowledge "of the highest importance to the practical man in the colonies."[36] Similarly, in "The Rationalization of Anthropology and Administration," which was in part a reply to the critical responses to "Practical Anthropology," he insisted, "The anthropology of the future will be concerned with the study of the 'changing' native and of the 'in-between' or 'barbarous' races; it will be as interested in the Hindu as in the Tasmanian, in the Chinese peasants as in the Australian aborigines, in the West Indian negro as in the Melanesian Trobriander, in the detribalized African of Harlem as in the Pygmy of Perak." Malinowski linked anthropology's status as a science to the study of the "changing native," implicitly challenging the epistemological categories of indirect rule in which the deracinated native figured as a dangerous excess. "Such anthropology," he contended, "will be not only practically more important but it will become, at the same time, real science."[37]

Malinowski's eagerness to obtain "first-hand information" from educated African informants reinforced their claims to insider knowledge. More radically, in a significant departure from the tendency to denigrate the perspectives of "detribalized" Africans, he insisted that the growing body of work produced by African intellectuals could not be ignored. By the 1910s, the British had "betrayed" creole and educated elites, as Bickford-Smith puts it, in favor of white settlers in southern and eastern Africa and "traditional" rulers in West Africa as partners in colonial administration.[38] Malinowski was critical of both the motives behind and the quality of ethnographies produced by African practitioners, but believed that they could not be dismissed. "The African," Malinowski wrote, "is becoming an anthropologist who turns our own weapons against us. He is studying European aims, pretenses, and all the real and imaginary acts of injustice." While "such an anthropology is no doubt mutilated and misguided, full of counter-prejudices, ... charged with bitter hostility, ... [and] often blind with intransigence and sweeping wholesale indictment," "it cannot be ignored by the man of science; and it would be better if the practical man did not treat it is as a joke or as an insignificant minor excrescence."[39] Malinowski may have had Kenyatta in mind when he wrote these words. His assistance to African intellectuals such as Kenyatta was part of his project for a new anthropology, but it came wrapped in a thinly veiled skepticism regarding the scientific quality of their work. Several of the black participants in his seminar noted that

Malinowski had clear favorites, all of whom were white, whom he consistently allowed and even encouraged to dominate the conversation. Kenyatta made the most of his association with the famed anthropologist but repeatedly expressed his suspicion of all whites during seminar meetings. On one occasion, Bunche noted in his diary that the seminar ended with Malinowski "'riding' Kenyatta about Indirect Rule and caustically telling him he doesn't know what Indirect Rule is." The latter, he added, "got plenty hot." Kenyatta had made "a 'technical error' in stating that D.C.'s 'appoint' the chiefs." If he misspoke, as Bunche understood, the statement captured the discrepancy between the theory and practice of British colonialism in Africa. "Malinowski," he wrote, was "talking of course about the 'pure, undefiled and highly virtuous' [British] colonial religion—indirect rule. If the practice deviated from the theory then it wasn't indirect rule, obviously." Ultimately, for Bunche, it was not ignorance of the workings of indirect rule, which Kenyatta comprehended in ways that Malinowski never would, that left Kenyatta "vulnerable" to the latter's reprobation but rather "his inability to handle the [English] language well."[40]

Succeeding generations of anthropologists have criticized Malinowski for his failure to account adequately for the dislocation engendered by colonialism within the functionalist method, and for his naiveté, if not disingenuousness, concerning the anthropologist's capacity to influence colonial policy and the "practical man" on the ground in the colonies.[41] Yet these critiques ignore the fact that black intellectuals gravitated to Malinowski and embraced his call for a "new branch of anthropology" focused on processes of cultural exchange and mixture. Many Africans and Afro-Caribbeans believed that the University of London and LSE offered a more amicable, stimulating, and, most important, international setting than Oxbridge and other elite institutions. Lewis told Bunche that there was "'informal' segregation of colored students (Indians and Negroes) in the Middle Temple dining room" in London,[42] Williams and others recounted similar stories based on their experiences at Oxford and Cambridge. As noted above, the WASU recommended the LSE, particularly Malinowski's seminar, to those interested in colonial studies and anthropology. In the 1930s, the faculty at the University of London and the LSE included an array of prominent scholars with international reputations, not only in anthropology but also in political science, sociology, economics, and history.[43] The WASU did not endorse the LSE solely on the merits of its curriculum and distinguished scholars, though it cited both; the union also stressed the school's commitment to internationalism and emphasis on intellectual cooperation. The LSE, an editorial in *Wāsù* claimed, "is not the hot-bed of Bolshevism as represented by A. A. B. of the *Evening Standard* and other fanatic imperialists. On the other hand it stands for sympathy, humanitarianism and internationalism and understanding among the various member States of the British Empire." The author singled out Malinowski for praise, noting that his ideas had influenced the union's members and vice versa. "From our own personal experience the course under Prof. Malinowski is very well taught. . . . The Professor very often interviews African students about problems in connection with his work, as a result he gets first-hand information."[44] Three years later, in 1936, the journal listed Malinowski among the recent "important visitors" to the union's hostel.[45] His dismissive, even pathologizing, attitude notwithstanding, black intellectuals found in his ideas support for their contention that, as Solanke phrased it in *United West Africa*, the British official in the colonies needed to work with the African intelligentsia and "give up the idea (if any) of regarding every educated element as his enemy."[46]

Africans and others of African descent often evaluated Malinowski more favorably than other anthropologists, particularly those in an emerging generation of women anthropologists. Some black intellectuals responded to the racist condescension that greeted their interventions in the field by disparaging the intelligence and physical appearance of the latter. After meeting Richards and Mair, Bunche noted in his diary, "Neither . . . appeared particularly impressive." His evaluation of the relative merits of these anthropologists seems to have been shared by many of his African peers. In striking contrast to the cosmopolitan—indeed, pan-African—atmosphere of Malinowski's seminar, those of his colleagues appear to have attracted far fewer non-European students. After a particularly "dull" seminar with Mair, at which a Chinese student was the only non-European participant aside from Bunche, he wrote in his diary: "I won't get to that one very often"; at the next seminar meeting, which Bunche attended only at Mair's invitation, there was "only one E. Indian in the class." The views that Mair expressed in class were more damning still in Bunche's eyes. "She discussed land policy," he noted, "and was amazingly apologetic for the [colonial governments], especially the British," adding that she "even tried to find a . . . [justification] for the land and segregation policies" in South Africa.[47] Similarly, in a review of *Native Policies in Africa*, Lewis argued that Mair's support of "Indirect Rule policy" demonstrated that she, "like all good Lugardites, . . . is suspicious of the educated African, who dares to have his own views as to how Africa should evolve." He warned, "Those who expect Africans to tolerate for generations a system in which every European, however ignorant or uncouth, is an aristocrat, and every African, however cultured, a subordinate, are dreaming a dangerous fantasy."[48] Black intellectuals criticized Mair and other anthropologists for producing a picture of unchanging difference in a politically and culturally fragmented Africa. As Lewis observed, such a view accorded nicely with the administrative structure of indirect rule and cast the emerging African intelligentsia as little more than a bothersome anomaly.

In the eyes of many black intellectuals, both Malinowski's willingness to engage with educated Africans and the substance of his ideas distinguished him from many of his peers. However, even those who directly engaged with or were influenced by his writings on cultural exchange were never disciples. Many ultimately found his functionalist method insufficient to capture the causes and complexities of the changes then taking place in colonial Africa. In the seminar room and their publications, they drew upon the concept of culture contact to legitimate and pursue their own intellectual and political concerns, but they also challenged key tenets of Malinowski's method and pushed anthropology in more interdisciplinary directions. Malinowski was particularly resistant to the inclusion of historical analysis, which he disparagingly characterized as a form of antiquarianism that emphasized stasis over cultural dynamism. The black intellectuals in his seminar, by contrast, insisted on the necessity of considering cultural ties, contemporary *and* historical, in relation to economic exploitation and political domination. When de Graft Johnson presented a paper on "culture contacts" in the Gold Coast, according to Bunche, "Malinowski said he was fascinated by [it] but on principle opposed to the historical aspects of it." Bunche, who spent a semester at Northwestern University with Herskovits before coming to London, pressed him on the point and asked about the "validity" of studying "African survivals among Negroes (necessarily relying on [history]) from [the] functionalist point of view." In response, Malinowski expounded on the principles of "applied or practical anthropology" and "denied [the] possibility of separating cultural origins in a cultural contact situation except for such formalized things as languages." Afterward, Lorenzo Turner, who was also present, commented to Bunche that Malinowski used some history himself, "but was really functionalist invested." A little more than a week later, Kenyatta delivered what Bunche deemed a "very good paper" on a new religious movement gaining popularity among the Kikuyu in Kenya. Bunche drew connections between Kenyatta's case study and similar examples of the development of racial consciousness in the face of colonial or semicolonial dispossession, such as the Watch Tower Movement, the African Church, and even Garveyism, which nevertheless "usually take on many aspects of European institutions." Of Malinowski's lecture later that afternoon, Bunche noted only that he finally accepted the "application of 'relevant' history," again illustrating the importance that the African American scholar, like many of his African friends, placed on this question.[49]

Writing in *Africana,* the Oxford-trained anthropologist Alex Kyerematen evaluated the relative merits of "three schools of thought" in this "comparatively new field of social research": the "historical school" of Mair and Monica Hunter, the "functional school" represented by Fortes and Schapera, and Malinowski's "three-column approach." He argued that Malinowski's recent work on "processes of culture change" represented the most promising current development in anthropology. Those associated with the "historical school," he wrote, "assume that when two cultures contact, they do not result in a new homogeneous culture, but in a 'mixture of partially fused elements, whose separate parent stock can and must be traced in any attempt to understand the new situation.'" Like Malinowski, Kyerematen viewed this as an essentially "profitless" task that would yield little insight into ongoing processes of cultural exchange. While Kyerematen saw the work of Fortes and Schapera as a useful corrective, he maintained that the "functional school" failed to adequately appreciate the role of conflict and power in cultural change. Only the "three-column approach of Malinowski," Kyerematen averred, "recognised three aspects of the problem, namely, the impinging culture with its institutions, intentions, and interests; the reservoir of indigenous custom, belief and living conditions . . . [;] and lastly the result of the impact, the actual processes of contact and change, in which members of the two cultures co-operate, conflict or compromise."[50] Kyerematen's reading of Malinowski appears to be based largely on the latter's "Introductory Essay" to *Methods of Study of Culture Contact in Africa* (1938), a collection of essays by leading anthropologists reprinted from *Africa,* and *The Dynamics of Culture Change: An Inquiry into Race Relations in Africa,* a compilation of his lectures on culture change between 1936 and 1938, which was published posthumously in 1945. In these publications, Malinowski devoted greater attention than in his earlier work to conflict, racism, and the "selective" withholding of cultural influence under colonial conditions. "To ignore the fact that there is a selective giving on the part of the Europeans," he argued, "makes for a distortion of evidence, and . . . a sin against science. Selective giving influences the process of change perhaps more than any other element in the situation." Malinowski asserted that European racism, not the reputedly primitive mind of backward races, represented the greatest obstacle to cultural exchange and mixture. "If power, wealth, and social amenities were given, culture change would be a comparatively easy and smooth process. It is the absence of these factors—our selective giving—which makes cultural change such a complicated and difficult process." Thus, he insisted, "the color bar, wherever it enters into the phases and details of culture change, has to be put on the methodological map, not as a political indictment but as a theoretical appreciation of an important force—perhaps the most important of all."[51] Malinowski not only provided a powerful set of analytical tools and established methodological procedures but also drew attention to the causal role of European racism and the power relations structuring the colonial situation.

Africans such as Kyerematen believed that these processes of "selective giving," epitomized by the color bar undergirding colonial rule, represented both an object worthy of intellectual scrutiny and "a political indictment." Kyerematen employed Malinowski's theoretical work on culture change and that of his former students and colleagues Firth and Siegfried F. Nadel to point anthropology in a direction quite different from that envisioned by the doyen of the field, but one intimately related to his own political concerns. According to him, West Africa was not only a political dream; shared and enduring patterns of cultural contact united the region and lent it wider significance as a site where anthropologists could study broader issues related to global integration. Following Malinowski, Kyerematen explained that "human institutions are not static, but are subject to constant modification or even extirpation, with the impact of foreign ideas, and as the people themselves develop new ideas due to changing conditions of living." He maintained that the dynamics of "culture change" "in which both cultures are active and each contributes its quota to the new culture content that emerges" belied the notion of a "civilizing mission" as well as the existence of static cultural units. British rule did not—indeed, could not—"uplift" colonized peoples through a one-way process of imposing ready-made cultural and political practices. However unequal, the colonial encounter inevitably entailed transformation for all parties. Kyerematen also drew on Nadel's work on urban migrants from the Nupe ethnic group in Nigeria, arguing that "separate communities with their own distinctive cultures . . . constitute sections of a single small commonwealth, 'a social symbiosis' as Nadel puts it," after an extended period of interaction.[52] On the basis of such examples, he asserted that West Africa "is unique as a cultural area for the study of culture contact and changes. For it has had contacts not only with modern European countries, dating from the fifteenth century, but also with the ancient civilizations of Carthage and Egypt." If "the problems concerned with culture contact ... are acute anywhere in the world today," he suggested, "it is in West Africa and some other parts of the continent."[53] Kyerematen combined the history of West Africa and contemporary problems introduced by colonialism within his analysis, and in identifying a long and shared history of cultural exchange as the region's defining characteristic, he implicitly legitimated the political aspirations for a United West Africa expressed by the WASU and other African intellectuals in Britain. Given Malinowski's objection to the inclusion of history in anthropological studies and his emphasis on long-term immersion and local observation, in all likelihood he would have rejected these arguments as well as their political implications. While Malinowski attempted to reorient anthropology toward the study of the "changing native" in an effort to make it both more practical and more scientific, Kyerematen had a more expansive view of its aims and objects of study.

Black intellectuals from the colonies, Africans above all, faced considerable obstacles in their pursuit of the trappings of expertise—advanced degrees, scholarly publications, induction into professional societies, and university appointments. Although colonial experts in Britain invited African intellectuals to act as "native informants" for their own analyses, many continued to believe that the latter were incapable of the dispassionate study undertaken by professional social scientists and greeted their attempts to draw conclusions based on their own experience with open skepticism. In some cases, European writers appropriated the work of African scholars without citing their sources. During a period when there were no opportunities for African scholars in British universities, Fadipe struggled to survive by working as a Yorùbá-language tutor, translator for the Ministry of Information, and clerk for the Unilever Corporation after earning his PhD. He continued to write prolifically, both in scholarly and journalistic veins, but was never able to publish his revised thesis as a monograph. Despite being the first major sociological study by an African, *The Sociology of the Yoruba* did not appear in print until the African American fraternity Alpha Phi Alpha funded its publication in 1970—a quarter of a century after the author's death in 1944.[54] As late as 1974, the anthropologist Malcolm MacLeod complained in a letter to *Africa* that Douglas Fraser's essay, "The

Symbols of Ashanti Kingship," in the recent edited collection *African Art and Leadership* drew heavily on Kyerematen's work without acknowledging this debt. MacLeod wrote, "The great majority of the data on which this whole chapter is built are taken, with the very minimum of alteration, from the Oxford doctoral dissertation of Dr. A. A. Y. Kyerematen. . . . So far almost nothing of this long and detailed work has appeared in print, and the fact that part of it has now appeared . . . under Professor Fraser's name makes it doubly important that it is used with due care and that readers should know its true source."[55] The fate of Kyerematen's dissertation underscores the long-term repercussions of the silencing of black voices within anthropology during this formative period. The immense difficulty that African intellectuals faced in getting published enabled the pilfering of their scholarship; indeed, Kyerematen's programmatic piece discussed above appeared not in one of the academic journals of the day, but in *Africana,* the short-lived journal of the West African Society.

Few outlets existed for black intellectuals to circulate work of a more analytical, rather than a purely descriptive or autobiographical, variety. Short pieces by African intellectuals appeared intermittently within the *Journal of the Royal African Society* (later *African Affairs*), *Man* (Royal Anthropological Institute of Great Britain and Ireland), and *Africa* during the interwar period and with greater frequency after World War II. However, in most cases, their contributions were distinguished from the rest of the journals' contents in various ways and limited to examples of African art and poetry or descriptions of African social and culture practices.[56] In addition to its quarterly, *Africa,* the International African Institute originally hoped to produce two other serial publications, *African Studies* and *African Documents.* Mirroring the distinction between the anthropologist and ethnographic subject, the executive committee envisioned the former as a scholarly journal that would publish "authoritative monographs by recognized experts," while the latter would feature "brochures or texts written or dictated by Africans preferably in their own language, translated into a European language." The institute never realized this more ambitious scheme, but a similar bifurcation separated a section of poems under the title "La Voix De L'Africain" (The Voice of the African) from the other contents of the inaugural issue of *Africa.*[57] When contributors to these journals reviewed books by Africans, they routinely questioned the authors' objectivity. For example, L. S. B. Leakey's review of Parmenas Gittendu Mockerie's *An African Speaks for His People* in the *Journal of the Royal African Society* stated that the "chief interest in his book lies in the

picture it gives us of the thoughts of politically-minded East African natives."
While conceding that Mockerie "is remarkably clever in putting his finger on
the weak points in the administrative and other services in East Africa," he
maintained that "his very brief chapter on Kikuyu tribal institutions loses
much of its value from being written in the style of communistic literature."[58]
The author of the review in *Man* of Prince Akiiki Nyabongo's *Africa Answers
Back* criticized the blending of fact and fiction in the text and suggested that
Nyabongo should focus his energies on providing a "living picture" of his
community.[59] In his review of *Facing Mount Kenya* in *Africa,* A. R. Barlow, a
former mission schoolteacher who had once taught Kenyatta, wrote, "The
facility with which Kenyatta, the ethnographer, merges into Kenyatta, the
general secretary of the Kikuyu Central Association, makes it difficult to
decide whether his book should be viewed primarily as a scientific study or as
a vehicle for propaganda."[60] While some, such as Kyerematen, were reduced
ex post facto to native informants at best, most of their European counterparts dismissed those who did publish ethnographic studies as overly political
and, hence, biased. Among established anthropologists in Britain, it appears
that only Malinowski praised Kenyatta's work for its analytical content. In his
introduction to *Facing Mount Kenya,* he described the book as "one of the
first really competent and instructive contributions to African ethnography
by a scholar of pure African parentage," adding: "As a first-hand account of a
representative African culture, as an invaluable document in the principles
underlying culture contact and change; last, not least, as a personal statement
of the new outlook of a progressive African, this book will rank as a pioneering achievement of outstanding merit."[61]

These African intellectuals anticipated a negative reaction to their perspectives from European experts, whose position of authority they linked to
the racial hierarchy sustaining colonial rule. Kenyatta expected his book to
provoke criticism from many quarters, and his inclusion of Malinowski's
foreword can be read as a preemptive, if ultimately unsuccessful, attempt to
defend the work against the inevitable charges of bias. As he stated bluntly:

> I am well aware that I could not do justice to the subject without offend-
> ing those "professional friends of the African" who are prepared to maintain
> their friendship for eternity as a sacred duty, provided only that the African
> will continue to play the part of an ignorant savage so that they can monopo-
> lise the office of interpreting his mind and speaking for him. To such people,
> an African who writes a study of this kind is encroaching on their preserves.
> He is a rabbit turned poacher.[62]

The work of the African scholar as a "rabbit turned poacher" represented a profound threat to the power relations structuring the empire and, in particular, to the privileged status of those who claimed to interpret and speak for the "native mind." C. L. R. James entitled his review of *Facing Mount Kenya* in the IASB's *International African Opinion*, "The Voice of Africa," underscoring this quality of table-turning. Appropriating the banner of the circumscribed space allotted to African perspectives in the journal of the International African Institute, James implicitly challenged the exclusive claims to knowledge of colonial experts in Britain and ascribed special significance to the voices of the African intellectuals.[63]

Like the contents of the *Journal of the Royal African Society/African Affairs, Man,* and *Africa,* the environs of Britain's top universities, down to the level of the seminar, reproduced the racial asymmetries and paternalism of empire. The color bar in academic book publishing was even more absolute. In 1940, Athlone Press of the University of London released the first in a new series of LSE monographs on social anthropology. The series would in the following decades include works by Firth, Evans-Pritchard, Green, Fortes, Mair, Leach, and other prominent anthropologists, but the first monograph by an African anthropologist (G. K. Nukunya's *Kinship and Marriage among the Anlo Ewe*) did not appear until 1969. *Trade and Politics in the Niger Delta, 1830–1890,* by the Nigerian Kenneth Onwuka Dike, who earned his PhD at the University of London in the 1940s, became in 1956 the first book by a professional African historian published in Britain. The first sociological work by an African author to make it into print, Busia's *Report on a Social Survey of Sekondi-Takoradi,* conducted under the auspices of the Gold Coast government, was published in 1951.[64]

THE POLITICS OF EXPERTISE

Echoing the sentiments of many black intellectuals in London, an editorial in *Wàsú* titled "*Our* Responsibilities" linked the work of "self-appointed colonial experts" to the racism undergirding colonial policy, as well as to class hierarchy and the color bar in British society:

> The perpetuation of the colonial status—a system of *herrenvolk,* of superiors and inferiors—has become with such experts a lucrative source of livelihood. To them also the possession of second-hand information on Africa is a

passport to glory, and entitles them to move in that section of English society which is separated by economic parasitism from the common mass. . . . Under such circumstances, it is more of a miracle that Africans do achieve academic successes in British Universities and other Institutions.[65]

The innumerable slights and insults that greeted Africans and Afro-Caribbeans, their scholarly interventions, and even their presence strengthened their resolve in intellectual and political pursuits. The case of Nnamdi Azikiwe is instructive in this regard. He spent nine years studying in the United States at Lincoln University and the University of Pennsylvania, where he earned a master's degree in anthropology for his thesis, "Mythology in Onitsha Society." Azikiwe recalled, "I based it on the theory, popularised by Professor Malinowski and his school at the time, that myths and folk-tales have functional values in non-literate societies." As luck would have it, Malinowski, who was in the United States on a speaking tour, attended a presentation by Azikiwe titled "The Origins of the State." Afterward, he invited Azikiwe to join the Royal Anthropological Society.[66] In anticipation of his trip to London in 1934, Azikiwe applied to the International African Institute for a fellowship to support his ethnographic work on the Igbo in southern Nigeria. The Nigerian education department and the institute were eager to give an African intellectual an award, and Azikiwe enjoyed the endorsement of both Perham and Malinowski. Yet, as Zachernuk notes, "Azikiwe's character was as much an issue here as his intellect." The institute's executive committee initially granted him funding for one year of training in London but soon began to retreat from its decision. There were concerns that Azikiwe was too "political," and some doubted the ability of an African to produce the same kinds of objective scholarship as a European could generate. Ultimately, the institute informed him that it lacked the financial resources to fund his project. Azikiwe's fate exposed the power imbalance between African intellectuals and European authorities on Africa. In much the same way as "the general atmosphere in interwar Britain constantly offered—but could never really allow—sustained cooperation between colonial and metropolitan intellectuals," this episode typifies the pattern of missed opportunities for intellectual dialogue and collaboration "between two communities keenly interested in understanding contemporary Africa." Such treatment not only hastened African intellectuals' politicization and alienation from Britain, but contributed to their interest in black unity as well. Azikiwe stayed in London for three months, spending most of his time either at the WASU House, with Nigerian friends such as Davies and

Mbanefo, or in the British Museum doing research for a manuscript entitled "The African in History," before he moved to the Gold Coast and became one of West Africa's most outspokenly anticolonial journalists.[67]

Racism also hindered Lewis early in his career. In 1938, while still completing his PhD under the liberal economist Arnold Plant and Labour Party economist Hugh Dalton, who later served as chancellor of the exchequer, Lewis received a post at the LSE, where he became the first black faculty member and designed the curriculum on colonial economics.[68] With little hope of advancement at the LSE, where younger and, thus, not soon to retire faculty dominated the economics department, Lewis applied to and was recommended unanimously by the selection committee for the prestigious Chaddock Chair of Economics at the University of Liverpool. Despite the wholehearted support of the head of his current department, A. H. Carr-Saunders, who wrote in his letter of recommendation that "few appointments which have been made in my time at the School have been better justified," the vice-chancellor at Liverpool, J. F. Mountford, rejected the candidate, citing "other considerations than high academic standing." Mountford identified racism outside the university—within the local business community and constituents who did not have the option of attending other universities in the area (as they did at the LSE)—as the reason for not hiring the West Indian economist. Carr-Saunders, however, saw the university community itself as the real source of resistance behind this obfuscation.[69]

While black intellectuals drew on the work of European scholars and even enjoyed the admiration of a few, personal rivalries and the racist climate in academia frustrated their quest for scholarly recognition and exacerbated differences of opinion. When disagreements arose, they often led to heated debates and competing claims to expertise and objectivity, which revealed political and philosophical differences between black intellectuals and their white interlocutors. From the 1930s, the African and West Indian members of the LCP and WASU became increasingly impatient with such defenders of the colonial regime as Margery Perham.[70] Davies recalled that Perham's visit to the WASU drew a large crowd of Africans and West Indians. Although "the address was duly delivered to a solemn and interested audience," he was forced to cut off the ensuing discussion because she "was bombarded with critical questions, and tirades on some of her past press publications." "The whole affair," Davies wrote, "seemed like a declaration of war against the most wanted critic of West Africans."[71] In 1941, Lewis, at the time a twenty-six-year-old junior faculty member at the LSE, contributed a damning review of Perham's *Africans and British Rule* to the *League of Coloured Peoples Newsletter*. "To Miss Perham," he wrote, "it is from his own savagery that the African needs protection; white exploitation is to be seen merely as the inevitable if unfortunate accompaniment of the effort to civilize him." Lewis was uncharacteristically severe in his assessment of the text. "Not merely smug and self satisfied," he charged, the book "reeks of that self-conceit which typifies the colonial Englishman and which is doing more than anything else to poison the relations between the races." "From the prosperous seclusion of Oxford," Lewis continued, "it is easy to ride the high horse of cultural superiority, to belittle the wrongs of a people and magnify their faults. . . . Africans fortunately are accustomed to being insulted. They will merely hope that Miss Perham will have learned a little manners before she settles down to write her next apology for imperialism." The subsequent issue of the *Newsletter* featured a defense of *Africans and British Rule* by the British anthropologist Margaret M. Green, a specialist on the Igbo of southern Nigeria and a friend of Perham. "Mr. Lewis," Green claimed, "writes . . . as though [the book] were a time bomb dropped by an enemy rather than a constructive piece of work by one of the most sincere and able of the champions of African advancement." In conclusion, she added, "The cause of African advancement demands and deserves responsible treatment and a review of this kind does Africans a grave disservice." Lewis, however, remained defiant in his reply to Green, stating, "I did not expect my review to please Miss Perham's friends any more than the book itself pleased me." "The burden of my criticism of the book," he explained, "was that it ignores [the exploitation of Africans in British territory], and is therefore almost useless . . . because it does not suggest to Africans how they might meet the exploitation, or consider the radical revision of British colonial policy and reconstruction of the British Colonial service which are necessary if British rule . . . is to cease to be a cloak for this exploitation."[72] For many holding views like Lewis's, Perham and other reputed experts were complicit in the ongoing impoverishment of colonial peoples, despite their ostensibly objective stance and expressions of empathy. The degree to which the activities of colonial experts blurred the distinction between scholarship and policy making seemed to confirm this assessment.

According to St. Clair Drake, news that L. S. B. Leakey was preparing a book on the Kikuyu "spurred Kenyatta to write *Facing Mount Kenya* to checkmate him." Leakey's father, Canon Leakey, was a missionary who had helped introduce the Anglican Church to Kenya at a time when forced labor practices and land alienation continued in Kikuyu areas. Raised in Kenya, L. S. B. Leakey, who later became a renowned anthropologist, claimed to have spoken Kikuyu better than English during his youth and, by the mid-1930s, to know "things about Gikuyu customs that no elders could tell young Gikuyus."[73] His previous books, *Kenya: Contrasts and Problems* (1936) and *White African* (1937), established his reputation in Britain as the foremost authority on the Kikuyu and on the Kenya colony in general. In the spring of 1936, he gave a series of lectures at Edinburgh University and soon thereafter received a grant from the Rhodes Trust to support his fieldwork among the Kikuyu for a minimum of two years. Around the same time, Peter Mbiyu Koinange, another Kikuyu intellectual, arrived from the United States to enroll at Saint John's College, Cambridge. There, he attended Raymond Firth's lectures alongside Leakey. Koinange, Ras Makonnen, and the English socialist Dinah Stock, who edited *Facing Mount Kenya,* helped Kenyatta get his book published before Leakey produced his own. Kenyatta acknowledged the influence of both Malinowski and Firth in his introduction but noted wryly, "I owe thanks also to my enemies, for stimulating discouragement which has kept up my spirits to persist in the task. Long life and health to them to go on with the good work."[74] When Drake met Koinange in the late 1940s, he had returned to London from Kenya and was working "in a half-hearted way" toward a PhD in anthropology under Richards at the LSE. Drake recalled that Koinange wanted the degree "very, very much as part of the game of one-upmanship on L. S. B. Leakey." The failure to realize this aspiration due to his work for the Kenya African Union "rankled him for the rest of his life."[75] Describing in his memoirs his motivation for producing a study of Kikuyu customs, Leakey detailed the shortcomings of previous works on the subject. He gave Kenyatta's book only a passing and rather dismissive reference: "At about this same time, while a student at the London School of Economics, Jomo Kenyatta, now President of Kenya, was writing a book entitled *Facing Mount Kenya*. It dealt with Kikuyu customs in general, but many aspects of Kikuyu life were covered either too superficially or not at all." Ironically, Leakey later served as a court translator when the government prosecuted Kenyatta on the charge of inciting rebellion.[76]

Like African anthropologists, the generation of Afro-Caribbean historians who were trained in Britain during the 1930s and 1940s often faced considerable resistance from established figures in the discipline. As F. Roy Augier and Elsa V. Goveia recalled years later, "The eagerness of the young colonial post-graduates after the Second World War to write the history of their own countries was a cause of concern to some of their English tutors."[77] In 1932, Eric Williams received the coveted island scholarship for Trinidad to attend Oxford. After completing his undergraduate studies, he earned a PhD in colonial history in 1938. Williams's innovative reading of the relationship between abolition and the growth of capitalism in his doctoral thesis, "The Economic Aspects of the Abolition of the West Indian Slave Trade and Slavery," targeted not only the prevailing "humanitarian thesis" within the historiography on abolition but also the historian most responsible for its ascendance in the interwar period, Reginald Coupland.[78]

In 1920, Coupland was appointed Beit Professor of Colonial History at Oxford, succeeding Hugh Egerton, who had occupied the chair since its inception in 1905. As his former student Frederick Madden notes, the choice of Coupland, who specialized in ancient history and the history of English "Greats," was not an obvious one. Indeed, when he succeeded Lionel Curtis as lecturer in colonial history in 1913, "he had little more than an amateur's interest" in the subject. Although Coupland was a relative newcomer to the field, the electors, according to Madden, "sought to give stature to the new discipline of imperial history" by selecting a prominent historian rather than a specialist—"a first-class scholar was better than a third-rate expert." The move, if measured in terms of the number of students who took their finals in colonial or Commonwealth history, was a resounding success. An insignificant subfield on the margins of the discipline during the early decades of the twentieth century, imperial history became one of the most popular subjects at Oxford during Coupland's nearly thirty years in the chair.[79]

Between 1935 and 1938, Williams studied in the shadow of Coupland and wrote explicitly against the renowned historian. "The subject I had selected," he later claimed, "was, of all the chapters in British colonial history, the least known." Nevertheless, the "general British view was that a band of humanitarians—The Saints, they had been nicknamed—had got together to abolish slavery, and . . . succeeded in arousing the conscience of the British people against man's greatest inhumanity to man." Employing terms like *conscience, repented,* and *redemption,* Williams highlighted the role of sentiment in this understanding of abolition, which he attributed to Coupland, in particular. He deemed Coupland's contention that Lord Mansfield's 1772 ruling in the case of James Somerset "marked the beginning of the end of slavery throughout the British Empire" nothing more than "poetic sentimentality translated into modern history."[80] For Williams, sentiment played a minimal role in abolition, far outweighed by economic and other considerations, but it had been essential to establishing the dominant humanitarian thesis. Writing in *The Keys,* he asserted, "The idea that the humanitarians, by the irresistible weight of their humanitarianism, would have abolished slavery is a pathological delusion. What turned the scale in favour of the Negroes was the attitude of the British industrialists."[81] Williams conceded the importance of the abolitionist movement, noting that "to ignore one of the greatest propaganda movements of all time" would be a "grave historical error," and admitted that his study "deliberately subordinated the inhumanity of the slave system and the humanitarianism which destroyed that system." Yet, if the "humanitarians were the spearhead of the onslaught which destroyed the West Indian system and freed the Negro," their significance, he argued, "has been seriously misunderstood and grossly exaggerated by men who have sacrificed scholarship to sentimentality." He noted that the connections between agents of the East India Company and the abolitionist movement have "not been fully appreciated," least of all by Coupland, who "understands the history of the abolition movement as little as his hero," Wilberforce.[82]

Williams perceived a link between racism, the economics of empire, and this blind faith in the tradition of British humanitarianism. As Colin Palmer notes, his "ferocious anticolonialism was honed during his sojourn in the metropolitan country."[83] Williams's failed bid for an All Souls Fellowship and a humiliating experience during his French exam, when the examiners erupted in laughter at a minor translation error the fluent French speaker committed, left him convinced that the "racial factor" was insurmountable at Oxford. "No 'native,' however detribalized, could fit socially into All Souls," he recalled. "What, for example, could I say, in the very midst of the Ethiopian War, shortly after the announcement of the infamous Hoare-Laval peace plan, in reply to a question as to whether advanced peoples have any right to assume tutelage over backward peoples?" These observations led Williams to suspect a "fundamentally political" dynamic at work within the "traditional view" of emancipation. The humanitarian thesis, he suggested, was not only the central trope of the historiography on abolitionism but also a fiction on which "Englishness" and the moral arguments for imperial expansion depended. Coupland was not merely an idealist producing poor scholarship. Due to his institutional power and public prominence, his work helped to mask the true face of imperial power. "Propounded by Coupland from his professional chair ... [with] all the authority of the British Government's special representative on commissions of inquiry in India, Palestine and East Africa," Williams maintained, the "traditional view not only involved large conclusions from no evidence at all; it also proceeded to draw still larger conclusions for imperialism in the twentieth century from its unsupported large conclusions about imperialism in the nineteenth."[84] In 1933, the same year that Coupland published *The British Anti-Slavery Movement,* he produced a pamphlet entitled *The British Empire: An Outline Sketch of Its Growth and Character* for the BBC.[85] He combined the life of a scholar, continuing to contribute to and have his books reviewed in journals like *Africa, African Affairs,* and *International Affairs,* with that of a part-time official, serving on the Royal Commission on Palestine, chaired by Lord Peel (1936–1937), and on Stafford Cripps's Mission to India, for which he produced the three-part *Report on the Constitutional Problem in India* (1942–1943). The various activities of an individual like Coupland demonstrated the connection between the production of knowledge and imperialism. "In a lecture at Oxford," Williams recalled, Coupland "stated that 'The British will do justice to Africa because they are heirs and guardians of a great tradition.' As it was clear to me that they had not and were not doing justice to the West Indians, as the Hoare-Laval peace plan seemed to me irreconcilable with justice to Ethiopia, it became imperative to analyse the great tradition."[86] Like many of his contemporaries, Williams believed that his intervention within the field of imperial history was an essential part of the fight against the apologists for empire, both within and outside the university.

Whereas Williams placed the Atlantic slave trade and slavery in the Caribbean at the heart of the development of capitalism and the British Empire, the Afro-Guyanese historian Elsa V. Goveia studied the colonial Caribbean as an interconnected totality in which the lives and agency of the region's black and mixed-race inhabitants loomed large. The daughter of a middling-rank family of mixed African and Portuguese descent, she won the competitive British Guiana scholarship in 1944, the first woman to do so, and traveled to Britain to attend the University College of London (UCL). She became the first Caribbean to receive the Pollard Prize for English history and graduated with First Class honors in 1948, at which point she entered the doctoral program in history at the University of London's Institute of Historical Research. Goveia remained in Britain until 1950, when she returned to the Caribbean to assume an assistant lecturer position at the new University College of the West Indies (UCWI) in Mona, Jamaica. She completed her PhD thesis, "Slave Society in the British Leeward Islands, 1780–1800," in 1952 and eventually published it in 1965. In the interim, she played the leading role in developing the Caribbean history curriculum at the UCWI.[87]

During her years in London, Goveia established lifelong intellectual friendships and began to think of the Caribbean as a discrete unit of analysis, a perspective that informed both her politics and her scholarship. Her dissertation topic and approach to it were strikingly new. The historians whom she encountered in Britain, including Vincent Harlow and her advisor, Eveline Martin, concentrated on metropolitan politicians, colonial officials, imperial policy and administration, or white elites in the colonies, while members of the new "school" of imperial history in the United States, including Frank W. Pitman and Lowell Joseph Ragatz, focused on the social and economic role of the planter classes of the early American colonies and the Caribbean. Goveia, by contrast, sought "to analyse how the society functioned and . . . its internal structure," "to find the principle of social organisation which gave coherence to the life of the community; and . . . to examine the influence of this principle upon the nature of the cultural contact between African and European—slave and master." She maintained that slavery, and the racial hierarchy and systematic political and economic disenfranchisement that sustained the institution and lived on after its demise, provided this overriding dynamic or "principle," later describing it as a "divisive kind of integration." She identified models for her sociocultural framework not in the work of other historians but rather in that of anthropologists, specifically Gilberto Freyre's *The Masters and the Slaves* (1946) and James Graham Leyburn's *The Haitian People* (1948). A former student of Boas, Freyre emphasized the mutual influence of indigenous, African, and Portuguese cultures and the role of racial gradations within the "social institution" of slavery in Brazil, while Leyburn, in Goveia's words, analyzed "Haitian society as a society of castes." She found Pitman's influential essay "Slavery in the British West Indian Plantations in the Eighteenth Century," published in 1926, both "inadequate and old fashioned" by comparison.[88]

Groundbreaking in conception and focus, Goveia's thesis helped set the agenda for historians of the Caribbean for years to come and anticipated the rise of social history and the introduction of theory and techniques from the social sciences to the discipline by more than a decade. In her eyes, the project not only addressed a glaring gap in the historiography but also traced the roots of an enduring political problem—the contradiction between intractable racial inequality and democratic, regional self-determination or, as she put it, the "inferiority/superiority premise on the one hand, and . . . the one man one vote premise on the other." Goveia presented history as a record of cultural adaptation and unfinished struggles to clarify the challenges facing the contemporary Caribbean. In the final paragraph of the published version of *Slave Society*, she expressed cautious optimism that "the forces of radicalism will prevail," but only if "the fragmented territories of the West Indies ... develop at last a new sense of community, transcending the geographical and political divisions and the alienations of caste and race that have so marked their common history."[89]

Because the racial order produced by slavery and colonialism marred the historiography on the Caribbean and remained an obstacle to political equality and collective liberation, for C. L. R. James, Williams, and Goveia, as Mary Chamberlain observes of Goveia, "history was both a social project and a mode of analysis." Goveia, in particular, insisted that political engagement and adherence to professional standards in the study and interpretation of sources were not mutually exclusive alternatives for the historian: "It might appear ... as if the desire to influence public opinion ... would be one of the great dangers to their impartiality; and those historians who have been actors in the history of their own times appear most open to this suspicion. But ... [i]nterest in contemporary affairs may indicate force of character or of intellect. ... The truth, is, [*sic*] that the basic assumptions of the historian are usually common to his life and work."[90] Challenging the historiographical status quo, these Caribbean historians focused on the underlying structures of and the interplay between different groups within the colonial situation, producing painstakingly researched scholarship with a purpose.

LONDON AND BLACK ATLANTIC INTELLECTUAL CULTURE

Ralph Bunche's detailed journal entries from 1937 provide a window on the early development of anthropology and colonial studies, the world of black intellectuals and activists in London, and the relation between the two. Bunche met with members of the Colonial Office, politicians, and nearly every colonial expert and anticolonial critic of note in the British Isles, and spent many hours reading at the British Museum and Colonial Office library.[91] He encountered students bound for the colonial service at the LSE and the University of London's Institute for Education, and became friends with the white South African lawyer Julius Lewin, who was the assistant secretary of the Royal African Society at the time. Lewin later held the posts of tutor and research assistant in the colonial department of the Institute of Education and lecturer in colonial administration at the LSE, on his way to becoming the foremost authority on African law and government in South Africa.[92] These contacts eased Bunche's entry into Britain's colonies in southern and eastern Africa, and provided invaluable insight into what awaited him there. However, Bunche's encounters with others of African descent in London had the greatest impact on him.

For Bunche, a typical day in London centered on the LSE. He usually arrived near midday, attended a seminar or two—on some days, Malinowski's lectures—and returned home in the evening. Before, after, or between seminars and lectures, Bunche enjoyed the company of what he affectionately termed the "Africa group," a revolving cast of African students which included Nathaniel Fadipe, Jomo Kenyatta, Peter Mbiyu Koinange, Louis Mbanefo, Adetokunbo Adegboyega Ademola, Cobina Kessie, Donald M'Timkulu, J. W. de Graft Johnson, and Akiiki Nyabongo.[93] They went to tea or lunch at Student Movement House on Russell Square, Aggrey House, and affordable eateries such as the Chinese restaurant on Buckingham Street that was a particular favorite of the group. Some days, Bunche dined with other black activists and intellectuals in the city, including George Padmore, Ras Makonnen, I. T. A. Wallace-Johnson, Lorenzo Turner, and Arthur Davis, with or without various members of the Africa group. After dark, Bunche and his wife, Ruth, went to the theater, the cinema, jazz clubs in Soho, parties in the homes of LSE faculty or African American musicians and actors, and several benefit concerts by Paul Robeson for refugees of the Spanish Civil War. But, more often than not, they merely talked or played games like Monopoly and Pell Mell with their African, Caribbean, and African American friends. Early in their stay, the Bunches hosted an evening "gab-fest" with an international group of black intellectuals that included Eric Williams, Kenyatta, Nyabongo, M'Timkulu, and Bunche's colleague and professor of English at Howard University, Arthur Davis. Bunche noted in his diary that they "had a jolly time" discussing "Africa, anti-imperialism and pan-blackism" over scotch, wine, and sherry until nearly midnight.[94] Two weeks later, he went to an "Africa party," where Turner, Davis, and ten Africans, mostly from the Gold Coast, were present. Other nights, Williams and his wife, Elsie, or Padmore, Makonnen, and C. L. R. James dropped by, often with some of these same Africans.

Bunche found both Kenyatta and M'Timkulu to be "very impressive," characterized James as a "brilliant young W. Indian writer," and noted in his diary that "Eric [Williams] is *such* a serious kid!" Kenyatta gave Bunche Swahili lessons, often before or after Malinowski's seminar; Bunche read and corrected drafts of Kenyatta's essay on Kikuyu social practices that was published in *Africa,* as well as another piece for the *New Leader.* Yet these interactions, like those in the seminar room, did not always lead to mutual agreement or even respect. After a visit from Koinange and another African student, Bunche noted in his diary that "both are bitter" against the British and "neither thinks much of Nyabongo." Bunche initially found Nyabongo to be "dumb, but sly and dangerous" and commented that he and Makonnen played "the lackey role" in relation to Padmore, but if the amount of time he spent with Nyabongo is any indication, he seems to have warmed to him gradually. Arguments often erupted between Afro-Caribbeans and Africans, East and West Africans, Gold Coasters and Nigerians—as when, at the aforementioned "African party," a group of Ghanaians insisted to the Nigerian Mbanefo that their compatriots were "much more independent and aggressive" and that Nigerians were, as Bunche paraphrased their arguments, "the cause of all Gold Coast troubles." Afterward, they told Bunche that "they don't see much possibility in any attempt at Pan-Africanism or unity among all Africans," even though most of them were heavily involved in black activist circles.[95] In short, familiarity by no means guaranteed unity or agreement. Yet different configurations of these black intellectuals and activists gathered in each other's homes or at the meetings of black internationalist organizations night after night.

These London encounters changed all parties involved. Relationships forged there nurtured fugitive and revolutionary thought, and furthered the personal ambitions and careers of these African, African American, and Afro-Caribbean intellectuals in significant but little-known ways. Frustration with white scholars and students led African American intellectuals to a closer engagement with Africans in the city and reinforced their desire to study African societies firsthand. Eslanda Goode Robeson recounted how her experience in the anthropology seminars of Firth and Malinowski at the LSE and of Arthur Hocart and W. J. Perry at the University of London motivated her first trip to Africa. She found them "very interesting and exciting and challenging," but "soon became fed up with white students and teachers 'interpreting' the Negro mind and character to me." When she protested, Goode Robeson recalled, "it went something like this: . . . 'Ah, no my dear, you're wrong. You see, you are European. You can't possibly know how the primitive mind works until you study it, as we have done.... [T]he primitive mind cannot grasp the kind of ideas we can.... You see, we've been out there for years and years . . . ; we've studied them, taught them, administered them, worked with them, and we know.[']" When she asked some of the Africans in these seminars and at the WASU, "What is all this about primitive minds and abstruse subjects [and] about only simple subjects and crafts in your schools?" they answered, "Oh, *that* . . . there's nothing primitive about our minds in their universities, is there? And how can we cope with any but simple subjects and crafts in our schools, when that is all they will allow us to have?" Because of these Africans in London, Goode Robeson wrote, "I began to see light.... We know we aren't essentially different from our fellow Negroes. We know also that others' merely saying we are different does not make us so." In 1936, she embarked on her own journey to Africa, traveling with her son to South Africa, Basutoland, Kenya, Uganda, and Egypt. Along the way, they visited Zach Matthews, whom she met in Malinowski's seminar, and African friends from London such as Nyabongo.[96]

Bunche's numerous chats over lunch, afternoon tea, and late-night drinks with Africans and Afro-Caribbeans led him to read and think in new directions. As Elliott Skinner suggests, his "experiences in Britain were probably as important as his early encounter with black intellectuals at Howard."[97] Fascinated as much by their idiosyncrasies and group dynamic as their unique insights, Bunche started a new "study of 'what the Educated African Thinks,'" developed a questionnaire with the assistance of Kenyatta, and skipped seminars to pose his questions to African friends. The differences between African Americans, Africans, and Afro-Caribbeans, in background and experience as well as training, encouraged them to think comparatively and to consider how race functioned in relation to economic and other structures internationally, across as well as within individual colonies or countries. During one of Williams's many visits to the Bunches' flat in Earl's Court, they compared the hierarchical organization of society around phenotypical gradations or "color caste[s]" in the Caribbean and South Africa to the more "rigid" racial lines found in the United States. Bunche read voraciously while in Britain. At the suggestion of his African and Caribbean friends, he poured over major texts in the imperialist canon, such as Lugard's *The Dual Mandate,* Perham's *Native Administration in Nigeria,* and Monica Hunter's *Reaction to Conquest,* and volunteered to review the latter two works for the *Journal of Negro Education.*[98] From Fadipe, he received a great deal of "interesting material," including a "large manuscript" on East Africa. Nyabongo gave Bunche a signed copy of his first book, *Africa Speaks Back,* and the unpublished manuscript of his second, *The "Bisoro" Stories,* which he also shared with Paul Robeson. Padmore, who had been Bunche's student at Howard, loaned him a number of books, including his most recent work, *Africa and World Peace,* and Cedric Dover's attack on eugenics and defense of the progeny of mixed-race unions, *Half-Caste.* Not two weeks later, Bunche met Dover. The latter asked him for advice about fellowships and other sources of funding in the United States, which Bunche gladly offered, and promised him "letters to Nehru and others in India." When the Bunches left Britain for Paris in late July 1937, Kenyatta, Makonnen, and Padmore met them at the train station to see them off; Padmore urged him to "look up" his old friend and former collaborator Tiemoko Garan Kouyaté, whose address he provided. Bunche's time in London cemented his "interest in imperialism and colonial policy." As he and his family traveled through southern and eastern Africa in late 1937 and early 1938, like Goode Robeson, they drew on the knowledge and connections of their London friends. M'Timkulu offered to travel around South Africa with them, and they stayed with Koinange's parents in Kenya.[99]

In turn, both during his time in London and after, Bunche assisted many of the Afro-Caribbean and African intellectuals he met. He helped Nyabongo, Kenyatta, and Fadipe either to revise pieces or to get them published. Bunche also played a major role in helping Williams secure a position at Howard University in Washington, D.C., in 1939, introducing him to colleagues Davis, Alain Locke, and the prominent sociologists Charles S. Johnson and E. Franklin Frazier and writing a glowing recommendation on his behalf to the dean of the College of Liberal Arts. The budding Caribbean historian spent the following decade as an assistant professor of social and political sciences at Howard, where he published *Capitalism and Slavery* in 1944.[100]

These relationships between black intellectuals from distance points around the Atlantic illustrate the importance of quotidian interactions to the progression of their thought and careers and, on a broader scale, to the formation of networks of intellectual discourse. A spate of new books by African and Afro-Caribbean intellectuals in the metropole, constituting "something of a golden age" for black publishing, emerged amid the tumult of political activity in the late 1930s.[101] The appearance and innovative quality of these works owed a great deal to collaboration within their ranks. Padmore's *How Britain Rules Africa* and *Africa and World Peace* were released in 1936 and 1937, respectively. James had published five book-length works by the time he left for the United States and staged his play *Toussaint L'Ouverture* at London's Westminster Theatre in 1936, with Robeson playing the starring role. *The Black Jacobins* and Kenyatta's *Facing Mount Kenya* both appeared in 1938, and later that year, *Fact,* a socialist monthly featuring a short monograph in each issue, published James's *A History of Negro Revolt.* In addition to *Labour in the West Indies* (1939), W. Arthur Lewis released *Economic Problems To-Day,* an introduction to the international economy for the uninitiated reader, in 1940.[102]

These black intellectuals wrote amid the resurgence of interimperial conflict and mounting resistance in Africa and the Caribbean, but intellectual friendships forged in the crucible of the imperial metropolis also shaped the content of their work. *The Black Jacobins* was a work of its times, written, as James famously put it in the original preface, "with something of the fever and fret" of the moment. Although he first decided to write a biography of Toussaint-Louverture while still in Trinidad, the events of the 1930s and his sojourn in London altered his approach to and his reasons for studying the Haitian Revolution in ways that shaped the final product. Reflecting on the circumstances surrounding the production of the book, James later wrote, "Historical in form, it drew its contemporaneousness ... from the living struggles around us, and particularly from the daily activity that centered around Padmore and the African Bureau. It represented in a specific form the general ideas that we held at the time."[103] Published on the centennial of the end of the "apprenticeship" period that deferred emancipation in the British Caribbean until 1838, *The Black Jacobins* returned to the only successful slave revolt in the Caribbean, in hopes of hastening African liberation. In the final chapter, James highlighted the historical parallels between the circumstances of enslaved insurgents of Saint Domingue, who "were closer to a modern proletariat than any group of workers in existence at the time," and those of colonial subjects in Africa: "The millions of blacks in Africa and the few of them who are educated are as much pariahs in that vast prison as the blacks and Mulattoes of San Domingo in the eighteenth century. The imperialists envisage an eternity of African exploitation. . . . They dream dreams."[104]

According to James, the book "created quite a stir" when it appeared in Britain in 1938. "By the time I settled down to write, I had reached the conclusion that the center of the Black revolution was Africa, not the Caribbean. If you read *The Black Jacobins* carefully you will see that time and time again it is Africa to which I am referring, . . . and that is how it got its reputation," he later recalled. "Nkrumah and others who read it were very much concerned because that placed the revolutionary struggle squarely in the hands of Africans." In James's telling, the Haitian Revolution provided historical lessons for present and future anticolonial struggles, and most Afro-Caribbean and African intellectuals read *The Black Jacobins* in precisely this light. The author of *The Keys'* review of the text opined, "This period in West Indian history provides many invaluable lessons in de-imperialisation, . . . for to the end we are faced with many of the symptoms that exist today and the writer strikes many parallels in today's imperial world, leaving the reader to draw the moral."[105] Even more than *The Black Jacobins, A History of Negro Revolt* connected the history of enslaved Africans and their descendants in the Americas to colonial Africa in a single frame of analysis. "This *History of Negro Revolt*," James remembered, "could be seen on all bookshops and railway stalls the month that it was published" in *Fact*. A global history of black resistance, the short book was groundbreaking in its scope; as James noted, "Such a book had never been done before." The ambitious undertaking would have been beyond his reach before his encounters with African intellectuals in London. In his brief discussion of the Women's War of 1929 in southeastern Nigeria, James acknowledged relying on his acquaintances from Nigeria for information regarding "the actual happenings in Aba [that] have been suppressed in all official reports."[106]

Williams met frequently with James, his former high-school teacher, while he was completing his doctoral thesis and James, *The Black Jacobins*. James's study of the Haitian Revolution and the ties that bound the Caribbean, Africa, and France, particularly the chapter the "The Owners," informed Williams's analysis of abolition in the British Empire and the rise of capitalism in Britain. *A History of Negro Revolt* foreshadowed Williams's arguments as well. "Slavery," James wrote, "made cotton king; cotton became the very life food of British industries, it built up New England factories. . . . What we are really witnessing [with abolition] . . . is not that sudden change in the conscience of mankind so beloved of romantic and reactionary historians, but the climax of a gradual transformation of world economy."[107] Williams and Bunche also discussed the former's project at length, both in person and in their correspondence, over the course of a year and a half. Williams enclosed a summary of his "case" in a letter to Bunche during the spring of 1937, soon after the latter's arrival in London, and later gave Bunche excerpts of the thesis for his input. The pair spent many afternoons and evenings mulling the particulars of Williams's argument. In a letter dated November 7, 1938, Williams briefly rehashed the most controversial part of it for Bunche:

Really everything seems quite clear—the B.W.I. in 1833 were remarkably unprofitable, chiefly from the competition of Brazilian & Cuban sugar, U.S. cotton, E.I. indigo, Ceylon coffee. The chronic evil was over-production, i.e. that the B.W.I. produced far more than was necessary for British consumption, & the surplus [could] not compete with [foreign] produce in the European market. Something had to be done to [ease] production—hence Emancipation. All this I hope to work out from the . . . documents.[108]

If, as discussed earlier, the pompous and racist confines of Oxford and the nationalist bent of British historiography helped to inspire Williams's critique, the less commanding spaces of black London nurtured the ideas therein. Williams's and Bunche's association was one of many friendships between black intellectuals that helped sustain their scholarly endeavors and that linked the centers of black activism and the university.

These intellectuals produced works of politically engaged scholarship, textual weapons in the struggle, and though their distribution was limited, their writings circulated through informal personal networks linking Africans and Afro-Caribbeans in London to one another and to others in the colonies and across the Atlantic as well as within groups on the British left. In Trinidad during the winter of 1940–1941, "wherever [Nancy Cunard] went, she found evidence that even if Padmore's writings were proscribed, nevertheless people were familiar with them." James later stated with pride "that many in Africa read [*The Black Jacobins*], and it passed about among them." When Wallace-Johnson arrived in Sierra Leone from London, customs officials confiscated the two thousand copies of the latest issue of the *African Sentinel*. Shortly after *The Black Jacobins*' release, Padmore wrote to Warburg and Seeker requesting that the publishers send a copy for him to review in the *West African Standard,* but colonial authorities seem to have intercepted it. In the spring of 1939, Wallace-Johnson wrote to Padmore to tell his friend that the copy of *The Black Jacobins* had never arrived and to ask that he place a second request with the publishers; he noted, however, that he had received a copy of *A History of Negro Revolt* from a friend. When Kwame Nkrumah arrived in London with a letter of introduction from James after the Second World War, Padmore gave him a tattered copy of *The Black Jacobins*.[109]

This stream of books by black authors appeared in print because of their connections to left-wing writers, publishers, and politicians in Britain. In 1933, Virginia and Leonard Woolf, pillars of the Bloomsbury literary set, Fabian Society, and Labour Party, published James's *The Case for West-Indian Self-Government* under their Hogarth Press imprint. The next year, Hogarth released the Kenyan Parmenas Githendu Mockerie's *An African Speaks for His People*. In the late 1930s, however, the IASB's most consistent allies on the British left—socialists such as Dinah Stock, A. Fenner Brockway, the novelist Ethel Mannin, and her husband, Reginald Reynolds—came from Maxton's ILP. James was one of the first authors associated with the party that Brockway introduced to Fredric Warburg, co-owner of the new-look Secker and Warburg press. Sales of his first book, the novel *Minty Alley*, were disappointing. According to Warburg, Padmore's *Africa and World Peace*, which appeared the same year, was similarly "a flop." However, James published "two important works" soon thereafter. His *World Revolution* (1937), Warburg remembered, "sold immediately well." The book offered a thoroughgoing history of the Communist International from 1864 to 1936, and a devastating critique of the reigning idealism concerning Stalin's Russia, exemplified by Beatrice and Sidney Webb's *Soviet Communism*. It helped establish its author as the leading intellectual in the ILP's "Marxist Group" and "became a kind of Bible of Trotskyism." The following year, Secker and Warburg published *The Black Jacobins*. The press also published Kenyatta's *Facing Mount Kenya*. Even before its completion, Warburg believed *Facing Mount Kenya* "would be an original and indeed unique contribution to African Studies," and after its release, he "was immensely proud of it." The book's sales were initially modest, amounting to only 517 copies. *Facing Mount Kenya* enjoyed much greater success when Warburg reprinted it amidst the British suppression of the Land and Freedom Army in Kenya, or "Mau Mau," selling some 8,000 additional copies.[110]

If Warburg distinguished himself from other radical publishers in Britain by publishing black authors, their access to the imprint remained dependent on his estimation of their books' sales potential and his personal judgment of their contents. Williams tried repeatedly to publish his PhD thesis, but "no one would buy." Even Warburg, whom Williams deemed "Britain's most revolutionary publisher," refused to publish the text, because of its un-British implications. Warburg told him, "Mr. Williams, are you trying to tell me that the slave trade and slavery were abolished for economic and not for humanitarian reasons? I would never publish such a book, for it would be contrary to the British tradition." As a result, Williams's central arguments, which became the backbone of his magnum opus, *Capitalism and Slavery*, first appeared in print when *The Keys* published excerpts from his thesis in 1939. The same year, the young historian contributed two pieces to the IASB's *International African Opinion*.[111]

Black organizations in London and their publications provided a rare space for Afro-Caribbean and African contributions to colonial studies. In contrast to the European anthropologists, former colonial officials, and other "professional friends of the African" whose writings dominated the leading academic journals of the day, the journals of the WASU, LCP, and IASB celebrated the combination of insider knowledge and scholarly acumen in the work of black intellectuals. The IASB published a series of affordable pamphlets, and *International African Opinion* advertised books by black authors alongside the works of white critics of imperialism. Although he disagreed with some of Kenyatta's conclusions, James declared in his review of *Facing Mount Kenya,* "Here, indeed, Africa speaks." The LCP lauded James, Lewis, and other individuals who balanced the demands of rigorous inquiry and political commitment. A piece in *The Keys* asserted that Lewis "has set a great standard before all African and West Indian students and . . . has shown that it is possible for a man of ability to serve his race as well as to achieve exploits in his examinations." The author expressed her or his hope "that young Africans and West Indians coming to this country will discover . . . [i]t is a duty that all of us owe to the future of our race." By 1948, the LCP's catalogue offered works by Kenyatta, Padmore, Moody, and Williams, as well as a multivolume collection of Marcus Garvey's writings.[112] *Wāsù* traced the contours of a distinctive African intellectual tradition through "pen portraits" of writers and public figures such as Kobina Sekyi and Herbert Macauley, celebrated the professional and educational achievements of black students and intellectuals in Britain and West Africa, and provided an outlet for new research on African culture and history. These black publications, which circulated alongside and often more broadly than black-authored books, served a dual function, publicizing those works that did make it into print or offering them for sale to readers and providing a forum for African and Afro-Caribbean intellectuals to publish short pieces based on their research.[113]

Black organizations not only pressured the Colonial Office to provide support for promising students and denounced gross inequalities in the awarding of resources, but also formed independent study groups as a critical supplement to students' university education. Besides hosting a regular lecture series and a number of conferences, the WASU launched a study group in 1941 that met biweekly.[114] Initially led by R. Kweku Atta Gardiner, it continued to meet throughout the decade under the direction of Ako Adjei, Max Iyalla, and Bankole Akpata, who was a student at the LSE at the time.[115] As Adjei explained in 1946, "The aim is to approach [the manifold problems that confront the peoples of Africa in their relations with the outside world] with as much scientific objectivity as it is practicable for a scholar, or any group of scholars, to attain." The study group, which included on average more than twenty participants, collaborated on research projects and joint memoranda to the Colonial Office and secretary of state, and invited speakers as diverse as Padmore, Wallace-Johnson, Peter Abrahams, Reverend Ransome-Kuti, and Rev. Dr. Edwin W. Smith, the former president of the Royal Anthropological Institute.[116]

The new organizations formed after World War II continued this tradition of fostering black scholarship. A group of West Africans led by Dr. Robert Wellesley Cole and his sister Irene Cole established the West Africa Society in London in 1947. Its journal, *Africana,* aspired to become a vehicle for "the spontaneous expression of national consciousness among West Africans, in the sphere of social and cultural activity," and "a common forum where we can all exchange ideas." It more closely approximated a scholarly publication than the other black publications of the time. During its brief existence, *Africana* featured contributions from such up-and-coming scholars as Kyerematen and the Ghanaian historian K. A. B. Jones-Quartey.[117] Founded in 1945, the West Indian Students' Union (WISU) included during its early years a number of future luminaries in the cultural, political, and intellectual life of the Caribbean, including a cohort of pathbreaking Afro-Caribbean artists, historians, and social scientists.[118] Elsa Goveia met the Jamaican Lucille Walrond (later Mathurin Mair), the daughter of the poet Eric Walrond, and worked alongside her in the WISU, while both studied English history at the UCL. Years later, she mentored Mathurin Mair as a PhD student at the UWI and supervised her seminal dissertation, "A Historical Study of Women in Jamaica, 1655–1844" (1974). In addition to publishing a biannual newsletter, the WISU organized a study group on the economic history and development of the region, led by Lewis.[119] As Goveia explained in the newsletter, this was a "field of study entirely new to most of us ... and we are more than ever convinced that a people must know something of its past in order to plan for the future."[120]

. . .

Black students and intellectuals gravitated toward the fields of anthropology and history in growing numbers in the decades before decolonization, embracing opportunities to engage European "experts" in a productive dialogue, while pursuing the trappings of expertise for themselves. As the political demands of Afro-Caribbeans and Africans expanded, the ideal of the activist-intellectual whose perspective transcended narrow sectional interests assumed a central place in their visions of development, international cooperation, and liberation. A commitment to intellectual culture and education, to rendering a more accurate picture of colonial encounters and of the histories, cultures, and struggles of people of African descent, linked the first generation of postcolonial political leaders in Africa and the Caribbean.

Scholars from the colonies faced significant difficulties in producing and disseminating their work and in attaining recognition (and the funding that accompanied it). The same inequities that characterized colonial rule marked their interactions with white anthropologists and historians. To the extent that it occurred at all, their limited inclusion within the academic establishment amounted, to borrow Goveia's phrase, to a partial and "divisive kind of integration." Within this context, personal ties between African, African American, and Afro-Caribbean intellectuals, and the organizations and publications they created in London, assumed intellectual as well as political importance. Their scholarly interventions and innovative studies emerged as much from relationships among black intellectuals and the city's spaces of black sociability as through the university. Black pressure groups disseminated the work of black authors and drew upon it in their protests and visions for a transformative future. The arrival of the black intellectual in the imperial metropolis was inseparable from the wider domain of black internationalist activity and the circulation of individuals and texts across the Afro-Atlantic world.

SEVEN

Pan-Africa in London, Empire Films, and the Imperial Imagination

ON JANUARY 16, 1948, the British Film Institute, in association with the Colonial Office, held a conference in London titled "The Film in Colonial Development." Participants included a mix of colonial officials and experts in filmmaking. Arthur Creech Jones, the Labour secretary of state for the colonies, delivered the opening address, and his parliamentary private secretary, Aidan Crawley, chaired the conference. John Grierson, the doyen of the documentary film movement in Britain and by this time the director of mass communications for UNESCO, spoke on the subject "Film and Primitive Peoples." The formal papers covered such diverse topics as the effects of commercial films, particularly American releases, on colonial populations; the logistical challenges of film production in colonial settings; and the use of films to educate the British public on the necessity of further development efforts. Taken together, the papers reflected a desire to exploit film as an integral part of (and a vehicle for propaganda on) colonial development—to, in other words, mobilize cinema as a heuristic tool and a means of publicity.

The conference organizers did not single out a specific region for special consideration, but the participants focused on sub-Saharan Africa. A number of African students and intellectuals attended and took part in the subsequent discussion. The speakers and discussants returned again and again to two fiction films in particular, *Sanders of the River* and *Men of Two Worlds*, to support their varying points of view. In his opening remarks, Creech Jones noted that there remained "abundant need for films of our colonial life in the education of the British public in colonial responsibility," and cited *Men of Two Worlds* as a potential model. Mr. Compton, representing the Union of South Africa, expressed concern over the suitability of motion pictures for "semi-literate African audience[s]," before referencing a notable exception:

"One thing I saw recently (it may be low brow), which might be shown was *Sanders of the River* in an African setting—it upheld British justice and the men were suitably punished, there was no silliness about officials not doing their job or anything of that kind." By contrast, the black Africans in attendance used these same films to discuss fissures in the empire and the racism that confronted them in their daily lives. Turning the conversation from the effects of cinema on colonial subjects to the impact of "films showing African life" on metropolitan viewers, Mr. Sunderland from Rhodesia discussed a recent conference on the causes of "colour discrimination" and explained, "We find the psychological effect on people is such that we are experiencing discrimination, because people who see that type of film think all dark men are like that." Ms. Baeta from the Gold Coast suggested a collaborative approach to producing films for use in Africa. "When a play is being made for showing in educational films, the company [should] ask Africans to write the script . . . because they have the background." For Baeta, this practice not only would produce better, more effective films but would also approximate more closely the spirit of partnership behind the larger project of colonial development.[1]

This final chapter returns to several of the book's overriding themes while introducing new actors and a newly important medium and site of negotiation over the meanings of race and the future of empire. It treats *Sanders of the River* and *Men of Two Worlds* as events that illuminate a changing imperial and international order. The films engaged multiple, overlapping imperial and transatlantic publics and connected heterogenous modes of public address and knowledge production. Like the empire itself, the completion of these two films depended on the active participation of those colonial subjects they claimed to represent. The production process involved significant numbers of black actors and extras, predominately Afro-Caribbeans and Africans residing in Britain, and considerable negotiation between the filmmakers and numerous outside parties. This is to say nothing of the black shipping workers and African carriers who transported film crews and their bulky equipment to distant locations on the African continent. The release of these films, in turn, provoked far-reaching discussions of racism and imperialism and a storm of protest among commentators on both sides of the Atlantic, revealing the heightened stakes of representing the colonial relationship on the screen. As Prem Chowdhry observes, "Empire cinema had emerged in the 1930s as an arena for debate and discussion on matters of imperialist concern and thus as a new site for the formation of public opinion." If the cinema became a powerful new propaganda tool, it was also capable of generating unforeseen and unintended consequences in the public arena. Imperial films were susceptible to anticolonial critiques, "a subversion of symbols and meanings," that potentially undermined their pro-British effects and "made them counter-productive."[2]

The films and the spirited debates surrounding them linked the filmmakers, colonial officials, members of Parliament, and black intellectuals, especially those in London, within a discordant community of discourse and dramaturgy. Assuming the posture of activist-intellectuals worthy of the full fruits of imperial citizenship, Africans and Caribbeans deployed countervailing performances of blackness in response to these imperialist narratives of a benighted Africa. In so doing, they demonstrated their fluency in the practices of democratic civil society and, thus, their suitability for self-government within the Commonwealth or for complete independence from it. At the same time, interactions on set and discussion of the films brought different groups and divergent visions of pan-African solidarity into dialogue and exposed differences in background, interests, and public stature. The responses of commentators of African descent to the films were neither identical nor unequivocal, but the often-heated exchanges in black periodicals contributed to and assumed a sense of common cause and coparticipation in a larger intellectual milieu and community of address—an oppositional and self-consciously black public.

Similarities in theme and purpose, as well as the participation of notable black Londoners, linked *Sanders of the River* and *Men of Two Worlds,* but the differences in their plots indexed a major alteration in the rationale for British rule in Africa during the decade between their releases. *Sanders of the River,* which premiered in 1935, is a hymn to the figure of the colonial district commissioner and the necessity for and beneficence of the British system of indirect rule in Africa. In *Men of Two Worlds,* the empire is reimagined through the lens of "development." In the face of mounting expressions of dissatisfaction and pressure for constitutional reform in the metropole as well as in the colonies, a particular model of colonial development attracted growing support as a way to identify and manage the sources of discontent, while enhancing the colonies' economic benefits for Britain and differentiating the British style of empire from that of its fascist counterparts.[3] At its core, this notion of development exalted technocratic paternalism and was based on the presumption, as British politicians, officials, and experts repeated endlessly, that social and economic measures took primacy over political questions. *Men of Two Worlds* mirrors not only the key features of the new developing mission but also, as Africans in London pointed out, the contradictions and lacunae in this reimagining of the British Empire. The film's release became part of a larger "indictment of British imperialism" and the limits of development, further evidence that the empire was beyond repair and that complete independence from Britain was the only answer.[4]

THE PROJECTION OF EMPIRE

Set in Nigeria, *Sanders of the River* is based on a short story by Edgar Wallace and bears the same title as the first book in the author's wildly popular *Sanders* series. The protagonist, played by Leslie Banks, is the archetype of the colonial administrator who rules by force of his personality over his childlike charges. The film's prologue neatly encapsulates its central message: "Sailors, soldiers and merchant adventurers were the pioneers who laid the foundations for the British Empire. Today their work is carried on by the civil servants—the Keepers of the King's Peace." Then, superimposed on a map of Africa, it continues: "Africa—tens of millions of natives, each tribe under its own chieftain, guarded and protected by a handful of white men, whose work is an unsung saga of courage and efficiency." Throughout, the subdued but decidedly authoritarian Sanders maintains order through an intuitive capacity to know—to distinguish, see through, and manipulate— the teeming thousands of Africans within his territory. The incident that leads to the film's central drama occurs when, after five years of uninter- rupted peace, Sanders travels to England to get married. Upon his departure from the scene, the European gunrunners Farini and Smith spread a rumor that "Lord Sandi" is dead, inciting the malevolent King Mofolaba to revolt. Commissioner Ferguson, Sanders's junior officer, confronts the old king alone and is murdered as a consequence. After Ferguson's disappearance, the missionary Father O'Leary cables the Colonial Office: "Send four battalions or Sanders." Cutting his honeymoon short, Sanders hastily returns and once again imposes his authority, which, for the first time, appears to depend on European technology; he is recalled over the telephone, returns by airplane, travels by paddle steamer to the old king's country, and subdues the latter's army with machine guns.

During the interwar period, officials in the Foreign Office and Department of Overseas Trade gradually convinced their colleagues and Parliament that government propaganda as a form of "national self-advertisement . . . was a necessary instrument of the modern state," particularly after the onset of the global economic depression.[5] As the secretary of the Empire Marketing Board, Stephen Tallents emerged as the best-known advocate of expanded public-relations efforts to advance British diplomatic interests and to promote commerce and imperial produce. Though reluctant to use the term *propaganda* in his influential pamphlet, *The Projection of England* (1932), Tallents argued that "we must master the art of national projection and must set ourselves to throw a fitting projection of England upon the world's screen."[6] It was within this context that the Colonial Office and the proimperial lobby in Britain began to take greater interest in the power of film to shape public opinion in multiple contexts. With *Sanders of the River,* the filmmakers and the colonial officials in Britain and multiple African colonies that assisted them sought to present a defense of the efficacy of indirect rule.

Many believed cinema could be applied more fruitfully as a propaganda tool among metropolitan and colonial populations as well as in foreign markets, and there were repeated calls at imperial conferences in the 1920s and 1930s for films promoting the empire. At the same time, the popularity of American films vis-à-vis homegrown productions both in Britain and the colonies represented a growing source of concern, particularly regarding the maintenance of British prestige in the latter. As Sir James Parr explained in an address to the Empire Film Institute, "It is horrible to think that the British Empire is receiving its education from a place called Hollywood. . . . Trade follows the film, not the flag."[7] Interest in the cinema as a technology of civic education and colonial control mixed with concerns over the fate of British films in domestic, imperial, and foreign markets.[8] As the social historian Ross McKibbin notes, the "cinema was the most important medium of popular culture" between the wars, "and the English went to the cinema more than any other people." Ever-growing numbers of British spectators flocked to cinemas offering few British products. At the start of World War I, British producers accounted for 25 percent of films shown in the British Isles, but that figure dropped to only 5 percent by 1925, leading the *Saturday Evening Post* in the United States to declare, "The sun never sets on the British Empire and the American motion picture."[9] In 1927, the *Daily Express* exclaimed, "We have several million people, mostly women, who, to all intents and purposes, are temporary American citizens." The same year, Parliament imposed a quota system under which 20 percent of all films released in the country had to be British productions by 1936.[10] To make matters worse, at a time when the diplomatic and economic support of the United States was increasingly vital, British inroads into the American market remained minimal. Among British releases, colonial epics were consistently the biggest box-office draws on the other side of the Atlantic throughout the interwar years and well into the postwar period. For filmmakers and cinemas in Britain and the United States, as Barbara Bush states, quoting a journalist from the *Daily Express,* "the empire was 'good business' and . . . films like *Sanders of the River* were 'far more successful at the box office than any equal amount of sophisticated sex nonsense.'"[11] For all of these reasons, Winifred Holmes wrote in *Sight and Sound* in 1936, "it is essential for the continued unity and good will of the Empire that more and better British films should be distributed everywhere and that these films should add to England's prestige and show more of her ideals and epic qualities than before."[12] In a memorandum on propaganda to Neville Chamberlain from April 1934, the deputy director of the government's National Publicity Bureau, Joseph Ball, suggested, "It should be possible to ensure the adoption by some of the more enlightened producers of scenarios dealing with . . . historical or imperial subjects in such a way as to enlist the sympathies of audiences on the side of the present government." By 1938, Ball could assure Chamberlain that "I have cultivated close links with the 'leaders' of the British film industry, and I am satisfied that I can count upon most of them for their full support."[13]

In this regard, the Hungarian filmmaker Alexander Korda fitted the bill perfectly, and he was probably one of the "leaders" of the British film industry of whom Ball wrote. Korda arrived in Britain in 1932 and soon thereafter formed London Films with the Conservative MP A. C. N. Dixey. The following year, his *Private Life of Henry VIII* (1933) became one of the first films produced in Britain to enjoy box-office success on an international level. For his next project Korda was eager to make a film that displayed the virtues of British rule in the colonies. Riding the wave created by his recent triumph, he transformed a low-budget "quota quickie" entitled *Congo Raid* into the "super-production" *Sanders of the River.* Korda dispatched two film crews under the direction of his brother, Zoltan, to shoot ethnographic footage in the Congo, Uganda, and Sudan. Upon Zoltan Korda's return from the six-month trip, during which he enjoyed the full support of the local colonial administration, he showed the African American actor and singer Paul Robeson excerpts from the nearly 60,000 feet of film, in the hope of persuading him to accept the lead role. Impressed by the footage of African landscapes and native African dances and rituals, Robeson enthusiastically agreed to participate, "certain," as his biographers put it, "that the film would offer blacks, in particular American blacks, a picture of the 'Dark Continent' in which they could take pride."[14]

A BLACK STAR IN LONDON

Shooting for the film in Britain began in the early summer of 1934 at Shepperton Studios in Middlesex. The set temporarily became a pan-African space on the western fringe of the metropolis. The film features two prominent African American actors: Robeson in the part of Bosambo and the twenty-year-old Nina Mae McKinney as his wife, Lilongo. Casting agents recruited nearly 250 extras from the ranks of black laborers, students, actors, and musicians in the port cities of Bristol, Liverpool, Cardiff, and London. At least twenty different African languages could be heard between takes. Jomo Kenyatta played one of the African chiefs in Sanders's district. Ernest Marke recalled first meeting him on the set; they met again at the 1945 Pan-African Congress in Manchester. Several black actors, including the Nigerian Orlando Martins and Afro-Caribbeans Robert Adams and Beresford Gale, appeared in minor roles, the latter delivering the last performance of his life, and a number of African students, such as H. O. Davies, as extras. The composition of the motley cast crossed not only ethnic and linguistic divides but also class differences. Most students from the Caribbean and Africa rarely interacted with black and mixed-race workers in the metropole, but for several weeks they mingled on a soundstage on the outskirts of London for the same daily pittance. An English electrician who worked for Sound City Film Studios during the making of the film recalled that they "were inclined to keep together."[15] Many others of African descent residing in London visited the studio during filming.

The Robesons' encounters with Africans and others of African descent in London kindled their growing interest in the history of African cultures. Eslanda, as previously discussed, studied anthropology at the LSE in preparation for her own trip to Africa; Paul studied African languages at the School of Oriental and African Studies, added African folk songs to his singing repertoire, and published a number of articles on black culture. As Schwarz observes, he "brought Harlem to London and, ... it was in London that, in his own words, he 'discovered Africa.'"[16] His son, Paul Jr., recalled, "He found his own African roots . . . and became radicalized by the African anti-colonial fighters of that time like Jomo Kenyatta."[17] In "I Want Negro Culture," an editorial published in the *New Statesman and Nation,* Robeson wrote, "I believe that Negro culture merits an honourable place amongst the cultures of the world. I believe that as soon as Negroes appreciate their own culture, and confine their interest in the European to learning his science and mechanics, they will be on the road to becoming one of the dominant races in the world."[18] In another piece, entitled "I Want to Be African," he declared, "in my music, my plays, my films I want to carry always the central idea: to be African."[19] Of the African students, artists, and workers on the set, Robeson became closest with Orlando Martins. Born in Lagos, Martins had first come to Britain to enlist in the British navy during the First World War. Rejected due to his young age, he joined the merchant marine instead and stayed in London after the war. He struggled to make ends meet for much of the inter-war period, working as a wrestler, a stagehand, a snake charmer, and an extra in several films. Martins encouraged the African American star's growing fascination with African oral traditions and culture. As Sheila Tully Boyle and Andrew Bunie note, he "gladly assisted Paul's 'research,' lending him books and entertaining him for hours with African folk tales."[20] Life on the set of *Sanders* contributed to a dramatic change in Robeson's self-presentation and politics, and it increased his zeal for the project. He believed, Marie Seton recalled, "that if he could portray an African chief on the screen with cultural accuracy, then he was making a contribution to the understanding of the tribal culture which he considered was a part of his own heritage." Despite clear signs within the script that the end result would reproduce a plethora of stereotypes of Africans, not least of which was his character's name (Bosambo), Robeson remained confident that the film would portray Africa "in a really magnificent way."[21]

If his interactions during the making of *Sanders of the River* inspired Robeson, they also revealed the limits of his own knowledge and experience, and exposed him to the differences and tensions among people of African descent in London. Robeson's longtime assistant Joe Andrews recalled an incident that demonstrated how little the couple understood of the regional differences and prejudices among Africans. Eslanda drove Paul to the set each morning and often picked up African cast members on the way. "More than once," Andrews recalled, "she had the East African Kenyatta and the West African Orlando Martins jammed with others into the car. Neither Kenyatta nor Martins was happy about the situation. When Paul realized there was a problem, he asked Essie simply not to pick up anyone. It never occurred to her whether they were East or West Africans before she let them in the car."[22] Robeson's costume, which consisted of a Tarzan-esque leopard skin and little else, drew criticism from some Africans who visited the set. Dame Flora Robson, Robeson's costar in the 1933 stage production of Eugene O'Neill's *All God's Chillun Got Wings,* remembered: "He . . . was ticked off by a Prince of the Ashanti who was up at Oxford and said 'What do you wear a leopard skin for?' So Paul said, 'Well, what do *you* wear in Africa? Tweeds?' And the Prince said 'Yes. We do.' They didn't like him. They thought as an educated man he shouldn't play these primitive parts."[23] These incidents were humbling for the Robesons and led them to take a greater interest in the diversity of, and complex relations among, African cultures and to seek out educated Africans in the city to serve as their guides. Eslanda later reflected on how, in their naiveté, they inadvertently perpetuated a bigoted image of Africans: "These Africans, these 'primitives,' make me feel humble and respectful. I blush with shame for the mental picture my fellow Negroes in America have of our African brothers: wild black savages in leopard skins, waving spears and eating raw meat. And we, with films like *Sanders of the River,* are unwittingly helping to perpetuate this misconception."[24]

By the end of 1934, Robeson had become more sensitive to the prevalence of racism in British society. In addition to the Africans, Afro-Caribbeans, and black Britons whom he encountered during the production of *Sanders of the River,* the Robesons became financial patrons of the WASU, joined the LCP, and mixed with C. L. R. James, George Padmore, Amy Ashwood Garvey, Kenyatta, and Peter Blackman, who later organized Paul's 1949 tour in Britain. When the Savoy Hotel denied Robeson service in 1929, Caribbeans and Africans were at the forefront of the ensuing protests. Despite this episode, Reginald Bridgeman of the League Against Imperialism reported that Robeson "startled many of those who heard him [at an LCP meeting in 1933] by denying that there was any discrimination against coloured persons in Britain. Any prejudice, he said, that may exist is due to the presence of Americans in this country."[25] By December 1934, when he delivered a speech entitled "The Negro in the Modern World" during a league meeting at Memorial Hall, his thinking had changed considerably. He focused on themes that had begun to preoccupy him—the cultural wealth of Africa and the need for people of African descent around the world to embrace this heritage. Robeson announced that he was "unquestionably leaving" Britain. Part of the reason, he explained, was that he could not ignore the extent to which his own position as a celebrity diverged from that of others of African descent in the country: "I want to be where I can be African and not have to be Mr. Paul Robeson every hour of the day." While he enjoyed "perfect freedom and peace" in Britain, "it has not been so with my friends—companions of my own race. Where I am welcome they are not. . . . I am tired of the burden of my race, which will be with me so long as I remain here."[26] Just months before *Sanders of the River* hit big screens across Britain and, soon thereafter, the United States and elsewhere, its star had made a dramatic volte-face in his public stance and personal politics as a result of his experiences in London.

As the Robesons developed ties to black agitators in the city, they became an important link between the latter and visiting African Americans. Martin Duberman suggests that the Barbadian leader of the Negro Welfare Association, Arnold Ward, first sparked Robeson's interest in communism and the Soviet Union. Goode Robeson arranged a meeting between the visiting African Americans Ralph Bunche and Max Yergan at the Robeson home in late April 1937; two days later, the Bunches hosted Yergan and his South African girlfriend as well as Padmore, Kenyatta, I. T. A. Wallace-Johnson, and several others to discuss the possibility of collaboration between their newly created organizations, the IASB and the International Committee on African Affairs, which Yergan headed in the United States. The Robesons became key policy makers and financial patrons of the organization they discussed that night in London, which became the Council on African Affairs from 1939. Bunche was also an active member, although he eventually left the group over its association with communism (due largely to the Robesons). The imperial metropolis exposed Bunche and the Robesons to new worlds of black experience, as well as racism, beyond the United States and deepened their engagement with Africa. These encounters challenged their assumptions and informed their evolving politics, even as their presence in London provided further channels and settings for dialogue among African Americans, Afro-Caribbeans, Africans, and black Britons.[27]

SANDERS OF THE RIVER AND THE
TRANSATLANTIC BLACK PUBLIC SPHERE

Sanders of the River was a commercial success even before its theatrical release. Publicity for the movie promised viewers both high adventure and a rare glimpse into an exotic Africa. The film shattered existing records for advanced ticket sales, and *Harper's Bazaar* proclaimed in the run up to the premiere on March 29, 1935, that "all the world is going."[28] James Agate of *Tatler* noted "the breathless interest it aroused" in a theater "packed from floor to ceiling by an audience of every height of brow." The aerial and panoramic footage of African landscapes and cultural practices were novel in the history of British cinema and lent a certain truth value to the film, and the filmmakers went to great lengths to give an authentic feel to the faux-African set constructed in Britain.[29] As one reviewer explained, it combined "a dramatic film with a 'documentary' authority" in "an illuminating study of a primitive civilization with full-blooded adventure to provide the maximum emotional thrill." Similarly, the *Daily Sketch* observed, "Sanders and his story are occasionally in danger of being ousted by something closely akin to a travelogue," but it is "a grand travelogue ... full of movement and primitive passion."[30] Not everyone in Britain held the film in such high regard, nor was the criticism limited to London's black residents. In a scathing review for *Cinema Quarterly,* the filmmaker Paul Rotha observed sardonically, "So this is Africa, ladies and gentlemen, wild, untamed Africa before your very eyes, where the White Man rules by kindness and the Union Jack means peace!" While excoriating Korda, Rotha expressed sympathy for the film's star, asked to "portray on the public screen one of your own people as a smiling but cunning rogue," and anticipated a hostile reception from those ostensibly represented in the film, who, he rightly surmised, would interpret it as "the disgrace of a Continent."[31]

After the film's release, *Sanders of the River* sparked a public outcry and recriminations from people of African descent in Britain, Britain's Caribbean and African colonies, and the United States. Black commentators on both sides of the Atlantic debated the significance and impact of Robeson's involvement, repeatedly questioning his judgment for participating in such a project. Many, though not all, concluded that he should have passed on *Sanders,* whatever the personal cost. In London, Afro-Caribbeans and Africans responded to it as a provocation and incitement to unity not unlike the campaigns against the Wembley Exhibition, for the release of the Scottsboro Boys, and in defense of Ethiopia. Though often critical of the film and its star, their diverse reactions also evidenced multiple, overlapping, and at times conflicting identifications and interests.

Robeson was a black entertainer with uniquely broad appeal. Indeed, his presence alone ensured that the debate over the film would cross the Atlantic. If the alluring images of Africa, including, as Rotha put it, the usual "snatched chances for black nudity," accounted for much of the film's popularity, the appearance of Robeson in his first British film was equally important.[32] Asked near the end of his life to write a short piece on the subject of "black intellectuals in Britain," C. L. R. James remarked, "I doubt if there are many black men who have made the impact on England that Paul Robeson has made. He . . . was one of the best-known and best-loved black men who ever was looked upon by British people as one of the blacks who had made it."[33] An African American celebrity who had become the most famous black man in Britain after his triumphant stints on the London stage in *Emperor Jones* (1925), *Show Boat* (1928), and *Othello* (1930), he was also an imperial star. In 1937, Bunche wrote to Robeson from South Africa: "Paul, you surely are an idol of the Bantu . . . when one mentions American Negroes they all chorus 'Paul Robeson and Joe Louis.' . . . The rumor still persists that you are coming down to the Union soon; if you do the black folk will mob you with enthusiasm."[34] A. Sivanandan recounted a story about a group of young boys gathered around a wireless radio in a bakery in northern Ceylon who were listening with rapt attention to Robeson "singing what sounded like a song of his people that sounded so much like their own."[35]

Released as Italian troops massed along the Ethiopian border, *Sanders of the River*, James recalled, "caused one hell of a row" among Afro-Caribbeans and Africans in London.[36] Nnamdi Azikiwe condemned it as racist propaganda. "Whoever sees this picture," he declared, "will be shocked at the exaggeration of African mentality, so far as superstitious beliefs are concerned, not to speak of the knavery and chicanery of some African chiefs. I feel what is being paraded in the world today as art or literature is nothing short of propaganda."[37] After a screening of the film in Cape Town, South Africa, the local correspondent for the *Chicago Defender* wondered: "Has Paul Robeson been tricked in his role of 'Bosambo'?" "This," the author noted, "is the all-engrossing subject of debate here."[38] Robeson also faced an onslaught of criticism when he returned to New York, where, he recalled in 1938, "I was met by a deputation who wanted to know how the hell I had come to play in a film which stood for everything they rightly thought I opposed."[39] During an interview in 1936 for the *Sunday Worker*, an African American journalist lambasted Robeson: "This picture . . . was a slanderous attack on African natives who were pictured as being satisfied with the 'benevolent' oppression of English imperialism. You yourself played the role of selling the natives out to the imperialists. . . . You became the tool of British imperialism and must be attacked and exposed whenever you act in such pictures or plays." In response, Robeson claimed that "the twist in the picture which was favorable to English imperialism was accomplished during the cutting of the picture after it was shot. I had no idea that it would have such a turn *after* I had acted in it." Ultimately, he conceded, "I think all the attacks against me and the film were correct."[40] These reactions indicate both the sense of betrayal provoked by Robeson's participation in the project and the extent to which the public debate on race and imperialism had become a transatlantic affair.

In London, more immediate concerns complicated this discussion. Quality roles for black thespians were nonexistent. Beresford Gale was a stalwart of the LCP and one of the few Caribbean members of the WASU, but from his first role in London, in the 1901 stage production of *In Dahomey,* to his last, he spent his career playing characters that contradicted his political activities. Poverty and want led many Africans and Afro-Caribbeans into work as film extras. Some, such as Kenyatta, remained silent on their involvement in *Sanders,* offering neither explanation nor justification. After six years without consistent employment, the St. Lucian actor Napoleon Florent, who played one of the evil King Mofolaba's lackeys, captured the attitude of many of the struggling performers and itinerant laborers on the set: "*Sanders of the River* pays the rent and puts food on the table."[41] For H. O. Davies, working as an extra on the film was a source of much-needed income for a cash-strapped student and a fun experience, but of little more significance. Davies, who was a major influence on the black internationalism espoused by the WASU from the mid-1930s, largely dismissed the criticism of his old friend Azikiwe. "None of us," he recalled, "worried about the article [by Azikiwe] because the fellows we met from day to day were decent and affectionate, and the crowd wage of two pounds a day was a little fortune in the pocket of overseas students in London. We all took the whole film, and acting in it, as great fun."[42]

People of African descent took pride in Robeson's successes, and for black organizations like the WASU and LCP, the publicity and financial resources that someone of his stature could provide attenuated their willingness to criticize him. In a review of the film in its journal, *The Keys,* the LCP's "Special Film Correspondent" offered a critical appraisal of the film's plot, while praising Robeson's gifts as an artist: "*Sanders of the River* ... is just the kind of film which will appeal to the average English audience in a Jubilee year. It portrays the good old myth of the strong, silent, white man quelling hordes of angry savages with his scowl, and peacefully and altruistically ruling his thousands of ignorant black children by the sheer strength of his personality." Although "Mr. Robeson's glorious voice is well recorded," the author maintained, "as Bosambo he is completely wasted. In fact the whole cast—many of whom you will recognize—has been sacrificed to make room for some news-reel pictures of Africa, and some fine opportunities for real Negro acting have been withheld." The league's unnamed correspondent dismissed the film as a work of propaganda and a missed opportunity for furthering black achievement and for fostering mutual recognition and understanding between black and white. "Still," the review concluded, "if only to hear Paul Robeson sing, and to see some good Negro dancing, you should see this film."[43]

As previously discussed, the WASU House in Camden Town had opened in 1933, but its future remained in doubt for much of the decade. Engaged in a campaign to raise funds for a freehold property, the union remained dependent on outside sources of funding as well as positive publicity. Robeson's ability to provide financial and cultural capital for the organization to continue its activities was of no small importance, leading to awkward apologetics at times. In 1935, the WASU honored him as a *babāsale*, or patron, in recognition of his financial contribution to the organization, and its journal published a group photograph of members seated around the Robesons, taken during the reception at its hostel.[44] In the subsequent issue, the editors defended Robeson against the mounting criticism directed toward him for *Sanders of the River*. They responded, in particular, to the recent accusations of Una Marson. She first met Robeson when she visited the set. "He told me," she recalled, "that he found it difficult to get suitable coloured plays" and introduced her to the work of the black Russian author Alexander Pushkin.[45] In the months after this initial meeting, however, Marson became increasingly embittered toward the famous African American artist as she read a series of articles in British papers in which he celebrated "the real but unknown glories of African culture." After "I Want Negro Culture" appeared in the *New Statesman and Nation,* a piece that the WASU's journal reprinted with glowing commentary, Marson published a response. "The cry for negro culture is putting the cart before the horse," she argued, "and the first task of the negro who has achieved is to teach his people the value of unity. The negro worries too much about what the white man thinks of him and too little about what he is himself in the eyes of people of his own race." Marson implied that Robeson placed his personal success and popularity before the collective interests of people of African descent, adding: "There is nothing the negro needs more than sound, wise leadership by men and women able and willing to sacrifice for the good of their own people."[46] His recent calls for the development of a distinct black culture, she suggested, represented little more than veiled attempts at self-aggrandizement. Worse still, these efforts had seduced many in London, including the members of the WASU.[47] The leaders of the union expressed agreement with Marson's call for black unity but dismissed her accusations: "If Miss Marson is insinuating that Mr. Robeson belongs to that class of successful Negroes who are 'boosting' the race in order to focus attention on themselves, we may tell her gently but firmly that she is mistaken."[48]

While Robeson's substantial celebrity and resources led the WASU to defend the star in the public realm, these same qualities fueled suspicion among others. Marcus Garvey emerged as the most vociferous critic of Robeson in London. Writing in the *Black Man,* Garvey exclaimed: "Anyone who has seen 'Sanders of the River' can readily grasp the significance of the surrender of the Negro to all that is cultural, civilized, lofty and high, which mark him as being unworthy for a competent place at the present time in the civilisation of the world." Identifying "the danger of Paul Robeson as an actor," Garvey noted, "A picture like this, shown to the majority of people of ordinary intelligence, can only tend to inflame them against the black man. There is no wonder . . . that cultured blacks and respectable people of colour find it difficult to secure courteous reception and accommodation in England."[49] Once again, the WASU rushed to respond to the charges leveled against Robeson. An editorial in *Wāsù* countered by questioning the motives of critics like Garvey and took the rather disingenuous position that *Sanders of the River* was a work of historical fiction with little connection to contemporary Africa. The WASU maintained that infighting among people of African descent was the most pressing problem, not the representation of Africans in imperialist films: "It is not what our ancestors wore nor the 'propaganda films' of the white man that is retarding our progress but such pointless criticism with which we have had to deal. It is not love of the race that has prompted its authors, but, we venture to think, it is a case of the Fox and the Sour Grapes."[50]

Citing the more critical views of other Africans in London and a recent photograph of Robeson at the WASU House, Garvey rejected the union's defense as youthful ignorance and gratitude for his support.[51] Garvey's insistence on the role of popular culture in warping Britons' perception of Africans accorded with views expressed by the WASU in other circumstances. Solanke's published denunciations of the portrayal of Africans at the 1924

Empire Exhibition had led to the union's creation in the first place. In this dispute, however, he and the WASU allied with Robeson against Garvey, stressing the need for racial unity and accusing the latter of "pointless criticism" motivated by petty jealousy. The WASU's members were not simply star-struck, naive, or, as Garvey suggested, lacking a "sense of racial integrity and pride." As even he recognized, other factors were at work. The group's position became both more established and more tenuous as it developed a more ambitious agenda. The WASU's response to the criticism directed at Robeson for *Sanders of the River* was a tactical move reflecting pragmatic concerns as well as its commitment to a united front. It also reflected the political differences between them. By the time Garvey returned to Britain in the early 1930s, with his credibility greatly diminished, he had little influence on and few ties to the centers of black activism in the city, and the WASU had become the most significant of the latter. Against the backdrop of the rising threat of fascism and a renewed bout of imperialist expansion by the fascist powers, the organization articulated a black internationalist perspective that it explicitly distinguished from Garveyite black nationalism.[52]

Robeson himself ultimately disavowed *Sanders of the River* and later cited the experience as an important turning point in his career. Exactly when (and the related question of why) remains unclear. He subsequently claimed that, "when it was shown at its premiere in London and I saw what it was, I was called to the stage and in protest refused to perform. Since that time I have refused to play in three films offered me by that same producer." However, in their recent biography, Boyle and Bunie point out: "By virtually all accounts (excepting Seton's) Robeson expressed no dissatisfaction with the film until faced with a storm of protest from . . . West Indians, Africans, native members of the India League, and white anti-imperialists."[53] Regardless, *Sanders of the River* marked a watershed in both his career and his political activities.

Robeson increasingly shunned the concert hall and drawing rooms of the British elite in favor of the popular stage and provincial town halls. His friend and early biographer, Marie Seton, noted, "Never before had a singer of Albert Hall stature appeared on these stages for three performances daily. . . . But to Robeson this was the way he could reach the British people." If for Robeson, as Schwarz suggests, "the connections binding Africa to the black experience of the New World were direct," he also searched for parallels among folk traditions around the globe. He began to articulate his own communist-informed brand of cultural internationalism, a "folk internationalism" that transcended "the inherited fixity between folk culture and a single, irreducibly conceived national-ethnic identity." In the folk tunes of Lancashire, he heard echoes of the African American's lament in the spirituals he performed and the African songs he encountered through his studies or through Africans in London.[54] He also became active in left-wing theater circles, especially the Unity Theatre. In 1935, he starred in director Andre van Gysengham's *Stevedore,* a play about the difficulty of fostering trade union solidarity across racial lines in the United States, and Ashwood Garvey and Padmore helped recruit black actors for the mostly nonprofessional cast. In January of the following year, he took the stage as Toussaint-Louverture in James's three-act drama. A correspondent for *The Keys* celebrated *Toussaint L'Ouverture* as a project finally comparable to his talents: "I have always wanted to see Paul Robeson in a play worthy of his powers. At long last my wish has been fulfilled . . . he does not fail to show what a great Negro actor can do, given the scope." Nevertheless, the author continued, "whether it will ever have the long run it deserves is a more doubtful matter. The play tells the truth about Negroes, and there are few white audiences which want to know the truth."

Orlando Martins, Robeson's Nigerian friend and fellow cast member in *Sanders,* appeared in both plays as well as in his next two films, *Song of Freedom* (1936) and *Jericho* (1937). Robeson demanded greater editorial control over these projects and considered them among his greatest accomplishments on screen because they portrayed black men as intelligent, courageous, and self-sacrificing. The film historian Kenneth Cameron suggests that his characters in these films established a "new archetype" that provided a model for the African protagonist in *Men of Two Worlds*—the educated African (or African American, in the case of *Jericho*) who returns to the continent and acts as an agent of progress. In *Song of Freedom,* he plays John Zinga, a black-British dockworker and heir to the rightful rulers of the fictional West African kingdom of Casenga. Zinga becomes an internationally renowned singer, rediscovers his Africanness through the dim memory of a song, and travels to Casenga, where he liberates the local population in thrall to a witch-doctor usurper. The film, as Philip Zachernuk observes, "is of a piece with longstanding African American, pan-Africanist traditions which argued the uplift of Africa could be achieved by the return of its civilised sons." In casting a diasporic African exposed to Western civilization abroad as the motive force behind Africa's entry into modernity, *Song of Freedom* reproduces a narrative of black exceptionalism that Robeson's African friends would have rejected, and the central drama in the film revolves around

Zinga's quest to dislodge the evil witch doctor, one of the most common symbols of African backwardness and superstition in imperial fantasies.[55]

During the Popular Front era, Robeson gravitated toward communism. He sang at a 1938 youth rally in London at which Blackman "appealed for unity with the colonial people." At an India League meeting welcoming Nehru the same year, Robeson declared, "The struggles that are going on in China, India, Abyssinia, and Spain are one. The struggle of the colonial peoples is a struggle for democracy and freedom for all." In 1949, he contributed the foreword to Amanke Okafor's short book, *Nigeria—Why We Fight for Freedom,* which the leadership of the CPGB urged West Africans to read instead of Padmore's extensive writings, and throughout the following decade, the party referred to its divisions in West Africa as "Robeson" branches.[56]

Robeson's turn to communism, particularly the timing of it, disappointed many of his associates in London. It was a failing that some linked to differences in background and experience. Attendees of an LCP meeting in 1937 criticized him for joining the Unity Theatre, and "it was agreed that steps should be taken to persuade him not to identify himself so closely with the Communist Party." The coverage of Robeson's activities in the next issue of *The Keys* was more sanguine. A short note congratulated him "on his decision not to act in any more films until he can get a 'cast-iron' part—one that cannot be distorted in the making," noting only that he had "joined Unity Theatre, the working-class theatre," and "done a great deal of singing lately in aid of the people of Spain and China."[57] James later attributed Robeson's failure to devote himself more fully to the pan-Africanist struggle against imperialism to his being an American rather than a colonial subject in the British Empire:

> Paul showed such intense interest in Africa during the early 1930s, I was sure he would eventually join us in the fight against British colonialism. He was such a giant, and we expected and hoped for so much from him. But, in truth, he was not a colonial and never really understood British imperialism. In fact, it took him a long time to grasp the damage done by a movie like *Sanders of the River.* . . . As an American I don't think he understood what the British had done in the colonies and how wrong it all was, even though it was so like his own situation in America.[58]

Meeting Robeson in London altered James's understanding of black identity, including black masculinity, in the modern world. Looking back in 1970, he lauded Robeson's great insight in his pieces in the *Spectator* and the *Observer* during the mid-1930s. "While he insisted that the Black man had something to contribute, something specially his own," which was the product "of his past in Africa and of his centuries of experience in the Western world," James explained, "he did not ... give the impression that it was impossible for whites to understand Blacks, or Blacks to understand whites." James insisted that the black star was a "man whose history is not to be understood unless seen in the context of the most profound historical movements of our century. And, at the same time, the most profound historical movements of the twentieth century cannot be understood without taking into consideration Paul Robeson."[59] However, the political distance between them, particularly Robeson's pro-Moscow stance, forced James to acknowledge the gulf between his friend's perspective as an African American and that of Africans and Afro-Caribbeans under British colonial rule.

Whatever disagreements emerged between them, Robeson's interactions with members of the LCP and WASU, as well as individuals such as James, Martins, and Kenyatta, played no small role in awakening his interest in Africa and spurring his turn to communist internationalism.[60] Like their Afro-Caribbean and African friends, if in their own way, the Robesons became internationalists while in the imperial metropolis. Conversely, the encounter with the African American star not only inspired black intellectuals from Africa and the Caribbean but also forced them to think in more global terms about both the consistency and mutability of racial subordination. The imperial networks that brought the Robesons, James, and the African and Caribbean members of the WASU and LCP together in London inadvertently helped to foster a sense of belonging to a larger black world, an object of identification and a community of address, that underpinned their discrepant reactions to *Sanders of the River*.

MEN OF TWO WORLDS AND THE INVENTION OF DEVELOPMENT

The responses that *Sanders of the River* triggered from Afro-Caribbean and African commentators reflected a growing struggle over the future of the British Empire and the bonds that held its diverse parts together. The film emerged at a moment when indirect rule seemed increasingly untenable as a means of securing Britain's ties to its African colonies. The film's appearance was a concomitant of wider efforts to market the empire at home, in the colonies, and abroad in the interwar period. Pressed into service as a technology of "empire-strengthening," the cinema also created new spaces for interaction, alliance building, and conflict among individuals of African descent in London and around the Atlantic, becoming an avenue and target of anti-imperialist critique and black public debate. A decade after the release of *Sanders of the River*, the portrayal of colonial Africa in *Men of Two Worlds* once again provided the occasion for both. However, the ideological content of the film and the debates into which it intervened were markedly different from those of the earlier film.

Directed by Thorold Dickinson, who was released from military service to make the film, *Men of Two Worlds* tells the story of Kisenga, a gifted composer and pianist who returns to the Litu people in Marashi, his home village in Tanganyika, after spending fifteen years in Britain. It is more subtle and nuanced, and more honest about the limits to British power in colonial Africa, than *Sanders of the River*. Film historian Peter Swaab suggests that "it's a film of two genres": "one of them a relatively traditional colonial melodrama not so very far upstream of *Sanders of the River*, but the other a more progressive, densely imagined Shavian debate on the intractabilities of political dirigism [*sic*] in far-off lands." Indeed, the filmmaker understood that people of African descent inevitably would compare *Men of Two Worlds* to Korda's earlier film. "Always," Dickinson wrote in 1947, "we had to prove to the coloured people that our film was to be no *Sanders of the River*, that bugbear of every educated person of colour."[61] The film opens with the conclusion of Kisenga's farewell performance at the National Gallery, which is greeted with rapturous applause from his British audience. Although the sequence acknowledges the growing presence of educated Africans and black music in Britain by showing that "the rhythms of Africa have found their way to the heart of the empire," it romanticizes their contributions and reception, glossing the effects of racism. In fact, Dickinson had to re-create the scene in the studio because Dame Myra Jess refused to permit a black man to perform at the National Gallery, even if only for the film. Against the protests of his acolytes, who tell him that British music "needs him," Kisenga leaves for Africa to serve as an educational officer and assist the local district commissioner with combating the spread of sleeping sickness. The scheme involves the wholesale relocation of the village and the introduction of concentrated agricultural production. Kisenga embraces these goals and the logic of development more generally. He insists that "knowledge is man's only weapon against his enemies": "disease," "superstition," and "fear."[62]

As unrest in both the Caribbean and Africa, echoed by the protests of people of African descent in the metropole, made the shortcomings of colonial policy more difficult to ignore, a new language of development, based on ostensibly universal standards of progress but, crucially, not substantive political reforms, began to take hold within official circles by the end of the 1930s. Many on the British left, an increasing number of self-appointed colonial "experts," and even some in the Colonial Office began to question the basic tenets of the conventional "pay your way" model of colonial governance. "Development" and "welfare" became the key terms of a new imperial imaginary, enshrined in the Colonial Development and Welfare Act, which went into effect in the summer of 1940. The decade that followed witnessed a major shift in the conceptualization and instruments of colonial rule as the civilizing mission was recast as what Wendy Webster terms a new "developing mission" focused on Africa. Rule by experts and "partnership" with educated Africans in the development project came to supplement, though not completely supplant, the Sanders archetype, "trusteeship," and indirect rule through native "chiefs."[63] This revised mandate combined greater centralized control from the Colonial Office with technocratic management by experts in a variety of fields; privileged measures of the relative health, educational attainment, and productive output of the population; and relied on a set of assumptions regarding the proper economic role of black labor in the colonies.[64] Although they conceded that self-government within the British Commonwealth must be the ultimate goal of colonial policy, British authorities on the empire increasingly argued that progress in the colonies and, by extension, the legitimacy of British rule should be judged by levels of economic development and social welfare, not the steps taken toward democracy and the Africanization of the state. Following the party's triumph in the 1945 general election, even Labour's staunchest advocates of colonial reform, individuals well known to Africans and Caribbeans in London, insisted that social and economic improvements had to precede self-government and envisioned a form of colonial development that privileged Britain's postwar economic needs.

Commissioned by the Ministry of Information at the urging of the Colonial Office in 1942 and released in 1946, *Men of Two Worlds* graphically captured the new imperatives of welfare and development in colonial administration. The international context and this changing imperial imaginary shaped the production of the film and its content. First and foremost, the film was a piece of propaganda intended to distinguish a benign British colonialism from Nazism, to justify government expenditure on development initiatives in the colonies, and to mollify an ostensibly anti-imperialist U.S. government in the wake of the Atlantic Charter. Soon after the start of the war, several interested parties had identified British scientists' battle against the tsetse fly in Africa as a fitting subject for propaganda. In 1940, the head of the Ministry of Information's empire division, Gervais Huxley, produced a script for a documentary film entitled "Man versus Fly," which he submitted to the Colonial Office. His wife, Elspeth Huxley, wrote the script for a BBC Home Service program called *War against the Locusts* as part of a series broadcast in 1943, which also included *Life of a District Officer* and *War against Superstition.*[65] *Men of Two Worlds* combined the main themes of "Man versus Fly" and these Home Service programs in what officials believed to be a more effective, melodramatic format. As one member of the Colonial Office put it, "For some time I have been convinced that the purely documentary type of Colonial film would not by itself serve the purpose . . . of stimulating interest about the Colonies in this country," citing the poor distribution and lackluster attendance of previous documentary films.[66] The desired effect, as a local newspaper in Tanganyika explained to its readers, was to combine "first-class entertainment value . . . with absolute authenticity and the presentation of a fair picture of the problems of African progress and development in Tanganyika."[67] Officials also hoped the film would appeal to and have a positive impact on American audiences. Mr. MacDougall of the British Information Service in New York viewed the project as an opportunity "for an imaginative presentation of our prime theme which is the march of the native peoples towards independence via rising standards of health and living, and political education in the village councils," adding, "What a chance we have to confront Americans with the nature, size and complexity of the problem and the efforts being made to solve it!"[68] In addition to "stimulating interest about the Colonies in this country," many officials hoped that the film, like *Sanders*, would provide a valuable service in the international arena by countering the arguments of anti-imperialist critics, including African Americans like Paul Robeson.[69]

Fittingly for a film intended to promote direct government intervention and investment in the colonies, official involvement in *Men of Two Worlds* was more direct than in Korda's film. The project was the brainchild of Noel Sabine, a public-relations officer in the Colonial Office. Sabine suggested a 1939 Empire Marketing Board documentary short (*Men of Africa*), whose message resembled that of *Sanders* in its broad outlines, as a model for an expanded Technicolor film. Based on his suggestions, the novelist Eileen Arnot Robertson wrote a treatment entitled *White Ants*. The story centers on District Officer Shearforth and his heroic battle against the twin obstacles of an inhospitable environment, epitomized by the eponymous ants, and superstition, embodied by a stock witch-doctor character. The village schoolteacher, Hale, who spent ten years at Achimota College in the Gold Coast, assists Shearforth in his efforts. Hale survives a witch doctor's curse thanks to the unyielding confidence and assistance of the Shearforths, despite revealing himself as "wholly African in his distress" over "age-old terrors." Following the ordeal, he tells the official: "What you can—and must do—is stand by us and make it possible for us to come forward; the African doctors and the African teachers; the new Africa that will fight the old evils with the science and the knowledge which you brought."[70]

White Ants was a hit with officials in the Colonial Office, and in 1942, they approached a titan of British cinema, Thorold Dickinson, to adapt it for the big screen. The director hired the former colonial official and author Joyce Cary to write the screenplay. Dickinson was a product of the antifascist left of the 1930s, and like many of his fellow travelers, believed firmly in the beneficial potential of a reformed colonialism guided by scientific expertise.[71] His directorial debut, *The High Command* (1937), included footage shot on location but used the Gold Coast mainly as the setting for "a battle ... between an old Britain and a newer one." During the war, he made several propaganda shorts for the Ministry of Information before assuming control of the Army Kinematograph Service, where he produced training films. Cary had served as a colonial officer in northern Nigeria and subsequently produced four novels based on his experiences, including *The African Witch* (1936), a foray into imperialist adventure fiction in which agents of progress and superstition compete for hearts and minds, and *Mister Johnson* (1939), the story of an African clerk who, like Kisenga in *Men of Two Worlds,* "embraces the opportunities of a modern colonial world" only to be done in as a result. The combination of his colonial-service experience and his books earned Cary a reputation as an Africa expert. The Colonial Office noted that he was "a writer of real distinction and an authority on African development."

Cary's ideas greatly influenced Dickinson. Both men viewed efforts to surmount the local barriers to development in Africa and the battle against fascism as parallel struggles between modernity and tradition, and this "ironic conflict between the old and the new," as Dickinson put it, remained the film's central theme through its various permutations. In his lengthy pamphlet *The Case for African Freedom* (1941), Cary dismissed the arguments of "racialists" and insisted that the devolution of self-government was a necessary component of effective economic development. At the same time, he castigated those who criticized the introduction of "modern economy" in Africa as naked exploitation, and compared anticolonial activists to fascist "dictators." In Cary's hands, enlightened colonial administration became the ultimate form of antifascism, simultaneously battling Nazism in Europe and superstition in the colonies. Discussing the making of *Men of Two Worlds* in 1945, Dickinson recapitulated Cary's arguments, noting that "there still survives, amongst the slow development of tribal society, the false racial pride, terrorism, and opposition to innovation which we in Europe recognise as Nazism."[72] Informed by this vision of progressive imperialism and the impediments to its success, the production process drew on the logic and tools of colonial development. Cary traveled with a film crew to East Africa for a "reconnaissance expedition" to conduct "intensive research on the subjects generally of Colonial development in Africa," with "every assistance and courtesy" from the Colonial Office and several colonial governments. To enhance the film's verisimilitude, Dickinson consulted with the anthropologist and musicologist Hans Cory on the music and ritual scenes, and claimed to have hired "a famous London psychiatrist" to make the portrayal of an educated African "who cracks up under strain . . . authentic from the current views on psychiatry."[73]

Men of Two Worlds reflects a changing colonial situation and an imperial imaginary in flux. Kisenga functions as both a symbol and an instrument of progress through development in Africa (and progress in Africa *as* development). Through his relationship with the district commissioner and scenes depicting the mobilization of the community's labor power for public works such as building a bridge, the film emphasizes hierarchical partnership in a joint venture. Yet the film repeatedly underscores Kisenga's status as a liminal figure who does not belong anywhere. Indeed, this is the only point on which the European and African characters in *Men of Two Worlds* agree. The local witch doctor Magole tells him bluntly, "We do not like a white man in black skin." In a conversation regarding Kisenga's difficulty reassimilating to the community, Professor Gollner says to District Commissioner Randall, "Big jump for him to make, the jump from the Stone Age to modern Europe." Randall replies, "Bigger jump for him to come back to the Stone Age." Even his adoring sister, Saburi, suggests, "This doesn't seem to be your country anymore," to which a dumbfounded Kisenga can only reply, "How can this not be my country? Africa?" Following his father's death, Kisenga confronts Magole, whose power over the villagers' minds presents the chief obstacle to the film's development project, and soon succumbs to superstition as his community before him. As his health and mental state worsen, he wonders aloud, "But what am I? I thought I had two worlds. Now I have none at all." Removed from the village to the district commissioner's house, Kisenga narrowly escapes death in the film's hallucinatory climax, a nightmare sequence in which he watches his arm turn white and his father tries to strangle him. He regains consciousness as the sound of his pupils in the children's orchestra performing his hybrid musical composition "Baraza" gradually supplants the ritual African drumming. Kisenga recovers and survives, and in the end, Commissioner Randall realizes "something like Cary's vision of progress, a utopian welfare state, with natives on trucks going over a new bridge to new lands under the guidance of a paternalistic colonial rule."[74] Nevertheless, a persistent undercurrent in *Men of Two Worlds* implies that intractable African backwardness will doom the project of modernization and development even when technoscience co-opts the educated new African and surmounts the challenges of disease and environment. Like the antifascist internationalist left of which Dickinson was a part and the colonial reformism that Cary represented, the film raises and then denies the possibility of equality and partnership across racial lines.

THE NEW AFRICAN AND INDEPENDENCE

Dickinson believed firmly in the greater authenticity of filming in situ and shot extensively in Tanganyika using scarce Technicolor film, but most of the footage did not survive the journey back to Britain. As a consequence, *Men of Two Worlds* combines snatches of atmospheric shots of Tanganyika with dramatic set pieces filmed in the studio in Britain. As with Korda's film, its cast included a number of Afro-Caribbeans and Africans residing in London. Whereas some had struggled for decades to find consistent work as professional actors, only to be limited to minor, stereotypical roles, others were making their first and only forays into film. Orlando Martins plays the witch doctor Magole, contributing the film's most powerful performance despite the role's stereotypical character. Napoleon Florent appears as Kisenga's father; the Sierra Leonean Viola Thompson as his mother; the Nigerian Tunji

Thompson as Ali, the local dispenser and Saburi's fiancé; the Jamaican Sam Blake as Chief Rafi; and Uriel Porter as Saidi, the local headman. The film crew discovered the Ugandan Eseza Makumbi while on location in East Africa and brought her to London to play the hero's sister, Saburi, at a time when African actresses were exceedingly rare in British cinema.[75] Dickinson also drew on black musicians and dancers in London. The musician and owner of the Caribbean Club, Rudy Evans, plays Akbram, the local African schoolmaster. The soprano Gladys Taylor is one of the local village women, and the Ghanaian musicians Harry Eben Quashie and Edmund Tagoe are shown drumming. As the *League of Coloured Peoples Newsletter* noted in advance of the film's release, the Jamaican dancer, choreographer, and cofounder of Britain's first black dance company, Berto Pasuka, can also be seen "doing his stuff" in the film.[76]

The filmmakers modeled their protagonist on familiar black musicians and considered several for the part of Kisenga. "Consciously or otherwise," Cameron suggests, the role "was clearly intended for Robeson," and the character has obvious similarities to Zinga in *Song of Freedom*.[77] The Nigerian organist, pianist, and composer Fela Sowande provided a second model. He earned a bachelor of music degree at the University of London, received a fellowship from the Trinity College of Music, and became a fellow of the Royal College of Organists in 1943, where he headed his class and garnered a litany of prizes and awards. Sowande was the first African composer to incorporate both African folk and popular material into the European classical idiom. While still a student and working as a nightclub musician, in 1939, he completed his *Africa Suite* for orchestra and harp, which would become his most widely known composition. In 1944, the BBC broadcast his *Africana* in Britain. Soon after he enlisted in the Royal Air Force in 1942, the *West African Pilot,* edited by Azikiwe, lionized him as "one of the most celebrated Negro musicians in the heart of the British Empire." During the war, he also served as music director for the Colonial Film Unit (CFU) and produced a number of works for the BBC's West African broadcasts. Sowande engaged in discussions with his fellow WASU members on how the CFU might better represent their concerns. Two years earlier, the union had protested the casting of a Guyanese actor, Robert Adams, as the lead in the unit's short film *An African in London* (1941), the first government production to deal with the African presence in the metropolis. Because of Sowande's efforts, *Nurse Ademola* (1943) and *An African in England* (1945) followed, both featuring WASU members. While circulating the film treatment, Noel Sabine introduced him to Dickinson and hired him as a consultant in June 1943. Sowande's orchestra performed at the London premiere of *Men of Two Worlds* in 1946.[78]

For the starring role of Kisenga, the filmmakers initially considered another musician and Sowande's close friend, the Guyanese W. Rudolph Dunbar, before finally opting for Robert Adams. Given that Dunbar was a black musician trained in the United States and Europe who was adept with both jazz and classical forms, Sabine thought him ideal for the role of Kisenga.[79] Dunbar had first been introduced to the clarinet in 1916 at the age of nine as an apprentice to the British Guiana Militia Band. He began his formal education as a clarinetist at the Institute of Musical Art in New York City, and he mixed with musicians in the vibrant Harlem scene between 1919 and 1924. He first traveled to Britain as a member of Will Vodery's Plantation Orchestra in *Blackbirds* of 1926 and lived in Paris during the late 1920s, where he was a pupil of the renowned clarinetist and composer Louis Cahuzac and associated with black jazz musicians from the United States and the Caribbean. Dunbar's debut as a clarinet recitalist before a "delighted" audience at the Salle D'Iena in 1930 received rave reviews in the French press. He returned to Britain later that year as part of a group under the direction of the African American jazz violinist Leon Abbey. In August 1931, *Melody Maker* declared him a "concert virtuoso of the clarinet," adding that he was "a saxophonist, too, and a hot one at that!" Like Sowande, before his greatest triumphs in the field of concert music, Dunbar spent years in the London jazz scene and led several all-black dance bands. On August 22 and 23, 1934, his band stood in for the BBC Dance Orchestra, becoming, as the *Topical Times* told readers, "the first all-British coloured band to be heard over the air," and, on December 7, 1934, his African Polyphony accompanied the British singer Gladys Keep on recordings of the popular jazz standards "Dinah" and "St. Louis Blues." Dunbar also wrote a regular column for *Melody Maker* for seven years and published a technical manual, *Treatise on Clarinet Playing* (1939), that remained the standard work of its type for years to come.[80]

After a decade of struggling to eke out an existence from teaching, writing, and playing in nightclubs, Dunbar's greatest achievements as an artist came in the 1940s. In 1942, he led the London Philharmonic Orchestra in a performance of works by Debussy, Dvořák, and the African American composer William Grant Still at Royal Albert Hall, a "triumph" that was followed by guest conductorships with some of Europe's leading symphony orchestras during the mid- to late 1940s.[81] He used the platform to expose

European audiences to experiments at incorporating African American music into the orchestral tradition and, in particular, the still-little-known works of black composers. In his choice of material, Dunbar linked his personal ambitions as a musician and conductor to a tradition of black musicianship as well as historical struggles for the recognition of black personhood and independence. He befriended Samuel Coleridge-Taylor's widow, Jessie Walmisley, and during one visit, she informed him of the existence of several "forgotten" compositions by her deceased husband. The *Star* reported that Dunbar would present one of these works, "Toussaint L'Overture" (*sic*), which had not been performed since 1901, at his upcoming performance with the London Symphony at Albert Hall on November 28, 1942.[82]

Dunbar was enthusiastic about the prospect of participating in *Men of Two Worlds*—as he had been about the presence of so many black actors in *Sanders of the River* a decade earlier—and acted as a mediator between the Colonial Office and black organizations in London when they petitioned for changes to the film's script. It is unclear from extant records why the filmmakers ultimately chose Adams, who was originally considered for the part of the Magole, over Dunbar, but it seems likely that Dunbar's public profile as a journalist figured heavily in the final decision. In addition to his music career, Dunbar was the London correspondent for the U.S.-based Associated Negro Press during the late 1930s and early 1940s. Reprinted in newspapers across the country, his copy reached millions of African American readers. He worked as a press officer at the Ministry of Information during the war, and his articles, which often celebrated the contributions of colonial soldiers and workers to the war effort, appeared in more than 120 papers in the Caribbean.[83] Officials in the Colonial Office repeatedly expressed concern over Dunbar's participation in the film, particularly the possibility that he would have to travel to Tanganyika. As the secretary of state explained to the governor of Tanganyika, "I believe him to be friendly, sincere and reliable, but I should like your assurance that his visit . . . would cause no undue embarrassment in the neighbourhood." Another official observed, "A visit by him to Tanganyinka . . . might raise rather awkward questions," adding, "I think that we could probably use our influence with the film company to prevent his going to Africa."[84] Colonial officials were, at best, reluctant to allow African Americans and Afro-Caribbeans to travel to British territories in Africa, fearing the impact of their mixing with the local population, and often attempted to block their passage. Dunbar's position as a journalist only deepened their apprehension.

A former heavyweight champion of the British Empire known as the Black Eagle, Adams had appeared in a number of stage productions in London as well as playing minor roles in several films, including alongside Robeson in *Song of Freedom* (1936), *King Solomon's Mines* (1937), and the play *Stevedore*.[85] With Robeson in the United States, he played the protagonist in the Unity Theatre's 1939 production of *Colony,* a timely drama about a strike in Jamaica. In 1944, he helped establish the short-lived Negro Arts Theatre, one of the earliest attempts to form a black theater company in London. Two years later, he joined the Unity's professional company and starred in its first production, a new run of Eugene O'Neill's *All God's Chillun Got Wings,* assuming the role that Robeson had made famous. Adams was also a founding member of the LCP and, by the early 1940s, sat on its executive committee. When the Fabian Colonial Bureau began contacting performers for a West Indian dance in 1946, the bureau's assistant secretary, Marjorie Nicholson, wrote first to Adams, after hearing him sing at the Indian Independence Day celebration in London.[86] Landing the part of Kisenga was a small coup, and the role would be the most prominent and controversial of Adams's career.

Controversy engulfed *Men of Two Worlds* while Dickinson was shooting in Tanganyika. When Two Cities Film approached the WASU for assistance in identifying suitable candidates to play African women in the film, Solanke requested a copy of the script before agreeing to help, and the company forwarded Cary's draft.[87] After reviewing it, Solanke informed Two Cities that the WASU was unwilling to assist owing to its "unrealistic and harmful" representation of African life. He objected, above all, to the emphasis on witchcraft in African society. In July 1943, the union's executive committee passed a resolution, which it enclosed with a letter of protest to the Colonial Office, stating that the script "casts a slur on the prestige of African peoples as a whole," "is in no way suggestive of real cooperation between white and black," and "prejudices future relations between the African peoples and the British Empire." The memorandum declared unequivocally, "There is no such thing as a witch doctor in African law and custom. It is an entirely European invention" and a distortion of African healing practices.[88] In a follow-up letter, Solanke cited the work of several African, European, and American scholars that supported this contention. He also offered substantive suggestions for revising the script, changes that, as officials in the Colonial Office recognized, would have modified the film's message considerably. The proposed changes pushed the setting back in time to the advent of British rule and altered the character Magole, in particular, recasting him as a counterpoint to Kisenga (at that point named Kijana) representative of a competing point of view among educated Africans. As Solanke explained:

> While the D.C. [district commissioner] Rende is trying . . . to secure British Imperial Rule . . . through the agency of that section of the educated African elements who are in favour of Direct Rule . . . which Kijana represents; the Magole, on the other hand, representing the opposite school of thought among the educated Africans, is advocating for [an] Indirect Rule system . . . [like] that of Egypt when the latter was still under the protection of Great Britain, namely, that within a definite and very short period, British rule and British imperialism in Africa should come to an end and complete self-government be granted to the African people.[89]

Solanke and the WASU attempted to transform a film about the noble efforts of British colonial officials, experts, and their African protégé in the battle between European science and African superstition into a film depicting the diversity of informed African opinion. The debate that they scripted for its African leads was one then raging within the group's ranks, in which the desire for political autonomy was a legitimate aspiration, though not the only option.

Although the union's efforts failed, the entire episode revealed the extent to which Africans and Afro-Caribbeans in London had secured a begrudging recognition from the Colonial Office. A. R. Thomas declared the WASU's revision of the script "unacceptable, partly because of the anti-imperialist tinge which it would give the film," but he asked Sabine to reach out to the West Africa Department regarding the script's accuracy and to inquire with Two Cities about "whether the filmmakers would consider recasting its theme fundamentally or adapting it . . . so as to take some account of these representations." Sabine, in turn, solicited the black British official Ivor Cummings's thoughts on the script, and officials in the West Africa Department mobilized the opinions of European experts and colonial officers in Africa to discredit the WASU's claims. T. K. Lloyd and C. Jeffries also met with a delegation composed of members of the WASU and LCP at the Colonial Office. Afterward, Lloyd noted that "they object . . . to any screen or other presentation which shows the primitive beliefs and habits of coloured peoples" and "argued, for example, that some of the native scenes in 'Sanders of the River' were an affront to the dignity of Africans." To his peers, Lloyd dismissed the delegation's criticisms, which he attributed to an unrealistic "attitude of mind" and an "inferiority complex." Nevertheless, he assured the organizations' representatives that the filmmakers were still revising the script, "not specifically to meet the Union's comments but in a way which will meet some of their points."[90]

Another official wrote that, "so far as the West African territories are concerned, W.A.S.U. has really limited political significance," citing, as always, local allegiance to the "native" rulers and their partners in indirect rule; but he added, "On the other hand, W.A.S.U. has considerable political influence in this country, especially among those Members of Parliament who take an interest in West Africa, as it is their main, if not their only, source of contact with West Africans over here."[91] The creation of the West African Parliamentary Committee in 1942 was particularly significant in this regard. The committee met weekly at Westminster Palace and consisted of Creech Jones and several other Labour MPs, the economist Rita Hinden of the Fabian Colonial Bureau (FCB), and West Africans from the WASU, including Solanke, R. W. Beoku-Betts, A. O. Thomas, R. K. Gardiner, F. O. Blaize, and later Joseph Appiah and Kwame Nkrumah. Reverend Reginald Sorensen, a peer in the House of Lords and one of the WASU's strongest supporters, chaired the committee and inquired twice into the affair, an intervention that likely helped persuade officials to meet with the delegation from the two organizations.[92]

The FCB had been established in 1940 as an independent department of the Fabian Society devoted to colonial issues, specifically to developing a socialist approach to colonial development. The bureau's executive and advisory committees were a who's who of socialist critics of colonial policy in Africa. Hinden served as its secretary for a decade, largely directing its activities; Creech Jones chaired its executive committee until 1945, when he assumed the post of assistant colonial secretary and then, two years later, that of colonial secretary. Professor W. Arthur Lewis and, later in the decade, Dr. Robert Wellesley Cole sat on the executive committee, and Hinden engaged with many other black intellectuals. Writing in *Wāsù* at the end of the war, Hinden proposed a "partnership . . . between progressive forces of Britain and their counterparts in the colonies." She raised "the possibility of a complete dissolution of the association between Britain and the colonial empire," only to dismiss it as impractical. "No responsible person, either in the Colonies or in Britain," she claimed, "is calling for that at this particular moment," advocating instead for the colonies "to remain inside some form of commonwealth or empire, but bearing a new status—and the phrase coined to describe the possible new status is 'partnership.'" Though not entirely uncritical of Labour politicians, the FCB remained closely tied to the party and defended the government's policies to black critics after 1945. WASU members dubbed it the "unofficial mouthpiece" of the Labour government.[93]

In light of such rhetoric and the negotiations between black organizations and the Colonial Office over the film, some within the black community in London expressed the hope that *Men of Two Worlds* would present a more nuanced portrait of colonial Africa befitting a new era of cooperation in the empire. Marson discussed the film on *Calling the West Indies* in early 1946. The LCP began publicizing it at about the same time, stating that it "typifies . . . the African of today whose desire is to become educated and help his peoples out of their misery and misunderstandings." When the film opened in London in July, the *League of Coloured Peoples Newsletter* noted of the Kisenga character: "It is one of the first roles played on the screen by a member of [the] race in which he is shown in [a] respectable and somewhat serious light, and it is one that few but Mr. Adams could play." The reviewer also drew readers' attention to other familiar faces in the cast, such as Viola Thompson, who had served on the organization's executive committee between 1934 and 1938, and appears in what seems to have been her only on-screen role.[94]

Despite—and, in part, because of—the presence of league members and others of African descent, *Men of Two Worlds* received a mixed but largely negative reception from black intellectuals and agitators in London, ranging from mild praise to outraged condemnation. Like *Sanders,* it also divided individuals and organizations, and became part of a much broader political discussion—in this case, over the choice between partnership and independence. This question hinged on the likelihood of securing fundamental political reforms and the economic benefits of development within the empire, and for many, the film provided further cause for skepticism. With Solanke in Nigeria on a fund-raising mission, the WASU's vice president, M. C. Peterside, led the group's campaign against the film with two letters published in the *Times.* In the first, he decried the filmmakers' persistence in "maintaining the fallacy of their plot" in the face of the union's "attempts at correction." They not only "projected the European concept of witchcraft into Africa" but also "invented a type of African who only exists in the imagination of some people, a man of two worlds, who cannot fit into European or African society because he has lived and studied in Britain." Peterside asked, "Is this type of film going to contribute towards creating the commonwealth of free peoples under the British Crown ... , or is it meant to postpone it?" In the second, longer letter, responding to correspondents' criticisms, he wrote, "I cannot see how our two peoples can cooperate together for common good in the new colonial partnership if we continue to misunderstand and misrepresent each other."[95] In November, Sydney Sandy noted in the *League of Coloured Peoples Newsletter* that the film had "caused quite a stir among my fellow colonials in this country" who "see in it a subtle attempt to hold them up to ridicule." He agreed that the film had flaws but suggested that, like the present historical conjuncture, it presented an opportunity, even an invitation, for black intellectuals to seize a greater role in the building of a new Africa. "Whatever the questionable motive behind its production ... ," Sandy argued, "there can be no denying the fact that there are two worlds of man's making [in colonial Africa]. ... The onus lies on us to bring about the fusion of these two worlds but we cannot do this by drifting aimlessly between them as so many of us are doing. ... Nor will it be done by sitting back and railing at ... our 'benefactors' who have proved altogether too dilatory."[96] In response to the controversy, Sandy issued a call for unity, as the WASU had in defending Robeson. He also used the occasion to lecture younger students about their responsibilities and their behavior in the metropole.

The war years and immediate postwar period saw the arrival or return of significant numbers of Caribbean and African students and political activists, many of whom became increasingly outspoken in their demand for immediate independence. Sandy spoke directly to these younger agitators, who vocally challenged both the British government and more established members of the WASU and LCP or split off into new groups. Both organizations assumed more assertive stances during the war. At a conference in 1942, the WASU passed a resolution demanding democratization and "Internal Self-Government Now, with a definite guarantee of Complete Self-Government within five years after the war." "We are convinced," the resolution asserted, "that only a realistic approach and a generous gesture on the part of the Imperial Government Now can save the Empire from collapse."[97] At a WASU conference the following year, before several representatives of the West African press, Kweku Bankole Awoonor-Renner raised the question of "whether West Africa would like to break away from the Empire." The answer, he argued, "depends upon the Policy of the British Government and indeed ... the attitude of the British people in the United Kingdom towards our national aspiration." He expressed "hope that with the aid of you, who appointed yourselves our Trustees, but now as partners, this most needed change will be realised," but warned, "it will be [realized] notwithstanding, for no nation or people can forestall the supreme march of history."[98] By decade's end, the number of Africans in London who expected either a "realistic approach" or "fundamental change" was dwindling.

Kwame Nkrumah arrived in London from the United States in 1945 with a letter of introduction from C. L. R. James. The previous year, he had participated in the Council on African Affairs' historic conference on Africa in New York alongside Ashwood Garvey and the Robesons. Appiah and Padmore met him at Euston station and took him directly to a railroad union meeting where Appiah was speaking. Afterward, they deposited him at the WASU's Africa House in Camden Town, where he spent his first days in the metropolis. Nkrumah immediately immersed himself in the union's activities and preparations for the upcoming Pan-African Congress in Manchester, serving as the regional secretary of the Pan-African Federation for southern England.[99] In his address to the gathering of activists and trade unionists from both sides of the Atlantic, Nkrumah declared that "the struggle for political power by colonial and subject peoples is the first step towards, and the necessary prerequisite to, complete social, economic and political emancipation." The *League of Coloured Peoples Newsletter* published Nkrumah's and W. E. B. Du Bois's speeches in early 1946, and they were included in *Colonial and . . . Coloured Unity: History of the Pan-African Congress,* edited by Padmore, which appeared the next year.[100]

The 1945 Pan-African Congress propelled Nkrumah to prominence in Britain and, via the printed word, West Africa. His time in Britain reunited or brought him into contact with individuals who later assumed important positions in his administration in Ghana (J. S. Annan, Kamkam Boadu, Eddie DuPlan, and Ako Adjei), as well as his friend and future political rival, Joseph Appiah. Soon after the Manchester conference, a group of West African radicals that included Bankole Akpata, G. Ashie Nikoi of the Gold Coast Aborigines' Rights Protection Society, Bankole Awoonor-Renner, and his wife, Olabisi, formed the West African National Secretariat (WANS) to serve as a vehicle for coordinating action in Britain and West Africa. I. T. A. Wallace-Johnson, who, after years of internment in West Africa, returned to London in 1945 to represent the Sierra Leone Trade Union Congress at the first meeting of the World Federation of Trade Unions, chaired it, but Nkrumah was its real driving force.

Most of the WANS's founders either had been or continued to be active members in the WASU. Nkrumah was elected vice president soon after his

FIGURE 14. Kwame Nkrumah. National Archives, Kew, United Kingdom, KV 2/1847 (1948).

arrival and remained on its executive committee until his departure in 1947. The belief that West Africa represented an organic entity and, thus, should share a political structure linked the two organizations. However, as the debate intensified within the WASU over whether self-governing dominion status or complete independence should be the immediate goal, this small group of communist-leaning West Africans launched the WANS to agitate for the latter. The group called "for unity and independence" or, in other words, "United West African National Independence."[101]

The differing reactions to *Men of Two Worlds* reflected not only generational and political divisions among black sojourners and migrants but also a growing and widely shared sense of frustration with the postwar Labour government. As early as May 1946, the FCB's journal, *Empire,* noted,

"Already we are being told that Labour is a disappointment. These elements come mainly from the colonial peoples, though also from some of the ranks of the Party at home."[102] Both the substance of constitutional reforms in Nigeria, which partitioned the colony into three regional units under a loose federated structure, and the way in which Governor Arthur Richards pushed them through the assembly angered Africa intellectuals there and in London. The government's guiding principle was, H. O. Davies observed, "discussion," not "greater *participation* by the Africans in theirs affairs.... No attempt is made to democratize ... bureaucrative [*sic*] rule or make it sensitive to public opinion." A pan-Nigerian delegation traveled to London to protest the Richards constitution and present an alternative. The Labour government's paternalistic response amounted, as the LCP's *Newsletter* reported, to an "admonition ... to go back home and give the Richard's Constitution a trial." Of particular note, the piece continued, was "the fact that it came from Mr. Arthur Creech Jones, ... one whom the Nigerian people in particular regarded as their friend." At an FCB conference on Britain's relationship to the colonies in April 1946, Elsa Goveia insisted that "British rule in Africa has arrested the evolutionary growth of African territory." The new Nigerian constitution, she argued, "has been unscientific and unreal. It was done by people who were scrambling for territory and had no thought about the good of the country." Nkrumah, Kenyatta, Padmore, Abrahams, Lewis, and a contingent from the WASU including Davies and Max Iyalla also took part; Robert Adams attended as well. Nkrumah restated the resolutions passed at the 1945 Pan-African Congress and declared, "We want absolute independence." Kenyatta rejected Hinden's plea for patience and a partnership for "social justice," remarking: "I am tired of talking about this. We are not asking the Labour Government to be revolutionary but to do certain things which it has promised to do. It is better food, housing, living conditions that we want. If we are to cooperate at all, it must be on an equal basis. ... We object to being treated as children." He charged that socialist "friends," as much as their Tory rivals, regularly attempted to silence black intellectuals from the colonies. "We have published books and our friends have reviewed them more critically than the books of our enemies. ... English socialists say that the Pan African Federation does not represent anything. Yet we are able to call a conference of our people from all the territories. Unless you change your attitude we cannot cooperate." For Kenyatta and his peers, partnership remained an impossibility "so long as someone sits on your back."[103]

Men of Two Worlds opened in theaters across Britain in early September 1946. In light of events in Nigeria and elsewhere, African and Caribbean critics of the film viewed it as another sign that Britons, even their newly empowered friends in the Labour Party, were unwilling to accept democratization and self-government. Nkrumah edited the WANS's monthly journal, the *New African,* and produced much of its copy. Lack of resources forced the group to stop publishing it after only five issues, but the *New African* re-emerged three months later in the fall of 1946 with an expanded sixth issue, which contained two pieces on *Men of Two Worlds.* The first, which Nkrumah presumably authored, characterized the film as "the last word of Africa's indictment against British imperialism." He denounced the representation of Africans as untrue and racist, merely an attempt "to support their [British imperialists'] contention that the African people are still incapable to administer their own affairs" and chastised "those Africans and peoples of African descent who have allowed themselves to be mixed up in this new imperialist method of deriding the African people." At the same time, like Peterside, he argued that, by portraying the poor conditions in Africa, the filmmakers had produced a damning portrait of the shortcomings of British colonial rule. "If after over two centuries of the so-called 'civilising mission' in Africa, the African remains as 'Men of Two Worlds' depicts him," he maintained, "then both the imperialists and their cohorts the missionary, the British anthropologist and educationalists might very well pack their things ... and leave Africa to the Africans." The film, the piece concluded, "should be ... a challenge to the present Labour Government, a challenge to the Colonial Office, to the Fabian Colonial Bureau and to Africans for that matter."[104] The second and longer piece by an unnamed "West African" noted that the film's overriding "lesson" regarding the nature of partnership and colonial development consisted of a "warning ... that even social and economic services are in such an elementary state that constitutional questions must be shelved or delayed till these are improved." The author insisted, "The fact is that social, economic, indeed, all progress, comes to a standstill once a country is occupied by a foreign invader." Referring to the health scheme at the center of the film, he opined, "when one looks at those flies, ... no African would hesitate to demand, as Indians are now rightly demanding, that Britain must quit Africa."[105] The *New African* situated the film within an ongoing history of colonial abuses and selectively rejected and appropriated elements of the movie to critique the new developing mission, turning a pro-empire propaganda piece into a catalog of British failings. The page layout linked the group's response to the film to its larger goals. A sidebar in the bottom right-hand corner beneath the longer piece listed the WANS's "aims and objects," which focused on "the struggle for West African National Unity and absolute independence," "combating the artificial territorial divisions now in existence," and promoting "Unity, Harmony and Understanding between Africans and peoples of African descent throughout the world."[106] The WANS's aims were similar to those of the WASU and the other black pressure groups created during the interwar period, but the demand for immediate independence marked a significant departure from the latter's prewar and wartime goals.

A growing awareness of the limits of the "development crusade," as Kyerematen put it, informed the reactions to *Men of Two Worlds*.[107] As Solanke had pointed out in his criticisms of the script in 1943, it perpetuated the "erroneous idea that modern progress among indigenous Africans is usually rendered abortive" by the hold of superstition on the African mind, personified in the racist caricature of the witch doctor.[108] By the time the film entered theaters, many black intellectuals and activists in London had concluded that the rhetoric of partnership within the Commonwealth, like the notion of trusteeship before it, represented little more than a pretext for the continuation of colonialism. Disillusionment with precisely those individuals and groups in Britain whom Africans and Afro-Caribbeans had once seen as potential allies led to their rejection of this political and ideational structure of the Commonwealth and to demands for complete independence. After his promotion to colonial secretary, in late October 1946, Creech Jones defended the Labour government's "constructive proposals" for colonial reform in the face of growing criticism. He noted that "fierce criticism" came not only from Moscow but also from the other side of the Atlantic where "Paul Robeson . . . was alleged to have said: 'The British Empire is one of the greatest enslavers of human beings.'" In response, Creech Jones declared: "We want less segregation and to get away from snobbery. It is a partnership we want to share with colonial peoples," Writing in the *New African*, Nkrumah observed: "Africans have from time to time heard these high sounding platitudes and declarations about economic and social justice, trusteeship, and partnership. We know that the applications of the stated colonial policies are in flat contradiction with actual colonial practices." "This is the reason," he continued, "why West Africans stand uncompromisingly for unity and complete and absolute independence for West Africa." In the same issue, "Gemini" characterized the "various Utopian schemes . . . put forward for the betterment of the Colonial peoples" as a mere cloak for keeping them within the "Colonial framework." Now that "the war has ended and they have seen the 'peace' which is being prepared," the author declared, the "Colonial peoples want no part of a British Commonwealth."[109] If their colonial overlords did not believe in their "utopian" development initiatives, as *Men of Two Worlds* seemed to suggest, then, increasing numbers of Africans and Caribbeans asked, why should they?

Nkrumah returned to the Gold Coast in 1947. Awoonor-Renner embarked on his own West African tour the following year to generate interest and support for a proposed West African National Congress. In Lagos, Nigeria, the Ghanaian urged his audience "to intensify their present activities" in pursuit of the "goal of West African, rather than Nigerian, nationalism." For a short time, the WANS continued to function as an extension of Nkrumah's efforts in the Gold Coast. Meanwhile, during Solanke's extended absence between 1944 and 1948, an internal struggle enveloped the WASU. After his return, younger West African radicals led by Appiah increasingly marginalized the longtime warden of Africa House and used the union to agitate for immediate independence.[110] "Public pronouncements by some of our leading 'comrades' in the new Labour Government such as Creech-Jones, Bevin, and Morrison," Appiah recalled in his autobiography, "left us in no doubt what the difference between Labour-in-office and Labour-in-opposition was." The shooting of ex-servicemen involved in a peaceful march in Accra on February 28, 1948, and the government's repressive response to the ensuing disturbances provoked outrage in London. The WANS and WASU led a protest march to Trafalgar Square a week later. Once the procession arrived, Awoonor-Renner, Padmore, and Edric Connor addressed a crowd of roughly four hundred demonstrators. For Appiah, the "coup-de-grace" came in 1949, when Creech Jones declared in the House of Commons, "I cannot foresee a point for a long time ahead when the work of the colonial service will come to an end because of the achievement of self-government."[111] Because of the racial paternalism of the British left and particularly Labour's failure to move forward with substantive political reforms in the colonies, by the end of the decade, mobilization around and for complete independence replaced appeals for self-government within a reformed Commonwealth. Although Nkrumah and others continued to envision the creation of "one united country" out of the territories of "British," "French," and "Portuguese" West Africa, the Congo region, and the Republic of Liberia, the aspiration for political freedom increasingly took the form of liberation movements within discrete colonial territories and the transformation of individual colonies into sovereign nation-states.[112]

. . .

When considered in terms of their content, the circumstances surrounding their production, and their subsequent reception, *Sanders of the River* and *Men of Two Worlds* can be seen as manifestations of a restructuring imperial social formation. Bookending a decade of turmoil in the colonies, transcolonial agitation, and fierce imperial rivals culminating in global war, the two films evidenced Britain's changing relationship to its African colonies and other empires, and as such, became weapons in the contest over empire. Alexander Korda's hugely successful imperial epic was an attempt to address new exigencies, including imperial Britain's postwar economic and political troubles and the need to compete in a growing, American-dominated, global cinema marketplace. The production brought together black artists and activists from around the Atlantic; its release sparked heated debates about race, representation, and colonial administration, and incited recriminations from black commentators addressing transatlantic, imperial, and local publics. A decade later, *Men of Two Worlds* was released as part of a concerted attempt to recast the empire in terms of development and captured the central tropes of this new imagining of the empire as well as its constitutive contradictions. Despite the high hopes for it, the film failed to move either British audiences or the Africans it claimed to represent, at least in the ways intended. As Zachernuk observes, "If the Colonial Office had intended to create a new image under its control it did not."[113] Ultimately, rather than instilling confidence in the new developing mission, the representation of Africa in *Men of Two Worlds* had the opposite effect, and intellectuals and activists from the colonies used it to shift discussion away from colonial reform and toward the cause of independence, which entailed its own blind spots and structural limitations.

Epilogue

The plain fact is that I became "black" in London, not Kingston.

STUART HALL, *"The Windrush Issue: Postscript" (1998)*

AMIDST SEVERAL UNPUBLISHED BOOK MANUSCRIPTS in the private papers of Dr. Robert Wellesley Cole at the School of Oriental and African Studies, I discovered "West Africa: an Outline of the History." More than four hundred pages in length, it traces some five hundred years of the region's development and interactions with the outside world.[1] Born in Freetown in 1907, Wellesley Cole came to Britain in 1928 to pursue a degree in medicine and, ultimately, a specialization in surgery, becoming the first African surgeon in Britain. He participated in a number of black organizations in the decades that followed. He remained a member and booster of the West African Students' Union for many years. In the early 1940s, he founded and served as president of the Society for the Cultural Advancement of Africa in Newcastle, where he settled and operated a surgical practice until 1950. As Wellesley Cole explained in a letter to the League of Coloured Peoples' president, Dr. Harold Moody, the society's aim was to "bind the students here, African, West Indian, and American negro, into a self-conscious and race-conscious unit."[2] He later served as the league's president after Moody's death. In 1947, Wellesley Cole founded the West African Society in London, and he edited the group's short-lived journal, *Africana*. He also served as a member of the advisory committee of the Fabian Colonial Bureau and three different Colonial Office committees in the late 1940s. A decade later, he helped sponsor a diverse, transnational cultural program, "Presenting the Negro World," held by the London branch of the Society of African Culture in 1959. Throughout these various activities and a successful career as a surgeon, he read widely and wrote prolifically.

Although Wellesley Cole was certainly an extraordinary individual in terms of his accomplishments, professional and otherwise, the scope of his ambitious history of West Africa and the political imaginary and goals that inspired it emerged from his years inhabiting the same circles as other Afro-Caribbean and African intellectuals in Britain and, like his political and philosophical eclecticism, were shared by many of them. The range of his interventions bespoke a particular understanding of what it meant to be a black intellectual in the imperial metropolis and a shared commitment to intellectual and cultural production as an extension of politics and an instrument of social change. Africans and Afro-Caribbeans wrote not simply to mobilize extant communities in opposition to colonial rule, but in order to constitute the extranational political collectivities that they presumed to address. The assiduous care and dedication evidenced in the yellowing pages of Wellesley Cole's sprawling history of West Africa attest to this unrealized vision's submerged quality as well as its persistence across time.

The assertion of a putative racial unity across barriers of colony, class, and region as a legitimate expression of internationalism was neither inevitable nor natural, but rather a fraught political project shaped by historically specific exigencies and by diasporic encounters in highly defined spaces. A series of interlocking developments after World War I informed the political struggles and the intellectual and creative work examined in this book: the broad political and administrative restructuring of the empire; the growing economic, political, and cultural influence of the United States; the emergence of an imperial actor that explicitly disavowed imperialism in the Soviet Union and the Third International; migratory patterns of non-European people and the racial populism and constraints on mobility that they elicited in response; the movements for and acquisition of the franchise by women in Britain, the white settler colonies, India, and the United States; and the surfeit of internationalist imagery, institutions, and movements that, to varying degrees, cut across all of these from the "Wilsonian moment" to the Popular Front. The thought and politics of Afro-Caribbeans and Africans in London developed within networks of exchange and debate connecting disparate movements, racial settings, and national and imperial formations—the effects, reach, and affective resonance of which they reconfigured and extended. Nested social relations and specific nodal points and centers of interaction in the city mediated the reception, domestication, and translation of ideas and cultural forms. In the basement of the imperial metropolis, black intellectuals and artists of distinct backgrounds forged novel conceptions of political community, and their divisions and differences emerged most starkly. Private spaces and the dance floors in Soho's black clubs or the

WASU's Africa House yielded evanescent collective solidarities as much as periodical culture and protest rallies. Above all, the fugitive landscape of black London reveals the potentially transformative effects of the intimate spaces of sociality and of webs of friendships and the situated knowledge generated from them.

This book is also meant to defamiliarize the genealogy of a global order of nation-states and to reveal its emergence as a contingent outcome of anticolonial struggles. When Wellesley Cole arrived in Britain, and for three decades thereafter, the world consisted mostly of empires, not "nation-states." The black intellectuals who fill these pages saw global black unity as part of the larger trend toward global coordination and cooperation. Although they focused predominantly on challenging the predations of British colonialism, their political and personal identifications, like the color bar and increasingly internationalized imperial order, extended beyond their homelands. Even their immediate, local or "national" ambitions took the form of internationalist proposals that transcended prevailing colonial divisions. Up to the late 1940s, most African and Afro-Caribbean intellectuals in London envisioned the possibility of a future *within* the institutional framework of a transformed imperial federation, demanding citizenship rights, internal self-government, and regional integration. The shifting demands of black critics of empire in the late 1940s and 1950s marked the relative decline of one vision of black internationalism and the rise of more conventionally nationalist projects in the years that followed. "Anticolonial movements from the 1930s onwards," Frederick Cooper explains, "were able to make the once-ordinary category of 'colony' into something unacceptable in international discourse largely because they linked activists in African towns and cities with principled groups in the metropoles, who in turn tied those issues to the self-conception of democracies."[3] The voices and agitation of Afro-Caribbeans and Africans played a crucial part in this epochal shift, but the story of decolonization is equally a history of persistent inequalities of power and unrealized and now largely forgotten political possibilities.

From the end of World War I to the 1950s, from the Wembley Exhibition to the Colonial Development and Welfare Acts, empire-strengthening initiatives, despite their changing form and scope, consistently sacrificed the needs and political aspirations of colonial subjects in Africa and the Caribbean to the maintenance of the racial status quo and Britain's economic interests. The very limited steps toward political devolution during the interwar period and at the end of the Second World War attempted to channel political mobilization into institutions at the local and colony level and, thus, to restrict its impact. At the same time, following a well-established divide-and-rule approach, the Colonial Office sought bulwarks against the democratizing demands of educated elites, nationalists, trade unionists, and their rapidly growing urban audiences by propping up and opposing the "traditional" authority and continued allegiance of "native" rulers to these restless constituencies. Groups such as the WASU in London responded with a double move, on the one hand, decrying the cynicism toward and betrayal of the colonial intelligentsia and, on the other, forming ties with sympathetic patrons among African rulers that belied the central opposition of indirect rule. British officials and experts devised the notion of colonial development, which explicitly disaggregated democratization from social and economic improvements, as a response to the daunting challenges of the 1930s. The Colonial Development and Welfare Acts raised the stakes for imperial governance, but, as an effort to defer indefinitely the question of political reform, they only ensconced it further as the goal of anticolonial agitation, and development proceeded only as monopoly capitalism. As the Caribbean and particularly Africa became focal points of the revised mandate for empire, black intellectuals' and agitators' frustration with the unwillingness of British officials and politicians, including longtime collaborators on the left, to take meaningful steps toward the creation of a more egalitarian British Commonwealth led them to focus their efforts from the late 1940s onward on attaining complete independence. They increasingly mobilized the colonial state's failures to improve social and economic conditions within an alternative interpretative framework in which those conditions became factors necessitating, not obstacles to be overcome before, political autonomy.

Negotiation on highly unequal terms and mutually informed but irreconcilable political imaginaries shaped the final act of formal colonial rule. As internal self-government and development became the avowed goals, the British searched for respectable partners and pupils in the 1950s. If, as Cooper observes, the transfer of power involved British officials and politicians reimagining "the Apostle[s] of Disorder" such as Nkrumah and Kenyatta as men of "Moderation and Modernity," it bears remembering that the brokers were not separated by a chasm of civilizational difference, representing African "tradition" and imposed imperial modernity, respectively, but rather were familiar interlocutors and antagonists engaged in a much longer conversation. The capacity of many key figures in the drive toward independence to address multiple audiences and to combine and move between different discourses and networks, including those connecting them to new genera-tions of student-agitators in London, played an important role in their politi-cal ascendency and the mass mobilizations of the 1950s.[4] Even as they became more insistent on the necessity of independence, many African and Afro-Caribbean anticolonialists accepted key aspects of the new development mission, especially the emphasis on concentrated investment in large-scale infrastructure initiatives and extractive industries. In the years that followed, postcolonial leaders and officials often extended colonial-era development projects under increasingly constrained, neocolonial circumstances, the dif-ference being that they focused on securing the benefits of such initiatives for nation-building and to produce national subjects. When they failed to deliver, their political power proved to be as tenuous and compromised as these projects. "In the end," as Pierre concludes, "European economic supremacy and structural privilege, and nativization in the form of persistent regionalism, were the true victors in the decolonization experiment. Perhaps a more important victory for neocolonialism was the fact that the reconsoli-dation of European power and influence on the ground were no longer treated as the major culprits . . . in economic and political marginalization on a global scale." The renewed and globalized "scramble" for African resources as well as "peace-keeping" and "anti-terrorism" operations by European pow-ers in their former African colonies today seems to confirm this chilling summation of the meager fruits of decolonization.[5]

Although most black activist-intellectuals left London for Africa or the Caribbean to lead or participate in movements for independence, others remained, becoming a living bridge between the small but vibrant interwar scene and an emerging post-imperial metropolis transformed by Com-monwealth migration. A striking number of individuals examined in these pages made their way to Ghana in the years before independence, for the celebrations marking it, or as advisors or officials in Nkrumah's government. Those who stayed in Britain became outsiders in a newly national space, while decolonization established national states roughly along the imposed territorial boundaries of colonization across the former empire, ending some forms of domination while deepening others and erecting new barri-ers.[6] Positioned at the nexus of the two defining developments of postwar Britain—the rise of the welfare state and the racist backlash against the growing black presence that culminated in immigration control—Dr. Wellesley Cole sold his general practice with the creation of the National Health Service in 1948 in order to apply for jobs as a surgical consultant.

However, the opposition of white doctors and administrators prevented him from obtaining a position at any of the hospitals and nursing homes in Newcastle, so in 1950, he relocated to Nottingham, a move that brought to an end his twenty-two-year marriage to his Scottish wife, Anna Law Brodie, who stayed behind. Wellesley Cole built a thriving new practice including a private nursing home in Nottingham, a hub of Afro-Caribbean and Asian settlement where white hostility to interracial mixing exploded in a race riot on August 23, 1958. In 1961, he attended a garden party at Buckingham Palace with his second wife, Amy Hotabah During, a nurse from Freetown. Later the same year, the government of newly independent Nigeria invited him to visit in a professional capacity as a senior surgical specialist. Although Wellesley had lived for thirty-three years in England, when he and his wife returned, customs officials changed the expiration date on their passports from February 1963 to August 1962 and the designation on them from "United Kingdom and Colonies citizen" to "Commonwealth citizen" in accordance with new restrictions imposed by the Commonwealth Immigration Act. Despite his vigorous and ongoing protests over the next twenty years, he and his family were denied British passports. Whenever Wellesley Cole returned to Britain after traveling abroad, officials registered him as a "visitor" and stamped "Admitted on condition that holder does not remain in the United Kingdom longer than six months" on his Sierra Leone passport.[7]

Contemporary globalization proceeds largely through old imperial economic structures of exploitation, engendering a context within which national sovereignty exists as a cruel fiction for many and a blunt instrument in the hands of others—a fate that many black internationalists foresaw and feared as early as the 1920s. Different articulations of black internationalism have remained a persistent, if at times muted, refrain from independence to the present, emerging alongside, in the interstitial spaces between, or from the ashes of nation-building projects. In some ways, the ideas and utopian dreams explored here constitute part of the prehistory of the Afro-Asian Conference in Bandung, Indonesia, in 1955 and the creation of the Organization of African Unity in 1963. Yet the latter developments also radically curtailed the scope of interwar articulations of black internationalism. These gatherings, after all, assumed and helped to naturalize the territorial nation-state as the building block of any broader unity or organization. If this book is in part a history of "the paths not taken," the visions of extranational community discussed within its pages appear prescient, if flawed, and as vital as ever from our vantage point in the early twentieth-first century.[8] Some contemporary West African intellectuals whose lives have followed comparably transnational trajectories have called for closer union in the region in strikingly similar terms. The Nigerian Nobel laureate Wole Soyinka marvels in his memoir at the "meaningless separation" of the "artificially divided peoples of West Africa." The "borders of such nation spaces," he observes, "... remained meaningless to a huge majority of those whom the borders enclose or separate. It was true of the preindependence entities, and it is still mostly true today." Born in Bamako, Mali, raised in Kankan, Guinea, and having lived for much of his adult life in Paris and New York City, the scholar and filmmaker Manthia Diawara argues that "the nation-state for which many Africans still fight, kill, and die, is no longer viable as a cultural and economic unit." "To survive in the postmodern world dominated by new regional economic powers and information systems," Diawara suggests, "West African states, too, must adopt a regional imaginary." For Diawara, as for many black intellectuals in London between the 1920s and 1940s, "what is urgent in West Africa today is less a contrived unity based on an innate cultural identity and heritage, but a regional identity in motion ... as defined by the similarities in political and cultural dispositions grounded in history."[9] Written in the belief that critical histories remain indispensable resources for imagining transformative futures, this book concludes with this recurring, perhaps resurgent dream of a united West Africa as an equal participant in a more humane world.

NOTES

INTRODUCTION

1. Eslanda Goode Robeson, *African Journey* (New York: John Day, 1945), 13.

2. C. L. Innes, *A History of Black and Asian Writing in Britain, 1700–2000* (Cambridge: Cambridge University Press, 2002), 167; Bill Schwarz, "Black Metropolis, White England," in *Modern Times: Reflections on a Century of English Modernity,* ed. Mica Nava and Alan O'Shea (London: Routledge, 1996), 177–178. See also Elleke Boehmer, *Empire, the National, and the Postcolonial, 1890–1920* (Oxford: Oxford University Press, 2002); Jonathan Schneer, *London 1900: The Imperial Metropolis* (New Haven: Yale University Press, 1999); Brent Hayes Edwards, *The Practice of Diaspora: Literature, Translation, and the Rise of Black Internationalism* (Cambridge, MA: Harvard University Press, 2003); idem, "Shadow of Shadows," *positions* 11, no. 1 (Spring 2003): 11–49; Raymond Williams, *The Politics of Modernism: Against the New Conformists* (London: Verso, 1989), 45; Steven M. Feierman, *Peasant Intellectuals: Anthropology and History in Tanzania* (Madison: University of Wisconsin Press, 1990).

3. Peter Abrahams, *The Coyoba Chronicles: Reflections on the Black Experience in the 20th Century* (Kingston, Jamaica: Ian Randle, 2000), 36; C. L. R. James, *Beyond a Boundary,* 2nd ed. (Durham, NC: Duke University Press, 1993), 80.

4. Michelle Ann Stephens, *Black Empire: The Masculine Global Imaginary of Caribbean Intellectuals in the United States, 1914–1962* (Durham, NC: Duke University Press, 2005), 5; Gary Wilder, "From Optic to Topic: The Foreclosure Effect of Historiographic Turns," *American Historical Review* 117, no. 3 (June 2012): 738.

5. Frederick Cooper, *Colonialism in Question: Theory, Knowledge, History* (Berkeley: University of California Press, 2005), 26, 32, 153–154; James Epstein, *Scandal of Colonial Rule: Power and Subversion in the British Atlantic during the Age of Revolution* (Cambridge: Cambridge University Press, 2012), 17; Gary Wilder, *The French Imperial Nation-State: Negritude and Colonial Humanism between the Two World Wars* (Chicago: University of Chicago Press, 2005), 196; John D. Kelly and Martha Kaplan, *Represented Communities: Fiji and World Decolonization* (Chicago:

University of Chicago Press, 2001), 4–6; Lynn Hollen Lees, "Being British in Malaya, 1890–1940," *Journal of British Studies* 48, 1 (January 2009): 76–101.

6. Kevin Grant, Philippa Levine, and Frank Trentmann, "Introduction," in *Beyond Sovereignty: Britain, Empire and Transnationalism, c.1880–1950*, ed. Frank Trentmann, Philippa Levine, and Kevin Grant (Basingstoke, UK: Palgrave Macmillan, 2007), 2–3.

7. Mrinalini Sinha, *Specters of Mother India: The Global Restructuring of an Empire* (Durham, NC: Duke University Press, 2006), 16–18.

8. Marilyn Lake and Henry Reynolds, *Drawing the Global Colour Line: White Men's Countries and the International Challenge of Racial Equality* (Cambridge: Cambridge University Press, 2008); Barbara Bush, *Imperialism, Race and Resistance: Africa and Britain, 1919–1945* (London: Routledge, 1999).

9. Gary Wilder, "Untimely Vision: Aimé Césaire, Decolonization, Utopia," *Public Culture* 21, no. 1 (Winter 2009): 103.

10. Winston James, "The Black Experience in Twentieth-Century Britain," in *Black Experience and the Empire,* ed. Philip D. Morgan and Sean Hawkins (Oxford: Oxford University Press, 2004), 348.

11. Paul Gilroy, *The Black Atlantic: Modernity and Double-Consciousness* (Cambridge, MA: Harvard University Press, 1993); Tiffany Ruby Patterson and Robin D. G. Kelley, "Unfinished Migrations: Reflections on the African Diaspora and the Making of the Modern World," *African Studies Review* 43, no. 1 (April 2000): 11–45; Brent Hayes Edwards, "The Uses of *Diaspora,*" *Social Text* 66, 19, no. 1 (Spring 2001): 45–73; Tina Campt, "The Crowded Space of Diaspora: Intercultural Address and the Tensions of Diasporic Relation," *Radical History Review* 83 (2002): 94–113; Sidney J. Lemelle and Robin D. G. Kelley, eds., *Imagining Home: Class, Culture and Nationalism in the African Diaspora* (London: Verso, 1994); Patrick Manning, *The African Diaspora: A History through Culture* (New York: Columbia University Press, 2009).

12. J. Lorand Matory, *Black Atlantic Religion: Tradition, Transnationalism, and Matriarchy in the Afro-Brazilian Candomblé* (Princeton: Princeton University Press, 2005), 15; James H. Sweet, *Domingos Álvares, African Healing, and the Intellectual History of the Atlantic World* (Chapel Hill: University of North Carolina Press, 2011), 5; Philip S. Zachernuk, *Colonial Subjects: An African Intelligentsia and Atlantic Ideas* (Charlottesville: University Press of Virginia, 2000); Hakim Adi, *West Africans in Britain, 1900–1960: Nationalism, Pan-Africanism and Communism* (London: Lawrence and Wishart, 1998).

13. Leela Gandhi, *Affective Communities: Anticolonial Thought, Fin-de-Siècle Radicalism, and the Politics of Friendship* (Durham, NC: Duke University Press, 2006).

14. Schwarz, "Black Metropolis, White England," 177.

15. Lauren Berlant and Lee Edelman, *Sex, or the Unbearable* (Durham, NC: Duke University Press, 2014), viii.

16. Peter Fryer, *Staying Power: The History of Black People in Britain* (London: Pluto Press, 1984); Gretchen Holbrook Gerzina, *Black London: Life before Emancipation* (New Brunswick, NJ: Rutgers University Press, 1995); Gretchen Holbrook

Gerzina, ed., *Black Victorians, Black Victoriana* (New Brunswick, NJ: Rutgers University Press, 2003); Jeffrey Green, *Black Edwardians: Black People in Britain, 1900–1914* (New York: Frank Cass, 1998); Laura Tabili, *"We Ask for British Justice": Workers and Racial Difference in Late Imperial Britain* (Ithaca, NY: Cornell University Press, 1994); Sukhdev Sandhu, *London Calling: How Black and Asian Writers Imagined a City* (London: Harper Collins, 2003).

17. Femi Franklin, with an introduction by Lola Young, "Nigeria-London Connections," in "Windrush Echoes," special issue, *Soundings* 10 (Autumn 1998): 114.

18. Joseph Appiah, *Joe Appiah: The Autobiography of an African Patriot,* foreword by Henry Louis Gates, Jr. (New York: Praeger, 1990), 164.

19. Steven Feld, *Jazz Cosmopolitanism: Five Musical Years in Ghana* (Durham, NC: Duke University Press, 2012), 49.

20. British Library, National Sound Archive, Oral History of Jazz in Britain Collection, Frank Deniz (T9910-T9912Y C1) and Clare Deniz (T9808-T9810Y C1); The National Archives, KV 2/1847.

21. John Chilton, *Who's Who of British Jazz,* 2nd ed. (London: Continuum, 2004), 198–199; Val Wilmer, "Cab Kaye: Musician Who Enlivened the British Jazz Scene and Rediscovered His African Roots," *Guardian* (March 20, 2000), www.guardian.co.uk/news/2000/mar/21/guardianobituaries2/print (accessed June 11, 2012); "Cab Kaye Launches All-Coloured Band," *Melody Maker* (March 12, 1955): 11.

22. Akira Iriye, *Cultural Internationalism and World Order* (Baltimore: Johns Hopkins University Press, 1997), 43; Wells quoted in ibid., 89. On the Universal Races Congress, see also Lake and Reynolds, *Drawing the Global Colour Line,* 251–262; and Robert John Holton, "Cosmopolitanism or Cosmopolitanisms? The Universal Races Congress of 1911," *Global Networks* 2, no. 2 (April 2002): 153–170.

23. John Coatman, *Magna Britannia* (London: Jonathan Cape, 1905), 18–19, 72, 89.

24. Frank Trentmann, "After the Nation-State: Citizenship, Empire and Global Coordination in the New Internationalism, 1914–1930," in Trentmann, Levine, and Grant, *Beyond Sovereignty,* 35, 37; David Long and Brian C. Schmidt, eds., *Imperialism and Internationalism in the Discipline of International Relations* (Albany: State University of New York Press, 2005); Casper Sylvest, "Continuity and Change in British Liberal Internationalism, c. 1900–1930," *Review of International Studies* 31 (2005): 263–283; Helen McCarthy, "The League of Nations, Public Ritual and National Identity in Britain, c. 1919–56," *History Workshop Journal* 70 (2010): 108–132; Mrinalini Sinha, Donna J. Guy, and Angela Woollacott, "Introduction: Why Feminisms and Internationalism?" *Gender & History* 10, 3 (November 1998): 345–357.

25. Lake and Reynolds, *Drawing the Global Colour Line;* Tony Ballantyne and Antoinette Burton, "Global Empires, Transnational Connections," in *A World Connecting, 1870–1945,* ed. Emily S. Rosenberg (Cambridge, MA: Belknap Press of Harvard University Press, 2012), 403–431.

26. See, for example, Tony Martin, *Race First: The Ideological and Organizational Struggles of Marcus Garvey and the Universal Negro Improvement Association,*

The New Marcus Garvey Library, No. 8 (Dover, MA: Majority Press, 1976); Winston James, *Holding Aloft the Banner of Ethiopia: Caribbean Radicalism in Early Twentieth-Century America* (London: Verso, 1998).

27. George Shepperson, "Pan-Africanism and 'Pan-Africanism': Some Historical Notes," *Phylon* 23 (Winter 1962): 349, 353; Edwards, *The Practice of Diaspora*, 3, 243; Lara Putnam, *Radical Moves: Caribbean Migrants and the Politics of Race in the Jazz Age* (Chapel Hill: University of North Carolina Press, 2013), 3, 6; Minkah Makalani, *In the Cause of Freedom: Radical Black Internationalism from Harlem to London, 1917–1939* (Chapel Hill: University of North Carolina Press, 2011); Michael O. West, William G. Martin, and Fanon Che Wilkins, eds., *From Toussaint to Tupac: The Black International since the Age of Revolution* (Chapel Hill: University of North Carolina Press, 2009); Erik S. McDuffie, *Sojourning for Freedom: Black Women, American Communism, and the Making of Black Left Feminism* (Durham, NC: Duke University Press, 2011); Hakim Adi, *Pan-Africanism and Communism: The Communist International, Africa, and the Diaspora, 1919–1939* (Trenton, NJ: Africa World Press, 2013); Marc Gallicchio, *The African American Encounter with Japan and China: Black Internationalism in Asia, 1895–1945* (Chapel Hill: University of North Carolina Press, 2000).

28. West, Martin, and Wilkins, *From Toussaint to Tupac*, xi; Edwards, "Shadow of Shadows," 14.

29. Michael Warner, "Publics and Counterpublics," *Public Culture* 14, no. 1 (Winter 2002): 81–82, 86–89. See also Gilroy, *Black Atlantic*, 200; Wilder, *French Imperial Nation-State*, 192–198; Putnam, *Radical Moves*, 126–152, 154; Black Public Sphere Collective, ed., *The Black Public Sphere: A Public Culture Book* (Chicago: University of Chicago Press); Ben Vinson III, "African (Black) Diaspora History, Latin American History," *The Americas* 63, no. 1 (July 2006): 1–18.

30. The term *colored internationalism* is Yuichiro Onishi's. See Onishi, *Transpacific Antiracism: Afro-Asian Solidarity in 20th-Century Black America* (New York: New York University Press, 2013).

31. James, "The Black Experience in Twentieth-Century Britain," 348; Edwards, *The Practice of Diaspora*, 5.

32. Berlant and Edelman, *Sex, or the Unbearable*, viii, xii.

33. The phrase is Alys Weinbaum's. Alys Eve Weinbaum, *Wayward Reproductions: Genealogies of Race and Nation in Transatlantic Modern Thought* (Durham, NC: Duke University Press, 2004), ch. 5.

34. Jacqueline Nassy Brown, *Dropping Anchor, Setting Sail: Geographies of Race in Black Liverpool* (Princeton: Princeton University Press, 2005), 42.

CHAPTER ONE

1. On the history of black workers in Britain, see Tabili, *"We Ask for British Justice"*; Caroline Bressey, "Looking for Work: The Black Presence in Britain, 1860–1920," *Immigrants and Minorities* 28, nos. 2–3 (July–November 2010): 164–

182; Marika Sherwood, *Many Struggles: West Indian Workers and Service Personnel in Britain, 1939–45* (London: Karia Press, 1985).

2. Schneer, *London 1900*, 203–226.

3. The 1921 census also included people from mandate territories under British control. Michael Banton, *The Coloured Quarter: Negro Immigrants in an English City* (London: Jonathan Cape, 1955), 67.

4. Tabili, *"We Ask for British Justice"*; Michael Rowe, "Sex, 'Race,' and Riot in Liverpool, 1919," *Immigrants and Minorities* 19, no. 2 (July 2000): 53–70; Jacqueline Jenkinson, "The 1919 Race Riots," in *Racial Violence in Britain in the Nineteenth and Twentieth Centuries,* ed. Panikos Panayi (London: Leicester University Press, 1996), 92–111.

5. *African Times and Orient Express* (February 1917): 36 and (December 1917): 113; James S. Coleman, *Nigeria: Background to Nationalism* (Berkeley: University of California Press, 1958), 203; Imanuel Geiss, *The Pan-African Movement: A History of Pan-Africanism in America, Europe and Africa,* trans. Ann Keep (New York: Africana, 1974), 295–297; James, "The Black Experience in Twentieth-Century Britain," 358; Adi, *West Africans in Britain,* 23–24.

6. Andrea Levy, *Small Island* (London: Review, 2004), 1; Daniel Mark Stephen, "'The White Man's Grave': British West Africa and the British Empire Exhibition of 1924–1925," *Journal of British Studies* 48, no. 1 (January 2009): 102, 105. See also Daniel Mark Stephen, *The Empire of Progress: West Africans, Indians, and Britons at the British Empire Exhibition, 1924–25* (Basingstoke, UK: Palgrave Macmillan, 2013).

7. Jayna Brown, *Babylon Girls: Black Female Performers and the Shaping of the Modern* (Durham, NC: Duke University Press, 2008), 93; Paul S. Landau, "Empires of the Visual: Photography and Colonial Administration in Africa," in *Images and Empires: Visuality in Colonial and Postcolonial Africa,* ed. Paul S. Landau and Deborah D. Kaspin (Berkeley: University of California Press, 2002), 141.

8. "An Outrage," *West Africa* (March 22, 1924): 247.

9. Stephen, "'The White Man's Grave,'" 123, 125; Charles Graves, "When West Africa Woos," *Sunday Express* (May 4, 1924), 7; "West Africa and the Empire Exhibition," *West Africa* (April 12, 1924): 322.

10. Stephen, "'The White Man's Grave,'" 103–104; "Manners Makyth Empire," *West Africa* (May 10, 1924): 1; "When West Africa Protests," *West Africa* (May 17, 1924): 484; "The Arts and Crafts of the Gold Coast and Asante," *West Africa* (August 2, 1924): 781, and (August 16, 1924): 830.

11. Quoted in Philip Garigue, "The West African Students' Union: A Study in Culture Contact," *Africa* 23, no. 1 (January 1953): 56.

12. "Mrs. Marcus Garvey in Jamaica," *Daily Gleaner* (September 25, 1924): 7; Ladipo Solanke, "Nigeria: Its Institutions and Customs," *Spokesman* (March 1925): 24–26; Solanke, "Open Letter to the Negroes of the World, Especially to Those in West Africa and America: A Comprehensive Survey of African Conditions, African Lands now Menaced," *Spokesman* (June 1925): 12–15; Hakim Adi, "Amy Ashwood Garvey and the Nigerian Progress Union," in *Gendering the African Diaspora:*

Women, Culture, and Historical Change in the Caribbean and Nigerian Hinterland, ed. Judith Byfield, LaRay Denzer, and Anthea Morrison (Bloomington: Indiana University Press, 2010), 199–218.

13. Frederick Cooper, *Africa since 1940: The Past of the Present* (Cambridge: Cambridge University Press, 2002), 25; Vivian Bickford-Smith, "The Betrayal of Creole Elites, 1880–1920," in Morgan and Hawkins, *Black Experience and the Empire,* 194–227; Jemima Pierre, *The Predicament of Blackness: Postcolonial Ghana and the Politics of Race* (Chicago: University of Chicago Press, 2013), 20, 33. See also Akintola J. G. Wyse, *H. C. Bankole-Bright and Politics in Colonial Sierra Leone, 1919–1958* (Cambridge: Cambridge University Press, 1990).

14. "Resolutions of the National Congress of British West Africa" and "Constitution of the National Congress of British West Africa," in *Ideologies of Liberation in Black Africa,* ed. J. Ayodele Langley (London: Rex Collings, 1979), 741–747, 753–757.

15. "Nationalism as a West African Ideal: Casely Hayford's Address to the Union on November 5, 1926," *Wāsù* 2 (December 1926): 23–34.

16. United Kingdom, The National Archives, CO 267/622/5, Dr. H. C. Bankole-Bright, "The Maladministration of British Justice in the Courts of Sierra Leone (The Assessors' Ordinance)," 3–5, 12.

17. Ibid.

18. Zachernuk, *Colonial Subjects,* 96.

19. "A Short History of W.A.S.U. and Its Organ 'Wasu,'" *Wāsù* 2, no. 1 (January 1933): 3.

20. H. J. L. Boston, "Fifty Years Hence," *Wāsù* 1 (March 1926): 15–19 (emphasis in original).

21. "The Union 'At Home': The Future of WASU," *Wāsù* 2 (December 1926): 49; Coleman, *Nigeria,* 210.

22. Robert A. Hill, ed., *The Marcus Garvey and Universal Negro Improvement Association Papers* (Berkeley: University of California Press, 1990), 12:734n8.

23. Alain Locke, "Who and What is 'Negro'?" in *The Philosophy of Alain Locke,* ed. Leonard Harris (1942; repr., Philadelphia: Temple University Press, 1989), 219, 225; Brad Evans, "Where Was Boas during the Harlem Renaissance? Diffusion, Race, and the Culture Paradigm in the History of Anthropology," in *Central Sites, Peripheral Visions: Cultural and Institutional Crossings in the History of Anthropology,* ed. Richard Handler (Madison: University of Wisconsin Press, 2006), 69–98.

24. Alain Locke, *Race Contacts and Interracial Relations,* ed. Jeffrey Stewart (Washington, DC: Howard University Press, 1992), 11.

25. Alain Locke, "Afro-Americans and West Africans: A New Understanding," *Wāsù* 8 (January 1929): 18–24; "Editorial," *Wāsù* 8 (January 1929): 2–3.

26. "Editorial," *Wāsù* 8 (January 1929).

27. Quoted in Adi, *West Africans in Britain,* 38.

28. See, for example, Solanke, *Yoruba Problems and How to Solve Them* (Ibadan, Nigeria, 1931), *Lectures Delivered at the Abeokuta Centenary Celebrations* (Lagos, Nigeria, 1931), and *A Special Lecture—Addressed to Mr. A. K. Ajisafe* (Lagos, Nigeria, 1931).

29. Ladipo Solanke, *United West Africa, or Africa at the Bar of the Family of Nations* (1927; repr., London: African Publication Society, 1969), 63–64; Philip S. Zachernuk, "Of Origins and Colonial Order: Southern Nigerian Historians and the 'Hamitic Hypothesis' c. 1870–1970," *Journal of African History* 35, no. 3 (1994): 44–45.

30. Matory, *Black Atlantic Religion*. On the Krios, or Creoles, of Sierra Leone, see Akintola J. G. Wyse, "The Sierra Leone Krios: A Reappraisal from the Perspective of the African Diaspora," *Global Dimensions of the African Diaspora,* ed. Joseph Harris (Washington, DC: Howard University Press, 1993), 339–368.

31. Ladipo Solanke, "Unity and Co-operation," *Wāsù* 5 (September 1927): 18–21; "A Short Review by Ladipo Solanke (a native of West Africa)," *Wāsù* 2, no. 1 (January 1933): 40–41.

32. A. Ade Ademola, "The Solidarity of the African Race," *Wāsù* 4, no. 2 (August 1935): 29–31.

33. Robert B. Cole, "West Africa in Evolution," *Wāsù* 2, no. 2 (April–June 1933): 30–34.

34. J. B. Danquah, "Is the Negro a Dead Letter?" *Wāsù* 1 (March 1926): 23–25.

35. Martin B. Duberman, *Paul Robeson: A Biography* (New York: Ballantine Books, 1989), 123–124; Ade Ademola, "Colour Bar Notoriety in Britain," in *Negro: Anthology Made by Nancy Cunard,* ed. Nancy Cunard (London: Nancy Cunard at Wishart and Co., 1934), 556–557.

36. Kenneth Little, *Negroes in Britain* (London: Routledge and Kegan Paul, 1947), 278–279.

37. Nyasilie Magxaka, "Colour Bar in South Africa," *The Keys* 2, no. 1 (July–September 1934): 13.

38. See C. E. C., "Mr. Ronald Moody," *The Keys* 5, no. 3 (January–March 1938): 68–69; David Killingray, "'To do something for the race': Harold Moody and the League of Coloured Peoples," in *West Indian Intellectuals in Britain,* ed. Bill Schwarz (Manchester, UK: Manchester University Press, 2003), 68n7.

39. Quoted in Killingray, "'To do something for the race,'" 54.

40. *West Africa* (December 17, 1927).

41. Killingray, "'To do something for the race,'" 60.

42. Quoted in ibid., 58.

43. Roderick J. Macdonald, "Introduction to *The Keys,*" in *The Keys: The Official Organ of the League of Coloured Peoples,* intro. and ed. Roderick J. Macdonald (Millwood, NY: Kraus-Thomson, 1976), 7; "Communications," *Journal of Negro History* 18, no. 1 (January 1933): 92–99; *The Keys* 1, no. 1 (July 1933), n.p.; David Vaughan, *Negro Victory: The Life Story of Dr. Harold Moody* (London: Independent Press, 1950), 55.

44. Green, *Black Edwardians,* 70–73, 266–267.

45. Killingray, "'To do something for the race,'" 62.

46. *The Keys* 1, no. 1 (July 1933): 1–2.

47. "The Wilberforce Centenary Celebrations, Hull, July 23rd–29th," *The Keys* 1, no. 2 (October 1933): 34–35.

48. See Frederick Hall, "The Negro in America," *The Keys* 2, no. 1 (July–September 1934): 9; Hall, *The Keys* 2, no. 2 (October–December 1934): 32–33.

49. "Play at Y.W.C.A.," *The Keys* 1, no. 2 (October 1933): 39–40; *The Keys* 1, no. 3 (January 1934): 47–50, 64; Susan D. Pennybacker, *From Scottsboro to Munich: Race and Political Culture in 1930s Britain* (Princeton: Princeton University Press, 2009), 47, 49, 58–59, 78, 123.

50. Eric Walrond, "Book Reviews," *The Keys* 2, no. 3 (January–March 1935): 61; H. W. Springer, "The Shroud of Colour: An Appreciation of Countee Cullen, *The Keys* 3, no. 4 (April–June 1936): 46–47, 62.

51. Sylvia Lowe, "Disillusionment," *The Keys* 1, no. 2 (October 1933): 28; Una Marson, "Nigger," *The Keys* 1, no. 1 (July 1933): 8–9.

52. Margaret Seon, "Vision," *The Keys* 1, no. 4 (April–June 1934); Sylvia Lowe, "The Stamp of Freedom," *The Keys* 3, no. 1 (July–September 1935): 7.

53. See Hakim Adi, "West Africans in the Communist Party in the 1950s," *Opening the Books: Essays in the Social and Cultural History of British Communism,* ed. Geoff Andrews, Nina Fishman, and Kevin Morgan (London: Pluto Press, 1995), 176–194. See also Adi, *Pan-Africanism and Communism;* Makalani, *In the Cause of Freedom;* Pennybacker, *From Scottsboro to Munich;* McDuffie, *Sojourning for Freedom.*

54. Hakim Adi, "The Negro Question: The Communist International and Black Liberation in the Interwar Years," in West, Martin, and Wilkins, *From Toussaint to Tupac,* 155; Hakim Adi, "Forgotten Comrade? Desmond Buckle, An African Communist," *Science & Society* 70, no. 1 (January 2006): 22.

55. "Smash the Lynching of Eight Young Negroes," *Negro Worker* 1, nos. 5–6 (June 1931): 8–11; "Lynch Justice in America: Story of the Scottsboro Case," *Negro Worker* 2, no. 7 (July 1932): 20–22; Pennybacker, *From Scottsboro to Munich,* 68; Bush, *Imperialism, Race and Resistance,* 238.

56. Wallace-Johnson published under the nom de guerre Wal. Daniels. Jonathan Derrick, *Africa's "Agitators": Militant Anti-colonialism in Africa and the West, 1918–1939* (New York: Columbia University Press, 2008), 207, 210, 213–214, 277–278; Pennybacker, *From Scottsboro to Munich,* 30. On the University of the Toilers of the East, see Irina Filatova, "Indoctrination or Scholarship? Education of Africans at the Communist University of the Toilers of the East in the Soviet Union, 1923–1937," *Paedagogica Historica: International Journal of the History of Education* 35, no. 1 (1999): 41–66.

57. See materials on Peter McFarren Blackman in The National Archives, KV 2/1838; Marika Sherwood, "Peter Blackman, 1909–1993," *History Workshop Journal* 37, no. 1 (1994): 266–267; Adi, "Forgotten Comrade?" 32.

58. Mrs. Carmel Haden Guest, the wife of Labour MP Leslie Haden Guest, Professor Hymie Levy, Eleanor Rathbone, and Naomi Mitchison served as the chair, president, and other vice presidents, respectively. "Event of the Season!" *Daily Worker* (July 7, 1933): 3; "Kentucky Minstrels on the Air Again," *Daily Worker* (June 24, 1934): 4; Pennybacker, *From Scottsboro to Munich,* 28–32, 47, 49, 58–59, 78, 123.

59. *The Keys* 1, no. 1 (July 1933): 2; *The Keys* 1, no. 3 (January 1934): 42.

60. "'Nigger' Hunting in America and Africa," *Wāsù* 3, no. 1 (March 1934): 4–5.

61. The National Archives, CO 96 714/21639.

62. Louis Mbanefo, "Seditious Offences," *The Keys* 3, no. 4 (April–June 1936): 49–50, 59; Derrick, *Africa's "Agitators,"* 310.

63. Bush, *Imperialism, Race and Resistance,* 114–118.

64. Dr. J. B. Danquah, "The Gold Coast and Asante Delegation: A Gesture and a Lesson," *The Keys* 2, no. 2 (October–December 1934): 23–26.

65. "African Progress Union," *African Telegraph* (December 1918), 89. On the APU, see J. Ayodele Langley, *Pan-Africanism and Nationalism in West Africa, 1900–1945* (Oxford: Clarendon Press, 1973); Geiss, *The Pan-African Movement,* 297; Jeffrey Green, "John Alcindor (1873–1924): A Migrant's Biography," *Immigrants and Minorities* 6, no. 2 (July 1987): 174–189.

66. The first item on the list of aims ratified at the WASU's founding was "to provide and maintain a hostel for students of African descent." *Wāsù,* nos. 6–7 (August 1928): 32–33.

67. Garigue, "The West African Students' Union," 58.

68. The educator Rev. I. O. Ransome-Kuti and his wife, Funmilayo Ransome-Kuti, headed the WASU branch in Abeokuta, Nigeria. Cheryl Johnson-Odim and Nina Emma Mba, *For Women and the Nation: Funmilayo Ransome-Kuti of Nigeria* (Urbana: University of Illinois Press, 1997), 125–129.

69. The WASU hostel opened to students on March 9, 1933. *Wāsù* 2, no. 2 (April–June 1933): 11, 13.

70. Ras Makonnen, *Pan-Africanism from Within,* ed. Kenneth King (London: Oxford University Press, 1973), 127.

71. Benjamin Nnamdi Azikiwe, *My Odyssey: An Autobiography* (New York: Praeger, 1970), 197.

72. "The Annual Report up to the Year Ended 31st December 1938," *Wāsù* 7, no. 1 (May 1940): 5, 10, 15.

73. When Victoria Omolara Bucknor returned to Nigeria in late 1935, the WASU held a farewell party to honor her contributions to the group and "commissioned" her "to do all she could in co-operating with the local W.A.S.U. Branch in Lagos, especially in the task of strengthening the Ladies' Section." See "News and Notes," *Wāsù* 4, no. 5 (November 1935): 76.

74. The artists and musicians present included "Arthur G. E. Barrett, Esq., L.R.A.M. (piano, organ, violin, etc. teacher), Señor Freederka (a famous Spanish dancer), Mr. Halford (pianist), and Mr. G. Biney (entertainer)." "The W.A.S.U. at Work and at Play," *Wāsù* 4, no. 2 (August 1935), 31.

75. Schomburg Center for Research on Black Culture, New York Public Library, New York City, "The Truth about Aggrey House: An Exposure of the Government Plan for the Control of African Students in Great Britain" (London: West African Student Union, March 1934).

76. Quoted in Adi, *West Africans in Britain,* 63; *Wāsù* 4, no. 3 (September 1935): 35 (emphasis in original).

77. Adi, *West Africans in Britain,* 59–61.

78. *Negro Worker* (August–September 1933): 17

79. "The Annual Report up to the Year Ended 31st December 1938," 5–7; *Wāsù* 6, no. 1 (January 1937): 5; The National Archives, CO 554/109/4 (1937–1938); Vischer quoted in Adi, *West Africans in Britain,* 42, 65; Dr. Robert Wellesley Cole, "Memorandum of the Claim of the West African Students' Union to Hostel known as Africa House at No. 1 South Villas, Camden Square, N.W. 1" (February 24, 1939); Cole, "Report on W.A.S.U. Hostel Submitted by Dr. R. B. Wellesley Cole," Papers of Dr. Robert Wellesley Cole (hereafter Wellesley Cole Papers), School of Oriental and African Studies Library, Archives and Special Collections, PP MS 35/6/1/14, File 157.

80. "The Annual Report for the year ended 31st December, 1939," *Wāsù* 7, no. 1 (May 1940): 14.

81. The WASU dances were held on a biweekly and, at times, weekly basis throughout most of the group's existence. "The Annual Report up to the Year Ended 31st December 1938," 4.

82. Chris Stapleton, "African Connections: London's Hidden Music Scene," in *Black Music in Britain: Essays on the Afro-Asian Contribution to Popular Music,* ed. Paul Oliver (Buckingham, UK: Open University Press, 1990), 92–93; *West African Review* (August 31, 1935), and (November 7, 1936): 1563.

83. "Installation of Mr. Paul Robeson as Babāsale (Patron) of W.A.S.U.," *Wāsù* 4, no. 1 (July 1935): 7–8.

84. Quoted in Adi, *West Africans in Britain,* 63.

85. "The Annual Report up to the Year Ended 31st December 1938," 17; Harris quoted in Adi, *West Africans in Britain,* 18; Simon quoted in Pennybacker, *From Scottsboro to Munich,* 137–139.

86. Wellesley Cole Papers, PP MS 35/6/1/14, File 157, "Memorandum of the Claim of the West African Students' Union to Hostel known as Africa House at No. 1 South Villas, Camden Square, N.W. 1" and "Minutes of First Meeting of Directors of W.A.S.U. Limited held on Friday the 3rd of March 1944 in No. 8 Committee Room, House of Commons, London S.W.1."

CHAPTER TWO

1. Kwame Nkrumah, *Ghana: The Autobiography of Kwame Nkrumah.* 2nd ed. (New York: International, 1971), 27.

2. Quoted in Stephen Bourne, *Mother Country: Britain's Black Community on the Home Front, 1939–1945* (Stroud, Gloucestershire, UK: History Press, 2010), 130.

3. "Fascist Terror against Negroes in Germany," *Negro Worker* 3, nos. 4–5 (April–May 1933): 1.

4. Pennybacker, *From Scottsboro to Munich,* 1; Makonnen, *Pan-Africanism from Within,* 147.

5. Cedric Robinson, *Black Marxism: The Making of the Black Radical Tradition* (London: Zed Press, 1983), 262–265, 312.

6. Makonnen, *Pan-Africanism from Within,* 152, 155.

7. "Meeting of White and Coloured Peoples in London Protests against Arms Embargo," *Daily Gleaner* (September 11, 1935): 18.

8. Makonnen, *Pan-Africanism from Within,* 113.

9. See, for example, George Padmore, "Ethiopia Today: The Making of a Modern State," in Cunard, *Negro,* 612–618.

10. Macmillan quoted in Bush, *Imperialism, Race and Resistance,* 257; McDuffie, *Sojourning for Freedom,* 95–96; Robeson quoted in Penny von Eschen, *Race against Empire: Black Americans and Anticolonialism, 1937–1957* (Ithaca, NY: Cornell University Press, 1997), 11; Makalani, *In the Cause of Freedom,* 203; Makonnen, *Pan-Africanism from Within,* 116; Coleman, *Nigeria,* 209–210; Derrick, *Africa's "Agitators,"* 332–334. See also Robin D.G. Kelley, *Race Rebels: Culture, Politics, and the Black Working Class* (New York: Free Press, 1996), 123–158; James H. Meriweather, *Proudly We Can Be Africans: Black Americans and Africa, 1935–1961* (Chapel Hill: University of North Carolina Press, 2002).

11. Jennifer Anne Boittin, *Colonial Metropolis: The Urban Grounds of Antiimperialism and Feminism in Interwar Paris* (Lincoln: University of Nebraska Press, 2010), 161–165; Edwards, *The Practice of Diaspora,* 298.

12. On Pankhurst's association with Claude McKay, see Winston James, "A Race Outcast from an Outcast Class: Claude McKay's Experience and Analysis of Britain," in Schwarz, *West Indian Intellectuals in Britain,* 75–76.

13. "The League, Italy and Abyssinia," *Wàsù* 4, no. 1 (July 1935): 3; *Wàsù* 4, no. 2 (August 1935): 21; *Wàsù* 4, no. 5 (November 1935): 70–71.

14. "Conference Report," *The Keys* 1, no. 1 (July 1933): 3–5; "The Second Mile-Stone," *The Keys* 1, no. 1 (July 1933): 17; C.L.R. James, "West Indies Self-Government," *The Keys* 1, no. 4 (April–June 1934): 72, 84.

15. C.L.R. James, "Lectures on the Black Jacobins," *Small Axe* 8 (September 2000): 69.

16. The founders initially referred to the group as the International African Friends of Abyssinia but quickly changed its name to the International African Friends of Ethiopia. The Grenadian T. Albert Marryshow had published in the *Negro Worker* while Padmore was its editor, and later became one of the architects of the short-lived West Indies Federation. J.M. Kenyatta, "Hands Off Abyssinia," *Labour Monthly* (September 1935): 536; Makalani, *In the Cause of Freedom,* 196, 203–207.

17. *Wàsù* 4, no. 5 (November 1935): 70.

18. Claude Cummings, "Italy and Abyssinia," *The Keys* 3, no. 1 (July–September 1935): 6–7.

19. "The Rape of a Black Empire," *The Keys* 4, no. 1 (June–September 1936): 2; C.L.R. James, "Abyssinia and the Imperialists," *The Keys* 3, no. 3 (January–March 1936): 32, 39–40; "Resolution re Abyssinia," ibid., 31; Brian Urquhart Collection on Ralph J. Bunche, Charles E. Young Library, University of California, Los Angeles, Collection 2051, Box 279, Folder 1, Ralph Bunche Diary (hereafter, Bunche Diary), March 23 and 24, 1937; British Library, London, League of Coloured Peoples,

"Abyssinia," *Seventh Annual Report* (1937–1938), 12; "Resolutions Passed by the Annual General Meeting," *The Keys* 5, no. 4 (April–June 1938): 85–86.

20. Bush, *Imperialism, Race and Resistance,* 222.

21. Hezekiah Oladipo Olagunju Davies, *Memoirs* (Ibadan, Nigeria: Evans Brothers, 1989), 70–72.

22. "Jamaican Girl Who Was Personal Secretary to Haile Selassie," *Daily Gleaner* (September 25, 1936): 17; "Racial Prejudice in London Not Improving Says Miss Marson," *Daily Gleaner* (September 28, 1936): 5; Una Marson, "A Call to Downing Street," *Public Opinion* (September 11, 1937): 5.

23. Una Marson, *The Moth and the Star,* intro. Philip M. Sherlock (Kingston, Jamaica: published by the author, 1937), 81.

24. See, for example, Robinson, *Black Marxism;* West and Martin, "Haiti, I'm Sorry," in West, Martin, and Wilkins, *From Toussaint to Tupac,* 72–104.

25. C. L. R. James, "George Padmore: Black Marxist Revolutionary" (1976), in *At the Rendezvous of Victory* (London: Allison and Busby, 1984), 254.

26. George Padmore, "Hitler, Mussolini and Africa," *The Crisis* (September 1937): 262; "Hitler Will Treat Jews like Blacks: Adopts South African Methods to Deal with Problem," *Chicago Defender* (November 13, 1937): 24.

27. On Padmore, James, and the circle of black radicals around them in London, see Leslie James, *George Padmore and Decolonization from Below: Pan-Africanism, the Cold War, and the End of Empire* (Houndmills, Basingstoke, Hampshire, UK: Palgrave MacMillan, 2014); Makalani, *In the Cause of Freedom*; Carol Polsgrove, *Ending British Rule in Africa: Writers in Common Cause* (Manchester, UK: Manchester University Press, 2009); Derrick, *Africa's "Agitators"*; Schwarz, *West Indian Intellectuals in Britain;* Fitzroy Baptiste and Rupert Lewis, eds., *George Padmore: Pan-African Revolutionary* (Kingston, Jamaica: Ian Randle, 2009); Pennybacker, *From Scottsboro to Munich;* and James R. Hooker, *Black Revolutionary: George Padmore's Path from Communism to Pan-Africanism* (New York: Praeger, 1967).

28. T. D. Burridge, *British Labour and Hitler's War* (London: Andre Deutsch, 1976), 17–18; Margery Perham, *Colonial Sequence, 1930–1949* (London: Methuen, 1967), 151; Lord Lugard, "The Claims to Colonies," *Journal of the Royal African Society* 35, no. 139 (April 1936): 115–122.

29. "The Third Annual Conference," *The Keys* 3, no. 4 (April–June 1936): 48.

30. McCarthy, "The League of Nations, Public Ritual and National Identity in Britain," 126; Adi, "Forgotten Comrade?" 30–31.

31. Helen McCarthy, *The British People and the League of Nations: Democracy, Citizenship, and Internationalism, c. 1918–45* (Manchester, UK: University of Manchester Press, 2011); Daniel Laqua, *Internationalism Reconfigured: Transnational Ideas and Movements between the World Wars* (London: Tauris, 2011); Donald S. Birn, *The League of Nations Union, 1918–1945* (Oxford: Oxford University Press, 1981).

32. MacDonald quoted in Derrick, *Africa's "Agitators,"* 405–406.

33. Labour Party statement quoted in Leonard Barnes, *Empire or Democracy?* (London: Victor Gollancz, 1939), 26–28; Pennybacker, *From Scottsboro to Munich,* 136, 142.

34. Pennybacker, *From Scottsboro to Munich*, 87–88, 129; Barnes, *Empire or Democracy?* 253–262; George Padmore, *How Britain Rules Africa* (London: Wishart and Co., 1936), 386, 393, 395–396.

35. George Padmore, "A New World War for Colonies," *The Crisis* (October 1937): 309, 318; Padmore, "Abyssinia Betrayed by the League of Nations," *The Crisis* (June 1937): 166–168, 178.

36. Quoted in Daniel Waley, *British Public Opinion and the Abyssinian War* (London: Maurice Temple Smith, 1975), 26; C. L. R. James, "Is This Worth a War? The League's Scheme to Rob Abyssinia of Its Independence," *New Leader* (October 4, 1935), http://www.marxistsfr.org/archive/james-clr/works/1935/new-leader.htm (accessed October 31, 2010); The National Archives, KV 2/1824; Fenner Brockway, *Inside the Left: Thirty Years of Platform, Press, Prison and Parliament* (London: George Allen and Unwin, 1942), 325–326.

37. James quoted in Makalani, *In the Cause of Freedom*, 192; Hooker, *Black Revolutionary*, 31; Padmore, "Abyssinia Betrayed by the League of Nations," 188; Pennybacker, *From Scottsboro to Munich*, 50.

38. Edwards, *The Practice of Diaspora*, 310 (emphasis in original).

39. Padmore quoted in Adi, *West Africans in Britain*, 77.

40. George Padmore, "The Missionary Racket in Africa," *The Crisis* (July 1935): 214; von Eschen, *Race against Empire*, 13. See also George Padmore, "Ethiopia and World Politics," *The Crisis* (May 1935): 138–139, 156–157.

41. Nyabongo was the eldest son of Mukama Daudi Kasagama of the Toro Kingdom in Uganda. He attended Yale University and Queen's College, Oxford, where he obtained a DPhil. The government of Uganda banned *Africa Answers Back* when it was released. James, "Is This Worth a War?"; C. L. R. James, "'Civilising' the 'Blacks'; Why Britain Needs to Maintain Her African Possessions," *New Leader* (May 29, 1936), http://www.marxistfr.org/archive/james-clr/works/1936/civilising-blacks.htm (accessed October 31, 2010).

42. Bunche Diary, April 7, 1937.

43. The group may have started as an offshoot of plans for the Negro World Congress. In June 1935, Colonial Secretary Sir Philip Cundiffe-Lister wrote to the governors of Britain's four West African colonies to warn them about a "Pan-African Brotherhood" formed by Padmore and Kouyaté, which issued a manifesto on Ethiopia. Special Branch reported that it was also known as the Pan-African Brotherhood, Pan African League, and Pan-Afro Group. H. Nye from East Africa and the Ugandan A. Natan also appear on its letterhead as treasurer and assistant secretary. Derrick, *Africa's "Agitators,"* 337–338, 387–389; The National Archives, KV 2/1787, Special Branch Reports (February 4, 1936, June 14, 1936, and July 3, 1936); New York Public Library, Schomburg Center for Research in Black Culture, Ralph Bunche Papers (hereafter Bunche Papers), General Correspondence (1937), Box 10b, Padmore to Bunche (n.d.; on Pan-African Federation letterhead).

44. Quoted in Derrick, *Africa's "Agitators,"* 383–385; The National Archives, CO 323/1610/2. On Wallace-Johnson, see Leo Spitzer and LaRay Denzer, "I. T. A. Wallace-Johnson and the West African Youth League," Parts I and

II, *International Journal of African Historical Studies* 6, nos. 3 and 4 (1973), 413–452, 565–601.

45. "Professor Azikiwe and Mr. Wallace Johnson," *Wāsù* 6, no. 2 (Coronation Number, 1937): 23; KV 2/1787, Special Branch Report, July 3, 1936 and April 24, 1937; The National Archives, CO 323/1610/2; Bunche Diary, March 27, April 5, and April 18, 1937.

46. C. L. R. James, *Nkrumah and the Ghana Revolution* (London: Allison and Busby, 1977), 65; James, "George Padmore," 256.

47. A Colonial Office report states that Tiemoko Garan Kouyaté (Sudan), Nnamdi Azikiwe (Nigeria), Chris Jones (Barbados), H. O. Cendrecourt (British Guiana), J. J. Ocquaye (West Africa), Louis Mbanafo (West Africa), Elsie Duncan (West Africa), F. A. Bruce (West Africa), K. Sallie Tamba (West Africa), O. Mandoh (West Africa), Gilbert Coka (South Africa), Aida Bastian (Jamaica), and E. Domanya (West Africa) were members of the IASB's executive committee. The National Archives, CO 323/1610/2.

48. Bunche Papers, General Correspondence (1937), Box 10b, IASB leaflet and Wallace-Johnson to Bunche (n.d.); "Editorial," *International African Service Bureau* 1, no. 1 (July 1938): 2–3; Edwards, *The Practice of Diaspora,* 300–304. On the *International African Opinion,* see also Carol Polsgrove, "George Padmore's Use of Periodicals to Build a Movement," and Matthew Quest, "George Padmore's and C. L. R. James's *International African Opinion,*" in Baptiste and Lewis, *George Padmore,* 97–132.

49. The National Archives, CO 323/1610/2; "A Brief Review of the Activities of the International Service Bureau for the Period May to December, 1937," *African Sentinel* 1, no. 4 (March–April 1938): 14, 20; Derrick, *Africa's "Agitators,"* 401; C. L. R. James, "Black Intellectuals in Britain," in *Color, Culture and Consciousness: Immigrant Intellectuals in Britain,* ed. Bhikhu Parekh (London: Allen and Unwin, 1974), 161.

50. Makonnen, *Pan-African from Within,* 120; George Padmore, *Pan-Africanism or Communism?* (1956; repr., New York: Doubleday, 1971), 123–124.

51. The National Archives, KV 2/1787; Bunche Diary. April 6, 7, 12, and 18, 1937; St. Clair Drake, "Mbiyu Koinange and the Pan-African Movement," in *Pan-African Biography,* ed. Robert A. Hill (Berkeley: University of California Press, 1987), 175–177; Jeremy Murray-Brown, *Kenyatta* (London: George Allen and Unwin, 1972), 118–121; Alan J. Mackenzie and C. L. R. James, "Radical Pan-Africanism in the 1930s: A Discussion with C. L. R. James," *Radical History Review* 24 (Fall 1980): 72–73.

52. "Racial Solidarity," *The Keys* 4, no. 2 (October–December 1936): 16.

53. The National Archives, KV 2/1824, Special Branch Report (February 2, 1937); Adi, *West Africans in Britain,* 77–78.

54. James, "Lectures on the Black Jacobins," 69; C. L. R. James, "The Voice of Africa," *International African Opinion* 1, no. 2 (August 1938): 3; "Editorial," *International African Service Bureau* 1, no. 1 (July 1938): 2–3; The National Archives, KV 2/1825, James to Padmore, June 22, 1953.

55. Mary Chamberlain, "George Lamming," in Schwarz, *West Indian Intellectuals in Britain,* 176. On the disturbances in the Caribbean, see O. Nigel Bolland, *On the March: Labour Rebellions in the British Caribbean, 1934–39* (London: James Currey, 1995); Martin Thomas, *Violence and Colonial Order: Police, Workers, and Protest in the European Colonial Empires, 1918–1940* (Cambridge: Cambridge University Press, 2012); Colin A. Palmer, *Freedom's Children: The 1938 Labor Rebellion and the Birth of Modern Jamaica* (Chapel Hill: University of North Carolina Press, 2014); Putnam, *Radical Moves,* 196–229.

56. Grier quoted in Robinson, *Black Marxism,* 400n171.

57. "The Wilberforce Centenary Celebrations, Hull," 22–23, 34–35; Modjaben Dowuna, "Reflections on the Wilberforce Centenary," *Wāsù* 3, no. 1 (March 1934): 26–27.

58. Marc Matera, "An Empire of Development: Africa and the Caribbean in *God's Chillun,*" *Twentieth Century British History* 23, no. 1 (March 2012): 12–37.

59. Macmillan quoted in Bush, *Imperialism, Race and Resistance,* 255.

60. William Miller Macmillan, *Warning from the West Indies: A Tract for Africa and the Empire* (London: Faber and Faber, 1936), 7.

61. Quoted in Derrick, *Africa's "Agitators,"* 393–394; Anthony Kirk-Greene, "The Emergence of an Africanist Community in the UK," in *The British Intellectual Engagement with Africa in the Twentieth Century,* ed. Douglas Rimmer and Anthony Kirk-Greene (Basingstoke, UK: Palgrave Macmillan, 2000), 23, 38.

62. Sir Malcolm Hailey, *An African Survey, Revised, 1956* (London: Oxford University Press, 1957), 202.

63. R. D. Pearce, *The Turning Point in Africa: British Colonial Policy, 1938–1948* (London: Frank Cass, 1982), 155–156. Bush, *Imperialism, Race and Resistance,* 263–264; Stephen Howe, *Anticolonialism in British Politics: The Left and the End of Empire, 1918–1964* (New York: Oxford University Press, 1993), 102.

64. Delia Jarrett-Macauley, *The Life of Una Marson, 1905–1965* (Manchester, UK: Manchester University Press, 1998), 109; W. Arthur Lewis, "A Forgotten Corner of the Empire," *The Keys* 3, no. 4 (April–June 1936), 66–67; W. Arthur Lewis, "African Economic Problems," *The Keys* 5, no. 1 (July–September 1937): 16.

65. H. W. Springer, "Labour Unrest in the Colonies," *The Keys* 5, no. 2 (October–December 1937): 45; "Labour Disturbances in the West Indies," *The Keys* 5, no. 3 (January–March 1938): 64–66; R. O. Thomas, "Revolt in the West Indies," *The Keys* 3, no. 3 (January–March 1936): 37–38; League of Coloured Peoples, "Disturbances in the West Indies: Special Meeting," *Seventh Annual Report* (1937–1938), 11.

66. The other speakers included Arnold Ward, Chris Braithwaite, and Reginald Bridgeman of the League Against Imperialism; T. Ras Makonnen, Surat Ali, and Nancy Cunard were also in attendance. See Special Branch Reports in The National Archives, KV 2/1787 and KV 2/1824.

67. George Padmore, "Fascism in the Colonies," *Controversy* 2, no. 17 (February 17, 1938); George Padmore, "An Outrageous Report," *Controversy* 2, no. 18 (March 1938); Wallace-Johnson, "The Trinidad Commission's Report: A Criticism," *African*

Sentinel 1, no. 4 (March–April 1938): 11; W. Arthur Lewis, "Notes on the Trinidad Report," *The Keys* 5, no. 4 (April–June 1938): 80–82.

68. George Padmore, "Parliament Upset by the West Indies," *Chicago Defender* (April 1938); "Activities of the League," *The Keys* 6, no. 1 (July-September 1938), 9–10; *Times* (May 26 and 30, June 9, 1938); "Activities of the Bureau," *International African Opinion* 1, no. 1 (July 1938): 16.

69. Macdonald, "Introduction to *The Keys*," 15; Peter Blackman, "Editorial; Royal Commission to the West Indies," *The Keys* 6, no. 2 (1938): 1–2.

70. The National Archives, CO 950/30, "Memorandum on the Economic, Political and Social Conditions in the West Indies and British Guiana Presented by the International African Service Bureau, The League of Coloured Peoples and the Negro Welfare Association" (September 9, 1938) (emphasis in original).

71. McCarthy, "The League of Nations, Public Ritual and National Identity in Britain," 125; Mark Gilbert, "Pacifist Attitudes to Nazi Germany," *Journal of Contemporary History* 27, no. 3 (July 1992): 493.

72. Bunche Papers, General Correspondence (1937), Wallace-Johnson to Bunche (n.d.); "Africa Speaks Out: Colonials Reply to Hitler's Demand for Colonies" and "International African Service Bureau," *African Sentinel* 1, no. 4 (March–April 1938): 5, 14; Derrick, *Africa's "Agitators,"* 419, 421; Wallace-Johnson, "'No Sir! No Colonies Back' for Germany," *Negro Worker* 7, no. 4 (April 1937): 3–4; "Africans and the Struggle for Peace," *The Keys* 6, no. 2 (October–December 1938): 3; "Annual Report," *Wāsù* 7, no. 1 (May 1940): 15; Margery Perham, "Colonies and European Peace," *The Keys* 3, no. 4 (April–June 1936), 60.

73. George Padmore, "White Workers and Black," *Controversy* 2, no. 20 (May 1938); George Padmore, "The Government's Betrayal of the Protectorates," *Controversy* 2, no. 21 (June 1938).

74. Quoted in Polsgrove, *Ending British Rule in Africa,* 80; James, "Black Intellectuals in Britain," 161.

75. Quoted in Polsgrove, *Ending British Rule in Africa,* 47; Padmore, *Pan-Africanism or Communism?* 304.

76. "Notes on the West Indies: Colonial Fascism," *International African Opinion* 1, no. 1 (July 1938): 3–5, 12–13.

77. "Greetings to Indian Congress Leader," *International African Opinion* 1, no. 1 (July 1939): 15; Pennybacker, *From Scottsboro to Munich,* 197.

78. The National Archives, KV 2/1787, "A Warning to the Colonial Peoples" (August 29, 1939); "Manifesto against War," *International African Opinion* 1, no. 4 (October 1938); George Padmore, *Africa and World Peace* (London: Secker and Warburg, 1937), 210.

79. Makonnen, *Pan-Africanism from Within,* 160–161.

80. Ibid., 117.

81. Harold Moody, "President's Message," *The Keys* 5, no. 4 (April–June 1938): 79.

82. The National Archives, KV 2/1824, Special Branch Report (n.d.); Padmore in the *New Leader* quoted in Hooker, *Black Revolutionary,* 61.

83. "Nationalism in Africa," *Wāsù* 6, no. 2 (Coronation Number, 1937): 22. Solanke's piece also appeared in *West Africa* (January 23, 1937). For Hailey's piece, see Malcolm Hailey, "Nationalism in Africa," *Journal of the African Society* 36 (April 1937): 146.

84. Hooker, *Black Revolutionary*, 53; "Manifesto against War."

85. Adi, *West Africans in Britain*, 80–81, 71–72.

86. Quoted in Zachernuk, *Colonial Subjects*, 112–113.

CHAPTER THREE

1. The National Archives, CO 318/412/3, "College Hall, London—Facilities for West Indian Women Students" (1933).

2. LaRay Denzer, "Yoruba Women: A Historiographical Study," *International Journal of African Historical Studies* 27, no. 1 (1994): 19–21; The National Archives, CO 537/5212, J. L. Keith to T. V. Scrivenor, "Welfare of Colonial Students—Liaison Officer for Women Students, West Africa (1949–1950)," August 25, 1950; Schomburg Center for Research in Black Culture, New York Public Library, St. Clair Drake Papers (hereafter Drake Papers), MG 309, Box 61, File 10; Banton, *The Coloured Quarter*, 67.

3. Constance Agatha Cummings-John, *Memoirs of a Krio Leader*, ed. LaRay Denzer (Ibadan, Nigeria· Humanities Research Centre, 1995), 17–18.

4. Boittin, *Colonial Metropolis*, 167, 156.

5. See Miriam Silverberg, "After the Grand Tour: The Modern Girl, the New Woman, and the Colonial Maiden," in *The Modern Girl around the World: Consumption, Modernity, and Globalization,* ed. Alys Eve Weinbaum et al. (Durham, NC: Duke University Press, 2008), 354–361.

6. Lynn M. Thomas, "The Modern Girl and Racial Respectability in 1930s South Africa," *Journal of African History* 47 (2006): 489, 461, 463–464; Oyinkan Abayomi, "Modern Womanhood," *Service* (December 1935): 14. On Mabel Dove and the "Women's Page" phenomenon in the Gold Coast, see Audrey Gadzekpo, "Gender Discourses and Representational Practices in Gold Coast Newspapers," *Jenda: A Journal of Culture and African Women Studies* 1, no. 2 (2001), www.jendajournal .com/jenda/vol1.2/gadzekpo.html (accessed September 13, 2003).

7. Mabel Dove, "What the Gold Coast People Said Recently about the W.A.S.U. Hostel Scheme," *Wāsù* 2, no. 1 (January 1933): 24–25.

8. See Adelaide M. Cromwell, *An African Victorian Feminist: Adelaide Smith Casely Hayford, 1868–1960* (London: Frank Cass, 1986); Barbara Bair, "Pan-Africanism in Process: Adelaide Casely Hayford, Garveyism, and the Cultural Roots of Nationalism," in Lemelle and Kelley, *Imagining Home,* 121–144; Folarin Coker, *A Lady: A Biography of Lady Oyinkan Abayomi* (Ibadan, Nigeria: Evans Brothers, 1987); Bolanle Awe, ed., *Nigerian Women in Historical Perspective* (Lagos: Sankore, 1992); Cheryl Johnson-Odim, "Grassroots Organizing in Anti-Colonial Activity in Southwestern Nigeria," *African Studies Review* 25, no. 2 (1982): 137–157; Johnson-Odim and

Mba, *For Women and the Nation*; LaRay Denzer, "Intersections: Nigerian Episodes in the Careers of Three West Indian Women," in Byfield, Denzer, and Morrison, *Gendering the African Diaspora,* 245–284.

9. See, for example, Efwa Kato, "What Women Can Do," *Wāsù* 3, no. 1 (March 1934): 13–14.

10. Titilola Folarin, "Our Native Dress," *Wāsù* 5 (Christmas Number, 1936): 56.

11. Sinha, Guy, and Woollacott, "Introduction: Why Feminisms and Internationalism?" 346, 350; Christine Bolt, *Sisterhood Questioned? Race, Class and Internationalism in the American and British Women's Movements, c. 1880s-1970s* (London: Routledge, 2004); Leila J. Rupp, *Worlds of Women: The Making of an International Women's Movement* (Princeton: Princeton University Press, 1997).

12. Adi, *West Africans in Britain,* 177; Putnam, *Radical Moves,* 4. For similar critiques, see also Bonnie Claudia Harrison, "Diasporadas: Black Women and the Fine Art of Activism," *Meridians: Feminism, Race, Transnationalism* 2, no. 2 (2002): 170; Patterson and Kelley, "Unfinished Migrations," 29; Ula Yvette Taylor, "Intellectual Pan-African Feminists: Amy Ashwood Garvey and Amy Jacques-Garvey," *Abafazi* 9 (1998): 10–18; Taylor, *The Veiled Garvey: The Life and Times of Amy Jacques Garvey* (Chapel Hill: University of North Carolina Press, 2001).

13. Elleke Boehmer and Bart Moore-Gilbert, "Introduction to Special Issue: Postcolonial Studies and Transnational Resistance," *interventions* 4, no. 1 (2002): 15.

14. George Padmore, ed., *Colonial and . . . Coloured Unity: History of the Pan-African Congress* (London: Hammersmith Bookshop Ltd., 1947), 52.

15. Tony Martin, "Amy Ashwood Garvey: Wife No. 1," *Jamaica Journal* 30 (August–October 1987): 36; Hakim Adi and Marika Sherwood, *Pan-African History: Political Figures from Africa and the Diaspora since 1787* (London: Routledge, 2003), 69.

16. Simon Gikandi, "Pan-Africanism and Cosmopolitanism: The Case of Jomo Kenyatta," *English Studies in Africa* 43, no. 1 (2000): 3; Alison Donnell, "Una Marson: Feminism, Anti-colonialism and a Forgotten Fight for Freedom," in Schwarz, *West Indian Intellectuals in Britain,* 129.

17. Tony Martin, *Amy Ashwood Garvey: Pan-Africanist, Feminist and Mrs. Garvey No. 1; or, A Tale of Two Amies,* The New Marcus Garvey Library, No. 4 (Dover, MA: Majority Press, 2007), 139–140; Martin, "Amy Ashwood Garvey," 36.

18. For Ashwood Garvey's account of the founding of the UNIA, see Tony Martin, *The Pan-African Connection: From Slavery to Garvey and Beyond,* The New Marcus Garvey Library, No. 6 (Dover, MA: Majority Press, 1983), 219–226. See also Lionel M. Yard, *Biography of Amy Ashwood Garvey, 1897–1969: Co-founder of the Universal Negro Improvement Association* (New York: Associated, 198?).

19. Denzer, "Intersections," 266; G. O. Olusanya, "Charlotte Olajumoke Obasa," in Awe, *Nigerian Women in Historical Perspective,* 105–120.

20. James, *Beyond a Boundary,* 258–259.

21. Makonnen, *Pan-Africanism from Within,* 130; James, "Black Intellectuals in Britain"; Padmore, *Pan-Africanism or Communism?* 123, 147; Abrahams, *The Coyoba Chronicles,* 36.

22. Quoted in Martin, *Amy Ashwood Garvey*, 168–170.

23. Quoted in Adi and Sherwood, *Pan-African History*, 72.

24. Padmore, *Colonial and . . . Coloured Unity*, 52.

25. On Ashwood Garvey's activities in Africa, see Denzer, "Intersections," and Martin, *Amy Ashwood Garvey*.

26. Martin, *Amy Ashwood Garvey*, 169.

27. Boehmer and Moore-Gilbert, "Introduction," 11.

28. Martin, *Amy Ashwood Garvey*, 238–244.

29. On Ashwood Garvey's relationship with Claudia Jones, see Carole Boyce Davies, *Left of Marx: The Political Life of Black Communist Claudia Jones* (Durham, NC: Duke University Press, 2007), 22, 66.

30. Adetokunbo Adegboyega Ademola, who was a member of the WASU at the time, may have written this piece. *Wāsù* 6–7 (August 1928): 17, 20.

31. Anthony Abiodun, "Education of Women and Employment in Africa," *Wāsù* 5 (Christmas Number, 1936): 57–59.

32. Pierre, *The Predicament of Blackness*, 19–20, 62.

33. "News and Notes," *Wāsù* 2, no. 2 (April–June 1933): 6–7, reprinted in Perham, *Colonial Sequence*, 109–110.

34. Kofoworola Aina Moore (now Lady Ademola), "The Story of Kofoworola Aina Moore, of the Yoruba Tribe, Nigeria," in *Ten Africans*, ed. Margery Perham (1936; repr., Evanston, IL: Northwestern University Press, 1971), 323–343; Denzer, "Yoruba Women," 21, 26.

35. *Wāsù* 4, no. 2 (August 1935): 29; 4, no. 4 (October 1935): 60; 6, no. 2 (Coronation Number, 1937): 27.

36. "The W.A.S.U. at Work," *Wāsù* 4, no. 1 (July 1935): 9; "Editorial Notes," *Wāsù* 4, no. 4 (October 1935): 49.

37. Cummings-John, *Memoirs of a Krio Leader*, 38.

38. British Library, London, League of Coloured Peoples, *Ninth Annual Report for the Year 1939–1940*; "Correspondence," *The Keys* 6, no. 2 (October–December 1938): 6–7.

39. *Wāsù* 12, no. 1 (March 1945): 8; "West Africans in Britain: Resolutions at a London Gathering," *West Africa* (September 14, 1946): 845; Enith [*sic*] H. Wallace-Johnson, "A Message to African Womanhood," *New African* 1, no. 1 (March 1946): 3; The National Archives, CO 964/24, "Gold Coast Commission of Enquiry Exhibits, Vol. 1."

40. See Irene Cole to her brother Dr. Robert Wellesley Cole, Wellesley Cole Papers, PP MS 35/1/1/7, File 7.

41. Irene Cole, "Social Problems in West Africa," *Wāsù* 10, no. 1 (May 1943): 24–25.

42. Wellesley Cole Papers, PP MS 35/1/1/7, File 7, Irene Cole to Dr. Wellesley Cole, January 29, 1946; The National Archives, KV 2/1840, "The West African Society."

43. LaRay Denzer, *Folayegbe M. Akintunde-Ighodalo: A Public Life* (Ibadan, Nigeria: Sam Bookman, 2001), 80–81.

44. Ogunlesi, Wuraola Esan, and Funmilayo Ransome-Kuti were the only Yorùbá women to participate in the discussions leading to constitutional reform in Nigeria. On Ekpo, see "The Lady Advisor from the East," *West Africa* (August 22, 1953): 773. On Ogunlesi, see "The Lady Advisor from the West," *West Africa* (August 15, 1953): 751. See also LaRay Denzer, "Yoruba Women," and Denzer, "Gender and Decolonization: A Study of Three Women Leaders in West African Public Life," *People and Empire in African History,* ed. J. D. Y. Peel and J. F. Ade Ajayi (London: Longman, 1992); Cheryl Johnson, "Class and Gender: A Consideration of Yoruba Women during the Colonial Period," in *Women and Class in Africa,* ed. Claire Robertson and Iris Berger (London: Africana, 1986).

45. Quoted in Denzer, *Folayegbe M. Akintunde-Ighodalo,* 85–86.

46. Ibid., 81–82. Several women in the WASU supported an earlier attempt in 1951 to remove the executive through a vote of no confidence. See House of Lords Record Office, London, UK, Papers of Reginald, Lord Sorensen (hereafter Sorensen Papers), SOR 168, "Petition" (December 30, 1951), 4.

47. *West Africa* (January 2, 1954): 1246; Denzer, *Folayegbe M. Akintunde-Ighodalo,* 89.

48. Folayegbe Akintunde-Ighodalo, "Votes for Women," *West Africa* (June 19, 1954): 564.

49. Between 1944 and 1948, Nigerians in London or Lagos formed the Ibo Federal Union and the rival Yorùbá organizations Egbe Omo Oduduwa and the Yoruba Federal Union, and by the early 1950s, there were separate student unions in London for each of the four British colonies in West Africa. See Richard Sklar, *Nigerian Political Parties: Power in an Emergent Nation* (1963; repr., Trenton, NJ: African World Press, 2004), 65, 67, 69–70, 85; Coleman, *Nigeria,* 228, 261–262, 340–341.

50. Denzer, *Folayegbe M. Akintunde-Ighodalo,* 34–35.

51. Wellesley Cole Papers, PP MS 35/1/1/7, File 7, Irene Cole to Dr. Wellesley Cole, February 11, 1948, and Samuel Ighodaro to Dr. Wellesley Cole, December 18, 1946.

52. Quoted in Adi and Sherwood, *Pan-African History,* 30. On black women in the CAA, see Jacqueline Castledine, *Cold War Progressives: Women's Interracial Organizing for Peace and Freedom* (Urbana: University of Illinois Press, 2012); Barbara Ransby, *Eslanda: The Large and Unconventional Life of Mrs. Paul Robeson* (New Haven: Yale University Press, 2013).

53. Adi and Sherwood, *Pan-African History,* 31–32; Wellesley Cole Papers, PP MS 35/6/1/11, File 155, invitation to Society of African Culture dinner reception, April 16, 1959; Magbaily C. Fyle, *Historical Dictionary of Sierra Leone* (Lanham, MD: Scarecrow Press, 2006), 40.

54. Jarrett-Macauley, *The Life of Una Marson,* 48. On Marson, see also Donnell, "Una Marson"; Donnell, "Una Marson and the Fractured Subjects of Modernity: Writing across the Black Atlantic," *Women: A Cultural Review* 22, no. 4 (Winter 2011): 345–369; Donnell *Twentieth-Century Caribbean Literature: Critical Moments in Anglophone Literary History* (London: Routledge, 2006); Anna Snaith, "'Little

Brown Girl' in a 'White, White City': Una Marson and London," *Tulsa Studies in Women's Literature* 27, no. 1 (Spring 2008): 93–114; Mary Lou Emery, *Modernism, the Visual, and Caribbean Literature* (Cambridge: Cambridge University Press, 2007); Giovanna Covi, "Una Marson: African-Caribbean New Woman Speaking Truth to Power," in *Modernist Women, Race, Nation: Networking Women, 1890–1950; Circum-Atlantic Connections,* ed. Giovanna Covi (London: Mango, 2005), 118–152; Innes, *A History of Black and Asian Writing in Britain.*

55. Erika J. Waters, "I like me black face and me kinky hair," *Women's Review of Books* 28, no. 6 (November–December 2011): 21.

56. *Cosmopolitan* 3, no. 1 (May 1930): 5; Una Marson, "The Age of Women," *Cosmopolitan* 1, no. 11 (March 1929): 65; Una Marson, "Jamaica's Victory," *Cosmopolitan* 2, no. 2 (June 1929): 66–67.

57. Honor Ford-Smith, "Unruly Virtues of the Spectacular: Performing Engendered Nationalisms in the UNIA in Jamaica," *interventions: International Journal of Postcolonial Studies* 6, no. 1 (2004): 31.

58. Quoted in Covi, "Una Marson," 128; Astley Clerk, "Empire Day," *Cosmopolitan* 2, no. 1 (May 1929): 10; Marson, "The Age of Women," 65; Jarrett-Macauley, *The Life of Una Marson,* 71.

59. "Play at Y.W.C.A.," *The Keys* 1, no. 2 (October 1933): 39–40; *The Keys* 1, no. 3 (January 1934): 47–50, 64.

60. Quoted in Jarrett-Macauley, *The Life of Una Marson,* 48, 70; "Editorial," *The Keys* 2, no. 3 (January–March 1935): 45–46.

61. Bolt, *Sisterhood Questioned?* 65, 84.

62. Jarrett-Macauley, *The Life of Una Marson,* 71–72, 76; Vera Brittain, *Testament of Friendship: The Story of Winifred Holtby* (New York: Macmillan, 1940), 355–356; Bush, *Imperialism, Race and Resistance,* 234–235.

63. Una M. Marson, "Education," *The Keys* 2, no. 3 (January–March 1935): 53.

64. The Women's Library, London, Margery Corbett Ashby Papers, 7MCA, Records of the International Alliance of Women, 2IAW/1/C/07, "Report of the Twelfth Congress of the International Alliance of Women for Suffrage and Equal Citizenship" (Istanbul, April 18–24, 1935), 15.

65. Jarrett-Macauley reconstructed the majority of Marson's remarks from excerpts published subsequently in the Turkish newspaper *Cumheriyet* and the *Daily Gleaner.* Quoted in Jarrett-Macauley, *The Life of Una Marson,* 91–92.

66. "Here and There," *The Keys* 3, no. 1 (June–September 1935): 13; A. A. Thompson, "Secretary's Notes," *League of Coloured Peoples Newsletter* 20 (May 1941): 47; Bolt, *Sisterhood Questioned?* 81, 84; Una Marson, "A Call to Downing Street," *Public Opinion* (September 11, 1937), 5.

67. Marson, "Little Brown Girl," "Winifred Holtby," "To the I.A.W.S.E.C.," and "To Joe and Ben," all in *The Moth and the Star,* 11–13, 79–83.

68. Quoted in Jarrett-Macauley, *The Life of Una Marson,* 103, 119.

69. Yale University, Beinecke Rare Book and Manuscript Library, James Weldon Johnson Collection (hereafter Weldon Johnson Collection), Marson to Weldon Johnson, January 27, 1938.

70. Jarrett-Macauley, *The Life of Una Marson,* 112–113.

71. Una Marson, "Feminism," *Public Opinion* (May 1, 1937): 10; Una Marson, "Should Our Women Enter Politics?" *Public Opinion* (February 20, 1937): 10.

72. Una Marson, "Coloured Contributions," *Public Opinion* (June 3, 1937): 10–11; Una Marson, "Readers and Writers Club," *Public Opinion* (July 31, 1937): 10.

73. Una Marson, "But My Own," *Public Opinion* (June 19, 1937): 15.

74. Emery, *Modernism, the Visual, and Caribbean Literature,* 116–121; Erika S. Smilowitz, "'Weary of Life and All My Heart's Dull Pain': The Poetry of Una Marson," *Critical Issues in West Indian Literature,* ed. Erika S. Smilowitz and Roberta Q. Knowles (Parkersburg, IA: Caribbean Books, 1984), 19–32. On the Romantics and South Asian thought and art, see Bonnie G. Smith, "Decentered Identities: The Case of the Romantics," *History and Theory* 50, no. 2 (May 2010): 210–219.

75. Emery, *Modernism, the Visual, and Caribbean Literature,* 121; Una M. Marson, "Nigger," *The Keys* 1, no. 1 (July 1933): 8–9.

76. Jamaican National Archives, Kingston, Una Marson Papers, Una Marson, "London Calling" (unpublished manuscript), Act 1, pp. 5, 7–9. For an example of the social interactions parodied by Marson, see "Social at Lady Proctor's," *The Keys* 2, no. 1 (July–September 1934): 7.

77. Marson, *London Calling,* Act 1, p. 11, 13.

78. Ibid., Act 2, p. 1; Act 3, p. 9.

79. Emery, *Modernism, the Visual, and Caribbean Literature,* 101, 123.

80. Marson, *The Moth and the Star,* 70–71, 76, 87–88, 91, 93, 97.

81. Angela Davis, *Blues Legacies and Black Feminism: Gertrude "Ma" Rainey, Bessie Smith, and Billie Holiday* (New York: Vintage Books, 1998), 41; Jarrett-Macauley, *The Life of Una Marson,* 123.

82. Weldon Johnson Collection, Marson to Weldon Johnson, January 27, 1938.

83. David Boxer, *Edna Manley, Sculptor* (Kingston: National Gallery of Jamaica and Edna Manley Foundation, 1990), 24.

84. Emery, *Modernism, the Visual, and Caribbean Literature,* 77–78, 80; Putnam, *Radical Moves,* 214, 218, 283n87; *Daily Gleaner* (December 9, 1935): 23; Jean Besson, "Religion as Resistance in Jamaican Peasant Life: The Baptist Church, Revival Worldview, and Rastafari Movement," in *Rastafari and Other African-Caribbean Worldviews,* ed. Barry Chevannes (The Hague, The Netherlands: Institute of Social Studies; Macmillan, 1995), 43–76.

85. Although reaction to the play in Jamaica was initially mixed, *Pocomania* introduced stylistic innovations and new thematic possibilities that informed the work of many subsequent Caribbean authors. Jarrett-Macauley, *The Life of Una Marson,* 136, 183.

86. Weldon Johnson Collection, Marson to Weldon Johnson, January 27, 1938.

87. British Broadcasting Corporation Written Archives Centre, Caversham Park, Reading, UK (hereafter BBC Written Archives), Una Marson, "Simple Facts—Jamaica" (August 1939).

88. BBC Written Archives, Marson interviewed by Victor Delumo, March 2, 1945.

89. Marson, *Pocomania,* Act 3, Scene 2, pp. 27, 34; Belinda Edmondson, *Making Men: Gender, Literary Authority, and Women's Writing in Caribbean Narrative* (Durham, NC: Duke University Press, 1999), 186.

90. Ford-Smith, "Unruly Virtues of the Spectacular," 30–32; Weldon Johnson Collection, Marson to Weldon Johnson, January 27, 1938.

91. Marson, *The Moth and the Star,* 85–86; Marson, "But My Own," 3.

92. "B.W.I. Affairs Topic of Talks at League Meeting in England," *Daily Gleaner* (October 1, 1938): 10; The National Archives, CO 950/36, "West India Royal Commission, Eleventh Session—30th September 1938," 348.

93. Una Marson, "The Convoy," *League of Coloured Peoples Newsletter* 12, no. 67 (April 1945): 8.

94. BBC Written Archives, E2/584 (Foreign General, West Indies, 1939–1950), John Grenfell Williams to Noel Sabine, Colonial Office (September 26, 1942). For the complete poem, see Una Marson, *Towards the Stars* (London: University of London Press, 1945), 58–60.

95. BBC Written Archives, Una Marson, "The Women's Institute," May 6, 1943, 5; Snaith, "'Little Brown Girl' in a 'White, White City,'" 108.

96. "Una Marson on Visit Home," *Daily Gleaner* (August, 18, 1945): 15.

97. Yevette Richards, "Race, Gender, and Anticommunism in the International Labor Movement: The Pan-African Connections of Maida Springer," *Journal of Women's History* 11, no. 2 (1999): 35.

98. Jarrett-Macauley, *The Life of Una Marson,* 147.

99. Quoted in Richards, "Race, Gender, and Anticommunism in the International Labor Movement," 44–45.

100. "Jamaican Technicians in Britain," *League of Coloured Peoples Newsletter* 24 (September 1941): 135.

101. Quoted in Jarrett-Macauley, *The Life of Una Marson,* 163.

102. BBC Written Archives, E2/584, Harold Nicolson to J. B. Clark, March 6, 1942; J. B. Clark to Nicolson, March 7, 1942; John Grenfall Williams, "Service to the West Indies: Lady Davson's Criticisms," March 11, 1942.

103. Before she left London, however, Marson realized another longtime goal when the University of London Press published *Towards the Stars* (1945), which included poetry from her previous collections, especially *The Moth and the Star.* The English poet and short-story writer Stella Mead helped Marson select the poems and get the book accepted for publication. Snaith, "'Little Brown Girl' in a 'White, White City,'" 108–109.

104. See, for example, Glyne Griffith, "Deconstructing Nationalisms: Henry Swanzy, *Caribbean Voices,* and the Development of West Indian Literature," *Small Axe* 10 (September 2001): 1–20.

105. Drake Papers, Box 61, File 5, March 2, 1948.

106. McDuffie, *Sojourning for Freedom,* 15; Hazel V. Carby, *Race Men* (Cambridge, MA: Harvard University Press, 1998), 113. Boyce Davies employs Audre Lorde's term *sister outsider* to describe Claudia Jones. Davies, *Left of Karl Marx,* 25.

107. Jean Allman, "The Disappearing of Hannah Kudjoe: Nationalism, Feminism, and the Tyrannies of History," *Journal of Women's History* 21, no. 3 (2009): 15–16, 30–31.

108. Dudley Thompson, with Margaret Cezair Thompson, *From Kingston to Kenya: The Making of a Pan-Africanist Lawyer,* foreword by Rex Nettleford (Dover, MA: Majority Press, 1993), 41.

109. A. A. Y. Kyerematen, "West Africa in Transition," *Africana* 1, no. 2 (April 1949): 3–4.

CHAPTER FOUR

1. The exact location of the Florence Mills Social Parlour remains something of a mystery. Following contemporary sources such as *Melody Maker,* Cowley places its location on Carnaby Street. However, one informant, Emile Chang of the Hackney Black Peoples Association, told Tony Martin that it was at the corner of Shaftsbury Avenue and Cambridge Circus, while Ernest Marke recalled that it was located near but not actually on Carnaby Street. See Martin, *Amy Ashwood Garvey,* 183n23.

2. Ibid., 63–64, 100–125, 188n16; "Dunbar and Manning Start New London Club," *Melody Maker* (July 4, 1936): 10. Martin reports that John Cowley found no evidence in contemporary sources to support Manning's claim to involvement in the production.

3. Martin, *Amy Ashwood Garvey,* 137–138.

4. C. L. R. James, quoted in ibid., 139–141; *Chicago Defender* (October 5, 1935): 24.

5. Yard, *Biography of Amy Ashwood Garvey,* 107–108.

6. "Dunbar Acts as Host," *Melody Maker* (June 20, 1936): 9; "Dunbar and Manning Start New London Club," *Melody Maker* (July 4, 1936): 10. See also John Cowley "Cultural 'Fusions': Aspects of British West Indian Music in the USA and Britain, 1918–1951," *Popular Music* 5 (1985): 85–86; Cowley, "West Indian Gramophone Records in Britain, 1927–1950," *Musical Traditions* 4 (Early 1985): 28–29.

7. Jarrett-Macauley, *The Life of Una Marson,* 84.

8. Yard, *Biography of Amy Ashwood Garvey,* 109–110; Makonnen, *Pan-Africanism from Within,* 130; *Ashanti Pioneer* (February 15, 1947).

9. Paul Gilroy, *"There Ain't No Black in the Union Jack": The Cultural Politics of Race and Nation* (1987; repr., Chicago: University of Chicago Press, 1991), 198, 209–210; Gilroy, *The Black Atlantic,* 16, 36–39; Edwards, *The Practice of Diaspora,* 67.

10. Indeed, as Jeffrey Green notes, Hylton's orchestra gained notoriety by touring with the African American tenor saxophonist Coleman Hawkins in the 1930s, and Heath "entered the jazz world through contacts with [Edmund] Jenkins in London." Green, "Spirituals to (Nearly) Swing, 1873–1938," in *Cross the Water Blues: African American Music in Europe,* ed. Neil A. Wynn (Jackson: University Press of Mississippi, 2007), 61; Jim Godbolt, *A History of Jazz in Britain, 1919–50* (1984; repr., London: Paladin, 1986), 185, 188.

11. Putnam, *Radical Moves,* 195.

12. Paul Oliver, "Introduction" to Oliver, *Black Music in Britain,* 82; Andrew Simons, "Black British Swing: The African Diaspora's Contribution to England's Own Jazz of the 1930s and 1940s," in *Aural History: Essays on Recorded Sound,* ed. Andy Linehan (London: British Library Sound Archive, 2001), 128; Leslie Thompson, with Jeffrey Green, *Swing from a Small Island: The Story of Leslie Thompson* (1985; repr., London: Northway, 2009), 84–85.

13. Alyn Shipton, *A New History of Jazz* (London: Continuum, 2001), 35. Although Eric Hobsbawm (under the pseudonym Francis Newton), Ross McKibbin, and others (including a number of musicians) also cite the importance of Louis Armstrong's first visit to London in 1932 (or 1934, the last year that American musicians could freely enter Britain, when Armstrong and Coleman Hawkins both visited the country), most histories of jazz in Britain follow the same trend. See Godbolt, *A History of Jazz in Britain;* Francis Newton, *The Jazz Scene* (New York: Monthly Review Press, 1960), 52, 229–230, 233, 245–246; Ross McKibbin, *Classes and Cultures: England, 1918–1951* (Oxford: Oxford University Press, 2000), 398.

14. Howard Rye, "Fearsome Means of Discord: Early Encounters with Black Jazz," in Oliver, *Black Music in Britain,* 50; Howard Rye, "Southern Syncopated Orchestra: The Roster," *Black Music Research Journal* 30, no. 1(2010): 19–70; Chris Stapleton, "African Connections: London's Hidden Music Scene," in ibid., 89.

15. Simons, "Black British Swing," 122; British Library Sound Archive, Oral History of Jazz in Britain Collection, Leslie Thompson (C122/33). On Dave Wilkins, see also "A Man and His Trumpet," *Checkers Magazine* 1, no. 4 (December 1948): 15.

16. Thompson (C122/33).

17. On black female performers in Britain, see Brown, *Babylon Girls.*

18. Thompson, *Swing from a Small Island,* 76–86, 93–94. On Johnson, see also Val Wilmer, "First Sultan of Swing," *Independent on Sunday* (February 24, 1991).

19. Thompson, *Swing from a Small Island,* 99.

20. Simons, "Black British Swing," 117–120; "New British Coloured Band," *Melody Maker* (April 18, 1936): 1.

21. Thompson, *Swing from a Small Island,* 94–98.

22. Frank Mort, *Capital Affairs: London and the Making of the Permissive Society* (New Haven: Yale University Press, 2010), 220; Charles Graves, *Champagne and Chandeliers: The Story of the Café de Paris* (London: Odhams Press, 1958), 9.

23. Simons, "Black British Swing," 124–126, 129; British Library Sound Archive, Oral History of Jazz Collection, Clare Deniz ('19808-T9810Y C1); Andrew Gray, "Getting the Real Low-Down on London's The Old Florida," *Melody Maker* (May 29, 1937): 2.

24. Simons, "Black British Swing," 126, 129–131.

25. See correspondence and program notes in BBC Written Archives, File E2/584 (Foreign General, West Indies, 1939–1950) and the transcripts from *Calling the West Indies.*

26. See "The Profession Mourns . . . ," *Melody Maker* (March 15, 1941): 1.

27. BBC Written Archives, BBC Scripts, *Calling the West Indies* (June 2, 1945).

28. Even in the exceptional case of the West Indian Dance Orchestra, as Simons notes, "one reason why Johnson was hired [at the Café de Paris] over other name bandleaders was his low price." Simons, "Black British Swing," 128.

29. Gus Newton had been active in the London music scene since 1929, when he performed with a trio led by pianist George Ruthland Clapham and the African American violinist Leon Abbey's band at the Deauville Restaurant on Regent Street, and, in the mid-1930s he was a member of Dunbar's band. Thompson recalled that Newton was from Trinidad originally, but Cowley claims that he was born in Britain. Tyree was a black British saxophonist from Birmingham. Cowley, "London Is the Place: Caribbean Music in the Context of Empire, 1900–60," in Oliver, *Black Music in Britain*, 64–69.

30. Thompson, *Swing from a Small Island,* 64, 66; British Library Sound Archive, Oral History of Jazz in Britain Collection, Frank Deniz (T9910-T9912Y C1) and Leslie Thompson (C122/33); "Hutchinson Leaves Geraldo," *Melody Maker* (March 4, 1944): 1; "'Colour Bar' May Cause Jiver Break-Up," *Melody Maker* (November 23, 1946): 1; "Colour Bar," *Melody Maker* (December 7, 1946): 5; Simons, "Black British Swing," 133–137; George McKay, *Circular Breathing: The Cultural Politics of Jazz in Britain* (Durham, NC: Duke University Press, 2005), 141–142; "'Jiver'—An Early Star of Jazz in Britain," *Melody Maker* (November 28, 1959): 4.

31. Clare Deniz (T9808-T9810Y C1) and Thompson (C122/33); Thompson, *Swing from a Small Island,* 94–95, 102; Simons, "Black British Swing," 121.

32. Simon, "Black British Swing," 131.

33. "Ace Frettist Found at Jig's," *Melody Maker* (April 26, 1941): 3; "Blake Leads New Jig's Band," *Melody Maker* (May 17, 1941): 1.

34. This is how the young jazz writer Leonard Feather described Happy Blake's band at the Shim Sham Club shortly after it opened. Leonard Feather, "London Lowdown," *New Amsterdam News* (October 19, 1935): 6.

35. Jack Glicco, *Madness after Midnight* (London: Elek Books, 1952), 132; Godbolt, *A History of Jazz in Britain,* 189–191.

36. British Library Sound Archive, Oral History of Jazz in Britain Collection, Beryl Bryden (C122/68–70).

37. Godbolt, *A History of Jazz in Britain,* 189–191.

38. The Parlophone record label first announced plans for a commercial release of the recordings, but in the end, Regal-Zonophone issued them. Cowley, "London Is the Place," 64; "Night-Club Recording on the Spot Is Parlophone Innovation," *Melody Maker* (December 13, 1941): 1; "Gin Mill on Wax: Parlophone's Unique Recording Session at Jig's Club," *Melody Maker* (December 27, 1941): 5; "Bargain-Price Swing on Regal-Zonophone," *Melody Maker* (January 24, 1942): 1.

39. Judith Walkowitz, "The 'Vision of Salome': Cosmopolitanism and Erotic Dancing in Central London, 1908–1918," *American Historical Review* 108, no. 2 (April 2003): 338–339. On cosmopolitanism, music, and Soho, see also Judith Walkowitz, *Nights Out: Life in Cosmopolitan London* (New Haven: Yale University Press, 2012); Mort, *Capital Affairs*; E.D. Mackerness, *A Social History of English Music* (1964; repr., Abingdon, UK: Routledge, 2007).

40. Brown, *Babylon Girls*, 131–132.

41. Martin Pugh, *"We Danced All Night": A Social History of Britain between the Wars* (London: Bodley Head, 2008), 220; Mica Nava, "Wider Horizons and Modern Desire: The Contradictions of America and Racial Difference in London, 1935–1945," *New Formations: A Journal of Culture/Theory/Politics* 37 (Spring 1999): 77; McKibbin, *Classes and Cultures*, 390–418.

42. Catherine Parsonage, "Fascination and Fear: Responses to Early Jazz in Britain," in Wynn, *Cross the Water Blues*, 89–105.

43. *Daily Mail* quoted in Pugh, *"We Danced All Night,"* 219; McKay, *Circular Breathing*, 107; S. A. Moseley, ed., *Brightest Spots in Brighter London: A Comprehensive Guide to London Amusements, Shopping Centres and Features of Interest to the Visitor* (London: Stanley Paul, 1924), 138; British Library Sound Archive, Oral History of Jazz in Britain Collection, Max Jones (H7318). On Valaida Snow, see Brown, *Babylon Girls*, 265–279.

44. Mort, *Capital Affairs*, 222.

45. Pugh, *"We Danced All Night,"* 218.

46. Jack Glicco recounts the story of Chan Nam, a migrant from Hong Kong whom he characterized as the "Dope King" and "Britain's biggest dealer in drugs," "through whose hands ran the bulk of the cocaine then being sold in . . . London." Jack Glicco, *Madness after Midnight* (London: Elek Books, 1952), 52–57. Others linked drug trafficking to "jazz crazy negroes." Like the extensive press coverage of him, books such as *Soho: London's Vicious Circle* and the *London after Dark* described the Jamaican Edgar Manning, a jazz drummer himself, as "a dope-pedlar [*sic*] and white slaver," "dope king," and "drug trafficker." Mort, *Capital Affairs*, 202; Brown, *Babylon Girls*, 107; Robert Fabian, *London after Dark: An Intimate Record of Night Life in London, and a Selection of Crime Stories from the Case Book of Ex-superintendent Robert Fabian* (New York: British Book Centre, 1954), 16, 32–33, 69; Parsonage, "Fascination and Fear," 95–96; Jeffrey Green, "Before the *Windrush*," *History Today* 50, no. 10 (2003): 32; Sandhu, *London Calling*, ch. 3.

47. Mort, *Capital Affairs*, 211, 221–222; Walkowitz, *Nights Out*, 243; John McLeod, *Postcolonial London: Rewriting the Metropolis* (London: Routledge, 2004), 27–28.

48. Glicco, *Madness after Midnight*, 10; Mort, *Capital Affairs*, 219–220.

49. Walkowitz, *Nights Out*, 221.

50. Fabian, *London after Dark*, 15; James, "A Race Outcast from an Outcast Class: Claude McKay's Experience and Analysis of Britain," in Schwarz, *West Indian Intellectuals in Britain*, 79.

51. Sandhu, *London Calling*, 120–121; police testimony quoted in Pugh, *"We Danced All Night,"* 218.

52. The map frontispiece of Glicco's book shows the Blue Lagoon on the corner of Carnaby and Beak Street. Leslie Thompson recalled that Frisco's was on Dean Street, which is one block west of Frith, but Walkowitz places both on Frith Street. Glicco, *Madness after Midnight*; Thompson, *Swing from a Small Island*, 90–91; Walkowitz, *Nights Out*, 230.

53. Joe Deniz quoted in Walkowitz, *Nights Out,* 239.

54. Simons, "Black British Swing," 121; Glicco, *Madness after Midnight,* 31; Fabian, *London after Dark,* 22; Thompson, *Swing from a Small Island,* 91.

55. Simons, Black British Swing," 123; Thompson (C122/33); Thompson, *Swing from a Small Island,* 86–87, 90.

56. Thompson, *Swing from a Small Island,* 66, 92; Glicco, *Madness after Midnight,* 40–41, 92, 132–133; Walkowitz, *Nights Out,* 231, 358n180.

57. Val Wilmer, "Tommy Thomas: Conga Drummer Who Graced London Clubs for 30 years," *Guardian* (September 22, 2005); Clare Deniz (T9808-T9810Y C1); Glicco, *Madness after Midnight,* 40–41, 92, 132–133; Fabian, *London after Dark,* 28.

58. Walkowitz, *Nights Out,* 232.

59. "Blake Goes West," *Melody Maker* (January 31, 1942): 3; "Jig's Club Closed," *Melody Maker* (April 4, 1942): 1.

60. Coleridge Goode and Roger Cotterrell, *Bass Lines: A Life in Jazz* (London: Northway, 2002), 62; Thompson, *Swing from a Small Island,* 92; Clare Deniz (T9808-T9810Y C1).

61. Glicco, *Madness after Midnight,* 131; Clare Deniz (T9808-T9810Y C1); Thompson, *Swing from a Small Island,* 85, 90, 92, 100–102; Godbolt, *A History of Jazz in Britain,* 118.

62. Kevin Morgan, "King Street Blues: Jazz and the Left in Britain in the 1930–1940s," in *A Weapon in the Struggle: The Cultural History of the Communist Party in Britain,* ed. Andy Croft (London: Pluto Press, 1998), 125. Harrison quoted in Walkowitz, *Nights Outs,* 240, 249; Max Jones (H7318).

63. Locke quoted in Paul Gilroy, *Between Camps: Nations, Cultures, and the Allure of Race* (London: Penguin, 2000), 297; Eric Porter, *What Is This Thing Called Jazz? African American Musicians as Artists, Critics, and Activists* (Berkeley: University of California Press, 2002), xv.

64. Rudolph Dunbar, "Harlem in London: Year of Advancement for Negroes," *Melody Maker* (March 7, 1936): 2; Davies, *Memoirs,* 61–64; Azikiwe, *My Odyssey,* 197, 203; Makonnen, *Pan-Africanism from Within,* 130; Bunche Diary (April 22, 1937); Abrahams, *The Coyoba Chronicles,* 31, 36.

65. Putnam, *Radical Moves,* 158–159.

66. *Wāsù* 6, no. 3 (Christmas Number, 1937): 44.

67. Dave Wilkins recalled attending Johnson's funeral at Aggrey House. Alistair Cooke, "Some Reflections on Jazz," *The Keys* 3, no. 1 (July–September 1935): 5–6; Stapleton, "African Connections," 94; British Library Sound Archive, Oral History of Jazz in Britain Collection, Dave Wilkins (C122/36).

68. From 1945 until 1952, Sowande was the organist at the West London Mission of the Methodist Church in Kingsway, performing weekly for a growing audience of African parishioners. His popularity as a church organist paved the way for Nigerian students after him to take up similar posts at venues such as London's Church of St. James-the-Less, where, in the 1950s, the organists Olaolu Omideyi, Akin Euba, and Ayo Banokole played in succession. Bode Omojola, *The Music of Fela Sowande: Encounters, African Identity and Creative Ethnomusicology* (Point Richmond, CA:

Music Research Institute Press, 2009), 9, 27, 47–57, 121; "Adelaide Hall and a New Coloured Band Hit London," *Melody Maker* 14, no. 291 (December 17, 1938): 1; Eileen Southern, "Conversation with Fela Sowande, High Priest of Music," *Black Perspective in Music* 4, no. 1 (Spring 1976): 91.

69. Omojola, *The Music of Fela Sowande*, 1–8; Fela Sowande, "A West African School of Music," *West African Review* (January 1944): 22–23.

70. "'Happy' Blake: Bandleader and Club Owner," *Checkers Magazine* 1, no. 3 (November 1948): 9; *League of Coloured Peoples Newsletter* 19 (April 1941): 24–27; 12, no. 68 (May 1945): 39; 12, no. 69 (June 1945): 57; 13, no. 78 (March 1946): 134; Wellesley Cole Papers, PP MS 35/6/1/14, File 151, M. Joseph Mitchell, "Report by the General & Travelling Secretary on the League of Coloured Peoples Seventeenth Annual General Meeting" (1948).

71. Jeffrey Green, "Spirituals to (Nearly) Swing, 1873–1938," in Wynn, *Cross the Water Blues*, 58; Goode and Cotterrell, *Bass Lines*, 26, 31–32, 38.

72. Max Jones (H7318); Simons, "Black British Swing," 131; McKay, *Circular Breathing*, 142; Makonnen, *Pan-Africanism from Within*, 130; "Caribbean Trio Leave the Caribbean," *Melody Maker* (November 16, 1946): 1; "Caribbean Trio for Rose Room," *Melody Maker* (December 14, 1946): 1; "The Ray Ellington Quartet," *Checkers* 1, no. 3 (November 1948): 14–15.

73. Goode and Cotterrell, *Bass Lines*, 45–48, 51; Val Wilmer, "Josie Miller Obituary," *Guardian* (April 29, 2010); Wilmer, "Harlem Nights in Deepest Mayfair," *Calling the West Indies* (January 16–17, 1945). On Lena Horne in London, see *Checkers* 1, no. 5 (January 1949), and The National Archives, CO 964/24, correspondence with Nkrumah, November 19, 22, and 29, 1947.

74. Quoted in "Ambrose Campbell: Nigerian-Born Musician Whose Relaxed African Rhythms and Harmonies Made a Stir in Drab Postwar Britain," *Sunday Times* (July 21, 2006); Val Wilmer, "Ambrose Campbell: Nigerian Musician Whose Career Took in the Postwar Soho of Colin MacInnes, Nashville—and Leon Russell," *Guardian* (July 8, 2006); Feld, *Jazz Cosmopolitanism*, 49; Goode and Cotterrell, *Bass Lines*, 51–52.

75. Goode and Cotterrell, *Bass Lines*, 51; John Cowley, "uBungca (Oxford Bags): Recordings in London of African and West Indian Music in the 1920s and 1930s," *Musical Traditions* 12 (Summer 1994; updated 1999), www.mustrad.org.uk/articles /ubunca.htm (accessed June 19, 2006).

76. Mike Phillips and Trevor Phillips, *Windrush: The Irresistible Rise of Multiracial Britain* (London: Harper Collins, 1998).

77. Dave Wilkins recalled performing, but not recording, with Lord Kitchener and other calypsonians at West Indian student dances. "Blake Leads New Jig's Band," 1; BBC Written Archives, File E2/584 (Foreign General, West Indies, 1939–1950), "Notes for Mr. Madden about Coloured Artists from Una Marson"; "War Time Radio Reviewed: Bouquet for Barreto, A Pan for Parry," *Melody Maker* (May 10, 1941): 9; "Calypsos On Air," *Melody Maker* (June 13, 1942): 2; Thompson, *Swing from a Small Island*, 64; Val Wilmer, "George Browne," *Guardian* (April 6, 2007); Wilkins (C122/36).

78. Thompson, *Swing from a Small Island,* 104–105; Cowley, "uBungca (Oxford Bags)," 12–13.

79. Frank Deniz (T9910-T9912Y C1); Paul Vernon Chester, "The Deniz Dynasty," www.paulvernonchester.com/DenizDynasty.htm (accessed June 11, 2012).

80. Feld, *Jazz Cosmopolitanism,* 49, 210–211, 219; Brown, *Babylon Girls,* 130.

81. See Robin D. G. Kelley, *Africa Speaks, America Answers: Modern Jazz in Revolutionary Times* (Cambridge, MA: Harvard University Press, 2012); Penny M. Von Eschen, *Satchmo Blows Up the World: Jazz Ambassadors Play the Cold War* (Cambridge, MA: Harvard University Press, 2006); Thomas Turino, *Nationalists, Cosmopolitans, and Popular Music in Zimbabwe* (Chicago: University of Chicago Press, 2000); Hermano Vianna, *The Mystery of Samba: Popular Music and National Identity in Brazil* (Chapel Hill: University of North Carolina Press, 1999); Michael George Hanchard, *Orpheus and Power: The* Movimento Negro *of Rio de Janeiro and São Paulo, Brazil, 1945–1988* (Princeton: Princeton University Press, 1998).

82. Feld, *Jazz Cosmopolitanism,* 243

83. Putnam, *Radical Moves,* 156; "Dunbar and Manning Start New London Club," 10.

84. Putnam, *Radical Moves,* 178–180; Thompson, *Swing from a Small Island,* 104.

85. Cowley, "uBungca (Oxford Bags)," 11; Cowley, "Cultural 'Fusions,'" 82–85; Cowley, "West Indian Gramophone Records in Britain, 1927–1950," 4.

86. Oliver, "Introduction," 82; "A Negro Sings . . . Millions Listen," *Checkers* 1, no. 4 (December 1948): 8–9; British Library Sound Archive, Oral History of Jazz in Britain Collection, Rupert Nurse (C122/154); liner notes to *London Is the Place for Me 6: Mento, Calypso, Jazz and Highlife from Young Black London* (London: Honest Jon's Records, 2013).

87. Christopher Alan Waterman, *Jùjú: A Social History and Ethnography of an African Popular Music* (Chicago: University of Chicago Press, 1990), 31–32, 39–40, 45–48; Cowley, "uBungca (Oxford Bags)," 6–7; Matory, *Black Atlantic Religion,* ch. 1.

88. Cowley, "uBungca (Oxford Bags)," 2; Stapleton, "African Connections," 89–90.

89. Paul Vernon, "Savannaphone: Talking Machines Hit West Africa," *Folk-ROOTS* (electronic edition, April 17, 1997), http://bolingo.org/audio/texts /fr122savanna.html (accessed March 28, 2013).

90. Little is known of Domingo Justus, but he was recording in London by 1925. Given their Portuguese names, he or Douglas Papafio, who recorded in Fanti for Zonophone, or both, may have been descendants of Afro-Brazilian traders on the West African coast or returnees from Brazil. Justus's recordings from 1928 have been reissued on *Domingo Justus: Roots of Juju* (West Sussex: Interstate Music Ltd., 1992).

91. "Installation of Mr. Paul Robeson as Babàsale (Patron) of W.A.S.U."; Pennybacker, *From Scottsboro to Munich,* 49; *The West African Instrumental Quintet, 1929* (West Sussex, UK: Interstate Music Ltd., 1992); Stapleton, "African Connec-

tions," 91–92. For an advertisement for Solanke's recordings, see the liner notes of *Living Is Hard: West African Music in Britain, 1927–1929* (London: Honest Jon's Records, 2008).

92. "EC's Gramophone Notes," *West Africa* (June 15, 1929). Recordings by a number of these artists have been rereleased on the recent compilations *Early Guitar Music from West Africa, 1927–1929* (West Sussex: Interstate Music Ltd., 2003) and *Living Is Hard*.

93. Andrew L. Kaye, "The Guitar in Africa," in *The Garland Handbook of African Music*, ed. Ruth M. Stone (New York: Garland, 2000), 79–80; liner notes for *Living Is Hard*; Janet Topp Fargion, *Out of Cuba: Latin American Music Takes Africa by Storm* (London: Topic Records/British Library Sound Archive, 2004).

94. *Illustrated Police News* (December 24, 1931): 7, quoted in Sandhu, *London Calling*, 120–121.

95. Stapleton, "African Connections," 93–97; *London Is the Place For Me 4: African Dreams and The Piccadilly High Life* (London: Honest Jon's Records, 2006).

96. Wilmer, "Ambrose Campbell"; Val Wilmer, "Hughes, Brewster," *Oxford Dictionary of National Biography* (Oxford: Oxford University Press, 2010; online ed., January 2012), http://www.oxforddnb.com/view/article/100490 (accessed September 3, 2014).

97. Waterman, *Jùjú*, 49–50, 64–65, 69, 96, 245; Michael E. Veal, *Fela: The Life and Times of an African Musical Icon* (Philadelphia: Temple University Press, 2000), 47.

98. Despite the involvement of such prominent investors as George Bernard Shaw, Aneurin Bevan, and Jennie Lee, financial difficulties forced Pasuka to close the company in 1953. "Negro Ballet Set to Open in London," *League of Coloured Peoples Newsletter* 13, no. 77 (February 1946): 111; Keith Watson, "They Were Britain's First Black Dance Company; How Come No One's Ever Heard of Them?" *Guardian* (August 4, 1999).

99. Noel Vaz, "Berto Pasuka and the Jamaican Ballet," *West African Review* (Spring 1947): 27–28; Pat Brand, "West African Witchery," *Melody Maker* (June 8, 1946): 6; *West African Review* (June 1946): 681.

100. Lloyd Bradley, *Sounds Like London: 100 Years of Black Music in the Capital* (London: Serpent's Tail, 2013), 135, 137, 140–141, 143.

101. *Wásù* 12, no. 2 (March 1946). 7; Wellesley Cole Papers, PP MS 35/6/1/14, File 157, H. L. O. George to Wellesley Cole (July 14, 1953).

102. Stapleton, "African Connections," 94; Wilmer, "Hughes, Brewster." On the lesser-known race riot of 1949, see Kevin Searle, "'Mixing of the Unmixables': The 1949 Causeway Green 'Riots' in Birmingham," *Race and Class* 54, no. 3 (January 2013): 44–64.

103. Omojola, *The Music of Fela Sowande,* 61; Bashorun quoted in Stapleton, "African Connections," 95.

104. Wilmer, "Ambrose Campbell"; Colin Macinnes, "City after Dark," *Twentieth Century* (December 1957): 571–573.

105. *The West African Instrumental Quintet, 1929*; Putnam, *Radical Moves,* 195; BBC Written Archives, BBC Scripts, Una Marson, "Greetings to Jamaica" (September 26, 1940); Cowley, "London Is the Place," 75.

106. Chris Stapleton and Chris May, *African Rock: The Pop Music of a Continent* (New York: Obelisk/Dutton, 1990), 297.

107. Veal, *Fela,* 47; "Jazz with a West African Accent," *West African Review* (November 1952): 1155; Bashorun quoted in Stapleton, "African Connections," 95.

108. Val Wilmer, liner notes to *London Is the Place For Me 3: Ambrose Adekoya Campbell* (London: Honest Jon's Records, 2006).

109. "Agwa's London Diary: Back from His Travels in the West Country, Agwa Brings News of West Africans About Town," *West African Review* (February 1954): 118–119.

110. Wilmer, "Hughes, Brewster."

111. Waterman, *Jùjú,* 96–97; Omojola, *The Music of Fela Sowande,* 60–62, 71; Veal, *Fela,* 12, 72, 136.

112. Kelley, *Africa Speaks, America Answers,* 18–22; Warren quoted in Mark Ainley, liner notes to *Marvelous Boy: Calypso from West Africa* (London: Honest Jon's Records, 2009); Feld, *Jazz Cosmopolitanism,* 58; John Collins, *E. T. Mensah, The King of Highlife* (London: Off The Record Press, 1986), 1–4; film interview clip with Mr. Aliyi Ekineh, *The WASU Project,* coordinated by Hakim Adi, http://wasuproject.org.uk/about-the-film/ (accessed June 2, 2012).

113. Feld, *Jazz Cosmopolitanism,* 212; Wilmer, "Hughes, Brewster"; Putnam, *Radical Moves,* 153.

114. Veal, *Fela,* 47; Ray Templeton, "Highlife Piccadilly: African Music on 45 rpm Records in the UK, 1954–1981," *Musical Traditions Internet Magazine* (May 1999), http://www.mustrad.org.uk/articles/african.htm (accessed June 19, 2006); Wilmer, "George Browne"; Feld, *Jazz Cosmopolitanism,* 213.

CHAPTER FIVE

1. For an introduction to critical approaches to intimacy, see Lauren Berlant, ed., *Intimacy* (Chicago: University of Chicago Press, 2000).

2. Robert Hyam, *Sexuality and Empire: The British Experience* (Manchester, UK: Manchester University Press, 1990), 58; Ann Laura Stoler, *Race and the Education of Desire: Foucault's* History of Sexuality *and the Colonial Order of Things* (Durham, NC: Duke University Press, 1995), 175–176; Robert Aldrich, *Colonialism and Homosexuality* (London: Routledge, 2003); Carina Ray, "Decrying White Peril: Interracial Sex and the Rise of Anticolonial Nationalism in the Gold Coast," *American Historical Review* 119, no. 1 (February 2014): 78–110.

3. Laura Tabili, "Women 'of a Low Type': Crossing Racial Boundaries in Imperial Britain," in *Gender and Class in Modern Europe,* ed. Laura L. Frader and Sonya O. Rose (Ithaca, NY: Cornell University Press, 1996), 165–190; Tabili, *"We Ask for British Justice"*; Brown, *Dropping Anchor, Setting Sail*; Susan Kingsley Kent, *After-*

shocks: Politics and Trauma in Britain, 1918–1931 (Basingstoke, UK: Palgrave Macmillan, 2009), ch. 2; Jon Lawrence, "Forging a Peaceable Kingdom: War, Violence and Fear of Brutalization in Post–World War I Britain," *Journal of Modern History* 75, no. 3 (September 2003): 557–589.

4. E. D. Morel, "Black Scourge in Europe," *Daily Herald* (April 10, 1920): 1; E. D. Morel, *The Horror on the Rhine* (London: Union of Democratic Control, August 1920), 9–10; Lucy Bland, "White Women and Men of Colour," *Gender and History* 17, no. 1 (April 2005): 32, 40–42; "A Black Man Replies," *Workers' Dreadnought* (April 24, 1920): 2; James, "A Race Outcast from an Outcast Class," 83. See also Iris Wigger, "'Black Shame': The Campaign against 'Racial Degeneration' and Female Degradation in Interwar Europe," *Race and Class* 51, no. 3 (2010): 33–46; Sally Marks, "Black Watch on the Rhine: A Study of Propaganda, Prejudice and Prurience," *European Studies Review* 13 (1983): 297–334; Keith Nelson, "The 'Black Horror on the Rhine': Race as a Factor in Post–World War I Diplomacy," *Journal of Modern History* 42 (1970): 606–627; Jock McCulloch, *Black Peril, White Virtue: Sexual Crime in Southern Rhodesia, 1902–1935* (Bloomington: Indiana University Press, 2000).

5. "*Our* Responsibilities," *Wāsù* 12, no. 1 (March 1945): 3–5.

6. St. Clair Drake, "Accommodative Leadership," Drake Papers, MG 309, Box 61, File 5.

7. As Lucy Bland notes, the voices and experiences of men of color, "the impact of prejudice upon them, and their strategies of support and survival" are largely absent from extant scholarship. Bland, "White Women and Men of Colour," 30, 32. See also Marcus Collins, "Pride and Prejudice: West Indian Men in Mid-Twentieth-Century Britain," *Journal of British Studies* 40, no. 3 (July 2001): 391–418; Carby, *Race Men,* 25; Stephens, *Black Empire.*

8. Their numbers only increased after the Second World War. In 1947 alone, the LCP hosted Drake, Richard Wright, and the sociologist and first black president of Fisk University, Dr. Charles S. Johnson. Bunche Diary, April 23, 1937; Mitchell, "Report by the General & Travelling Secretary on the League of Coloured Peoples Seventeenth Annual General Meeting."

9. Bunche Diary, April 18, 1937.

10. See Lloyd Braithwaite, *Colonial West Indian Students in Britain* (Mona, Jamaica: University of the West Indies Press, 2001), ch. 5; Wellesley Cole Papers, PP MS 35/73/15, File 20, "Spring in Nigeria" (unpublished manuscript, 1959), esp. ch. 22, and PP MS 35/73/14, File 180, "Sex and Society or the Problem of Sex" (unpublished manuscript, 1961); Azikiwe, *My Odyssey,* 202–203.

11. St. Clair Drake, "Sex and Family Relationship," Drake Papers, MG 309, Box 61, File 10.

12. Ibid.

13. Sigmund Freud, *The Joke and Its Relation to the Unconscious* (1905; repr., London: Penguin, 2002), 98, 100, 106–109, 145, 148; Ralph Ellison, *Shadow and Act* (1953; repr., New York: Quality Paperback Book Club, 1994), 45. See also Shoshana Felman, *Testimony: Crises of Witnessing in Literature, Psychoanalysis and History*

(London: Routledge, 1991); Cathy Caruth, "Trauma and Experience: Introduction," in *Trauma: Explorations in Memory,* ed. Cathy Caruth (Baltimore: John Hopkins University Press, 1995), 3–13; Dominick LaCapra, *Writing History, Writing Trauma* (Baltimore: John Hopkins University Press, 2001), 145–150.

14. Dominick LaCapra, *History in Transit: Experience, Identity, Critical Theory* (Ithaca, NY: Cornell University Press, 2007), 58–60; Braithwaite, *Colonial West Indian Students in Britain,* 58; Berlant and Edelman, *Sex, or the Unbearable,* viii.

15. Berlant and Edelman, *Sex, or the Unbearable,* viii, xii.

16. Abrahams, *The Coyoba Chronicles,* 31–34.

17. Makonnen, *Pan-Africanism from Within,* 131–132.

18. Schwarz, "Black Metropolis, White England," 198; Bunche Diary, April 18, 1937; Drake, "Accommodative Leadership.".

19. Schwarz, "Black Metropolis, White England," 197; Bunche Diary (April 18, 1937); Drake, "Sex and Family Relationship"; Collins, "Pride and Prejudice," 406–407. See also Sonya O. Rose, *Which People's War? National Identity and Citizenship in Wartime Britain, 1939–1945* (Oxford: Oxford University Press, 2003), ch. 3; Graham Smith, *When Jim Crow Met John Bull: Black American Soldiers in World War II Britain* (London: I. B. Tauris, 1987), 188.

20. See "The Case of Mr. E. S. Ajayi," *Wāsù* 2, no. 1 (January 1933), 22–23; Carina E. Ray, "The 'White Wife Problem': Sex, Race, and the Contested Politics of Repatriation to Interwar British West Africa," *Gender and History* 21, no. 3 (November 2009): 628–646.

21. Adi, *West Africans in Britain,* 14, 18–19; Derrick, *Africa's "Agitators,"* 404; Bush, *Imperialism, Race and Resistance,* 25.

22. The National Archives, CO 554/109/4 (1937–8) (emphasis in original).

23. The National Archives, CO 554/109/4, Metropolitan Police Report, Somers Town Station, N. Division (September 5, 1937).

24. The National Archives, CO 554/114/4 (1938), Mr. Jones, Minutes to internal Colonial Office correspondence.

25. The National Archives, CO 859/21/1 (1940), Vischer to Keith, April 17, 1940; "Minute of Interview with Dr. Moody," by J. L. Keith, Colonial Office. April 30, 1940.

26. Ibid., Colonial Office to Mr. Hodson, Ministry of Information, May 14, 1940.

27. The expelled Caribbean student was Mr. Wilkins. Ibid., Lloyd to colonial governors in Africa and the Caribbean, May 23, 1940.

28. "'Moral Issue' Closes Club, Coloured Students' Only Social Centre," *Evening Standard* (May 4, 1940); "Students' Club Closed by Trustees," *Daily Worker* (May 6, 1940); The National Archives, CO 859/21/1, "Memorandum by Harold A. Moody," May 3, 1940, and Minute by J. L. Keith, July 25, 1940.

29. Stoler, *Race and the Education of Desire,* 176, 184.

30. Makonnen, *Pan-Africanism from Within,* 146–147; Drake, "Sex and Family Relationship."

31. Bunche Diary, March 28 and April 2, 1937; Abrahams, *The Coyoba Chronicles,* 37.

32. Mass Observation respondent quoted in Pennybacker, *From Scottsboro to Munich,* 254.

33. Drake, "Sex and Family Relationship."

34. Ibid.

35. Black male characters appear as markers of transgressive desire in the period's two most important works of queer literature, Radclyffe Hall's seminal work of lesbian-and-transgender fiction, *The Well of Loneliness* (1928), and Reginald Underwood's *Flame of Freedom* (1936). Radclyffe Hall, *The Well of Loneliness* (1928; repr., New York: Doubleday, 1956), 361–365; Reginald Underwood, *Flame of Freedom* (London: Fortune Press, 1936), 184–185; Matt Houlbrook, *Queer London: Perils and Pleasures in the Sexual Metropolis, 1918–1957* (Chicago: University of Chicago Press, 2005), 248–249.

36. Mort, *Capital Affairs,* 228; McLeod, *Postcolonial London,* 27, 41–42; Ové, Farson, and Wyndham quoted in Tony Gould, *Insider Outsider: The Life and Times of Colin MacInnes* (London: Allison and Busby, 1983), 220, 141, 116; Colin MacInnes, *City of Spades* (1957; repr., New York: E. P. Dutton, 1985), 203, 207–223; Wendy Webster, *Imagining Home: Gender, Race and National Identity, 1945–1964* (New York: Routledge, 1998), 48–49, 51–52, 104.

37. Appiah, *Joe Appiah,* 152–153; Bunche Diary, May 2, 1937; Val Wilmer, "Christmas Cake and Calypso," *Soundings: A Journal of Politics and Culture* 10 (Autumn 1998): 182.

38. Bourne, *Mother Country,* 105–106; Trevor Chepstow, "Ras Prince Monolulu, 1880–1965," *My Brighton and Hove,* http://www.mybrightonandhove.org.uk /page_id__8823_path__op117p155p.aspx (accessed August 12, 2012); Drake, "Sex and Family Relationship."

39. Ernest Marke, *In Troubled Waters: Memoirs of My Seventy Years in England* (London: Karia Press, 1986), 101–102, 106–107.

40. Appiah, *Joe Appiah,* 152–153; Ulf Hannerz, *Soulside: Inquiries into Ghetto Culture and Community* (New York: Columbia University Press, 1969), 105–107.

41. Appiah, *Joe Appiah,* 152; Bunche Diary, March 28 and April 23, 1937; *Daily Herald* (August 26, 1935): 3; *Times* (September 24, 1935): 11; Makalani, *In the Cause of Freedom,* 206, 208.

42. The student may have been Peter Koinange, with whom Drake developed a friendship. Drake, "Sex and Family Relationship."

43. Braithwaite, *Colonial West Indian Students in Britain,* 89–91, 95; Makonnen, *Pan-Africanism from Within,* 131–132; C. L. R. James, *Letters from London: Seven Essays by C. L. R. James* (1932; repr., Port of Spain, Trinidad and Tobago: Prospect Press, 2003), 102–106.

44. Hooper and Barlow quoted in Murray-Brown, *Kenyatta,* 118–119, 129, 216.

45. Bunche Diary, March 21, April 7, and May 24, 1937.

46. Carolyn Martin Shaw, *Colonial Inscriptions: Race, Sex, and Class in Kenya* (Minneapolis: University of Minnesota Press, 1995), 123–125; Murray-Brown,

Kenyatta, 91; Gikandi, "Pan-Africanism and Cosmopolitanism," 6, 24; John Lonsdale, "Jomo Kenyatta, God and the Modern World," in *African Modernities: Entangled Meanings in Current Debate,* ed. Jan-Georg Deutsch, Peter Probst, and Heike Schmidt (Portsmouth, NH: Heinemann, 2002), 32–33, 38. On dandyism as a model and black internationalist masculinity, see Monica L. Miller, *Slaves to Fashion: Black Dandyism and the Styling of Black Diasporic Identity* (Durham, NC: Duke University Press, 2009), ch. 3.

47. Bunche Diary, March 21, April 7, and May 24, 1937.

48. "Editorial," *International African Service Bureau* 1, no. 1 (July 1938): 2–3; LaCapra, *History in Transit,* 60 (emphasis in original).

49. Carby, *Race Men,* 113.

50. On white women's involvement with antiracism and anticolonialism, see Caroline Bressey, "Victorian 'Anti-racism' and Feminism in Britain," *Women: A Cultural Review* 21, no. 3 (December 2010): 279–291; Laura Tabili, "Empire Is the Enemy of Love: Edith Noor's Progress and Other Stories," *Gender and History* 17, no. 1 (April 2005): 5–28; Barbara Bush, "'Britain's Conscience on Africa': White Women, Race and Imperial Politics in Inter-war Britain," in *Gender and Imperialism,* ed. Clare Midgley (Manchester, UK: Manchester University Press, 1998), 200–223.

51. Braithwaite, *Colonial West Indian Students in Britain,* 90; Hercules quoted in Bland, "White Women and Men of Colour," 52; Rowe, "Sex, 'Race,' and Riot in Liverpool, 1919," 60; Abrahams, *The Coyoba Chronicles,* 42; Appiah, *Joe Appiah,* 154–155.

52. Bunche Diary, June 26, 1937; Makonnen, *Pan-Africanism from Within,* 146–147; Nkrumah, *Ghana,* 56; Basin Clarke, *Taking What Comes: A Biography of A. G. Stock (Dinah),* ed. Surjit Hans (Chandigarh, India: Panjab University Press, 1999), 83; Murray-Brown, *Kenyatta,* 156, 199–200.

53. Bunche Diary, July 17, 1937; Braithwaite, *Colonial West Indian Students in Britain,* 91–92, 95.

54. Bunche Diary, April 29, 1937.

55. Braithwaite, *Colonial West Indian Students in Britain,* 85–86; Drake "Sex and Family Relationship"; Derrick, *Africa's "Agitators,"* 336n197; Cole, "Spring in Nigeria," 303.

56. Bunche Diary, March 28, 1937.

57. Drake, "Sex and Family Relationship."

58. Braithwaite, *Colonial West Indian Students in Britain,* 86–87; Drake, "Sex and Family Relationship."

59. Makonnen, *Pan-Africanism from Within,* 160; *Negro Worker* 2, no. 3 (March 1932): 2–3; *Negro Worker* (August–September 1933): 17; Bunche Diary, April 12 and July 15, 1937.

60. Bunche Diary, April 12, June 4 and 8, July 1, 1937.

61. Drake, "Sex and Family Relationship."

62. Makonnen, *Pan-Africanism from Within,* 147.

63. Abrahams, *The Coyoba Chronicles,* 42, 39.

64. Adi, *West Africans in Britain,* 27.

65. Ernest Marke disputed this characterization of Nkrumah. Appiah, *Joe Appiah,* 164; Marke quoted in Marika Sherwood, "Kwame Nkrumah: The London Years, 1945–47," in *Africans in Britain,* ed. David Killingray (London: Frank Cass, 1994), 181–182.

66. Nkrumah, *Ghana,* 42; Jean Allman, "Phantoms of the Archive: Kwame Nkrumah, a Nazi Pilot Named Hanna, and the Contingencies of Postcolonial History-Writing," *American Historical Review* 118, no. 1 (2013): 129.

67. Drake, "Accommodative Leadership."

68. Mackenzie and James, "Radical Pan-Africanism in the 1930s," 72.

69. Peter Abrahams, *A Wreath for Udomo* (London: Faber and Faber, 1956), 20–21, 28.

70. Paul Mabi was based most likely on the Nigerian artist Benedict Chukwu-kadibia Enwonwu, who attended Goldsmith College, London, in 1944; Ruskin College, Oxford, from 1944 to 1946; and Slade School of Fine Arts at the University of London from 1946 to 1948. Sylvester Okwunodu Ogbechie, *Ben Enwonwu: The Making of an African Modernist* (Rochester, NY: University of Rochester Press, 2008).

71. Although Padmore's biographer calls Abrahams's characterization of him "a cruel travesty," he uncritically accepts the portrayal of Pizer, noting that it "seems to square with others' observations." Abrahams, *A Wreath for Udomo,* 41, 45–48; Hooker, *Black Revolutionary,* 48.

72. Abrahams, *A Wreath for Udomo,* 132, 193–194.

73. The National Archives, CO 964/24, correspondence from Bankole Akpata, Margot Parrish, and Florence Manley to Nkrumah (November 22 and 29, 1947; January 8, 1948; n.d.).

CHAPTER SIX

1. See Robert H. Bates, V. Y. Mudimbe, and Jean F. O'Barr, eds., *Africa and the Disciplines: The Contributions of Research in Africa to the Social Sciences and Humanities* (Chicago: University of Chicago Press, 1993); Rimmer and Kirk-Greene, *The British Intellectual Engagement with Africa in the Twentieth Century*; Helen Tilley, *Africa as a Living Laboratory: Empire, Development, and the Scientific Problem of Knowledge, 1870–1950* (Chicago: University of Chicago Press, 2011). On the centrality of Africa to the development of anthropology in Britain, see Henrika Kuklick, *The Savage Within: The Social History of British Anthropology, 1885–1945* (Cambridge: Cambridge University Press, 1992); Sally Falk Moore, *Anthropology and Africa: Changing Perspectives on a Changing Scene* (Charlottesville: University of Virginia Press, 1994); Jack Goody, *The Expansive Moment: Anthropology in Britain and Africa, 1918–1970* Cambridge: Cambridge University Press 1995); David Mills, *Difficult Folk: A Political History of Social Anthropology* (Oxford: Berghahn Books, 2008); Helen Tilley, ed., with Robert J. Gordon, *Ordering Africa: Anthropology,*

European Imperialism and the Politics of Knowledge (Manchester: Manchester University Press, 2011).

2. For rare exceptions to this tendency, see George Shepperson, "Notes on Negro American Influences on the Emergence of African Nationalism," *Journal of African History* 1, no. 2 (1960): 299–312; P.-J. Ezeh, "Anthropology in Post-colonial Africa: The Nigerian Case," in *African Anthropologies: History, Critique and Practice,* ed. Mwenda Ntarangwi, David Mills, and Mustafa Babiker (London: Zed Books, 2006); William G. Martin and Michael O. West, eds., *Out of One, Many Africas: Reconstructing the Study and Meaning of Africa* (Urbana: University of Illinois Press, 1999).

3. Cooper, *Colonialism in Question,* 43.

4. "Editorial," *Wāsù* 2, no. 2 (April–June 1933): 1–2.

5. David Long and Brian C. Schmidt, "Introduction," in Long and Schmidt, *Imperialism and Internationalism,* 1–2, 10.

6. Quoted in Peter Lamb, "Harold Laski (1893–1950): Political Theorist of a World in Crisis," *Review of International Relations* 25 (1999), 330, 332–333.

7. *Wāsù* 3, no. 1 (March 1934): 37; Padmore, *Pan-Africanism or Communism?* 164.

8. H. O. Davies, "The Royal Road to Independence," *Wāsù* 5, nos. 2–3 (June–July 1936): 38–40; H. O. Davies, "Looking Ahead," *Wāsù* 12, no. 2 (March 1946): 13–15.

9. James, *Beyond a Boundary,* 18.

10. Ben Carrington, "Improbable Grounds: The Emergence of the Black British Intellectual," *South Atlantic Quarterly* 109, no. 2 (Spring 2010): 369–389.

11. Véronique Dimier, "Three Universities and the British Elite: A Science of Colonial Administration in the UK," *Public Administration* 84, no. 2 (2006): 337–366; David Killingray, "Colonial Studies," in Rimmer and Kirk-Greene, *The British Intellectual Engagement with Africa,* 42–43. On Margery Perham, see Alison Smith and Mary Bull, eds., *Margery Perham and British Rule in Africa* (London, 1991).

12. Zachernuk, *Colonial Subjects,* 97–101.

13. "This Business of Trusteeship," *West African Review* 7 (August 1936): 13.

14. Gladstone E. Mills, "Foreword," in Braithwaite, *Colonial West Indian Students in Britain,* viii–ix.

15. Azikiwe became the first governor-general of Nigeria in 1960 and, in 1963, the country's first president under the new federal system. On Kenyatta's ethnographic work, see esp. Shaw, *Colonial Inscriptions,* and Gaurav Desai, *Subject to Colonialism: African Self-Fashioning and the Colonial Library* (Durham, NC: Duke University Press, 2001).

16. Malcolm McLeod, "Letters to *Africa,*" *Africa* 44, no. 3 (July 1974): 300.

17. *Wāsù* 12, no. 3 (Summer 1947): 12.

18. Alex T. Carey, *Colonial Students: A Study of Social Adaptation of Colonial Students* (London: Secker and Warburg, 1956), 29; Sheila Patterson, *Dark Strangers: A Sociological Study of the Absorption of a Recent West Indian Migrant Group in Brixton, South London* (London: Tavistock, 1963), 37–38.

19. The vast majority, some 170 students, were Nigerians, Sierra Leoneans, or Ghanaians, while the remainder came from the Gambia, East Africa, or Northern Rhodesia. The new scholarships were funded by public and private sources, including money provided under the Colonial Development and Welfare Act and contributions from some colonial governments, the British Council, and the United Africa Company. J. L. Keith, "African Students in Great Britain," *African Affairs* 45 (1946): 65–66; *Wāsù* 12, no. 1 (March 1945): 34.

20. Mills, "Foreword," vii.

21. J. C. de Graft Johnson became a distinguished academic, publishing *African Glory: The Story of Vanished Negro Civilizations* (1954) and *An Introduction to the African Economy* (1959), and later served as Ghana's ambassador to the European Community. *League of Coloured Peoples Newsletter* 12, no. 72 (September 1945): 113; Ogbechie, *Ben Enwonwu,* 67, and 243n43. For a critical assessment of the British Council's activities by an African commentator, see "British Council and the Students," *West Africa* (January 21, 1950): 36.

22. Davies, *Memoirs,* 67–68, 76–78.

23. Eric Williams, *Inward Hunger: The Education of a Prime Minister* (London: Andre Deutsch, 1969), 53–54.

24. Moore, *Anthropology and Africa,* 18–19, 21; W. E. F. Ward, "The International Institute of African Languages and Cultures: A Memory of Its Beginnings," *Africa* 60, no. 1 (1990): 132–133.

25. Kirk-Greene, "The Emergence of an Africanist Community in the UK," 17–18; Goody, *The Expansive Moment,* 26–27, 73.

26. "African Prince awarded PhD. (Oxon)," *League of Coloured Peoples' News Notes* 8 (May 1940): 35.

27. Nyabongo returned to the United States in the 1940s, where he was a professor at the University of Alabama and later North Carolina A&T University. Busia joined the faculty at the University of the Gold Coast from 1949 to 1954. In the late 1950s, he became Nkrumah's chief political rival and, later, prime minister from 1969 until January 1972. Kirk-Greene, "The Emergence of an Africanist Community in the UK," 19; Goody, *The Expansive Moment,* 9–10, 27, 84–85, 87, 205.

28. Nkrumah subsequently enrolled at Gray's Inn to become a barrister and as a PhD student in philosophy at University College London, where he proposed to write his dissertation on the topic "Knowledge and Logical Positivism," but never completed either program of study. Sherwood, "Kwame Nkrumah," 182; Nkrumah, *Ghana,* 51.

29. "Distinguished Visitors," *Wāsù* 9 (December 1932): 5.

30. Adi and Sherwood, *Pan-African History,* 59.

31. Turner studied Africanisms in the Gullah dialect of coastal Georgia and South Carolina. St. Clair Drake, "Mbiyu Koinange and the Pan-African Movement," in *Pan-African Biography,* ed. Robert A. Hill (Los Angeles: African Studies Center, UCLA; Crossroads Press, 1987), 175.

32. Jomo Kenyatta, "Kikuyu Religion, Ancestor-Worship, and Sacrificial Practices," *Africa* 10, no. 3 (1937): 308–328.

33. Bunche Diary, May 21, 1937.

34. Ladipo Solanke, "Editorial," *Wāsù* 4, no. 5 (November 1935): 69–72; Nnamdi Azikiwe, "Ethics of Colonial Imperialism," *Journal of Negro History* 16 (1931): 308; Azikiwe, *Liberia in World Politics* (1934; repr., Westport, CT: Greenwood, 1970), 217. For a list of other anthropologists whose work influenced Azikiwe's thinking during this period, see Azikiwe, *My Odyssey*, 156.

35. Nkrumah, *Ghana,* 44.

36. Bronislaw Malinowski, "Practical Anthropology," *Africa* 2, no. 1 (January 1929): 24, 26, 36–37.

37. Bronislaw Malinowski, "The Rationalization of Anthropology and Administration," *Africa* 3, no. 4 (October 1930): 407.

38. Vivian Bickford-Smith, "The Betrayal of Creole Elites, 1880–1920," in *Black Experience and the Empire,* ed. Philip D. Morgan and Sean Hawkins, Oxford History of the British Empire Companion Series (Oxford: Oxford University Press, 2004), 194–227.

39. In a footnote, Malinowski argued, "The literature produced by the educated Africans . . . constitutes a body of evidence on which scientific work by a White anthropologist must sooner or later be undertaken." Bronislaw Malinowski, *The Dynamics of Culture Change: An Inquiry into Race Relations in Africa,* ed. Phyllis M. Kaberry (New Haven: Yale University Press, 1945), 58–59.

40. Bunche Diary, June 3, 1937.

41. See Max Gluckman, "Malinowski's 'Functional' Analysis of Social Change," *Africa* 17, no. 1 (1947): 105, 111. For more recent critiques, see Talal Asad, ed., *Anthropology and the Colonial Encounter* (Atlantic Heights, NJ: Humanities, 1973); Jairus Banaji, "The Crisis of British Anthropology," *New Left Review* 64 (1970): 70–85.

42. See Bunche Diary, May 31, 1937.

43. In anthropology and sociology, Malinowski, Mair, Firth, and Charles Gabriel Seligman; in economics, Arnold Plant, Lionel Robbins, Friedrich Hayek, and John Coatman (professor of imperial economic relations); in colonial, world, and economic history, Arnold Toynbee, T. S. Ashton, and R. H. Tawney; and, by the end of the 1930s, specialists in African languages such as Ida Ward, L. S. Ward, E. O. Ashton, and R. C. Abraham at the SOAS.

44. *Wāsù* 2, no. 2 (April–June 1933): 1–2.

45. *Wāsù* 5, no. 1 (May 1936): 7.

46. Solanke, *United West Africa, or Africa at the Bar of the Family of Nations,* 50.

47. Bunche Diary, March 3, May 3, and May 5, 1937.

48. W. Arthur Lewis, "Europe's Impact on Africa," *The Keys* 4, no. 2 (October–December 1936): 23–25.

49. Bunche Diary, May 27 and June 24, 1937.

50. A. A. Y. Kyerematen, "West Africa in Transition," *Africana* 1, no. 2 (April 1949): 3–4.

51. In addition to the Boasian concept of "diffusion," Malinowski adopted Don Fernando Ortiz's term *transculturation* as a synonym for "culture change" because it entailed "no implications of one standard dominating all the phases (of culture change),

but a transition in which both sides are active, each contributing its quota, each merging into a new reality of civilization." Malinowski, *The Dynamics of Culture Change*, vii, 58–59; Bronislaw Malinowski, "The Present State of Studies in Culture Contact: Some Comments on an American Approach," *Africa* 12, no. 1 (January 1939): 27–47.

52. In 1932, Nadel received a Rockefeller Fellowship to conduct fieldwork in Nigeria the following year, and completed his PhD in anthropology at the LSE under Malinowski. He famously experimented with combining psychology and anthropology or "culture psychology" in his analysis. See S. F. Nadel, "Experiments on Culture Psychology," *Africa* 10, no. 4 (1937): 421–435, and Nadel, *A Black Byzantium* (London: Oxford University Press, 1942).

53. Kyerematen, "West Africa in Transition," 3–4.

54. Adi and Sherwood, *Pan-African History*, 59, 63.

55. In the book's preface, Fraser and Cole mentioned Kyerematen among a long list of "those who have also helped develop the ideas expressed here," and Fraser included a note in his chapter stating that it "was compiled from information supplied by the Honourable A. A. Y. Kyerematen, Ph.D., Director, Ghana National Cultural Centre." However, Fraser did not cite the latter's PhD thesis or subsequent publications as sources of or influences on his analysis. McLeod, "Letters to *Africa*," 300; Douglas Fraser, "The Symbols of Ashanti Kingship," in *African Art and Leadership*, ed. Douglas Fraser and Herbert M. Cole (Madison: University of Wisconsin Press, 1972), xvi, 137.

56. Between 1902 and 1951, the *Journal of the Royal African Society* included fifty-two articles or works of art by Africans, but more than half of them appeared after World War II. See "Fifty Years of a British African Society," *African Affairs* 50, no. 200 (July 1951): 194–195.

57. Kirk-Greene, "The Emergence of an Africanist Community in the UK," 17–18; *Africa* 1, no. 1 (January 1928): 132–133.

58. L. S. B. Leakey, *Journal of the Royal African Society* 34, no. 135 (April 1935): 218–219.

59. E. B. H., *Man* 36 (December 1936): 214–215.

60. A. R. Barlow, *Africa* 12, 1 (January 1939): 114–116.

61. Bronislaw Malinowski, "Introduction," in Jomo Kenyatta, *Facing Mount Kenya* (1938; repr., New York: Vintage Books, 1965), xiii.

62. Malinowski, "Introduction," xviii.

63. James, "The Voice of Africa," 3; Louis Mbanefo, "Africa Speaks for Herself," *The Keys* 4, no. 2 (October–December 1936): 25–26.

64. K. A. Busia, *Report on a Social Survey of Sekondi-Takoradi* (London: Hazel, Watson and Viney, 1951).

65. *Wāsù* 12, no. 1 (March 1945): 3–5.

66. Azikiwe, *My Odyssey*, 156, 187; Ezeh, "Anthropology in Post-colonial Africa," 207.

67. Zachernuk, *Colonial Subjects*, 98–99; Azikiwe, *My Odyssey*, 193.

68. When Lewis was a given a professorship at Manchester University in 1948, he became the first person of African descent to hold a named chair at a British

university, before leaving to serve briefly as the chief economic advisor to Nkrumah in a newly independent Ghana. Lewis later became the first black principal of the University College of the West Indies and the first vice-chancellor of the University of the West Indies. In 1979, he won the Nobel Prize for his seminal influence on the field of development economics, especially through his essay "Economic Development with Unlimited Supplies of Labour" (1954), making him the first economist of African descent to receive the honor. See "Britain's First Negro Professor," *League of Coloured Peoples Newsletter* 17, no. 99 (January–March 1948): 14.

69. Robert Tignor, *W. Arthur Lewis and the Birth of Development Economics* (Princeton: Princeton University Press, 2006), 37–38.

70. In her influential book, *Native Administration in Nigeria* (1937), Perham rejected the notion of integrating educated Africans into the "scaffold" of colonial administration and suggested instead that an effort should be made "to find or create opportunities for them within the Native Administrations." Margery Perham, *Native Administration in Nigeria* (London: Oxford University Press, 1937), 361.

71. Davies, *Memoirs,* 85.

72. The same issue that contained Lewis's review of Perham's book also included reviews of Norman Leys's *The Colour Bar in East Africa* and Joyce Cary's *The Case for African Freedom. League of Coloured Peoples Newsletter* 24 (September 1941): 128–129, and 25 (October 1941): 7–10.

73. L.S.B. Leakey, *By the Evidence: Memoirs, 1932–1951* (London: Harcourt Brace, 1974), 74.

74. Malinowski, "Introduction," xvii.

75. Koinange, Drake writes, "mistrusted [Richards's] motives and was dubious about his own ability to keep up in the classes on theory at the London School of Economics, because of the amount of time he had to spend on his political work." Drake, "Mbiyu Koinange and the Pan-African Movement," 174–177.

76. Leakey, *By the Evidence,* 77.

77. Elsa V. Goveia and F.R. Augier, "Colonialism from Within," *Times Literary Supplement* (July 28, 1966).

78. Frederick Madden, "The Commonwealth, Commonwealth History, and Oxford, 1905–1971," in *Oxford and the Idea Commonwealth: Essays Presented to Sir Edgar Williams,* ed. Frederick Madden and D.K. Fieldhouse (London: Croom Helm, 1982), 13.

79. Ibid., 11–14. On the rise of imperial history at the University of London, see Richard Drayton, "Imperial History and the Human Future," *History Workshop Journal* 74, no. 1 (Autumn 2012): 156–172.

80. Williams, *Inward Hunger,* 49–50.

81. Eric Williams, "The Abolition of the Slave System in Britain," *The Keys* 7, no. 1 (July–September 1939): 11–13.

82. Eric Williams, *Capitalism and Slavery,* intro. Colin A. Palmer (1944; Chapel Hill: University of North Carolina Press, 1994), 45, 178, 188, 211, 253.

83. Colin A. Palmer, *Eric Williams and the Making of the Modern Caribbean* (Chapel Hill: University of North Carolina Press, 2006), 26.

84. Williams, *Inward Hunger*, 45–46, 50.

85. Reginald Coupland, *The British Anti-slavery Movement* (1933; London: Frank Cass, 1964); Coupland, *The British Empire: An Outline Sketch of Its Growth and Character* (London: British Broadcasting Corporation, 1933).

86. Williams, *Inward Hunger*, 50.

87. Goveia was promoted to senior lecturer in 1958, becoming the first professor of West Indian history and, in 1961, the first woman to hold a chair at the University College of the West Indies. Mary Chamberlain, "Elsa Goveia: History and Nation," *History Workshop Journal* 58, no. 1 (Autumn 2004): 170; Philip Sherlock and Rex Nettleford, *The University of the West Indies: A Caribbean Response to the Challenge of Change* (London: Macmillan Caribbean, 1990), 206.

88. Elsa Vesta Goveia, "Slave Society in the British Leeward Islands, 1780–1800" (PhD thesis, University of London, 1952), 1–3; Goveia, quoted in Chamberlain, "Elsa Goveia," 185.

89. Elsa V. Goveia, "The Social Framework," *Savacou: A Journal of the Caribbean Artists Movement* 2 (September 1970): 14; Elsa V. Goveia, *Slave Society in the British Leeward Islands at the End of the Eighteenth Century* (New Haven: Yale University Press, 1965), 338.

90. Chamberlain, "Elsa Goveia," 168; Elsa V. Goveia, *A Study on the Historiography of the British West Indies to the End of the Nineteenth Century* (1956; Washington, DC: Howard University Press, 1980), 168–169.

91. For example, Bunche met Harold Laski, William Macmillan, Leonard Barnes, Stafford Cripps, Reginald Reynolds, and politicians Ellen Wilkenson, Charles Roden Buxton, and Colonial Secretary Malcolm Macdonald in London. He also traveled to Oxford to meet Evans-Pritchard and Perham. See Bunche Diary, various dates.

92. On Julius Lewin, see "Professor Julius Lewin," *African Studies* 27, no. 1 (1968): 45–46; on his relationship with Bunche, see Bunche Diary.

93. Bunche Papers, Box 10b, Nathaniel A. Fadipe to Ralph Bunche, March 2, 1937.

94. Bunche Diary, March 16, 1937.

95. Ibid., March 21, 23, 31, and April 6, 1937).

96. Goode Robeson, *African Journey*, 14–15. On Goode Robeson, see Maureen Mahon, "Eslanda Goode Robeson's African Journey: The Politics of Identification and Representation in the African Diaspora," in *Transnational Blackness: Navigating the Global Color Line*, ed. Manning Marable and Vanesa Agard-Jones (New York: Palgrave Macmillan, 2008); and Ransby, *Eslanda*.

97. Elliott P. Skinner, "Ralph Bunche and the Decolonization of African Studies," in *The Trustee for the Human Community: Ralph J. Bunche, the United Nations, and Decolonization in Africa*, ed. Robert A. Hill and Edmond J. Keller (Athens: Ohio State University Press, 2010), 58.

98. Bunche Diary, May 28, June 14, and June 21, 1937; Bunche Papers, Box 10b, Hortense Moon, *Journal of Negro Education*, to Bunche, July 1, 1937.

99. Bunche Diary, March 10, 16, April 23, May 6, 15, 18, and 21, 1937); Bunche Papers, Box 10b, Prince Nyabongo to Bunche, May 24, 1937; George Padmore to

Bunche (April 13 and July 27, 1937); Mbiyu Koinange to Bunche, February 20, 1938. On Cedric Dover, see Nico Slate, *Colored Cosmopolitanism: The Shared Struggle for Freedom in the United States and India* (Cambridge, MA: Harvard University Press, 2012), 83–87.

100. Bunche Papers, Box 10b, Moon to Bunche (July 1, 1937); Bunche to Dr. Dean, Dean, College of Liberal Arts, Howard University, n.d.; Williams to Bunche (May 27, 1937).

101. Christian Høgsbjerg, "Black Books," *History Workshop Journal* 70 (Autumn 2010): 252.

102. W. Arthur Lewis, *Labour in the West Indies: The Birth of a Workers' Movement,* preface by Arthur Creech Jones (Fabian Society, Research Series no. 44, 1939; repr., London: New Beacon Books, 1977).

103. C. L. R. James, *The Black Jacobins: Toussaint L'Ouverture and the San Domingo Revolution,* 2nd ed. (New York: Random House, 1963), xi; James quoted in Robert A. Hill, "In England, 1932–1938," *Urgent Tasks* 12 (Summer 1981): 26.

104. James, *The Black Jacobins,* 86, 375–376.

105. C. L. R. James, "Lectures on *The Black Jacobins,*" *Small Axe* 8 (September 2000): 67; Mackenzie and James, "Radical Pan-Africanism in the 1930s," 69–70; K. A., "Black Jacobins by C. L. R. James," *The Keys* 6, no. 2 (October-December 1938), 12–13; Dorothy Pizer, "A Lesson in Revolution," *Controversy* 28 (January 1939).

106. James later republished it in a slightly expanded form as *A History of Pan-African Revolt.* C. L. R. James, *A History of Negro Revolt, Fact* (September 1938). C. L. R. James, "Black Intellectuals in Britain," in *Colour, Culture and Consciousness: Immigrant Intellectuals in Britain,* ed. Bhikhu Parekh (London: Allen and Unwin, 1974), 160; James, "Lectures on *The Black Jacobins,*" 72–73; C. L. R. James, "Revolts in Africa," in *The Future in the Present* (London: Allison and Busby, 1977), 70, 75.

107. James, *A History of Pan-African Revolt,* 14, 36, 38–39, 59.

108. Bunche Diary, May 4, 1937; Bunche Papers, Box 10b, Williams to Bunche (n.d., May 27 and November 7, 1937).

109. Hooker, *Black Revolutionary,* 61; James, "Lectures on *The Black Jacobins,*" 73; The National Archives, KV 2/1824, Special Branch Reports (October 8, 1938, and April 4, 1939).

110. Fredric Warburg, *An Occupation for Gentlemen* (London: Hutchinson and Co., 1959), 185, 206, 211, 213, 215, 251–254, 270. See also Polsgrove, *Ending British Rule in Africa,* 23–42; Ivar Oxaal, *Black Intellectuals Come to Power: The Rise of Creole Nationalism in Trinidad and Tobago* (Cambridge, MA: Schenkman, 1968), 69–72.

111. Williams, *Inward Hunger,* 52–53; Eric Williams, "The Abolition of the Slave System in Britain," *The Keys* 7, no. 1 (July–September 1939), 11–13; E. E. [Eric E. Williams], "Child Labour in the British West Indies," *International African Opinion* 1, no. 7 (May–June 1939): 8–11.

112. "The Literary Scene," *International African Opinion* 1, no. 1 (July 1938): 14–16; James, "The Voice of Africa," 3; K. A., "Black Jacobins by C. L. R. James,"

12–13; "Outstanding Student Success," *The Keys* 5, no. 1 (July–September 1937): 6; "'Economic Problems of To-day,' by W. Arthur Lewis," *League of Coloured Peoples Newsletter* 9 (June 1940): 42; back cover of *League of Coloured Peoples Newsletter* 17, no. 100 (January–March 1948).

113. See Cobina Kessie, "Pen Portrait of Kobina Sekyi, Esq.," *Wāsù* 9 (December 1932); Olu Alakija, "A Short Pen Portrait of Herbert Macauley, Esq., C.E.," *Wāsù* 2, no. 1 (January 1933): 10–11.

114. *Wāsù* 9, no. 1 (May 1942): 3.

115. *Wāsù* 12, no. 2 (March 1946): 1, 5.

116. Ako Adjei, "Extract from the Report of the Activities of the Study Group of the West African Students' Union during the year 1944–1945," *Wāsù* 12, no. 2 (March 1946): 9–10.

117. Quoted in "Africana: A Quarterly Magazine, Vol. 1, No. 1," *Venture* (February 1949).

118. Early members of the WISU included politicians such as Michael Manley, Errol Barrow, Linden Forbes Burnham, Maurice Bishop, and Lee Llewellyn Moore; the sociologist Lloyd Braithwaite; and the historians Elsa V. Goveia, F. Roy Augier, and Lucille Mathurin Mair. Errol Barrow and Linden Forbes Burnham later became the first prime ministers of Barbados and Guyana, respectively; Maurice Bishop served as the prime minister of Grenada from 1979 to 1983. Lee Llewellyn Moore was a prominent figure within the Labour Party in St. Kitts and served as premier in 1979. On the WISU, see David Clover, "Dispersed and Destroyed: Archives, The West Indian Students' Union, and Public Memory," *The Society for Caribbean Studies Annual Conference Papers* 6 (2005), ed. Sandra Courtman, http://www .caribbeanstudies.org.uk/papers/2005/olvol6p10.PDF (accessed February 5, 2014): 1–14; Braithwaite, *Colonial West Indian Students in Britain*.

119. Clover, "Dispersed and Destroyed," 6–7.

120. Quoted in Anne Walmsley, *The Caribbean Artists Movement, 1966–1972: A Literary and Cultural History* (London: New Beacon Books, 1992), 5.

CHAPTER SEVEN

1. *The Film in Colonial Development: A Report of a Conference* (London: British Film Institute, 1948), 6–7, 40, 45–46, 50–51.

2. Prem Chowdhry, *Colonial India and the Making of Empire Cinema: Image, Ideology, and Identity* (Manchester, UK: Manchester University Press, 2000), 45.

3. Cooper, *Africa since 1940*, 88; Stephen Constantine, *The Making of British Colonial Development Policy, 1914–1940* (London: Routledge, 1984); Frederick Cooper and Randall Packard, eds., *International Development and the Social Sciences: Essays on the History and Politics of Knowledge* (Berkeley: University of California Press, 1997); Pearce, *The Turning Point in Africa*.

4. "Men of Two Worlds," *New African* 1, no. 6 (August–December 1946): 46.

5. Philip M. Taylor, *The Projection of Britain: British Overseas Publicity and Propaganda, 1919–39* (Cambridge: Cambridge University Press, 1981), 103.

6. Stephen G. Tallents, *The Projection of England* (1932; repr., London: Olen Press, 1955), 39–40. See also Scott Anthony, *Public Relations and the Making of Modern Britain: Stephen Tallents and the Birth of a Progressive Media Profession* (Manchester, UK: Manchester University Press, 2011).

7. Parr quoted in Paul Swann, *The British Documentary Film Movement, 1926–46* (Cambridge: Cambridge University Press, 1989), 125.

8. Madhavi Kale, "Screening Empire from Itself: Imperial Preference, Represented Communities, and the Decent Burial of the Indian Cinematograph Committee Report (1927–8)," in Trentmann, Levine, and Grant, *Beyond Sovereignty,* 191–213.

9. McKibbin, *Classes and Cultures,* 419; *Saturday Evening Post* quoted in Melani McAlister, *Epic Encounters: Culture, Medi, and U.S. Interests in the Middle East Since 1945* (2001; repr., Berkeley: University of California Press, 2005), 31.

10. McKibbin, *Classes and Cultures,* 427.

11. Bush, *Imperialism, Race and Resistance,* 25.

12. Winifred Holmes, *Sight and Sound* 5 (1936): 74, quoted in Anthony Aldgate and Jeffrey Richards, *Best of British Cinema and Society from 1930 to the Present* (London: I. B. Tauris, 1999), 30.

13. The National Archives, NC 8/21/9, April 14, 1934 and June 1938, quoted in Aldgate and Richards, *Best of British Cinema,* 30–31.

14. Charles Drazin, *Korda: Britain's Movie Mogul* (New York: I. B. Tauris, 2002), 107–108; McKibbin, *Classes and Cultures,* 435; Sheila Tully Boyle and Andrew Bunie, *Paul Robeson: The Years of Promise and Achievement* (Amherst: University of Massachusetts Press, 2001), 292–293.

15. Marke, *In Troubled Waters,* 136; "Here and There," *The Keys* 3, no. 2 (October–December 1935): 13; Davies, *Memoirs,* 61–62; English electrician Charles Packham, quoted in Stephen Bourne, *Black in the British Frame: The Black Experience in British Film and Television,* 2nd ed. (London: Continuum, 2001), 230.

16. Schwarz, "Black Metropolis, White England," 180; Philip S. Foner, ed., *Paul Robeson Speaks: Writings, Speeches, Interviews, 1918–74* (London: Quartet Books, 1978), 351.

17. Paul Robeson Jr., interviewed in Channel Four Television, *Songs of Freedom: Paul Robeson and the Black American Struggle* (London, broadcast June 30, 1986).

18. "I Want Negro Culture Says Paul Robeson Discussing His Plans for a Negro Theatre in London," *Wāsù* 4, no. 1 (July 1935): 11.

19. Paul Robeson, "I Want to Be African," in Foner, *Paul Robeson Speaks,* 91.

20. Boyle and Bunie, *Paul Robeson,* 294. Later in life, Martins became a well-known stage and radio personality back in Nigeria. On Martins, see Bourne, *Black in the British Frame.*

21. Marie Seton, *Paul Robeson* (London: Dennis Dobson, 1958), 78, 300.

22. Quoted in Boyle and Bunie, *Paul Robeson,* 298.

23. Flora Robson, interviewed in BBC Television, *Paul Robeson* (November 26, 1978).

24. Goode Robeson, *African Journey*, 49.

25. The National Archives, KV 2/1829, Reginald Bridgeman to Arnold Ward, September 15, 1933.

26. Quoted in *Manchester Guardian* (December 14, 1934); "The 21st General Meeting," *The Keys* 2, no. 3 (January–March 1935): 52.

27. Duberman, *Paul Robeson*, 628n59; Bunche Diary, April 23, 1937; von Eschen, *Race against Empire*, 16–19. On Yergan, see David Henry Anthony III, *Max Yergan: Race Man, Internationalist, Cold Warrior* (New York: New York University Press, 2006).

28. *Harper's Bazaar* (March 1935).

29. On the extravagant and costly set constructed in Britain, which included more than fifty reed-thatched huts, see Boyle and Bunie, *Paul Robeson*, 296–297.

30. *Film World* (April 13, 1935); *Daily Sketch* (April 10, 1935); James Agate, "The Cinema: Lighted Africa," *Tatler*, no. 1,764 (April 17, 1935).

31. Paul Rotha, "Sanders of the River," in *Rotha on the Film: a Selection of Writings about the Cinema* (Fair Lawn, NJ: Essential Books, 1958), 139–40.

32. Rotha, "Sanders of the River," 139.

33. C.L.R. James, "Black Intellectuals in Britain," in Parekh, *Colour, Culture and Consciousness,* 154.

34. Quoted in Robert Edgar, "The Making of an Africanist: Ralph Bunche in South Africa, 1937," in Hill and Keller, *Trustee for the Human Community*, 31.

35. A. Sivanandan, *A Different Hunger: Writings on Black Resistance* (London: Pluto, 1982), 79–80.

36. Quoted in Boyle and Bunie, *Paul Robeson,* 324.

37. Nnamdi Azikiwe, *Renascent Africa* (1937; repr., London: Frank Cass, 1968), 153–155.

38. "Africans Believe Paul Robeson Was Tricked in British Film," *Chicago Defender* (October 5, 1935): 24.

39. *Cine-Technician* (September–October 1938): 74–75.

40. Ben Davis Jr., "U.S.S.R.—The Land for Me," *Sunday Worker* (May 10, 1936), reprinted in Foner, *Paul Robeson Speaks,* 107–108.

41. Florent quoted in Sean Creighton, "Paul Robeson's British Journey," in Wynn, *Cross the Water Blues,* 136.

42. Davies, *Memoirs,* 61–62.

43. G.M., *The Keys* 2, no. 4 (April–June 1935): 83.

44. "Installation of Mr. Paul Robeson as Babāsale (patron) of W.A.S.U.," 6–8.

45. Una Marson, "Coloured Contributions," *Public Opinion* (July 3, 1937): 20.

46. *News Chronicle* (June 8, 1935).

47. Jarrett-Macauley attributes Marson's attack to envy. She undoubtedly felt upstaged by Robeson, who appeared to be usurping some of her central concerns, such as the creation of a theater for plays by black authors in London, and receiving all the credit for advancing them. Indeed, she tried (unsuccessfully) to establish a London-based black theater group that, as she told the *Daily Gleaner* in 1936, could "produce Empire plays by native people." Yet, if the motivation for Marson's

intervention was in part personal, she also articulated concerns shared by other Afro-Caribbeans and Africans in London. "Racial Prejudice in London Not Improving Says Miss Marson," *Daily Gleaner* (September 28, 1936): 5; Jarrett-Macauley, *The Life of Una Marson,* 95.

48. "Race Enemy No. 1," *Wāsù* 4, no. 2 (August 1935): 18.

49. Marcus Garvey, "Paul Robeson as Actor," *Black Man* 1, no. 2 (June 1935): 8–9.

50. "Mr. Paul Robeson and His Critics," *Wāsù* 5 (Christmas Number, 1936): 49–51.

51. Marcus Garvey, "Paul Robeson and His Mission," *Black Man* 2, no. 5 (January 1937): 2–3. "Ogboni and Iyafin Paul Robeson and W.A.S.U. Members and Their Friends at the W.A.S.U. Day Celebrations at the African Hostel in London, on the 31st of October, 1936," *Wāsù* 5 (Christmas Number, 1936): 60.

52. See "Nationalism in Africa," *Wāsù* 6, no. 2 (Coronation Number, 1937): 22.

53. Davis, "U.S.S.R.—The Land for Me," 107–108; Boyle and Bunie, *Paul Robeson,* 324.

54. Seton quoted in Bourne, *Black in the British Frame,* 225–226; Schwarz, "Black Metropolis, White England," 180, 185; Creighton, "Paul Robeson's British Journey," 126.

55. Nancy Cunard, "Stevedore in London," *The Crisis* (August 1935): 238; G. M., "Toussaint L'Ouverture; Westminster Theatre (Stage Society)," *The Keys* 3, no. 4 (April–June 1936): 68–69; Kenneth M. Cameron, *Africa on Film: Beyond Black and White* (New York: Continuum, 1994), 66, 105; Philip S. Zachernuk, "Who Needs a Witch Doctor? Refiguring British Colonial Cinema in the 1940s," in *Film and the End of Empire,* ed. Lee Grieveson and Colin MacCabe (Basingstoke, UK: British Film Institute; Palgrave Macmillan, 2011), 97. On the Unity Theatre, see Colin Chambers, *The Story of Unity Theatre* (New York: St. Martin's, 1989).

56. Creighton, "Paul's Robeson's British Journey," 136. For Okafor's *Nigeria—Why We Fight for Freedom,* see The National Archives, KV 2/1853. On Robeson's political activities and associates in London, see Duberman, *Paul Robeson,* 171, 192–200.

57. The National Archives, KV 2/1829, October 26, 1937; "News Items," *The Keys* 5, no. 3 (January–March 1938): 71.

58. James quoted in Boyle and Bunie, *Paul Robeson,* 365–366.

59. C. L. R. James, "Paul Robeson: Black Star," in *Spheres of Existence: Selected Writings* (London: Allison & Busby, 1980), 256, 260–261.

60. Von Eschen, *Race against Empire,* 17.

61. Peter Swaab, "Dickinson's Africa: *The High Command* and *Men of Two Worlds,*" in *Thorold Dickinson: A World of Film,* ed. Philip Horne and Peter Swaab (Manchester, UK: Manchester University Press, 2008) 188; Thorold Dickinson, "Search for Music," *Penguin Film Review* 2 (1947): 13.

62. Swaab, "Dickinson's Africa," 186n90.

63. Wendy Webster, *Englishness and Empire, 1939–1965* (New York: Oxford University Press, 2005), ch. 3.

64. James Vernon, *Hunger: A Modern History* (Cambridge: Harvard University Press, 2007), 112.

65. Webster, *Englishness and Empire,* 69–70.

66. The National Archives, CO 875/17/6, Minutes of Correspondence, August 18, 1945. On the empire, the General Post Office (GPO) Film Unit, and the British documentary more generally, see Scott Anthony and James Mansell, eds., *The Projection of Britain: A History of the GPO Film Unit* (Basingstoke, UK: Palgrave Macmillan, 2011); Swann, *The British Documentary Film Movement*; Matera, "An Empire of Development."

67. The National Archives, CO 875/17/6, "Authentic Africa on the Screen at Last?"

68. Ibid., "Extract from Letter of Mr. MacDougall, British Information Service, New York," February 24, 1943.

69. "Colonial News and Oddities," *New African* 1, no. 6 (August–December 1946): 52.

70. Zachernuk, "Who Needs a Witch Doctor?" 101; *White Ants* character Hale quoted in ibid., 99. On the British fascination with witchcraft in Africa and Africans' participation in debates on the subject, see also Tilley, *Africa as a Living Laboratory,* 293–308.

71. On Dickinson, see Jeffrey Richards, *Thorold Dickinson: The Man and His Films* (London: Croom Helm, 1986), reissued in the United States as *Thorold Dickinson and the British Cinema* (Scarecrow Filmmakers Series, 1997); Horne and Swaab, *Thorold Dickinson.*

72. Swaab, "Dickinson's Africa," 178, 180, 185–186; Joyce Cary, *The Case for African Freedom* (1941; repr., Austin: University of Texas Press, 1962) 37, 39, 41; Thorold Dickinson, "Africa Has a Lesson for Britain" (1945), in Horne and Swaab, *Thorold Dickinson,* 70–72.

73. The National Archives, CO 875/17/6, "General Progress Report on 'The White Ants' (Tentative Title)"; Dickinson quoted in Swaab, "Dickinson's Africa," 186.

74. Swaab, "Dickinson's Africa," 186.

75. Although viewers voted Martins one of England's fifteen favorite actors in a poll conducted in 1947, his film roles were limited almost exclusively to that of "chiefs" and other stock African characters throughout his thirty-year career. Al Monroe, "Swinging the News," *Chicago Defender* (October 18, 1947): 19.

76. "Negro Ballet Set to Open in London," *League of Coloured Peoples Newsletter* 13, no. 77 (February 1946): 111.

77. Cameron, *Africa on Film,* 66, 105; Zachernuk, "Who Needs a Witch Doctor?" 113n40.

78. "Celebrated Nigerian Joins the Royal Air Force," *West African Pilot* (January 28, 1942); Zachernuk, "Who Needs a Witch Doctor?" 97, 114n14, 117n94; Jeffrey Green, "Afro-American Symphony: Popular Concert Hall Performers, 1900–1940," in Oliver, *Black Music in Britain,* 40.

79. The National Archives, CO 875/17/6, Two Cities Films Ltd. to Noel J.B. Sabine, April 21, 1943.

80. Cowley, "London Is the Place," 62; Amon Saba Saakana, "Culture, Concept, Aesthetics: The Phenomenon of the African Musical Universe in Western Musical Culture," *African American Review* 29, no. 2 (Summer 1995): 337; "W. Rudolph Dunbar: Pioneering Orchestra Conductor," *Black Perspective in Music* 9, no. 2 (Fall 1981): 193–225; Gilroy, *Between Two Camps*, 324–325

81. "Dunbar's Albert Hall Triumph," *Melody Maker* (May 2, 1942): 1.

82. Reprinted in "W. Rudolph Dunbar," 198–202.

83. BBC Written Archives, E2/584, Cecil Madden to O. P. P., December 11, 1940.

84. The National Archives, CO 875/17/6, Secretary of State for the Colonies to Governor of Tanganyika, May 27, 1943; Minutes to Colonial Office Correspondence, May 1, 1943.

85. Adams was also Robeson's stunt double in *The Proud Valley* in 1940. See Bourne, *Black in the British Frame*, 72–76.

86. *League of Coloured Peoples Newsletter* 14, no. 79 (April 1946): 19; Chambers, *The Story of Unity Theatre*, 182; United Kingdom, Oxford University, Bodleian Library of Commonwealth and African Studies at Rhodes House, Fabian Colonial Bureau Papers (hereafter FCB Papers), MSS Brit. Emp. S. 365, Box 69, Nicholson to Adams, January 7, 1946; Adams to Nicholson, January 11, 1946. The *League of Coloured Peoples Newsletter* published in serial form his lengthy address on the history of black music in the Americas at an LCP conference. See Robert Adams, "Some Thoughts on Negro Music," *League of Coloured Peoples Newsletter* 14, no. 83 (August 1946): 107–109; 14, no. 84 (September 1946): 131–134; 15, no. 85 (October 1946): 11–14.

87. Two Cities Film was created to produce Anglo-Italian films (the two cities of its title being London and Rome), but in 1938, Filippo Del Giudice, a wealthy refugee from Fascist Italy, effectively assumed control of the company. The next year, it released *French without Tears* (1939), "one of the most successful British films of the 1930s." McKibbin, *Classes and Cultures*, 439.

88. The National Archives, CO 875/17/6, WASU Memorandum on "A Proposed Film Entitled 'The Men of Two Worlds,'" July 27, 1943.

89. Ibid., Solanke to the Under Secretary of State for the Colonies, September 11, 1943.

90. Ibid., Minutes of Correspondence, August 20, 1943.

91. Ibid., Minutes of Correspondence, August 14, 1943.

92. Ibid., Reginald Sorensen to Oliver Stanley, Secretary of State for the Colonies, July 30, 1943. On the West African Parliamentary Committee, see Appiah, *Joe Appiah*, 149–150; "The West African Parliamentary Committee Report," *Wāsù* 12, no. 1 (March 1945): 21–22; and The National Archives, CO 554/127/11.

93. Rita Hinden, "Partnership and What It Means," *Wāsù* 12, no. 1 (March 1945): 9–10; "Produce and Politics," *Wāsù* 12, no. 3 (Summer 1947): 5.

94. BBC Written Archives, BBC Scripts, *Calling the West Indies*, January 16–17, 1945; "Men of Two Worlds," *League of Coloured Peoples Newsletter* 13, no. 77 (February 1946): 116; "Secretary's Notes," *League of Coloured Peoples Newsletter* 12, no. 70

(July 1945): 107. On Thompson and other Sierra Leonean women in the League of Coloured Peoples, see LaRay Denzer, "Women in Freetown Politics, 1914–1961: A Preliminary Study," *Africa* 57, no. 4 (1987): 439–456.

95. M. C. Peterside, "Men of Two Worlds," *Times* (September 11, 1946): 5; Peterside, "Africa and the Africans," *Times* (September 27, 1946): 7. The *Times'* own review of the film was laced with allusions to "darkest Africa." "Men of Two Worlds," *Times* (July 18, 1946).

96. Sydney O. Sandy, "Some Reflections on 'Men of Two Worlds,'" *League of Coloured Peoples Newsletter* 16, no. 86 (November 1946): 27–28.

97. *Wāsù* 10, no. 1 (May 1943): 1–2, 7–8.

98. Reprinted from *Chicago Defender* (October 30, 1943) in Bankole Awoonor-Renner, *West African Soviet Union* (London: WANS Press, 1946), 25.

99. In his now-infamous letter of introduction to Padmore, James described Nkrumah as talking "a lot about imperialism and Leninism and export capital, and talk[ing] a lot of nonsense." "This young man," he wrote, "is coming to you. He is not very bright, but nevertheless do what you can for him because he's determined to throw the Europeans out of Africa." On Nkrumah's first days in London, see Appiah, *Joe Appiah,* 163; Peter Abrahams, "Nkrumah, Kenyatta and the Old Order," in *African Heritage,* ed. Jacob Drachler (New York: Crowell-Collier, 1963), 138; Sherwood, "Kwame Nkrumah," 167–169, 179–181.

100. "Fifth Pan-African Congress," *League of Coloured Peoples Newsletter* 13, no. 76 (January 1946): 77–78; Padmore, *Colonial and . . . Coloured Unity.* See also Hakim Adi and Marika Sherwood, *The 1945 Manchester Pan-African Congress Revisited* (London: New Beacon Books, 1995).

101. "Aims and Objects of the West African National Secretariat," *New African* 1, no. 6 (August–December 1946): 50.

102. *Empire* 9, no. 1 (May–June 1946).

103. Davies quoted in Coleman, *Nigeria,* 277–278; "The Pan-Nigerian Delegation—Its Mission to London," *League of Coloured Peoples Newsletter* 16, no. 96 (October 1947): 190–192; FCB Papers, MSS Brit. Emp. S. 365, Box 69, File 3, Conference on the Relationship between the British and Colonial Peoples, Clacton-on-Sea, April 12–14, 1946.

104. "Men of Two Worlds," *New African* 1, no. 6 (August–December 1946): 46–47.

105. Ibid., 50; "A West African," *New African* 1, no. 6 (August–December 1946): 50.

106. "Aims and Objects of the West African National Secretariat," 50.

107. Wellesley Cole Papers, PP MS 35/6/1/12, File 156, A. A. Y. Kyerematen, draft review of Dr. Rita Hinden, *Empire and After: A Story of British Imperial Attitudes* (1949).

108. The National Archives, CO 875 17/6, Ladipo Solanke to Under Secretary of State for the Colonies, July 27, 1943.

109. "Editor's Note," and Gemini, "Red Roses for Africa," *New African* 1, no. 6 (August–December 1946): 52, 43.

110. The National Archives, KV 2/1840, police commissioner of Lagos, Nigeria, to police commissioner of Accra, Gold Coast, August 26, 1948; United Kingdom, London, House of Lords Record Office, Papers of Rev. Reginald Sorensen, SOR 168, Solanke to Sorensen (October 29, 1951).

111. The National Archives, KV 2/1840, Special Branch report, March 7, 1948; Appiah, *Joe Appiah,* 162–163.

112. "West Africa," *New African* 1, no. 6 (August–December 1946): 51.

113. Zachernuk, "Who Needs a Witch Doctor?" 109.

EPILOGUE

Stuart Hall, "The Windrush Issue: Postscript," in "Windrush Echoes," special issue, *Soundings* 10 (Autumn 1998): 190.

1. Wellesley Cole Papers, PP MS 35/7/3/17, File 184, Dr. Robert Wellesley Cole, "West Africa: An Outline of the History."

2. Wellesley Cole Papers, PP MS 35/6/1/7, File 151, Dr. Wellesley Cole to Dr. Harold Moody (June 2, 1942). For discussion of his activities for the Colonial Office and Fabian Colonial Bureau, respectively, see PP MS 35/3/1, File 86, and PP MS 35/6/1/5, File 149.

3. Cooper, *Colonialism in Question,* p. 110.

4. Cooper, *Africa since 1940,* p. 52. See also Frederick Cooper, "Networks, Moral Discourse, and History," in *Intervention and Transnationalism in Africa: Global-Local Networks of Power,* ed. Thomas M. Callaghy, Ronald Kassimir, and Robert Latham (Cambridge: Cambridge University Press), 23–46; Frederick Cooper, "Reconstructing Empire in British and French Africa," *Past & Present* 210, supp. 6 (2011): 196–210.

5. Pierre, *The Predicament of Blackness,* 63.

6. See, especially, Jordanna Bailkin, *The Afterlife of Empire* (Berkeley: University of California Press, 2012).

7. "Dr. Robert Benjamin Ageh Wellesley Cole," introduction to Wellesley Cole Papers, PP MS 35.

8. Cooper, *Colonialism in Question,* 18.

9. Wole Soyinka, *You Must Set Forth at Dawn: A Memoir* (New York: Random House, 2006), 47; Manthia Diawara, "Toward a Regional Imaginary in Africa," in *The Cultures of Globalization,* ed. Fredric Jameson and Masao Miyoshi (Durham, NC: Duke University Press, 1998), 124.

BIBLIOGRAPHY

ARCHIVAL COLLECTIONS

Bodleian Library of Commonwealth and African Studies at Rhodes House, Oxford University, United Kingdom

Papers of Arthur Creech Jones
Papers of the Fabian Colonial Bureau
Papers of Margery Perham

British Broadcasting Corporation Written Archives Centre, Caversham Park, Reading, United Kingdom

British Library, London, United Kingdom

Oral History of Jazz in Britain Collection, British Library Sound Archive

Charles E. Young Library, University of California, Los Angeles

Brian Urquhart Collection on Ralph J. Bunche

The Women's Library (formerly Fawcett Library), London, United Kingdom

British Commonwealth League Papers
Margery Corbett Ashby Papers

House of Lords Record Office, London, United Kingdom

Papers of Reginald, Lord Sorensen (Rev. R. W. Sorensen, MP) (SOR)

National Library of Jamaica, Kingston, Jamaica

Una Marson Papers

The National Archives, Kew, United Kingdom

Colonial Office Files (CO)
Ministry of Information Files (INF)
Security Service Files (KV)

Schomburg Center for Research on Black Culture,
New York Public Library, New York City, NY

Ralph Bunche Papers
St. Clair Drake Papers

School of Oriental and African Studies Library,
Archives and Special Collections, London, United Kingdom

Papers of Dr. Robert Benjamin Ageh Wellesley Cole Papers (PP MS 35)

Yale University, Beinecke Rare Book and
Manuscript Library, New Haven, CT

James Weldon Johnson Collection

NEWSPAPERS, MAGAZINES, AND JOURNALS

Africa (Journal of the International Institute of African Languages and Cultures)
Africana
African Affairs
African Sentinel
African Telegraph
African Times and Orient Review
Ashanti Pioneer
Black Man
Checkers Magazine
Chicago Defender
Cine-Technician
Controversy
Cosmopolitan
The Crisis

Daily Gleaner
Daily Herald
Daily Sketch
Daily Worker
Empire
Evening Standard
Fact
Film World
Harper's Bazaar
International African Opinion
International African Service Bureau
Jamaican Standard
Journal of the Royal African Society
The Keys
Labour Monthly
Lagos Standard
League of Coloured Peoples Newsletter
League of Coloured Peoples' News Notes
Man
Manchester Guardian
Melody Maker
Negro Worker
New African
New Amsterdam News
New Leader
New Statesman and Nation
Nigerian Daily Telegraph
News Chronicle
Pan-Africa
Penguin Film Review
Public Opinion
Service
Sight and Sound
Spokesman
Sunday Express
(London) Times
Tatler
Twentieth Century
Venture
Wāsù/WASU
West Africa
West African Pilot
West African Review
Workers' Dreadnought

Abrahams, Peter. *The Coyoba Chronicles: Reflections on the Black Experience in the 20th Century*. Kingston, Jamaica: Ian Randle, 2000.

———. *A Wreath for Udomo*. London: Faber and Faber, 1956.

Adi, Hakim. *Pan-Africanism and Communism: The Communist International, Africa, and the Diaspora, 1919–1939*. Trenton, NJ: Africa World Press, 2013.

———. *West Africans in Britain, 1900–1960: Nationalism, Pan-Africanism and Communism*. London: Lawrence and Wishart, 1998.

Adi, Hakim, and Marika Sherwood. *The 1945 Manchester Pan-African Congress Revisited*. London: New Beacon Books, 1995.

———. *Pan-African History: Political Figures from Africa and the Diaspora since 1787*. London: Routledge, 2003.

Aldgate, Anthony, and Jeffrey Richards. *Best of British Cinema and Society from 1930 to the Present*. London: I. B. Tauris, 1999.

Appiah, Joseph. *Joe Appiah: The Autobiography of an African Patriot*. Foreword by Henry Louis Gates, Jr. New York: Praeger, 1990.

Awoonor-Renner, Bankole. *West African Soviet Union*. London: WANS Press, 1946.

Azikiwe, Nnamdi. *My Odyssey: An Autobiography*. New York: Praeger, 1970.

———. *Renascent Africa*. 1937. Reprinted, London: Frank Cass, 1968.

Bailkin, Jordanna, *The Afterlife of Empire*. Berkeley: University of California Press, 2012.

Banton, Michael. *The Coloured Quarter: Negro Immigrants in an English City*. London: Jonathan Cape, 1955.

Baptiste, Fitzroy, and Rupert Lewis, eds. *George Padmore: Pan-African Revolutionary*. Kingston, Jamaica: Ian Randle, 2009.

Bates, Robert H., V. Y. Mudimbe, and Jean F. O'Barr, eds. *Africa and the Disciplines: The Contributions of Research in Africa to the Social Sciences and Humanities*. Chicago: University of Chicago Press, 1993.

Berlant, Lauren, and Lee Edelman, *Sex, or the Unbearable*. Durham, NC: Duke University Press, 2014.

Bland, Lucy. "White Women and Men of Colour," *Gender and History* 17, no. 1 (April 2005): 29–61.

Boehmer, Elleke. *Empire, the National, and the Postcolonial, 1890–1920*. Oxford: Oxford University Press, 2002.

Boittin, Jennifer Anne. *Colonial Metropolis: The Urban Grounds of Anti-imperialism and Feminism in Interwar Paris*. Lincoln: University of Nebraska Press, 2010.

Bolland, O. Nigel. *On the March: Labour Rebellions in the British Caribbean, 1934–39*. London: James Currey, 1995.

Bolt, Christine. *Sisterhood Questioned? Race, Class and Internationalism in the American and British Women's Movements, c. 1880s-1970s*. London: Routledge, 2004.

Bourne, Stephen. *Black in the British Frame: The Black Experience in British Film and Television,* 2nd ed. London: Continuum, 2001.

————. *Mother Country: Britain's Black Community on the Home Front, 1939–1945.* Stroud, Gloucestershire, UK: History Press, 2010.

Boyle, Sheila Tully, and Andrew Bunie. *Paul Robeson: The Years of Promise and Achievement.* Amherst: University of Massachusetts Press, 2001.

Braithwaite, Lloyd. *Colonial West Indian Students in Britain.* Foreword by Gladstone E. Mills. Mona, Jamaica: University of the West Indies Press, 2001.

Brittain, Vera. *Testament of Friendship: The Story of Winifred Holtby.* New York: Macmillan, 1940.

Brockway, Fenner. *Inside the Left: Thirty Years of Platform, Press, Prison and Parliament.* London: George Allen and Unwin, 1942.

Brown, Jacqueline Nassy. *Dropping Anchor, Setting Sail Geographies of Race in Black Liverpool.* Princeton: Princeton University Press, 2005.

Brown, Jayna. *Babylon Girls: Black Female Performers and the Shaping of the Modern.* Durham, NC: Duke University Press, 2008.

Brown, Judith, and Wm. Roger Louis, eds. *The Oxford History of the British Empire,* Volume 4: *The Twentieth Century.* Oxford: Oxford University Press, 1999.

Bush, Barbara. *Imperialism, Race and Resistance: Africa and Britain, 1919–1945.* London: Routledge, 1999.

Byfield, Judith, LaRay Denzer, and Anthea Morrison, eds. *Gendering the African Diaspora: Women, Culture, and Historical Change in the Caribbean and Nigerian Hinterland.* Bloomington: Indiana University Press, 2010.

Cameron, Kenneth M. *Africa on Film: Beyond Black and White.* New York: Continuum, 1994.

Carby, Hazel V. *Race Men.* Cambridge, MA: Harvard University Press, 1998.

Carrington, Ben. "Improbable Grounds: The Emergence of the Black British Intellectual." *South Atlantic Quarterly* 109, no. 2 (Spring 2010): 369–389.

Cary, Joyce. *The Case for African Freedom.* 1941. Reprinted, Austin: University of Texas Press, 1962.

Chamberlain, Mary. "Elsa Goveia: History and Nation." *History Workshop Journal* 58, no. 1 (Autumn 2004): 167–190.

Chowdhry, Prem. *Colonial India and the Making of Empire Cinema: Image, Ideology, and Identity.* Manchester, UK: Manchester University Press, 2000.

Clarke, Basil. *Taking What Comes. A Biography of A. G. Stock (Dinah).* Edited by Surjit Hans. Chandigarh, India: Panjab University Press, 1999.

Clover, David. "Dispersed and Destroyed: Archives, The West Indian Students' Union, and Public Memory." In *The Society for Caribbean Studies Annual Conference Papers* 6 (2005), 1–14. Edited by Sandra Courtman. http://www.caribbeanstudies.org.uk/papers/2005/olvol6p10.pdf.

Coleman, James S. *Nigeria: Background to Nationalism.* Berkeley: University of California Press, 1958.

Collins, Marcus. "Pride and Prejudice: West Indian Men in Mid-Twentieth-Century Britain." *Journal of British Studies* 40, no. 3 (July 2001): 391–418.

Constantine, Stephen. *The Making of British Colonial Development Policy, 1914–1940.* London: Routledge, 1984.

Cooper, Frederick. *Africa since 1940: The Past of the Present*. Cambridge: Cambridge University Press, 2002.

———. *Colonialism in Question: Theory, Knowledge, History*. Berkeley: University of California Press, 2005.

———. "Conflict and Connection: Rethinking Colonial African History." *American Historical Review* 99, no. 5 (December 1994): 1516–1545.

———. *Decolonization and African Society: The Labour Question in French and British Africa*. New York: Cambridge University Press, 1996.

Cooper, Frederick, and Randall Packard, eds. *International Development and the Social Sciences: Essays on the History and Politics of Knowledge*. Berkeley: University of California Press, 1997.

Covi, Giovanna, ed. *Modernist Women, Race, Nation: Networking Women, 1890–1950; Circum-Atlantic Connections*. London: Mango, 2005.

Cowley, John. "Cultural 'Fusions': Aspects of British West Indian Music in the USA and Britain, 1918–1951," *Popular Music* 5 (1985): 81–96.

———. "uBungca (Oxford Bags): Recordings in London of African and West Indian Music in the 1920s and 1930s," *Musical Traditions* 12 (Summer 1994; updated 1999). www.mustrad.org.uk/articles/ubunca.htm.

———. "West Indian Gramophone Records in Britain, 1927–1950." Occasional Papers in Ethnic Relations, No. 1. Coventry, UK: Centre for Research in Ethnic Relations, University of Warwick, February 1985: 1–17.

Cummings-John, Constance Agatha. *Memoirs of a Krio Leader*. Edited, with introduction and annotation, by LaRay Denzer. Ibadan, Nigeria: Humanities Research Centre, 1995.

Cunard, Nancy, ed. *Negro: Anthology Made by Nancy Cunard, 1931–1933*. London: Nancy Cunard at Wishart and Co., 1934.

———. *Essays on Race and Empire*. Edited by Maureen Moynagh. 1942. Reprinted, Ontario: Broadview Press, 2002.

Davies, Carole Boyce. *Left of Marx: The Political Life of Black Communist Claudia Jones*. Durham, NC: Duke University Press, 2007.

Davies, Hezekiah Oladipo Olagunju. *Memoirs*. Ibadan, Nigeria: Evans Brothers, 1989.

Davis, Angela. *Blues Legacies and Black Feminism: Gertrude "Ma" Rainey, Bessie Smith, and Billie Holiday*. New York: Vintage Books, 1998.

Denzer, LaRay. *Folayegbe M. Akintunde-Ighodalo: A Public Life*. Ibadan, Nigeria: Sam Bookman, 2001.

———. "Gender and Decolonization: A Study of Three Women Leaders in West African Public Life." In *People and Empire in African History*. Edited by J. D. Y. Peel and J. F. Ade Ajayi. London: Longman, 1992.

———. "Yoruba Women: A Historiographical Study." *International Journal of African Historical Studies* 27, no. 1 (1994): 1–39.

Derrick, Jonathan. *Africa's "Agitators": Militant Anti-colonialism in Africa and the West, 1918–1939*. New York: Columbia University Press, 2008.

Desai, Gaurav. *Subject to Colonialism: African Self-Fashioning and the Colonial Library*. Durham, NC: Duke University Press, 2001.

Deutsch, Jan-Georg, Peter Probst, and Heike Schmidt, eds. *African Modernities: Entangled Meanings in Current Debate*. Portsmouth, NH: Heinemann, 2002.

Douglas, R. M. *The Labour Party, Nationalism and Internationalism, 1939–1951*. London: Routledge, 2004.

Drachler, Jacob, ed. *African Heritage*. New York: Crowell-Collier, 1963.

Duberman, Martin B. *Paul Robeson: A Biography*. New York: Ballantine Books, 1989.

Edmondson, Belinda. *Making Men: Gender, Literary Authority, and Women's Writing in Caribbean Narrative*. Durham, NC: Duke University Press, 1999.

Edwards, Brent Hayes. "The Uses of *Diaspora*." *Social Text* 66, 19, no. 1 (Spring 2001): 45–73.

———. *The Practice of Diaspora: Literature, Translation, and the Rise of Black Internationalism*. Cambridge: Harvard University Press, 2003.

———. "Shadow of Shadows," *positions* 11, no. 1 (Spring 2003): 11–49.

Emery, Mary Lou. *Modernism, the Visual, and Caribbean Literature*. Cambridge: Cambridge University Press, 2007.

Feld, Steven. *Jazz Cosmopolitanism: Five Musical Years in Ghana*. Durham, NC: Duke University Press, 2012.

Foner, Philip S. ed. *Paul Robeson Speaks: Writings, Speeches, Interviews, 1918–74*. London: Quartet Books, 1978.

Ford-Smith, Honor. "Unruly Virtues of the Spectacular: Performing Engendered Nationalisms in the UNIA in Jamaica." *interventions: International Journal of Postcolonial Studies* 6, no. 1 (2004): 18–44.

Freud, Sigmund. *The Joke and Its Relation to the Unconscious*. 1905. Reprinted, London: Penguin, 2002.

Fryer, Peter. *Staying Power: The History of Black People in Britain*. London: Pluto Press, 1984.

Garigue, Philip. "The West African Students' Union: A Study in Culture Contact," *Africa* 23, no. 1 (January 1953): 55–69.

Geiss, Imanuel. *The Pan-African Movement: A History of Pan-Africanism in America, Europe and Africa*. Translated by Ann Keep. New York: Africana, 1974.

Gerzina, Gretchen Holbrook. *Black London: Life before Emancipation*. New Brunswick, NJ: Rutgers University Press, 1995.

Gerzina, Gretchen Holbrook, ed. *Black Victorians, Black Victoriana*. New Brunswick, NJ: Rutgers University Press, 2003.

Gikandi, Simon. "Pan-Africanism and Cosmopolitanism: The Case of Jomo Kenyatta." *English Studies in Africa* 43, no. 1 (2000): 3–27.

Goode Robeson, Eslanda. *African Journey*. New York: John Day, 1945.

Gilroy, Paul. *Between Camps: Nations, Cultures, and the Allure of Race*. London: Penguin, 2000.

———. *The Black Atlantic: Modernity and Double-Consciousness*. Cambridge: Harvard University Press, 1993.

———. *"There Ain't No Black in the Union Jack": The Cultural Politics of Race and Nation*. Foreword by Houston A. Baker Jr. 1987. Reprinted, Chicago: University of Chicago Press, 1991.

Glicco, Jack. *Madness after Midnight*. London: Elek Books, 1952.

Godbolt, Jim. *A History of Jazz in Britain, 1919–50*. 1984. Reprinted, London: Paladin, 1986.

Goode, Coleridge, and Roger Cotterrell. *Bass Lines: A Life in Jazz*. London: Northway, 2002.

Goody, Jack. *The Expansive Moment: Anthropology in Britain and Africa, 1918–1970*. Cambridge: Cambridge University Press, 1995.

Green, Jeffrey. *Black Edwardians: Black People in Britain, 1900–1914*. New York: Frank Cass, 1998.

———. "John Alcindor (1873–1924): A Migrant's Biography." *Immigrants and Minorities* 6, no. 2 (July 1987): 174–189.

———. "West Indian Doctors in London: John Alcindor (1873–1924); James Jackson Brown (1882–1953)." *Journal of Caribbean History* 20, no. 1 (1985–1986): 49–70.

Grieveson, Lee, and Colin MacCabe, eds. *Film and the End of Empire*. Basingstoke, UK: British Film Institute; Palgrave Macmillan.

Gundara, Jagdish S., and Ian Duffield, eds. *Essays on the History of Blacks in Britain*. Aldershot: Avebury, 1992.

Hailey, Sir Malcolm. *An African Survey: A Study of Problems Arising in Africa South of the Sahara,* 2nd ed. London: Oxford University Press, 1945.

———. *An African Survey, Revised, 1956*. London: Oxford University Press, 1957.

Harris, Joseph, ed. *Global Dimensions of the African Diaspora*. Washington, DC: Howard University Press, 1993.

Hall, Stuart. "Break Bread with History: C. L. R. James and *The Black Jacobins*." Interviewed by Bill Schwarz. *History Workshop Journal* 46 (Autumn 1998): 17–31.

Hill, Robert A. "In England, 1932–1938." Special Issue, "C. L. R. James: His Life and Work." *Urgent Tasks* 12 (Summer 1981): 19–27.

Hill, Robert A., ed. *Pan-African Biography*. Introduction by George A. Shepperson. Los Angeles: African Studies Center, University of California, Los Angeles; Crossroads Press, 1987.

Hooker, James R. *Black Revolutionary: George Padmore's Path from Communism to Pan-Africanism*. New York: Praeger, 1967.

Horne, Philip, and Peter Swaab, eds. *Thorold Dickinson: A World of Film*. Manchester, UK: Manchester University Press, 2008.

Howe, Stephen. *Anticolonialism in British Politics: The Left and the End of Empire, 1918–1964*. New York: Oxford University Press, 1993.

Innes, C. L. *A History of Black and Asian Writing in Britain, 1700–2000*. Cambridge: Cambridge University Press, 2002.

Iriye, Akira. *Cultural Internationalism and World Order*. Baltimore: Johns Hopkins University Press, 1997.

James, C. L. R. *At the Rendezvous of Victory*. London: Allison and Busby, 1984.

———. *Beyond a Boundary*. 2nd ed. Introduction by Robert Lipsyte. Durham, NC: Duke University Press, 1993.

———. *The Black Jacobins: Toussaint L'Ouverture and the San Domingo Revolution*. 2nd ed. New York: Random House, 1963

————. "The Black Scholar Interview: C. L. R. James." *The Black Scholar* 2, no. 1 (September 1970): 35–43.

————. *Case for West Indian Self-Government*. London: Hogarth Press, 1933.

————. *The Future in the Present*. London: Allison and Busby, 1977.

————. *A History of Negro Revolt. Fact* (September 1938).

————. *Letters from London: Seven Essays by C. L. R. James*. Edited by Nicholas Laughlin. Introduction by Kenneth Ramchand. 1932. Reprinted, Port of Spain, Trinidad and Tobago: Prospect Press, 2003

————. *Nkrumah and the Ghana Revolution*. London: Allison and Busby, 1977.

Jameson, Fredric and Masao Miyoshi, eds. *The Cultures of Globalization*. Durham, NC: Duke University Press, 1998.

Jarrett-Macauley, Delia. *The Life of Una Marson, 1905–1965*. Manchester, UK: Manchester University Press, 1998.

Jenkins, Ray. "Gold Coasters Overseas, 1880–1919: With Specific Reference to Their Activities in Britain." *Immigrants and Minorities* 4, no. 3 (1985): 5–52.

Kelly, John D., and Martha Kaplan. *Represented Communities: Fiji and World Decolonization*. Chicago: University of Chicago Press, 2001.

Kelley, Robin D. G. *Africa Speaks, America Answers: Modern Jazz in Revolutionary Times*. Cambridge, MA: Harvard University Press, 2012.

Kenyatta, Jomo. *Facing Mount Kenya*. Introduction by Bronislaw Malinowski. 1938. Reprinted, New York: Vintage Books, 1965.

Killingray, David, ed. *Africans in Britain*. London: Frank Cass, 1994.

Kuklick, Henrika. *The Savage Within. The Social History of British Anthropology, 1885–1945*. Cambridge: Cambridge University Press, 1992.

LaCapra, Dominick. *History in Transit: Experience, Identity, Critical Theory*. Ithaca: Cornell University Press, 2007.

————. *Writing History, Writing Trauma*. Baltimore: John Hopkins University Press, 2001.

Lake, Marilyn, and Henry Reynolds. *Drawing the Global Colour Line: White Men's Countries and the International Challenge of Racial Equality*. Cambridge: Cambridge University Press, 2008.

Langley, J. Ayodele. *Pan-Africanism and Nationalism in West Africa, 1900–1945: A Study of Ideology and Social Classes*. Oxford: Oxford University Press, 1973.

Langley, J. Ayodele, ed. *Ideologies of Liberation in Black Africa*. London: Rex Collings, 1979.

Laski, Harold. A *Grammar of Politics*. London: George Allen and Unwin, 1925.

Lemelle, Sidney J., and Robin D. G. Kelley, eds. *Imagining Home: Class, Culture and Nationalism in the African Diaspora*. London: Verso, 1994.

Levy, Andrea. *Small Island*. London: Review, 2004.

Lewis, W. Arthur. *Labour in the West Indies: The Birth of a Workers' Movement*. Preface by Arthur Creech Jones. Fabian Society, Research Series no. 44, 1939. Reprinted, London: New Beacon Books, 1977.

Little, Kenneth. *Negroes in Britain: A Study of Race Relations in English Society*. London: Routledge and Kegan Paul, 1947.

Locke, Alain. *The Philosophy of Alain Locke.* Edited by Leonard Harris. 1942. Reprinted, Philadelphia: Temple University Press, 1989.

———. *Race Contacts and Interracial Relations.* Edited by Jeffrey Stewart. Washington, DC: Howard University Press, 1992.

Long, David, and Brian C. Schmidt, eds. *Imperialism and Internationalism in the Discipline of International Relations.* Albany: State University of New York Press, 2005.

Macdonald, Roderick J. "Dr. Harold Arundel Moody and the League of Coloured Peoples, 1931–1947: A Retrospective View." *Race* 14, no. 3 (1973): 291–307.

Mackenzie, Alan J., and C. L. R. James. "Radical Pan-Africanism in the 1930s: A Discussion with C. L. R. James." *Radical History Review* 24 (Fall 1980): 68–75.

Macmillan, William Miller. *Africa Emergent: A Survey of Social, Political and Economic Trends in British Africa.* London: Faber and Faber, 1938.

———. *Warning from the West Indies: A Tract for Africa and the Empire.* London: Faber and Faber, 1936.

Madden, Frederick, and D. K. Fieldhouse, eds. *Oxford and the Idea Commonwealth: Essays Presented to Sir Edgar Williams.* London: Croom Helm, 1982.

Makalani, Minkah. *In the Cause of Freedom: Radical Black Internationalism from Harlem to London, 1917–1939.* Chapel Hill: University of North Carolina Press, 2011.

Makonnen, Ras. *Pan-Africanism from Within.* Edited by Kenneth King. London: Oxford University Press, 1973.

Malinowski, Bronislaw. *The Dynamics of Culture Change: An Inquiry into Race Relations in Africa.* Ed. Phyllis M. Kaberry. New Haven: Yale University Press, 1945.

———. "Practical Anthropology." *Africa: Journal of the International Institute of African Languages and Cultures* 2, no. 1 (January 1929): 22–38.

———. "The Rationalization of Anthropology and Administration." *Africa* 3, no. 4 (October 1930): 405–430.

Marke, Ernest. *In Troubled Waters: Memoirs of My Seventy Years in England.* London: Karia Press, 1986.

Marson, Una. *The Moth and the Star.* Introduction by Philip M. Sherlock. Kingston: published by the author, 1937.

———. *Towards the Stars.* Foreword by L. A. G. Strong. London: University of London Press, 1945.

Martin, Tony. *Amy Ashwood Garvey: Pan-Africanist, Feminist and Mrs. Garvey No. 1; or, A Tale of Two Amies.* The New Marcus Garvey Library, No. 4. Dover, MA: Majority Press, 2007.

———. *Pan-African Connection: From Slavery to Garvey and Beyond.* The New Marcus Garvey Library, No. 6. Dover, MA: Majority Press, 1983.

Martin, William G., and Michael O. West, eds. *Out of One, Many Africas: Reconstructing the Study and Meaning of Africa.* Urbana: University of Illinois Press, 1999.

Matory, J. Lorand. *Black Atlantic Religion: Tradition, Transnationalism, and Matriarchy in the Afro-Brazilian Candomblé*. Princeton: Princeton University Press, 2005.

McClellan, Woodford. "Africans and Black Americans in Comintern Schools, 1925–1934." *International Journal of African Historical Studies* 26, no. 2 (1993): 371–390.

McDuffie, Erik S. *Sojourning for Freedom: Black Women, American Communism, and the Making of Black Left Feminism*. Durham, NC: Duke University Press, 2011.

McKay, George. *Circular Breathing: The Cultural Politics of Jazz in Britain*. Durham, NC: Duke University Press, 2005.

McKibbin, Ross. *Classes and Cultures: England, 1918–1951*. Oxford: Oxford University Press, 2000.

McLeod, John. "A Night at 'The Cosmopolitan': Axes of Transnational Encounter in the 1930s and 1940s." *interventions: International Journal of Postcolonial Studies* 4, no. 1 (2002): 53–67.

———. *Postcolonial London: Rewriting the Metropolis*. London: Routledge, 2004.

Meriweather, James H. *Proudly We Can Be Africans: Black Americans and Africa, 1935–1961*. Chapel Hill: University of North Carolina Press, 2002.

Miller, Monica L. *Slaves to Fashion: Black Dandyism and the Styling of Black Diasporic Identity*. Durham, NC: Duke University Press, 2009.

Mills, David. *Difficult Folk: A Political History of Social Anthropology*. Oxford: Berghahn Books, 2008.

Moody, Harold A. *Colour Bar*. London: New Mildmay Press, 1944.

Moore, Sally Falk. *Anthropology and Africa: Changing Perspectives on a Changing Scene*. Charlottesville: University Press of Virginia, 1994.

Morgan, Philip D., and Sean Hawkins, eds. *Black Experience and the Empire*. Oxford History of the British Empire Companion Series. Oxford: Oxford University Press, 2004

Mort, Frank. *Capital Affairs: London and the Making of the Permissive Society*. New Haven: Yale University Press, 2010.

Murray-Brown, Jeremy. *Kenyatta*. London: George Allen and Unwin, 1972.

Nava, Mica. "Wider Horizons and Modern Desire: The Contradictions of America and Racial Difference in London, 1935–1945." *New Formations: A Journal of Culture/Theory/Politics* 37 (Spring 1999): 71–91.

Newton, Francis. *The Jazz Scene*. New York: Monthly Review Press, 1960.

Ntarangwi, Mwenda, David Mills, and Mustafa Babiker, eds. *African Anthropologies: History, Critique and Practice*. London: Zed Books, 2006.

Nkrumah, Kwame. *Towards Colonial Freedom*. London: WANS Press, 1947.

———. *Ghana: The Autobiography of Kwame Nkrumah*. 2nd ed. New York: International, 1971.

Ntarangwi, Mwenda, David Mills, and Mustafa Babiker, eds. *African Anthropologies: History, Critique and Practice*. London: Zed Books, 2006.

Oliver, Paul, ed. *Black Music in Britain: Essays on the Afro-Asian Contribution to Popular Music*. Buckingham, UK: Open University Press, 1990.

Olusanya, Gabriel Olakunle. *The West African Students' Union and the Politics of Decolonisation, 1925–1958.* Ibadan, Nigeria: Daystar, 1982.

Omojola, Bode. *The Music of Fela Sowande: Encounters, African Identity, and Creative Ethnomusicology.* Point Richmond: Music Research Institute Press, 2009.

Oxaal, Ivar. *Black Intellectuals Come to Power: The Rise of Creole Nationalism in Trinidad and Tobago.* Cambridge, MA: Schenkman, 1968.

Padmore, George. *Africa and World Peace.* London: Secker and Warburg, 1937.

———. *How Britain Rules Africa.* London: Wishart and Co., 1936.

———. *Pan-Africanism or Communism?* 1956. Reprinted, New York: Doubleday, 1971.

Padmore, George, ed. *Colonial and . . . Coloured Unity: History of the Pan-African Congress.* London: Hammersmith Bookshop Ltd., 1947.

———. *The Voice of Coloured Labour.* Manchester: PanAf Service Ltd., 1945.

Palmer, Colin A. *Freedom's Children: The 1938 Labor Rebellion and the Birth of Modern Jamaica.* Chapel Hill: University of North Carolina Press, 2014.

Parekh, Bhikhu, ed. *Colour, Culture and Consciousness: Immigrant Intellectuals in Britain.* London: George Allen and Unwin, 1974.

Pearce, R. D. *The Turning Point. British Colonial Policy, 1938–1948.* London: Frank Cass, 1982.

Pennybacker, Susan D. *From Scottsboro to Munich: Race and Political Culture in 1930s Britain.* Princeton: Princeton University Press, 2009.

Perham, Margery. *Colonial Sequence, 1930–1949.* London: Methuen, 1967.

Perham, Margery, ed. *Ten Africans.* 1936. Reprinted, Evanston, IL: Northwestern University Press, 1971.

Phillips, Mike, and Trevor Phillips. *Windrush: The Irresistible Rise of Multi-racial Britain.* London: Harper Collins, 1998.

Pierre, Jemima. *The Predicament of Blackness: Postcolonial Ghana and the Politics of Race.* Chicago: University of Chicago Press, 2013.

Polsgrove, Carol. *Ending British Rule in Africa: Writers in Common Cause.* Manchester, UK: Manchester University Press, 2009.

Porter, Bernard. *Critics of Empire.* London: Macmillan, 1968.

Porter, Eric. *What Is This Thing Called Jazz? African American Musicians as Artists, Critics, and Activists.* Berkeley: University of California Press, 2002.

Posnock, Ross. *Color and Culture: Black Writers and the Making of the Modern Intellectual.* Cambridge, MA: Harvard University Press, 1998.

Pugh, Martin. *"We Danced All Night": A Social History of Britain between the Wars.* London: Bodley Head, 2008.

Putnam, Lara. *Radical Moves: Caribbean Migrants and the Politics of Race in the Jazz Age.* Chapel Hill: University of North Carolina Press, 2013.

Ransby, Barbara. *Eslanda: The Large and Unconventional Life of Mrs. Paul Robeson.* New Haven: Yale University Press, 2013.

Ray, Carina. "Decrying White Peril: Interracial Sex and the Rise of Anticolonial Nationalism in the Gold Coast." *American Historical Review* 119, no. 1 (February 2014): 78–110.

———. "The 'White Wife Problem': Sex, Race, and the Contested Politics of Repatriation to Interwar British West Africa." *Gender and History* 21, no. 3 (November 2009): 628–646.

Rich, Paul. *Race and Empire in British Politics*. Cambridge: Cambridge University Press, 1986.

Richards, Yevette. "Race, Gender, and Anticommunism in the International Labor Movement: The Pan-African Connections of Maida Springer." *Journal of Women's History* 11, no. 2 (1999).

Rimmer, Douglas, and Anthony Kirk-Greene, eds. *The British Intellectual Engagement with Africa in the Twentieth Century*. Basingstoke, UK: Palgrave Macmillan, 2000.

Robinson, Cedric. *Black Marxism: The Making of the Black Radical Tradition*. London: Zed Press, 1983.

Rose, Sonya O. *Which People's War? National Identity and Citizenship in Wartime Britain, 1939–1945*. Oxford: Oxford University Press, 2003.

Rupp, Leila J. *Worlds of Women: The Making of an International Women's Movement*. Princeton: Princeton University Press, 1997.

Sandhu, Sukhdev. *London Calling: How Black and Asian Writers Imagined a City*. London: Harper Collins, 2003.

Schneer, Jonathan. *London 1900: The Imperial Metropolis*. New Haven: Yale University Press, 1999.

Schwarz, Bill. "Black Metropolis, White England." In *Modern Times: Reflections on a Century of English Modernity*. Edited by Mica Nava and Alan O'Shea. London: Routledge, 1996.

Schwarz, Bill, ed. *West Indian Intellectuals in Britain*. Manchester: Manchester University Press, 2003.

Shaw, Carolyn Martin. *Colonial Inscriptions: Race, Sex, and Class in Kenya*. Minneapolis: University of Minnesota Press, 1995.

Shipton, Alyn. *A New History of Jazz*. London: Bloomsbury Academic, 2001.

Simons, Andrew. "Black British Swing: The African Diaspora's Contribution to England's Own Jazz of the 1930s and 1940s." In *Aural History: Essays on Recorded Sound*, 117–138. Edited by Andy Linehan. London: British Library Sound Archive, 2001.

Sinha, Mrinalini. *Specters of Mother India: The Global Restructuring of an Empire*. (Durham, NC: Duke University Press, 2006).

Snaith, Anna. "'Little Brown Girl' in a 'White, White City': Una Marson and London." *Tulsa Studies in Women's Literature* 27, no. 1 (Spring 2008): 93–114.

Solanke, Ladipo. *United West Africa, or Africa at the Bar of the Family of Nations*. 1927. Reprinted, London: African Publication Society, 1969.

Spitzer, Leo, and LaRay Denzer. "I. T. A. Wallace-Johnson and the West African Youth League." Parts I and II. *International Journal of African Historical Studies* 6, nos. 3 and 4 (1973): 413–452, 565–601.

Stapleton, Chris, and Chris May. *African Rock: The Pop Music of a Continent*. New York: Obelisk/Dutton, 1990.

Stephen, Daniel Mark. *The Empire of Progress: West Africans, Indians, and Britons at the British Empire Exhibition, 1924–25*. Basingstoke, UK: Palgrave Macmillan, 2013.

Stephens, Michelle Ann. *Black Empire: The Masculine Global Imaginary of Caribbean Intellectuals in the United States, 1914–1962*. Durham, NC: Duke University Press, 2005.

Stoler, Ann Laura. *Race and the Education of Desire: Foucault's* History of Sexuality *and the Colonial Order of Things* (Durham, NC: Duke University Press, 1995

Sweet, James H. *Domingos Álvares, African Healing, and the Intellectual History of the Atlantic World*. Chapel Hill: University of North Carolina Press, 2011.

Tabili, Laura. *"We Ask for British Justice": Workers and Racial Difference in Late Imperial Britain*. Ithaca, NY: Cornell University Press, 1994.

Tallents, Stephen G. *The Projection of England*. 1932. Reprinted, London: Olen Press, 1955.

Taylor, Philip M. *The Projection of Britain: British Overseas Publicity and Propaganda, 1919–39*. Cambridge: Cambridge University Press, 1981.

Thomas, Martin. *Violence and Colonial Order: Police, Workers, and Protest in the European Colonial Empires, 1918–1940*. Cambridge: Cambridge University Press, 2012.

Thompson, Dudley, with Margaret Cezair Thompson. *From Kingston to Kenya: The Making of a Pan-Africanist Lawyer*. Foreword by Rex Nettleford. Dover, MA: Majority Press, 1993.

Thompson, Leslie, with Jeffrey Green. *Swing from a Small Island: The Story of Leslie Thompson*. 1985. Reprinted, London: Northway, 2009.

Tignor, Robert. *W. Arthur Lewis and the Birth of Development Economics*. Princeton: Princeton University Press, 2006.

Tilley, Helen. *Africa as a Living Laboratory: Empire, Development, and the Scientific Problem of Knowledge, 1870–1950*. Chicago: University of Chicago Press, 2011.

Tilley, Helen, ed., with Robert J. Gordon. *Ordering Africa: Anthropology, European Imperialism and the Politics of Knowledge*. Manchester, UK: Manchester University Press, 2011.

Trentmann, Frank, Philippa Levine, and Kevin Grant, eds. *Beyond Sovereignty: Britain, Empire and Transnationalism, c. 1860–1950*. Basingstoke, UK: Palgrave Macmillan, 2007.

Vaughan, David A. *Negro Victory: The Life Story of Dr. Harold Moody*. London: Independent Press, 1950.

Veal, Michael E. *Fela: The Life and Times of an African Musical Icon*. Philadelphia: Temple University Press, 2000.

Von Eschen, Penny M. *Race against Empire: Black Americans and Anticolonialism, 1937–1957*. Ithaca, NY: Cornell University Press, 1997.

Walkowitz, Judith. *Nights Out: Life in Cosmopolitan London*. New Haven: Yale University Press, 2012.

Walmsley, Anne. *The Caribbean Artists Movement, 1966–1972: A Literary and Cultural History*. London: New Beacon Books, 1992.

Warburg, Frederic. *An Occupation for Gentlemen*. London: Hutchinson and Co., 1959.

Warner, Michael. "Publics and Counterpublics." *Public Culture* 14, no. 1 (2002): 49–90.

Waterman, Christopher Alan. *Jùjú: A Social History and Ethnography of an African Popular Music*. Chicago: University of Chicago Press, 1990.

Webster, Wendy. *Englishness and Empire, 1939–1965*. New York: Oxford University Press, 2005.

———. *Imagining Home: Gender, Race and National Identity, 1945–1964*. London: Routledge, 1998.

Weinbaum, Alys Eve. *Wayward Reproductions: Genealogies of Race and Nation in Transatlantic Modern Thought*. Durham, NC: Duke University Press, 2004.

Weinbaum, Alys Eve, Lynn M. Thomas, Priti Ramamurthy, Uta G. Poiger, Madeleine Yue Dong, and Tani E. Barlow (The Modern Girl Around the World Research Group), eds. *The Modern Girl around the World: Consumption, Modernity, and Globalization*. Durham, NC: Duke University Press, 2008.

West, Michael O., William G. Martin, and Fanon Che Wilkins, eds. *From Toussaint to Tupac: The Black International since the Age of Revolution*. Chapel Hill: University of North Carolina Press, 2009.

Wilder, Gary. *The French Imperial Nation-State: Negritude and Colonial Humanism between the Two World Wars*. Chicago: University of Chicago Press, 2005.

———. "Untimely Vision: Aimé Césaire, Decolonization, Utopia." *Public Culture* 21, no. 1 (Winter 2009): 101–149.

Williams, Eric. *Capitalism and Slavery*. Introduction by Colin A. Palmer. 1944. Reprinted, Chapel Hill: University of North Carolina Press, 1994.

———. *Inward Hunger: The Education of a Prime Minister*. London: Andre Deutsch, 1969.

Williams, Raymond. *The Politics of Modernism: Against the New Conformists*. London: Verso, 1989.

Wynn, Neil A., ed. *Cross the Water Blues: African American Music in Europe*. Jackson: University Press of Mississippi, 2007.

Yard, Lionel M. *Biography of Amy Ashwood Garvey, 1897–1969: Co-founder of the Universal Negro Improvement Association*. New York: Associated, 198–?.

Zachernuk, Philip S. *Colonial Subjects: An African Intelligentsia and Atlantic Ideas*. Charlottesville: University Press of Virginia, 2000.

INDEX

American Council for African Education (ACAE), 120
Amery, Leo, 14–15
Amore, Reg, 155
Amstell, Billy, 167, 173
Andrews, Joe, 287–88
Annan, J. S., 313
anthropology, 81, 143, 238, 240–41, 268, 270, 278, 286; and West Africa, 245–59, 263
antifacism, 16, 61, 63, 75, 87, 96, 173, 303
Anti-Slavery and Aborigines' Protection Society (ASAPS), 15, 39–40, 60, 76, 77, 88, 201, 210
Appiah, Nana Joseph Emmanuel, 8, 9, 118, 216–19, 225, 231–32, 310, 313, 318
Appleton, Joe, 152, 154, 155, 159
Araba, Julius Oredola, 196
Archer, John R., 52
Armstrong, Dulcina, 41
Armstrong, Lil Hardin, 170
Armstrong, Louis, 154, 162, 163, 170, 172
Asante (or Ashanti), 26, 27, 50, 36, 50, 124, 190, 242, 246, 257, 288
Asare, Kwame, 189
Ashby, Margery Corbett, 125–27
Ashwood Garvey, Amy, 20, 28–29, 50, 82, 106*fig.*, 145–48, 183, 288, 296; and Italo-Ethiopian conflict, 62–63, 65, 67–69, 72–73, 219; and Pan-Africanism, 104–110, 143–44, 313; *See also* Florence Mills Social Parlour
Atta, Nana Ofori, 50, 124, 131
At What a Price (Marson), 44–45, 122, 124
Auerbach, Frank, 179
Augier, F. Roy, 243, 263
Awoonor-Renner, Kweku Bankole, 47, 115, 196, 312, 313, 318
Azikiwe, Benjamin Nnamdi, 53–54, 81, 82, 174, 233, 242, 248, 260–61, 291–92, 305

Baa, Akosua "Princess," 26–27
Bag O' Nails, 168, 169, 171
Bailey, Amy, 129
Baker, Noel, 84
Ball, Joseph, 285
Ballets Nègres, Les, 191–92

Ballinger, William, 126
Bankole-Bright, H. C. (Herbert Christian), 29, 30–31
Banks, Leslie, 283
Baptiste, Mona, 12, 181
Barbadians in London, 8, 37, 40, 41, 46, 47, 91, 151, 152, 169, 195, 214, 289. *See also* Blackman, Peter; Braithwaite, Chris
Barbados, 47, 88, 92, 93, 110, 145, 160, 243
Barbour James, Amy, 41, 44
Barbour James, John Alexander, 40–41, 43
Barlow, Arthur Ruffell, 223, 258
Barnes, Leonard, 75
Barreto, Don Marino, 12, 181
Barrett, James, 93
Barriteau, Carl, 152, 154, 156
Barrow, Errol, 161
Bashorun, Ade, 180, 192, 195
Bass, Charlotta, 120
Bastian, Aida, 82
Basutoland, 94, 95, 271
Bates, Frank, 151
BBC (British Broadcasting Corporation), 27, 122, 136, 138, 141, 157, 266, 301, 305; and black music, 156, 158, 161, 178, 180, 181, 191, 306. See also *Calling the West Indies; Caribbean Voices*
Bechet, Sidney, 11
Bechuanaland, 95
Beckett, Harry, 195
Belasco, Lionel, 146, 183–84, 194
Belize. *See* British Honduras
Bennett, Louise, 181
Benson, Bobby, 195–97
Beoku-Betts, R. W., 310
Berlant, Lauren, 19, 206
Bermuda, 43
Bickford-Smith, Vivian, 30, 250
Big Apple, 167, 168, 170
Biney, J. Kwesi, 58, 187, 188
Bingham, Frisco, 169
black Atlantic, 5, 32, 104–111; intellectual culture of the, 268–79; music of the, 9–11, 177–99
Blackbirds, 9, 146, 165, 306
black internationalism, 4–5, 15–17, 23–24, 98; and African Americans, 15, 32, 39; as

part of broader internationalisms, 13–15; and communism, 13–14, 85–86, 96; defined, 17; diversity of, 18–19; and feminism, 20–21, 104–111; interracial support for, 37–40, 60–61, 67–68, 109, 226–33; sexual politics of, 19–20, 236–37; and South Asia, 18, 40, 77, 94, 297. *See also* Pan-Africanism

Black Jacobins, The (James), 273–75, 276

black masculinity, 19–20, 142–43, 161, 202–7, 216, 221, 227, 229, 232–33, 235–37, 297. *See also* gender, interracial sex

Black, Stanley, 182

Blackman, Peter, 8, 47–48, 75, 92–93, 95, 141, 212, 288, 297

Blaize, F. O., 310

Blake, Cyril, 151–52, 154, 156, 158, 160–63, 169, 171, 175, 180–81

Blake, George "Happy," 151–52, 154, 160, 161–63, 169, 172, 176–77, 180–81

Blake, Sam, 305

Bloomsbury, 10, 11, 80, 275

Blue Lagoon, 168, 169

Blyden, Edward Wilmot, 30, 34

Boadu, Kankam, 9, 313

Boas, Franz, 32, 248, 249, 267

Bochmer, Elleke, 104

Boi, Rans, 189

Boittin, Jennifer, 101

Bolt, Christine, 127

Bond, Geoffrey, 176

Boston, H. J. L., 31–32

Boucher, James Horton, 151

Bourne, Stephen, 216

Bowen, Wally, 155

Boyle, Sheila Tully, 287, 295

Bradley, Ben, 93

Bradley, Buddy, 154

Braithwaite, Chris (pseud. Chris Jones), 45–46, 72, 82, 85, 94, 219

Braithwaite, Lloyd, 203, 205, 221–22, 225, 227, 242

Bridgeman, Reginald, 46–48, 81, 93, 288

Bright, Gerald Walcan "Geraldo," 158–60

British Centre Against Imperialism, 96, 226

British Commonwealth, 4, 15, 51, 75, 96, 99, 127; ideal of, 75–76, 127

British Commonwealth League (BCL), 15, 125–26

British Empire, 3–4, 14–16, 26, 51, 73–77, 94–99, 127, 236, 322; and film, 281–83, 319; and imperial propaganda, 56, 86, 138, 289, 282, 284–85, 293–94, 300–302; and music, 149–60; sexual politics of, 236; and universities, 240–42

British Empire Exhibition, 24–29, 94, 152, 290, 294–95, 322; criticism of, 27–28

British Guiana (Guyana), 40, 42, 43, 65, 69, 88, 145, 151, 154, 160, 161, 266, 306

British Honduras (Belize), 42, 88

Broadhurst, Robert, 80, 82

Brockway, A. Fenner, 77–78, 96, 276

Bromley, Tommy, 157

Brown, George, 75, 244

Brown, Gordon, 246

Brown, Harry, 178

Brown, Lawrence, 82

Browne, George (aka Young Tiger), 181, 185, 188

Browne, T. K., 188

Bryden, Beryl, 162

Buchanan, George, 78

Buckle, Desmond, 40, 47, 75, 98, 212

Bucknor, Victoria Omolara, 55

Buddy Pipp's Highlifers, 196

Buell, Raymond Leslie, 90, 239

Bunche, Ralph, 70, 81, 85, 174, 289, 291; and academia, 247–48, 251–54, 268–72, 274–75; and sexual politics, 203, 208, 217, 219, 224, 225, 227, 230

Bunche, Ruth, 174, 219, 269

Bunie, Andrew, 287, 295

Bush, Barbara, 126, 210, 285

Busia, Kofi Abrefa, 242, 246, 259

Butler, Uriah, 93

Buxton, Roden, 94

Byne, Bliff Radie, 198

Café de Paris, 12, 156–58, 171

Cahuzac, Louis, 306

Calling the West Indies (BBC), 138–39, 158, 311

Calloway, Cab, 172

calypso, 10, 62, 135, 145–48, 158, 161, 167, 173, 177, 180–85, 189, 194–99

Gold Coast Students Association (GCSA), 75, 94, 98
Gold Coast Students' Union, 29
Gollancz, Victor, 84
Goode, Coleridge, 159, 171, 177–80
Goode Robeson, Eslanda, 1, 58, 62, 108, 247, 270, 286–88
Goody, Jack, 246
Goring, Edith Rita, 41
Goveia, Elsa V., 242, 263–64, 266–68, 278, 279, 315
Graham, Kenny, 190, 193, 196
Grant, Freddy, 152, 158, 181
Grant, Kevin, 3
Grant, Ulric, 93
Grappelli, Stephen, 172, 178
Green, Jeffrey P., 122, 149
Green, Margaret M., 171, 259, 262
Greenslade, Freddie, 155
Grier, Selsyn, 88
Grierson, John, 280
Griffiths, Thomas. See Makonnen, T. Ras
Guyana. See British Guiana
Guyanese in London, 44, 49, 53, 82, 124, 128, 147, 196, 198, 305, 306. See also Makonnen, T. Ras

Hailey, Malcolm, 89–91, 98, 238
Haitian Revolution, 273–74
Hall, Adelaide, 172, 176
Hamilton-Hazeley, Lottie, 116, 121
Harlem, 15, 46, 66, 82, 105, 108, 124, 139, 154, 194, 250, 286, 306
Harlem Renaissance, 123, 228
Harlow, Vincent, 267
Harriott, Joe, 178
Harris, John, 57, 60–61, 76, 201, 210, 211
Harrison, Juan, 184
Harrison, Tom, 173
Harrison, William, 82–83
Hart, Rannie, 198
Hatch, Isaac "Ike," 44, 48–49, 168–69, 174, 188
Hausa, 26, 186, 188
Hawariat, Tekle, 72
Hawkins, Coleman, 172
Hayes, Roland, 188
Hayford, J. Ephraim Casely, 29, 30–31

Headley, James, 82
Hearne, John, 243
Heath, Ted, 149
Heather, Patrick, 209
Heer, Nicholas de, 187
Henderson, Fletcher, 154
Hercules, Felix, 225
Hermanos Deniz Cuban Rhythm Band, 182
Herskovits, Melville J., 248, 249, 253
Hicks, Bert, 176
highlife, 10, 12, 55, 148, 176–77, 182, 186, 188–90, 192, 195–99
Hinden, Rita, 310–11, 315
His Master's Voice (HMV), 157, 175, 188–89
History of Negro Revolt, A (James), 273–75
Hoare-Laval peace plan, 66, 265, 266
Hobson, John A., 80, 239
Hocart, Arthur, 270
Holmes, Winifred, 125–28, 285
homosexuality, 106, 149, 162, 166, 208, 214–16, 236; See also same-sex relations
Hooper, Handley, 223
Horne, Lena, 179
Horton, Asadata Dafora. See Dafora, Asadata
Horton, Constance, 43, 82, 113. See also Cummings-John, Constance
Horton, James Africanus Beale, 30, 34, 171
Houdini, Wilmoth, 184
Howard University, 39, 46, 249, 269, 272
Howe, Irene, 55
Hughes, Brewster (Ignatius Abiodun Oke), 10, 189–92, 194–98
Hughes, Langston, 124
Hunter, Alberta, 172
Hunter, Monica, 271
Hunton, Alphaeus, 210
Hurston, Zora Neale, 123, 124, 135
Hutchinson, Leslie "Jiver," 12, 152, 154, 155, 159–60, 177, 181, 185, 216
Hutchinson's All-Coloured Orchestra, 12, 159
Hutchinson's West Indian Orchestra, 181
Hutton-Mills, Thomas, Sr., 30
Huxley, Elspeth, 301
Huxley, Gervais, 301
Huxley, Julian, 56

Katz, Dick, 178

Keane, Ellsworth McGranahan "Shake," 178, 196

Keep, Gladys, 305, 306

Keith, J. L., 212

Kelley, Joe, 196

Ken Johnson and His Rhythm Swingers, 156

Kenya, 8, 31, 39, 47, 88, 92, 123, 226, 227, 242, 253, 263, 271

Kenyans in London, 8, 220. *See also* Kenyatta, Johnstone (Jomo)

Kenyatta, Johnstone (Jomo), 8, 41, 47–48, 57, 96, 125, 141, 143, 270–73, 286–89, 292, 298, 315, 323; and anthropology, 242, 246–48, 250–53, 258, 262–63, 276–77; and International African Service Bureau, 82–83, 85–87, 92; and Italo-Ethiopian conflict, 65, 69, 79–80; and sexual politics, 223–24, 226–27, 230, 234

Kessie, Ohenenana Cobina, 34, 48, 248, 269

Keys, The, 42–45, 48–49, 50, 51, 69, 70, 71*fig.*, 86, 87, 90, 91–93, 95, 175, 244, 265, 274, 276, 277, 296, 297; edited by Una Marson, 123–24, 125, 126, 131

Khama, Sereste, 179

Kidd, Ronald, 93

Kikuyu, 86, 123, 223–24, 247, 253, 258, 262–63, 270

Kikuyu Central Association (KCA), 8, 47, 223–24

Killingray, David, 38

King, Abdulrafiu Babatunde "Tunde," 190

King, Bertie, 152, 154, 157, 159, 172, 181, 194

Kingston, 104, 122, 129, 135, 141, 143, 152, 177, 183, 320

Kipling, Rudyard, 25

Kisch, Martin S., 35

Koinange, Peter Mbiyu, 11, 227, 242, 248, 263, 269, 270, 272

Korda, Alexander, 285, 290, 299, 301, 304, 319

Korda, Zoltan, 285

Kouyaté, Tiemoko Garan, 67, 79, 82, 272

Krio, 5, 35–36, 113, 115–16

Kru, 186, 190

Kuti, Fela, 187, 196

KUTVU (Communist University of the Toilers of the East), 8, 47

Kyerematen, Alex Atta Yaw, 143, 242, 246, 254–58, 278, 317

Labour Party, 69, 74–76, 84, 93–94, 98, 117, 121, 217, 226, 239, 275, 316

Lacton, Frank, 151

Lagos, 5, 22, 35, 47, 67, 72, 106, 120, 136, 175–76, 186, 189–90, 197, 287, 318

Landau, Paul, 25

Laski, Harold J., 238–40, 246

LCP. *See* League of Coloured Peoples

Leach, Edmund, 246

League Against Imperialism (LAI), 14, 46, 74, 288

League of Coloured Peoples (LCP), 23–24, 39–45, 90–93, 229–30, 244, 277, 298; and black clubs, 175–76, 191; criticism of *Men of Two Worlds,* 309, 311–12, 315; dance band, 176; dances, 44, 219; and Italo-Ethiopian War, 70, 73–75, 229; newsletter, 262, 305, 311, 312, 313; and politics of respectability, 163, 204–5, 208, 219–20; relationship with British left, 47–50, 52–53; relationship with WASU, 45, 47–50, 58–59; women's involvement in, 100, 112–13, 116, 122–27, 137. *See also* Moody, Harold

League of Nations Union, 15, 70, 75, 76, 84, 88, 94

League of Nations, 15–16, 125, 129; and Italo-Ethiopian conflict, 65–67, 70, 72, 75–76, 80

Leakey, Canon, 262–63

Leakey, L. S. B., 257, 262–63

Leslie, Lew, 146

Levine, Philippa, 3

Levy, Andres, 24

Lewin, Julius, 268–69

Lewis, W. Arthur, 69, 82, 90–91, 92, 124, 244, 245*fig.*, 310, 315; and academia, 242, 248, 251, 252–53, 262, 273, 277, 278

Leyburn, James Graham, 267

Leys, Norman, 47, 56, 75, 89

Liberia, 30, 109, 110, 186, 197, 244, 318

Lightbourne, Hyacinth, 43

Quaye, Caleb Jonas Kwamlah (aka Mope Desmond), 11

race riots, 22, 192, 201, 325
Radio Rhythm Club Sextet, 160, 161
Ragatz, Lowell Joseph, 267
Ramblers' Dance Band, 12
Ransome-Kuti, J. J., 187, 278
Rathbone, Hugo, 46, 47
Rattray, Robert Sutherland, 26–27
Ray Ellington Quartet, 178
Read, Margaret, 247
Regal-Zonophone, 163, 186–88, 217
Reinhardt, Django, 160, 179
Renner, O. Alakija, 115, 226
Rhodesia, 88, 127, 281
Richards, Audrey, 246, 247, 252, 263
Richards, Yevette, 139
Roachford, Willy, 195
Roberts, George, 40, 156
Robertson, Eileen Arnot, 302
Robeson, Paul, 1, 37, 41, 44, 58, 62, 66, 108, 120, 124, 172, 188, 269, 273, 317; and *Man of Two Worlds*, 305, 308, 312; and *Sanders of the River*, 174, 285–301
Robeson, Paul, Jr., 285–86
Robinson, Cedric, 63–64
Rockefeller Foundation, 241, 245, 246
Rodgers, Jimmie, 186
Roosevelt, Eleanor, 120
Ros, Edmundo, 158, 173, 181, 184, 190, 195
Ross, Isabel and William McGregor, 47, 226
Rotha, Paul, 290–91
Royal Anthropological Society, 257, 260, 278
Russell Square, 8, 11, 27, 187, 269

Sabine, Noel, 301, 305–6, 309
Said, Mohamed, 80
Saint Domingue, 78, 273
Saklatvala, Shapurji, 52
Salvation Army bands, 152, 186
same-sex relations, 162, 167, 170, 214. *See also* homosexuality
Sanders of the River, 8, 124, 174, 224, 238, 280–301, 307, 309, 311, 319
Sankoh, Laminah, 82

Saro, 35, 120, 190, 191
Scala Theatre, 44, 124
Schapera, Isaac, 246, 254
School or Oriental and African Studies (SOAS), 193, 247, 286, 320
Schwarz, Bill, 6, 208–9, 286, 295
Scott, Ronnie, 193
Scottsboro Boys, 8, 42, 45–51, 62, 75, 123, 188, 225, 290
seamen, 23, 40, 41, 46, 47, 94, 123, 153, 177, 179, 210
Sekyi, Kobina, 30, 41, 277
Selassie, Haile, 63, 66, 67, 71–72, 78, 129, 143
Seon, Margaret R., 44
Seton, Marie, 62, 287, 295
sexual politics, 19–20, 130, 141, 142–43, 165–66, 170–71, 200–237; and representations of Africa, 54, 73. *See also* interracial sex, homosexuality, same-sex relations
Shaw, Carolyn Martin, 224
Shelley, Percy Bysshe, 131
Shepperson, George, 15
Sherwood, Marika, 105
Shim Sham Club, 11, 154, 168–74
Shipton, Alyn, 151
Sholanke, Billy Olu, 9, 181, 189, 196
Sierra Leone, 26, 31, 42, 115–16, 120–21, 275
Sierra Leoneans in London, 30–31, 36, 43, 82, 113, 146; musicians, 151, 185, 190, 198, 218, 304. *See also* Cole, Robert Wellesley; Dunbar, W. Rudolph; Wallace-Johnson, Isaac Theophilus Akunna
Sierra Leone Women's Movement (SLWM), 121
Simmons, Ben, 187, 189
Simon, Kathleen, 60–61
Simons, Andrew, 150, 171
Singha, Shoran, 40
Sinha, Mrinalini, 4
Sivanandan, A., 291
Small Island (Levy), 24
Smith, Bessie, 134
Smith, Joe "Manny," 151, 152
Smith, Norris, 169
Snaith, Anna, 128, 141
Society of Friends, 39, 56

THE CALIFORNIA WORLD HISTORY LIBRARY

Edited by Edmund Burke III, Kenneth Pomeranz, and Patricia Seed